Social Trends & Indicators USA

Volume 2:
Community & Education

Social Trends & Indicators USA

Volume 2: Community & Education

Arsen J. Darnay, Managing Editor

Joyce Piwowarski, Editor

Helen S. Fisher, Robert Lazich,
Monique D. Magee, and Linda Schmittroth,
Assistant Editors

GALE®

THOMSON

GALE

Detroit • New York • San Diego • San Francisco • Cleveland • New Haven, Conn. • Waterville, Maine • London • Munich

Social Trends & Indicators USA
Community & Education

Joyce Piwowarski, Editor

Project Editor
Amanda C. Quick

Editorial
Arsen J. Darnay, Helen S. Fisher, Robert Lazich,
Monique D. Magee, Linda Schmittroth

Product Design
Pamela A. E. Galbreath

Manufacturing
NeKita McKee

ISBN 0-7876-5906-1 (set)
ISBN 0-7876-5907-X (v.1)
ISBN 0-7876-5908-8 (v.2)
ISBN 0-7876-5909-6 (v.3)
ISBN 0-7876-5910-X (v.4)
Library of Congress Control Number: 2002117074

TABLE OF CONTENTS

Introduction

Upon this gifted age, in its dark hour,
Rains from the sky a meteoric shower
Of facts ... they lie unquestioned, uncombined.
Wisdom enough to leech us of our ill
Is daily spun; but there exists no loom
To weave it into fabric.
                          Edna St. Vincent Millay

Social Trends & Indicators – The Concept

The idea for this series, *Social Trends & Indicators USA*, arose because we are inundated by statistics, but the meaning of the numbers is often elusive. We are getting outrageously obese, for instance, yet we are living longer. Layoffs are devastating sectors, yet the economy seems to be booming. We are the most educated society on earth, yet Johnny can't read. The crime rate is dropping, but we do not feel safe. The workweek is shrinking, yet we never have time.

The Federal Government's many statistical agencies produce a great wealth of superb data. We are undoubtedly the best documented and most measured society that has ever existed. Newspapers attractively box factoids to amaze or to alarm us. Competing interests marshal their data to make their cases, often omitting numbers that do not bolster the argument. Statistics become catch-phrases. The rich fabric of our national experience is thinned by the speed and noise of the mass media attempting to "infotain" us.

But statistics out of context — and without historical background — are often less than informative. They can be confusing and lead to wrong conclusions. Whereas a properly developed presentation on an issue, using what numbers are available, is often very revealing, at times sobering, and frequently reassuring. A balanced presentation of facts within context can serve the public by illuminating hidden facets of an issue and, as often happens, show that beneath the hoopla and the hype is a deeper-lying demographic movement.

This series was born from such considerations, and from our long experience in dealing with, and publishing, statistics. The idea, simply, was to present statistics in context, with as much historical background as possible, in order to answer questions and to pinpoint trends.

Organization of the Series

Work & Leisure deals with the whole economic realm — work, productivity, employment, unemployment, income, and fringe benefits — and with how we organize our leisure time. *Community & Education*, the current volume in the series, covers who we are, where we live, all kinds of family structures, race and ethnicity, politics, religion, and the vast subject of education and the many issues it encompasses. *Crime & Justice* attempts to shine a statistical light into the darker woods of our nature — victimization, crime, law enforcement, the drug war, terrorism, the justice system, and how all these matters affect us. *Health & Sickness* takes on the body and the mind and what can go wrong with us — our state of health and illness, old and emerging diseases, risky behaviors, prevention and treatment, our preoccupation with drugs, disability, sexuality, and the people and institutions that deal with us when we are ailing.

Each volume, of course, is divided into chapters. In their totality, the chapters present a fairly complete picture of the subject in each volume. But the objective is not to create a compendium on health and sickness, for instance, but to deal with issues of current concern. Dealing with the issues of today, of course, often causes us to look backwards — all the way back to the 19th century sometimes. But the focus is on current trends and on indicators of what is likely to happen tomorrow.

Each chapter is divided into several so-called "panels" (see below). Panels tend to come in two flavors: those that provide background information on a subject, including general trends, and those aimed specifically at answering a question: "Is government really growing? Which parts? Why?" "Will future jobs all require an advanced degree? No? Why not?" "Why are today's children suddenly so frequently 'learning disabled'?"

The Mode of Presentation: The Panel and the Tables

Each volume in the series presents statistical information in two forms. In Part I of the book, data are presented in graphic format followed by explanations and commentaries.

The principal unit of presentation in Part I is thus a "panel" — one topic, one main graphic, and a commentary of usually no more than two pages. Panels sometimes also feature additional graphics and statistics laid out in tabular format. The text is a discussion of the topic. It may feature footnotes for additional comment. A source note concludes each panel citing the sources used. In most instances, web addresses are provided pointing to sites where the user can obtain additional information.

Sometimes a single panel is not sufficient to develop a subject. In that case, the discussion continues with another panel, with its own graphic. Groups of panels form chapters, and each chapter has a brief introduction.

Users of such works as *Social Trends & Indicators USA* find graphics a vivid way to show data, but they want to see the actual numbers as well. For this reason, *Community & Education* produces all of the data graphed in Part II, the Data Presentation. Here, statistical data are presented in tabular format. Frequently only the data used to create the graphics are shown. Sometimes, however, additional time series are provided as well for a more comprehensive documentation of the subject. Tables in Part II are organized by chapters for rapid access. These chapters are organized to correspond to panels in Part I. The tables are also fully indexed.

Accessing Information

Each volume of *Social Trends & Indicators USA* provides a Table of Contents and an Index. The Table of Contents will guide the user to appropriate chapters. The Index lists important concepts, names, institutions, and issues. Page numbers cited refer to the pages where text or data can be found under the topic listed.

Sources of Information

Data presented in *Community & Education*, and in the other volumes, come predominantly, but not exclusively, from Federal or State statistical agencies. Data from not-for-profit organizations and from commercial sources are also sometimes shown. Sources of data are always referenced in footnotes or source notes. Where such data are copyrighted, the copyright notice is provided.

An important feature of this series is that data from different sources are analytically combined and presented together. A typical example might be to show birth data in combination with population data on women of child-bearing age. Another might be to show a flow of expenditures but rendered in constant dollars (for comparability year to year) — for which purpose index data from the Consumer Price Index (or the Gross Domestic Product deflator) may have been used to transform the dollar quantities. Data on alcohol, tobacco, and illegal drug consumption — derived from three sources — might be shown together.

Data were obtained using the Internet or from print sources. Web-based data are "sourced" showing the web site from which they were obtained. The links shown, however, are not guaranteed to be functioning at some later date. Most will be accessible because they are predominantly governmental sites. Historical data were obtained from the *Historical Statistics of the United States, Colonial Times to 1970*, published by the Bureau of the Census.

Authorship and Presentation

Community & Education was prepared by five individuals (three women, two men), each responsible for chapter-length segments of the book. The authors are all skilled statistical analysts but none is an expert on the subject presented. All members of the editorial group reviewed and discussed every panel contained in this work. Changes, revisions, and augmentation of the material took place as a consequence of these reviews. Finally, all materials were reviewed and edited by the senior editor in charge. However, no attempts were made — or thought to be desirable — to conform the presentational style of the authors to produce a uniform (and possibly bureaucratic-sounding) voice.

Our aim is to present often complicated and difficult subjects — as these are seen by the educated layperson — the view of the proverbial "man on the street." To the extent that expert opinion was required, it was obtained from the literature and is quoted in the panels. We made a serious effort to present as balanced a view as possible, resisting both the temptation to be politically correct and the temptation to range far off the reservation. No doubt people of all persuasions will find fault with something in these panels, all will find something to applaud.

How to Use this Book

Although *Community & Education* is, above all, a reference work, it is best approached by actually *reading* a chapter. Within a chapter, the different panels are closely related to develop the subject. The panels are relatively short. It is not difficult to peruse a chapter from beginning to end.

Use of a panel should begin with a close study of the graphic presented (only very few panels lack a graphic). Each graphic has a title. The meaning of the curves and bars is indicated in legends (or shown in the graph itself). Sometimes both the left and the right scale of the graphic is used to measure data sets that would not otherwise be visible. Please note that some of the graphics are in logarithmic scale. The log scale is used when the lowest value charted would be all but invisible — or in cases where the slope of curves is important to show how one set of data is growing more or less than the other. Some graphics are quite "busy," but a little study will well repay the effort. The general message is usually contained in the chart, although, in a few instances, the graphic is just a way of enticing the user to read the text.

Once the graphic is understood, the text will be more accessible. The objective of the text is to make clear what is depicted and then to add other information to put the subject into perspective. Sometimes parts of the information charted are also shown in tabular form in the text itself. This is done in those cases where the numerical values — not merely the pattern that they form — is of great importance. Sometimes additional, smaller graphics are shown to highlight additional aspects of the data or to present new information.

The user who wishes to look at the numbers charted can immediately refer to Part II, which presents data in tabular format.

The source note at the end of the panel may list one or more web sites for more information. The user might wish to be "distracted" into checking out those web sites — or continue on to the next panel until the entire subject is fully developed.

Introduction to this Volume – *Community & Education*

Community & Education divides into two halves as the title suggest. The principal aim of this volume is to look at trends and indicators in the way in which we live — as a community — at our ethnic composition, our settlement patterns, at our family arrangements, at our political behavior and our systems of beliefs. On the one hand. And then, on the other hand, we look at the manner in which we organize and conduct our preparation for life — education, not least our continuing education. Education, if taken at all levels, is truly the single largest common activity in which we engage as a people.

This volume leaves aside work and play, two subjects covered in *Work & Leisure*. The subject of our health is left for *Health & Sickness*, and that aspect of our community life which deals with law and order has its own volume titled *Crime & Justice*.

In one sense *Community & Education* is a snapshot of ourselves as we pass from the 20th into the 21st century. It sums up what we have become after a century that saw World War I, the Great Depression, World War II, the Baby Boom, the Civil Rights Movement, the Vietnam War, the coming of the cyber age, major shifts in our population, and changes in our ways of forming and maintaining a family.

In the first six chapters of this volume we grapple with some very fascinating matters. We're looking at ourselves as *people*, hence the stress is on demographics, on fertility, ethnicity and race, immigration, and the family. We note that among the developed nations, our reproductive energy is high. Our population has greatly increased — despite legalized abortion — not least by the most fundamental phenomenon of the 20th century, the post-war Baby Boom. The Baby Boom has left an indelible imprint on all aspects of American life, especially its demographic patterns.

We were much more urban — or, rather, *suburban* — at the dawn of the 21st century. We were very, very rural at the dawn of the 20th. But the density of our settlement patterns does not as yet approach those found in Europe or other densely populated parts of the world. We also have a lot more square footage of hearth and home — especially if we've recently moved into new housing.

The family has undergone a revolutionary transformation — with important consequences for our children. We deal with this subject extensively — although we leave some aspects of the discussion (our reproductive practices and sexuality) to the volume on *Health & Sickness*.

Has there been a meaningful "diversification" in our ethnic and racial makeup? To some extent. We are slightly less white — but only by a smidgen. Our ads are much more multi-racial than our neighborhoods. Changes in immigration law have brought into prominence people of Hispanic origin. We look in some detail at the way we live together — and apart — along racial and ethnic lines. We cover a time which saw the Civil Rights Movement come into its own — and yet pressures for integration have faded. In our politics, we have seen some interesting transformations along gender lines, which we present. The American genius has always been to find the middle. It may be flavored a little more left sometimes, a little more right at others, but the majority is in the center. Hardcore liberals and conservatives are strictly limited minorities.

Next we turn to education. By any measure, Education is *the* industry of the U.S.A. It employs more people than any other sector — and its impact on our culture and, ultimately, on our economy, is enormous. Education is really rather difficult to squeeze into the seven chapters that we were able to allocate to it. We touch on all of the major aspects of the subject — our educational attainment, teachers and teaching, money, how the school are doing, SAT scores, grade schools, high schools, college. Throughout, in line with the mission we pursue in this series, we focus on *issues*. Can Johnny read? And if not, will smaller class sizes and smarter teachers (being paid a lot more) make a difference? We deal with homework, the Federal Governments numerous intrusions (for good or ill) into the local business of educating children. We also touch upon the education of the gifted and the handicapped.

Important issues in education are performance — and how we test for it. Scores are flat. Money is rising. Classes are getting smaller. Are teachers underpaid — underqualified? We present surprising conclusions. The cost of higher education? You have to shield your eyes when you look that high up. Vouchers, anyone? Should we teach children in English — or in the language of their choice?

Education is a vast morass of theory and practice, politics, dedication, commercialism, and contention. All this makes for interesting study, reading, and some odd surprises.

If you, the reader, do the homework, we promise that you will be rewarded.

Comments and Suggestions

Those of us who have labored on *Community & Education* — and those who have suffered us while we did so — welcome your comments and suggestions. We have made every effort to be accurate, fair, and complete. No doubt we succeeded only in trying. Should errors have occurred, despite best efforts, they will be corrected in future editions. We shall be pleased to incorporate users' suggestions to the extent possible. To reach authors directly, please call Editorial Code and Data, Inc. at (248) 356-6990.

Please address other communications to:

Editor
Social Trends & Indicators USA
Community & Education
Gale
27500 Drake Road
Farmington Hills, MI 48331-3535
248-699-GALE
BusinessProducts@gale.com

Chapter 1

Who Are We?

We begin this volume on our community of peoples and our education by answering some questions about who we are. We are, first of all, more numerous. Using several panels, we look at population growth over the span of a century. We examine the birth rate, fertility, abortions, and contraceptive practices, and attempt to answer the question: Are we reproducing enough? Fertility is dropping all over the world. What about the United States? Panels are devoted to looking at differences between and among the races and also at different rates of reproduction between and among ethnicities.

Next we look at our age structure and note that we're increasingly older. And not just with every passing day. The age structure of the population is changing. We explore the subject of life expectancy, an aging population, and the implied issue of "dependency" that arises from a "top heavy" population structure. The question we're pursuing is controversial: Are we living *too* long? Will the young be willing to support us when we're no longer able to work? We supply what looks like a hopeful answer. Whether or not we are *enjoying* the long lifespan provided us by science and technology will be answered more fully in another volume in this series, *Health & Sickness*.

We end this chapter by looking briefly at our racial and ethnic composition. We have become much more diverse over the last 100 years — at least as measured by racial and ethnic origins. But the degree to which we have changed is not as dramatic as would appear from the intensity of our political discussions or the color-scape of the advertisements beamed at us. Aspects of our racial/ethnic composition are further explored in virtually every chapter in the remainder of this volume. Here we present an interesting overview — and a forecast some decades out. Change, we note, will be quite gradual.

Births of a Nation

**Live Births, Fertility Rate, and Birth Rate
1909 to 2000**

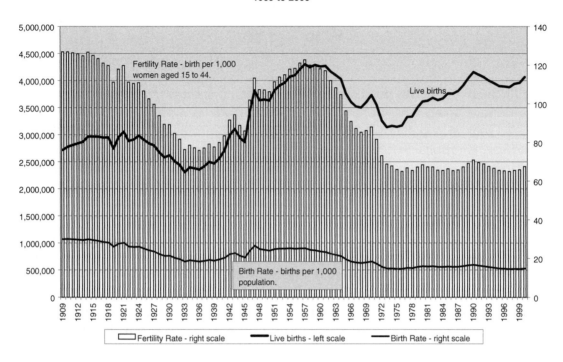

In 1909, 2.7 million babies were born. In that year the birth rate stood at 30 live births for every 1,000 people; and the fertility was 126.8 babies for every 1,000 women aged 15 to 44 years. At that time World Wars I and II were still in the future. So was the great Depression. And anyone saying "Baby Boom" would have received strange looks from his or her neighbor.

Nearly a century later, in 2000, just shy of 4.1 million babies were born. The birth rate had dropped to less than half of its 1909 rate — 14.8 births per 1,000 people. The fertility rate had declined to 67.6 babies per 1,000 women in the childbearing cohorts of the population. The nation had seen a long, sustained period of prosperity and, in recent years, a great upsurge in wealth and general well being. The troubles of 2001 were still ahead, and anyone talking of 9/11 wouldn't have been understood.

Grand sweeps of demographic data, such as the one shown above, vaguely hint at the interplay of good times and of troubles as they — along with culture, ethnic and racial composition, and many other factors — affect the birth rate.

The Roaring 20s produced a slide in fertility and births. Births began to climb in the dark days of the Depression as people began to live once again according to basic values. The birth rate flattened briefly as Johnny marched off to war and Rosie the Riveter went to the factory. Then came the Baby Boom, the defining demographic event of the 20th century — and with us to this day. It stands like a mountain in the center of this century of births. As the 1960s began, fertility began to drop to levels never seen before. Births continued rising — but the population, of course, had by then increased from around 92 million in 1910 to 178 million in 1960 — due to new births but also due to immigration and a lengthening life span.

Several things are worth noting in these data[1]. The birth rate, while declining, is staying relatively flat. This measure, which relates births to *total* population, indirectly reflects increasing longevity. People remain in the population longer and longer. If the life expectancy of 1909 had prevailed in 2000, the birth rate would have been higher.

The fertility rate — births for each 1,000 women of childbearing age — fluctuates much more. It responds to many factors — not least income, education, divorce rates, abortion practices, general levels of confidence, women's participation in the workforce (much higher as time moves forward), and so on. Since about the 1970s, the fertility rate has been relatively stable.

Generations echo one another. Note that the peak reached in 1921 is "echoed" in 1943 — a new generation is settling down to breed. Similarly, the peak reached in 1947, after World War II wound down, is echoed by another peak 23 years later in 1970 — and again, 20 years later, in 1990. Thus fertility rates are influenced by the past and shape the future. Troughs are also echoed. Deployment of troops in large-scale wars produce dips in births.

This is the overall picture. In the next three panels, we shall take a closer look at the driving force behind the births of a nation — fertility — and the factors that influence it.

Source: U.S. Department of Health and Human Services. National Center for Health Statistics (NCHS). "Vital Statistics of the United States, 1998," Volume I, *Natality,* updated from later issues of *National Vital Statistics Reports* and *Monthly Vital Statistics Report* also published by NCHS.

---

[1] In this volume, as in all others, the numerical values charted may be found in Part II.

Are Births Replacing Deaths?

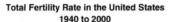

Total Fertility Rate in the United States
1940 to 2000

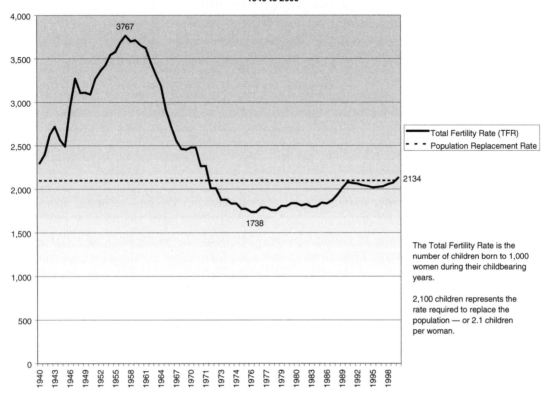

The Total Fertility Rate is the number of children born to 1,000 women during their childbearing years.

2,100 children represents the rate required to replace the population — or 2.1 children per woman.

All over the world, development has been accompanied by a drop in the reproductive rate, usually expressed as the "Total Fertility Rate" or TFR. The TFR is defined as the total number of children a woman will have in her childbearing years if current fertility rates continue. The value is usually expressed as children per 1,000 women in the 15 to 44 age group — or as children per woman. A population will replace itself if this rate is 2,100 children per 1,000 women or 2.1 children per woman, on average[2]. This is known as the replacement rate. In 2000, this value was 2,134 for the United States, or 2.13 children per woman. A comparison with other countries/regions will put this into perspective. The data shown are for 1996:

---

[2] The slight increase over 2 — husband and wife each replaced — is dictated by the need to replace also infertile women and to account for children who die in infancy.

Total Fertility Rate the World Over – 1998

Children born to women during fertile years[3]

United States	2.0
European community (1996)	1.4
Bulgaria, Hong Kong, Latvia (world's lowest)	1.1
Niger (world's highest)	7.3
Japan	1.4
India	3.2
China	1.9
Russia	1.2
Malaysia	3.1

Based on these data, the total fertility rate in the United States is one of the higher rates for a developed country — above replacement level in 2000. During the period shown in the graphic, the TFR has been above replacement rate in the 1940 to 1970 period, below it in the 1971 through 1999 period, and has just peaked above the line in 2000 for the first time in 29 years.

In the next panel, we look more closely at the total fertility rate, examining first the differences between African Americans and whites and, in the next panel, between all of the racial/ethnic groups for a more recent period.

Source: U.S. Department of Health and Human Services. National Center for Health Statistics (NCHS). "Vital Statistics of the United States, 1998," Volume I, *Natality*, updated from later issues of *National Vital Statistics Reports* and *Monthly Vital Statistics Report* also published by NCHS.

---

[3] "2000 World Development Indicators," The World Bank, Washington, D.C., March 2000.

Total Fertility: Blacks and Whites

Total Fertility Rate - Blacks and Whites

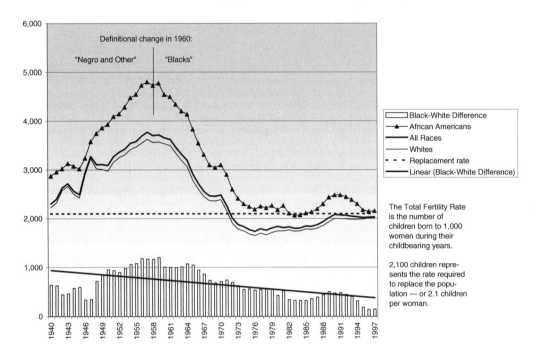

The Total Fertility Rate is the number of children born to 1,000 women during their childbearing years.

2,100 children represents the rate required to replace the population — or 2.1 children per woman.

The total fertility rate is not available for all of the racial and ethnic groups into which, in the early 21st century, demographers like to divide the American population. Data for whites and African Americans are available back to 1960 together with a series called "All other races" (not shown). In the 1940 to 1960 period, the only category other than white was "Negro and Other."

These series are shown in the graphic above together with the composite total fertility rate (TFR). The movement of this measure, over time, makes several interesting points.

The African American fertility rate is higher than the TFR for whites, reflecting the general observation that populations with higher income have lower fertility rates. The black population's income, throughout this period, was lower than that of the white population taken as a whole.

Black and white fertility rates show the same pattern of change — indicating that the same overall national and economic experiences produce very much the same kind of behavior.

Shown at the bottom of the chart, as bars, is the difference between the African American and the white TFR. Differences are most pronounced in the period of the Baby Boom — where everything, it seems, was exaggerated.

The straight line traversing the bars is the linear trend of these data. It clearly shows that blacks' total fertility rate is trending down — undoubtedly as a consequence of diminishing economic differences between the two groups. Note that the black TFR dips below the replacement rate in 1983 and 1984 and hovers just above the replacement rate toward the end of the 58-year period shown.

The white TFR closely matches — indeed defines — the overall TFR for all races. Whites represent the majority of the population. In this presentation, Hispanics are included either in the African American rate (if the Hispanic women were black) or in the white rate (if they were white). Asian Americans, Pacific Islanders, and Native North Americans are reflected only in the "Negro and Other" portion of the curve for the 1940 to 1960 period.

In the next panel, for a more recent 9-year period, we shall look at these racial/ethnic components in more detail.

Source: U.S. Department of Health and Human Services. National Center for Health Statistics. "Total Fertility Rates and Birth Rates by Race, 1940-1980 and 1981-1997." Online. 2002. National Center for Health Statistics. Available: http://www.cdc.gov/nchs/default.htm.

Total Fertility: Ethnic and Racial Detail

Total Fertility Rate, by Race/Ethnicity

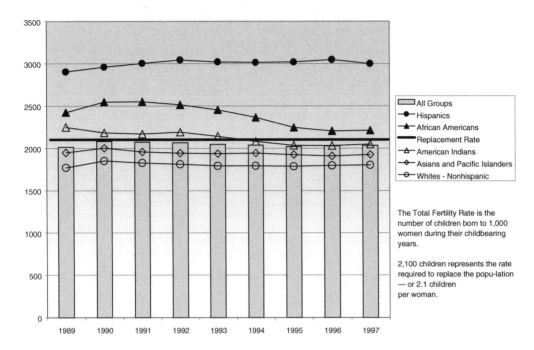

Legend:
- All Groups
- Hispanics
- African Americans
- Replacement Rate
- American Indians
- Asians and Pacific Islanders
- Whites - Nonhispanic

The Total Fertility Rate is the number of children born to 1,000 women during their childbearing years.

2,100 children represents the rate required to replace the popu-lation — or 2.1 children per woman.

This graphic displays the total fertility rate (TFR) by ethnic/racial groups for the 9-year period 1989 through 1997. Demographic focus on fine differences between ethnicities and racial groups goes back 40 years as it relates to African Americans and 20 years as it relates to Hispanics, Asian Americans, and Pacific Islanders. Therefore a consistent comparison between racial and ethnic groups as shown here can only be shown for recent years. Detailed measurements, as these relate to the age groups of women in their period of fertility, were not reported.

The chart shows that Hispanics have the highest total fertility rate, followed, in order, by African Americans, American Indians, Asians and Pacific Islanders, and whites.

The first two populations reproduce "above" the replacement rate — meaning that their birth rate, if it continues at current levels, will completely replace the current population and, in these cases, produce net growth. But both the Hispanic and African American total fertility rates show a downtrending tendency.

The other four populations are "below" replacement rate. This means that, over the long term — again, if the TFRs continue at current levels — these groups will lose population share.

As shown in the last panel, the total fertility rate in the developed world is below replacement. In practice this means that the population will remain stable or will decline — unless fertility rates change. In the less developed regions of the world, especially the so-called "third world," fertility is high. This is true in most of Africa, India, and Malaysia.

It is generally assumed that as development proceeds, total fertility will drop below replacement level in those regions as well. It is well to note, however, that these trends are not likely to signal the gradual disappearance of humankind. Populations respond to the environment — whether human-made or natural — in surprisingly adaptive ways.

Source: U.S. Department of Health and Human Services. National Center for Health Statistics. *National Vital Statistics Reports.* Vol. 47. No. 18, April 29, 1999. Online. 2002. Available: www.cdc.gov/nchs/data/nvsr/nvsr47/nvs47_18.pdf.

Births and Abortions: A Relationship?

Live Births and Abortions
(1975 to 1997, in Thousands)

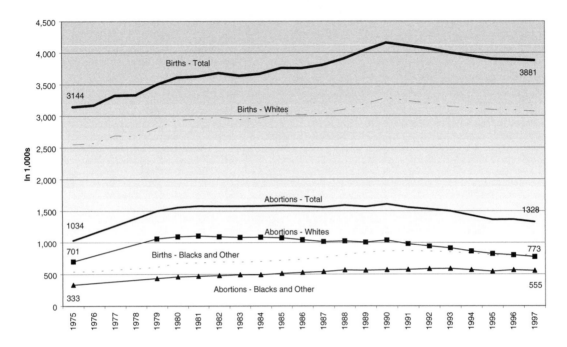

The graphic shows data for live births and abortions for the 1975 to 1997 period. Data are shown for the entire population and for two of its subdivisions — whites and "blacks and other." "Other" includes American Indians, Asians, and Pacific Islanders. Hispanics are accounted for in each group, depending on race (most Hispanics are white).

Both live births and abortions are trending up for the population as a whole — births more than abortions. Abortions for whites have decreased slightly from the beginning to the end of this period. Abortions for the "blacks and other" population category have increased. The net effect is a slight increase from 1975 to 1997, with a slight bulge in the middle.

The abortion *rate* for both subgroups is trending down, as shown further in the next panel. The small increase in total abortions is due to the *decline* in the number of white women in the childbearing age group (15 to 44) and an *increase* in childbearing-age women in the black and other population. Whites have a lower abortion rate overall. The net effect is a slight increase in total abortions.

The gradual down-trend in the rate of abortions, for both populations group, somewhat obscures what appears to be a pattern — namely that as births rise, so do abortions, and as births fall, so do abortions. The abortion rate in 1997 was 16.1 abortions per 1,000 women in the childbearing age group for whites and 47.8 for the black and other category. The difference between these two groups — about 32 abortions per 1,000 women, has not changed significantly in the 22 years of this period.

Births clearly reflect the size of the female population cohort capable of bearing children. Abortions appear to do so as well. Some proportion of pregnancies is not wanted. In 1997 this number corresponded to 250 pregnancies per 1,000 live births for whites and 680 pregnancies per 1,000 live births for the black and other population. Nearly 80% of all abortions are sought by unmarried women. The specific age stratification of the child-bearing female population may be the explanation for the falling abortion rate in this period, as discussed in the next panel.

Source: U.S. Bureau of the Census. *Statistical Abstract of the United States*, 2001. 121st ed. Washington, DC: U.S. Government Printing Office, 2001, p. 71, Table 92. Data are originally from the Centers for Disease Control. Abortions in 1983 and 1986 are extrapolations. Data for 1976-1978 are not available. The trend line between 1975 and 1979, however, is shown in the graph. All birth data, from National Center for Health Statistics, show actual counts.

Declining Abortion Rate? – A Closer Look

Abortion Rates - Two Populations
(Number of abortions per 1,000 women in the 15 to 44 age group)

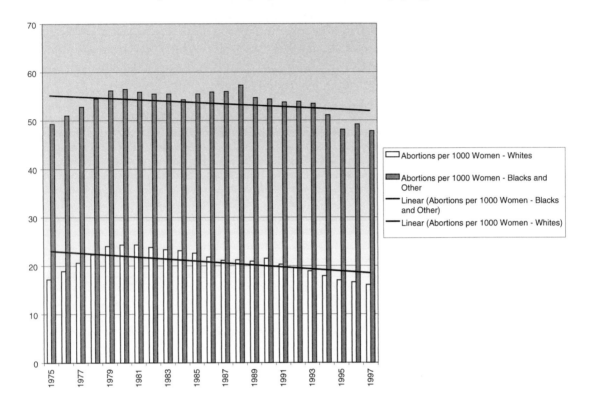

The abortion rate is trending down — as shown here for two population groups: whites and the "blacks and other" category. "Other" includes American Indians, Asians, and Pacific Islanders. Hispanics are included in both groups depending on their race.

Rates for selected years are shown in the following table in numerical format:

Abortions per 1,000 Women Aged 15 to 44

	1975	1980	1990	1997
All Races	21.7	29.3	27.4	22.2
Whites	17.2	24.3	20.9	16.1
Blacks and Other	49.3	56.5	54.4	47.8

In the graphic above, the straight lines indicate the linear trend of the data, and trends are down for both whites and the "black and other" population. Raw numbers show more fluctuations, rising uniformly from 1975 to 1980, declining until 1990, and again until 1997. It is these later periods that the trend reflects.

Another measure is abortions per 1,000 live births. This measure shows much the same pattern for All Races and whites but a growing rate for the black and other population. The next table provides the milestone numbers:

Abortions per 1,000 Live Births

	1975	1980	1990	1997
All Races	331	428	389	340
Whites	276	376	318	250
Blacks and Other	565	642	655	680

In situations such as this one, it is worthwhile to look more closely at the underlying factors that influence the abortion rate. As pointed out in the last panel, 80.9% of abortions are sought by unmarried women — who tend to be predominantly young. This is borne out by the age structure of women getting abortions. Those in the 15 to 24 age group accounted, in 1997, for 50.7%, those in the 24 to 34 a group for 37.8%, and those aged 35 to 44 for 11.5% of all abortions. Thus abortions appear to be influenced by the age stratification of the childbearing cohort of the population.

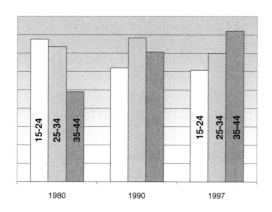

Indeed, the downward trend in abortions seems to be due to changes in the age composition of fertile females. The two age groups that usually account for more than 80% of all abortions — the two largest in 1980 — have become the two smallest by 1997.

Source: U.S. Bureau of the Census. *Statistical Abstract of the United States*, 2001. 121st ed. Washington, DC: U.S. Government Printing Office, 2001, p. 71, Table 92. Data are originally from the Centers of Disease Control. Abortions in 1983 and 1986 are extrapolations. Data for 1976-1978 are not available. Trend data between 1975 and 1979 have been inserted into the graph. Population data are from the U.S. Bureau of the Census.

Contraceptive Patterns

Contraceptive Status of Women in 1995
(In Percent, by Age Group)

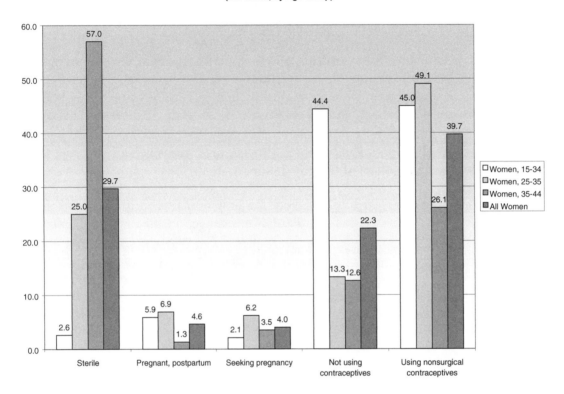

The contraceptive practices of women in the childbearing years — ages 15 to 44 — is another factor that affects the nation's overall fertility rate. The graphic above profiles these practices for a single year, 1995.

Data are shown for three age groups and for the entire childbearing group of women in 1995, 60.2 million in that year, roughly in equal distribution, but skewed toward the oldest age group:

Women 15-24:	18.00 million	29.9%
Women 25-34:	20.76 million	34.5
Women 35-44:	21.44 million	35.4

Among those who are classified as sterile, nearly 94% are surgically sterile; the rest are sterile because of congenital conditions, illness, accidents, or because the male is sterile for non-reported reasons. Fifty-seven percent of the oldest age group are classified as sterile (12.2 million women), and nearly 30% of all women (17.9 million).

The two smallest groups (together 8.6% of childbearing age women), are either pregnant or postpartum or reported that they were attempting to become pregnant — a group of 5.2 million women.

Slightly more than 22% of women in these age groups were not using contraceptives of any kind. Of these, nearly half (48.9% or 6.6 million) reported never having had intercourse. 44.4% of the 15-24 year old women reported that they did not use contraceptives; and of these, 69.4% had never had intercourse.

Nearly 39.7% of all women of childbearing age reported using non-surgical forms of contraception — 23.9 million women. Forty-five percent of the youngest and 49% of the middle age group reported such practice. The form of non-surgical contraception used by all age groups combined is shown in the following pie chart:

Contraceptives Used - All Women

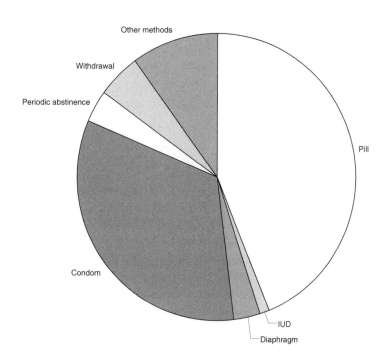

The Pill had the largest share of such contraceptives (43.6%) followed by condoms (33%), and by "Other methods" (9.8%). "Other methods" includes implants, injectables, morning-after pills, suppositories, Today ™ sponge, and less frequently used methods.

Source: U.S. Bureau of the Census. *Statistical Abstract of the United States*, 2001. 121ˢᵗ ed. Washington, DC: U.S. Government Printing Office, 2001, Table 87, p. 69. The source indicates that the data were developed by the National Center for Health Statistics in a special tabulation from the 1995 National Survey of Family Growth.

Life Expectancy Basics

Life Expectancy at Birth
(In years, 1900-1998)

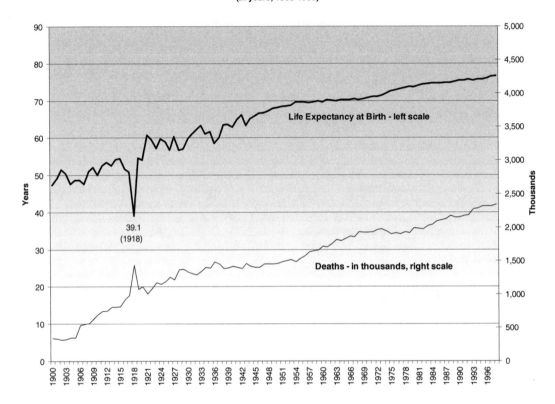

Life expectancy has been on a steady increase throughout the last century. In 1900, life expectancy at birth was just a shade over 47 years. In 1998, it reached nearly 77 years.

This life-affirming indicator of general well-being and social progress is closely linked with — indeed based upon — the death rate. It was 17.2 deaths per 1,000 population in 1900 and 8.6 in 1998. In the graphic above, Life Expectancy is shown on top, and total deaths (in thousands, right scale) are shown below. Note the sharp dip in 1918 — when life expectancy dipped to its lowest level in the 20th century (39 years) and deaths peaked; the death rate that year, 18.1 per 1,000 population (not shown), was also the highest in the century. More comment will follow below.

Life expectancy is calculated by looking at age-specific death rates in any given year. The death rate is simply the number of people who die per 1,000 population. These data are categorized by age. The rates are applied to a hypothetical population of 100,000 newborn babies. Some die in infancy. They are removed from the hypothetical population. The rest "go on living," but at each age some die, of course. The number used is determined by the measured rate taken from registries of death. Thus individuals are removed from the population at each age, using the age-specific death rates prevailing in the year of calculation. Years actually lived by each individual are cumulated. In 1997, for example, the death rates for that year indicated that 100,000 newborns would, altogether, live 7,650,789 years. This number, divided by 100,000, produces 76.5 — which was the life expectancy at birth, in years, for 1997.

This means that, in effect, life expectancy is not something achieved once and for all and "locked in" for all time. The measure is simply another way of depicting the mortality rate in a given year. This is illustrated by the data for the year 1918. The cause of the dip, that year (and in the spike in deaths) was not World War I but the so-called "Spanish Influenza." The sickness extracted some 20 million lives across the globe — and nearly 500,000 in the United States. For a while, after that, children sang a little ditty:

> I had a little bird
> And its name was Enza
> I opened the door
> And in-flew-Enza.

The death rates of children and young adults were especially affected in 1918 — as shown in the following table.

Increase in Death Rate, 1917 to 1918, in %

Age	Male	Female
<1	51.4	57.9
1-4	217.7	264.7
5-14	560.6	716.3
15-24	1273.7	1659.6
25-34	1438.1	1924.4
35-44	428.4	551.4
45-54	118.7	164.4
55-64	34.2	37.8
65-74	7.8	2.5
75-84	-18.7	-23.7
>84	-30.3	-29.8

Increases of more than 1,000% in the death rate produce dramatic results in life expectancy. But note that, in 1919, life expectancy had climbed again. This brings home the character of the life expectancy measurements — which are based on the death rates in a *single* year.

Note that, in the first half of the 20th century, life expectancy seesaws a good deal. These were times before modern medicine and sanitation took hold; tuberculosis stalked the land. After about World War II, life expectancy — and also total deaths — show a less dramatic up-down fluctuation.

We look at more detail on this interesting subject in the following three panels.

Source: U.S. Department of Health and Human Services. National Center for Health Statistics. *National Vital Statistics Reports*. Vol. 47. No. 28. December 13, 1999. Online. 2002. Available: www.cdc.gov/nchs/data/nvsr/nvsr47/nvs47_28.pdf.

Women Live Longer

Women's and Men's Life Expectancy at Birth
(In years - 1900 to 1998)

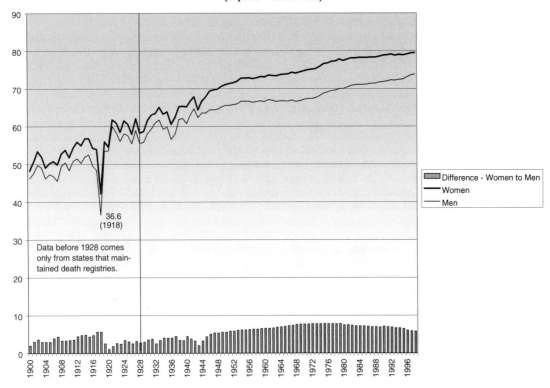

Life expectancy data for the 1900 to 1998 period are shown on this graph for women and men. The bars on the bottom of the graph show the difference between women's and men's life expectancy. In 1900 women were expected to live 2 years longer than men, in 1998 5.7 years longer; the smallest difference, one year longer, still in favor of women, came in 1920 and was most likely a consequence of the flu epidemic of 1918.

Women live longer than men. Various explanations have been offered.[4] These explanations usually involve behavioral and physical differences. Males exhibit more reckless and violent behavior after the onset of puberty. The male death rate flares up in the 15 to 24 age group because of traffic deaths, homicides, suicides, cancer, and drowning. "Bad" cholesterol (low-density lipoprotein) is increased in the blood by testosterone and leads to higher rates of heart disease and stroke. Estrogen, on the other hand, lowers LDL cholesterol and increases high-density lipoproteins, which are beneficial.

Males have an advantage at the beginning; 115 are conceived for every 100 females, but "their numbers are preferentially whittled down thereafter. Just 104 boys are born for

---

[4] See especially Perls, Thomas T. and Ruth C. Fretts, "Why Women Live Longer than Men," *Scientific American*, June 1998, accessible at sciam.com/1998/0698womens/0698perls.html.

every 100 girls because of the disproportionate rate of spontaneous abortions, stillbirths and miscarriages of male fetuses" [Perls].

Evidently the differential in favor of women is of long standing, going back at least as far as 1500. Swedish records (the earliest mortality data for a nation) show that in the second half of the 18th century similar differences prevailed.

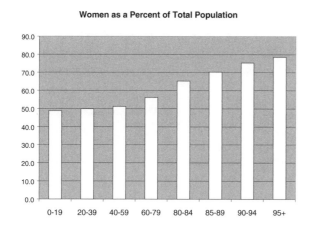

Women as a Percent of Total Population

The population aged 40 years and older becomes increasingly more female — as shown in the graphic on the left, which is based on 1990 data. Sixty-five of 100 people aged 80 and older were women. This percentage reaches almost 80% among nonagenarians.

Biological differences become much more pronounced in the period following World War II. In the 45 years before then, women were more prone to die in childbirth and were as much subject to epidemics — not yet brought under control by modern medicine — as men.

High life expectancy is, of course, a consequence of collective social and economic success. Growth in life expectancy may slow and stop as the natural life span is reached under optimal conditions — and conditions can change.

In the next panel we touch on this subject by examining differences between whites and other races.

Source: U.S. Department of Health and Human Services. National Center for Health Statistics. *National Vital Statistics Reports*. Vol. 47. No. 28. December 13, 1999. Online. 2002. Available: www.cdc.gov/nchs/data/nvsr/nvsr47/nvs47_28.pdf. Population data from the U.S. Bureau of the Census.

Life Expectancy by Race

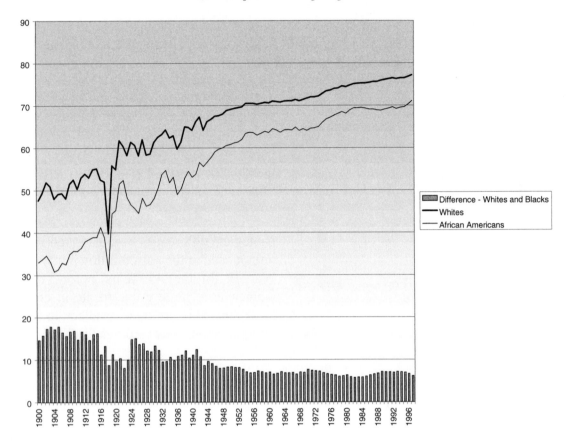

Life expectancy for whites and African Americans is shown in the graphic. The bars at the bottom show the difference between whites and blacks. In 1997, the last year for these series, whites had a life expectancy 6 years more than blacks. In 1900 the difference was 14.6 years. There are some points to be made before we attempt to report the explanation for these persistent differences between white-black life expectancy at birth.

Note that the curves for both populations have very similar overall patterns. Life expectancy rises and falls more or less in parallel. The impact of the 1918 flu epidemic has the same shape. Life expectancy for both groups rises over time. The gap between whites and African Americans narrows until about 1954. Thereafter it remains essentially flat, rising in the Vietnam years, dropping in the middle-1980s, then rising again to the levels of the 1950s.

Why is there a persistent gap between the life expectancies of these two groups? At a technical level, it is due to higher black age-specific mortality rates; these underlie life expectancy calculations. As mentioned in the first panel on this subject, life expectancy mirrors the death rate. Blacks have a higher mortality rate in every age category except the oldest, those 85 years old or older. This is shown on the next page for 1998.

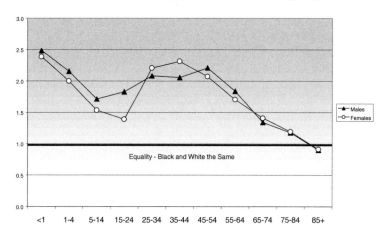

Ratio: Black Death Rate to White Death Rate, 1998

Equality - Black and White the Same

Males
Females

<1 1-4 5-14 15-24 25-34 35-44 45-54 55-64 65-74 75-84 85+

The graph shows, for example, that African American male children less than 1 year old have a death rate 2.5 times the rate for whites of the same age. Females have just a slightly lower multiple of the white rate. Women in the prime child-bearing age of 25 to 34 have twice the death rate of white women in the same age group.

African Americans have a much higher rate of infant mortality. In 1998, for every white child who died before age 1 (in a group of 1,000 live births), 2.4 black infants died. Blacks have a much higher maternal death rate. In 1997, for every white woman who died in childbirth (in a group of 100,000 live births), 3.6 black women died. Please note here that early deaths have a disproportionate impact on life expectancy calculations.

African Americans experience more accidents and violence, as the following table shows:

Death Rates per 100,000 Population in 1998

Cause of Death	White Male	Black Male	White Female	Black Female
Motor vehicle accident	21.9	22.2	10.7	**9.4**
All other accidents	26.0	29.3	15.5	12.8
Suicide	20.3	**10.2**	4.8	**1.8**
Homicide	6.1	42.1	2.2	8.6

Bold items indicate categories in which African Americans have lower death rates than whites; they are less prone to commit suicide, and fewer black women die in auto accidents.

The African American population had a median household income, in 1999, of $27,910 — versus a median household income for whites of $42,504. The blacks' income was 65.7% that of whites. These are *average* incomes. Many, many households earned much less. The black population, on average, is poorer. The income differential is the most obvious overall explanation for the gap in life expectancy — because it translates into less disposable income available for the more expensive medical, nutritional, care-providing, and educational services that produce health, safety, and well being for the larger population of the U.S. It should be noted that *per capita* income differentials are smaller.

Source: *Source*: U.S. Department of Health and Human Services. National Center for Health Statistics. *National Vital Statistics Reports*. Vol. 47. No. 28. December 13, 1999. Online. 2002. Available: www.cdc.gov/nchs/data/nvsr/nvsr47/nvs47_28.pdf. Death rates due to accidents and violence are also from NCHS but were obtained from *Statistical Abstract of the United States*, 2001, Table 113, p. 86.

More Elders, Fewer Children

Elderly and Young as Percent of the Population
1850, 1900, 1950, and 2000

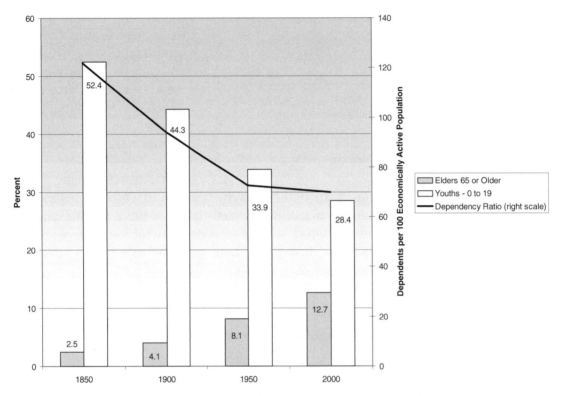

Growing life expectancy and decreasing fertility (discussed under the last topic), have resulted in an increase in the elderly population (those 65 years old and older) and a smaller population of children and youths (the cohorts aged 0 to 19 years).

The graphic charts this phenomenon over a period of 150 years.

We are now ready to answer the question posed in the introduction to this topic. Are we living too long? Will the support of masses of dependents — the young and the old — bankrupt those who are in the middle?

It appears that the answer is "No." Demographers speak of a dependency ratio. This is the number of people — the young and the old — whom the economically active population in the middle must support. The ratio in 2000 was 70, i.e., 100 economically active people had to support 70 others, a mixture of children, youths, and the retired.

In 1850, the dependency ratio was much higher — 122. Translated to the household level, this meant (roughly) that a couple had to care for two children and an elderly person. Dependents were overwhelmingly the young, in those days, not the elderly. Pneumonia carried off the old in the days before sulfa drugs were invented. By 2000 the situation had changed. The elderly population had risen to 12.7% of the total population, up from 2.5% in 1850 and 4.1% in 1900. But children and youths, who had been more than half of the population in the middle of the 19th century, were less than a third of total population in 2000. In effect, the number of dependents per economically active adult had declined from 1.22 to less than one person (0.7).

What has changed — whether we look back 100 or 150 years — is that care of the elderly has become an institutionalized social endeavor, with cross-generational transfer payments (Social Security) having a recognizable budgetary form at the national level. Another change is that improvements in pharmaceutical and medical interventions have significantly increased the costs of caring for the elderly. Finally, the Baby Boom, which began in the late 1940s, will significantly increase the number of those retiring in the early part of the 21st century. Will *that* have a severe impact?

A good deal of discussion surrounds the subject now and will in coming years. But the dependency ratio, although it is predicted to rise (after a drop by 2010 and again by 2020) to 86 per 100 economically active by 2030 — this number is well below the level that the 19th century took in its stride.

May you live long and have many children.

Source: U.S. Bureau of the Census. *Population Estimates,* and *Historical Statistics of the United States.*

Racial Profile of a Century

U.S. Population by Race
(Percent of Total Population, 1900 to 2000)

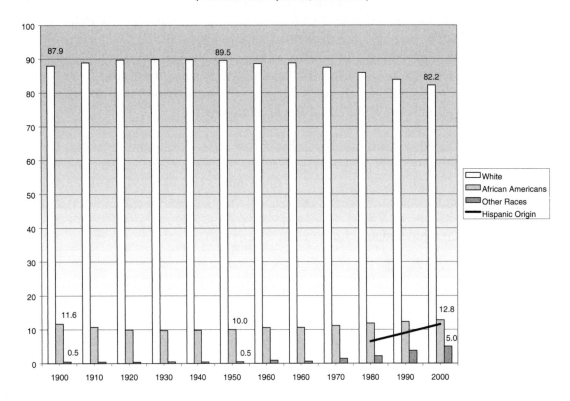

During the 20th century, the population of the United States was predominantly of the Caucasian race — people of European origin. Whites had the highest population share in 1930 and 1940. In both of those census years, whites had an 89.8% share — 90% in round numbers. African Americans, the second largest racial group, declined in population share from 1900 (11.6%) to 1950 (10%). Thereafter, this population has grown, peaking in 2000 at just under 13%.

In 2000, 226 million whites, 35 million blacks, and nearly 14 million people classified as Asians or Native North Americans made up humanity in the United States.

"Other Races," shown in the graphic, includes American Indians, Eskimos, Aleuts, Asians, and Pacific Islanders.[5] These Other Races were around 0.5% of the population for the first half of the century. They increased ten-fold in the second half, reaching 5% of the population in 2000. Of this population, 13.6 million people, 82% were Asians and Pacific Islanders and 18% American Indians, Eskimos, and Aleuts. The growth of this racial group was stimulated by immigration from Asia.

---

[5] This terminology dates from 1980. In earlier times, American Indians, Japanese, and Chinese were specifically identified; other groups were summed; the largest element within that group was Filipinos.

Beginning in 1980, population came to be regarded through yet another lens. Ethnicity was added to the definition to identify, specifically, a population that had predominantly Latin American origins. Thus race *and* ethnicity are usually reported in demographic and health statistics. This is the Hispanic category and refers to people with origins in Latin America. The majority of Hispanics are of Caucasian race; some are black. The government's statistical reports always state that "Persons of Hispanic origin may be of any race." This category, while not racial in character, is recognized in the graphic with a curve from 1980 to 2000. The population of Hispanic origin was 6.4, 9, and 11.5% of the population in 1980, 1990, and 2000, respectively. Hispanics represent a population just over 23 million people.

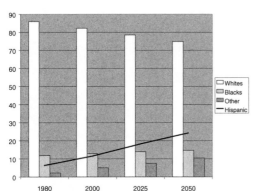

Future trends, based on population projections, indicate that the white population will continue to lose its share of the total population. To show the trend from past into future, data for 1980, 2000, 2025, and 2050 are shown in the inset. Future years, of course, are estimates, and could be affected by future policies relating to immigration.

Note in this projection that the non-racial group, the Hispanic population, shown by the curve, becomes the dominant "minority" population soon after 2000.

Source: U.S. Bureau of the Census. Historical data from *Historical Statistics of the United States,* published by the same agency.

Chapter 2

Where Do We Live?

In answering the question posed in this chapter, we go a bit back and start at a time when we had a total population of under 4 million, in 1790. At that time the entire urban population of the United States was smaller than the population of Amarillo, Texas, is today. Then we lived in the country. Now we live in the cities. In fact, the largest single population concentration is in the suburbs that surround our cities.

We explore this subject in two panels and also look at the density of our settlement. We are now 80% urbanized, but we still have lots and lots of room, especially in comparison with other countries around the world.

We turn next to housing and, in three panels, examine trends in housing stock. The big trend is that we are building ever-bigger homes, but that most of us are still living in fairly small amounts of space. The dream of home ownership continues, but some groupings still rent more than they own.

We look next at the interesting change in our regional distribution across the United States and examine how settlement patterns have changed over the period of a century. These patterns of population shift led to the examination of our mobility. We have certainly moved about a great deal during our history. Are we still doing it? The last panel in this chapter presents some information on our restless to and fro.

Town and Country, Now and Then

Rural and Urban Population
1790 to 2000

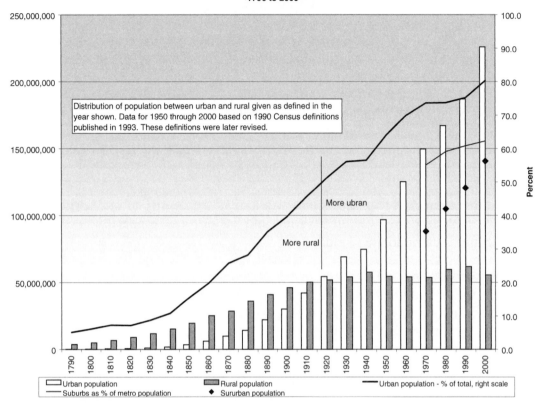

The graphic depicts how we have lived for most of the history of the United States. Until somewhere in the late 1910s, we were predominantly a rural country living on farms or in small towns. Since 1920, we've become ever more urban. In 2000, 80% of us lived in large metropolitan areas. Within those areas, the majority of us (62.2% — just shy of two-thirds) lived in areas classified by the government as suburbs. A more exact subdivision is shown in the following table:

Where the Population Lived (% of total population)

Areas	In 1970	In 2000	Change, 1970 to 2000
Metropolitan areas	78.70	80.30	1.6
Central cities	35.35	30.32	-5.0
Suburbs	43.37	49.97	6.6
Nonmetropolitan areas	21.28	19.70	-1.6

The table shows that the population is growing in the urbanized areas (or moving there) and that within the metro areas, the growth is in the suburbs, whether by increase or by relocation.

While these data show "share of the living space," and two of the categories show losses in "share," all of these sectors had positive population increase as shown in the next table.

Annual Rate of Population growth, 1970 to 2000 - %

Areas	Growth
Total population	1.09
Metropolitan areas	1.16
Central cities	0.57
Suburbs	1.57
Nonmetropolitan areas	0.83

Population grew at a faster rate in the nonmetropolitan areas than in central cities. The strongest growth was experienced in the suburbs.

Note, please, that the concept "metropolitan area" first came to be officially fixed in 1949 by the Bureau of the Budget, predecessor of the U.S. Office of Management and Budget (part of the Office of the President) an office that still defines the standards for city designations. Since that time, the definition of an urban area has changed at regular intervals. The last change was made in 1999.

Under the current definition, a Metropolitan Statistical Areas (MSAs) must be a city with 50,000 or more people or an urbanized core area, e.g., a county, of the same size and a total area population of 100,000 (75,000 in New England). Within these areas, the central city or county is the densely urbanized core; areas beyond it are suburbs. The suburbs, of course, are usually incorporated places with distinct names of their own.[1]

We make these necessary distinctions by way of indicating that the "nonmetropolitan" areas should not be visualized as lonely farms in the country. They are sometimes that. They are also small towns with small-to-moderate- populations.

In the next panel we look more closely at recent years in the context of population density.

Source: U.S. Bureau of the Census, 1990 Census Tabulations, "Population and Housing Unit Counts," and "Population Change and Distribution," Census Bureau 2000 Brief, April 2001 for historical and 2000 population data. Data on suburbs from the SOCDS database, distributed by U.S. Department of Housing and Urban Development. Online. Available: socds.huduser.org/index.html and from *Statistical Abstract of the United States*, 2001, 121st ed. Washington, DC: U.S. Government Printing Office, 2001, Appendix II, p. 892.

---

[1] MSAs are sometimes freestanding, sometimes parts of larger aggregates. CMSAs are consolidated metropolitan statistical areas that have a number of MSAs. These components are then called PMSAs or primary metropolitan statistical areas. The hierarchy is freestanding MSA; next comes the PMSA which is part of a larger aggregate; the larger aggregate, holding multiple PMSAs, is the CMSA.

Urbanization and Density

Metro and Nonmetro Population and Population Density

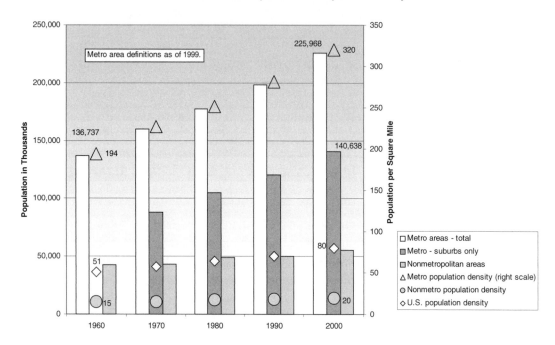

As we crowd into metro areas, are we getting more crowded? It seems that we are. The graphic shows population distribution by the urban, suburban, and nonmetropolitan categories for the more recent 40 years along with population density, measured as the number of people per square mile of land areas (bodies of water, including rivers, are excluded).

In 1960 the national density was 51 persons per square mile; by 2000 this value was up to 80 people. We need not be alarmed. In India, the density is more than a hundred times greater (897) and it is three-and-a-half times higher in France (283) — a romantic tourist destination.[2]

In our metropolitan areas, density increased from 194 people per square mile to 320 in 2000. The 2000 value provides a half an acre for each child, woman, and man — which seems a generous amount of space, even after streets, schools, churches, offices, hotels, ball fields, and factories are deducted. Averages, of course, are just that. Most core cities have substantially higher density. The population density of New York City is 26,402, Los Angeles is 7,877, and Houston is 3,372. Overseas, metropolitan density in some lo-

---

[2] The highest in the world is Macao at 73,448, followed by Monaco with 41,235. China has 354. The lowest density reported is 2 for Western Sahara, followed by Mongolia with 4.

cations is even greater. To give an example, Hong Kong, one of the world's denser places, has a density of 18,883 people per square mile of territory.

Rising densities signal that more people are settling into the same areas or that the bounds of metropolitan settlement are not expanding as fast as the population (sprawl). This is supported by patterns of population increase. The fastest growing groups are those with the lowest median family incomes, the Hispanic population and African Americans — populations with high density of settlement (see Chapter 4 – *Ethnicity & Immigration*).

Source: U.S. Bureau of the Census. *Statistical Abstract of the United States, 2001.* 121st ed. Washington, DC: U.S. Government Printing Office, 2001. Data on suburbs are from the SOCDS database, distributed by U.S. Department of Housing and Urban Development. Online. Available: www.socds.huduser.org/index.html.

Housing Trends: Big is Beautiful

The 1997 Housing Stock - Smallest and Largest

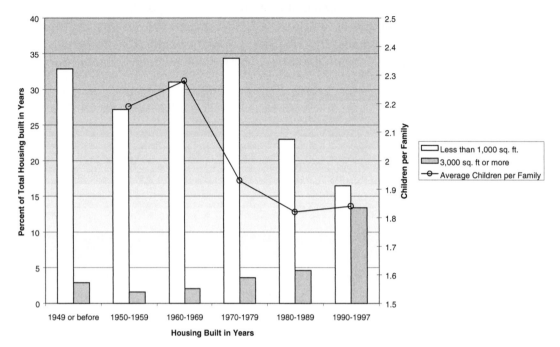

We may live at greater densities in our urban areas, but the trend in housing is toward more room rather than less.

The graph above illustrates trends in construction based on the 1997 residential housing survey conducted by the U.S. Department of Energy. It provides a partial picture of the housing stock in that year, divided by periods in which the housing was constructed. Only the smallest dwelling units (those less than 1,000 square feet of heated floor space) and the largest dwelling units (those with 3,000 square feet or more of heated floor space) are shown.

The idea is to show how construction at the two extremes has fared over a period of 50 years or more. Data are shown as units in these size ranges built in each decade as a percentage of total units built. Units include all kinds of residential construction. The total universe is more than 100,000 dwellings.

The trend is quite striking. Fewer and fewer small dwelling units were built since the 1970s and, since the 1950s, more and more large homes.

The upsurge in the construction of smaller dwellings in the 1960s and 1970s may reflect economic woes, particularly in the 1970s. There was a recession spanning 1960-1961 and another that began in 1969; there were two recessions in the 1970s, the first beginning in 1969 and lasting through almost all of 1970. Another lasted 17 months, beginning in November 1973 and ending in March of 1975. The early 1980s also saw two recessions, but these apparently did not cause a continued gain in the construction of small-footprint dwellings. The 1990s were almost cloudless except for an eight-month downturn in the economy in 1990-1991. Recessions apparently did not dampen our enthusiasm for large homes.

Generally, dwellings with more square footage have increased their share of the housing stock, those with less have dropped in share. This is shown in the table below:

Change in Share, between 1949 or before and 1990-1997

Square Footage Category	Change in Share - %
No estimate provided	-7.48
<1000	-16.36
1,000 to 1,599	2.41
1,600 to 1,999	1.75
2,000 to 2,399	2.78
2,400 to 2,999	6.39
3,000 or more	10.51

Note that in the categories above 1,000 square feet, the greater the square footage, the greater the gain in share. The only exception is in the 1,600 to 1,999 category (about 15% of the housing stock). The trend is clearly toward more space. The decisive loser is the small home.

Other data bear this out. A look at new privately owned one-family houses completed in the 1970 to 1999 period indicates that average floor area has increased from 1,500 to 2,225 square feet in the period. Large homes (2,400 sq. feet and larger), which had a 15% share of this category in 1980, had earned a 34% (and largest) share in 1999.

Economics — rather than an increase in the size of families — has been driving this trend. Since the 1965, when children per family reached a peak of 2.42, the number of children has been in decline, reaching 1.84 in 1997; by 2000, the number had further dropped to 1.75.

Source: U.S. Department of Energy. Energy Information Administration. Office of Energy Markets and End Use. "A Look at Residential Energy Consumption in 1997." (November 1999). Washington, DC: U.S. Government Printing Office. 1999. New construction data are from *Statistical Abstract of the United States, 2001*. Table 938, p. 597.

Housing Trends: But Small Must Do

Square Foot Distribution of 1997 Housing Stock
(Percent of Total Units by Square Footage Category)

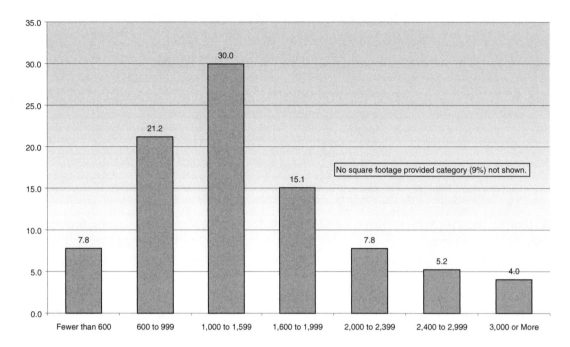

Trends are towards bigger houses, but most of the population continues to live in the housing built over many decades of the past. The graphic displays the 1997 housing stock (built at any time) by percent of total units. Some 9% of the units were reported without square footage; they are omitted.

Using a household size of 2.64 persons, the average in 1997, around 20 million people lived in units 600 square feet or less, 56 million in 600 to 999 square feet, and 80 million in 1,000 to 1,599 square foot units. These three groups, around 157 million people, were about 59% of the population.[3]

The two most spacious groupings — 2,400 to 2,999 square feet and 3,000 square feet and over — represent populations of 13.9 and 10.8 million, together comprising 9% of the population.

Source: U.S. Department of Energy. Energy Information Administration. Office of Energy Markets and End Use. "A Look at Residential Energy Consumption in 1997." (November 1999). Washington, DC: U.S. Government Printing Office. 1999. New construction data are from *Statistical Abstract of the United States, 2001*. Table 938, p. 597.

---

[3] The actual number may be somewhat less. Those with the lowest incomes — presumably living in the less expensive, low-square footage dwellings — have a lower than average number of household members.

Housing Trends: Home Ownership, Yes and No

Owners and Renters in 1999
(Percent of Total Within Each Group)

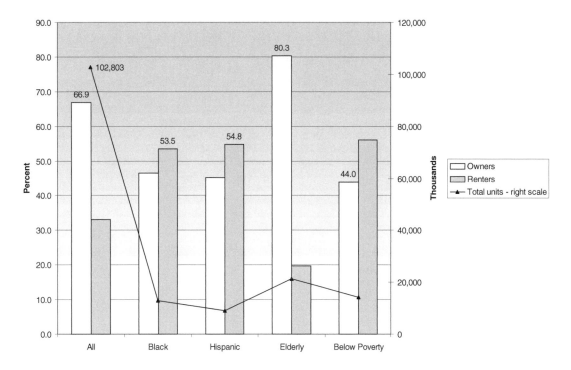

In this last panel on housing trends, we take a look at one important element of the "American Dream" — owning your own home. The dream is far from dead. The percent of households that own their own homes has been increasing at a relentless but slow rate. In 1985, 63.9% of all households owned their own home; this value had increased to 64.7% ten years later and reached 67.4% in 2000.

Significant populations in the United States, however, still lag the overall pattern — as shown in the graphic. It shows that more African American households rent their dwelling (53.5%) than own it. The same is true of the smaller Hispanic population, where the rental rate is 54.8%. The highest homeownership rate is exhibited by those classified as elderly (65 years of age or older). Surprisingly, 44% of all households classified in 1999 as living below the poverty line owned their own home. It can only happen in America. Poverty households were 14.3 million of a total of 102.8 million in 1999.

In 1999, blacks and Hispanics accounted for nearly 35% of total renters, whites and other groups for 65%. Black and Hispanic households that year were 21.4% of total households.

Source: U.S. Bureau of the Census. *Statistical Abstract of the United States, 2001*. 121ˢᵗ ed., Washington, DC: U.S. Government Printing Office, 2001. Table 961, p. 609. Data are drawn from U.S. Bureau of the Census. *Current Housing Reports*.

Living Geographically

Regional Shares of the Population - 1900 to 2000
(Perfent of total population)

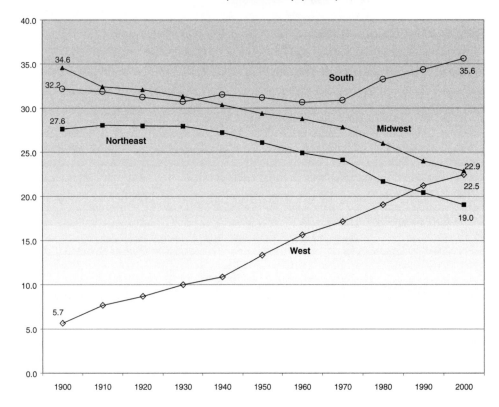

Where do we like to live? Where did our grandparents live? The graphic provides some answers. It shows the geographical location of the population from 1900 to 2000 in ten-year intervals.

In 2000, nearly 36% of people lived in the South and 19% in the Northeast. The Midwest and West each had just shy of 23% of the population, the Midwest edging out the West by a nose — but, based on the growth patterns shown, not for long. The leading states were California (33.9 million) and Texas (20.9 million).

A century earlier, the West had just a sprinkling of people, although a man with the ringing name of John Babsone Lane Soule had written the famous words, "Go west, young man," some 49 years before[4]. California then had a population of 1.48 million. At that time the Midwest was the most populous region, the South a close second, and the Northeast already losing its early dominance — although the two leading states were New York (7.26 million) and Pennsylvania (6.3 million).

---

[4] In the *Terre Haute (Indiana) Express*. The statement is usually credited to Horace Greeley, *New York Tribune*, but Greeley was quoting Soule, whose article he printed in his paper.

During the first half of the century, growth rates were much higher than in the second and set the patterns early. They haven't changed much, although the rates have dropped, as shown in the following table. Periods of most rapid growth are shown in bold.

Annual Population Growth Rates, % per annum, and 2000 Population

Region/Area	1900-1950	1950-2000	1980-2000	1900-2000	Population, Millions.
Northeast	**1.266**	0.613	0.435	0.939	53.6
Midwest	**1.053**	0.744	0.450	0.898	64.4
South	1.318	**1.518**	1.436	1.418	100.2
West	**3.137**	2.308	1.924	2.722	63.2
United States	**1.381**	1.249	1.091	1.314	281.4

From the beginning, the South was a center of agricultural power, beginning with indigo, then tobacco and cotton. Beginning in mid-century, the New South rose and began attracting modern industry. The Midwest drew people with its fertile lands and "amber waves of grain" — also by its stockyards, its "city of big shoulders," Chicago, and the dream of the automobile. The West was gold, frontier, dreams of fame and Hollywood fortune, an enormously productive California agricultural sector and the aerospace industry. And the Northeast began it all with mills of cloth and paper, its mines and shipyards. The Northeast sent forth its children, received new immigrant waves, and still rules the bastions of finance and empires of media.

The land is fairly evenly populated, the West and South expanding their population shares. And everywhere beautiful places beckon — from "sea to shining sea" and places in between.

Source: U.S. Bureau of the Census. "Population and Housing Unit Counts." August 27, 1993, and *Census 2000*.

Moving? We Move About Less

Mobility of the U.S. Population
(People moving as a percent of total population)

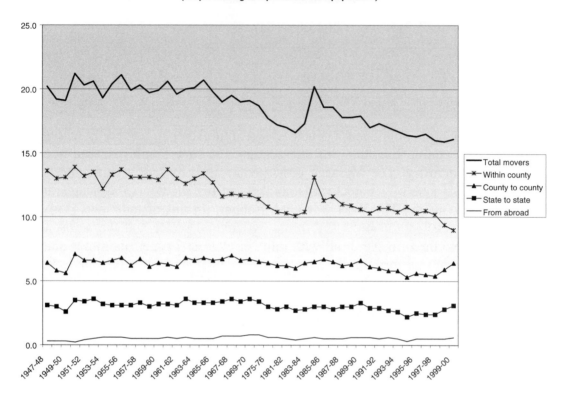

As the last panel suggested, people in the U.S. move a great deal — otherwise the shares of the various regions would not have changed so much over the last century. Americans also like to move at shorter distances. In 2000, 43.4 million people changed their residence (16.1% of the population). Of these 24.4 million (well over half) moved within the same county. 8.4 million (3.2% of the population) moved to another state. Less than a percent of the population moved to the U.S. from abroad.

Overall trends in mobility are down, strongly echoed by local moves within the same county, which constitute the majority of moves. Trends in county-to-county and state-to-state moves are also down, but much less. And the trend in moves from abroad are essentially flat since the midpoint of the last century.

Mobility is influenced by many factors, especially economic. Thus in the recessionary 1970s, moves diminished. In the early 1980s, interest rates were high and mortgages unattractive. The Census Bureau explains the peak in the 1984 to 1985 period as due to the easing of interest rates. A pent-up demand for better housing was vocalized, and the peak is, indirectly, a reflection of the decline in mobility in the previous decade or so.

Who is most likely to move? This is answered by looking at the "moving rate." In the most recent period, 1999 to 2000, Asians and Pacific Islanders had the highest moving rate; 18.4% of them moved. They were closely followed by Hispanics (18.1%) and by African Americans (17.1%). Non-Hispanic whites came last with a 14.4% moving rate.

To quote from the U.S. Census Bureau's *Current Population Reports* (May 2001): "Among people who moved, Hispanics and Blacks were most likely to have moved within the same county (63 and 61 percent, respectively), while White non-Hispanics were most likely to have made intercounty and interstate moves (44 percent)... Asians and Pacific Islanders and Hispanics were much more likely than Blacks or White non-Hispanics to have come to the United States from Abroad."

The regional pattern of moves for the 1999 to 2000 period is depicted in the following table. The South has been the biggest net gainer, the Northeast the biggest net loser of population:

Population Changes by Region (in thousands)

Region	Gains	Losses	Net
Northeast	363	615	-252
Midwest	722	640	82
South	1,258	1,031	227
West	763	820	-57

In this more recent period, greater numbers of poor people have moved than wealthier — perhaps because those big-footprint homes are comfortable, at last. Central cities have lost population to the suburbs and rural areas to the cities.

Source: U.S. Bureau of the Census. *Annual Geographical Mobility Rates, By Type of Movement: 1947-2000*. July 12, 2000. Online. Available: http://www.census.gov/population/www/socdemo/migrate.html.

Chapter 3

The Family

Early in the 20th century, the Census Bureau used to keep track of families with their own households and those who lived with others. Young couples were often living with one of the parents in the ancestral household — the farm. As the century closed out and the Census Bureau took the 2000 census, bureaucrats recorded same-sex partner households for the first time ever. Things have changed a great deal in a hundred years, indeed, in 50 years. And there might be a return to the older ways as well. In the 12 panels of this chapter, we attempt, briefly, to encapsulate a lot of change, a lot of trends.

We start by looking at households — how they have changed in definition and why. Non-family households (predominantly single people) are a new and growing phenomenon — of which the gay-couple household is a tiny subset. Next we look more closely at family households and note the rise of the single-parent phenomenon. Most affected by these changes are children — and so we look at how children are distributed across the family spectrum.

The dramatic rise in single-parent families prompted a searching look at the state of marriage — and what has become, of late, its lengthening shadow: divorce. The demographics of marriage show interesting patterns — in the exploration of which we look at *when* people marry. Why do we, these days, marry as late as people did in the late 18th century? Are the same factors at work — or new ones? Rather startling differences in the view of marriage show up between whites and blacks. We explore these next. And then we look at marriages between members of different races — which is on the rise.

While, on the whole, marriage appears to be alive and well, how we reach that state — and why some of us never do — is the subject of some panels. We look at cohabitation, single-parent families, and the prevalence of same-sex households across the nation.

Throughout, we report on children and how they fare. The final panel gets right down to business. How much does it cost to raise a child? Have costs gone up? Where does our money go, now as opposed to a few years ago?

Households in the U.S.

Average Number of People per U. S. Household in the 20th Century

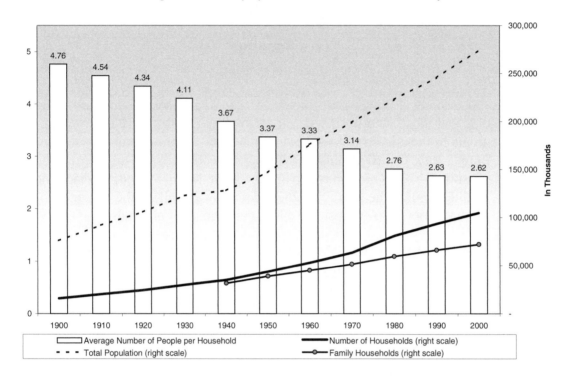

The household is the most basic building block of society. Our living arrangements, and the ways in which we organize our households, tell us a great deal about society's organization, too. Household statistics over the last century reveal dramatic changes. Household sizes are down — and a new kind of household has emerged — recognized for the first time in 1940 by the U.S. Bureau of the Census: Non-Family Households[1]. Even the definition of what "household" means has changed during the century.

The chart presents an overview of households from 1900 to 2000 by decade. The bars present the average number of individuals in a household. The lines present overall population, total number of households, and the number of family households. By inferences, the number of non-family households is the difference between the number of family households and the total number of households.

A family household consists of two or more people related by blood, marriage, or adoption. A non-family household can be a person living alone or an individual living with others to whom he or she is not related. In 1940, the first year in which this bifurcation in households was officially noted, non-family households accounted for 10% (3,458,000) of all households. Sixty years later, non-family households accounted for 31%

---

[1] Interestingly, the U.S. Bureau of the Census used to keep track of another division of households. It differentiated between married couples with their own households and those without their own households.

(32,680,000) of households. Of these, 82% (26,724,000) were households made up of single individuals — nearly a quarter of all households in 2000! This fact alone accounts for much of the decline in the average number of persons per hearth.

A clear trend towards smaller households is apparent[2]. What explains this trend? We saw in Chapter 1 that the fertility rate has been declining. We're not having as many children. We're also living longer. The elderly often live alone or with a spouse. Thus the number of single and two-person households is bolstered by our increasing life expectancy. We marry later; the divorce rate is up. Both of these factors mean that people live on their own longer. As women have entered the workforce in ever-greater numbers — and as their incomes have increased (although still shy of men's incomes on average) — women have been economically able to maintain households on their own.

There is also the matter of rising prosperity. In the early part of the century, households spent much more of income on the residence itself than they do today. We can afford the luxury of having our own places now. And many of us do.

In the next panels we look at the groups that form our family and non-family households and begin to try and answer the question: What's happening with the family?

Source: U.S. Bureau of the Census. *Current Population Reports.* Series P20-537. "America's Families and Living Arrangements: March 2000."; *Households by Type: 1940 to Present* (an historical compilation table). Online. Available: http://www.census.gov/population/socdemo/hh-fam/tabHH-1.txt June 29, 2001; *Historical Statistics of the United States — Colonial Times to 1970,* page 15; Statistical *Abstract of the United States 2001.* 121ˢᵗ ed. p. 14 and 15.

---

[2] The trend in housing size, however, is going in the opposite direction, towards larger houses. For more on that subject, please see the previous chapter.

Family Households With Children

Family Households with Their Own Children Under 18, 1970 -- 2000 by Decade

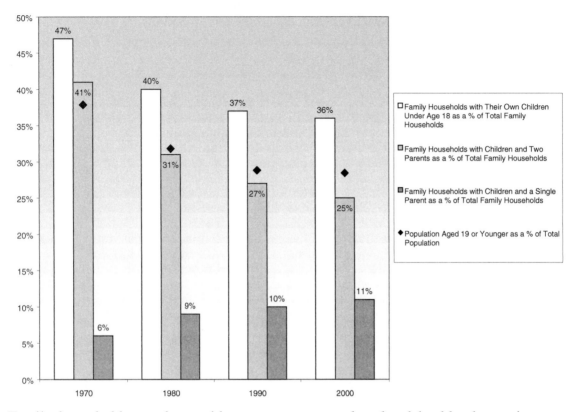

Family households are those with two or more people related by blood, marriage, or adoption. This chart presents data on family households that include unmarried children under the age of 18 years. The first bar is all families with children under 18. The second and third bars disaggregate this total into married-couple and single-parent households, both with children under 18.

As we saw in the previous panel, the number of households that fit the "family household" category has declined. The number of family households with children is also declining as a percentage of all family households.

In part this decline is due to the fact that the under-18 age group has dropped as a percent of population. The diamond-shaped markers indicate the percentage of the population aged 19 years or younger[3]. Young people have declined as a percentage of total popula-

---

[3] The figures for those 17 and younger (numbers that would more directly correlate to the family households with children under 18) are not easily available. Nonetheless, the 19 and under percentage of the population indicates the general decline in the youngest cohort of our society.

tion between 1970 and 1980 — from 38 to 32%. In the 1970s the last of the Baby Boom generation was still in its teens. By the 1980s, boomers were all into their twenties. Not surprisingly, families with children under 18 are down.

The number of families made up of Mom, Dad, and children also has declined. Single-parent households have almost doubled — from 6% to 11% — in the 30-year period presented here. If we look at married couples and single-parent households as a percentage of family households with children, instead of as a percentage of all family households (including those without children), the rise in single-parent households is even more pronounced.

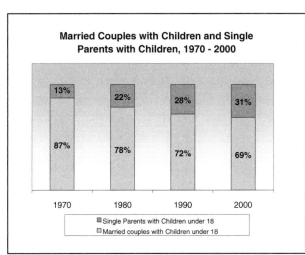

The top portion of each of the bars to the left represents that percentage of households with children under 18 and a single parent — 13% in 1970, just over a tenth of families with children. In 2000 that figure had risen to 31%, just shy of one-third of all families with children under 18.

Many factors influence the rise in single-parent households. To name two: children born to unwed mothers have risen in number; the number of divorcing couples who have children has increased[4]. In the next panel, we will look at children living in various arrangements. Here, we limit the discussion to the percentage of households and not the number of children involved.

Households in the United States have lost "membership," as we have seen: fewer people per household. In this panel we have seen the decline in both percent of the population age 19 or younger and percent of family households raising young children. Has the number of children per family also declined? How many children are living in single-parent versus two-parent households? These are the questions we turn to next.

Source: U.S. Bureau of the Census. *All Parent Child Situations by Type, Race, and Hispanic Origin of Householder or Reference Person, 1970 to Present.* Online. Available: http://www.census.gov/population/socdemo/hh-fam/tabHH-1.txt. June 29, 2001. Data are based on the *Current Population Survey*; *America's Families and Living Arrangements 2000. Current Population Report* issued in June 2001.

---

[4] Primary reasons for increase in the number of single parent households comes from the "America's Families and Living Arrangements." See source note for a full citation.

Mom, Dad, and Two Children — Does the Pattern Still Hold?

Number of Children, Under the Age of 18, by Living Arrangement in 2000

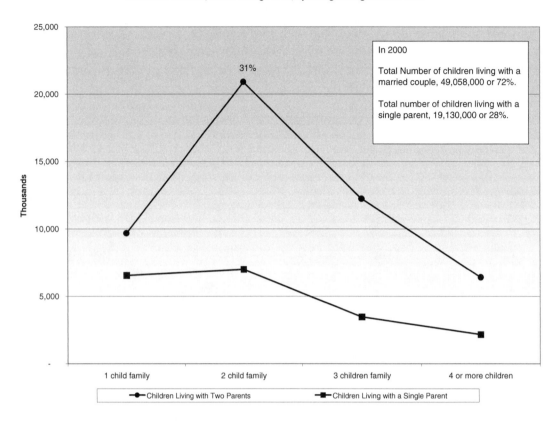

In 2000

Total Number of children living with a married couple, 49,058,000 or 72%.

Total number of children living with a single parent, 19,130,000 or 28%.

Since the 1970s, more and more children are being raised in single-parent homes. Nonetheless, as the graphic shows, most children are being raised in two-parent families — at least for a part of their childhood. The graphic is a snapshot of the year 2000 and does not attempt to illustrate a trend.

The top line shows the number of children, by size of family, in two-parent households. Despite the impression that the "typical" family of four is no longer with us, data suggest that it's a standard that has yet to be displaced. The greatest number of children in any of the eight family arrangements listed above is in a "traditional" family of four. In the year 2000, 31% of children were living with two parents and a sibling; 72% were living with two parents.

This having been said, it is true that as we enter the 21st century, many more children in the United States are being raised by a single parent than ever before. This is of the greatest importance — at least for the well-being of the children. Two parents have more money than one — and other resources as well. In turn, family resources have a direct bearing on the children's prospects.

Single-parent homes run by women are far more likely to live below the poverty line than any two-parent households (women typically earn less than men). In 2000, 32% of single-mother households lived below the poverty line. While this is a high number, it represents a 12% improvement over the situation that existed just ten years before. The corresponding figures for married-couple families with children were 7.8% living below poverty in 1990 and 6% in 2000.

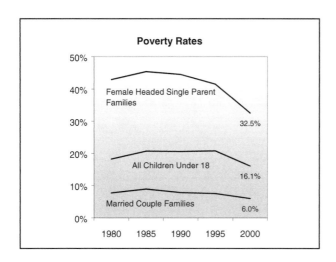

Although the *decline* in poverty rate for single-parent, female-headed households with children has been greater than that experienced by married couples raising children, as can be seen in the graphic, the poverty rate itself remains much higher. Two parents, even if both work, are better able to provide financially — and some would argue emotionally — for children. If both work, they are more likely to be able to afford daycare. If one stays at home — that *is* daycare.

More than 55% of all children living below the poverty line were in households headed by a single mom. Single-parent households accounted for 28% of all children. A child, therefore, is four times more likely to live below the poverty line if he or she lives with mother only.

This fact is part of the motivation behind the George W. Bush Administration's marriage initiative — a sort of marriage education and promotion program — a key element of any reauthorized Welfare Reform Act. The idea is clear enough. If children reared in two-parent homes have better outcomes (fewer live in poverty, fewer drop out of school) then one way to address the problem is to increase the number of children living in two-parent homes. Get young mothers and fathers to the chapel.

Many circles have cried Foul at the Bush Administration's marriage initiative. Some groups fear that it's an attack on women's independence and would force poor, young women into unwanted marriages with irresponsible or even violent men. Others argue that the real problem is early, out-of-wedlock births and that, therefore, sex education and birth control are better areas in which to invest than is the promotion of marriage.

It is not clear whether or not the marriage initiative will become a part of the next Welfare Reform Act. What is clear is the fact that the decline in the number of marriages is seen by some as a cause for problems in the social order. How much has the rate of marriage declined over the last decades? This is what we will address in the next panel.

Source: U. S. Bureau of the Census. *America's Families and Living Arrangements 2000. Current Population Reports.* Issued June 2001.

Marriage in the 20th Century

Marriages and Divorces Annually, 1900 -- 2000

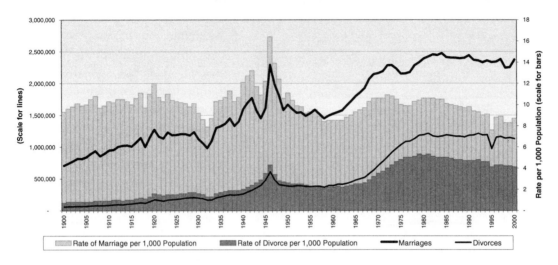

For people making a living in the "wedding business" — wedding planners, banquet halls, and the like — business has been good. The later half of the 20th century saw a lot of weddings. The peak year was 1984 when 2,477,000 couples were united in holy matrimony. The rate of marriage per thousand population that year was 10.5, just over the century average of 10.14. The bars on this chart show rates of marriage and divorce per thousand population, a measure that allows for greater trend analysis as it corrects for changes in population.

There has been a slight decline in the rate at which we married during the 20th century. We started the century with a rate of 9.3 and ended it with a rate of 8.7; both rates are below the century average. Notable peaks occurred in post-war eras. The sharpest of these was immediately following World War II when our rate of marriage per thousand population shot up to 16.4, 162% of the century average. It was this peak in marriages that lead directly to the Baby Boom and the demographic shock wave that the Boom has

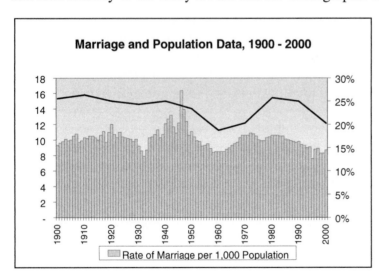

been to all aspects of social life in the second half of the century.

A chart showing annual marriage figures and population data only can be useful in identifying some of the dynamics behind the decline in the marriage rate. This chart presents the annual marriage rate per thousand population in the form of bars and a line for the percentage of the population made up of those in the "prime" marriage years, between the ages of 20 and 34. The patterns produced by the two data series are remarkably similar, suggesting that the rate at which we marry is directly linked with the age demographic of our society. Worth noting is the fact that the marriage rate listed here includes not only first marriages but second, third, fourth, and, in the case Elizabeth Taylor, eighth marriages too. Which leads us to divorce.

The rate of divorce, which can be seen on the main graph, has a similar pattern to that of marriage. The divorce rate rose throughout the first four-fifths of the century, peaking in 1979 and 1981 and declining thereafter. The rate of divorce shows less fluctuation, the peaks being lower and the valleys shallower but the overall pattern is very similar to that produced by the marriage rate. The century started with many fewer divorces annually than marriages. It ended with these two rates having come much closer together. In the year 2000, the rate of marriage was 8.7 per thousand population and the rate of divorce was 4.1, almost half that of marriage[5].

Marriage has not gone out of style. We are still as likely to marry in a lifetime as we were a century ago, the odds being 9 to 1 in favor of a person marrying by middle age. However, we are marrying later in life and although the institution of marriage seems to have a lasting appeal the marriages themselves are not lasting as long.

Source: U.S. Centers for Disease Control. National Center for Health Statistics. *Fast Stats A to Z Marriage.* Online. Available: http://www.cdc.gov/nchs/fastats/marriage.htm; National Vital Statistics Report. August 22, 2001. *Births, Marriages, Divorces, and Deaths: Provisional Data for January-December 2000*; National Vital Statistics Report. July 6, 1999. *Births, Marriages, Divorces, and Deaths: Provisional Data for 1998.* U.S. Bureau of the Census. *Statistical Abstract of the United States 2001.* 121st ed. Washington, DC: U.S. Government Printing Office. 2001, p. 59, table 68; U.S. Department of Health, Education and Welfare. Public Health Service. Vital and Health Statistics Series 21. No. 24. December 1973. *Marriages, divorces, and rates: United States, 1867—1967.*

---

[5] It is from an analysis of a single year's worth of Census Bureau data on marriage and divorce that the following erroneous but often-quoted statement comes — "50% of all marriages end in divorce." For a number of years — 1976, 1977, 1979, 1981, 1991-5, 1998 and 1999 — the number of divorces filed equaled half or more of the number of marriages entered into in that year. If this pattern were to continue unabated than the quoted statement would become true in about the year 2030.

Older Grooms, Older Brides

Median Age at First Marriage

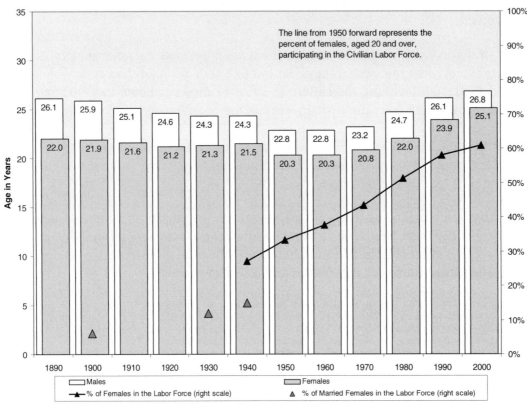

This chart shows the median age (half are younger and half are older) at which men and women in the United States have been entering a first marriage since 1890. Men marry a bit later in life than do women on average, but this difference in age has diminished from 4 years in 1900 to 1.7 years in 2000.

The pattern over the last century suggests that in the late 1800s people entered marriage later in life than was the norm for most of the 20th century. As we enter the 21st century we are again delaying marriage. The median age at first marriage for women has seen a greater change over the period than has that for men. The rate for men started at 26.1 and was, 100 years later, again 26.1 having dipped during the intervening years. In the year 2000 the age reached a high of 26.8 years.

Women started the period shown with a median age at first marriage of 22 years. Like men, women saw that age drop during most of the following decades. The rate again reached 22 years in 1980. In the following 20 years, women delayed marriage at ever-greater rates and, by the year 2000, the median age at first marriage had reached a high of 25.1 years. The change for women has been greater than for men. What's behind this change?

The two most cited reasons for the delay in marriage are, first, increased participation of women in the workforce and diminished economic dependence on men. The chart provides a line that shows the participation of women in the labor force as a percentage of all women aged 20 years or older. As the women of the Baby Boom generation reached maturity they began in ever-greater numbers to pursue college degrees[6]. In many cases these degrees led to employment opportunities in careers and jobs that placed greater demands on time than the traditional 9-to-5 occupation. In the pursuit of these activities many women put off marriage and child bearing.

The second factor commonly cited for the delay of marriage is the sexual revolution that dates to the mid-1960s and coincides with the advent of highly dependable methods of birth control.

Although we are entering first marriages a bit later in life, an estimated half of these marriages are proceeded by an extended period of cohabitation. The number of couples cohabiting has increased dramatically over the last 40 years, from under half a million in 1960 to over 4.7 million in 2000. Various theories explaining the rise in cohabitation among the young suggest that cohabitation, although appearing to be an alternative to marriage, is more often entered *not* as an

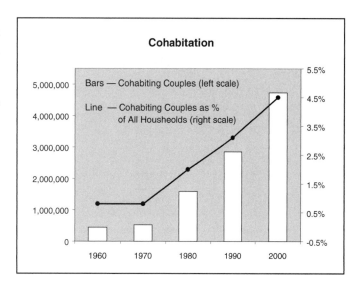

alternative to marriage but rather as a precursor to marriage (Kenney). Cohabitation is another factor delaying the entrée to first marriage.

The factors involved in deciding whether or not to marry and, if so, when, are complex. Disentangling them is not a simple matter. What is remarkable is the resilience and persistence of the institution of marriage in the face of dramatic changes in the economic role of marriage in our society.

How much do the trends in marriage differ by race? That is what we will look at next.

Sources: U.S. Bureau of the Census. *America's Families and Living Arrangements 2000. Current Population Reports.* June 2001; *Estimated Age at First Marriage: by Sex, 1890 to Present.* Online. Available: http://www.census.gov/population/socdemo/ms-la/tabms-2.txt. January 1999. Kenney, Catherine T. "Marriage Delayed or Marriage Forgone? New Cohort Forecasts of First Marriage for U.S. Women." *American Sociological Review.* (August 2001) vol. 66, pp. 506-519.

---

[6] In the early 1980s women began to earn more bachelor degrees than men and have done so ever since. For more on this subject see the Trends in Post-Secondary Education chapter of the Community and Education volume of this series.

Racial Differences on Marriage

Adult Population Never Married, 1950 -- 2000

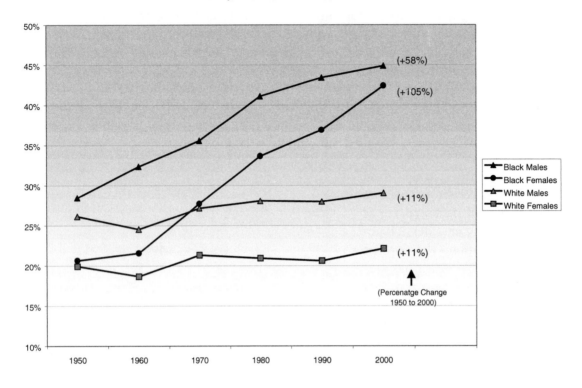

The chart shows the number of adults (defined here as anyone over 15) who have never been married. The figures for white and black males and females are charted. Changes in the percentages of adults never married over the last half of the 20th century are much greater for blacks than for whites, although for all categories there are more of us who have never married at the end of the period than at the beginning.

As we saw in the previous panel, much of this change can be attributed to later entry into a first marriage. But the striking rise in the number of black men and women who have never married is worth further exploration.

A look at demographic data by gender shows a large difference between whites and blacks in the age range at which most of us marry. There are fewer black men in the age range 20 to 53 than there are black women. This fact, in combination with higher rates of murder, accidental death, incarceration, and chronic unemployment for black men as compared with white men accounts to some extent for the difference in the numbers of blacks and whites who have

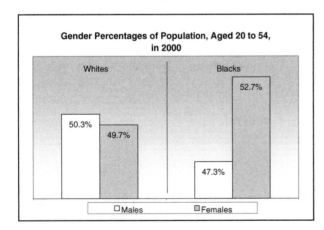

never married. However, because almost the same sex ratios existed in the year 1950 as did in the year 2000, these gender balance differences alone do not explain the sharp increase in never-married blacks versus never-married whites in the last 50 years of the 20th century.

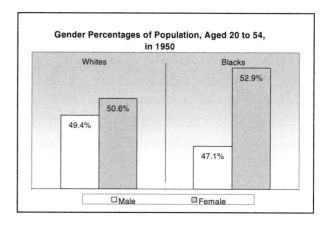

Explanations for the rapid decline in marriage among blacks come in two primary flavors: economic and cultural.

In his influential 1987 book, *The Truly Disadvantaged*, Dr. William Julius Wilson presents the economic argument. He makes the case that the truly disadvantaged (the new underclass made up primarily of black unmarried mothers and the jobless fathers of their children) are largely the result of the deindustrialization of the inner city. As high-paying manufacturing jobs left the urban centers, young unskilled men were left with few employment opportunities and young women refused to marry financially unstable men.

The cultural argument is one that associates the decline in the marriage rate to a breakdown of social norms, expectations, and institutions generally. The fact that the black community has seen its rate of marriage decline faster than rates overall merely means that the social norms and expectations supporting marriage in the black community have deteriorated more quickly than they appear to have done so in the society at large.

Some proponents of both economic and cultural causation point to 40 years of social welfare policies as an additional cause for the decline in marriages among the poor. It is said that social welfare policies intended to assist single mothers inadvertently served to encourage single motherhood and further undermined the institution of marriage.

In 1998 a group of prominent black leaders gathered at Morehouse College in Atlanta, Georgia, to confer on the subject of African-American fathers and families. The resulting statement paper entitled *Turning the Corner on Father Absence in Black America* rejects the economic versus cultural dichotomy in favor of a call to action. Co-author of the statement, Enola G. Aird, put it this way: "The heartrending crisis of black father absence that African-American children suffer has cultural, economic and spiritual roots. Addressing all of these to strengthen marriage and fatherhood in the Black community should be our most urgent priority."

Source: U.S. Bureau of the Census. *Marital Status of the Population 15 Years Old and Over by Sex and Race: 1950 to Present*. Online. June 29, 2001; *Race and Hispanic or Latino Origin by Age and Sex for the United States: 2000*. Online. Available: http://www.census.gov/population/www/cen2000/briefs.html. The quote from Enola G. Aird is from a press release issued by the Institute for American Values. Their web site is accessible at http://www.americanvalues. org/index.html

Interracial Marriages Are Becoming More Common

Interracial Married Couples, 1960 -- 2000

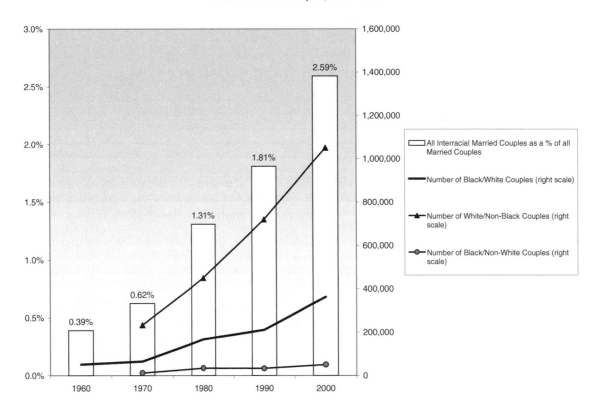

Over the 40 years covered by the chart above, the United States has seen its population of interracial married couples grow sharply, from 157,000 couples in 1960 to 1,464,000 in 2000. This is not surprising when one considers that until 1967 interracial marriage was illegal in more than 20 states. In 1967 the U.S. Supreme Court ruled in *Loving v. Virginia*, a case brought by an interracial married couple attempting to live freely and openly in Virginia. The court found that a ban on interracial marriage was unconstitutional. In the years that followed, there was a predictable increase in the number of mixed marriages.

The total number of married couples in the U.S. increased by 40% between the years 1960 and 2000. The increase in interracial marriages was an astounding 832%. Although still a small percentage of all couples (2.59% in 2000), interracial couples are becoming somewhat more common, and they certainly no longer have to skirt the law or cross a state border in order to wed.

The chart uses bars to show the percent of all married couples that is composed of interracial couples and lines to present data on the number of interracial couples by race combinations[7].

Race breakdown of Interracial Couples
(Presented as a percentage of all interracial couples)

Racial Categories	1970	1980	1990	2000	% Change
Black and White	21.0%	25.7%	21.9%	24.8%	18.3%
White and Asian/Pacific Islander or Native American	75.2%	69.1%	74.7%	71.8%	-4.5%
Black and Asian/Pacific Islander or Native American	3.9%	5.2%	3.4%	3.4%	-11.8%

The number of black/white couples has risen most over the period. However, the group that represents the largest number of mixed marriages is the white partnered with a non-black, i.e. white/Asian or Pacific Islander or white/Native American. Although this category has seen a slight decline, it still represents almost three-fourths of interracial couples.

One interesting aspect of interracial marriages is the husband/wife/race disparity. One quarter of mixed marriages are black/white couples. Of these, however, nearly three-fourths are black men and white women. Supreme Court Justice Clarence Thomas and his wife Virginia Lamp Thomas are a prominent example of such a couple, not to mention Sidney Poitier and his wife Joanna Shimkus. The exact opposite is true when we look at white/Asian mixed couples. In 1990[8] 72% of white/Asian marriages were like that of Maury Povich and Connie Chung, or John Lennon and Yoko Ono, white males and Asian females.

This situation has led to a growing disapproval of interracial marriage among Asian men and black women[9]. According to Steven Sailer, in an article titled *Is Love Colorblind?* "the heart of the problem is that intermarriage does not treat every sex/race combination equally. On average it offers black men and Asian women new opportunities to find mates among whites, while exposing Asian men and black women to greater competition from whites."

The fact that new groups (Asian men and black women) are joining those opposed to interracial marriage just as interracial marriages become more common suggests that this is a social phenomenon for which predictions are difficult to make. Complicating an already complex subject is the fact that recent studies suggest that our rates of interracial cohabi-

---

[7] Data on the racial combinations of interracial couples was incomplete for 1960.

[8] 1990 is the most recent year for which federal, detailed data on white/Asian couples is available.

[9] As we've seen in the previous panel, there are more young black women than there are black men. Is it any wonder that black women look disapprovingly on anything that reduces further the already small pool of potential same race mates? Read the next panel for more on this subject.

tation are higher than our rates of interracial marriage. Could this portend a continuation or even increased growth rate for interracial marriages? We will have to watch and see.

Sources: U.S. Bureau of the Census. Race of Wife by Race of Husband: 1960, 1970, 1980, 1991 and 1992. Online. Available: http://www.census.gov/population/socdemo/race/interracttab1.txt. (For data for the chart and table*); America's Families and Living Arrangements 2000.* Current Population Reports. June 2001. (for figures for 2000); Sailer, Steven. "Is Love Colorblind?" *National Review*, 14 July 1997. Online. Available: http://www.isteve.com/IsLoveColorblind.htm. ; University of Michigan. "Intimate relationships between the races more common than thought." 23 March 2000. Online. Available: http://www.umich.edu/~newsinfo/Releases/2000/Mar00/r032300a.html. (for cohabitation study data).

Cohabitation: All Part of the New Dating Scene?

Cohabitation

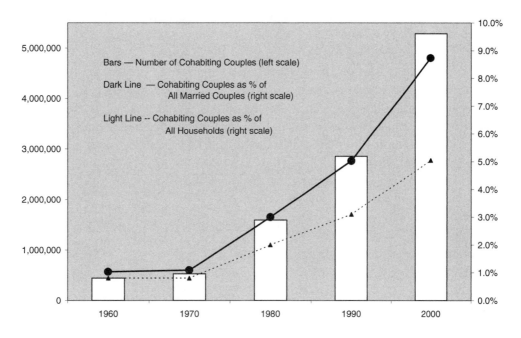

Bars — Number of Cohabiting Couples (left scale)

Dark Line — Cohabiting Couples as % of
All Married Couples (right scale)

Light Line -- Cohabiting Couples as % of
All Households (right scale)

Living in sin is what cohabitation was once routinely called. That time was not so long ago. The last 30 years of the 20th century saw a dramatic rise in the number of couples living together out of wedlock and a growing acceptance of this practice by society at large. This represents a striking change from earlier times. The trend is very clear. We are choosing to cohabit instead of, or in anticipation of, marrying at a rate 12 times higher in 2000 than we did in 1960. Fully 5% of all households are now made up of an unmarried couple living together.

Because cohabitation has only slowly gained acceptance over the period presented on the chart, it is only recently that data are being gathered on the phenomenon in a systematic manner. Only since 1995 has the Census Bureau begun to collect such data consistently. "Unmarried partner" appeared for the first time on the 2000 Census of the U.S. as a relationship category. Once the detailed figures from this census are available, we will have far better statistical data with which to work in gaining an understanding of who exactly cohabits. The data available to date suggests that cohabitation is a very generalized practice.

University of Michigan sociologist Pamela J. Smock, who has studied and written on this subject extensively, offers the following observations. First, and rather predictably, those who choose cohabitation tend to have a "slightly lower" socioeconomic status, be "slightly less" religious, have "slightly more" liberal views and support non-traditional gender and family roles.

What is more interesting is the fact that, according to Dr. Smock, only about 17% of co-habiting couples live together, unmarried, for more than three years. Cohabitation seems to be a short-term arrangement and in more than half the cases it is a prelude to marriage.

An estimated 55% of cohabiting couples will marry their partner within three years. In fact, between the years 1990 and 1994 56% of all marriages were preceded by a period of cohabitation. This suggests that for at least half of those living together, cohabitation can be seen as an intimate extension of old dating patterns. Some argue that the children of divorced parents are particularly concerned with avoiding divorce themselves. They believe that by living together they can more accurately gauge their compatibility with a prospective mate and thus be more "sure" before entering marriage. Sadly, as a widely quoted study found, couples that cohabit prior to marriage actually have a higher risk of divorce than those who do not.

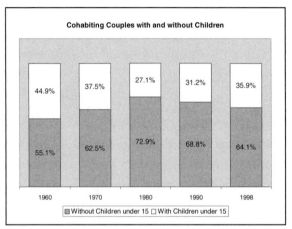

Another aspect of cohabitation that is generating great interest is that a large number of cohabiting couple households include children. The U.S. Census Bureau data for 1998 show a decline in the percentage of cohabiting couples living with children under the age of 15 since 1960. Of course, in 1960, 44.9% of co-habiting households was only 197,000. In 1998, although the percentage of un-married couples living together with children is down, the number of house-holds involved has risen substantially to 1,520,000.

One final point should be made about cohabiting couples and children. Dr. Smock has written, "a large share of children born to supposedly 'single' mothers today are born into two-parent households. Moreover, the widely cited increase in recent years in nonmarital childbearing is largely due to cohabitation, and not to births to women living without partners." Here is an area of great interest to anyone studying the steady rise in single-mother households.

Clearly, cohabitation patterns have changed the look of the American family landscape in the last 30 years. Statistical data collection has not kept pace, but as it catches up we will be better able to understand the present and future significance of this practice on our living arrangements and patterns of family formation.

Source: U.S. Bureau of the Census. *Unmarried-Couple Households, by Presence of Children, 1960 to Present.* Online. Available: http://www.census.gov/population/socdemo/ms-la/tabad-2.txt. January 7, 1999 (for chart data*); Census 2000 Supplementary Survey Profile.* Table 1. Online. Available: http://www.cen- sus.gov/c2ss/www/Profiles/2000/Tabular/010/01000US1.htm. (for 2000 data). Eric Nagourney. "Study Finds Families Bypassing Marriage." *New York Times on the Web,* 15 February 2000, http://www.unl.edu/rhames/courses/212/family_trends/familytrends.htm. (for information about Dr. Pamela Smock's research).

Single-Parent Households

Children in Single Parent Households and Marital Status of Parent, 1960 -- 2000

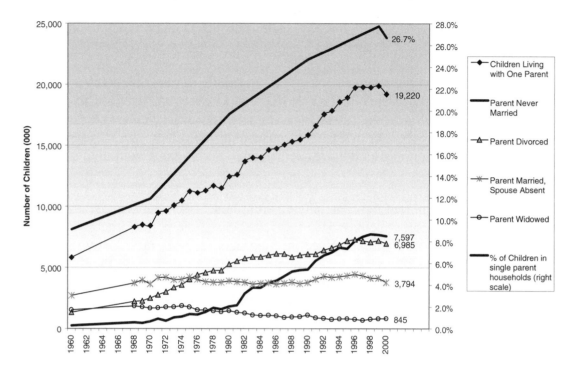

Children in Single Parent Households and Marital Status of Parent, 1960 -- 2000

Earlier in this chapter we saw that 72% of households with children are two-parent households. Now we turn to the 26.7% of households with children being raised by a single parent.[10] Single-parent households have been the subject of much discussion, debate, and study as their numbers have risen over the last 40 years. In 1999 the number of children being raised by a single parent reached a high of 19,899,000, or 27.75% of children under the age of 18.

The chart presents data on the number of children living with one parent only. The top line on the chart presents data as a percentage, the percentage of all children being raised in a single-parent home. The four lines running along the bottom of the chart show the number of children by the marital status of the parent in the household.[11]

The two categories that have seen the most dramatic rise over the period shown and the two that account for the rise in single-parent households are divorced parents (rising 422%) and those who have never married (rising 3,026%). This explains, to some extent,

---

[10] There are also 1.3% of children under the age of 18 being raised by neither parent or in institutional settings.

[11] The use of the term "single parent" in the context of single-parent household means only that one parent is raising the child and does not refer to the marital status of the parent. In some cases the parent is married but the spouse is not present.

why the subject of never-married parents dominates the debate about single-parent households, most of which are single-mother households (84%). This is not to say that divorce escaped great scrutiny during the 1990s. Many popular books like Barbara Dafoe Whitehead's *The Divorce Culture: Rethinking Our Commitments to Marriage and Family*, present a stark picture of the negative impact that divorce has on the children in the families being separated. The question now being raised frequently is: "Should you stay together for the kids?"

Further fueling these discussions have been the sad results of several studies done on the outcomes of children raised in single-parent families. On average, the economic and social well-being of children being raised by a single parent was shown to be lower than that of children being raised in two-parent households. To many, these findings would seem self-evident. It is simply harder for one person to do the same work that two people working together are able to do.

The poverty rate for children living in single-parent homes is five times greater than for children living in two-parent homes. This fact has focused the political debate surrounding welfare reform squarely on the subject of marriage. In 1996, after many false starts, the Personal Responsibility Work Opportunities Reconciliation Act (PRWORA) was signed into law. Under this law the focus of welfare shifted from cash assistance for women and their children to an emphasis on self-sufficiency through work and enhanced financial support and involvement by fathers. One clearly stated intention of this legislation is to reduce out-of-wedlock births and encourage the formation of two-parent families.

Some argue that the solution to poor single-mother households is to go after fathers and make them pay. Others say that preventing out-of-wedlock births in the first place, especially those born to teenaged mothers, is a far better course of action particularly since immature, unprepared, and uneducated teenagers tend to make poor parents whether or not they are married.

The number of single-parent households fell between 1999 and 2000. The number of never-married single parents fell as did the number of divorced single parents. Could this be the beginning of a new trend?

Next we will look at the rates of single-parent families by race. Are there notable differences between the races and ethnicities in this area? Yes.

Source: U.S. Bureau of the Census. *Unmarried-Couple Households, by Presence of Children, 1960 to Present.* Online. Available: http://www.census.gov/population/socdemo/ms-la/tabad-2.txt. (for chart data); *Census 2000 Supplementary Survey Profile.* Table 1. Online. Available: http://www.cen- sus.gov/c2ss/www/Profiles/2000/Tabular/010/01000US1.htm. (for 2000 data); Eric Nagourney. "Study Finds Families Bypassing Marriage." *New York Times on the Web,* 15 February 2000. http://www.unl.edu/rhames/ courses/212/family_trends/familytrends.htm. (for information about Dr. Pamela Smock's research).

Racial Breakdown of Families with Children

Children's Living Arrangements by Race

(Number of children under 18 years of age by race presented at the top of each section)

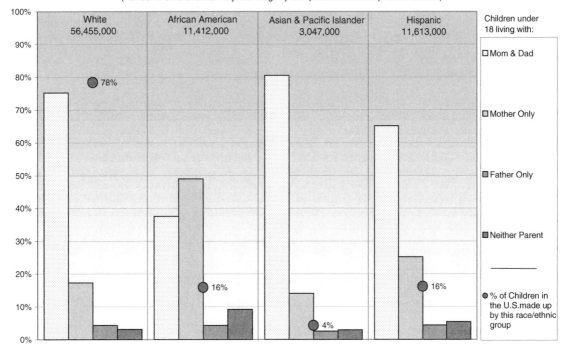

In this panel we take a look at the distribution of single-parent households by race and ethnicity for the most recent period available, March 2000. Four bars are presented for each race as well as for Hispanics[12]. The light bar stands for the percentage of households raising children with two parents in the home. The other bars show the percentages of single-parent households by head of household, mother, father, or neither parent.

Other than for African Americans, two-parent households are by far the most common. Within the black community, this is no longer the case. More than half of all black children are being raised in single-parent households — 49% are being raised exclusively by their mothers and 4% by their fathers. An additional 9% live with neither parent. This leaves only 38% who are being raised in two-parent households.

This situation has caused growing concern among community leaders. The "Million Man March" in Washington D.C. (10/95) gathered black men for a day-long rally. The Promise Keepers, a Christian group, also had a large gathering of men in the capital (10/97). Both gatherings, although *very* different in nature, had one common aim: to rededicate men to basic moral, social, cultural, and political ethics — as fathers, brothers, husbands, and members of their communities. In 1998 a conference was held at Morehouse College in Atlanta, Georgia. It brought together prominent black leaders and was designed to ad-

---

[12] Hispanics may be of any race. They may appear in the race groupings as well as under "Hispanics."

dress the issue of African American fathers. The statement paper that was issued at the conclusion of the conference, and summarizes its finding, says:

> "In the eyes of the sponsors, and for many participants, the Morehouse Conference was an important moment. The group did not agree on everything, but it did agree unequivocally that African American children deserve strong and positive relationships with their fathers and that reversing the trend of father absence must rise to the top of the agenda for African Americans and for the nation. We agreed that both the economic structures, the cultural values, and the private and public sector policies that discourage many black men from becoming active in their children's lives demand urgent attention."

A new consensus was forming. In the 90s, research came out showing that failed marriages and poor single-parent families produce extremely high social costs. The resulting "family friendly" consensus was not yet visible when in 1992 Dan Quayle blasted the popular sit-com "Murphy Brown" for its casual attitude towards fatherless childbearing. His comments ignited a firestorm of protest and a national debate. By the late 1990s, however, the mood had changed. In an interview, Candice Bergen, the actress who played Murphy Brown, told the *Los Angeles Times* that Dan Quayle had picked the right theme to support. She said of the show's single-parenting plot, "I didn't think it was a good message to be sending out." (Popenoe).

Government policies were also changing. Passage of a welfare reform act in 1996, discussed in the last panel, was yet another sign of both changing attitudes and policies regarding out-of-wedlock childbearing. These changes appear to be having an impact.

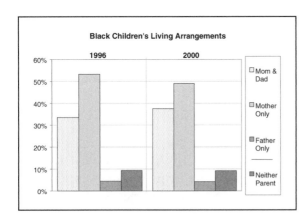

Between March 1996 and March 2000 the percentage of children who were living with just one parent declined. This change was most dramatic within the black community. As striking as the figures in the initial chart are, they are an improvement over the situation that existed just four years earlier in 1996. As a percentage, two-parent homes in the African American community increased from 34% in 1996 to 38% in 2000.

The percentage of children being raised by single parents has stopped growing. Changing public policies and attitudes about the healthiest environment for children make it easy to imagine that the decline in single-parent households, in favor of two-parent households, may mark the beginning of a new trend. Time will tell.

Source: U.S. Bureau of the Census. *Household Relationship and Living Arrangements of Children under 18*. Online. Available: http://www.census.gov/population/socdemo/hh-fam/p20-537/2000/tabC2.txt. March 2000; *Household Relationship and Presence of Parents for Persons Under 18 Years*. March 1996; Morehouse Research Institute & Institute for American Values. *Turning the Corner on Father Absence in Black America*. p.1. David Popenoe. " New Day Dawnin? In the struggle over the family, foundations make the difference." *Philanthropy Magazine* (March/April 2002). Online. Available: http://www.philanthropyroundtable.org/ magazines/2002/March/.

Gay Couples Now Being Counted, For the First Time

Top 20 States by Number of Gay Couples Reported in the 2000 Census

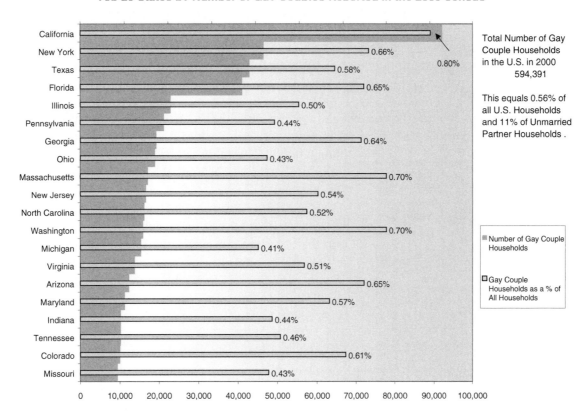

Total Number of Gay Couple Households in the U.S. in 2000
594,391

This equals 0.56% of all U.S. Households and 11% of Unmarried Partner Households .

■ Number of Gay Couple Households

□ Gay Couple Households as a % of All Households

Counting the number of gays and lesbians in the United States is a difficult undertaking. By definition, gays and lesbians are categorized by their sexual orientation — they are attracted to members of the same sex. Gays and lesbians must wish to be categorized as gay or lesbian; they must, in the vernacular, "come out" of the closet. Because it is difficult to be a member of a minority, and because they sometimes experience intolerance, many gays and lesbians prefer to keep their sexual preference private. For that reason, counting gays and lesbians has been more a matter of guesswork than science for most of history.

In 2000, for the first time ever, the U.S. Bureau of the Census has made an effort to begin to collect information on same-sex couples. The count is not based on sexual orientation but rather on living arrangements. This is a breakthrough is many ways.

This initial count of gay and lesbian couples is not, of course, a count of all gays and lesbians. It is the first nationwide, full census in which couples who identified themselves as same-sex partners were left in that category instead of being arbitrarily assigned to other categories by the Bureau of Census upon compilation of the data. Gay men and lesbian women living alone or listing their living arrangements as including a roommate or friend were not, of course, included in the unmarried same-sex partner category. In fact, they would not have been identified by sexual preference whatsoever.

Now that we have collected at least some census data on same-sex partners, what do they tell us? There are at least 594,743 same-sex couples living in the United States. Gay and lesbian couples were reported in all 50 states and the District of Columbia, dispelling the notion that they live almost exclusively in New York City and San Francisco. Lesbian couples make up 49.4% of the same-sex partners counted and gay men 50.6%.

The chart on the previous page presents figures for the top 20 states. Also shown is the percentage of same-sex partners are of all households. California has the largest number of such couples (92,138). In that state they represent 0.8% of all households.

Another way of looking at the early state-by-state 2000 census data is to rank the top states by the percentage that their respective same-sex partner households represent of all households. The table to the left does just that. Any state that appears in both the chart and the table is highlighted.

State	Percent of Households made up of Same-Sex Partners
Washington DC	1.481
Vermont	0.803
California	0.801
Massachusetts	0.700
Washington	0.700
Oregon	0.670
New Mexico	0.663
Nevada	0.662
New York	0.659
Maine	0.655
Arizona	0.649
Florida	0.648
Georgia	0.642
Delaware	0.625
Colorado	0.606
Rhode Island	0.605
Hawaii	0.592
Texas	0.580
New Hampshire	0.570
Maryland	0.568

The states that appear in the table and did not appear on the chart are less populous states that have a relatively high concentration of gay and lesbian couples. Even, however, where the percent of households made up of same-sex couples is highest, the District of Columbia, that percentage is small (1.48%).

It is difficult to say with any certainty whether the number of same-sex partner households is growing. The 2000 Census is the first to attempt to count these households. However, the estimates done by the Bureau, based on partial counts in previous years, suggest that gay and lesbian partner households are very much on the rise, or at least that the self identification of these couples is on the rise.

We will have far better data with which to assess trends in same-sex partner households as more years' worth of data are collected, as more accurate counts are taken, and as more same-sex partners choose to declare their partnerships to government officials.

Worth noting in any discussion of same-sex partnerships are the trends in formalizing these unions. It is interesting that in an era when marriage is commonly assumed to be on the wane,[13] there is a growing movement within the gay and lesbian communities to formalize their unions and to benefit from the same legal obligations and privileges accorded married couples. In 2000, the state of Vermont passed a civil unions law that offers same-sex couples the right to join in a civil union, a legal status parallel to marriage

---

[13] See the panel entitled "Racial Breakdown of Families with Children" for a further discussion of whether or not marriage is really on the wane.

for the purpose of state law.[14] State civil union laws and domestic partnership laws do not, however, make those covered by the laws eligible for any of the federal protections offered married couples. These include such things as family-related social security benefits, the right to inherit, the ability to participate in the provisions of the federal Family and Medical Leave Act, to name just a few.

The passage of Vermont's civil unions law sparked a wave of new legislation the following year. According to an in depth report issued by the Human Rights Campaign Foundation, about half of the proposed legislation in 2001 was in support of legalizing same-sex partnerships and half designed to bar their formation under law. As the legal and political systems grapple with the desires of same-sex couples to formalize and legalize their unions, it will probably become easier to follow the demographic measures of this community.

Source: U.S. Bureau of the Census. *Profile of General Demographic Characteristics: 2000 and Unmarried-Partner Households by Sex of Partners.* Census 2000 Summary File 1. Human Rights Campaign Foundation. *The State of the Family*, p. 13.

---

[14] The State of Vermont is the only state to have passed civil unions law, as of July 2002.

Does Raising A Child Cost More These Days?

Cost of Raising a Child, 1960 and 2000

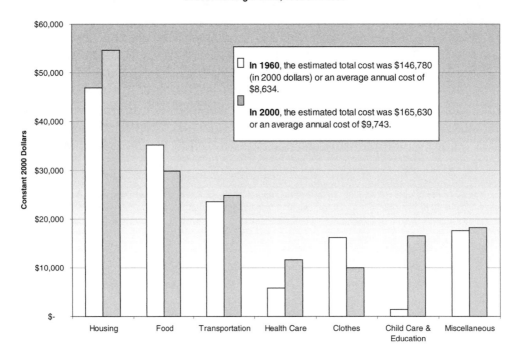

The short answer to the question posed in the title is, Yes. It costs about $1,110 more per year (constant dollars), for 17 years, to raise a child in 2000 than it did in 1960.

The data charted above come from a detailed annual report produced by the U.S. Department of Agriculture's Center for Nutrition Policy and Promotion. The figures charted are based on the costs for a middle-income family with two parents to raise one child.

When looking at the change in expenditures from 1960 to 2000 by category, several things are worth noting. In all but two categories, the cost was up over the period. This was most notable for the category "child care and education" which went from being a minor portion (1%) of the overall expenditure to a not insignificant 10% of the cost to raise a child. This is the result of rising day care costs associated with the entry of women into the workforce in large numbers.

The other expense categories that rose are housing, transportation (our love of large sport utility vehicles might plays a role here), health care, and the catch-all category "miscellaneous" which includes such things as toys, video games, movies, sporting equipment, and the like.

The cost of feeding a child fell between 1960 and 2000. It is still, however, the second largest cost category representing 18% of the total cost to raise a child. Surprisingly, the cost of keeping the little one clothed also fell. The common belief is that children's "styles" and desire for name brand clothes is making it ever more expensive to buy clothes for children. It turns out that this impression is wrong. In 1960 we spent $365 more every year to clothe a child than we do in 2000. It should be noted that the figures in the chart do not include the value of any gifts received, like a new pair of tennis shoes from grandma and grandpa, or the baby clothes passed on from your big sister.

The table below gives a more details.

Family Type & Income (000 annually)	Housing	Food	Trans-port	Clothes	Health Care	Child Care	Misc.	TOTAL
Two Parent < $38	39,900	23,820	17,550	9,120	8,970	9,480	12,390	121,230
Single Parent < $38	44,550	23,880	12,570	9,330	7,050	8,310	9,450	115,140
Two Parent > $38 < $64	55,170	28,650	24,420	10,680	11,640	16,560	18,510	165,630
Single Parent > $38	89,290	35,940	38,820	12,690	14,070	21,630	30,480	242,910
Two Parent > $64	89,580	35,670	32,760	13,770	13,380	26,520	30,090	241,770

The Center for Nutrition Policy and Promotion does not offer the same income break-downs for both single-parent households and two-parent households[15]. This makes it difficult to compare single-parent and two-parent households other than for those in the first two lines, with a before-tax income below $38,000 annually.

For the categories that cover life's most urgent needs, food and shelter (here we can include clothes and health care) we see little differences between what is spent by a single-parent family and a two-parent family. In the other categories, the differences are greater. Of particular interest is the fact that the single-parent household spends more on housing for a child than does a two-parent household. Could this be the difference between renting and owning? Probably.

Finally, these data stop as soon as children reach their 18th birhtdays. Yet it is at this point that another cost of raising children arises, college. For information on trends in the cost of a college education, see Chapter 12 in the volume on Community and Education.

Source: U.S. Department of Agriculture. Center for Nutrition Policy and Promotion. *Expenditures on Children by Familes, 2001.* Annual Report, pps. 19 and 25.

---

[15] Most single-parent households in the sample surveyed have an annual before-tax income at or below $38,000 (83%). The sample was weighted to reflect the population it represents. The remaining 17% of single-parent households are presented in the single category — before-tax annual income of more than $38,000. Because this category includes a few single-parent households with high income, the data in this line of the table is not strictly comparable with the line above it, two parents with an income before taxes of between $38,000 and $64,000 annually.

Chapter 4

Ethnicity & Immigration

We are many colors, speak in many tongues, and we come from all over the world. In this chapter we look at some of the indicators of our diversity. We look at our racial and ethnic makeup in somewhat more detail than we could do in Chapter 1, *Who Are We?* In a way, this chapter continues that theme.

In the first four panels we look at racial and linguistic minorities, beginning with an overview, *Minorities within Minorities*, in which we report on the ways in which the Bureau of the Census counts and classifies individuals. This produces some interesting findings not often noted when minorities are discussed. The next two panels examine two of the smaller racial groupings — American Indians and Asians. No specific focus is given to whites and African Americans — two groups about which the Census reports very extensively in any case —, as do we, in many of the panels. This section concludes with a look at the interesting subject of our many linguistic minorities.

The latter half of the 20th century saw the Civil Rights movement and legislation (and court decisions) aimed at making us live closer to one another. The data show that this just hasn't happened. The five panels in the middle of this chapter provide some interesting views of how the races in the U.S. live together. To do this, we look at two segregation measures and use them to examine the settlement patterns of African Americans, Hispanics, Asians, and American Indians. The data are ten years old but still "the latest" available — nor are patterns likely to have changed a great deal in the last ten to twelve years. These indicators show how we choose to live, or, perhaps, how some of us are forced to live. But no really hard conclusion can be drawn. At the level where we live, we live largely segregated lives.

We conclude the chapter by looking at the seesawing nature of immigration over time. We note that the foreign-born population is much more Latin or Asian in origin. We trace the history of changes in migration — and conclude with a look at illegal immigration, once more a hot topic after the events of 9/11.

Minorities within Minorities: An Overview

Racial and Ethnic Minorities
(Population counts in 2000)

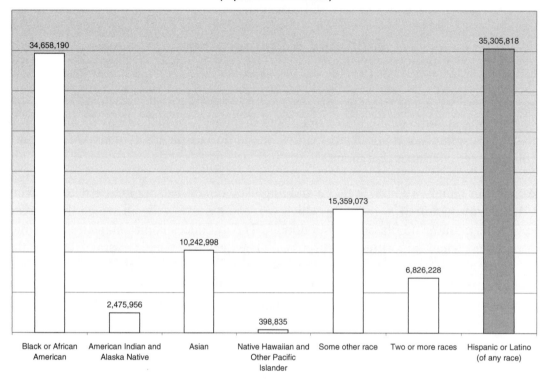

This panel will serve as an overview of the complexities that underlie public discussions of "minorities." The graphic shows the major racial groups and, at the right, in shaded form, the only official ethnic category that is based not on race but country of origin, the Hispanic or Latino population.

The **African American** population, the largest *racial* minority, is well understood and needs no special comment. In the 2000 census, this group was 34.7 million people in the United States. Some, of course, were also Hispanic in origin (see below).

American Indians and Alaskan Natives, although numerically small, represent a great diversity of cultures. As of the 1990 census, American Indians and Alaskan Natives were classified into 379 distinct, named tribes, not counting smaller scattered groups. These peoples spoke more than 18 languages. The largest tribe, the Cherokees, had a population of nearly 370,000 in 1990. In 2000, this entire racial group had a population of just under 2.5 million.

Asians are the third largest defined racial group, with 10.2 million people in 2000. Although classified as a racial grouping, they are not racially homogeneous. Like Hispanics, they are peoples who originated in a defined geographical region — Asia. As the Census Bureau informs us, Asians are people who trace their origins to the Far East, Southeast

Asia, or the Indian subcontinent including, e.g., Cambodia, China, India, Japan, Korea, Malaysia, Pakistan, the Philippines, Thailand, and Vietnam. Also included are Bangladeshis, Bhutanese, Burmese, Indochinese, Indonesians, Iwo Jiman, Madagascarians, Malaysians, Maldivians, Nepalese, Okinawans, Pakistanis, Singaporeans, Sri Lankans, or people originating from elsewhere in Asia. Arabs, Near Easterners, and Lebanese are classified as whites. The largest Asian component in 2000 was Chinese (2.3 million).

Native Hawaiians and Other Pacific Islanders, together the smallest racial group, are usually reported with Asians as "Asians and Pacific Islanders." This group had a population of under 400,000 in 2000. The group includes descendants of the original peoples of Hawaii, Guam, Samoa, or other Pacific Islands.

The next grouping in the Census — some 15.4 million — are those classified as **Some other race**. This population is, in effect, the creation of bureaucratic or data-collection formalism. All those people who designate themselves as "multiracial," "mixed," "interracial," or use some equivalent term are classified here. So, also, are people who write "Mexican" or "Cuban" or "Puerto Rican" on their form. Given the prevailing orthodoxy that "Hispanics may be of any race," people who write such words are classified as "some other race" if the race is not specifically indicated on the Census forms. To this group might be added the next category, **Two or more races**, 6.8 million people. The people counted in this category provided more than one racial designation. If those could not be grouped under one of the other major categories, if the person, for instance checked *both* white and Asian or *both* Asian and black, the Census Bureau reports them under this category (some 57 such combinations are possible). Combined, the two groups make rather a large block (22.2 million). But they are clearly heterogeneous and do not express themselves politically — else there would be a good deal more awareness of them.

The final category shown, **Hispanics or Latinos**, the largest *ethnic* minority (36.3 million, slightly larger than African Americans) is another "land of origin" classification, like Asians — but while in the case of Asians the multi-racial composition of that group is *not* constantly emphasized, the multi-racial character of Hispanics is always footnoted by the government.[1] Hispanics are enumerated as a separate group in the Census but "overlay" the racial composition. To add them to other races is to *double count*. They are of white, American Indian, African, Polynesian, and Asian origins. People are classified as Hispanics if they report their place of origin as Spain or Latin American countries or if they classify themselves as Hispanics or Latinos. People are asked to classify themselves by race as well.

Source: U.S. Bureau of the Census. *2000 Census of Population and Housing. Definitions*. Summary File 1. March 2002.

---

[1] Asians are always listed as a *racial* group, although they include Mongolian, Polynesian, Indonesian, Caucasian, Asian Indian, and other racial groupings.

Minorities: American Indians

Top 10 American Indian Tribes, 1980 and 1990
(Percent of total Indian population)

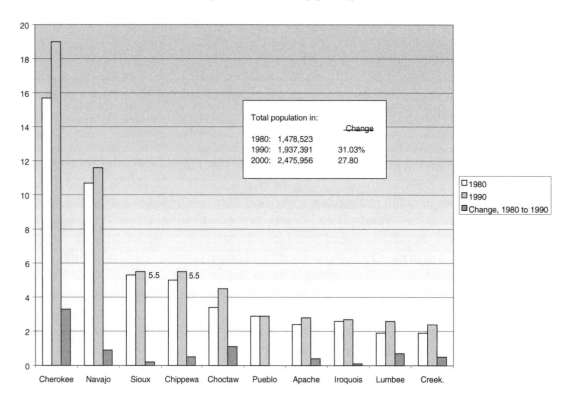

Total population in:		Change
1980:	1,478,523	
1990:	1,937,391	31.03%
2000:	2,475,956	27.80

Legend:
□ 1980
▨ 1990
■ Change, 1980 to 1990

The Cherokee Indians, with a population of just shy of 370,000 people, were the largest tribe in that part of the U.S. population designated as American Indians and Alaskan Natives. In 1990 this group was part of a total population of just over 1.93 million, the smallest racial group in the country if Hawaiian Natives and Other Pacific Islanders are grouped with Asians, as is the custom.

Data on such small populations are not usually available, in detail, until some years after each decennial census. Thus we show data for the years 1980 and 1990, which were first published in 1995, five years after the 1990 census. The graphic shows the top ten tribes within this racial category as a percent of the American Indian population. The last bar shows the change between the two census dates. Population data for 1990 are shown in the table on the next page, illustrating the fact that we are dealing with rather small groups. Only four tribes had populations greater than 100,000.

Considering that, in 1990, the Census Bureau identified some 379 tribes by name, it is easily seen that some of these are just a few families in extent.

1990 Populations of 10 Leading Tribes

Tribe	1990 Population	% increase, 1980 to 1990
Cherokee	369,035	59.0
Navajo	225,298	42.0
Sioux	107,321	36.5
Chippewa	105,988	44.0
Choctaw	86,231	71.7
Pueblo	55,330	30.0
Apache	53,330	48.7
Iroquois	52,557	37.5
Lumbee	50,888	77.7
Creek	45,872	62.2

The Indian population increased, 1980 to 1990, by 31% over all. All of the tribes shown here had higher rates of increase, suggesting that the big get bigger, the small perhaps shrink. In the 1990 to 2000 period, the Indian population increased by 27.8%, growing at a lower rate in this last period, to 2.48 million. Details about tribal groups and their increases or declines are not yet available.

Census data on the Indian population before 1980 were summed under the category "Other Races." This makes it difficult to establish a trend in the population, but it is clearly up from 1930, when details were published by the Census Bureau and the total population reported, in that year, was 332,397.

Source: U.S. Bureau of the Census. *1990 and 2000 Census of the Population*, and "Top 25 American Indian Tribes for the United States, 1990 and 1980." Online. Available: http://www.census.gov/population/www/socdemo/race/indian.html. Data on 1930 population are from Dr. Leon E. Truesdell, *The Indian Population of the United States and Alaska, Fifteenth Census of the United States: 1930*. U.S. Bureau of the Census.

Minorities: Asians

Top Ten Asian Groups in the U.S.
(Population in 2000 and % of Asian population)

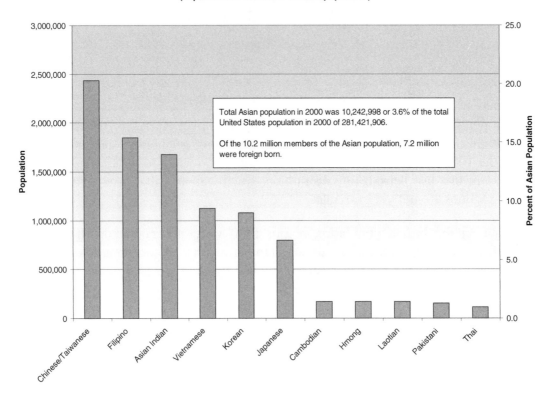

Total Asian population in 2000 was 10,242,998 or 3.6% of the total United States population in 2000 of 281,421,906.

Of the 10.2 million members of the Asian population, 7.2 million were foreign born.

This panel shows some detail on Asian Americans. In the 2000 Census, this group was 3.6% of the total population, some 10.2 million people. Shown here are the top 11 groups that comprise 95% of the Asian population.

Some clarifications. This category is often reported as Asians and Pacific Islanders. That population, in 2000, as reported in *Current Population Reports*, was 10.8 million and was 3.8% of the population. The Census also reports a higher number of Asians, 11.9 million. This number includes people of combined race or combined Asian origin, e.g., "Pakistani *and* Nepalese." The lower number is more accurate, because the combined population is, in effect, tallied twice or more times, because a person reporting as in the example above, is counted twice, once as a Pakistani, once as a Nepalese.

The Asian population increased 48.3% between 1990 and 2000 (an increase nearly 4 times as high as that of the U.S. population as a whole, which increased 13.2%). Population growth was most dramatic in the 1970s and 1980s (see Chapter 1, *Who We Are*).

Some 7.2 million of the Asian population is foreign born; it has a high citizenship rate (47%) second only to those born in Europe (52%).

Top ranking concentrations of Asians, by region and states is shown in the table:

Leading Region and Top Three States in Asian Population

Area	Population 1990	Population 2000	Change in Population	% of Total 2000 popul.
West	3,734,191	5,003,611	1,269,420	7.9
California	2,735,060	3,697,513	962,453	10.9
New York State	689,303	1,044,976	355,673	5.5
Texas	311,918	562,319	250,401	2.7

The four states with the lowest percent of Asians were West Virginia and Montana (both 0.5%) and North Dakota and Wyoming (both 0.6%) in 2000.

The five cities with the most Asians were New York, Los Angeles, San Jose, San Francisco, and Honolulu. These cities, with a combined population of 1.8 million Asians in 2000, hosted 18% of the Asian population in the United States.

Source: U.S. Bureau of the Census. "The Asian Population: 2000." *Census 2000 Brief*. United States Census 2000. Note: The source separately lists populations of those originating in Mainland China and on Taiwan.

Minorities: Linguistic

Selected Foreign Languages Spoken in the U.S.
(Number of speakers)

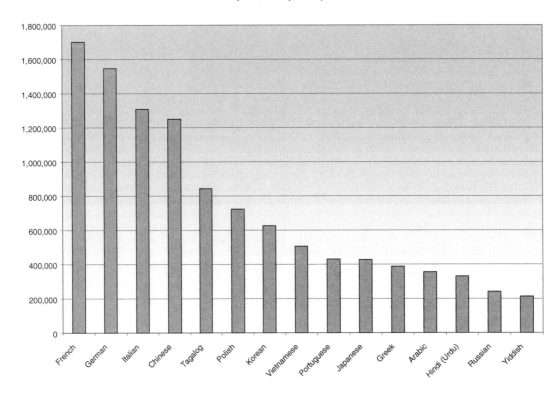

Language is another lens through which we may view minorities. Many languages are spoken daily in the United States. Shown in the graphic are foreign tongues ranked second to 16th. The 50th ranked language, Amharic (spoken in Ethiopia) had 31,505 speakers as of the 1990 Census.

The language most common, after English, is Spanish. Spanish is not shown on the graphic so that the other languages can be made more visible — but a view of the proportion of Spanish to the other foreign languages can be seen in the inset graphic. While 17.3 million people speak Spanish, the next largest language group, French, only has 1.7 million speakers, one tenth that of the language of the Conquistadors.

Languages of Europe hold the first four spots — Spanish, French, German, and Italian. Virtually all European languages appear in the list of the first 50. A complete list is provided in Part II of this volume. There were, for instance, nearly 36,000 Danish speakers, 54,000 Finnish speakers, and 148,000 Hungarian speakers in 1990.

Asian languages — Chinese, Tagalog (spoken in the Philippines), Korean, Vietnamese, and Japanese comprise the top 16.

Data of this type are collected every 10 years in the Census of the Population. Data for the 2000 Census are not yet available; hence we are looking here at old photographs of the linguistic landscape. In 1990, however, 31.8 million people spoke a foreign language, 13.8% of the population.

The Census identifies the English-speaking ability of these people as part of its data collection effort. Seventy-nine percent of these people speak English well or very well; 5.8% do not speak English at all, some 1.8 million people.

The linguistic groups with the highest English-language skills are, in order of rank, speakers of Kru, Danish, Dutch, Swedish, and Hebrew. Kru is spoken in Liberia. 97.5% of Kru speakers speak English well or very well.

The five groups with the lowest English skills are (arranged from the bottom up) speakers of Miao (the Hmong), Mon-Khmer (Cambodians), Korean, Chinese, and Vietnamese. Only 53.7% of Miao speakers speak English well or very well.

Among Spanish speakers, the largest linguistic minority, 74% speak English well or very well and 6.2% do not speak English at all, a group of some 1.46 million people. This, perhaps, is the root of pressures to teach school, in certain areas, in the native tongue of those attending.

Some concluding notes: French does not include French Creole (spoken by more than 187,000 people) or Cajun (nearly 34,000 people); these languages have their own classifications. Individuals reporting three languages, e.g., Russian, French, and Yiddish, will be counted three times in this survey.

Source: U.S. Bureau of the Census. 1990 Census of Population. CPHL-133. "Detailed Language Spoken at Home and Ability to Speak English for Persons 5 Years and Over - 50 Languages with Greatest Number of Speakers: United States, 1990."

Measuring Segregation

Measures of Segregation - Blacks - 1990

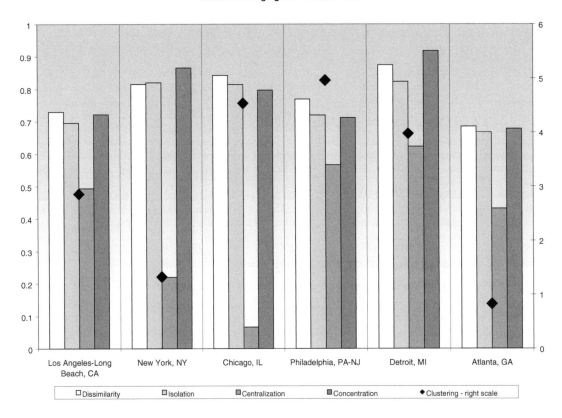

| □ Dissimilarity | ▣ Isolation | ▣ Centralization | ▣ Concentration | ◆ Clustering - right scale |

Measuring segregation is no easy matter. The U.S. Census Bureau publishes some 19 measures. Of these, five are shown, for six major U.S. metro areas and for African Americans only — by way of an introduction to this subject.

Please bear with us... We shall attempt to explain each measure first and then explain why we shall use two of these in the analyses and presentations that follow.

Dissimilarity. If a racial minority is segregated from the majority in a spatial sense, how many people would have to move to mix the two populations evenly? This number is expressed as a proportion, from 0 to 1. If the value is zero, nobody would have to move. If it is 1 all would have to move. Dissimilarity measures this "need to move" to achieve desegregation. If the values on the left axis are multiplied by 100, the percent that would have to move is given. In the case of Detroit, in this graphic, the value for dissimilarity is .874 — suggesting that 87.4% of the African Americans in Detroit would have to move to achieve complete desegregation.

Isolation. This is another spatial measure. It shows the relationship between minority and majority group members in an area. If the index is 1 (i.e., 100%), all the people are of the minority. A number like 0.823 (Detroit's "isolation" index) means that 82.3 percent of the minority population lives with 17.7% of the majority population. The higher the value, the fewer whites are present, in the data shown here — hence the more "isolated" the minority population is. The lowest value in this display is for Atlanta, 0.667, suggesting that in Atlanta one third of residents are of the majority population.

Both *Dissimilarity* and *Isolation* implicitly assume the value of a desegregated society rather than, say, a multicultural society.

Centralization. This index measures how close to the central business district (CBD) the minority population is located. A high value means a strong aggregation of the minority population in the city's center. In New York and in Chicago this value is low for blacks, no doubt indicating the high value of real estate in Lower Manhattan and on Chicago's lakefront (which is surrounded by enclaves with names like Greektown, Chinatown, and Ukrainian Village). It is high in Detroit where redevelopment of central areas has been sporadic and isolated. The measure is inapplicable to cities with no well-defined CBD.

Concentration. This index measures density relative to the white population. It measures how small an area a minority occupies relative to the majority population, all other things equal (normalized for population size). Relative concentration, the measure used here, means that if the average density for the minority is the same as for the majority, the index is zero. The higher the index, the more densely settled the minority is. If the measure drops below zero, it means that the majority is more densely settled, the minority more dispersed (often the case with Indians, as we shall see). The upper bound of this measure is 1 — maximum density. The lower bound, expressed in negative numbers, can be quite high (negative), with populations spread thinly over an area. The underlying assumption is that a one-acre lot is better than a two-room flat for a family of five. It's difficult to argue.

Clustering. This indicator is high if minority neighborhoods are adjoining. The more neighborhoods are clustered, without intervening white neighborhoods, the higher the index. We show "relative clustering," a measure based on the average distance between minority members compared with the average distance between majority members. High values indicate close clustering of minority enclaves. Negative values signal dispersion of settlements. Values plotted are on the right scale. High concentration combined with high clustering suggests dense, adjoining neighborhoods. If concentration is high but clustering low, there are many dense neighborhoods but separated by majority settlements.

In the following panels, we shall use "relative concentration" as our measure of choice, illuminated, where meaningful, by the isolation measure. Concentration has a certain objective quality. Minorities might wish to live together. How densely must they live to do so — that is the issue. It is also useful for showing situations where minorities are dispersed. We shall encounter such cases. Isolation is one of the traditional measures of segregation. It shows the degree to which races and ethnicities are in contact with the majority white population.

Source: U.S. Bureau of the Census. Housing and Household and Economic Statistics Division. Online. Available: census.gov/hhes. www.housing/ resseg/def.htm. Presentation is from the work of Roderick J. Harrison and Daniel H. Weinberg. *Racial and Ethnic Residential Segregation: 1990.*

African American Settlement Patterns[2]

Cities with the Lowest and Highest African American Population
(Measures of Concentration and Isolation)

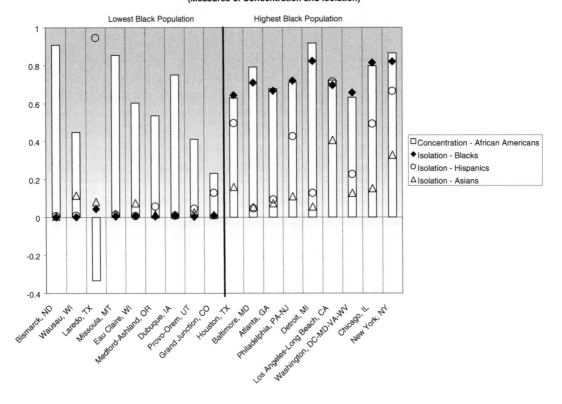

In this and the following three charts, we shall examine how racial minorities, and the Hispanic population, are settled in metro areas where they have the smallest and the largest numbers. Each group has its own panel. In this panel we shall examine African American patterns of settlement.

The Concentration measure indicates space occupied (density) relative to whites, by the same number of people. The Isolation measure indicates the proportion of African Americans within each area relative to whites. A value of 0.6 (60%), for instance, means that 6 blacks live in the same area with 4 whites. Isolation measures are provided for blacks, Hispanics, and Asians and Pacific Islanders. The left part of the graphic shows cities with the smallest black populations, the right part cities with the largest black populations. Absolute counts were used for ranking so that patterns encountered in small as well as very large metro areas can be shown side by side. All data are for 1990. Such measures for the 2000 census have been announced but have not been issued.

---

[2] All cities shown are Metropolitan Statistical Areas (MSAs) as defined by the Office of Management and Budget, the Office of the President. Rankings are by population of African Americans in each MSA, the lowest population being the left-most, the highest the right-most on the graphic.

Values close to the zero line indicate equivalency with the majority white population. A concentration level at or near zero means that the relative space occupied by the minority is the same as that of whites. Higher values indicate more density, negative values indicate less density. An isolation measure at or near zero indicates that as many whites as minorities are living in the same neighborhood.

Looking at two pairs of cities will illustrate what these measures can tell us. Note first that levels of concentration can be quite high even when the minority population is quite low. This means that the same numbers occupy less physical space than whites. Thus Bismarck, North Dakota, has a concentration measure of 0.908, second only to Detroit, MI, with a measure of 0.918. But while African Americans in Bismarck live as densely (in as little space) as in Detroit, they are not as isolated. They are in neighborhoods where an equal number of whites live. Detroit, by contrast, has the highest isolation measure, 0.823, of any city shown. Isolation is related to population size; the races/ethnicities live together, for whatever reasons. In Bismarck, blacks were less than 0.1% of the population in 1990; in Detroit they were 22%.

Another pattern is shown by Laredo, Texas. In that city African Americans occupy much more space than an equivalent group of whites. They are less densely settled, are less concentrated. The concentration measure is negative. Their isolation level is low — lower than that of Asians and Pacific Islanders. In the same city, Hispanics live in very high isolation and have, based on this measure, only minimal contact with the non-Hispanic white population. This is easily understood when one notes that, in Laredo, Hispanics were nearly 94% of the total population in 1990.

Data for the large metro areas, which have large populations of African Americans, show both high concentrations and high isolation. The races separate into their own enclaves where the populations are large. Note that Hispanics and Asians have lower isolation measurements in these large cities than blacks. The one exception is Los Angeles-Long Beach, CA, where large Hispanic numbers produce isolated settlement patterns. In that metro area, Hispanics represented nearly 38% of total population in 1990, versus 11% for African Americans.

African Americans were less than 1% of total population in all of the smaller metro areas and significantly higher (19 to 20%) in the large metro areas; the only exception was Los Angeles-Long Beach, where the black population had an 11% share in 1990.

Source: U.S. Bureau of the Census. Housing and Household and Economic Statistics Division. Online. Available: census.gov/hhes. www.housing/ resseg/def.htm. Presentation is from the work of Roderick J. Harrison and Daniel H. Weinberg. "Racial and Ethnic Residential Segregation: 1990."

Hispanic Settlement Patterns[3]

Cities with the Lowest and Highest Hispanic Population
(Measures of Concentration and Isolation)

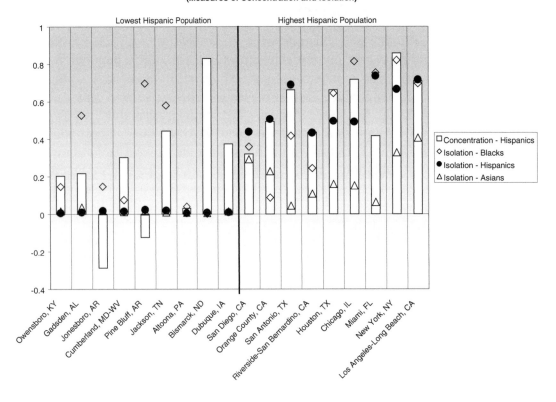

Hispanic concentration and isolation measures for cities with the lowest and highest Hispanic populations are shown in the graphic. For an explanation of "concentration" and "isolation," please see earlier panels titled *Measuring Segregation* and *African American Settlement Patterns*.

Hispanics generally have higher concentration levels (take up less space) than equivalent non-Hispanic whites, the comparison group. Density is an indirect measure of wealth. With increasing wealth people in urban areas — and the data shown here are for the largest U.S. metropolitan aggregations — attempt to have more space. Using these measures, a population living predominantly in apartment blocks and in small houses, clustered close together, will have a higher density than the majority population living in large houses with larger lots.

---

[3] All cities shown are Metropolitan Statistical Areas (MSAs) as defined by the Office of Management and Budget, the Office of the President. Rankings are by population of Hispanics in each MSA, the lowest population being the left-most, the highest the right-most on the graphic.

In two metro areas, Jonesboro and Pine Bluff, AR, Hispanics occupy *more* room than equivalent non-Hispanic whites.

Isolation measures the relative integration of neighborhoods. Low values show high degrees of mixing between the minority and the majority, in this case Hispanics and non-Hispanic whites. Isolation reflects the size of the population. The smaller the population of a minority, the less likely it is to be isolated. Note, in this chart, that seven of the cities with lowest Hispanic populations have much higher isolation measures for African Americans. In each of those cases, the black population was higher and in some cases significantly higher, than the Hispanic population in 1990: in Pine Bluff, Arkansas, blacks were 43% and in Jackson, Tennessee 28% of the population, versus a 0.5% Hispanic population in both cities. Not surprisingly, these two metro areas had the highest black isolation measures.

Looking at metro areas with the highest populations of Hispanics, we note that, again, with high populations, the isolation measure goes up. In these areas, Hispanics largely interact with one another in their own neighborhoods, not with non-Hispanic whites. They outnumber blacks in every large metro area shown except Chicago and New York. In those cities black isolation was measurably higher in 1990 — also in Houston, where the Hispanic population was only slightly larger than the African American. The pattern suggests that while Hispanics congregate in enclaves, like all minority groups, they are somewhat more "mixed" with the majority population. Latent habits of active segregation may affect this population less than they do with blacks. Hispanics may see themselves as less restricted in where they choose to live.

Note, finally, the uniformly low isolation level of Asians and Pacific Islanders. They have much smaller populations than blacks in all but two locations, San Diego and Orange County, California.

Source: U.S. Bureau of the Census. Housing and Household and Economic Statistics Division. Online. Available: census.gov/hhes. www.housing/ resseg/def.htm. Presentation is from the work of Roderick J. Harrison and Daniel H. Weinberg, "Racial and Ethnic Residential Segregation: 1990."

Asian and Pacific Islander Settlement Patterns[4]

Cities with the Lowest and Highest Asian/Pacific Islander Population
(Measures of Concentration and Isolation)

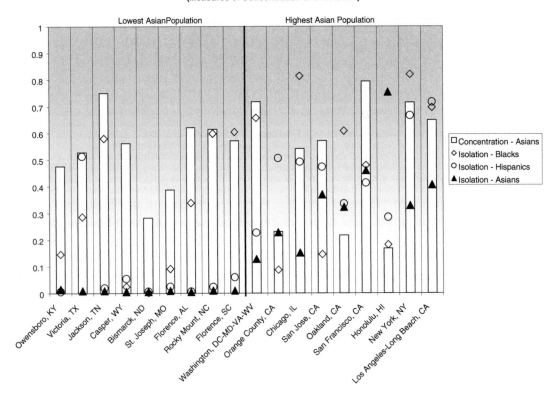

Asians and Pacific Islanders (APIs) have relatively high concentration levels vis-à-vis whites in this sample of cities — nine with the lowest, and nine with the highest API population. Isolation, a measure of segregation, was low in metro areas with small populations and variable in metro areas where APIs have the largest relative share of population. (For an explanation of "concentration" and "isolation," please see earlier panels titled *Measuring Segregation* and *African American Settlement Patterns*.)

APIs are a small racial/ethnic minority. In the cities shown, they constitute the majority of all races (indeed of the total population) only in Honolulu, HI, which is, of course, on a Pacific Island. They have a larger population than blacks only in Bismarck, San Jose, San Francisco, and Honolulu. They also have a larger population than Hispanics in those cities, but in San Jose and San Francisco, the combined black/Hispanic population is higher than the API population. Not so in Honolulu.

---

[4] All cities shown are Metropolitan Statistical Areas (MSAs) as defined by the Office of Management and Budget, the Office of the President. Rankings are by population of Asians and Pacific Islanders in each MSA, the lowest population being the left-most, the highest the right-most on the graphic.

Concentration levels — consistently higher than that for whites — appear to reflect cultural predilections. Concentration is an indirect measure of wealth. But APIs have the highest median family income of any group ($56,316 in 2000). Their ability to afford spacious housing is undisputed. The lowest concentration measure is for Honolulu, where APIs are the majority population.

Isolation levels are, again, very low where the population is low. Where the population is high, isolation measures closely reflect population, being highest in Honolulu, where APIs interact mostly with APIs. API neighborhoods are most closely clustered in New York, Los Angeles-Long Beach, Oakland, CA. and Orange County, CA (in that order). Clustering patterns, therefore (not shown) cannot be predicted strictly from API population density.

Asian and Pacific Islander settlement patterns show a tendency toward density (which is not necessitated by poverty) and the same inclination to live in cultural enclaves as exhibited by other races/ethnicities.

Source: U.S. Bureau of the Census. Housing and Household and Economic Statistics Division. Online. Available: census.gov/hhes. www.housing/ resseg/def.htm. Presentation is from the work of Roderick J. Harrison and Daniel H. Weinberg, "Racial and Ethnic Residential Segregation: 1990."

American Indian Settlement Patterns[5]

Cities with Lowest and Highest Populations of American Indians
(Measures of Concentration and Isolation)

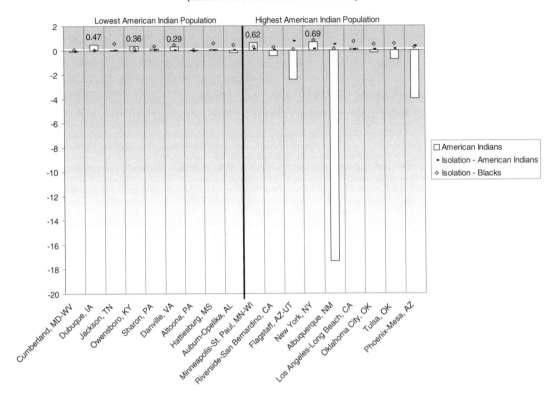

"American Indians," as discussed in this panel, include Eskimos and Aleuts. Data on their concentration (density of settlement) and isolation (segregation from whites) are shown in this graphic, for 1990, for the nine metro areas with the smallest and the nine with the greatest American Indian population. (For more of an explanation of "concentration" and "isolation," please see earlier panels titled *Measuring Segregation* and *African American Settlement Patterns*.)

The American Indian population is the smallest racial grouping in the United States. In this sample (lowest and highest populations in metropolitan statistical areas), American Indians are only a significant percent of total population (5% or higher) in Flagstaff, AZ, (27.8%), Tulsa, OK, (6.8%), Albuquerque, NM, (5.1%), and Oklahoma City, OK, (4.8%).

This population shows a concentration pattern unusual for a racial group. American Indians have a low concentration generally, and where they are most populous, there they oc-

---

[5] All cities shown are Metropolitan Statistical Areas (MSAs) as defined by the Office of Management and Budget, the Office of the President. Rankings are by population of American Indians in each MSA, the lowest population being the left-most, the highest the right-most on the graphic.

cupy much more space than does the white population, which is used as the point of reference. For this reason, the scale, as shown, is somewhat distorted, but concentration values are shown in numerical format for reference. An enlargement of the upper portion of the graphic is inserted below. In this population, eight of 18 cities show less concentration than whites; three are close to zero, the rest range from 0.1 to 0.69, the level shown in New York.

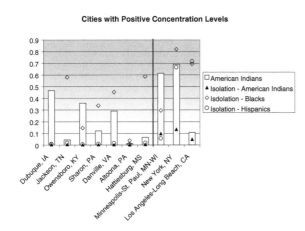

Cities with Positive Concentration Levels

□ American Indians
▲ Isolation - American Indians
◇ Isdolation - Blacks
○ Isolation - Hispanics

Low concentration levels indicate the inclusion in metro areas of areas of tourism with extensive lands but low levels of settlement, as well as spatially separated households, often housed in trailers, living on relatively poor land. Low concentration, in this instance, does not necessarily equal wealth. Albuquerque, with a very low-concentration American Indian population, in this sample, is the center of the Pueblo Indian culture, ringed by some 19 Pueblo reservations.

Minneapolis-St. Paul shows another pattern. This metro area had slightly over 24,000 American Indians (less than 1% of the Twin Cities' population) living at high concentration (0.615), comparable to that encountered in New York City (0.691).

The isolation measure for American Indians also follows the usual pattern: it is higher where the population is greater.

Source: U.S. Bureau of the Census. Housing and Household and Economic Statistics Division. Online. Available: census.gov/hhes. www.housing/ resseg/def.htm. Presentation is from the work of Roderick J. Harrison and Daniel H. Weinberg, "Racial and Ethnic Residential Segregation: 1990."

Immigration: The Trend is Up

U.S. Foreign-born Population

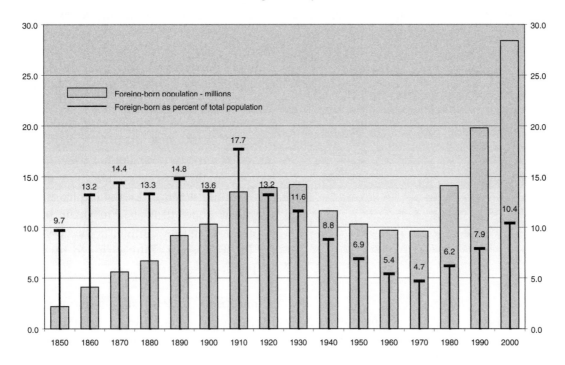

In 2000, the foreign-born population of the United States was 28.4 million people, the highest number of people ever, but a relatively low percentage of the total population, 10.4%. In the latter part of the 19th and the early part of the 20th centuries, the foreign population was well above 10%, peaking at 17.7% in 1910.

Immigration to the United States — and hence the size of the foreign-born population in the country — is influenced equally by what might be called "natural" phenomena (wars and economic trends) and by legislation. War and poor economic conditions inhibit immigration. Legislation may be repressive or stimulative. The two periods of steady increase in the foreign population in this 150-year period, 1850 to 1920 and 1970 to 2000, were periods of permissive legislation. The period of downturn was in part the result of legislation passed in 1921 and 1924, then renewed in 1952, which imposed a nation-of-origin quota system, restricted immigration, and favored immigration from Europe. No quota system existed before 1921, and this policy was removed in legislation passed in 1965; subsequent acts of Congress further liberalized immigration policy. The recent increase in the foreign-born population, consequently, is the result of changes in national policy — which may, of course, also reverse again.

One person in ten was born in a foreign country. The foreign-born may be citizens or non-citizens, and may be in the United States legally or illegally. What is the profile of this population?

Let us compare the regions of origin of these populations in 1960, 1980 and in 2000. The following table provides the particulars.

Foreign-Born Population of the United States, 1960, 1980, and 2000

Region of origin	% of Foreign-Born Population			Change between periods	
	1960	1980	2000	1960-1980	1980-2000
North America	9.8	6.8	2.5	-3.3	-4.0
Europe	75.0	39.0	15.3	-36.0	-23.7
Latin America	9.4	33.1	51.0	23.7	17.9
Asia	5.1	19.3	25.5	14.2	6.2
Other Area	0.7	2.1	5.7	1.4	3.6

As a percent of the foreign-born population, Europeans have been displaced from their leading position by a combination of Latin Americans and Asians in the 40-year span between 1960 and 2000. This, of course, is the origin of the rising Hispanic ethnicity and of the new prominence enjoyed by the Asian/Pacific Islander group of the population. North America, as a point of origin, means Canada. "Other Area" includes the Middle East, Africa, and Australia.

The two major trends in immigration, thus, are a strong increase in the population of those born non-citizens of the U.S. and a shift toward foreigners born in Latin America and Asia. In the next panel, we examine the citizenship status of this foreign-born group. In the last panel, we look briefly at illegal immigrants.

Source: U.S. Bureau of the Census. Current Population Reports. Series P23-206. Schmidley, A. Dianne, *Profile of the Foreign-Born Population in the United States:2000*. Washington, DC: U.S. Government Printing Office, 2001.

Citizenship of Immigrants: The Trend is Down

Percent of All Foreign-Born who are Naturalized Citizens

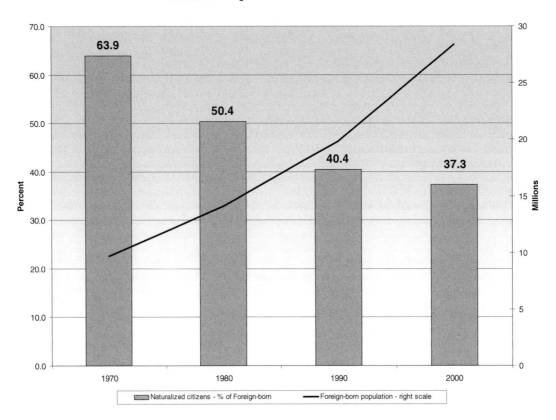

In the period 1970 to 2000, the foreign-born population of the United States increased from 9.7 to 28.4 million people, nearly a tripling of numbers (a 192% increase). In the same period, foreign-born residents who were naturalized citizens increased from 6.2 to 10.6 million (a 71% increase).

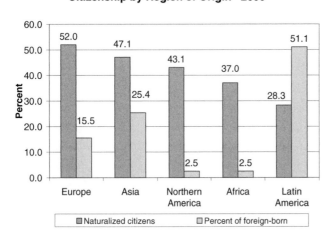

A look at citizenship rates by region of origin is provided in the inset graphic. Note that the Latin American group, with more than half of the foreign-born population, has the lowest rate of citizenship. At the same time, the second most rapidly growing group, the Asians, has the second highest naturalization rate. The overall citizenship rate of the foreign-born population is thus a composite of these two factors.

The highest rates of citizenship are associated with those groups that have been in the United States for the longest time. Due to the rapid increase in immigration during recent decades, the median length of residence of foreign-born individuals has dropped. It was 20.3 years in 1970 and 14.4 years in 2000. It may be assumed that, as these newcomers spend more time in the United States, the citizenship rate also will increase.

Non-citizens cannot vote. In courting the new minorities, are politicians taking this fact into account? Most likely they are. At the margins, every vote counts.

Source: U.S. Bureau of the Census. Current Population Reports. Series P23-206. Schmidley, A. Dianne, *Profile of the Foreign-Born Population in the United States:2000*. Washington, DC: U.S. Government Printing Office, 2001.

Illegal Aliens: Best Estimate

Foreign-Born Population and Illegal Immigrants - 2000

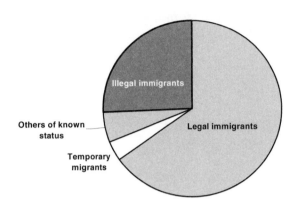

Based on the best estimates of the U.S. Census Bureau, derived by careful analysis of 2000 Census results, adjusted in various ways for undercounts, in 2000 some 8.5 million illegal immigrants lived in the U.S., accounting for slightly more than 1 in 4 for some 33.1 million foreign-born individuals. The 33.1 million figure for the foreign-born population is some 4.7 million higher than shown in the last panel, which was based on March 2000 *Current Population Survey* data, not 2000 Census results.

These data are obtained by taking Census results for the foreign-born, deducting the population which can be independently enumerated from the records of the Immigration and Naturalization Service (adjusted for mortality) and for the emigration (exit) of legal immigrants. Temporary migrants are deducted next (foreign students, temporary workers, etc.). Finally, deducting foreign-born residents who have a quasi-legal status — asylum-seekers and others in the INS processing backlog further reduces the residual. This leaves a group of people whom the Census Bureau labels "implied unauthorized migrants." This population was some 8.5 million in 2000.

In a final note to the data, the 8.5 million were not all physically counted in the Census. A substantial number were assumed to be "undercounted" — missed for some reason, probably because they were not willing to respond to questionnaires or avoided census takers. Estimating the level of undercount depends, to some extent, on the more or less arbitrary choice of some percentile figure, however well justified. The 8.5 million value is based on an assumption that legal immigrants had an undercount rate of 2% (twice that of the population as a whole), temporary migrants of 35%, others of known status 5%, and unauthorized migrants of 12%. The undercount rate for the total population was about 1%, for Hispanic renters just under 5%. In fact one wonders why 88% of illegal aliens actually filled out the forms; they must feel that the Census doesn't talk much to "La Migra."

The INS web site reports an illegal alien population of 5.0 million for 1996 and an estimate that the number increases at the rate of 275,000 people a year. This is a net figure; more come in, but a substantial number also leave again; some die here; etc. If the INS estimates are correct, the 2000 illegal alien population should be 6.1 million, substantially below the 8.5 million figure reported by the Census Bureau study.

Other figures are also offered by other sources, suggesting that, ultimately, the number of illegal immigrants is not what might be called a very "hard" figure.

Given these estimates, the foreign-born population increased by 13.3 million between 1990 (19.8 million) and 2000 (33.1 million). If 25.7% of the foreign-born population is made up of illegal immigrants, the rate of net in-migration of undocumented foreigners was around 342,000 a year.

Source: U.S. Bureau of the Census and *1999 Statistical Yearbook of the Immigration and Naturalization Service*. Robinson, J. Gregory, "ESCAP II – Demographic Analysis Results." Executive Steering Committee for A.C.E. Policy II. Report No. 1, 13 October 2001. Online. Available: http://www.ins.usdoj.gov/graphics/aboutins/statistics/Illegals.htm.

Chapter 5

The Political World: Voting, Tolerance, and Civility

In the most recent election, less than half the voting age population cast a vote for president. What persuades us to cast a vote? What keeps us away from the polls? These are some of the questions that will be examined in this chapter.

The initial panels in this section will look at the political parties. The two major political parties have rich histories, to be sure. But just who is a Democrat? Who is a Republican? One of the most exciting trends has been the growing power of Independent candidates. How much influence do they wield?

We'll also identify major demographic trends in the political world. More women are registered and voting than men. What effect will this have, if any? We'll also see that seniors are out voting while the younger generation shrugs and stays at home. Indeed, over 20 million registered voters sat out the last election. How will these people be reached?

There is an important theme to many of these panels: what exactly influences our vote? Do we no longer vote along party lines, but instead vote based on certain issues or the charisma of a certain candidate? Some would argue that there is only one factor that shapes our voting: the pocket book.

The final panels in the chapter will shift the focus slightly. How we vote is influenced by what kind of people we are. Are we more tolerant than we used to be? Many feel that we have lost our manners and our ability to respect each other — to "agree to disagree." The chapter will look at our manners. It will also look at our attitudes. In spite of all the dialogue about gender roles in this country, do we still cling to some old ideas about the roles played by the sexes? We'll also look at how the races are getting along. Final panels in the section will look at the rise of domestic partnership laws and gays in the military.

Electing a President

Voting in Presidential Elections, 1932-2000

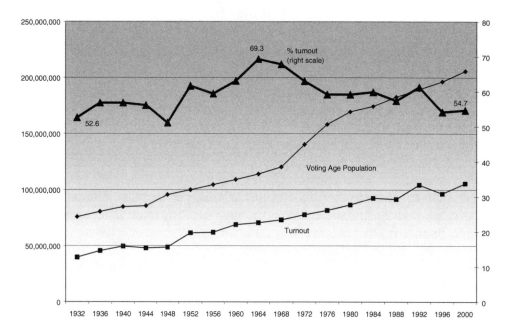

Voter turnout is measured as a percentage of those eligible to vote, not the percentage of those registered.

In 1932, nearly 53% of the voting-age population cast a vote for president. Turnout remained constant during World War II and then increased through the 1950s and 1960s. People had faith in their government and leaders. The war was over. People were working, getting married, buying homes, and going to school. Voters typically were employed, married, homeowners, and educated.

The highest turnout came in 1964. The public was still caught up in the enchantment of Camelot. President Kennedy championed social causes and encouraged us to ask, "what we could do for our country." Many people become more civic minded and joined groups like the newly formed Peace Corps. The 1960s was also the time of great social unrest. Blacks registered to vote in record numbers. The Voting Rights Act passed in 1965. It expanded the number of government agencies that could act to register voters. Before 1965, only 23% of voting-age blacks had registered to vote; by 1969, 61% had done so.

Things then began to change as government stances and policies were called into question. The country began sending troops to Vietnam in 1965. The Watergate scandal served to further disillusion the public. The rest of the 1970s brought additional frustrations for potential voters: a government that could not control gas prices or bring home hostages from Iran. Another dip in voting took place between 1984 and 1988. Perhaps some people were tired of government, budget cuts, and situations like the Iran-Contra scandal.

Turnout increased in 1992, hitting 61.3%. The country had entered the Gulf War in 1991. The economy was suffering. People were looking for a change in leadership. The country turned to Bill Clinton.

There are many other factors that influence voting, of course. Many people still feel that their vote doesn't count. Clinton was favored for re-election in 1996. Could the attitudes of people who simply shrugged their shoulders and said, "It's four more years of him, so why should I bother?" account for the fall in voter turnout between 1992 and 1996? In addition, the top reason given for not voting is lack of time. While our lives have certainly grown busier over the years, is this really an excuse?

The next panels will look at party affiliation.

Source: U.S. Bureau of the Census. Current Population Reports. *Voting and Registration in the Election of November 2000.* "Committee for the Study of the American Electorate." February 2002, p. 12. Online. Available: http://wwww.gspm.org/csae/cgans12.html, for chart data.

Are We Loyal to Our Party?

Party Identification, 1952-2000

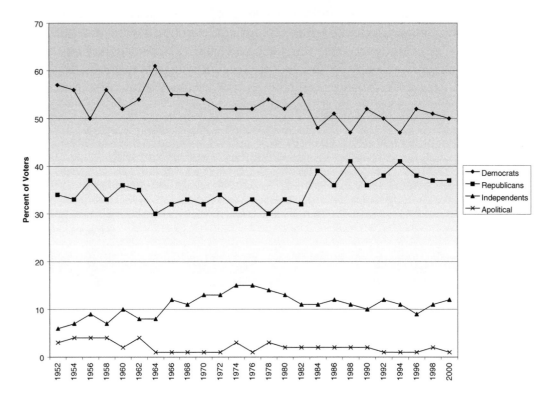

The graphic shows the results of a survey of political-party affiliation conducted by National Election Studies at the University of Michigan. Figures include "leaners" — people inclined to favor a particular party.

More people identified themselves as Democrats than as adherents to any other party. Democrats are seen as the party of social change that best represents the interests of the "common man." The early 1960s saw the first televised presidential candidate debates, which helped to put Kennedy in the White House. The election of 1964 was seen as a battle over true issues, such as social security and civil rights (Goldwater wanted to cut spending and support; Johnson supported them and won by a landslide). We still seemed to have faith in our government and leaders to do the "the right thing." A few years later, after Vietnam and Watergate, and the resignation of a president, our views must have become far more jaundiced (seeing politicians as crooked or self-serving dates back to years far earlier than seen on this panel, of course!). Certainly this played some role in the rise of those seeing themselves as "independents" — not affiliated with either party.

Republicans saw a return to power in the 1980s — and a rise in affiliation, as well. Reagan's charisma won over voters, even as others blamed him for trade deficits and "trickle down economics." The level of those who view themselves as apolitical has remained nearly constant for 40 years.

So who is mostly like to vote for a particular party? According to the survey, 61% of union households were Democrats in 2000, down from 66% in 1952. In 1952, more men were Democrats than women (58 versus 56%) were. In 1966, women surpassed men in the party for the first time. By 2000, 53% of women claimed to be Democrats, while men had dropped back to 46%.

Roughly 60% of those with just a grade-school education aligned with the Democrats over recent years; more than 50% of those with a high-school diploma did. For African Americans, the identification rates increased during the civil rights struggles of the 1960s. In 1952, 63% claimed to be Democrats; 82% did so in 1964, 91% did in 1968. By 2000, the percentage had fallen back to 83% (just 44% of all whites claim such an affiliation).

Those who identify with the Republicans are more likely to be educated white males. Thirty-three percent of men identified with the party in 1952; 41% did in 2000. Thirty-five percent of women saw themselves as members in 1952, 34% of them did so in 2000. By education, the highest rates were for college and post-graduate degree holders. Fifty-three percent claimed to embrace Republican ideals in 1952, compared to 48% in 2000.

More people began thinking of themselves as Independents in the 1960s. Recently, independent candidates have become formidable powers in elections. John Anderson garnered 7% of the final vote in 1980; H. Ross Perot received 19% of the vote in 1992, and 8% in 1996. Ralph Nader's 2% in 2000 is seen by many as having cost Gore the election.

Some points worth making here: most states ask voters when they register to express a party preference. Registration lists help the parties in mobilizing voters for Election Day. However, simply because one identifies with a party doesn't mean that one has to vote that way; voters often split tickets and do not vote a straight-party ticket. Note also that curves of affiliation tend to mirror each other. As Democratic affiliation drops, Republican affiliation rises. And vice-versa.

Source: "The NES Guide to Public Opinion and Electoral Behavior." Online. Available: http://www.umich.edu. April 4, 2002.

How Men and Women Vote

Party Identification Between the Sexes

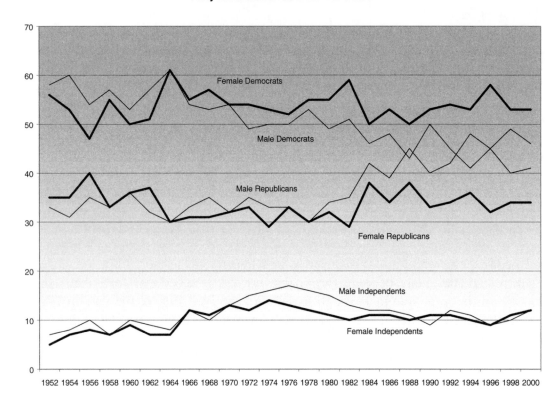

The panel shows the results of a study of political-party affiliation by the National Election Services at the University of Michigan. Figures include those leaning toward a particular party. The graphic charts the change in party affiliation for the sexes from 1952-2000. Why has this happened?

In the late 1950s and early 1960s, more men identified themselves as Democrats. But the panel shows that, with time passing, an increasing number of men saw themselves as more conservative and voted Republican. These years featured the rise of Corporate America, where men were under pressure to be "company men" — that is, to be conservative and to fit in. Sloan Wilson's 1956 novel *The Man in the Grey Flannel Suit,* addresses the conflict of men trying to balance personal and work lives and to fit in with this new culture. The protagonist, Tom Rath, as he climbs the corporate ladder, notes this: "I really don't know what I was looking for when I got back from the war, but it seemed as though all I could see was a lot of bright young men in grey flannel suits rushing around New York in a frantic parade to nowhere. They seemed to me to be pursuing neither ideals nor happiness — they were pursuing a routine. For a long while I thought I was on the sidelines watching the parade, and it was quite a shock to glance down and see that I too was wearing a grey flannel suit." Union members, who traditionally vote Democratic, were growing fewer in number as well. Membership hit 30.4% of the American workforce in 1963 and has been declining since (it currently stands at 13.5%).

In presidential elections, the share of men voting Democratic fell steadily: 61% in 1964, 53% in 1968, 49% in 1972, and 46% in 1984. More men either voted Republican or saw themselves as wild cards — Independents.

Women frequently vote Democratic or Independent. Perhaps women embrace the social issues championed by these parties, such as health care, social spending, and higher wages achieved by government intervention. Women Democrats wielded considerable power in 1964 and have been the leading segment of the voting population, according to the survey. Indeed, the female population in general has surpassed the male population, with 108 million over the age of 18 in the year 2000, compared to 100 million men.

Interestingly, both sexes were more inclined to vote Democratic in nonpresidential elections, perhaps suggesting our wish for balance: a bigger, more liberal local government and a smaller, conservative federal one. A Republican president may get a Democratic Congress.

Every analysis of elections brings up the issue of the gender gap. Included in the blizzard of voter surveys that are conducted during these periods, are those that show that men and women often agree more than they don't. One recent ABC News Poll shows that the sexes differ on some issues such as gun control and gay rights, but the gap on other issues is quite small.

	Men Favor (%)	Women Favor (%)	Gap
Stricter gun control	51	76	25
Death penalty	73	56	17
Gays in the military	59	75	16
Increased education spending	57	72	15
Raise minimum wage	78	88	10
Cut funding in failing schools	39	34	5
Strengthen Social Security before giving a tax cut	69	64	4
Abortion rights	55	58	3
Stricter campaign finance laws	65	66	1
After school prayer	67	67	0

There has been, on average, a 14 point-gap between the male and female vote over recent elections. Is it just a handful of issues that sway how the sexes vote? Do women prefer bigger government, as some have argued, because it offers social programs they prefer? Is it perhaps related to the fact that men are less likely to vote Democratic? Will the fact that more women are registered and voting (and make up more of the population) balance this trend?

Source: "The NES Guide to Public Opinion and Electoral Behavior." Online. Available: http://www.www.umich. edu. April 4, 2002; Daniel Merkle, "The Gender Gap's Back." Online. Available: http://abcnews.go.com; "Union Trends and Data." Online. Available: http://www.laborresearch.org;. April 26, 2002. The quote from *The Man in the Grey Flannel Suit* was included in Robert A. Brawer's *Fictions of Business: Insights on Management from Great Literature*.

Who Votes: Women

Voting in Presidential Elections, 1968-2000

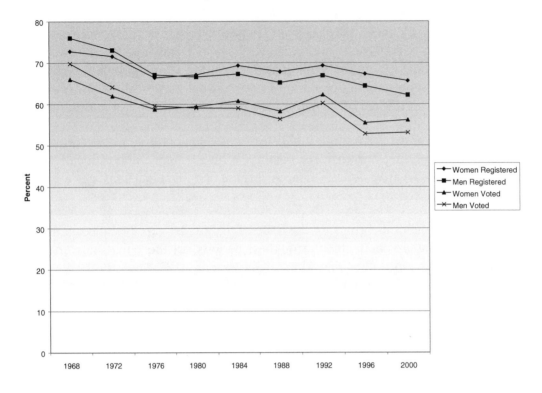

In 1984, women's voting rates in presidential elections surpassed men's rates for the first since the Census Bureau began tracking voting data in 1964. More women continue to register and vote than men do. While the panel above shows only presidential elections, their rates in congressional elections are higher than men's as well: 46.1% of women voted in 1986, while 45.8% of men did; in 1998, 42.4% of women voted in 1998, while 41.4% of men did. Recalling the suffragettes of long ago, one is tempted to say: "You've come a long way, baby!"

In the 1984 presidential election, 60.8% of women voted in the election, compared to 59% of men. This was the year of Reagan's re-election. Both sexes favored him over Mondale, with 62% of men and 56% of women supporting his continued presidency.

The media have increasingly looked at recent presidential elections through the lens of gender. According to several sources, the term "gender gap," the difference between the way men and women vote, seems to have appeared about 1980. Anna Greenberg of Harvard's Kennedy School of Government analyzed recent elections this way: 1980 was the gender gap; 1992 was the Year of the Woman; 1994 was the angry, white young man, 1996 was the soccer mom; 1998 was the waitress mom.

What has brought more women to the polls? As we have seen in this book and its companion volume *Work and Leisure*, women have increasingly pursued advanced degrees. Their participation in the labor force has been on the rise. Education and workforce participation have traditionally been correlates of voting. An educated, employed person will more likely be concerned about issues that affect him or her — tax cuts, social security, health care — and will vote accordingly. In short, the "waitress mom" of the 1998 election, most likely a single woman who has children and who holds a low-wage job, will vote for the candidate most likely interested in issues like tax cuts, higher wages, and childcare.

Women are concerned with other issues as well. The field of women's health — research, funding, access, contraception — is a top concern. A candidate's viewpoint on abortion rights continues to be a vital concern for many voters (of both genders). Women, as mothers, are often concerned with education.

The next panel looks at turnout by age.

Source: U.S. Bureau of the Census. "Reported Voting and Registration by Race, Hispanic Origin, Sex and Age Groups." Online. Available: http://www.census.gov.

Who Votes: Turnout by Age

Voting in Presidential Elections by Age, 1964-2000

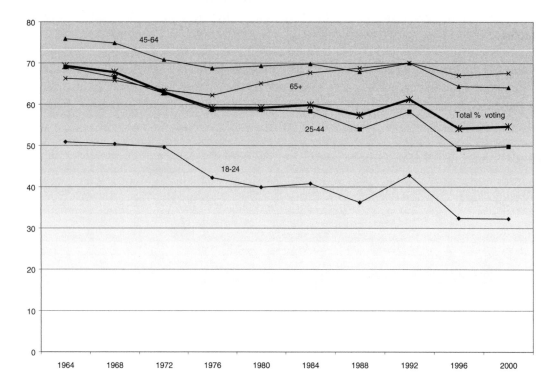

With the exception of seniors, every age group has seen declining rates of voter participation since 1964.

In 1964, the U.S. had 110.6 million people of voting age; 69.3% of them voted. Nearly four decades later, the population had increased 83% to 202.5 million people. But the number of people voting had fallen to 54.7% of the population.

The 18-24 year old category saw the lowest rates, with less than half of that population voting. The decline began after 1971 — curiously after the 26th Amendment lowered the voting age to 21. The cliché is that young people are apathetic about the public sphere, particularly government and politics. There have been drives to mobilize the young voting public, such as the Rock the Vote and Choose or Lose campaigns, which, according to their Web site, registered more than 850,000 young people in 1992 and 1996. But this age group has lost momentum since the 1992 election.

Those aged 25-64 were more inclined to vote, although both groups saw a drop in their rates. Seniors have seen their rates rise and fall over the period, from a low of 62.2% in 1972 to a high of 70.1% in 1992. They have seen an increase in their 2000 turnout compared to 1964. In that year, 66.3% reported voting; by 2000, the rate had increased slightly to 67.6%. Why? Senior citizens have developed into a formidable force, and are voting on issues that matter to them, such as health care and social security. Some explanation may be found in simple lifestyle habits: they vote because they have *always* voted.

They have a stronger sense of history and the power to cast a vote. They may also have deeper convictions about the role of government in their lives.

The 1992 election appeared to galvanize voters. The economy was suffering. Voters responded to Bill Clinton's charisma and his promises of bringing change to the country. H. Ross Perot offered a serious challenge to the two-party system. Voters were motivated — or simply fed up with state of things — to turn out on Election Day. Every age bracket saw a jump in voter turnout. There was a 20% increase in youth-voter rates, thanks to voter registration programs (and no doubt Clinton's man-of-the-people tactics, from playing his saxophone to discussing his underwear preferences on national television).

The next panels will examine how minorities vote.

Source: U.S. Bureau of the Census. Current Population Reports. *Voting and Registration in the Election of November 2000*. Washington, DC: U.S. Government Printing Office, February 2002, p.12.

Who Votes: Minorities

Percent of Each Race that Reported Voting

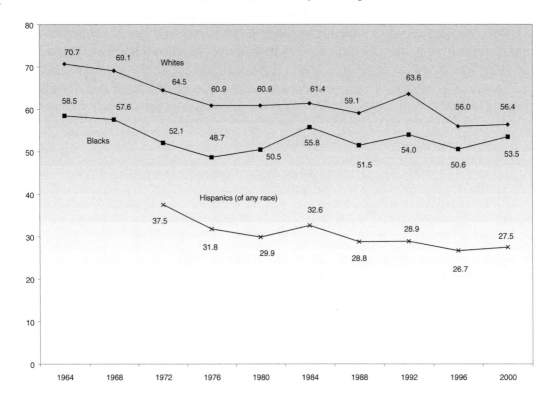

The graphic shows how the races reported voting from 1964–2000. Whites, blacks, and Hispanics are all voting at lower rates than they were in 1964.

Whites enjoy the highest voting rates. A little more than 70% went to the polls in 1964. Their rates fell gradually over the following presidential elections. More whites went to the polls in the 1992 election, when 63% of them cast a vote. The country was looking for a change in leadership and direction, and more people turned out to cast a vote. It was the highest turnout for a presidential election since 1968. According to Voter Research and Surveys, ballots cast by whites in the 1992 election were nearly evenly split between the two major candidates: 40% favored Bush, 39% favored Clinton, 20% favored Perot. The voting rate of whites fell to 56.2% in 2000, a fall of 20% over the 1964 election.

Blacks followed similar patterns. Their rate was the highest in 1964 (other races were included in the statistics for this year). Fewer of them visited the polls in the following years. More African Americans turned out to vote in the 1980 and 1984 elections. This was the beginning of the Reagan years, and blacks, who largely vote Democratic, may have felt compelled to vote for the Democratic candidate. Their rates improved in 1992 and 1996 when Clinton was seeking the nomination and re-election. 83% and 84% of blacks supported him in these elections, respectively.

Hispanics were not tracked until 1972. While their rates are low, they represent a significant portion of the population. The majority of them live in key electoral states such as New York, Florida, California, and Texas. Any potential candidate in a presidential or state election knows that they wield tremendous influence.

What are some possible reasons for the voting rates? Those most likely to vote are older individuals, homeowners, married couples, people with more education, higher income, and good jobs. We've seen in other chapters in this book and its companion volumes that whites are more likely to fit into these categories.

We've looked at their level of voting. How do minorities vote?

Sources: Connelley, Marjorie. "Who Voted: A Portrait of American Politics, 1976-2000." *New York Times*, 12 November 2000, p. 4; U.S. Bureau. of the Census. Current Population Reports. *Voting and Registration in the Election of November 2000*. Washington, DC: U.S. Government Printing Office. February 2002, p. 12.

Who Votes Democrat? Who Votes Republican?

How the Races Voted, 1980-2000

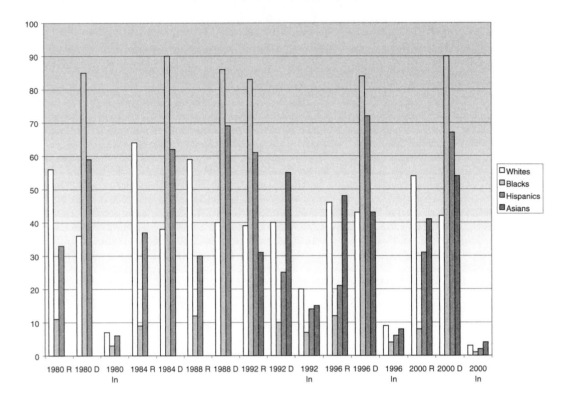

The common belief is that minorities vote Democratic. The party claims that it is more compassionate and more willing to support and spend money on social programs aimed at helping people. The Democrats are for women, minorities, middle-class to lower income working families, and union members. Is this an accurate assumption?

The data track how minorities voted in presidential elections from 1980-2000. During the 1980s, whites favored Reagan, a president widely regarded as favoring big business and wealthy families. Fifty-six percent voted Republican vs. 36% Democratic in 1980; 64% vs. 35% in 1984. White votes were split rather evenly between Clinton and his challengers (43% vs. 44% in 1996), but whites strongly favored Bush over Gore in 2000 (54% to 42%). Perhaps some just did not like Gore. After the scandals of the Clinton presidency, perhaps some felt the country needed a more conservative presence in the White House.

Blacks and Hispanics routinely vote Democratic, in some cases overwhelmingly so. In 1984, 64% of whites voted for Reagan and 35% for Mondale; however, 90% of blacks and 62% of Hispanics voted for Mondale. Eighty-five percent of blacks supported Carter in 1980, as did 59% of Hispanics but only 36% of whites.

Age did not play much of a role in voting either. Ninety percent of African Americans between ages 18-29 voted for Carter in 1980; 84% of blacks between 45-59 did. In 1988, 86% of 18-29 year olds cast a vote for Mondale; so did 86% of men 45 to 59.

Asian voting patterns were more evenly distributed. They were slightly more inclined to vote Republican, a party that perhaps most accurately reflects their conservative principles: 55% supported Bush in 1992, compared to 31% for Clinton. In 1996, 46% supported Dole compared to 43% for Clinton. However, 54% supported Gore in the 2000 election, compared to 41% for Bush.

Some questions to be raised here: what, or who, influences our vote? Do we vote a straight ticket ("I always vote Republican")? Are we shaped by our upbringing and our parents' voting preferences? ("This is a democratic house.") How much are we persuaded by a candidate's record and performance? What really influences our vote?

Source: Connelley, Marjorie. "Who Voted: A Portrait of American Politics, 1976-2000." *New York Times*. 12 November 2000, p. 4. Data for 2000 were collected by Voter News Service based on questionnaires completed by 13,279 voters leaving 300 polling places on Election Day. 1996 data came from a survey of 16,627 voters. 1992 data came from a survey of 15,490 voters. Data from 1980 – 1988 came from the New York Times and CBS News: 11,645 in 1998, 9,174 in 1984, 15,201 in 1980.

Religion and Voting

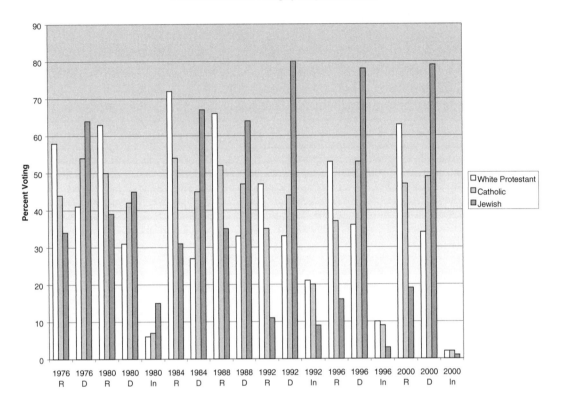

There is another persistent notion about elections: those of a specific religious affiliation will vote consistently for a specific party. Is this true?

Data suggest that it is, more or less. The panel displays the voting patterns of the top religions in recent presidential elections. Jews consistently favor the Democratic candidate, in some cases in overwhelming numbers: they favored Mondale over Reagan in 1984 (67% to 31%) and Gore over Bush in 2000 (79% to 19%). In the 1992 and 1996 elections, there was a gap of 69% and 62% between their votes for the major parties (80% and 11%; 78% and 16%). Why the preference? One important factor could be the Democratic Party's image as more inclusive and tolerant.

How do Protestants vote? The members of this faith tend to be white, of middle or upper middle class income. They tend to support traditional values, and a conservative government that values the personal liberties of its citizens. They consistently vote Republican. They voted for Reagan over Mondale (72% to 27%), George Bush over Clinton (47% to 33%) and George W. Bush over Gore (63% to 34%).

Catholics have followed a different path. They voted for Carter in 1976, switched to the Republican ticket in 1980, 1984, and 1988 (creating the term "Reagan Democrats"), then voted Democratic again in 1992 and 1996. They voted Democratic in the year 2000, but by a slim margin (49% to 47%). Catholics are often seen as more socially conservative

---

than other religions, with issues such as contraception, abortion, and gay rights continuing to polarize segments of their community. But Catholics also have a long history of social activism and caring for the poor, traits popularly associated with Democrats. Many come from working-class and union households, also a Democratic characteristic The group seems equally at home in both Republican and Democratic parties. As a result, Catholics have become something of a swing vote, with every candidate courting them — and none of them being entirely able to count on their support.

Our religious background is, of course, a key factor in shaping our attitudes about the world. But many of us have views differing from the official tenets of our faith. More to the point, few elections are ever won or lost on social issues. A Catholic may be against abortion, for example, but he well may vote on what matters most: his pocketbook or personal security.

Source: Connelley, Marjorie. "Who Voted: A Portrait of American Politics, 1976-2000." *New York Times*. 12 November, p. 4. Data for 2000 were collected by Voter News Service based on questionnaires completed by 13,279 voters leaving 300 polling places on Election Day. 1996 data came from a survey of 16,627 voters. 1992 came from a survey of 15,490 voters. Data from 1980 – 1988 came from the New York Times and CBS News: 11,645 in 1998, 9,174 in 1984, 15,201 in 1980.

Why Don't We Vote?

Top Reasons for Not Voting, 2000

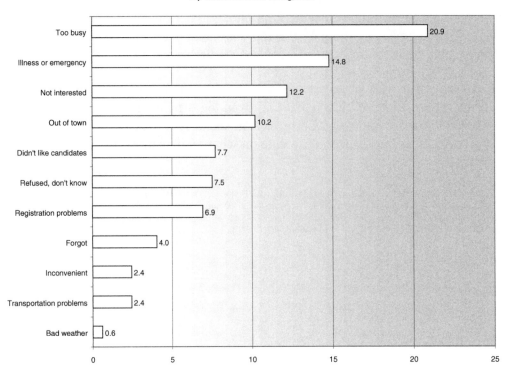

Too busy	20.9
Illness or emergency	14.8
Not interested	12.2
Out of town	10.2
Didn't like candidates	7.7
Refused, don't know	7.5
Registration problems	6.9
Forgot	4.0
Inconvenient	2.4
Transportation problems	2.4
Bad weather	0.6

Of the 130 million people registered to vote, 19 million (14%) did not do so in the 2000 election. Why? The top reasons for not voting cited by registered non-voters are shown above. The data come from the Census Bureau.

The main reason given for not voting was being too busy or experiencing a conflict with work or school schedules. Nearly 21% of non-voters, or 4 million people, offered this reason. Those who reported such a problem were usually men, the educated, and younger adults (18 to 44). Hispanics also gave this reason.

Another 15% reported being ill, disabled or having a family emergency. These respondents were more likely to be women, the elderly, and those with less education. Those who claimed not to be interested or that their vote would not count tended to have a high school education or less. Men, white non-Hispanics, and more educated people were more likely to be out of town.

What can be done to combat voter apathy — for whatever reasons? One of the main reasons people did not vote was a timing issue: they were too busy, polling hours were too inconvenient, they forgot, or had transportation problems. Many of the ideas posed to increase voter turnout could alleviate these issues: longer poll hours, voting on a weekend, more polling places and voting over multiple days. Chances are that behavior will change only a little in response to such mechanical fixes.

How can you combat apathy? 12.2% of people claimed not to be interested, 7.7% claimed not to like the candidates, 7.5% simply refused to do so. Those who do not vote multiply the votes of those who do. You can lead a horse to the water, but you cannot make him drink.

Source: U.S. Bureau of the Census. Current Population Reports. *Voting and Registration in the Election of November 2000*. Washington, DC: U.S. Government Printing Office, February 2002, p.12.

You Ultra-Conservative Liberal!

We're Pretty Fair-Minded: How We See Ourselves

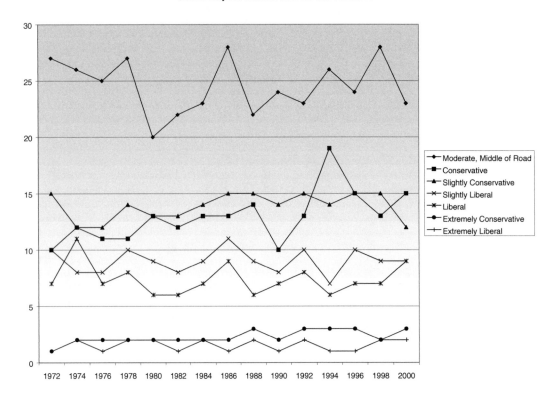

The terms are frequently thrown around: liberals, moderates, ultra-conservatives. How do we see ourselves? The panel shows the results of a survey conducted by the National Election Studies at the University of Michigan. People were asked: "Here is a 7-point scale on which the political views that people might hold are arranged from extremely liberal to extremely conservative. Where would you place yourself on this scale, or haven't you thought much about this?" (Roughly a quarter of respondents every year claimed not to have thought about it.)

Roughly a quarter of the people polled identified themselves as moderates in the 1972 to 2000 period. There is a steady segment of the population that is open to compromise, willing to "live and let live." Over recent years, people seem to be embracing slightly more conservative views. There was a strong rebound in those seeing themselves as conservatives in 1992, with percentages jumping from 13% to 19% in 1994. However, a balance will always be struck: those seeing themselves as moderates increased from 23% to 26% from 1992 to 1994 and from 24% in 1996 to 28% in 1998. The liberal category increased from 1998 to 2000.

What accounts for some of these recent changes? In part, it was the Clinton presidency. Some criticized the man. Some criticized the policies. Conservatives feasted on scandals such as Whitewater and Monica Lewinsky. Some were turned off by Newt Gingrich or Pat Buchanan and shifted their views slightly to the left.

The survey also points at a consistent base of people with extreme views. Roughly 2 to 3% of the respondents consistently labeled themselves as extremely liberal or conservative, suggesting there is a segment of the population that will not change its thinking for any reason. (Has anyone *listened* to talk radio lately?)

Of course, people's views are affected by such things as their upbringing and current events. The survey raises some interesting questions. What characteristics defined liberals and conservatives in 1972 compared with today? What are we still fighting about? People are still polarized by issues such as abortion and the death penalty. In some matters, there has been great change. Gays have attained increased visibility and acceptance in our culture. Few people raise an eyebrow at mixed-race couples. As some social changes become more mainstream, however, there will always be a subset of the population that resists the change.

The next panels are going to look at our attitudes more closely. How do we feel about certain issues? Are we more tolerant? Do we still hold on to certain perceptions about each other?

Source: "The NES Guide to Public Opinion and Electoral Behavior." Online. Available: http://www.umich.edu. April 4, 2002.

Where Are Our Manners?

The Major Causes of Rudeness and Disrespect in Our Society
(percent agreeing)

Cause	Percent
Too many parents are failing to teach respect to their kids	84
Values and morality are in decline in our society. People less likely to be polite and respectful	62
Even when parents try to raise their kids right, there are too many negative role models	60
People are often in overcrowded place or long lines - they get frustrated	50
Life is so hectic and people so busy, they forget to be polite	47
There is a declining sense of community	47
Fewer people are willing to question rude behavior	45
Rude behavior so common people stop being nice	41

In a recent study by Public Agenda, 78% of Americans insisted that "a lack of respect and courtesy is a serious problem and we should try to address it." How people treat each other is one of the basic components of any civilized society. The source singles out two questions: (1) Will people take steps to be respectful of one another? (2) Are they willing to moderate their own desires and comforts to accommodate the needs of others? Recent news stories on the issue range from the curious to the tragic: In April 2000, Steven Clevenger of Michigan faced a possible three-months jail term and $100 fine for swearing in the presence of children (a man faced similar charges in 1998 and was convicted). In January 2002, Thomas Junta, father of a hockey-playing youngster, was convicted of involuntary manslaughter for beating another father to death at the kids' hockey practice in Massachusetts.

Only 12% of people claim that they "practically never" encounter people who are rude or disrespectful; the remainder sees them either "often" (34%) or "sometimes" (54%). The study found this to be true regardless of the demographic background of the respondents — by region of the country, income, or size of the town. What causes rudeness? Respondents to the survey say the main reason is that parents are failing to teach values to their children. Those that do, the respondents assert, have to compete with a crude, sexually explicit pop culture.

Another major influence seems to be our hectic lives. We're forced to balance work and family. The process overwhelms some. Also, there are just too many people in some places. Social scientists have long pointed to the connection between population density and stress levels — although density in the U.S. is still rather moderate. Still, in some places, there are more people now and also much more aggravation. Many of us face these things daily: we wait in long lines or drive on overcrowded highways that weren't designed for creep and crawl. The other major factor is a theme that has appeared elsewhere in this book: a lack of community. We live in the suburbs instead cities. We don't know our neighbors; our children do not play together. More of us live alone. Related families no longer live close to one another. Many of us don't volunteer. In short, it is easier to be impolite and disrespectful to total strangers.

Another very interesting statistic in the study: 41% of the respondents confessed to being rude or disrespectful themselves. We all have moments when we lose our cool. But is rudeness in our culture an epidemic? Can courtesy, to quote the old golden rule of civility, ever be contagious?

Has the way we treat each other improved at all? The next panel addresses this question.

Source: Public Agenda. *Aggravating Circumstances: A Status Report on Rudeness in America.* Online. Available: http://www.publicagenda.org. April 28, 2002. Figures come from a random survey of 2,013 adults conducted January 2002.

Our Perception of the Sexes

How Do We See Men and Women?

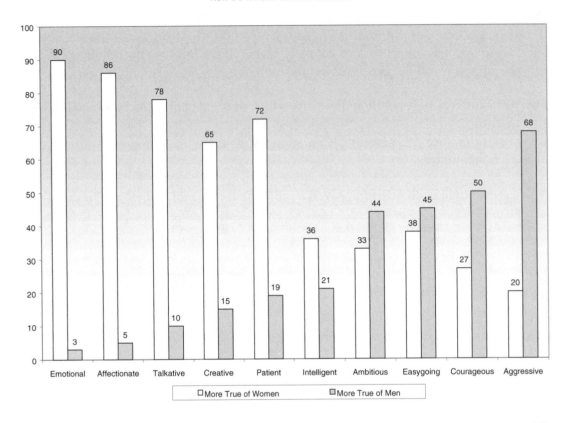

Popular culture tells us about the changing roles of men and women. True, significant changes *have* taken place: more women hold jobs traditionally held by men. Men have been increasingly encouraged to "get in touch with their feminine side." For all this talk of changing roles, however, are we seeing men and women any differently?

The panel shows the results of a Gallup Poll in which respondents were asked to identify characteristics that were truer of a certain sex. Men are still seen in traditional masculine, active terms. Sixty-eight percent saw men as aggressive, while less than half saw women with the same characteristic. Men are thought to be courageous, ambitious, and easygoing; in short, men are still seen as the strong, silent Gary Cooper type, climbing the corporate ladder in their gray flannel suits. Respondents believe that men are not supposed to be affectionate (5%) or emotional (3%). They also believe that under no circumstances should men be talkative (10%).

If a man is typically *doing* things, a woman is typically *feeling* them. A woman is still seen as an emotional creature. Ninety percent of respondents assigned this trait to women. They are often seen as possessing the qualities of a good wife or mother: women are affectionate and patient. Few people assigned such qualities to men. Women were seen as talkative (78%). They still are seen as leaning over their neighbor's fence, exchanging gossip as they hang up laundry.

Professor Henry Higgins in *My Fair Lady* posed the question: "Why can't a woman be more like a man?" In some areas, she is. Men and women were seen as ambitious at fairly similar levels: (44% and 33%, respectively). More women were viewed as intelligent than men (36% to 21%). This makes sense. More women are pursuing degrees and obtaining high-level, well-paying jobs. Many own their own businesses. Many men have women bosses.

Source: "Americans See Women as Emotional and Affectionate, Men as More Aggressive." Online. Available: http://www.gallup.com. April 17, 2002.

The Rise of Domestic Partner Benefits

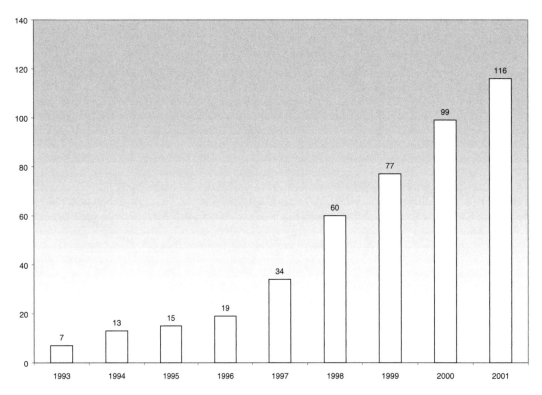

Fortune 500 Firms Offering Domestic Partner Benefits

Once seen as scandalous, living together is increasingly seen as an acceptable stage in a relationship. Terms such as girlfriend, boyfriend, or lover have come to signify more than one half of a couple. These are often serious, long-term relationships, valued by the heart and, increasingly, by Corporate America. In a sign of how society is changing, the Census created the category of "unmarried partner" just in 1990 and began to track these couples. They discovered that the number of unmarried partner households increased 72% in the 1990s, from 3.18 million to 5.47 million households.

Over 4,200 employers around the country, including colleges and universities, offer domestic partnership benefits, including General Motors, Ford, Boeing, AT&T and IBM. The panel shows the growing number of Fortune 500 companies that offer benefits to domestic partner benefits to unmarried and same-sex couples. The number increased 1,314.2% from 1993-2000, from 7 firms to 99.

How does this fit into a bigger picture? The share of large U.S. companies offering domestic partner benefits has more than doubled from 10% in 1997 to 22% in 2000, according to Hewitt Associates. According to their study, 76% of these companies offered these benefits to attract and retain employees, 30% to comply with a nondiscrimination policy, and 17% to comply with local government regulations. In short, some of these companies offered these benefits because they wanted to, some did it because they *had* to.

San Francisco was the first city in the nation to insist that all companies holding contracts with the city institute same-sex benefits. It's one thing to have such an ordinance, another to enforce it. In 1997, the city stalled approval of a lease agreement with San Francisco International Airport's largest tenant, United Airlines, for the company's failure to provide domestic partner benefits. (The company did not offer them in the United States, but did so in the Netherlands, Australia, and New Zealand, where it is required by law.) That same year, the city reported its contracting business strangled under a mountain of red tape. The San Francisco *Chronicle* reported that the situation had become so bad three supervisors who backed the law proposed amending it to allow individual city departments to issue wavers so the city could properly function. In a few cases, the city was forced to award contracts to competitive bidders, none of which offered same-sex benefits.

The next panel will look at the military's "Don't Ask, Don't Tell" policy.

Source: "Unmarried, with Benefits." *U.S. News & World Report.* 26 February 2001, p. 10; "Domestic Partner Benefits Doubled From 1997." *Research Alert*, 26 February 2001, p. 8; "San Francisco DP Enforcement Overwhelmed." Online. Available: http://www.datalounge.com. April 25, 2002. Data for 2001 are as of February 2001.

The State of Don't Ask, Don't Tell

Gay and in the Military

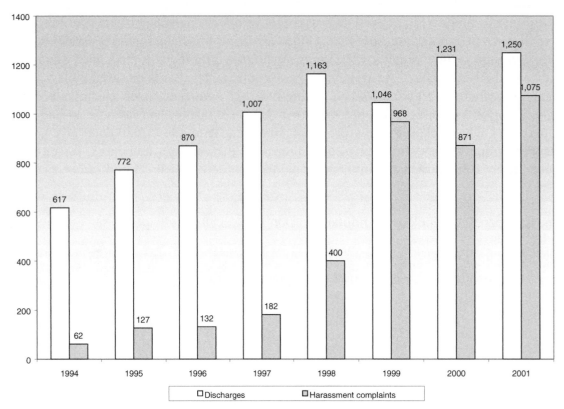

The number of harassment complaints and discharges of gay service members reached record levels in 2001, according to the Servicemembers Legal Defense Fund.

The policy of Don't Ask, Don't Tell allowed homosexuals to serve in the military as long as they did not identify their orientation. President Clinton approved the policy in 1993 after he failed to end the ban on gay and lesbian service members in the early days of his presidency. Both discharges and complaints have risen nearly every year since the policy's implementation.

The number of discharges rose 102.5% from 1994 to 2001. The number of harassment complaints is up 1,633.8%. From 2000 to 2001, while discharges increased slightly, the number of complaints increased 23.4%. Why did numbers drop in 1999? In part, tolerance programs are thought to have had some effect. But the beating death of gay soldier Barry Winchell at Fort Campbell, Kentucky, is thought to have played a part as well. After the investigation into this case, the military added "don't harass" to its policy of "don't ask, don't tell, don't pursue."

The Army discharges the most soldiers, the Coast Guard the fewest. According to the Army, 92% of the separations involved soldiers identifying themselves as gay, violating the policy. Gay activists claim soldiers step forward and identify themselves as gay or lesbian to escape continued harassment. The Navy was the only branch to see their number of discharges fall in 2001. The service discharged 314 sailors, compared to 358 the year before. Women were discharged at twice their rate of service. Women make up 14% of the military and 30% of the discharged in 2001.

Homosexuals have long had a battle with the U.S. military. In 1942, the Armed Forces issued instructions to military psychiatrists to make distinctions between homosexual and "normal" service members. Homosexuals were labeled unsuitable for military service. In 1957, however, a 639-page Navy document called the Crittenden Report concluded there is "no sound basis" for the charge that homosexuals in the military pose a security risk. The Pentagon denied the existence of such a report for nearly 20 years. In 1975, Sgt. Leonard Matlovich, after being dismissed from the Air Force for being gay, sued to be reinstated. Five years later a federal judge ordered just that, but Matlovich accepted a financial settlement instead. A series of high-profile cases followed challenging the policy, involving such figures as Perry Watkins and Miriam Ben-Shalom. In 1992, the General Accounting Office reported that between 1981 and 1990 nearly 17,000 men and women had been dismissed for being homosexual, and that it had cost $493.19 million to replace them.

Keep in mind that these are reported incidents. How many go unreported?

Sources: Stone, Andrea. "Military Discharges of Gays, Rising, Report Says." *USA Today*, 14 March 14 2002, p. 10A. "Gays and the Military Timeline." Online. Available: http://www.glimm.com. April 24, 2002; "Army Base Acknowledges Under-Reporting Gay Discharges." Online. Available: http://www.sldn.org.

Are Things Getting Better?

Percent Who Say Things Have Gotten Better

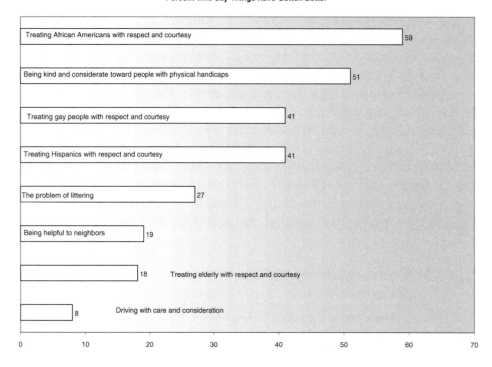

Treating African Americans with respect and courtesy	59
Being kind and considerate toward people with physical handicaps	51
Treating gay people with respect and courtesy	41
Treating Hispanics with respect and courtesy	41
The problem of littering	27
Being helpful to neighbors	19
Treating elderly with respect and courtesy	18
Driving with care and consideration	8

Are things improving in some areas? The Public Agenda survey asked respondents in what areas they thought things had gotten better, worse, or stayed the same when compared to the past.

We have made some progress in being more respectful to segments of our population. Blacks, Hispanics, gays and handicapped people have become powerful forces in our society, influencing our culture and shaping political debate and policy. What accounts for our improving attitudes? Some may argue it is simply a case of political correctness or "thought police." There may be some element of this. But perhaps we are more tolerant because the diverse elements of society mix more. More African-Americans and Hispanics are attending college and working at higher-paying jobs than in previous years. Gays are increasingly open and visible, with many of us having a gay friend or coworker. In short, we are learning about and from each other.

Some people in the survey saw great improvements. Over 60% rated the treatment of the handicapped as good or excellent compared to their treatment in the past. Some attitudes are still in transition, however: only 31% of the respondents felt Americans' treatment of gay people was good or excellent.

While respondents were willing to give Americans good marks in some of their attitudes, members of these minorities felt that they were not given reasons to be so charitable. For example, only 26% of African-Americans felt the respect and courtesy given to them by their fellow citizens was excellent or good. Sixty-four percent claimed that demonstrations of respect and courtesy "needed improvement." Many confessed to experiencing chronic racial-bias issues: from being followed in stores to prevent shoplifting to racial profiling.

There are some issues we have yet to address. We still disrespect our planet with litter and pollution. Many of us still don't value our seniors. Cases of road rage seem to be getting deadlier.

Where are things headed? Are things better? Are we getting angrier as a society? Will we get along with each other in public, but not in private?

Source: Public Agenda. *Aggravating Circumstances: A Status Report on Rudeness in America*. Online. Available: http://www.publicagenda.org. April 28,2002. Figures come from a random survey of 2,013 adults conducted January 2002.

Chapter 6

Religion in America

The United States of America: A religiously diverse nation. Or is it? The First Amendment to the Constitution, in part, states: "Congress shall make no law respecting an establishment of religion, or prohibiting the free exercise thereof...." We have freedom to choose religions (or no religion) and, in 2001, 76% of us chose some branch of Christianity. Not surprising, since Christianity has the most adherents throughout the world. The first panel presents an overview of religious affiliation in the United States and in the world. The next panel shows the 10 largest religions in the United States based on adult adherents.

The next two panels explain growth (or decline) in religious membership. First, we look at the phenomenon of switching religions. About 1 in 6 Americans say that they've switched religious affiliation (or have become non-religious). Many are leaving the traditional religions in favor of the newer religions (or those that are newer to America). Second, we look at the top 20 religions based on growth rate. Many New Age, Evangelical Christian, and Eastern religions are growing faster than are traditional religions. The Wiccan religion grew an astounding 1,575% from 1990 to 2001!

Where do we worship? The next panel discusses Christian houses of worship and tracks the change in the number of churches compared to the change in the number of adherents. The following panel discusses the effects this has had on the size of these congregations. Next, we look at some of the non-Christian houses of worship and where they are concentrated in the United States. Some states do not have any houses of worship for a particular religion.

The Internet has touched nearly every aspect of our lives, and our spiritual life is no exception. The next panel discusses the top 10 activities of the 28 million Americans in 2001 who used the Internet to supplement their spiritual life. More of us are attending church online. More churches are Web-casting their services and the faithful are flocking (or surfing) to them. Cyber-churches don't have physical buildings, but they do offer sermons, inspirational music, multimedia Bibles, and "virtual" sanctuaries. The cyber-church is not just for Christians, either. Muslims, Buddhists, and Jews also have sites dedicated to helping adherents in their spiritual quest.

Religious Affiliation

Religious Affiliation in the United States, 1990 and 2001
(% of Adult Population)

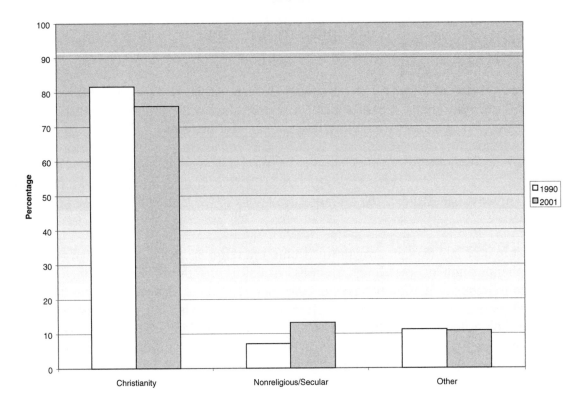

The chart shows the religious affiliation of the adult population[1] in the United States for two years: 1990 and 2001. Adherents to Christianity made up a majority in both years. In 1990, the number of Christians exceeded those who claimed no religious affiliation. By 2001 this had changed. Those without an affiliation made up a higher percentage of the adult population (2.4% higher) than did the total non-Christian religious population. The latter stood at 10.8%.

The following table breaks down the graphed data into the 15 religions (in the U.S., of course) with the highest adult populations in 2001. Ratios are shown to the adult population as reported in the year 2000 census of population. Individually, except for Judaism, each non-Christian religion shown made up less than 1% of the U.S. adult population in 2001. But these religions have been the most dynamic in terms of growth from 1990 to 2001. A later panel will discuss these growth rates.

---

[1] Agnostic, atheist, and humanist are a part of the "Other" category in the graph.

Top 15 Religions in the United States by Adult Population, 2001

	% of adult pop.	Est. adult pop.
Christian	76.00	159,030,000
Nonreligious/secular	13.20	27,539,000
Jewish[2]	1.40	2,831,000
Islamic	0.50	1,104,000
Buddhist	0.50	1,082,000
Agnostic	0.50	991,000
Atheist	0.40	902,000
Hindu	0.40	766,000
Unitarian Universalist	0.30	629,000
Wiccan/Pagan/Druid	0.10	307,000
Spiritualist	0.06	116,000
Native American Religion	0.05	103,000
Baha'i	0.04	84,000
New Age beliefs	0.03	68,000
Sikh	0.03	57,000

Christianity has the highest percentage of adherents in both the United States and in the world. But the United States is slightly more secular or unbelieving than the world. Combining the nonreligious, secular, atheistic, and agnostic values, 14.1% of the U.S. population falls into these categories, 14.0% of the world's adult population. The following table shows the top 15 religions of the world, by percentage of world population[3] and by number of adherents.

Top 15 Religions in the World, by Number of Adherents, 2001

	% of world pop.	Est. adherents
Christian	33.00	2,000,000,000
Islamic	22.00	1,300,000,000
Hindu	15.00	900,000,000
Secular/Nonreligious/Agnostic/Atheist beliefs	14.00	850,000,000
Buddhist	6.00	360,000,000
Chinese traditional religion	4.00	225,000,000
Primal-indigenous beliefs	3.00	190,000,000
Sikh	0.38	23,000,000
Yoruba Religion	0.33	20,000,000
Juche	0.32	19,000,000
Spiritist	0.23	14,000,000
Jewish[2]	0.23	14,000,000
Baha'i	0.10	6,000,000
Jainist	0.07	4,000,000
Shinto	0.05	3,000,000

In the next panel, we look at the 10 largest denominational families in the United States.

Sources: "Top 20 Religions in the United States." Online. Available: http://www.adherents.com/rel_USA.html. February 28, 2002. 1990 and 2000 Population data: U.S. Bureau of the Census. World Religion data: "Major Religions of the World Ranked by Number of Adherents." Online. Available: http://www.adherents.com/Religions_By_Adherents.html. November 28, 2001.

[2] Only includes adherents to Judaism.

[3] Some data in the table extrapolated using a world population of 6 billion.

Traditional...

10 Largest Denominational Families, 1990 and 2001
(% of the U.S. Population)

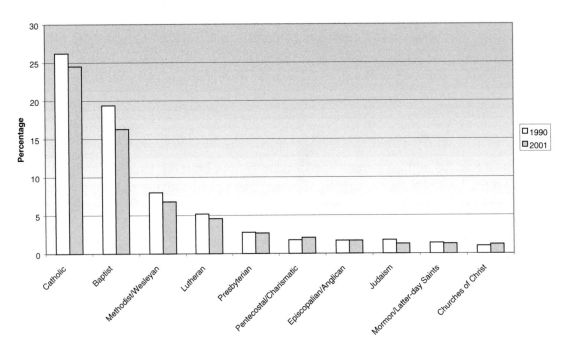

The chart shows, as a percentage of the adult population, those who identify with a religious denomination[4]. The largest denominations are shown. As might be expected, these are also the oldest ones. Most are Christian religions, but Judaism is also in the top 10. No one denomination has a majority of the population. Many of the denominations shown have seen a decline in the percentage of adult adherents. Despite this, Catholics maintained the highest percentage of the population (24.5% in 2001), followed by Baptists (16.3%). The Churches of Christ was tenth in rank (1.2%). Adherents.com reports that Islam, the third-largest major religion in the United States "is smaller than about 15 of the country's largest Christian denominations."

The table on the next page shows gains and losses between 1990 and 2001. The table also shows the number of adults identifying with each of the denominations. Decline in a denomination's share of total population doesn't mean absolute decline. Many groups have gained adherents. Exceptions are Methodists/Wesleyans, Baptists, and the adherents of Judaism.

---

[4] Although Judaism consists of many branches (Orthodox, Conservative, Reform, etc.), the source cites it as a single religion.

Change in Population by Denomination, 1990-2001 and

Estimated Adult Population by Denomination, 1990 and 2001

	Change, 1990-2001	1990	2001
Catholic	4,869,000	46,004,000	50,873,000
Pentecostal/Charismatic	1,216,000	3,191,000	4,407,000
Churches of Christ	824,000	1,769,000	2,593,000
Presbyterian	611,000	4,985,000	5,596,000
Lutheran	470,000	9,110,000	9,580,000
Episcopalian/Anglican	409,000	3,042,000	3,451,000
Mormon/Latter-day Saints	210,000	2,487,000	2,697,000
Methodist/Wesleyan	-24,000	14,174,000	14,150,000
Baptist	-134,000	33,964,000	33,830,000
Judaism	-306,000	3,137,000	2,831,000

Why are many of the traditional religions experiencing a decline in the share of the U.S. adult population? Why are the numbers of adult members declining in some religious denominations? We look at this phenomenon in the next panel.

Source: "Largest Religious Groups in the United States of America." Online. Available: http://www.adherents.com/ rel_USA.html. February 28, 2002. Tracey Rich. "Judaism 101." Online. Available: http://www.jewfaq.org. March 13, 2002.

... to Nontraditional...

Net % Gain or Loss of Members Due to Switching Religions, 2001

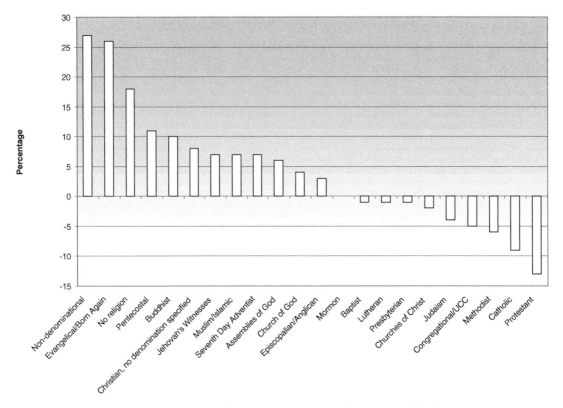

About 1 in 6 American adults say they've switched religious affiliation or have become non-religious. The chart shows groups gaining adherents on the left, those losing members[5] on the right. Many newer religions (or those that are newer to America) gained membership by converting outsiders. Traditional religions lost members who have gone to worship elsewhere or have stopped worshipping. Non-denominational groups show the highest gains (27%). Protestant religions have lost the highest percentage of members due to conversion: 13% fewer people converted to Protestant religions than Protestants who switched to another religion or became non-religious.

The following table shows the numbers of members gained and lost as illustrated in the graph. In terms of numbers, those that consider themselves as having no religion saw the biggest increase: more than 5.5 million adults switched from being affiliated with a religion to having no religion. Catholicism, on the other hand, saw the largest number of members convert to another religion (or no religion at all): over 5.2 million fewer adults converted to Catholicism than Catholic adults who converted to another religion did.

---

[5] In this panel, members refer to those who are affiliated with a religious group. Percentages were derived by subtracting the percentage of adults who switched out of a religion from the percentage of adults who switched into a religion. Data obtained from *American Religious Identification Survey*.

Catholicism, being the largest single Christian grouping, also lost the most numbers in a time where non-belief appears to be on the increase.

Net Gain or Loss of Adult Members Due to Switching Religions, 2001

	Net gain or loss of members
No religion	5,504,413
Christian, no denomination specified	1,386,541
Non-denominational	678,135
Pentecostal	610,043
Evangelical/Born Again	306,290
Episcopalian/Anglican	154,532
Jehovah's Witnesses	136,557
Buddhist	119,488
Muslim/Islamic	84,526
Assemblies of God	76,884
Seventh Day Adventist	70,145
Church of God	45,563
Mormon	-4,683
Churches of Christ	-53,519
Congregational/UCC	-85,860
Lutheran	-102,231
Presbyterian	-116,050
Judaism	-119,943
Baptist	-218,066
Protestant	-771,822
Methodist	-1,144,374
Catholic	-5,211,003

With the number of people who consider themselves non-religious growing (from 14 million in 1999 to 29 million in 2001), does this mean that more and more people are rejecting religion? Not necessarily. According to Barna Research Group, in 1999 2% of atheists and agnostics attended Christian church services on Sunday (12% did so on Easter Sunday that year). 60% own a Bible, about 34% read it at least occasionally, and 19% pray to God during a typical week. Atheists may be just as ambivalent as the believers...

Conversion isn't the only way religious congregations grow in membership. Other factors include birth rates and immigration. In the next panel we look at the top 20 religions in the United States that showed the most growth overall from 1990 to 2001.

Sources: "Exhibit 7: Number of Adults by Current and Prior Religious Identification, 2001." *American Religious Identification Survey.* Online. Available: http://www.gc.cuny.edu/studies/images/image019.gif. March 5, 2002. Barna Research data: "One in 15 Adults Atheist, Agnostic." *Research Alert,* 3 December 1999.

... to Pagan?

Top 20 Religions in the United States Based on Growth Rate, 1990-2001
(% change, 1990-2001)

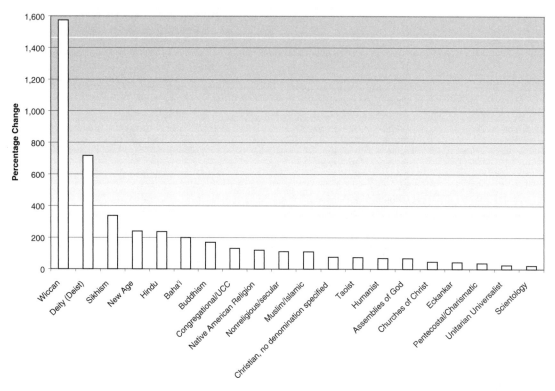

The chart shows the 20 religions with the highest growth rates from 1990 to 2001. Most are non-Christian religions, with a pagan religion, Wiccan, having the highest growth rate (1,575%!). The top 20 growing religions present mostly a mix of New Age, Evangelical Christian, and Eastern religions. The growth of the nonreligious/secular group is also in the top 20 (110% growth between 1990 and 2001).

Growth in the Eastern religions (Sikhism, Hinduism, Buddhism, and Taoism) could be due, in part, to immigration from India and China (more than 700,000 people from India and China immigrated to the United States from 1991-2000). The New Age movement also has contributed to the popularity of these religions. New Age takes some of its beliefs and practices from Eastern religions. Immigration from traditionally Muslim countries may contribute, in part, to the growth of members of the Muslim/Islamic faith also. But, as the previous panel showed, the Islamic faith is also popular among those seeking a new religion. In 2001, more than 84,000 adults in the United States converted to Islam.

The New Age movement became popular in the 1960s and continues strong 40 years later. A backlash against traditionally God-centered, organized religion spurred this movement which seeks more of a personal spirituality: a oneness with nature, the universe, and society. The modern Wiccan movement essentially grew out of this tradition also. Wiccan religion also emphasizes personal freedom within the community as evidenced by its central creed: "If it harms none, do what you will" (PEN)[6].

Evangelical Christian denominations, still traditionally Christian, have a diversity of worship styles according to the needs and desires of the individual congregation, not a uniform worship style across the religion as some traditional organized religions do, such as Catholicism.

With the huge growth in non-traditional religions (and in those professing to be of no religion) does this mean that traditional religion is fading away? Hardly. As we've seen in an earlier panel, traditional organized religions still make up a sizeable portion of the American population. The following table shows that despite the huge growth rates, the non-traditional religions each make up only a relatively small fraction of the total religious population of the United States. In terms of the number of adherents, only those professing no religion and those who consider themselves Pentecostal/Charismatic are in the top 10. The rest of the religions in the top 10 are the traditional organized religions, with Catholics and Baptists having the largest numbers of adherents.[7]

Adult Religious Affiliation, 2001

Catholic	*50,873,000*	Muslim/Islamic	1,104,000
Baptist	*33,830,000*	Buddhism	1,082,000
Nonreligious/secular	27,539,000	Hindu	766,000
Christian, no denomination specified	14,190,000	Unitarian Universalist	629,000
Methodist/Wesleyan	*14,140,000*	Wiccan	134,000
Lutheran	*9,580,000*	Native American Religion	103,000
Presbyterian	*5,596,000*	Baha'i	84,000
Protestant, no religion specified	*4,647,000*	New Age	68,000
Pentecostal/Charismatic	4,407,000	Sikhism	57,000
Episcopalian/Anglican	*3,451,000*	Scientology	55,000
Judaism	*2,831,000*	Deity (Deist)	49,000
Churches of Christ	2,593,000	Humanist	49,000
Congregational/UCC	1,378,000	Taoist	40,000
Assemblies of God	1,106,000	Eckankar	26,000

Sources: "Top Twenty Religions in the United States, 2001." Online. Available: http://www.adherents.com/ rel_USA.html. February 28, 2002; DeBarros, Anthony B. and Cathy Lynn Grossman. "A Measure of Faith: By the numbers." *USA Today, 24 December* 2001. B. A. Robinson. "New Age Spirituality." Online. Available: http://www.religioustolerance.org/newage.htm. March 13, 2002. Immigration data: U.S. Immigration and Naturalization Service. *2000 Statistical Yearbook of the Immigration and Naturalization Service.* Online. Available: http://www.ins.gov. March 5, 2002. Wiccan data: Pagan Educational Network. "Contemporary Witchcraft." Online. Available: http://www.bloomington.in.us/~pen/Wicca.pdf. March 5, 2002. Pagan Educational Network. "Contemporary Paganism." Online. Available: http://www.bloomington.in.us/~pen/mpagan.html. March 5, 2002.

---

[6] PEN stands for Pagan Educational Network.

[7] Lines in italics are the traditional organized religions. "Protestant, no religion specified" was italicized because it could include the traditional Protestant religions. "Christian, no religion specified" was not italicized because it appears in the graph, but may also include traditional Christian religions.

Christian Houses of Worship

Denominations With the Most Churches in 1999

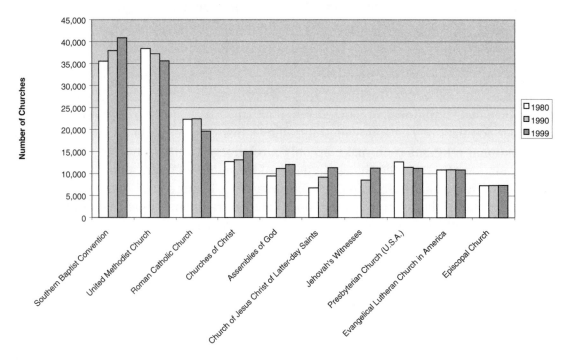

Religious affiliation in the United States is overwhelmingly Christian. Therefore, as expected, the top 10 denominations with the most churches in the United States in 1999 are all Christian. The chart above shows the number of churches by denomination for the years 1980, 1990, and 1999. Although The Church of God in Christ reported having more churches than the Churches of Christ, that denomination was not included here because data were from 1991 and no comparable data were available for 1980 or 1999.

Most of the denominations report having more churches in 1999 than in 1980. Only the United Methodist Church, the Catholic Church, and the Presbyterian Church (U.S.A.) report having fewer. The number of churches belonging to the Evangelical Church in America and the Episcopal Church have remained essentially unchanged in those 19 years.

Does the growth (or decline) in churches parallel a growth (or decline) in membership? The following table shows that this is not always the case. The number of United Methodist and Presbyterian (U.S.A.) churches declined in accordance with the decline in adherents. The number of Assembly of God churches and the number of Latter-Day Saint churches increased in accordance with an increase in adherents. However, the rest (except for the Catholic Church) had declines in adherents but increases in the number of churches, suggesting more but smaller congregations.

Percentage Change in Adherents vs. Percentage Change in Number of Churches, 1980-1999

	Adherents (% change)	Churches (% change)
Southern Baptist Convention	-3.4	14.9
United Methodist Church	-27.5	-7.4
Roman Catholic Church	31.3	-12.2
Churches of Christ	-6.3	17.9
Assemblies of God	59.7	27.6
Church of Jesus Christ of Latter-day Saints	90.4	67.1
Jehovah's Witnesses[8]	-28.3	31.7
Presbyterian Church (U.S.A.)	-11.3	-11.6
Evangelical Lutheran Church in America	-4.3	0.1
Episcopal Church	-17.9	1.4

We turn next to the effects of the growth or decline in the number of churches on the congregation.

Sources: U.S. Bureau of the Census. *Statistical Abstract of the United States 2001.* American Religion Data Archive. "Denominational Groupings: Full U.S. Report." Online. Available: http://www.thearda.com. March 6, 2002. "Top 10 Religious Bodies with Most Churches in the U.S., 1990." Online. Available: http://www.adherents.com/rel_USA.html. February 28, 2002.

---

[8] Percentage change is from 1990-1999. No data was available for 1980.

Adherents Per Church

Denominations With the Most Churches in 1999: Average Adherents per Church

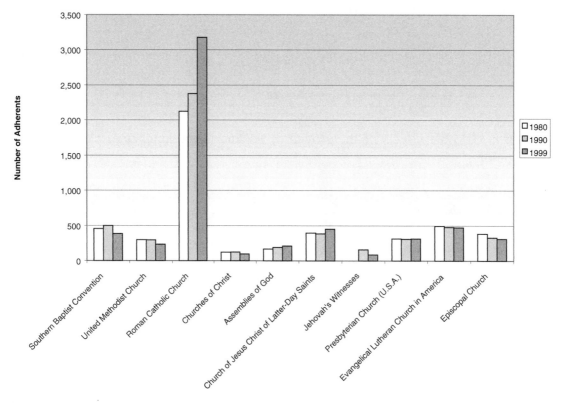

The chart shows the average number of adherents per church. Churches with the most church structures in 1999 are shown. Most denominations have seen a decline in the number of adherents per church. In most cases this was due to an increase in the number of churches built. Two exceptions were the Assemblies of God and the Church of Jesus Christ of Latter-Day Saints. These two denominations saw the number of adherents per church rise while, simultaneously, the number of churches increased. In these cases, the number of churches built did not keep up with the demand. In the Assemblies of God denomination, the number of adherents increased by 59.7% from 1980 to 1999, while the percentage of churches increased 27.6%. In the case of the Church of Jesus Christ of Latter-Day Saints, the number of adherents went up 90.4% since 1980, but the number of churches increased only 67.1%. The United Methodist Church saw declines in the average number of adherents per church even though the number of churches declined also. Adherents dropped at a faster rate than the percentage of churches closing.

The Catholic Church was the only denomination in the group that closed churches despite having gained members. More than 2,700 Catholic churches closed, 1980 to 1999, but slightly more than 15 million more Catholics populated the church. Why? A major reason is the shortage of priests. According to the Center for Applied Research at Georgetown University, 1 out of 6 parishes in the U.S. (3,151) has no resident priest. That's up from 1 in 30 (549) back in 1965. The Catholic Church has been seeing a decline in all religious vocations, except permanent deacons. The number of priests declined by 13,441 from

1965 to 2001 and the number of priest ordinations in 2001 was 485 fewer than in 1965. The number of religious sisters declined by more than 101,000 in the same time period.

The next panel shows non-Christian houses of worship in the United States.

Sources: U.S. Bureau of the Census. *Statistical Abstract of the United States 2001.* American Religion Data Archive. "Denominational Groupings: Full U.S. Report." Online. Available: http://www.thearda.com. March 6, 2002. "Top 10 Religious Bodies with Most Churches in the U.S., 1990." Online. Available: http://www.adherents.com/rel_USA.html. February 28, 2002. Belluck, Pam. "Maine Parish Agonizes Over a Priest's Confession." *New York Times,* 5 March 2002. Religious vocation data: Center for Applied Research in the Apostolate. "Frequently Requested Church Statistics." Online. Available: http://cara.georgetown.edu/bulletin/index.htm. March 6, 2002.

Non-Christian Houses of Worship

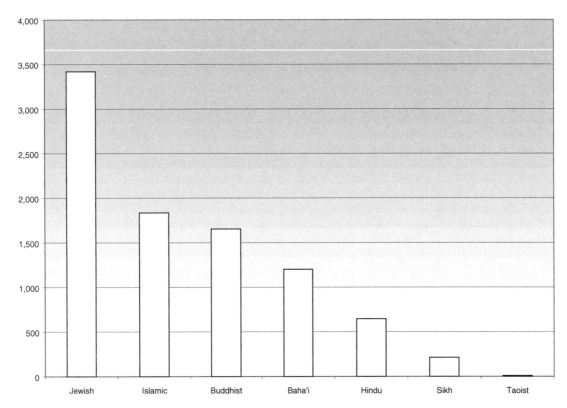

The chart shows the number of synagogues and religious centers for a selection of major non-Christian faiths. Data for Jewish synagogues are from 1990. Data for the Baha'i faith are from 2001. The Baha'i faith has one House of Worship in the United States (in Illinois); however, each local Baha'i community has an elected Spiritual Assembly. The data shown are the approximate number of Spiritual Assemblies in the United States. The data for the remaining religions are from January 2002.

The number of synagogues and religious centers corresponds to the number of adherents in each of the religions. Adherents to Judaism made up the largest population (2.8 million in 2001) and they also had the most houses of worship (more than 3,400 synagogues). Taoists had the lowest population (40,000 in 2001) and had the fewest houses of worship in the United States (9 Temples[9]).

Where is each of these populations concentrated? The following table shows the states in which the most houses of worship can be found. In the case of Taoism, however, the

---

[9] There were an additional 46 other Taoist institutions, spread over 18 states and the District of Columbia, where the Taoist beliefs and practices were taught.

states listed are the only states where Taoist Temples can be found, according to ReligionQuest.com.

Concentrations of Non-Christian Houses of Worship, 2002

	States with the most houses of worship	States with no houses of worship
Jewish Synagogues	NY, CA, FL, PA, IL, MA, Washington D.C.[10]	-
Islamic Religious Centers	100+: CA, IL, NY 50-99: MI, OH, NJ, MD, VA, NC, GA, FL	-
Buddhist Religious Centers	100+: CA, NY 50-99: WA, CO, TX, IL, MA, HI	WY, ND, SD
Baha'i Spiritual Assemblies	Data not available	Data not available
Hindu Religious Centers	100+: CA 50-99: NY, NJ 25-49: TX, FL, MD, IL	MT, WY, ND, SD, IN, AR
Sikh Religious Centers	50-99: CA 10-24: TX, OH, NY	ID, WY, ND, SD, NE, AR, KY, WV, SC, RI, NH, VT, ME
Taoist Temples	7: CA 1: CO, TX	Rest of the United States

The next panel discusses the impact the Internet has on our religious life.

Sources: U.S. Bureau of the Census. *Statistical Abstract of the United States 1994.* The Pluralism Project. "Geographic Distribution of Religious Centers in the U.S." Online. Available: http://www.pluralism.org/resources/statistics/distribution.php. March 6, 2002. "Welcome to The Baha'i Faith — Community." Online. Available: http://www.us.bahai.org/community/index.html. March 6, 2002. "Taoist Temples and Centers in the West." Online. Available: http://www.ReligionQuest.com. March 7, 2002. World ORT. *Antisemitism World Report 1997.* Online. Available: http://www.ess.uwe.ac.uk/documents/antsemus.htm. March 7, 2002.

---

[10] Based on a listing of cities with the highest concentration of the Jewish population. Those cities were: New York, Los Angeles, Miami, Philadelphia, Chicago, Boston, San Francisco, Washington D.C. Data taken from World ORT.

Religion Online

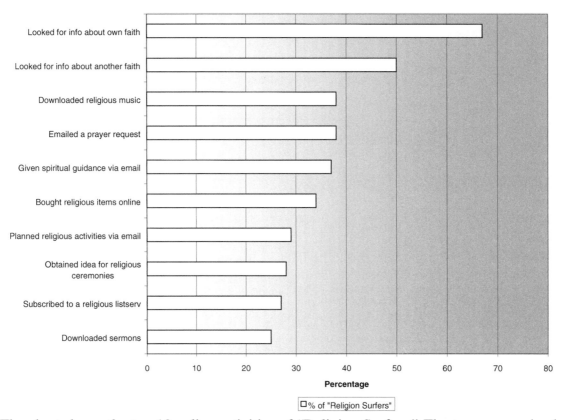

Top 10 Online Activities of "Religion Surfers", 2001

- Looked for info about own faith
- Looked for info about another faith
- Downloaded religious music
- Emailed a prayer request
- Given spiritual guidance via email
- Bought religious items online
- Planned religious activities via email
- Obtained idea for religious ceremonies
- Subscribed to a religious listserv
- Downloaded sermons

Percentage

☐ % of "Religion Surfers"

The chart shows the top 10 online activities of "Religion Surfers." The term was coined by Elena Larsen of the Pew Internet & American Life Project to describe the 28 million Americans in 2001 (up from 19-20 million in 2000) who have used the Internet to get religious and spiritual information or to interact with the faithful. Most of these "Surfers" used the Internet as a spiritual library: searching for information on their own faith or the faith of others. But not all activities were of a solitary nature. Many also requested prayers or offered spiritual advice online — activities that promote socialization and helping their fellow human beings. This is not surprising: 81% say their faith is very strong, 74% attend religious services at least once a week, and 86% pray or meditate daily. In fact, "Religious Surfers" put a higher priority on "real world" interactions.

Percent of "Religion Surfers" Who Say These Activities Are Important To Them

Solitary meditation or prayer	85%
Volunteering to help others	71%
Regular worship or prayer	70%
Conversation with fellow worshippers	69%
Group celebration of holidays	55%
Small group study	50%
Regular confession	44%
Speaking with clergy or other advisors	43%
Going online for religious information	13%

On any given day in 2001, 3 million Americans sought spiritual information on the Internet. This activity was more popular than online gambling, online banking and investing, online auction participation, and Internet-dating services.

What about the clergy? Are they seeking divine inspiration on the web? The following table presents the top 5 online activities of the clergy. Besides these activities, more than half of the clergy who use the Internet did so to get information on other denominations or faiths and have sought information on matters of their own faith.

Top 5 Online Activities by the Clergy, 2000

Obtained information for worship services	81%
Sought information on the Bible, Torah, or other scriptures	77%
Obtained devotional resources	72%
Gathered information for educational programs	72%
Looked for information on matters of doctrine	59%

The next panel discusses religious congregations online.

Source: Larsen, Elena. *CyberFaith: How Americans Pursue Religion Online.* Pew Internet & American Life Project: Washington D.C., December 23, 2001. Online. Available: http://www.pewinternet.org. Elena Larsen, et. al. *Wired churches, wired temples: Taking congregations and missions into cyberspace.* Pew Internet & American Life Project: Washington D.C., December 20, 2000. Online. Available: http://www.pewinternet.org.

Congregations in Cyberspace

Top 10 Things Congregations Do With Their Web Sites, 2000

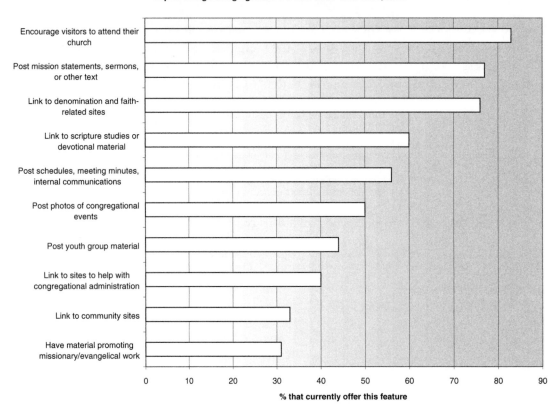

Depicted here are the top 10 features offered by congregational Web sites. There are more than 99,000 congregational Web sites on the Internet. Most don't intend to displace the physical church. They offer visitors insight into their faith community and invite people to come and worship — in the flesh. Posting mission statements, sermons, other texts, links to denominational and faith-related sites, and photos of congregational events all aid in welcoming the visitor. Congregational Web sites keep current members informed. Sermons, photos, and calendars are posted. Church administration can also keep up to date, by exchanging minutes and so on. Posting links to community sites and posting materials on missionary and evangelical work is a way for the congregation to be a part of the community.

These Web sites are meant to supplement the "brick and mortar" church. What about virtual congregations and virtual churches? Will we ever want to set foot in a real church building again?

Harvest Christian Fellowship, in Southern California, was one of the first churches to go online in 1995. In 1997, they became one of the first to broadcast services via the Web. "Every service has been Web-cast live and archived on the site [for future viewing]. The site has audio and video presentations on Christianity, MP3s with daily devotional messages, Christian music, and even live online counseling so visitors can chat in real time with a church counselor about matters of faith. According to Harvest, about 4 million people visit their site annually with 250,000 "attending their church services online" (ACFnewsource). The Crystal Cathedral in Garden Grove, California, has live web-casts of Sunday sermons. This site has about 10,000 people tuning in by Internet each Sunday. Non-denominational churches aren't the only ones web-casting. Atlanta's Peachtree Presbyterian Church also web-casts its services. At a service in 1999, 1,600 people watched via the Internet.

Both of these churches have buildings, and hold services there. What about cyber-churches? They have no building. They exist totally in cyberspace. The First Church of Cyberspace (www.godweb.org) is one such church. It was organized in 1994 by a Pres-byterian minister, Charles Henderson, "as an attempt to bring Christianity online with thoughtfulness, humor and a willingness to address more controversial questions that tend to be avoided in the traditional church" (godweb.org). The site offers sermons, inspira-tional music, a multimedia Bible, and a "virtual" sanctuary with a "virtual" eternal flame. Cyber-churches are not just for the Christian. IslamiCity (www.islam.org), based in Southern California, is a virtual mosque that serves the worldwide Muslim community. Buddhists have BuddhaNet (www.buddhanet.org) to help in their spiritual life. Jews have The Wall.org (www.aish.com/wallcam/). This site allows the faithful to type out mes-sages, which students in Jerusalem print out and place in the Western Wall.

What will the future bring? Will cyber-churches (and mosques, and temples, etc.) become more popular than physical places of worship? In 1998, 1 in 6 teenagers said they rely on the Internet to augment their spiritual needs and expect to stop attending a physical church altogether sometime in the future. By 2010, researchers predict that between 10% and 20% of American Internet users will rely on the Web for all of their worship and faith-related endeavors. Of course, a lot can change in eight years…

Sources: Larsen, Elena, et. al. *Wired churches, wired temples: Taking congregations and missions into cyberspace.* Pew Internet & American Life Project: Washington D.C., December 20, 2000 (chart data). "High Tech Religion." *ACFnewsource,* February 16, 2001(congregation and cyber-church data); "Holy Log-on." *ACFnewsource,* various dates 1999. Online. Available: http://www.acfnewsource.org. March 7, 2002. Andrew Careaga. "Cyber Congregations Go Fishing on the Net." *Church Business* (October 2000). Online. Available: http://www.churchbusiness.com. March 7, 2002. P.J. Huffstutter. "God is Everywhere on the Net." *Los Angeles Times,* 14 December 1998. Abraham McLaughlin. "Onward Online Soldiers." *ABCNEWS.com*, 22 April 1999.

Chapter 7

How Educated Are We?

How educated are we? The answer seems to change depending upon your point of view.

First, we look at graduation rates and educational attainment. We see that the high school graduation rates have soared since the 1870s. And, although rates have fallen off in the last 30 years of the 20th Century, by 2000, the percentage of graduates was the highest it had been since 1960. The number of college students has also been on the rise since the 1870s, with a dramatic increase from 1950-2000.

Educational attainment for all racial groups has been rising steadily since 1960. The simple literacy rate for adults has been going up ever since the 1870s, reaching a rate of 99.3% in 1979. "Functional literacy" became a concept after 1980. How do educational attainment and employment relate to a person's level of functional literacy?

Next, we examine the reading and math skills of children in the United States. The test scores of the National Assessment of Educational Progress (NAEP) varied little in the past 30 years. Are students proficient in reading and math according to these tests? How do our children compare to others in the world? In reading, the United States ranks in the top 10. In math, we still rank in the top 10 for 4th graders, but we drop in the rankings for 8th and 12th graders. Why aren't the students in the U.S. keeping up with students from other nations?

Standardized testing became a tool for measuring school performance in the 1970s, just as Federal spending on education increased. Has the rise in per-pupil funding correlated to a rise in standardized test scores? Since the late 1980s, Federal and State governments tied funding to standardized test scores. This added emphasis has created some unintended consequences. The next panel discusses some of the issues opponents of standardized testing have with the system. Standardized tests are not just for assessing student progress throughout grades K-12. The next two panels discuss the SAT and the ACT, standardized tests used for college entrance.

Test results show that most students have learned "the basics" by graduation. Professors and employers think otherwise. We look at disparities between test results and the opinions of professors and employers. With employers saying that 61% of students graduate without learning "the basics," is a high school diploma worth anything? The last panel takes a look at this issue.

High School Graduates

Percentage of High School Graduates, 1870-2000

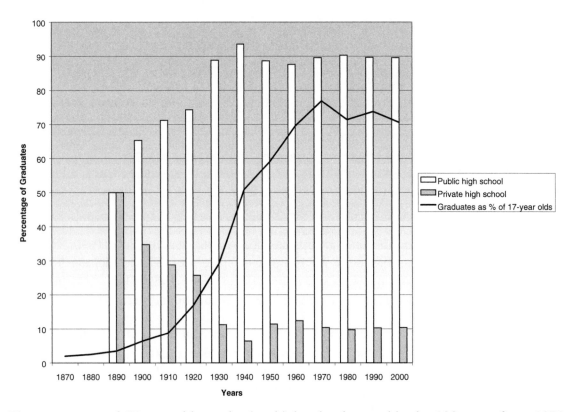

The percentage of 17-year olds graduating high school soared in the 100 years from 1870 to 1970, reaching a peak of 76.9%[1] in 1970. Since then, the percentage of graduates has fallen to 70.6%. The fluctuations in the percentage of graduates from 1970 to 2000 could be explained by the fluctuations in the number of dropouts during this time period. From 1970 to1980, the number of dropouts increased by nearly 550,000. From 1980 to 1990, nearly 1.4 million fewer students dropped out. But, there was another slight increase in the number of dropouts (112,000) from 1990 to 1999[2].

Before 1874, high schools were rare. In the colonial days, Latin grammar schools were the secondary schools. They taught Latin and Greek grammar to prepare a few boys to attend Harvard. The first Latin grammar school was established in 1635. In the early 19th century, Latin grammar schools lost favor. Academies replaced them. These were private secondary schools that taught more varied and "practical" courses. Public high schools became more popular after the Kalamazoo case of 1874: the Supreme Court of Michigan

---

[1] The actual peak was in 1969 (not shown), when the percentage of 17-year olds who graduated high school was 77.1% The lowest percentage since then was in 1998 when 69.3% graduated.

[2] 1999 was the last year data were available.

held that school districts should support high schools with taxes. Because high schools were free and trained students for jobs in our industrializing society, more and more students (who may not have been able to attend private schools for economic reasons) attended these public high schools.

The rise in graduation rates coincided with new laws mandating school attendance and curbing child labor. In 1842, Connecticut enacted a law prohibiting the employment of any child under 15 without proof of school attendance. By 1918, all states had enacted compulsory attendance laws. Later legislation expanded these early statues. Most states now make it mandatory to attend school until at least age 16. The Fair Labor Standards Act also restricts the hours and type of work done by children under 18. As the 20th century progressed, so did economic prosperity. Families needed fewer hands to support the common enterprise. As a result dropout rates decreased and graduation rates soared. The drop in graduation rates in the last 30 years may have been due to a belief that getting a General Education Development certificate (GED) was equivalent to getting a high school diploma. States that made it easier for students to take the GED experienced higher dropout rates[3].

Starting around 1900, the percentage of students graduating from public high schools was much greater than the percentage of those graduating from private schools. The popularity of private high schools was still high — nearly 35% of graduates came from such institutions. But this waned in the next 40 years to a low of 6.4% in 1940. The 14% decline from 1920 to 1930 may have been due to the stock market crash of 1929 and the ensuing Great Depression. Fewer people had money to spend on private education. After World War II, economic prosperity was on the rise, but most of us still sent our children to public schools. During the 1950s and 1960s, the percentage of graduates from private high schools saw a slight increase (11.4% in 1950 and 12.4% in 1960). In the 1970 to 2000 period, it has been about 10%.

Next we'll look at college and university graduates.

Sources: U.S. Department of Education. National Center for Education Statistics. *Digest of Education Statistics 2000.* Online. Available: http://nces.ed.gov. March 19,2002. Education history data: College of Education Online. University of Arkansas at Little Rock. "American Education." Online. Available: http://www.ualr.edu. March 20, 2002. U.S. Department of Labor. Employment Standards Administration. Wage and Hour Division. "Child Labor Provisions of the Fair Labor Standards (FLSA) For Nonagricultural Occupations." Online. Available: http://www.dol.gov. November 29, 2001. Vicky Grocke. "Compulsory Education." *History of American Education Project.* Online. Available: http://www.nd.edu/~rbarger/www7/compulso.html. March 21, 2002. Jay P. Greene. "GED proves it's not equivalent to high school degree." *Detroit News,* 7 April 2002.

---

[3] Unfortunately, later studies have shown that getting a GED is not equivalent to a high school diploma. Of the 60% of GED holders who try to get a higher education, nearly 75% drop out of community colleges (compared to 44% of high school graduates) and 95% drop out of 4-year colleges (compared to 25% of high school graduates). Source: *The Detroit News,* April 7, 2002. Full citation in source note above.

College[4] Graduates

Higher Education: Enrollment and Degrees Conferred, 1870-1998

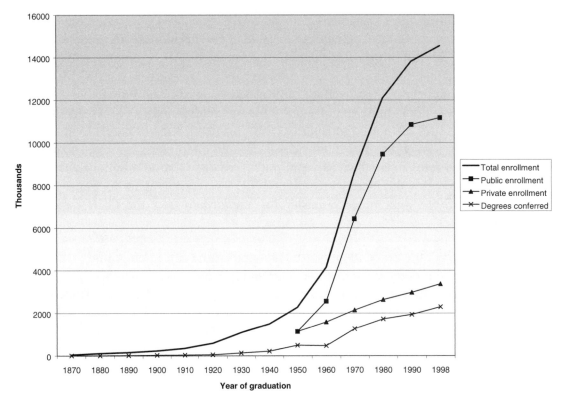

The chart above shows college enrollment for the years 1870-1998. Total enrollment is then broken down into public and private college enrollment. The chart also shows the number of degrees conferred for all higher education institutions. Just as high school education was once for the wealthy, so too was higher education. But, in the latter half of the 20th century, this changed. As the number of high school graduates rose, so too did the number of people attending college. In 1960, 45.1% of high school graduates went on to college. In 1998, 65.6% did.

The number of people attending colleges started to increase dramatically after World War II. The Servicemen's Readjustment Act of 1944 allowed millions of veterans (regardless of race or social class) to attend college. Of the 7.8 million veterans eligible, 2.2 million used the benefits to attend colleges and universities. By 1947, half of all college students were veterans. The demand for more practical coursework led to a greater emphasis in higher education on degree programs. This contributed to the rise in degrees conferred after 1940.

---

[4] In this panel, "college" means all degree-granting institutions of higher learning.

Later, more and more women started to go to college. The percentage of women students in 1950 was 31.6%; by 1970 it was 40.8%. In 1998, the percentage of women enrolled in colleges and universities was greater than the percentage of men enrolled: 56.8%. More minorities started to attend college as well. This coincided with the increased minority enrollment in public elementary and secondary schools (in 1972, 22% of public school students were part of a minority group; by 1999, 38% were). The following table shows the change in the number of students attending college by race/ethnicity from 1980 to 1997.

Change in Number of Students Attending College, by Race/Ethnicity, 1980-1997

	Total enrollment (1997)	Change in enrollment (1980-1997)	% Change (1980-1997)
White	10,266,100	433,100	4.4
Black	1,551,000	444,200	40.1
Hispanic	1,218,500	746,800	158.3
American Indian	142,500	58,600	69.8
Asian	859,200	572,800	200.0
Nonresident alien	465,000	160,000	52.4

The dramatic rise in public college enrollment may be attributed to the cost. Tuition at public institutions continued to be much lower than at private institutions. In 1970, the cost of tuition at a public institution was about 21% of the cost of tuition at a private college. In 2000, tuition at a public college was less than 18% that of a private college. The next table shows the annual tuition cost of both public and private institutions and the median family income in current dollars. A more in-depth discussion about tuition costs can be found in a later chapter, *Trends in Postsecondary Education*.

Annual Tuition Cost, 1970-2000

	Public tuition per year ($)	Public tuition as % of income	Private tuition per year ($)	Private tuition as % of income	Median Family Income[5] ($)
1970	323	3.3	1,533	15.5	9,867
1980	583	2.8	3,130	14.9	21,023
1990	1,356	3.8	8,174	23.1	35,353
2000	2,507	5.1	14,175	29.0	48,950

In the next panel we look at the educational attainment of the population by race.

Sources: U.S. Bureau of the Census. *Historical Statistics of the United States: Colonial Years to 1970* and *Statistical Abstract of the United States: 1994, 1996* and *2001*. U.S. Department of Education. National Center for Education Statistics. *Digest of Education Statistics: 1992* and *1999* and "Racial/Ethnic Distribution of Public School Students." *The Condition of Education: 2001*. Online. Available: http://nces.ed.gov. March 21, 2002. "G.I. Bill." *West's Encyclopedia of American Law*. Online. Available: http://www.wld.com/conbus/weal/wgibill.htm. March 21, 2000. Chart data: Enrollment data for 1960 is actually enrollment data for 1961. Source did not provide data for 1960. Enrollment data for 1950-1998: *Digest of Education Statistics*. Degree-conferred data for 1870-1960: *Historical Statistics*. Degree-conferred data for 1970-1998: *Statistical Abstract of the United States 2001*.

---

[5] Current dollars. Year 2000 data are from 1999. 1970 data from *Historical Statistics of the United States*, Table G189-204. 1980-2000 data from *Statistical Abstract of the United States: 2001*, Table 673. Full citations are in the source note.

Educational Attainment

**Percentage of 25+ Year Olds Who Have Completed
At Least 4 Years of High School, 1960-2000**

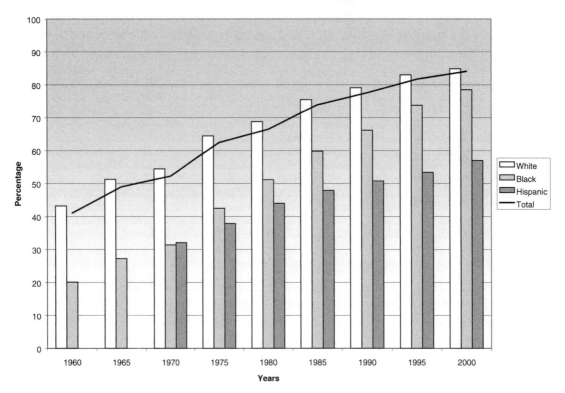

The chart shows the percentage of people 25 years old and over who have completed at least 4 years of high school. Data are broken down by race. Asians and Pacific Islanders, not shown in the graph, maintained the highest educational attainment. In 1990, more than 80% completed at least 4 years of high school (as compared to 78% of the population as a whole). In 2000, nearly 86% completed at least a high school education (as compared to 84% of the general population).

In all cases, the educational attainment level of the population rose. Whites maintained the highest percentage (except for Asians and Pacific Islanders). Blacks increased their educational attainment level at a faster rate than did Hispanics. In 2000, there was only a 6.4% difference in the educational attainment of blacks and whites. Hispanics differed the most: 27.9% fewer Hispanics than whites completed at least 4 years of high school.

Do we see the same pattern among those completing at least 4 years of college?

As the next chart shows, at the college level, the same pattern applies. Educational attainment at the college level has risen. Asians and Pacific Islanders have the highest percentage of the educated population with at least 4 years of college, followed by whites, blacks and Hispanics. However, at this level, the percentage differences between the racial/ethnic groups are greater. In 2000, 18.3% more Asians and Pacific Islanders had a college education than did the population as a whole. The percentage of whites with a college education was 0.5% greater than the percentage in the total population. 9.6% fewer blacks had a college education than whites. Hispanics had 15.5% fewer.

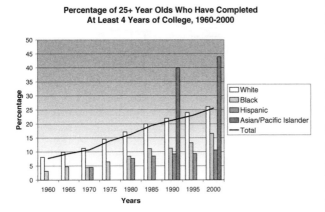

Percentage of 25+ Year Olds Who Have Completed
At Least 4 Years of College, 1960-2000

As the educational attainment levels rise, how educated are we? We begin with a discussion of literacy.

Source: U.S. Bureau of the Census. *Statistical Abstract of the United States 1994* and *2001*.

Literacy Rates: The Early Years

Literacy Rates in the United States, by Race, 1870-1979

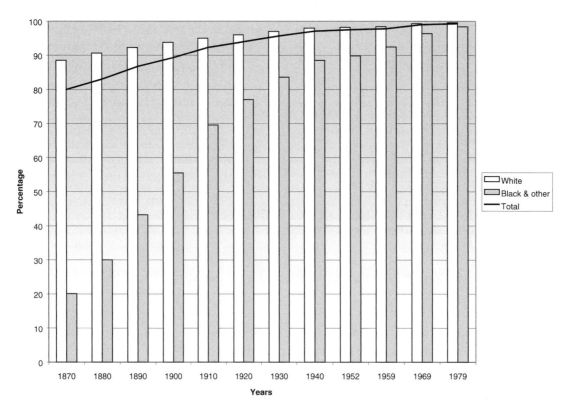

The chart shows the literacy rates for those aged 14 years old and older, by race, for the years 1870-1979. Literacy rates increased for all races over this period. By 1979, the overall literacy rate was 99.3%. By far, the biggest *gain* in literacy has been in the non-white population. In 1870, only 20.1% of non-whites were literate. In 1979, the percentage increased to 98.4%. By comparison, in 1870, 88.5% of whites were literate. In 1979 99.6% of whites were literate.

What happened in the 1980s? The focus of literacy changed. Starting with the 1985 *Young Adult Literacy Survey*, statisticians concentrated on functional literacy. Prior to 1985, literacy was defined as the ability to read and write, either in English or some other language. Today, this is called "simple literacy." This survey (and later the National Literacy Act of 1991), defined literacy as "an individual's ability to read, write, and speak in English, and compute and solve problems at levels of proficiency necessary to function on the job, to function in society, to achieve one's goals, and to develop one's knowledge and potential." The next panel will discuss this type of literacy.

Sources: Chart data: U.S. Department of Education. National Center for Education Statistics. "Literacy from 1870 to 1979: Illiteracy." *National Assessment of Adult Literacy*. Online. Available: http://nces.ed.gov/. March 21, 2002. Data for 1969 and 1979 "Black and other" include only the rate for blacks. Functional literacy definition: U.S. Department of Education. National Center for Education Statistics. *How Much Literacy is Enough*, March 2000. Online. Available: http://www. nces.ed.gov. March 21, 2002.

Functional Literacy and Educational Attainment

Adult Functional Literacy in the United States, by Educational Attainment, 1992

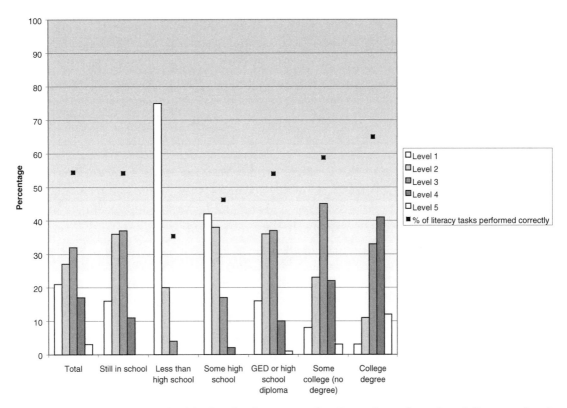

According to Mike Rose in his book, *Lives on the Boundary*, functional literacy in the 1930s meant having three or more years of schooling. During World War II it meant completion of the fourth grade, in 1960, completion of the eighth grade. In the late 1970s, some defined functional literacy as completion of high school. In later years, this definition proved too simplistic. Statisticians now define functional literacy on many skill levels.

Literacy Proficiency Levels as Defined in *Digest of Education Statistics, 1992*

Level 1: Able to follow brief written directions and select phrases to describe pictures.
   Example: Locate time or place of a meeting on a form

Level 2: Able to understand combined ideas and make references based on short uncomplicated passages about specific or sequentially related information.
   Example: Enter background information on an employment form

Level 3: Able to search for specific information, interrelate ideas, and make generalizations about literature, science and social studies materials.
   Example: Integrate information from long, dense texts or documents

Level 4: Able to find, understand, summarize, and explain relatively complicated literary and informational material.
   Example: Research and write a college-level term paper with footnote references.

Level 5: Able to understand the links between ideas even when those links are not explicitly stated and to make appropriate generalizations even when the texts lack clear instructions or explanations.
   Example: Read and comprehend the themes in a classical play or novel such as *Hamlet* or *War and Peace*.

The chart on the previous page shows the proficiency level of the adult population by educational attainment level. The chart also shows the percent of literacy tasks performed correctly by the various groups that took the *National Adult Literacy Survey*[6] in 1992. As expected, functional literacy goes up when educational attainment goes up. Those with less than a high school diploma performed 35% of the literacy tasks correctly; those with a college degree performed 65% of the tasks correctly. Ninety-five percent of those with less than a high school diploma functioned at the two lowest levels. This group had less than 1% functioning at the highest levels. Those with a college degree had the highest percentage functioning at the highest two levels (53%). However, 14% of those with a college degree function at the two lowest levels of proficiency. Surprising! Adults who are proficient at levels one and two are considered, by some, to be functionally illiterate. In 1992, this included 90 million adults (48% of the adult population).

According to a 1993 *Education Week* article on the *National Adult Literacy Survey*, this meant that "nearly half of all adult Americans cannot read, write, and calculate well enough to function fully in today's society...." Is this an accurate picture of nearly half of all the adults in America? Not necessarily. In the *Literacy Survey,* these adults were asked to rate their own literacy skills. Sixty-six percent to seventy-five percent of those functioning at Level 1[7] described themselves as being able to read and write English "well" or "very well". At Level 2, 93% to 97% described themselves this way. Some of those in these groups do get help from family and friends to perform everyday tasks, but the number is low: 14-25% of those at Level 1 and 4-12% at Level 2. This suggests that although 48% of the adult population is classified as "functionally illiterate," this doesn't prevent most of them from functioning in their personal and professional lives.

The next panel looks at functional literacy from an employment perspective.

Sources: Carl F. Kaestle et. al,. "Adult Literacy and Education in America." *Education Statistics Quarterly* (Winter 2001). Online. Available: http://nces.ed.gov. March 21, 2002. Irwin Kirsch et. al., "Executive Summary of Adult Literacy in America: A First Look at the Results of the National Adult Literacy Survey." Online. Available: http://nces.ed.gov. March 21, 2002. U.S. Department of Education. National Center for Education Statistics. *Digest of Education Statistics, 1992.* U.S. Department of Education. National Center for Education Statistics. *How Much Literacy is Enough?* March 2000. Quote from Mike Rose's book *Lives on the Boundary,* from "Literacy and Computers." Online. Available: http://www.mansfield.ohio-state.edu/writing/E993/literacy.htm. (March 22, 2002). 1979 simple literacy data: U.S. Department of Education. National Center for Education Statistics. "Literacy from 1870 to 1979: Illiteracy." *National Assessment of Adult Literacy.* Online. Available: http://nces.ed.gov/naal/historicaldata/illiteracy.asp. March 22, 2002. 1980 population data: U.S. Bureau of the Census. *Statistical Abstract of the United States, 1994.*

---

[6] The survey involved 25,750 adults. 13,600 were randomly selected; 1,150 were inmates in federal and state prisons; and 11,000 were interviewed based on their participation in a concurrent survey that provided comparable results. The survey involved various tasks using the kinds of materials they would encounter in their daily lives. The results were scored on a 500-point scale. The "% of literacy tasks performed correctly" in the graph on the previous page is based on the average scores of the participants.

[7] Level 1 also includes those who cannot read and write at all. In 1979, the most recent year available, this was 0.7% of the population 14 years old and older. In 1980, when the decennial census was taken, this included over 12 million people. (Figures based on the 15 year old and older population in 1980, approximately 175.3 million.)

Functional Literacy and Employment

Adult Functional Literacy in the United States, by Employment Status, 1992

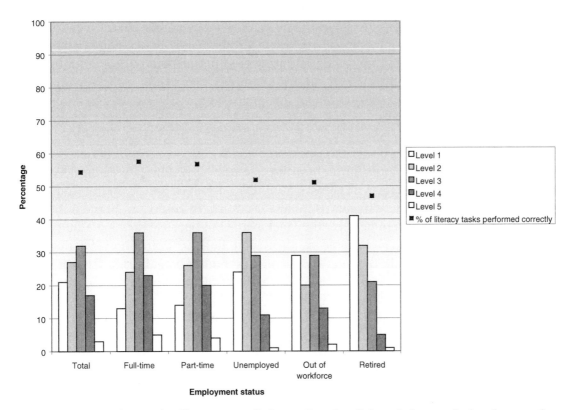

The chart above shows the literacy proficiency levels of the adult population by employment status. The graph also shows the percentage of literacy tasks that were performed correctly by those taking the *National Adult Literacy Survey, 1992*. For a discussion of the literacy levels and the *Literacy Survey*, see the preceding panel. Those employed full time performed the highest percentage of literacy tasks correctly (57.6%). Those in retirement averaged lowest (47%). This is not surprising. People who are employed full time had the highest percentage among the group who function at a Level 3 proficiency or higher. Those who are retired had the lowest percentage among the group of those who function at Level 3 and above.

Overall, most of the population functions at Level 3 proficiency[8] or above (52%). This is true for the employed; 64% of those working full time and 60% of those working part time function at a Level 3 proficiency or higher. The unemployed and the retired score lower. Most in these categories function at the two lowest levels of literacy proficiency — 60% of the unemployed and 73% of the retired.

---

[8] As cited in the previous panel, some suggest that those functioning at the two lowest levels of literacy are "functionally illiterate."

Most of the retired grew up in the first half of the 20th century. During that time, many had to quit school and go to work in order to help support the family. Many jobs in those days did not require a high school diploma.

Low literacy rates imply difficulty in getting work. Data on the chart suggest that the unemployed function at the two lowest levels of literacy. They cannot read, write, or calculate well enough to function in our society. Between 18% and 37% of adults at these two levels admit to getting help from family and friends to perform daily tasks. But low literacy proficiency cannot be the only reason for unemployment: 40% of those with a Level 3 proficiency or higher were also unemployed. Economic slowdowns and individual work habits play a role.

Those who are classified as out of the workforce are nearly evenly split between those in the lowest two levels and those in the top three levels (49% function at the lowest two levels, 51% function at Level 3 or above). Why the near-even split? One reason may be that the mix of people in this category is more varied than in any other. Some may choose to be out of the workforce not because they lack skills but because they have other priorities — housewives and stay-at-home mothers and fathers. Some may be out of the workforce temporarily while they go to school. Some may be suffering from mental or physical disabilities. (In 1998, more than 11.9 million of those aged 16-64 with a work disability were out of the workforce). Therefore, we see a pattern similar to the total adult population for Levels 3-5; but we also see a higher percentage functioning at a Level 1 proficiency.

The next panel examines children's reading proficiency.

Sources: Carl F. Kaestle, et. al. "Adult Literacy and Education in America." *Education Statistics Quarterly* (Winter 2001). Online. Available: http://nces.ed.gov. U.S. Bureau of the Census. March 21, 2002. "Table 2. Labor Force Status – Work Disability Status of Civilians 16 to 74 Years Old, by Educational Attainment and Sex: 1998." Online. Available: http://www.census.gov. April 2, 2002.

Children's Reading Skills

Average 17-Year-Old Reading Proficiency Scores, by Race, 1971-1999

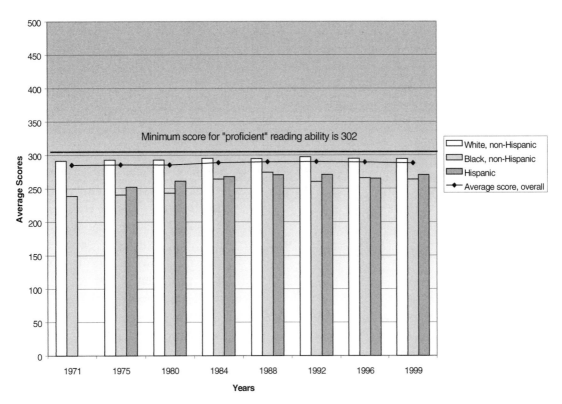

The test scores for 17-year-olds from 1971-1999 are charted here. These are average test scores from the National Assessment of Educational Progress (NAEP) survey. During this entire period, average scores failed to reach "proficient" levels of reading. After 1992, average scores have even declined. Belief in universal progress may be premature.

White students scored the highest throughout these years. Except for 1988 and 1996, Hispanic students outscored black students. But scores for black students have risen the most since 1971: 25.2 points. Hispanic students' scores rose 18.3 points. White students' scores have risen only 3.4 points. In 1984, Hispanic students scored within the "basic" reading proficiency level[9] for the first time. They were scoring in the "below basic" proficiency level throughout the 1970s and early 1980s. Black students did not reach the "basic" level until 1988. White and Hispanic students have remained at this level ever since. Black students dropped back to the "below basic" level in 1999.

---

[9] The minimum "basic" proficiency level score is 265. In 1984, Hispanic students scored 268.1. In 1988, black students scored 274.4. Since then, scores for Hispanics have increased to 270.7 and declined for blacks to 263.9 in 1999.

What do all these scores mean? According to the NAEP, the average 17-year-old student was barely able to follow directions in order to completely fill out an employment application and would not be able to explain the relevance of a major issue in a political speech.

What about the younger students? The next chart shows the NAEP average test scores for 13-year-olds. At this level also, on average, students have not been able to achieve a "proficient" level of reading ability. In fact, scores for 13-year-olds are more below the minimum proficiency level than are scores for 17-year-olds. In 1999, the average score for a 13-year-old was 21.6 points lower than the minimum 281 points needed to obtain a rating of "proficient." The average 17-year-old had a score 13.9 points lower than the minimum score of 302. Overall, students scored in the "basic" proficiency range. However, black students' scores, on average, have remained in the "below basic" range throughout this time period. Hispanic students reached the "basic" level only in 1999, when their average score was 243.8. The minimum score for "basic" proficiency is 243.0. White students consistently scored within the "basic" range. In 1999, their average score was 266.7.

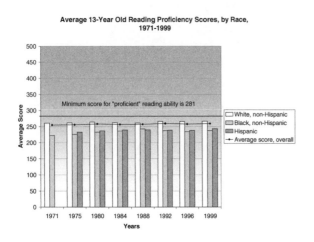

A Nation At Risk: The Imperative for Educational Reform, a report by the National Commission on Excellence in Education (NCEE), was published in April 1983. It outlined the reasons the NCEE believed that students in the United States were falling behind students from other nations academically. The report also gave suggestions on how to improve our educational system. Many of the suggestions, such as increased emphasis on the "New Basic" curriculum[10] and standardized testing, were implemented. In the nearly 20 years since this report, student reading test scores on the NAEP exams do not seem to reflect the level of improvement envisioned by the NCEE.

Next we'll take a look at children's mathematics proficiency.

Sources: U.S. Department of Education. National Center for Education Statistics. *Digest of Education Statistics 2001*. National Commission on Excellence in Education. *A Nation At Risk: The Imperative for Educational Reform* (April 1983). Online. Available: http://www.ed.gov/pubs/NatAtRisk/ April 11, 2002. U.S. Department of Education. National Center for Education Statistics.. National Assessment of Educational Progress (NAEP). "Item Map of Selected Item Descriptions on the NAEP Reading Scale for Grade 8" and "Item Map of Selected Item Descriptions on the NAEP Reading Scale for Grade 12." Online. Available: http://nces.ed.gov. April 12, 2002.

---

[10] 4 years of English, 3 years of mathematics, 3 years of science, 3 years of social studies, and one half-year of computer science. For college-bound students, 2 years of a foreign language was recommended also.

Children's Math Skills

Average Student Mathematics Proficiency Scores for 17-Year-Olds, 1973-2000

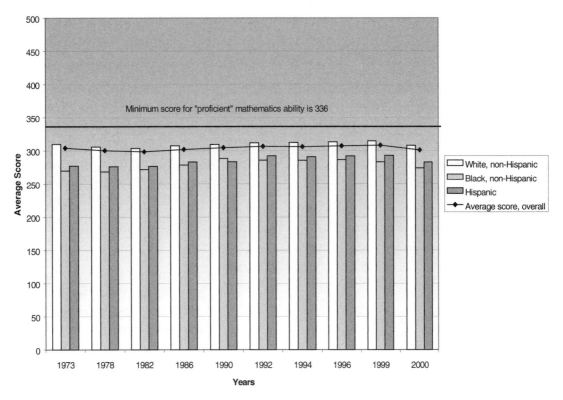

In this panel we turn to mathematics. The chart shows test scores of the National Assessment of Educational Progress (NAEP) for 17-year-olds from 1973 to 2000. Students did not perform well enough to be considered proficient in mathematics over this time period. In fact, from 1999 to 2000, scores declined. Scores had been increasing for the 17 years before 1999.

White students consistently scored higher than did African American and Hispanic students. Except for 1990, Hispanic students scored higher than did black students did. Hispanic students' scores also rose 16 points from 1982-1999: 16 points. Black students' scores rose 11.5 points. White students' scores rose 11.1 points. Unfortunately, Hispanic students' scores also declined the most, 9.7 points, from 1999 to 2000. Black students' scores followed with a drop of 9.3 points. White students' scores dropped 6.8 points.

Hispanic students scored within the "basic" mathematics proficiency level[11] for the first time in 1992 and scores stayed there until 2000, when they slipped to "below basic" proficiency level. Black students scored within the "basic" level in 1990; however, this was

---

[11] The minimum "basic" proficiency level score is 288.

the only time their scores have been at this level. Since then, the average black students' score has fallen into the "below basic" range.

What do these scores mean in a nonacademic setting? According to the NAEP, the average 17-year-old student is able to determine the cost of renting a car given the per day and mileage charges. However, he would not be able to calculate the distance between two cities on a map.

What about those students preparing to enter high school? The next chart shows the NAEP average test scores for 13-year-olds. Again, students have not been able to achieve mathematics proficiency according to the NAEP. But 13-year-olds are faring better than 17-year-olds. In 2000, the average score for a 13-year-old was 24 points below what is needed for a "proficient" rating. Seventeen-year-olds scored 35 points below this level. Overall, students scored in the "basic" proficiency range. Black and Hispanic students' scores never reached this level. They have consistently scored within the "below basic" range throughout this time period.

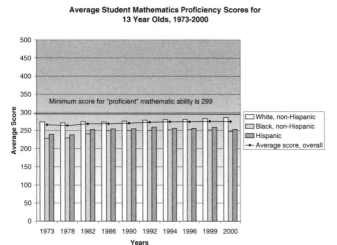

Average Student Mathematics Proficiency Scores for 13 Year Olds, 1973-2000

What does this mean? The overall score for the year 2000 was 275. According to the NAEP, this means that the average 13-year-old was able to calculate how many of a certain item he could buy at a given amount, but he was unable to determine how much change he would be owed.

Despite the changes brought about in the 19 years since *A Nation At Risk* was published, NAEP mathematics scores have not improved to a level envisioned by the National Commission on Education. In January 2002, President George W. Bush signed the No Child Left Behind Act of 2001. This law mandates changes in the educational system: from funding expenditures for qualified teachers and community learning centers, to implementation of research-based teaching methods, to standardized testing for accountability. Will these mandates improve the education of our 46.8 million public school children?

The next panel will look at how the children of the United States rank internationally in reading.

Sources: U.S. Department of Education. National Center for Education Statistics. *Digest of Education Statistics, 2001* and *The Nation's Report Card: Mathematics 2000.* "President Bush Signs Landmark Education Reforms Into Law." Online. Available: http://www.whitehouse.gov. April 16, 2002. "The Facts About…21st Century Learning." Online. Available: http://www.NoChildLeftBehind.gov. , April 16, 2002. "NAEP Mathematics – Grade 12 Item Map" and "NAEP Mathematics – Grade 8 Item Map." Online. Available: http://nces.ed.gov/nationsreportcard/mathematics. April 12, 2002.

International Literacy Comparisons

Top 10 Countries in Reading Proficiency, 1992

Rank	9-year-olds	14-year-olds
1	Finland	Finland
2	**United States**	France
3	Sweden	Sweden
4	France	New Zealand
5	Italy	Hungary
6	New Zealand	Iceland
7	Norway	Switzerland
8	Iceland	Hong Kong
9	Hong Kong	**United States**
10	Singapore	Singapore

The table above shows the 10 countries whose 9- and 14-year-olds had the highest reading literacy test scores. The United States is in the top 10 both times. But its ranking drops from 2 (for 9-year-olds) to 9 (for 14-year-olds). Italy and Norway also drop in the rankings. Italy fell to 18th in the 14-year-old age group; Norway dropped to 17th. All other countries showed an increase in rank. Hungary showed the biggest increase (from 19th to 5th).

What about 17-year-olds? There were no data available, suggesting that the literacy levels of this age group were grouped with the total adult literacy rate. The next table presents the countries with the highest adult literacy rates. The data are taken from the Central Intelligence Agency's publication *The World Factbook 2001*. The most recent simple literacy data are shown. As a result, the data are from various years. The most recent simple literacy data from the United States is from 1979. The U.S. Census Bureau reported a simple literacy rate of 99.3% for 1979, thereby ranking the United States 2nd (6 countries had higher literacy rates). The CIA, however, ranks the United States 7th (37 countries had higher rates).

Adult Simple Literacy Rates

Rank	Countries	Literacy rate (%)
1	Australia, Denmark, Estonia, Finland, Latvia, Norway	100.0
2	Czech Republic, Armenia, France, Georgia, Germany, Hungary, Japan, North Korea, Netherlands, New Zealand, Poland, Slovenia, Sweden, Switzerland, United Kingdom, Uzbekistan	99.0
3	Guyana	98.1
4	Austria, Belarus, Belgium, Bulgaria, Ireland, Italy, Kazakhstan, South Korea, Lithuania, Russian Federation, Tajikistan, Turkmenistan, Ukraine	98.0
5	Trinidad and Tobago	97.9
6	Uruguay	97.3
7	Azerbaijan, Canada, Croatia, Kyrgyzstan, Romania, Spain, **United States**	97.0
8	Argentina	96.2
9	Moldova	96.0
10	Cuba	95.7

The next panel looks at international mathematics proficiency.

Sources: U.S. Department of Education. National Center for Education Statistics. *Digest of Education Statistics, 2000.* Central Intelligence Agency. *The World Factbook 2001.* Literacy for 9- and 14-year-olds was measured by the International Association for the Evaluation of Educational Achievement (IEA) Reading Literacy Study.

International Mathematics Proficiency Comparisons

Top 10 Countries in Mathematics Proficiency, 1994-1995

Rank	4th grade	8th grade	12th grade[12]
1	Korea, Singapore	Singapore	Netherlands
2	Japan	Japan	Sweden
3	Hong Kong	Korea	Denmark
4	Netherlands	Hong Kong	Switzerland
5	Czech Republic	Belgium (Flemish), Czech Republic	Iceland
6	Austria	Austria, Hungary, Slovak Republic, Switzerland	Norway
7	Hungary, Slovenia	France, Slovenia	France
8	Australia, Ireland, **United States**	Bulgaria, Netherlands, Russian Federation	Australia, New Zealand
9	Canada	Belgium (French), Canada, Ireland	Canada
10	Israel, Latvia (Latvian-speaking)	Australia	Austria
		14. England, **United States**	19. **United States**

The table shows the top 10 countries in mathematics proficiency according to the Third International Mathematics and Science Study (TIMSS). 4th graders in the United States rank 8th internationally in mathematics proficiency. For grades 8 and 12, the United States fell to 14 and 19, respectively.

Why haven't the students of the United States been able to keep up with others? The table on the next page compares class size, teaching styles, and average hours math is taught per week for the 8th grade. The countries listed are the same as those listed above. No data were available for Bulgaria, however.

As the table shows, the United States does not differ from most other countries with higher rankings. Many in this country are calling for smaller class sizes. They say this will help teachers provide more individualized attention and students will be educated better. But the class size in the United States is comparable to class size in most countries that rank above us. In fact, the countries with the highest ranking in mathematics proficiency have larger class sizes on average than the United States. Singapore, Japan, and Hong Kong have an average of 31-40 students per math class. The United States has an average of 21-30. Korea, ranked 3rd, averages 41 or more students per class.

Perhaps the teaching techniques of other countries have something to do with the mathematics proficiency rankings. This is not necessarily the case. Teaching techniques do not vary that much between the U.S. and other higher-ranking countries. Most countries have students working in groups while the teacher instructs the whole class for some of the time. At other times, the students work individually with teachers providing assistance.

Could the difference in the number of hours per week devoted to math teaching account for the rankings? No. Half of the countries that rank above the United States teach math

---

[12] Completion of secondary school. Not all countries from the 4th and 8th grade lists had data available for the 12th grade.

for the same number of hours a week. The other half teach math for fewer hours than the United States does.

8th Grade International Comparisons of Mathematics Classes, 1994-1995[13]

Rank	Country	Math class size (no. of students)		Teaching techniques		Hours teaching math per week	
		21-30	31-40	Work together, teacher teaches whole class	Individual work, teacher assistance	At least 2 but less than 3.5 hours	At least 3.5 but less than 5 hours
1	Singapore		x	x		x	
2	Japan		x	x		x	
3	Korea		41+	x		x	
4	Hong Kong		x		x		x
5	Belgium (Flemish)	x		x	x	x	x
5	Czech Republic	x			x		x
6	Austria	NA	NA	x	x	x	
6	Hungary	x		x	x	x	
6	Slovak Republic	x		x	x		x
6	Switzerland	< 20			x		x
7	France	x		x	x		x
7	Slovenia	x			x	x	
8	Netherlands	x		x	x	x	
8	Russian Federation	x		x	x		x
9	Belgium (French)	x		x	x		x
9	Canada	x			x		x
9	Ireland	x		x		x	
10	Australia	x			x	x	x
14	England	x		x	x	NA	NA
14	**United States**	**x**		**x**	**x**		**x**

Perhaps the amount of homework is greater in countries that rank higher than the United States. This is not the case. Most of the countries assign homework three or more times a week with average assignment lengths of 30 minutes or less each. There are also many countries that assign math homework less frequently. In fact, except for Singapore, the countries ranked from second to fifth places only assign math homework once or twice a week with assignment lengths of 30 minutes or less. Singapore assigns math homework three or more times a week with the average assignment length of 30 minutes or more.

Maybe the disparity comes from what is taught in our schools. In 2001, researchers involved with the Survey of Enacted Curriculum Project discovered that what teachers teach and what states' assessment tests measure vary. More and more states are using standardized tests to improve academic standards. But how useful are these tests in tracking student progress if the subjects on the test are not those that are taught in the classroom? Should the tests be changed or should the curriculum be changed?

The next panel presents an overview of standardized testing in the United States.

Sources: U.S. Department of Education. National Center for Education Statistics. *Digest of Education Statistics, 2000.* David Hoff. "Teaching, Standards, Tests Found Not Aligned." *Education Week,* 31 October 2001. Online. Available: http://www.ed- week.org. April 3, 2002.

---

[13] NA stands for not available.

Accountability

Expenditures per Pupil at the Elementary and Secondary Levels and Student Test Scores, 1970-2000

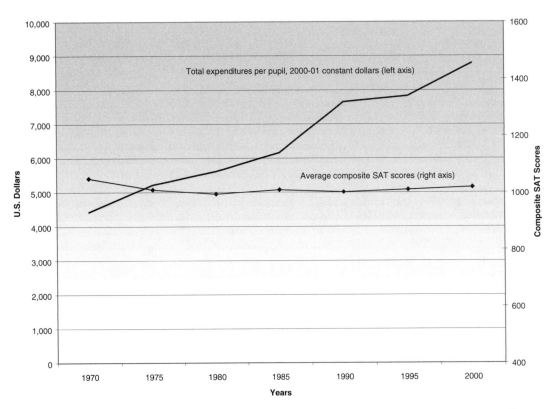

From 1965-1970, the Federal government increased its funding to elementary and secondary schools by nearly $4 billion (from $1.9 billion in 1965 to $5.8 billion in 1970)[14]. In 1970, possibly to determine if the money spent was yielding tangible results, standardized testing became a tool for measuring school performance. And, as the graph above shows, despite the fact that the average amount spent per pupil was on the rise, the average test results from the Scholastic Assessment Test (SAT)[15], taken by nearly half of all graduating high school students, has remained fairly steady. In recent years, test scores have been rising but they still are not at the level they were in 1970, when spending per pupil was at its lowest in the past 30 years. The National Assessment of Educational Progress (NAEP) test scores (as seen in previous panels) showed a similar pattern. At all grade levels where the test is administered, test scores have varied little in the past 30 years.

---

[14] In fiscal year 2000-01 dollars, the increase would equal nearly $15 billion, from $10.4 billion in 1965 to $25.1 billion in 1970.

[15] The Scholastic Assessment Test existed before 1970. The scores shown in the graph were included to show a national sampling of high school student performance. Most standardized testing is administered on a state-by-state basis.

In 1970, testing school-aged children was not a new idea. Early in the 20th century, however, testing was used to segregate students into different courses of study according to ability. In 1912, the first IQ test was created. Over the course of the next 20 years, 250,000 students took the test. It was given to test innate ability. In the 1920s, most high schools switched from the traditional college-prep curriculum to career tracking. The Philadelphia school system, for example, switched to four courses of study: academic, commercial, mechanical, and industrial.

The testing controversy isn't a recent phenomenon, either. In 1922, Harlan C. Hines, a professor at the University of Washington, wrote a criticism of testing in the *American School Board Journal.* He felt "that a test loses its value and becomes a dangerous weapon in the hand of the untrained." The following year, Lewis Terman, one of the creators of the IQ test, created subject area Achievement Tests. And in 1932, 75% of large U.S. cities reported using standardized intelligence testing for career tracking.

In the 1970s, the Back to Basics movement took hold. States instituted minimum competency tests to ensure that high school graduates had mastered basic reading, writing, and math skills. In the 1980s and 1990s new technologies were eliminating many of the unskilled jobs. Well-educated workers were in high demand. State governments pushed for higher educational standards to attract new industries and jobs. In 1983, the National Commission on Excellence in Education released the report *A Nation At Risk.* It outlined the problems of the U.S. educational system and encouraged reform. Many states enacted laws to increase graduation standards. In 1988, state governors adopted Goals 2000. The major purpose of Goals 2000 was for all American students to become "first in the world" in math and science. Student assessment was a key feature of Goals 2000. Although participation was voluntary, states that participated in this initiative received federal funding. In January 2002, President George W. Bush signed the No Child Left Behind Act of 2001. A key feature of this legislation is standardized testing to "create a system of accountability" so that "federal spending on schools [can be] a federal investment in improved student performance."[16]

One can almost feel the rising demand of the public, expressed by various institutions. But resistance to testing is fierce. Critics of standardized testing have argued that these tests are used less for determining student achievement and more for determining school funding and teacher raises. The next panel will discuss some of the criticism levied in recent years on the use of standardized testing.

Sources: U.S. Department of Education. National Center for Education Statistics. *Digest of Education Statistics, 2001.* "Timeline: Testing and Standards Controversy." Online. Available: ://www.pbs.org. April 19, 2002. "President Bush Signs Landmark Education Reforms into Law." Online. Available: http://www.whitehouse.gov. April 16, 2002. Ann Blackman et. al. "Is That Your Final Answer?" *Time,* 19 June 2000.

---

[16] Source: "President Bush Signs Landmark Education Reforms into Law." Retrieved April 16, 2002 from http://www.whitehouse.gov.

Assessing the Tests

Parents' Opinions on Higher Academic Standards and Standardized Tests, 2000

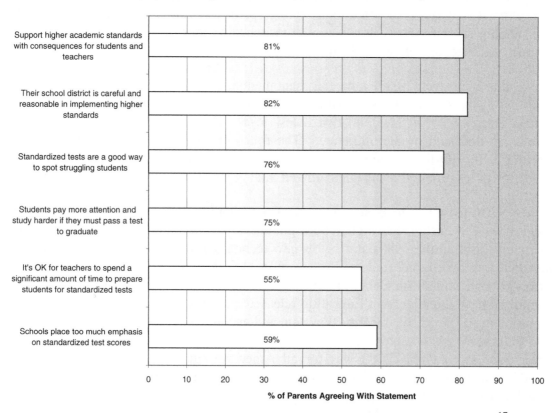

The data in the graph were taken from a 2000 national Public Agenda survey[17]. As the graph shows, most parents surveyed support school districts that implement higher academic standards with consequences for students and teachers. Interestingly, 19% of parents say that academic standards are high enough. Seventy-six percent of parents are in favor of standardized testing, believing that test scores help the teacher spot struggling students. Tests, they say, also help students stay focused. Seventy-five percent of parents say that tests given for graduation motivate children to study more and pay attention in class. According to this survey, most parents (55%) also believe that there is nothing wrong with teaching to the test because they believe that the test measures important skills and knowledge. But, despite the agreement by most parents agreeing that standardized tests are a good idea, a majority of parents also believe that schools rely too much on standardized test scores.

---

[17] The survey is based on a national telephone sampling of 803 parents of public school students in grades K-12. The margin of error is +/- 3%. Fifty-six percent of parents questioned had at most a high school diploma or some college with no degree. Seventy-four percent were white, 12% African-American, 8% Hispanic, 3% Asian. Fifty-one percent lived in a suburban area, 29% in an urban area, and 20% in a rural area.

Why this discrepancy? Perhaps it has something to do with the use of the tests. Parents see the tests as a gauge for individual student performance. Failing students should be provided opportunities such as summer school, tutoring, and if necessary, repeating a grade in order to help the child catch up academically. Teachers who consistently have a majority of their students fail the test should be retrained — say the survey respondents.

The Federal and State governments have a different perspective. In most cases, test scores are used to gauge the individual schools and districts. The goal of standardized testing is to ensure that students are becoming proficient in the subjects tested, but the incentives provided for districts and students to pass the test put too much pressure on teachers and students — say the critics.

In many cases state monies and school district reputations are riding on the results of the tests. For example, in Michigan, where 500,000 students take the Michigan Educational Assessment Program test (MEAP), schools can earn $50,000 grants if their students score well or demonstrate improvement. Eighth graders can win $500 college scholarships if they pass the test. Eleventh graders can win $2,500 scholarships. Many newspapers across the state also publish school district test results. The comparisons of districts may not take into consideration academic progress over the years or the demographic make-up of the district, possibly making the districts with lower passing rates look worse than they really are.

Nationally, failing districts also may lose money. According to the No Child Left Behind Act of 2001, if a school fails to make progress after two years and continues to fail even after special resources are provided, students in that school can transfer to another public school with transportation provided. With the average per-pupil expenditure at $8,787 in 2000, this could add up to a substantial amount of funding loss[18], especially in disadvantaged districts where the percentage of students failing the tests tends to be higher.

How are teachers handling the pressure? In some classrooms, teachers are teaching to the test. In Longfellow School in the Mount Vernon, New York, school district, class lessons were changed to focus on the skills required for the English language arts test (E.L.A.). Before this curriculum change, only 13% of students passed this test. After the change, and after students took many sample tests, 82% of students passed the E.L.A. test. At Davis Middle School, also in the Mount Vernon school district, an 8th-grade language arts textbook is designed specifically for standardized test-taking with chapters such as "Test," "Pre-test," and "Exam Overview."

If the test is supposed to assess the skill level of students, what is so harmful about teaching to the test so students can score higher (and thus demonstrate skills they are supposed to have)? Sometimes, the test standards may be beneath the level of the student's abilities. In the Scarsdale, New York, school district, teachers, preparing students to take the year 2000 state assessment test in science, taught their students how to use a

---

[18] This amount is an average. Some districts spend less per-pupil; some more. Only a portion of the funding that would normally go for the student's education in his own district is given to the school of choice.

triple-beam balance (an outdated measurement tool) while their state-of-the-art digital science equipment sat unused. Standardized testing, according to its proponents, is supposed to be a tool for helping to maintain high standards in schools, but "parents in Scarsdale have trouble understanding how they can benefit from standards lower than the ones they apply to themselves" (Traub).

The pressure to pass the test can also lead to abuses. In 2000, schools in California, Florida, Maryland, New York, and Ohio, were accused of teacher-assisted cheating. In 2001, 67 districts in Michigan (more than 8%) were accused of cheating on the state tests.

How are the students handling the pressure? Surprisingly well. According to students surveyed for Public Agenda's report *Reality Check 2001*, 67% of students say that they "get nervous when [they] take [standardized] tests, but [they] can handle it." Another 28% say that they don't get nervous at all. They also don't feel overwhelmed by too many tests. Sixty-seven percent think they are taking the right number of tests.

Maybe this calm attitude has something to do with the attitude some teachers and schools are taking. At Sampson Middle School in Detroit, Michigan, for example, every year before the MEAP test, students hold a pep rally, T-shirt design contest, and parade. Encouraging MEAP messages are also posted around the school. Does this approach pay off? In the Detroit school district, 8% more students on average passed the MEAP in 2001 than in 2000. There is no way of measuring how much of this increase was due to better teaching strategies and how much was due to getting the students motivated (rather than afraid) to take the test. However, the strategy seems to be popular, and other districts in the state also have been trying to take the pressure off of students in various ways.

Standardized test scores are also used in college admissions. The next panel discusses the Scholastic Assessment Test (more commonly known as the SAT).

Sources: Chart data: "Survey Finds Little Sign of Backlash against Academic Standards or Standardized Tests." Online. Available: http://www.publicagenda.org. April 24, 2002. James Traub. "The Test Mess." *The New York Times Magazine*, 7 April 2002. "The Facts About...Getting Results." Online. Available: http://www.NoChildLeftBehind.gov. 24 April 2002. Hall, Sheri. "Pupils, schools feel pressure to pass MEAP." *Detroit News*, 21 January 2002. Mercer, Tenisha. "Detroit: Positive messages pump up students for tests." *Detroit News*, 21 January 2002. "Is That Your Final Answer?" *Time*, 19 June 2000. "Public Agenda: *Reality Check 2001*." *Education Week*, 21 February 2001. U.S. Department of Education. National Center for Education Statistics. *Digest of Education Statistics, 2001*. Cascade Policy Institute. *School Choice Basics*. Online. Available: http://www.cascadepolicy.org/pdf/edref/SCB. pdf. May 1, 2002.

The Scholastic Assessment Test (SAT)

Average Scholastic Assessment Test (SAT) Scores For College-Bound High School Seniors, 1967-2001

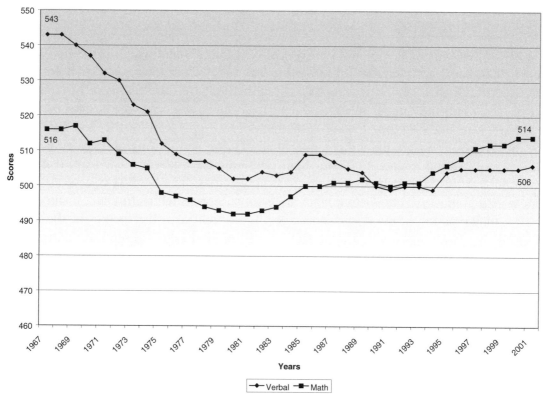

The Scholastic Assessment Test (SAT) was known as the Scholastic Aptitude Test prior to 1993. In 2001, more than 1.2 million students took the SAT. This was up from 1996 when nearly 1.1 million students sat for SAT.

The test consists of a verbal section and a mathematics section. Each section is scored on a scale from 200 to 800. Prior to 1995, the scores for the verbal and the math section were misaligned. A score of 420 on the verbal section, for example, would equal a score of 470 on the math section. In order to align the verbal and math scales, the SAT scale was "re-centered" in 1995 using the 1990 scores as a reference. This had the effect of establishing the average score near the center of the 200-800 scale. The chart above shows the average SAT verbal and math scores for 1967-2001 on the recentered scale. As the chart shows, in 1990, the recentered average verbal and math scores are nearly identical.

Overall, the scores have decreased since 1967. The verbal scores have decreased the most, 37 points, from a high of 543 in 1967 to 506 points in 2001. The mathematics scores decreased considerably in the 1970s and early 1980s, but they have recovered since then to nearly the level they were in 1967. Although both scores are lower than they were in 1967, the scores have been on the rise during the 1990s. Math scores have been on the rise since 1984.

But does the SAT do an adequate job of predicting future college performance? Some say no. The SAT is a reasoning test. It measures the verbal and mathematical problem-solving abilities of the student. A core knowledge base is needed to perform well, but the test is not meant to assess a student's knowledge in a range of subjects. However, the test has been (and continues to be) used by many colleges and universities admissions programs.

In 2001, at the American Council on Education's annual meeting, Richard C. Atkinson, president of the University of California system and former visiting scholar for ETS[19], proposed eliminating the SAT scores as a requirement for admissions at his university. Before attending the annual meeting, he visited "an upscale private school where 12-year-olds were studying long lists of verbal analogies to prepare for the SAT" (Gehring). The emphasis on test-taking ability rather than reading and writing ability disturbed him and led to his announcement. Rather than eliminating standardized tests altogether, he proposed that the SAT II be used in college admissions. The SAT II is a series of one-hour tests that measure knowledge in a variety of subjects such as English, history, social studies, mathematics, science, and languages. Later that year, the faculty of the University of California proposed that applicants for admission take a three-hour achievement test in math, reading, and writing.

In reaction to this announcement, in 2002, the College Board proposed revamping the SAT to align it better with what is taught in high school classrooms. The test would dispense with vocabulary-based analogy questions; new Algebra II and trigonometry questions would be introduced. A writing section would also be included (taken from the SAT II writing test). Proponents in California say that a curriculum-based test would improve teaching in high-poverty schools. Also, they say, this type of test will narrow the performance gap between those who can afford expensive test-prep courses and those who can't. The true test-prep for the new tests will be daily class attendance and participation. Opponents say that the racial gaps will persist with this type of test and the writing sample will test skills that are the most difficult to learn.[20] They say that doing well in high school should have more weight in the admissions process than test scores.

We take a look at the ACT exam next. ACT stands for American College Testing Program.

Source: Chart data: Gams, Janice et. al. *"2001 College Bound Seniors Are The Largest, Most Diverse Group in History." The College Board.* Online. Available: http://www.collegeboard.com/sat/cbsenior/yr2001/pdf/CompleteCBSReport.pdf. April 11, 2002. "Recentering." and "Taking the SAT II Subject Tests 2002." Online. Available: http://www.collegeboard.com. April 4, 2002. "Scholastic Assessment Test (SAT)." Online. Available: http://www.csuchico.edu/test/sat.html. April 4, 2002. Gehring, John.. "UC President Pitches Plan to End Use of SAT in Admissions." *Education Week,* 28 February 2001. *2001 College-Bound Seniors: A Profile of SAT Program Test Takers.* Online. Available: http://www.collegeboard.com. April 29, 2002. "SAT Program Information – 1996 Profile of College-Bound Seniors." Online. Available: http://www.collegeboard.com/sat/cbsenior/yr1996/nat/cbtgen96.html. April 29, 2002. Kronholz, June. "Math, Verbal – and Writing." *Wall Street Journal,* 5 June 2002.

---

[19] ETS stands for Educational Testing System. ETS administers the SAT for the College Board.

[20] A 1998 U.S. Department of Education writing exam given to 4th, 8th, and 12th graders showed that only about 25% of students wrote at grade level. Source: *Wall Street Journal,* 5 June 2002.

American College Testing (ACT) Program

American College Testing (ACT) Average Scores, 1967-2001

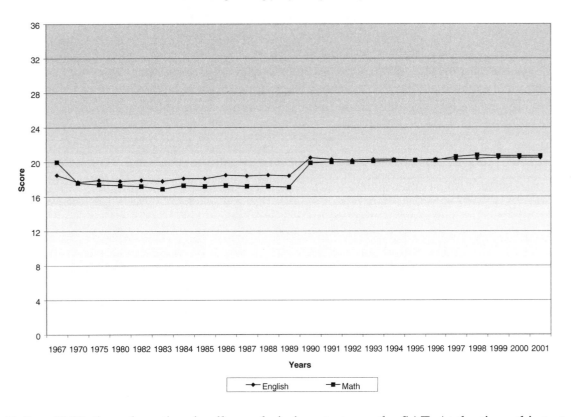

Before 1959, the only national college admissions test was the SAT. At the time, this test was used to identify the best students — mainly for elite colleges. Other college-bound students took entrance exams offered by individual colleges and universities. In the 1950s, large numbers of students were attending college. Colleges were growing. More and more students were receiving financial aid. To keep up with the growth and the need for new curricula, colleges needed more data about students than the SAT could provide. To answer this need, the American College Testing Program (ACT) was established in 1959. Colleges use the scores for admissions and course placement — also in academic advising and career counseling. Some scholarship and financial aid agencies also use ACT scores. In 2000, more than 1 million students took this exam (an increase of 250,000 since 1990).

The chart above shows the average English and mathematics ACT Assessment scores for college-bound seniors from 1967 to 2001. The English test scores during this period fell from 1967 to 1970, then increased slightly after 1970. The mathematics scores declined from 1967 to 1983 and then increased slightly. But what contributed to the higher test scores from 1990 onward, when a new version of the test was introduced[21]?

---

[21] The new version of the test was first administered in October 1989.

Before the late 1980s, ACT scores were adjusted for grade level. In 1970, a score of 18 was given to 11th graders if they answered 35 of the 75 questions correctly. Twelfth graders had to answer 37 or 38 questions to get a score of 18. Growth adjustments were eliminated in the new version of the test. In order to make the scoring equal for all students, the new scoring system may have lowered the minimum requirements for 12th graders. This could be one reason why the scores jumped in 1990.

Another reason (and the rise in scores from 1996 onward) could be improving academic preparedness of the students. Not surprisingly, those with a higher grade point average score higher. The grade point average of test takers has risen from 3.14 in 1996[22] to 3.22 in 2001. The percentage of test takers who have completed core curriculum classes has also increased, from 48.4% in 1990 to 63.2% in 2000. The core curriculum includes at least four years of English and three years each of math (algebra and above), social sciences, and natural sciences. These students averaged a composite score of 21.9 in 2001, as opposed to an average composite score of 19.2 for students not completing the core curriculum. Nationally, the average composite score was 21.0.

In 2001, 28% of those who did not take the core curriculum had a composite score of 16 or below. Colleges with open admissions policies (the most lenient of all admissions standards) require a composite score of at least 17[23] for admission. According to the American College Testing Program, those scoring 16 or below are not ready for college-level courses. They do not comprehend the main ideas in a paragraph; they cannot solve one-step mathematics problems; they can't read tables and graphs. The core curriculum, however, is not a silver bullet. Overall, in 2001, 18% of test takers (nearly 200,000 students[24]) had a score of 16 or below. This included both those who did and did not take the core curriculum. But, all those who take the ACT have aspirations of getting a college education.

What about those who do have scores of 17 or higher? Does this mean that they are ready for college level courses? The next panel discusses the relationship between test scores and performance in the college classroom and in the workforce.

Sources: Chart data: U.S. Department of Education. National Center for Education Statistics. *Digest of Education Statistics, 1992* and *2001* editions. *ACT Newsroom: National Press Release,* 15 and 17 August 2001. Online. Available: http://www.act.org. April 8, 2002. "ACT Average Composite Scores by State: 2001 ACT-Tested Graduates." Online. Available: http://www.act.org. April 25, 2002. "Facts About Scoring the ACT Assessment," "History of the ACT," and "How High Schools and Colleges Use ACT Results." Online. Available: http://www.act.org May 1, 2002.

---

[22] Data for previous years were not available.

[23] Those with selective admissions standards require 22 or higher, which is higher than the national average. Those with highly selective admissions standards, such as Harvard or Yale, require a 27 or above.

[24] Based on 1,065,000 test takers in 2000.

Academic Standards

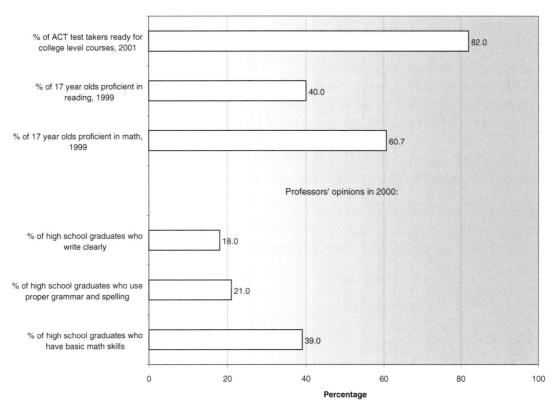

The chart above shows students' test results and professors' opinions of the academic achievement of high school graduates. Data for the "Percentage of ACT test takers who are ready for college level courses, 2001" are based on a 2001 American College Testing Program news release that revealed 18% of test takers' scores suggested that they were not ready for college level courses. "Percentage of 17-year olds proficient in reading, 1999" and "Percentage of 17-year olds proficient in math, 1999" data were taken from the *Digest of Education Statistics, 2001*. The test results were based on an exam administered by the National Assessment of Educational Progress (NAEP)[25]. The data include all those who had reading and math scores at or above 300 on a 500-point scale.

There is a wide disparity between what the ACT, NAEP, and college professors assess as student proficiency. If we look at ACT's standards, we see that 82% of those taking the ACT scored high enough to enter a college or university with liberal admissions policies, at the least. If we look at reading proficiency among high school graduates according to

---

[25] The NAEP is also known as "The Nation's Report Card." The Commissioner of Education Statistics in the U.S. Department of Education is responsible, by law, for carrying out this assessment. The assessment has been done periodically since 1969 in reading, mathematics, science, writing, U.S. history, civics, geography, and the arts.

the NAEP assessments, only 40% of the high school graduates are proficient in reading (meaning at or above a level set by the U.S. Department of Education). In mathematics proficiency, this is about 61% of graduates.

College professors, however, do not think that the mathematics proficiency of most of the students is that high. According to them, only about 40% possess at least a basic knowledge of mathematics; all others fall short. And when it comes to writing clearly and using proper grammar and spelling, only about 20% of students are perceived to have these skills. This mirrors a 2002 survey of high school teachers in which only 20% said that students in their schools learn to speak and write well. One possible cause for the perceived shortcoming in mathematics and reading proficiency could be that schools of education don't stress these skills. A survey by Public Agenda found that only 19% of education professors said that it was "absolutely essential to produce teachers who 'stress correct spelling, grammar, and punctuation for their students."

What about non-academic skills that are useful for college and employment success? The picture isn't much brighter in many cases. According to college professors and employers, in 2002, few high school graduates have many of the skills it takes to succeed.

Percentage of Recent High School Graduates Who Possess These Traits

According to College Professors and Employers, 2002

	% of graduates (according to professors)	% of graduates (according to employers)
Being organized and on time	26	31
Being motivated and conscientious	44	28
Being curious, interested in learning	49	47
Working with others effectively	69	53
Being respectful and polite	63	51
Honesty	65	56

The "standards movement" has been around since the 1980s. This movement, a reaction to the 1983 report *A Nation At Risk,* set out to increase academic standards in our nation's schools. Part of this reform was to emphasize standardized testing as a way of tracking students' learning. But is this an accurate way of assessing student academic progress when there are such disparities between test results and the perceptions of college professors and employers?

With the perceived lack of basic education obtained by high school graduates, is a high school diploma worth anything? We will attempt to answer this question in the next panel.

Sources: Chart data: "Reality Check 2000." *Education Week*, 16 February 2000. Online. Available: http://www.edweek.org; April 3, 2002. U.S. Department of Education. National Center for Education Statistics. *Digest of Education Statistics, 2001*. "Reality Check 2002." *Education Week,* 6 March 2002. Online. Available: http://www.edweek.org. April 3, 2002. "What is NAEP?" Online. Available: http://nces.ed.gov/nationsreportcard/about. April 8, 2002. Jeffrey M. Jones, M.D. Ph.D. "The Standards Movement – Past and Present." Online. Available: http://www.execpc.com/~presswis/stndmvt.html. April 8, 2002. "Item Map of Selected Item Descriptions on the NAEP Reading Scale for Grade 12." Online. Available: http://nces.ed.gov. April 8, 2002.

The Value of a High School Diploma

Median Annual Income by Educational Attainment, 1965-2000

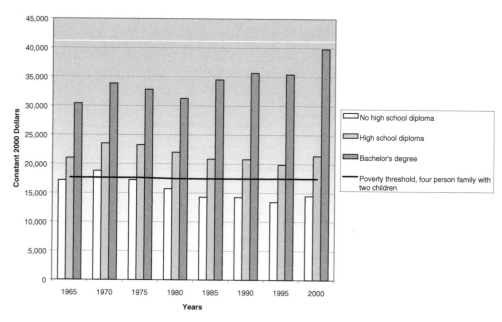

In 2000, Public Agenda's survey, *Reality Check 2000,* found that only 39% of employers thought that having a high school diploma meant that the student "has at least learned the basics." Despite employers' apparent dissatisfaction with the level of education high school graduates have, employers still value a high school diploma. As the chart above shows, those without a high school diploma on average make less than those with a diploma. And those who go on to obtain a bachelor's degree earn a greater amount than those with only a high school diploma do. Only those without a high school diploma earn less than the poverty threshold for a family of four.

Does this mean that those with high school diplomas will be able to get jobs and support themselves, even if the employers believe that they have learned less than the basics? Not necessarily. As we saw in an earlier panel, most of the unemployed function at the two lowest levels of literacy. But, most of the employed function at higher levels, suggesting they have knowledge beyond just "the basics." Most jobs (75.8% in 2000) do not require a college degree, suggesting that those who take advantage of educational opportunities in high school will be prepared to enter the workforce. Unfortunately, *Reality Check 2002* found that most students surveyed admitted that the prevailing attitude was to get by with the least effort possible: 56% of students admitted that they themselves "could try a little harder" in school.

Sources: U.S. Bureau of the Census. "Table P-16. Educational Attainment – People 25 Years Old and Over by Median Income and Sex: 1991 to 2000", "Table P-17. Years of School Completed – People 25 Years Old and Over by Median Income and Sex: 1958 to 1990." and "Table 1. Weighted Average Poverty Thresholds for Families of Specified Size 1959 to 2000." Online. Available: http://www.census.gov. "Reality Check 2000." *Education Week, 16* February 2000 and "Public Agenda: Reality Check 2002." *Education Week,* 6 March 2002. Online. Available: http://www.edweek.org. April 3, 2002. Hecker, Daniel E. "Occupational employment projections to 2010." *Monthly Labor Review,* November 2001.

Chapter 8

Teachers and Teaching

The number of teachers has been increasing since the 1870s. So has the number of students. Pupil-teacher ratios have fallen considerably in the last 130 years, suggesting that the number of teachers is increasing at a faster rate than is the number of students. Who are these teachers? Most of them are women. In the 1870s, the ratio of female to male teachers was 1.6 to 1. In 1996, the ratio increased to 2.9 to 1. Until the 1970s, the number of male teachers had been increasing. What happened in the 1970s? The second panel will attempt to answer this question.

Teachers today are highly educated. Since 1961, the percentage of teachers with a master's or specialist degree has soared, while the percentage of those with less than a bachelor's degree has dropped. The percentage of those with a doctorate grew by 557% since 1961. The third panel will discuss the educational attainment of teachers.

A highly educated teacher workforce may not be enough. Many judge the abilities of teachers by their certification. The fourth panel will discuss certification and the problem of the growing number of uncertified teachers. Why are there so many uncertified teachers? Teacher shortages. The fifth panel discusses this problem and the next panel provides an in-depth discussion of teacher turnover.

The top complaint among teachers is low salaries, but in the year 2000, the average public school teacher salary was between 1.7 and 3.0 times the poverty level for a family of four. So, why the complaint? The next panel compares teacher salaries to those of other professions in an attempt to answer that question.

The Class Size Reduction Initiative is a part of the education reform package entitled The No Child Left Behind Act of 2001. The initiative is based on studies showing that smaller class size improves student achievement. The next panel looks at a couple of these programs to see if they really work.

Not many will argue that America's schools need improvement. But, what are the top problems in our schools today? You may be surprised to find out that teachers and the general public have different opinions.

What should we be teaching children and how should we be teaching it? The debate has been going on since the middle of the 19th century. We begin the discussion with the whole language vs. phonics debate. Then we move on to the different methods of mathematics instruction. We end this chapter with a discussion of character education.

Teachers and Students

Number of Teachers, Number of Students, and Pupil-Teacher Ratio
(Public Elementary and Secondary Schools)

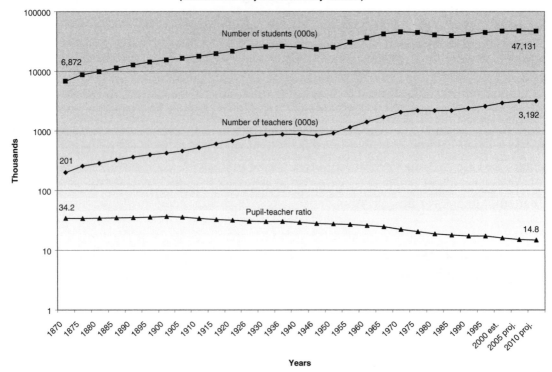

The chart above shows the number of teachers, the number of students and the pupil-teacher ratio for public elementary and secondary schools from 1870-2010. Data for 2000 are estimated. Data for 2005 to 2010 are projections. The fluctuation in the number of teachers mirrors the fluctuation in the number of students. When the number of students increases, the number of teachers increases. From 1936 to 1946, however, enrollment was decreasing, but the number of teachers remained steady. This pattern is seen again from 1975 to 1985. Why doesn't the number of teachers decline when student enrollment declines? Protests from the teachers' unions, parents, and students discourage the practice. When teachers are laid off, it is usually due to budget constraints within the individual districts.

The decline in the pupil-teacher ratio suggests that the number of teachers has increased at a greater rate than the number of students. Pupil-teacher ratios have been steadily dropping since the early 1900s. With the pupil-teacher ratio dropping to a projected 14.8 students per teacher in 2010 (down about 20 students since the 1870s), why is there an effort by the government and school districts to decrease class size?

The pupil-teacher ratio is an average taken by dividing the number of enrolled students by the number of teachers. If all schools and classrooms were equal, all teachers would have had 16 students per classroom in 2000. However, not all schools and classrooms are equal. Some classrooms have fewer students; some have more. In practice, the average public school class size in 1996[1] was 24 — well above the ideal of 17 that some states are striving for. A later panel will have a more in-depth discussion of class size.

The next two panels will discuss the characteristics of teachers in the United States.

Sources: U.S. Bureau of the Census. *Historical Statistics of the United States: Colonial Times to 1970.* U.S. Department of Education. National Center for Education Statistics. *Digest of Education Statistics, 2001.* U.S. Department of Education. National Center for Education Statistics. *Projections of Education Statistics to 2011.* Joan M. Haas. "Hundreds of teachers face layoffs." Online. Available: http://www.weac.org/BARGAIN/2001-02/march02/layoffs.htm. May 2, 2002. U.S. Department of Education. *Local Success Stories: Reducing Class Size*, November 1999. Online. Available: http://www.ed.gov/offices/OESE/ClassSize/localsuccess.html. April 29, 2002.

---

[1] The last year for which data were available.

Teaching's Gender Gap

Teachers by Gender, 1870-1996

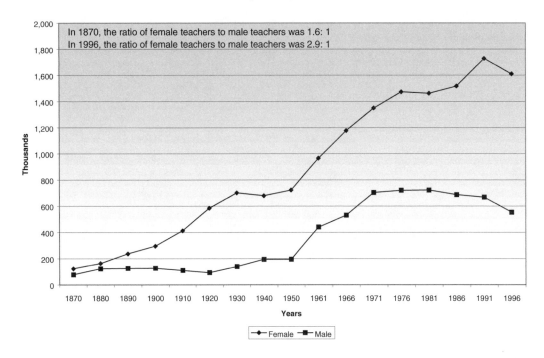

In 1870, the ratio of female teachers to male teachers was 1.6: 1
In 1996, the ratio of female teachers to male teachers was 2.9: 1

Throughout the period shown in the graphic, female teachers outnumbered male teachers. There were nearly as many women in front of the blackboard as there were men from 1870 to 1880. But from 1880 onward, the classroom grew increasingly more feminine. By 1996, there were nearly three times as many female as male teachers.

The rise in the number of women in teaching remained fairly steady throughout the years. However, from 1930 to 1940, the number of female teachers declined by 22,000. This same decade, the number of male teachers increased by 55,000. This continued the increase in male teachers that started in 1920. There were 47,000 more male teachers in 1930 than in 1920. Another period that saw a drop in the number of female teachers was from 1976 to 1981. During this 5-year period, 12,000 fewer women worked as teachers. Again, more men became teachers from 1976 to 1981, but the numbers were smaller than they were in the 1920s and 1930s. There were only 1,000 more male teachers in 1981 than there were in 1976. From 1991 to 1996, both male and female teachers saw a decline in their numbers (about 110,000 each). However, the numbers of male teachers had been declining since 1981.

Increases in the number of male teachers came after both World Wars. There was an increase from 1920 to 1940, and a second increase from 1950 to 1971. There were 102,000 more male teachers in 1940 than there were in 1920. This increase coincided with an increase in college enrollment that started in 1910[2]. Just over 1 million more students at-

---

[2] For more information on college enrollments, see Chapter 7.

tended college in 1940 than did in 1910. This is a nearly 5-fold increase from the previous 30 years (1880-1910), when student enrollment went up by only 241,000. The second increase in the number of male teachers was more dramatic. In the 21 years from 1950 to 1971, the number of male teachers increased by 609,000. During these two decades the number of college students also rose dramatically: 6.3 million more students attended college in 1970 than in 1950.

However, the relationship between the growth in college enrollment and more men choosing the teaching profession doesn't seem to hold for the years after 1971. College enrollment continued to rise dramatically, but the number of men choosing to teach either remained steady or declined during this period. (The number of female teachers fluctuated during this period, but trended upward.)

Why did teaching suddenly become unappealing to men? Perhaps men prefer to advance into supervisory roles. Male principals outnumbered female principals in the 1980s and 1990s. In 1988, the ratio was 3.1 to 1 (58,585 men compared to 19,118 women). By 1994, the ratio dropped to nearly 2 to 1 (52,114 men compared to 27,505 women). Therefore, this may only partially explain the drop in the number of male teachers over this time period. There was no drop in the number of female teachers even though more were moving into supervisory roles.

As we will see in the next panel, more and more teachers held advanced degrees during the 1980s and 1990s. However, some men may feel that the rewards of the private sector are much greater for those with an advanced degree. The next table touches on the issue of salaries for teachers. Salary data are in 2000-2001 constant dollars.

Teacher Salaries and Supplemental Income, 1988 and 1994[3]

	1988		1994	
Age	< 30	30-39	< 30	30-39
Average base salary	28,812	36,577	29,117	34,452
Hours spent on teaching duties per wk.	49		49	
Supplemental school year contract				
Salary	2,814	3,182	2,092	2,546
% of teachers	41.5	35.4	44.0	39.5
Supplemental summer contract				
Salary	2,813	2,635	2,141	2,286
% of teachers	19.0	18.0	20.0	19.8
Non-school employment (% of teachers)	36.7	22.6	18.6	18.2

Sources: U.S. Department of Education. National Center for Education Statistics. Digest of Education Statistics, 1992, 1996, 1999 and 2001.U.S. Bureau of the Census. Historical Statistics of the United States: Colonial Years to 1970. U.S. Bureau of the Census. *Statistical Abstract of the United States, 2001.*

---

[3] Data for hours spent on teaching duties per week are from 1986 and 1996, respectively. An example of a supplemental school year contract: coach of the football team. An example of a supplemental summer contract: summer school teacher. Supplemental contract jobs are done in addition to regular teaching duties.

Educational Attainment of Teachers

Number of Public School Teachers by Highest Degree Held, 1961-1996

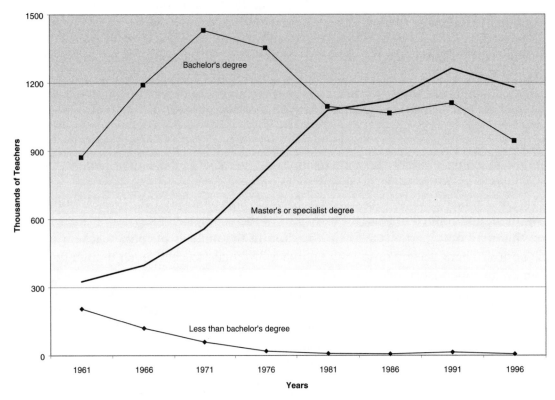

The graphed data are based upon sample surveys conducted by the National Education Association[4]. Not all teachers surveyed are certified, however. The number of teachers with less than a bachelor's degree dropped substantially. In 1961, more than 205,000 teachers had less than a bachelor's degree (14.6%). In 1996, the number dropped to 6,500 (0.3%).

The number of teachers with master's or specialist degrees soared. Starting in the early 1980s, the number of teachers with a master's or specialist degree outnumbered those with a bachelor's degree! The number of those with a bachelor's degree rose dramatically from 1961 to 1971, but the number has trended downward ever since. There was a slight increase in 1991, but the number dropped again for 1996. The drop in numbers for bachelor's, master's, and specialist degrees between 1991 and 1996 may partially be explained by the drop in the percentage of teachers surveyed (86% in 1991 compared to 70% in 1996).

---

[4] The percentage of public elementary and secondary teachers surveyed was between 85% and 89%, except for 1996, when 70% of the teachers were surveyed.

Although not shown in the graph, the number of teachers with a doctorate has also increased. In 1961, 5,600 teachers had doctorates. In 1996, 36,800 had doctorates. The next table shows the growth in the levels of educational attainment among teachers.

Growth in Educational Attainment Among Teachers, 1961-1996

	% growth in the number of teachers holding degrees (1961-1996)
Less than bachelor's degree	-97
Bachelor's degree	8
Master's or specialist degree	263
Doctor's degree	557

The educational attainment of teachers has risen dramatically. Many people, however, judge teacher competency by certification status. Certification typically requires taking courses in teacher education followed by passing certification tests. These examinations test the applicant's skill in pedagogical subjects. If the teacher is a subject-matter specialist, special certification tests related to the subject must also be passed.

In recent years, there has been an outcry among parents and those in government about the number of uncertified teachers across the United States. The next panel will discuss elementary and secondary teacher certification.

Source: U.S. Department of Education. National Center for Education Statistics. *Digest of Education Statistics, 2001.*

Teacher Certification

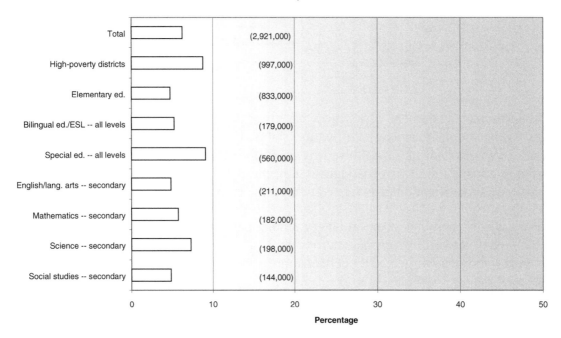

Percentage of Public Elementary and Secondary Teachers Not Certified, School Year 2000
(number in parentheses indicates the estimated number of students being taught by uncertified teachers)

Total	(2,921,000)
High-poverty districts	(997,000)
Elementary ed.	(833,000)
Bilingual ed./ESL -- all levels	(179,000)
Special ed. -- all levels	(560,000)
English/lang. arts -- secondary	(211,000)
Mathematics -- secondary	(182,000)
Science -- secondary	(198,000)
Social studies -- secondary	(144,000)

Percentage

The chart above shows the percentage of teachers who are uncertified. The data were taken from individual state reports required by Title II of the 1998 Amendments to the Higher Education Act. The numbers in parentheses are estimates of the number of students who were being taught by uncertified teachers. The estimates were extrapolated using the pupil-teacher ratio (16.0) for the year 2000.

An estimated 2.9 million students (of the 47.2 million students enrolled) were being taught by uncertified teachers in 2000. What does this mean? In some states (Arkansas, Georgia, Nebraska, Oregon, and West Virginia[5]), 100% of uncertified teachers demonstrated subject content expertise in their area of teaching. This means that they held at least a bachelor's degree. They completed an academic major in each of the subject areas they were teaching or they passed the state's assessments of subject area knowledge "however a state chooses to define 'passing' for this purpose."[6] What they lacked were the necessary teacher preparation courses required for certification. They also did not take (or did not pass) the certification exams administered by the state in which they were working.

---

[5] Not all states reported data for school year 2000. Because of this, there may be more states in which 100% of their uncertified teachers have demonstrated subject-area knowledge.

[6] Definition retrieved May 9, 2002 from http://www.title2.org/scripts/statereports/waiverdef.asp.

Unfortunately, the five states mentioned on the previous page were the exception. In most states, only a fraction of uncertified teachers were able to demonstrate subject content expertise in their area of instruction, as defined by Title II. The next table shows the five states with the highest and the five states with the lowest percentage of uncertified teachers who lacked subject content expertise in the subjects they teach. The table also lists the number of students being taught by these teachers. As the table shows, even when the percentage of uncertified teachers without subject-area expertise is low, the number of students affected can be relatively high. This indicates a high number of uncertified teachers in those states. Overall, the percentage of students being taught by uncertified teachers who lack subject area expertise is very small. Some may argue, however, that even one poorly taught child is one too many.

Percentage of Uncertified Teachers Without Subject Content Expertise and

The Students Taught by Them, School Year 2000

	% of uncertified teachers without subject content expertise	Number of students taught by uncertified teachers without subject content expertise[7]	Students taught by uncertified teachers without subject content expertise as a % of total student population
Top 5			
Michigan	99.0	36,240	2.12
Delaware	97.8	7,264	6.35
Idaho	96.1	5,072	2.06
Illinois	88.5	49,840	2.43
Kentucky	75.5	4,528	0.73
Bottom 5			
New Jersey	24.5	7,120	0.54
West Virginia	24.0	3,568	1.25
New Hampshire	22.9	352	0.17
Virginia	15.4	14,384	1.26
Minnesota	13.7	672	0.08

There is a "but" here. Is teaching by certified teachers much better than is teaching by uncertified teachers? The first annual report to Congress on the state of teacher quality was submitted in 2001. It found that teacher certification standards were quite low. On one teacher certification exam — used in 29 states — only one state sets the passing score near the national average in reading. Fifteen set their passing scores below the 25th percentile. Illiterate teachers? On math and writing, only one state sets its passing score above the national average.

The report called for states to require teachers to pass rigorous exams in the subject they plan to teach in order to meet the goal of having a highly qualified teacher in every classroom by 2005-06. It also called for the elimination of many of the pedagogy courses needed for certification, saying that extensive training in these courses does little to improve teacher quality.

---

[7] Estimate.

How do we fare internationally? Singapore, a country in which students in the 4th and 8th grades ranked first in the world on the Third International Mathematics and Science Study (TIMSS) in 1994-1995[8], also employs teachers to teach outside of their core subject expertise. However, according to the Ministry of Education, this is accepted practice, and teachers who are chosen are encouraged to "take this as a challenge and use this opportunity to prove [their] ability and potential to undertake greater responsibility."[9]

Whether full-time teachers in Singapore teach their subject of expertise or not, they have to be certified. In Singapore, this involves having a university degree in a teaching subject (i.e., math, English, science, etc.). Then, students must attend the National Institute of Education (NIE) for a year of teacher training. This institute is highly selective (even though there is a high demand for teachers in Singapore also). Acceptance is based on an interview, Entrance Proficiency Test scores[10], academic and non-academic achievements. After the NIE training, beginning teachers are given a workload of 80% of their normal responsibility during their first year. The remaining time allows for on-the-job learning from experienced teachers (mentoring, co-teaching). To ensure that teachers are familiar with new developments in their area of expertise, Singapore teachers are entitled to 100 hours of training a year. These are normally taken during their 12-week school vacation.

Are there uncertified teachers teaching in Singapore? Yes. University graduates who are thinking of becoming teachers are encouraged to become relief teachers before applying to the NIE. Relief teachers are expected to be responsible for teaching duties. But it is up to the individual school to assign those duties. This could range from the equivalent of full-time teacher to the equivalent of teacher assistant.

What leads U.S. school districts to hire uncertified teachers and, in some cases, uncertified teachers who haven't demonstrated an in-depth knowledge of the subject matter they will be teaching? The answer is simple: teacher shortages. Shortages are exacerbated by legislation forcing a certain class size. The next panel will discuss this issue.

Sources: "Title II State Report 2001 -- Waivers," all states and Washington D.C. Online. Available: http://www.title2.org. May 9, 2002. U.S. Department of Education. National Center for Education Statistics. *Digest of Education Statistics, 2000* and *2001*. Singapore teacher data: Ministry of Education, Singapore. "Teach. Mould the future of our nation." Online. Available: http://www1.moe.edu.sg/teach/; May 22, 2002. Ministry of Education, Singapore. "A Summary Report from the Steering Committee on the Review of the Teacher Training System," 16 March 1999. Online. Available: http://www1.moe.edu.sg/press/1999/pr170399.html. U.S. Department of Education. "Paige Releases Report to Congress that Calls for Overhaul of State Teacher Certification Systems," June 11, 2002. Online. Available: http://www.ed.gov.

---

[8] The United States ranked 8th and 14th, respectively. For more information on test scores see Chapter 7.

[9] Source: Ministry of Education, Singapore. "Those Who Can, Teach." Online. Available: http://www1.moe.edu.sg/teach/those_who_can_teach.html. May 22, 2002.

[10] This test must be passed the first time it is taken to be eligible for NIE.

Teacher Shortages

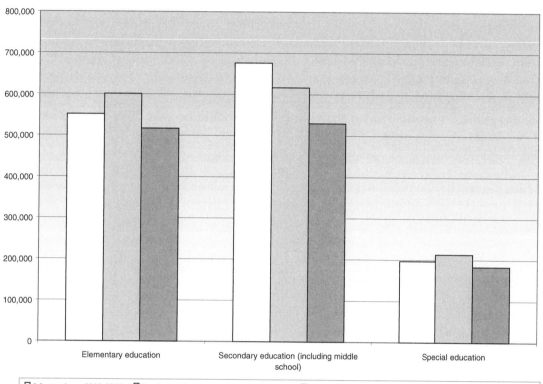

The chart above shows the projected number of job openings for teachers (due to growth, retirement, and teachers leaving the profession) and the projected number of degrees conferred for the years 2000 to 2010[11]. The chart also shows estimates of the number of graduates during this time period expected to continue teaching after one year in the profession. This last number was based on the average percentage of teachers who leave the profession after one year (14.05% in 1995) and the assumption that for each degree conferred, one person will be employed as a teacher.

If we look at the number of degrees conferred, colleges will be graduating more than enough potential elementary and special education teachers. However, after a year, many of these teachers will leave the profession, causing a shortage of teachers. Not enough students are preparing to teach at the secondary school level. The problem of teacher shortages at this level becomes worse after one year when some of those that were employed decide to leave the profession. The table on the next page lists the teacher shortfalls if the percentage of teachers leaving after the first year remains at the 1995 level.

---

[11] Projections based on the number of degrees conferred from 1993-1998. Data retrieved from *Digest of Education Statistics, 1996-2001.*

Teacher Shortfalls, 2000-2010

Elementary school	-34,422
Secondary school (including middle school)	-146,041
Special education – all levels	-13,564

Over the course of a career (25 years or more), a little over 60% of teachers leave the profession for reasons other than retirement. Why is this? One reason might be the money and benefits offered by private industry. Tracey Gunn, a fully certified teacher in California with a master's degree, admits that most of her friends who work in private industry make two or three times what she makes. "It's very difficult to say… proudly [that I'm a teacher] when I know that I don't get paid what I should be paid. …It's very seductive, a lot of money. Stock options are huge [in the private sector]. That's a long term investment that I don't necessarily have."[12]

Another problem could be general teacher dissatisfaction (dissatisfaction with salaries is a part of this). In sample surveys of public school teachers conducted by the National Education Association, teachers were asked if they would be willing to teach again. In 1961, 76.8% said that they would. In 1996, this dropped to 62.6%. The percentage of teachers who said that they would not teach nearly doubled within this time frame: from 10.9% in 1961 to 20.1% in 1996.[13]

What are school districts doing to attract and retain certified teachers? Some are offering signing bonuses, student loan forgiveness, and subsidies for low-cost day care. In the Santa Clara Unified School District in California, state-of-the-art apartments were built in 2000 to house teachers (many who left complained about lack of affordable housing). But will these measures work? Professor Richard M. Ingersoll, who analyzed teacher turnover for the Fall 2001 issue of *American Educational Research Journal,* doesn't think so. He states: "None of these will solve the problem because recruiting more teachers into schools will not work … if teachers then leave." He believes that the schools have to address all of the reasons for the high turnover rate, not just the financial ones. At Edison Charter School in San Francisco (a corporately run charter school), teachers were paid slightly higher than public school teachers and given stock options and other corporate perks. However, due to long work-hours, a longer school year, and a rigid, uniform teaching structure, three-quarters of the teachers left after the first year. In the next panel we'll take an in-depth look at the issue of teacher turnover.

Sources: U.S. Department of Education. National Center for Education Statistics. *Digest of Education Statistics,* 1996-2001 editions. "Wanted: Teachers." *Online NewsHour,* September 6, 2000. Online. Available: http://www.pbs.org. May 15, 2002. American Educational Research Association. "Teacher Shortages: Myth or Reality." *AERA News,* December 10, 2001. Online. Available: http://www.aera.net/communications/news/011210.htm. May 16, 2002. Joan Walsh. "The shame of San Francisco." *Salon.com News,* March 29, 2001. Online. Available: http://www.salon.com/news/feature/2001/03/29/edison/index2.html. May 16, 2002.

---

[12] Source: "Wanted: Teachers" *Online NewsHour,* September 6, 2000. Online. Available: http://www.pbs.org. May 15, 2002.

[13] The percentage who said that the chances would be even that they would teach again went up from 12.5 in 1961 to 17.3 in 1996.

Teacher Turnover

Top Reasons for Teachers Leaving the Profession and Ranking by School Type, 1993-1994

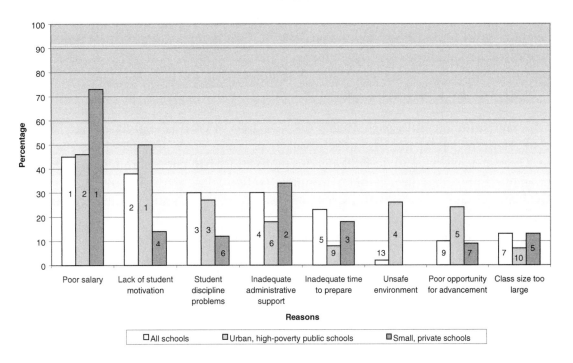

Nationwide, about 20% of teachers leave the profession after 5 years. In the 1993-94 school year, 212,908 teachers left the profession (up from 172,645 in the 1987-1988 school year).[14] How are school districts responding? John Merrow, a public television commentator, in an article for *Education Week,* likened the teaching workforce to "a swimming pool with a serious leak." Merrow states: "'You wouldn't expect that pouring more and more water into the pool would in time fix the leak, but that's precisely the approach we are taking to the so-called teacher shortage. We're misdiagnosing the problem as 'recruitment' when it's really 'retention.' Simply put, we train teachers poorly and then treat them badly — and so they leave in droves'" (Borsuk).

The chart above shows the top reasons teachers left the profession in 1993-1994. The data were originally taken from the Schools and Staffing Survey and the Teacher Followup Survey administered by the National Center for Education Statistics. The surveys encompassed a total of 6,733 teachers (most still in the teaching profession, but 1,962 who left). The numbers in the bars are the rankings.

Overall, the top reason given for leaving the teaching profession was low salary. However, among teachers in urban, high-poverty schools, lack of student motivation ranked first, with half of those leaving citing this as the top reason for quitting the profession.

---

[14] For comparison, 50,242 teachers retired in 1993-1994. In 1998-1989, 35,179 retired.

Poor salary ranked second among teachers in this group. Student discipline ranked third, overall. Next came inadequate administrative support and insufficient time to prepare. Teachers in urban, high-poverty schools feared for their safety and complained about lack of advancement. In small private schools, inadequate administrative support ranked second behind low salaries — followed by inadequate time to prepare, lack of student motivation, and large classes. Teachers in small, private schools indicated that large class size ranks high as a reason for leaving the profession. This is interesting. Private schools tend to have smaller pupil-teacher ratios than do public schools. And, yet, in urban, high-poverty schools, where class size tends to be higher than average, this class size ranked 10th in reasons given for leaving the profession.

As we saw in the previous panel, many districts zero in on financial incentives to attract and to retain their teachers. Big money "out there" lures many teachers from the profession. Other reasons have to do with student motivation, behavior, administrative support, time management, and the school environment (safety, class size). Not much information is available to show that school districts are paying much attention to these other problems. But Hawley Elementary School in Milwaukee, Wisconsin, provides mentors for first-year teachers to help them cope with job pressures. Hawley started this program after learning from a federal study that teachers are nearly twice as likely to quit after their first three years if they don't have mentoring at the start of their careers. Universities and colleges also are responding. There's a drive to make teacher training more practical. More classroom training helps first-year teachers feel less ill prepared.

The next panel will focus on the top reason for teacher dissatisfaction: low salaries. Are teachers really underpaid?

Sources: Ingersoll, Richard M. Center for the Study of Teaching and Policy. University of Washington. *Teacher Turnover, Teacher Shortages, and the Organization of Schools,* January 2001. Alan J. Borsuk. "Halting teacher turnover remains challenge at MPS." *Milwaukee Journal Sentinel*, March 2, 2000.

Teacher Salary Trends

Comparisons of Salaries: Teachers, All Workers, and All Government Workers, 1956-2000

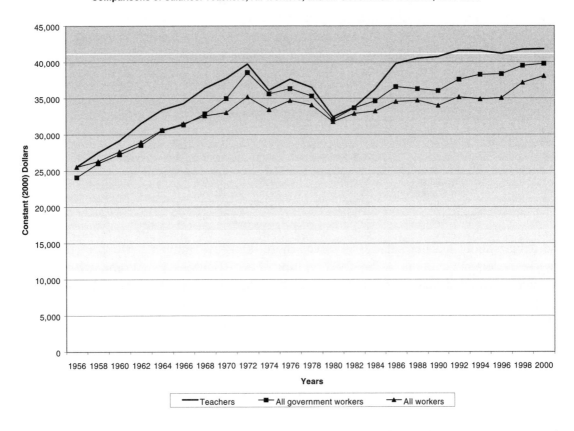

Teachers are paid more than the average worker and more than other government workers. The data shown are averages. Some teachers make more than average, some obviously less. In some cases, their salaries are far less than the year 2000 average of $41,820. In the 1999-2000 school year, the average salary in 35 states (70%) fell below the national average. The lowest average teacher salary was in South Dakota: $29,072. The highest in this group of 35 was Ohio's $41,713. The state that pays its teachers the highest salary overall was Connecticut. The average teacher salary in that state was $52,410.

Average salaries for public school teachers, in 2000, range from approximately 1.7 to 3.0 times the poverty level for a family of four ($17,463 in 2000). What is the basis for the claim of low teacher salaries?

Is it that teacher salary increases fall below the rate of inflation? No. In most cases since the 1987-1988 school year, salary increases have been at or above the rate of inflation. When they did fall below the inflation rate, the percentage difference was from 0.2% to 1.1%. Since the mid-1990s, annual raises have been increasing: from a low of 2.2% in the 1995-1996 school year up to 3.2% in 1999-2000 school year. However, this was a considerable drop from earlier years. In the 1960s, 1970s, and early 1980s, raises were between 5% and 9% annually (the rate of inflation fluctuated, however, between 1% and 13.3%).

The complaint about low teacher pay is based on comparisons to salaries in other occupations. The next table compares the average beginning teacher salary to the average beginning salary in some of the occupations that have gained employees due to teacher turnover. As a comparison: In the 1999-2000 school year, the average maximum salary for a teacher (not a beginning teacher) with a master's degree was $49,264. This is just a little more than $2,500 above the average beginning salary for someone in a mathematics or statistics profession, who may only have a bachelor's degree.

Average Beginning Salaries

(Constant 2000 dollars)

	1980		2000	
	Salary	$ above teacher salary	Salary	$ above teacher salary
Liberal arts	26,808	5,321	36,201	8,212
Math or statistics	35,494	14,007	46,744	18,755
Chemistry	34,526	13,039	38,210	10,221
Teaching	**21,487**	-	**27,989**	-

The debate about teacher salaries involves more than raw numbers. Much of the debate involves adequate compensation for handling the difficulties that come with the job. Teachers argue that their role involves more than educating their students. In the process of educating, they must also be motivators, social workers, and disciplinarians to 30 to 150 students[15] a year — each student having his own learning style, level of knowledge, and maturity. And some bring with them physical or emotional needs that may hamper their ability to learn.

In the next panel we'll discuss another teacher complaint: large class sizes.

Sources: Nelson, F. Howard. The Research & Information Services Department. American Federation of Teachers, AFL-CIO. *Survey & Analysis of Teacher Salary Trends 2000.* "Annualized Inflation Rates." Online. Available: http://www.fintrend.com. May 22, 2002. U.S. Bureau of the Census. "Poverty 2000." Online. Available: http://www.census.gov/hhes/poverty/threshld/thresh00.html. May 22, 2002.

---

[15] At the junior high and high school level. Number based on a typical average of 30 students per class, 5 classes taught per day.

Smaller Class Sizes and the Consequences

Average Class Sizes, by School Type, 1987-2000

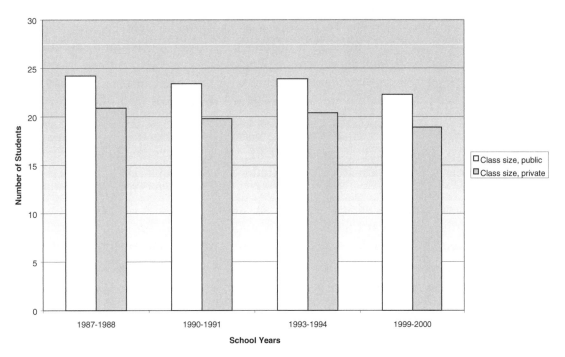

The chart compares average class sizes in public and private schools. How many students are there in a class, on average? That is the question.

In response to results from a few controlled studies in various states showing that smaller class size improves student achievement, Congress incorporated the Class Size Reduction Program into the Title II Teacher Quality block grant. These, in turn, became part of the No Child Left Behind Act of 2001. This initiative gave school districts $1.6 billion to recruit, hire, and train 30,000 new teachers for the 2001-02 school year in order to reduce class sizes. According to the Class Size Reduction Program's web site, some school districts supplement the funding and hire even more teachers. As a result, class sizes continue to decrease. Class sizes have been decreasing since the 1993-1994 school year. But, will class size reduction boost student achievement? In countries that tested in the top 5 in mathematics proficiency on the Third International Mathematics and Science Study, 1994-1995 (TIMSS), average mathematics class sizes were equal to or higher than the U.S. average for that year. In Korea (ranked 3rd), the average math class had more than 41 students. The average U.S. math class had 21-30 students.[16]

---

[16] The United States ranked 14th. For more information about TIMSS score rankings, see Chapter 7 of the current volume.

Class size reduction programs in Tennessee and California have yielded mixed results. Tennessee's *Project STAR*[17] included 79 schools, more than 300 classrooms, and 7,000 students. The project followed students for four years. A follow-up study was done in 1989 after the students had returned to larger classes. The study found that students in the smaller classes "substantially outperformed"[18] students in the larger classes on standardized and curriculum-based tests. They were less likely to be held back a grade. The higher achievement persisted (although at increasingly lower levels) until the 8th grade. Low income and minority students experienced gains twice as high as those of other students did. An added benefit: 4th grade students who had been in smaller classes from kindergarten through 3rd grade were better behaved than those from the larger classes were.

California's Class Size Reduction initiative (CSR) involves all schools in the state (voluntarily) and nearly 1.9 million students in kindergarten through 3rd grade (K-3) in the 2000-2001 school year. CSR, a part of S.B. 1777, passed in 1995. It mandated that there should be no more than 20 students per K-3 classroom. Although the program is voluntary, the school district receives $850 for each student in a reduced-sized classroom. By the 2000-2001 school year, about 95% of K-3 classrooms had implemented this program. With what results? Behavior problems decreased. Student test scores rose. From the 1997-1998 to 2000-2001 school years, standardized test scores[19] rose 13.4 points for the 2nd grade cohort, 12.1 points for the 3rd grade cohort. Test scores rose for those in 4th through 6th grades also: 8.7, 5.1, and 4.9 points, respectively. The positive effect of lower class sizes seems to carry over when students return to larger classes. (The Tennessee study had similar results.) But, can this be attributed to CSR? During the years of CSR's implementation, many other educational reforms were taking place in California. Reading initiatives and the Standardized Testing and Reporting System (STAR) were both implemented the same year. "Evidence from other states indicates that test scores rise as teachers and students become more familiar with the test. An increase equivalent to 2-5 points on the SAT-9 (Stanford Achievement Test — 9) scale has been observed in other states that have implemented the test under conditions where stakes were lower than they are in California. The gains in SAT-9 scores in California are well within the range that might be associated with 'normal' score inflation" (Stecher).

Tennessee's *Project STAR* program was a controlled study with adequate space for small class sizes. Qualified teachers were on hand to implement the experiment. California school districts lack these two ingredients. So do many districts in the country. Before the

---

[17] This was a 4-year controlled study of kindergarten through 3rd grade classrooms starting in 1985. It compared classes of 13-17 students with classes of 22-26 students, both with and without an instructional aide in the larger classrooms. Students were randomly assigned to three different types of classrooms. Teachers did not receive additional training for teaching smaller classes.

[18] Source: Pritchard, Ivor. *Reducing Class Size: What Do We Know?* March 1999. Full citation in source note.

[19] Stanford Achievement Test – 9. Testing was first implemented in the 1997-1998 school year. No standardized testing is given to kindergarten or 1st graders.

implementation of CSR (1995-1996), nearly 30% of California schools reported taking space from Special Education to make room for K-3 classrooms. After CSR, in the 1999-2000 school year, nearly 45% of schools reported raiding Special Education; nearly 40% of schools reported taking space from music and art classrooms to make room for smaller K-3 classes. Before CSR (1995-1996), 1.8% of K-3 teachers were not fully certified. By 2000-2001, the fifth year of the CSR, the percentage of K-3 teachers without full certification had soared to 13.3%.

Overcrowding and more underqualified teachers? Is this the real consequence of lower class sizes? Some California principals and superintendents seem to think so. In a survey conducted by the CSR Research Consortium in Spring 2000, principals and superintendents in California were asked whether they would prefer "none," "some," or "a lot" of the $1.5 billion now spent for CSR to be channeled into other programs. Over 50% of principals and close to 40% of superintendents supported having "some" or "a lot" of the CSR funds used to "hire more reading and math specialists" and to "upgrade teacher training" (Stecher). What do California teachers think about CSR? Eighty-three and one-half percent of teachers in reduced-size 3rd grade classrooms say that they would like to give more individualized attention to their students — but they don't have the time to do it. And 69.8% of teachers in reduced-size 3rd grade classrooms find it difficult to meet the instructional needs of their students[20]. Two of the arguments in favor of smaller class sizes are that smaller classes will allow teachers to provide more individualized instruction and that the needs of students will be met better than in larger classrooms. According to the teachers surveyed, smaller class sizes *are* an improvement (6.5% and 22.0% more K-3 students are benefiting, respectively). But is this enough?

The next panel discusses the most serious problems in schools according to teachers.

Sources: U.S. Department of Education. National Center for Education Statistics. *The Condition of Education, 1997* and *2002* editions and *Digest of Education Statistics, 2000* and *2001* editions. Stecher, Brian M. and George W. Bohrnstedt. *Class Size Reduction in California: Findings from 1999-00 and 2000-01,* February 2002. Charles M. Achilles. "The Difference between Class Size and Pupil/Teacher Ratio." Online. Available: http://www.heros-inc.org/pupil-teacher%20ratio.pdf. June 5, 2002. Pritchard, Ivor. National Institute on Student Achievement, Curriculum and Assessment. U.S. Department of Education. *Reducing Class Size: What Do We Know?* March 1999. "Class Size Reduction Program." Online. Available: http://www.ed.gov/offices/OESE/ClassSize/. April 26, 2002.

---

[20] By comparison, 100% of teachers in large 3rd grade classrooms said that they would like to give more individualized attention, but they don't have the time, and 91.8% of teachers in large 3rd grade classrooms said that they find it difficult to meet the educational needs of all their students.

Top School Problems

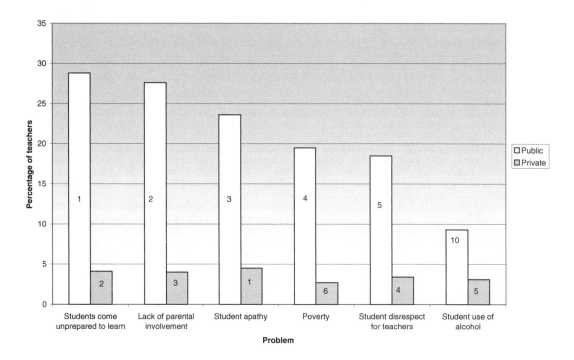

The charted data — top problems facing schools according to teachers — were originally taken from the Schools and Staffing Survey administered by the National Center for Education Statistics. The survey polled 68,000 teachers (56,736 public and 11,548 private). A higher percentage of teachers in public schools perceived serious problems than those in private schools, but, essentially, the problems were the same in both types of schools. Four out of the six problems listed have to do with student attitudes and behaviors.

Teachers saw lack of parental involvement as a serious problem. According to the National Coalition for Parent Involvement in Education (NCPIE), when a parent becomes involved, the child does better in school and in life. Low-income and minority students benefit most. Even in poverty-stricken homes, parental involvement in a child's school experience can help to eliminate problems. Parental involvement can reduce apathy, student unpreparedness, drinking problems — and increase respect for teachers.[21]

Ordinary people cite other major problems in public schools. The next table lists the top five issues facing public schools — as the public sees it[22]. The public only lists two

---

[21] For a more in-depth discussion on parental involvement see Chapter 13, the panel entitled "How Involved Are Parents in Schools?"

[22] Keep in mind that the percentage of responses were quite low: 1 – 18%, 2 – 13%, 3 – 11%, 4 – 8%, 5 – 7%.

---

problems relating to behavior: fighting/violence/gangs and use of drugs. Students' attitudes towards school and schoolwork are not singled out. Lack of financial support and standards/quality of education also rank high on the list. These two problems have been in the forefront since *A Nation At Risk*[23] was published. Congress also addressed both issues in the revisions of the Elementary and Secondary Education Act (ESEA), now called the No Child Left Behind Act of 2001. Large schools and overcrowding ranked 5th among the problems in public schools named by the general public in 1994. A Department of Education study, *The Condition of America's Schools: 1999* concluded that 22% of U.S. schools (more than 17,000) are overcrowded. A year after this study, the general public ranked this problem third.

Problems Facing Public Schools According to the General Public, with Rankings, 1994

	Ranking among general public	Ranking among public school teachers
Lack of discipline & fighting/violence/gangs	1	11
Lack of financial support	2	NA[24]
Use of drugs	3	16
Standards/quality of education	4	14
Large schools/overcrowding	5	NA

The next series of panels will focus on what should be taught. We begin with the language vs. phonics debate.

Sources: U.S. Department of Education. National Center for Education Statistics. *Digest of Education Statistics, 2001* and *An Overview of the Schools and Staffing Survey (SASS)*, July 1996. National Coalition for Parent Involvement in Education. "The Benefits of Family-School Partnerships." Online. Available: http://www.ncpie.org/AboutNCPIE/AboutPartnerships.html. June 6, 2002. Neighborhood Capital Budget Group. "Overcrowding: A National Problem/A National Solution." Online. Available: http://www.ncbg.org/documents/nationalcrowding.html. June 6, 2002.

---

[23] This report by the National Commission on Excellence in Education (NCEE) was published in April 1983. It outlined the reasons, according to the NCEE, that students in the United States were falling behind students from other nations academically. The report also gave suggestions on how to improve the educational system. Two of the suggestions were to improve the curriculum and increase the use of standardized testing.

[24] NA stands for not available.

Teaching Johnny to Read

National Assessment of Educational Progress (NAEP) Reading Achievement for 4th Graders, 1992-2000

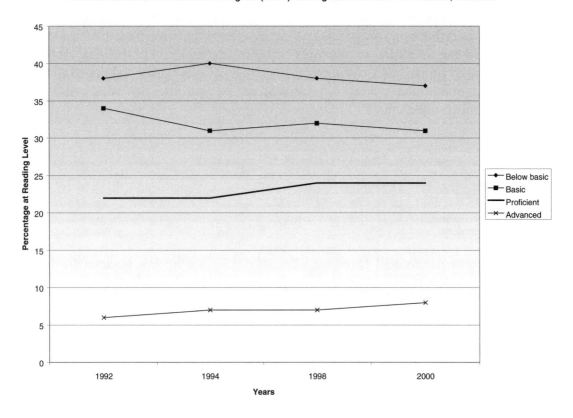

In 2000, 68% of fourth graders read at less than a proficient level. What does this mean? They could not identify the main message in a story or explain an author's statements within a text selection. The percentage of students who were proficient or advanced increased since the mid-1990s, but the numbers of those who did not reach this level far outweighed the numbers of those who did.

The debate over the most effective method of teaching children to read has been going on for more than a century. Traditionalists believe that the most effective way to teach reading is to have students learn the alphabet, learn the sounds each letter makes, and then learn to blend the sounds in order to form words. Only when the student masters this decoding, they say, is he ready to learn to read. This practice is called systematic phonics. In the mid-nineteenth century, Horace Mann, the secretary of the Massachusetts Board of Education, challenged the effectiveness of this method. He stated that the letters of the alphabet are "bloodless, ghostly apparitions" responsible for "steeping [children's] faculties in lethargy" (Levine). He promoted the "look-say" method[25] dominant in American

---

[25] The method was first developed by Thomas Hopkins Gallaudet around 1810 in order to teach deaf mutes to read. Since the deaf have no concept of putting sounds to letters (phonics), this method involved matching pictures to words.

education from the 1920s to the 1950s. This method taught children whole words instead of component sounds.

In the 1950s, Rudolf Flesch challenged Mann's method in his book *Why Johnny Can't Read.* Many new studies followed. Each attacked the "look-say" method. The conclusion of the studies: systematic phonics was the best method to teach children to read. By the 1970s, most schools had again adopted phonics over "look-say." But critics countered that systematic phonics, with its worksheet drills and Dick-and-Jane-type stories, squelched children's interest in reading. They also argued that reading groups that organize children by ability stigmatize children and promote failure. Ken Goodman, a professor of education at the University of Arizona, and a leading academic in the whole-language movement, claimed that children learn to read by figuring out the meaning of words in context. The Whole Language Teacher's Newsletter recommends teaching children confronted by an unfamiliar word to "skip it, use prior information...or put in another word that makes sense. Don't sound-it-out" (Levine). (Is it any wonder then that most 4th graders would not be able to explain the author's statements in a text selection, if they are taught to skip over or substitute words?[26])

As of December 1994, the whole language method was used by a fifth of all reading teachers despite a 1990 study by the U.S. Department of Education, *Beginning to Read.* The study concluded that "explicit phonics resulted in comprehension skills that are at least comparable to, and word recognition and spelling skills that are significantly better than ... [methods] that do not [include phonics]" (Levine). In 1997, Congress asked the Director of the National Institute of Child Health and Human Development (NICHD) to convene a national panel. It would study researched methods of reading instruction and conclude which method was the most effective. The panel of 14 included "leading scientists in reading research, representatives of colleges of education, reading teachers, educational administrators, and parents."[27] In a report published in April 2000, they concluded that systematic phonics was a necessary component in an overall method for teaching reading. They also concluded that this method was ready for implementation in the classroom since "systematic phonics instruction has been widely used over a long period of time with positive results, and a variety of systematic phonics programs have proven effective with children of different ages, abilities, and socioeconomic backgrounds." The National Reading Panel also emphasized that phonics is only one compo-

---

[26] The New York State Education Department recently changed its decades-old policy of deleting or altering "offensive" words or phrases from its literature selections on its Regents exam. In a letter to the education commissioner, those opposing the policy (including authors whose work was "edited" for the exam) wrote: "Testing students on inaccurate literary passages is an odd approach to measuring academic achievement." Source: *New York Times.* For full citation, see source note at the end of the panel.

[27] The types of participants on the panel were specified by Congress. Source: National Institute of Child Health and Human Development. Report of the National Reading Panel. *Teaching Children to Read: An Evidence-Based Assessment of the Scientific Research Literature on Reading and Its Implications for Reading Instruction,* 2000.

nent in an effective teaching strategy. Other components include "phonemic awareness, fluency, and comprehension strategies."[28]

Using this study as a guide, phonemic awareness, phonics, fluency, vocabulary, and comprehension were incorporated into the No Child Left Behind Act of 2001. The Act provides grants to districts in which students are "systematically and explicitly" taught these skills. The Act (and the press releases and fact sheets about it) emphasizes the "solid scientific research" to support these teaching strategies as opposed to the "many unproven fads and fashions in reading instruction... that have hurt our kids" in the past.

Who can argue with "solid scientific research"? The supporters of the whole language method can. Supporters of this method of teaching criticize the National Reading Panel for having excluded certain studies from their analysis. The critics say that by limiting their analysis to studies that yield measurable results, they exclude valid research and case studies that could provide insight into other methods that may be effective in the classroom (Manzo).

Educators also criticize the stringent guidelines, saying that in order to meet the requirements for funding, they will have to follow commercially packaged reading programs, leaving little leeway to tailor their teaching to the students' needs. Their concerns are not totally unfounded. In the late 1960s, Seigfried Engelmann, then a professor at the University of Illinois, founded the Direct Instruction movement. The curriculum requires teachers to adhere to scripted, sequenced lessons. Despite criticisms of this method by educators, in 1999, 1,100 schools in the U.S. used this method to teach reading.

Will systematic phonics instruction boost student testing scores and put the United States on top in reading achievement? We may have to wait until the results of next NAEP reading test are published. But, given the history of this debate, the results still may not provide any clear answers. Underlying this debate are two opposing philosophies of how children learn, the adherents of each strongly committed.

The next panel will examine the controversy over Whole Math.

Sources: U.S. Department of Education. National Center for Education Statistics. *The Nation's Report Card: Fourth Grade Reading Highlights 2000.* Online. Available: http://nces.ed.gov/nationsreportcard/pdf/main2000/2001513.pdf. June 6, 2002. National Institute of Child Health and Human Development. Report of the National Reading Panel. *Teaching Children to Read: An Evidence-Based Assessment of the Scientific Research Literature on Reading and Its Implications for Reading Instruction,* 2000. Online. Available: http://www.nichd.nih.gov/publications/nrp/smallbook.pdf. June 6, 2002. "The Facts About Reading Achievement." Online. Available: http://www.NoChildLeftBehind.gov. "Phonics & Whole Language." June 7, 2002. *Education Week on the Web,* June 5, 2002. Online. Available: //www.edweek.org. June 7, 2002. Kathleen Kennedy Manzo. "Some Educators See Reading Rules as Too Restrictive." *Education Week on the Web,* February 20, 2002. Online. Available: http://www.edweek.org. June 7, 2002. "A Direct Challenge." *Education Week,* 17 March 1999. Kleinfield, N.R. "The Elderly Man and the Sea? Test Sanitizes Literary Texts." *New York Times,* 2 June 2002. Art Levine. "The Great Debate Revisited." *The Atlantic Monthly Online,* December 1994. Online. Available: http://www.theatlantic.com/politics/educatio/levine.htm. June 12, 2002.

---

[28] Phonemic awareness refers to the student's ability to break words down into their constituent sounds. Fluency refers to the ability to read with speed, accuracy, and proper expression (a skill that is often neglected in the classroom, according to the Panel).

The Three R's: Reading, 'riting, and... Mathematics?

National Assessment of Educational Progress (NAEP) Mathematics Achievement for 12th Graders, 1990-2000

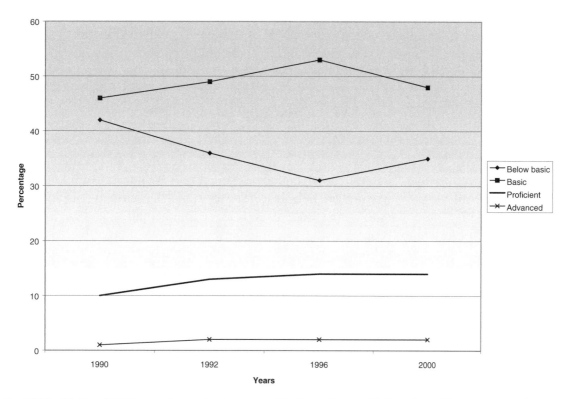

In 2000, 83% of 12th-grade students scored below the proficient level in mathematics on the National Assessment of Educational Progress (NAEP) exam. What does this mean? They could not calculate the distance between two cities on a map or analyze percentage data. The percentage of students who reached the proficient level increased since 1990, but the percentage of those who did not reach this level far outweighed those who did.

The debate over the best method for teaching mathematics has been going on since the nineteenth century[29]. Jean Piaget's research in child psychology led him to the theory that children "have real understanding only of that which they invent themselves, and each time that we try to teach them something too quickly, we keep them from reinventing it themselves."[30] John Dewey believed that education was a lifelong process, not a process in *preparation* for life. He advocated that teachers adopt a "hands-off" approach. They should only guide the students' experiences. Dewey believed that all subjects should be learned in the context of the "real world." He advocated classes in cooking, sewing, and

---

[29] The U.S. does not have a mandatory set of guidelines for teaching mathematics. Some teachers have a traditional classroom, some reformed, some blend the "best" of both systems.

[30] Jean Piaget wasn't an educator and never formally advocated an educational reform movement. Source: Papert, Seymour. "Child Psychologist: Jean Piaget." *Time 100 Online.*

---

manual arts to provide "real world" circumstances in which subjects like mathematics can be taught.[31]

William Heard Kilpatrick, who studied and worked with Dewey, invented the "project method" of teaching. Students were to work collectively on a project tailored to students' interests. During this process it was believed that students would learn all that they needed to know to become productive members of society. He believed that only subjects that had direct practical value (or student interest) should be taught. Kilpatrick's style of education was popular from the 1920s to the 1950s. As a result, the percentage of students in high school algebra dropped from 56.9% in 1909-10 to 24.8% in 1954-55. But the meaning of "direct practical value" changed during these years. Math became important.

After the Soviets launched Sputnik in 1957, math teaching received an overhaul. David Snedden's[32] premise that "algebra...is a...valueless subject for 90 percent of all boys and 99 percent of all girls..."[33] no longer held true. The National Defense Act (1958) provided almost a billion dollars to attract students to science, mathematics, and engineering. The new math curriculum proposed was labeled "New Math." No longer were students only told how — they must discover why. The use of manipulatives, such as Cuisenaire rods[34], became prevalent. The rods would teach students the relationship among numbers and arithmetic. According to Lynn Steen, a math professor at St. Olaf College in Northfield, Minnesota, the "New Math" led to "absurd lessons in which students were drilled on how to spell such terms as 'commutative,' as in the 'commutative property' – which simply means 2 + 3 = 3 + 2" (Colvin).

By 1966 "New Math" had lost favor and the "Back to Basics" movement was taking hold. Traditionalists argued that students weren't learning basic skills. Traditionalists believe that children learn by memorization and by learning to use algorithms to solve problems in math. (Many of us probably remember the "invert and multiply" rule for doing division with fractions. But how many of us know why it works?) Arithmetic drills and multiplication tables were back in the classroom during the late 1960s and 1970s.

Then *A Nation At Risk* appeared in 1983. It chronicled the failures of the American school system. The Reform movement proposed changes in the way math was taught.

---

[31] His views on education were first published in "My Pedagogic Creed." *The School Journal*, January 16, 1897.

[32] An educational psychologist who spent some of his career as Massachusetts Commissioner of Education.

[33] Source: Klein, David. *A Brief History of American K-12 Mathematics Education in the 20th Century*, August 21, 2001.

[34] Developed by Emile-Georges Cuisenaire in France in the 1950s. The rods are different colors based on the numbers 1 to 10. The rods were used to help children learn the basic properties of numbers and arithmetic. For example, by stacking two 2-unit rods and then putting them next to a 4-unit rod, the student can see that 2 + 2 = 4. These manipulatives are still in use today.

Traditional "Back to Basics" was out again. Discovery Learning was back in the saddle. This time it was called Whole Math[35]. The National Council of Teachers of Mathematics (NCTM) released standards in 1989. They called for decreased emphasis on rote practice and memorization and increased emphasis on manipulatives, problem solving, and use of calculators and computers.

In 1997, Jerry Rosen, a math professor at Cal State Northridge said: "Things the average student would know backward and forward 12 years ago, these students don't know at all." Elaine McEwan, an Arizona-based author and educator, stated: "…when you turn kids loose to constructivist math and you haven't taught them any of the basics, you have chaos." To counter the critics, Lee V. Stiff, president of the NCTM, stated that "we need to uncover math to show how it works. If there were nothing wrong with the traditional math of the '70s and '80s, our kids would be at the top of the pack, and adults wouldn't be lamenting the fact that they hated fractions or don't know algebra."[36]

But is Whole Math any better? The NCTM's 1989 *Principles and Standards for School Mathematics* shows examples of what students should be learning. A basic NCTM skill 9-12th grade students should be able to demonstrate: given a fixed interest rate, students (using a calculator) should know how to determine the amount of money in an account over a 10-year period by applying a simplified version of the formula for compound interest. An NAEP advanced skill for 12th-graders: "given a table of interest rates, students should be able to determine which bank account would have the most money after two years."[37] In the year 2000, 11 years after the NCTM standards were published, only 2% of 12th-grade students were able to demonstrate this skill on the NAEP exam.

The next panel will discuss character education.

Sources: U.S. Department of Education. National Center for Education Statistics. "The Nation's Report Card: National Mathematics Achievement-Level Results, Grade 12: 1990-2000." Online. Available: http://nces.ed.gov/nationsreportcard/mathematics/results/natachieve-g12-pf.asp. June 11, 2002. and "The Nation's Report Card: Grade 12 Item Map." Online. Available: http://nces.ed.gov/nationsreportcard/mathematics/itemmapgrade12.asp. June 11, 2002. John Dewey. "My Pedagogic Creed." *informal education*. Online. Available: http://www.infed.org/archives/e-texts/e-dew-pc.html. June 18, 2002. Beyer, Landon E. "William Heard Kilpatrick." *PROSPECTS*, vol. XXVII, no. 3, (September 1997). "Slates, Slide Rules, and Software: Teaching Math in America." Online. Available: http://american-history.si.edu/teachingmath/. June 19, 2002. Marilyn Burns. "Math for the 21st Century – Back to Basics?" *Math Solutions Online,* Spring/Summer 1998. Online. Available: http://www.mathsolutions.com. June 18, 2002. National Council of Teachers of Mathematics. *Principles and Standards for School Mathematics*, 1989. Online. Available: http://standards.nctm.org. June 18, 2002. Richard Lee Colvin. "Formulas For Math Problems." *Los Angeles Times,* January 5, 1997. Online. Available: http://www.intres.com/math/Colvin.html. June 19, 2002. Jennifer K. Corvino. "Math Wars: Old vs. New." *District Administrator*. Online. Available: http://www.ca-magazine.org/SpecialReports/Math-Science/mathwars.html. May 17, 2002. Seymour Papert. "Child Psychologist: Jean Piaget." *Time 100*. Online. Available: http://www.time.com/time/time100/scientist/profile/. June 18, 2002. High school algebra participation data and David Sneeden's quote: David Klein. *A Brief History of American K-12 Mathematics Education in the 20th Century,* August 21, 2001. Online. Available: http://www.csun.edu/ ~vcmth00m/AHistory.html. June 18, 2002.

[35] Also called constructivist math or "new-new math".

[36] Source: Covina, Jennifer K. "Math Wars: Old vs. New." *District Administration*. Online. Available: http://www.ca-magazine.com/SpecialReports/MathScience/mathwars.html. May 17, 2002.

[37] Source: "Grade 12 Item Map." *The Nation's Report Card: Mathematics*. Online. Available: http://nces.ed.gov. June 11, 2002.

Character Education

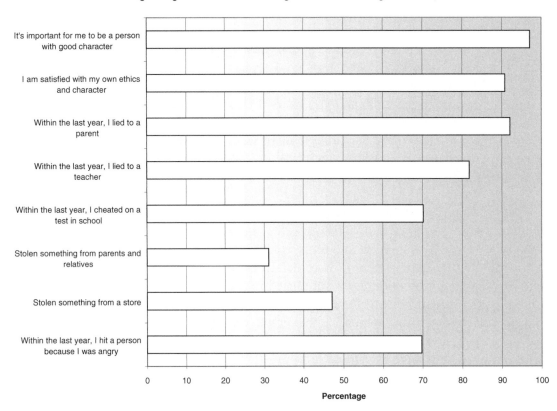

The chart shows the results from a 1998 survey of more than 10,000 randomly selected high school students. Almost all high school students agreed that it is important for them to have good character. Over 90% said that they are satisfied with their own ethics and character.[38] But, as the rest of the data show, most students lied, cheated, and exhibited violent behavior in the year before the survey was taken. A sizeable minority of students stole from parents, relatives, or a store. Judging from the nearly 10% of students who are not satisfied with their own ethics and character, some students do find their behavior ethically wrong. But that leaves 21.1% to 82.1% of high school students believing that it is permissible to lie, cheat, steal, and hit another person.[39]

---

[38] A troubling side note: 2.9% of high school students said that being a person with good character is unimportant. If this percentage is applied to the high school student population at large, this translates to over 380,000 students.

[39] Actually, the students may believe that it's wrong to lie, cheat, steal, and hit another person, but their actions run contrary to their beliefs. In another survey question, 78% of students agreed that "it's not worth it to lie or cheat because it hurts your character," however, 92.1% lied to a parent, 81.8% lied to a teacher, and 70.2% cheated on a test at least once in the past year.

Do students think that adults are doing enough to teach them ethical behavior? Most students believe that their parents are: 83.2% said that their "parents always want them to do the ethically right thing, no matter what the cost." (But, 16.8% of parents, more than 5.8 million, believe it's sometimes permissible to do something ethically wrong.) Fewer students believe that their school is trying hard to instill ethics in students. Fewer still believe that their teachers set a good example.

In response to the perceived moral decline of youth in recent years (increasing dishonesty, violence, self-destructive behaviors, and decreasing work ethic), character education programs in the schools have become popular again. Until the middle of the 20th century, people believed that character education was an essential part of schooling. Early on, teachers used the Bible to instill moral values. But, as the country grew and continued to diversify, disputes arose. Which Bible should be used? The McGuffey Reader offered an alternative, although references to biblical teachings were included.

In the 1800s and early 1900s, the McGuffey reader had a dual purpose: teach children to read and teach them morals. Each story in the book contained lessons to be learned, such as "honesty, hard work, thriftiness, kindness, patriotism, and courage."[40] One such story in *McGuffey's Third Eclectic Reader, Revised Edition*, tells of a boy, Rob, who was bullied by a classmate Jack. Rob got angry and chased after Jack intending to fight him. Suddenly Rob remembered one of the Commandments: "return good for evil". Upon remembering this, Rob decided to do the "right thing" and abruptly stopped chasing Jack. Just then he suddenly twisted his ankle and ended up on crutches for two weeks. Upon lamenting the fact that he did the "right thing" but still ended up injured, his friend Genie offered this advice: "If one must stumble at [the Commandments], it is a good thing to fall on the right side."

Character education fell out of favor in the middle of the 20th century. The Vienna Circle, an informal meeting of mathematicians, scientists, and philosophers that convened after World War I, influenced moral thinking. Participants in the Circle advocated that all human knowledge had logical and scientific foundations. From an ethical perspective, this meant that there was no objective right or wrong. Each person should be free to choose his or her own values and should not impose those values on others. Society was also becoming more secular: some feared that teaching morality in schools would lead to teaching religion.

By the 1960s and 1970s, character education was back in schools. Teachers, however, did not teach students "right from wrong" in the traditional sense. Students were encouraged to think about, clarify, reason, and decide on what was right or wrong in a given situation.

In the past 20 years, traditional character education has made a comeback. Various organizations such as The Josephson Institute of Ethics published guidelines on what should be taught. To answer critics who say that teaching ethics is the same as teaching

---

[40] Source: Center For The 4th and 5th Rs. "What is the History of Character Education?" Retrieved June 20, 2002 from http://www.cortland.edu/c4n5rs/history.htm.

religious values or values espoused by one group of people, a universally agreed-upon set of values is a part of all programs. These values include trustworthiness, respect, responsibility, fairness, caring, and citizenship.[41] The Character Education Partnership (CEP) endorses 11 principles that all character education programs should contain. Some of these include:

- ▯③ "Define core ethical values... and hold all school members accountable to standards of conduct consistent with those behaviors."
- ▯③ "Integrate character development into all aspects of school life...[do not wait] for opportunities to present themselves."
- ▯③ "Provide students with real-life challenges to help them develop a practical understanding of the moral requirements of the core ethical values."
- ▯③ "Require strong moral leadership from both staff and students."
- ▯③ "Develop students' intrinsic commitment both to core values and to the academic curriculum." (Starr).

Are the programs working? The Child Development Program (CDP), a character education program in California in the early 1980s, used children's literature to reflect on values and provide students regular opportunities to work together. Students shared the responsibility of creating a respectful classroom. The school offered service programs such as cross-grade tutoring and mentoring. Families were required to take part in "family homework" every two to three weeks. Sessions were intended to help parents discuss ethical issues with their children. At the end of a longitudinal study, students who had completed the program were more considerate and cooperative, more likely to feel accepted by peers, better able to solve interpersonal problems, and more tolerant of others. A follow-up study of 8th graders found that positive effects lingered: students had higher self-esteem, participated more in extracurricular activities and were less likely to use drugs and alcohol. Similar results were found in South Dakota after Character Counts! was implemented. Crime decreased by 31% to 56% between 1998 and 2000. Suspensions dropped 28%.

Title X, Part A, of The No Child Left Behind Act of 2001 provides funds to states to implement character education programs in their schools. In 2002, 37 states took advantage of these funds. Will more states implement character education programs? Is character education likely to impede the decline in students' ethical behavior?

Sources: Josephson Institute of Ethics. *1998 Report Card on the Ethics of American Youth*, October 1998. Bureau of the Census. *Statistical Abstract of the United States, 2001*. Tom Lickona et. al. The Character Education Partnership. "11 Principles of Effective Character Education." Online. Available: http://www.character.org/principles/Files/ElevenPrinciples.pdf. Starr, Linda. "Is Character Education the Answer?" *Education World*, 1 February 1999. Center For The 4th and 5th Rs. "Signs of a National Crisis of Character," "What is the History of Character Education?" and "The Child Development Project."Online. Available: http://www.cortland.edu/c4n5rs. Department of Education. "The Partnerships in Character Education Pilot Project Program." Online. Available: http://www.ed.gov/offices/OERI/ORAD/fie.html. Josephson Institute of Ethics. "The Six Pillars of Character." *Making Ethical Decisions*. Online. Available: http://www. josephsoninstitute.org/MED/MED-6pillars.htm. Josephson Institute of Ethics. "The Evidence for Character Counts!" Online. Available: http://www.charactercounts.org. Various pages from *McGuffey's Third Eclectic Reader, Revised Edition*, 1920. Online. Available: http://members.aol.com/ shoresshc/ pages/mcguffey3.html.

---

[41] These guidelines are from the Josephson Institute of Ethics. These are also the six elements of character adopted by the No Child Left Behind Act of 2001 as a requirement in any character education program a state wishes to fund with Federal monies.

Chapter 9

Trends in Educational Funding

Few Americans would argue against the desirability of a publicly funded education for every child. In fact, most state constitutions guarantee an education, and they use phrases like "equal," "appropriate," "uniform," and "thorough and efficient" to describe the type of education every child should receive.

Despite the loftiness of the states' intentions, there have always been inequities in the funding of public schools. The U.S. Supreme Court took a stand with Brown *v* Board of Education (1954), ruling that "separate but equal" schools for African-Americans were inherently unequal. Movies, books, and television programs with titles like *Blackboard Jungle, Dangerous Minds,* and *Savage Inequalities: Children in America's Schools,* graphically depict the problems faced by the large numbers of children who attend America's poorest schools.

Fair-minded people asked: Was it just or appropriate for some children to attend schools that resembled country clubs, while poor children settled for so much less? Lawsuits were filed on behalf of poor students, demanding fairness in the taxation system used to support education. It began with California's Serrano *v* Priest (1971), in which the high court ruled that a child's access to public education could not be based on the wealth of his or her parents. By 2000 poor school districts in more than 40 states had challenged the constitutionality of their states' school financing system. The lawsuits are still being filed and fought. State courts say repeatedly that education is the duty of the state and legislatures must find ways to make sure every child has an equal chance at an adequate education.

Bob Chase, President, National Education Association, describes the issue this way: "That some children are more equal than others in American public schools is an abomination, a national disgrace, and an ugly pustule on democracy's fair visage."[1]

In theory, equal educational opportunity sounds like the American way. But what about parents who want more than what the states are willing to provide? Should they be allowed to spend their own money to make their childrens' schools better? One such parent, novelist John Irving, calls legislation to equalize education funding "Marxism." "It's

---

[1] Quote retrieved May 6, 2002, from http://www.nea.org/nr/sp970411.html

leveling everything by decimating what works... It's that vindictive 'We've suffered, and now we're going to take money from your kid and watch you squirm.'"[2]

In the panels that follow, we will look at how our schools are funded and where the money goes. We will look at the issue of whether schools allocate their funds wisely. We will examine Americans' willingness to tax themselves to pay to educate their own children versus the unknown child in some other part of the state.

Americans have always regarded education as important, whether it was for the purpose of teaching people how to think, for the survival of democracy, or for the productivity of the economy. Throughout American history there has been an emphasis on providing at least a rudimentary education for the poor.

Education used to be a parental responsibility. As society became more complex, education became a local responsibility. When the public perceived a failure of the education system to meet the increasing demands placed on it, with test scores falling or flat, remedies were sought. A major shift in education funding resulted in the second half of the twentieth century, with state and federal governments playing an increasingly larger role in support of schooling. This is evident in state equalization efforts and in federal programs for the poor such as Title I, Head Start, and after-school programs. We will close this chapter with a look at trends in preprimary education and funding for Head Start and latchkey programs.

---

[2] Tamala E. Edwards, "Revolt of the gentry: in Vermont a new law meant to equalize public school funding has set off a ferocious class war," *Time,* June 15, 1998 v151 n23 p34 (2).

Public Schools: Where Does the Money Come From?

General Revenue Sources for Public Elementary and Secondary School Systems: 1997-98

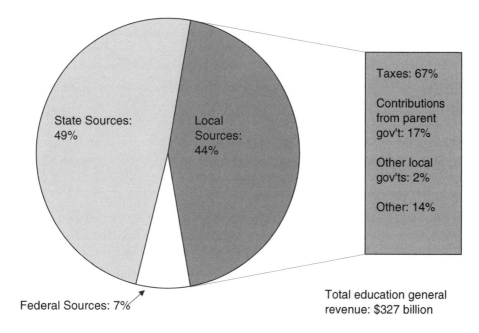

State Sources: 49%

Local Sources: 44%

Taxes: 67%

Contributions from parent gov't: 17%

Other local gov'ts: 2%

Other: 14%

Federal Sources: 7%

Total education general revenue: $327 billion

The chart shows the three major sources of general revenue for the nation's more than 14,000 public elementary and secondary school districts: Federal, state, and local governments. According to the National Center for Education Statistics, expenditures for education rose from $213.4 billion in 1985-86 to $311.6 billion in 1998-99, a 46% increase (constant 1999-2000 dollars).

The share of revenue that comes from the federal government, practically non-existent before the 1970s, hovered near 7% throughout the 1990s. Title I is the largest federal program for elementary/secondary education; it helps disadvantaged children. Federal spending on education between 1965-2000 approached $200 billion.[3]

State and local funds account for 93% of education expenditures. These governments spend more money on public education than on any other item. According to *Public Administration Review*, the trend has been for states to assume more control of education funding (from an average of 41% in 1960 to 50% in 1992). The major sources of state funds are sales and income taxes (personal and corporate). At the local level, property taxes are the revenue source of choice.

There are regional differences in the way revenue is generated (whether more comes from state or local sources), as the table below shows. The only significant increases in

---

[3] The Leave No Child Behind Act of 2001 increased federal education funding to an estimated $10.4 billion for the Title I program, an 18% increase over 2001 and a 30% increase over 2000 levels.

local funding were in the West between 1991-92 and 1994-95, largely because the California state budget permanently transferred $3.6 billion of local property tax revenues to schools from other local entities. The only significant decreases in local funding occurred in the Midwest between 1993-94 and 1994-95. This was largely due to events in Michigan, a subject we shall discuss later in this chapter (see "Litigating School Funding").

Percentage Distribution of Education Revenues by Region: 1991-92 to 1996-97

Region	1991-92	1992-93	1993-94	1994-95	1995-96	1996-97
			Local sources			
Northeast	55.4	55.8	56.3	56.3	56.3	56.5
Midwest	56.2	55.5	55.0	48.3	47.6	47.4
South	43.8	43.7	43.5	43.9	43.4	43.4
West	32.0	33.4	36.1	36.6	35.6	33.9
			State sources			
Northeast	39.5	38.8	38.4	39.0	38.7	38.6
Midwest	37.9	38.5	39.0	45.8	46.7	46.8
South	48.5	48.0	48.0	48.1	49.0	48.9
West	60.7	59.0	55.7	54.9	56.3	58.4

States' ability to fund education varies. Richer states can provide more funding. At least 45 states rely heavily on sales taxes to fund education. When sales tax revenues go down, school funding can suffer. This reality is behind the current trend to push for collection of sales taxes from online purchases of merchandise. The National Education Association estimates the revenue losses to states from online purchases could be as much as $45.2 billion by 2006.

Historically, local property taxes have been the major source of education revenue. Declining cities with less wealth and a smaller tax base now tend to rely on high income taxes to fund education. Wealthy communities raise more money from property taxes. Only state legislatures can fix the inequity, and they have usually done so only after being ordered to by state courts. (See "Litigating School Funding Equity," later in this chapter.)

Other sources of revenue are PTAs, booster clubs, state lotteries, school-business partnerships (businesses supply the vending machines that make our children obese), tobacco settlement money,[4] and one of the hottest trends, Local Education Foundations. LEFs are non-profit groups that raise funds from private sources to benefit local public schools. They took off in the late 1980s in California. In 1992, California LEFs raised $28.9 million, compared to PTAs at $27.7 million and booster clubs at $19.3 million.

Sources: Chart: U.S. Bureau of the Census. *Statistical Abstract of the United States: 2001*, Table 241. Online. Available: http://www.census.gov/govs/www/school.html. Table: NCES, *The Condition of Education 2000*, Table 63-1, Online. Available: http://nces.ed.gov. May 2, 2002. National Education Association, "Public Education Embroiled in a Taxing Situation," Online. Available: www.nea.org/neatoday. May 1, 2002. "Study Results on Local Education Foundations," Online. Available: www.rand.org/publications/MR/MR1429/MR1429.appd.pdf. May 6, 2002. Johnston, Jocelyn M. and William Duncombe, "Balancing Conflicting Policy Objectives: the Case of School Finance Reform. *Public Administration Review* (March/April 1998) v58. n2. p145, page 1.

---

[4] In 1998 the attorneys general of most states and the major tobacco companies agreed to settle more than 40 pending lawsuits brought by states against the tobacco industry. In exchange for dropping their lawsuits and agreeing not to sue in the future, the states would receive billions of dollars in payments from the tobacco companies.

Public Financial Support of Education

**Per-capita Personal Income (Constant 1998 dollars) and
Revenue per Elementary/Secondary Student: 1930-1997**

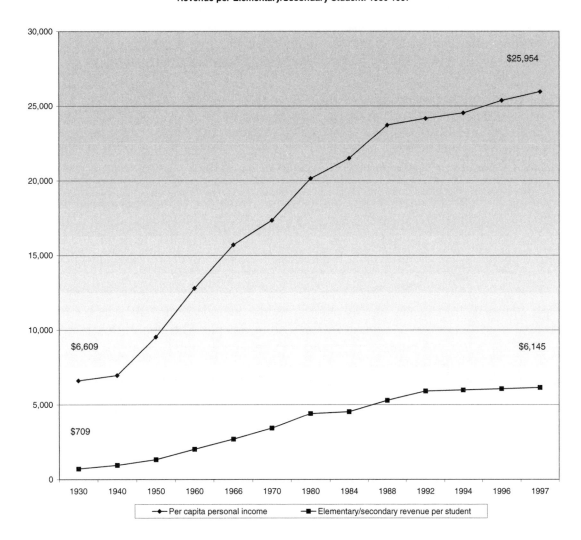

How willing are we to tax ourselves to pay for education? Fairly willing, according to the chart. Revenues per elementary/secondary student generally rose between 1930 and 1997. There was a leveling-off period in the early 1980s, a time of recession, and funding per pupil increased only about 0.14% annually in the 1990s. Per capita personal income rose at a faster rate than per-pupil expenditures. In 1930, revenue per student equaled 11% of per capita personal income. In 1997, the figure was 24%.

Michael F. Addonizio[5] describes a "nearly 100-fold increase" in education spending between 1890 and 1990, "more than triple the growth of the U.S. gross national product

---

[5] See Source notes.

(GNP) over this period, with K-12 public school expenditures increasing from less than 1 percent of GNP in 1890 to 3.4 percent in 1990."

Fervent antitax sentiment led in 1978 to the passage of Proposition 13 in California. This was just the beginning of a national revolt against the high property taxes that were a major source of school funding. Public support for education funding remains high, however, and other sources of school revenue were found (discussed later in this chapter).

The National Opinion Research Center (NORC) at the University of Chicago reports that support for education rose to the top of America's priority list in the 1990s. Support for education continues even though the number of families with school-aged children (under 18) fell from 55% of 1972 households to 38% of 1998 households. In 1973 and 1975, education spending ranked sixth out of 11 in Americans' list of spending priorities.

According to NORC, women (69%), African-Americans (81%) and the college-educated (67%) are most likely to support increases in education spending.[6] According to the General Accounting Office, people in poor communities are generally more willing than are wealthy people to tax themselves at high rates to finance education; their problem is an inadequate tax base.

People opposed to increases in education spending include senior citizens on fixed incomes who no longer have children in the system, people who oppose tax increases of any kind, and a sizeable number of people who believe it would simply be folly to pour any more money into poorly managed school systems.

Sources: Chart: NCES, *The Condition of Education 2000,* Table 62-1. *Digest of Education Statistics 1999* and 120 Years of American Education: A Statistical Portrait. Online. Available: http://nces.ed.gov. May 2, 2002. National Education Association, Legislative Action Center, "School Modernization." Online. Available: http://www.nea.org/lac/modern/. May 2, 2002. "Dramatic shifts in spending priorities favor education." The University of Chicago News Office. 17 August 1999. Online. Available: http://www-news.uchicago.edu/releases/99/990817.spending.shtml. May 6, 2002. Michael F. Addonizio, "New Revenues for Public Schools: Alternatives to Broad-Based Taxes." Online. Available: http://nces.ed.gov/pubs99. May 6, 2002. Frank Johnson, "Revenues and Expenditures for Public Elementary and Secondary Education: School Year 1998-99. Online. Available: http://nces.ed.gov/pubs2002/. May 8, 2002.

---

[6] The NORC survey was part of the General Social Survey, a study begun in 1972. Sample size is 3000 cases.

Public Schools: Where Does the Money Go?

Expenditures of Public Elementary and Secondary School Systems: 1997-98

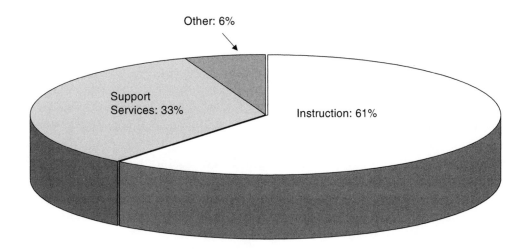

The chart shows how America's school districts spend their money: 61% goes for instruction and 33% goes for support services. The statistics are not very enlightening. It would be more valuable to know how schools actually allocate their resources. Do they spend money on smaller classes and better-educated teachers — or do they mismanage and waste it, as news headlines allege? ("Bad bookkeeping: Missing and misspent school money," says the *Detroit News*. "Mismanagement and wrong priorities top issues for schools," says the *Seattle Post Intelligencer.*[7])

The table below shows that more than 14,000 school districts are in operation and are allocating their resources in different ways. Margaret Hadderman cited studies of resource allocation.[8] One found that the New York State system increased spending on special education by 55% between 1983 and 1992, while spending on science and math teachers increased only modestly. A study of 1,000 California schools revealed a similar pattern. A Chicago study found that thriving schools spent more for instruction, while poorer schools spent more on noninstructional items like security.

---

[7] www.detnews/schools; http://seattlepi.nwsource.com/opinion/ringop.shtml

[8] "Trends and Issues"; see Source notes.

Hadderman says that teacher salaries (more than 60% of most school budgets), increased nearly 21% from 1981 to 1990, then declined for most of the 1990s. She reports that money spent on maintenance declined from 14% of budgets in 1920 to 9.6% in 1960 and 3% in 1992. This trend cannot continue. The average age of America's public schools is 42, says the NEA. The General Accounting Office estimates that more than 14 million children are being taught in schools that need major repairs, especially schools in inner cities and those with more than 50% minority enrollment. NEA estimates $322 billion is needed to update and repair schools. Major construction projects are already underway in DC ($2 billion) and Detroit ($1.5 billion).

California, home to the nation's largest school system, must contend with an enrollment of one-quarter limited-English-proficient students (the number of these students, most of them Hispanic, doubled to 5 million in the 1990s). All school districts say new technology drives up costs. The number of special education students is growing faster than that of general students, and federal law requires that every special education student must be provided with a free, appropriate education regardless of cost to the district.

School administrators complain that after mandating special help for children with disabilities, neither federal nor state governments provided sufficient funds. The Center for Special Education Finance estimates that it costs 128% more to educate a special ed student. Expenditures rose from $19.3 billion in 1987 to $32.6 billion in 1995. In school year 1998-99, $49.2 billion was spent (Hadderman; states paid 38.8% and local districts paid 53.9%). (See Chapter 13, "Special Needs.) Spending for technology nearly doubled between 1991-92 and 1996-97, from $2.1 to $4.1 billion.

School District Expenditures per Student: 1996-97

District characteristic	Total	Instruction	Support services	Capital outlay	Other	Number of districts
Total	6,555	3,473	1,876	617	589	14,493
Metropolitan status						
Primarily serves a central city	6,742	3,607	1,958	567	610	709
Serves a metro area, not a central city	6,711	3,526	1,920	677	588	5,751
Does not serve a metro area	5,952	3,168	1,663	558	564	8,033
Children in district below poverty level						
Less than 2%	7,080	3,753	2,074	639	614	3,535
2%-9%	6,912	3,631	1,961	701	618	3,623
10%-19%	6,075	3,184	1,729	619	544	3,618
More than 19%	6,422	3,459	1,844	529	590	3,717

The table shows how public school expenditures vary depending upon the district's poverty level and metropolitan status. School districts with the smallest percentage of students below the poverty level spend more on their students than districts with more poor students. Expenditures are highest in central cities, where living costs are higher.

Sources: U.S. Bureau of the Census. *Statistical Abstract of the United States 2001*. 121st ed. Table 241. Online. Available: http://www.census.gov/govs/www/school.html. Margaret Hadderman. "Trends and Issues: School Finance." Online. Available: http://eric.uoregon.edu/trends_issues/finance/. May 1, 2002. Jay G. Chambers et al., "What are we spending on special education in the U.S.? Center for Special Education Finance Brief No. 8 (February 1998). Online. Available: http://csef.air.org/papers/brief8. May 1, 2002. "School Facilities: America's Schools Report Differing Conditions (Letter report)." 14 June 1996. GAO/HEHS-96-103. Online. Available: http://frwebgate6.access.gpo.gov/. May 6, 2002.

Does More Money Equal Better Student Achievement?

**Top 10 States According to Per-pupil Expenditure (1998-99)
and Their RAND NAEP Ranking (1996)**

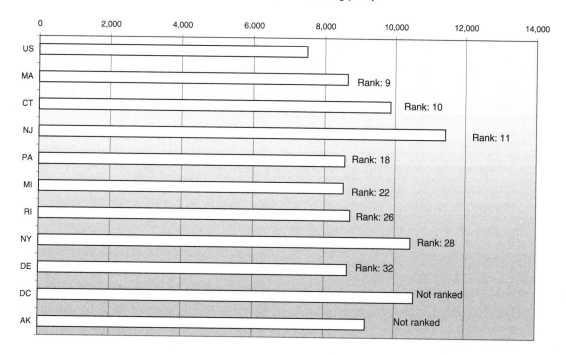

Whether more money leads to better student achievement is one of the most hotly debated topics in American education. What we do know is that students in high-poverty schools are, according to a Congressional study, "least able to demonstrate the expected levels of academic proficiency."[9]

Schools may have money, but their SAT scores may be lower than those of schools with less money. Schools may have money, but their NAEP[10] scores may show little improvement from one year to the next.

---

[9] "Prospects: The Congressionally Mandated Study of Educational growth and Opportunity," cited by Maris A. Vinovskis; see Source notes.

[10] National Assessment of Educational Progress; see Chapter 7

**RAND's Top 8 States Ranked for Improvement on
NAEP Scores, Their Per-pupil Expenditures and SAT Scores**

State	1998-99 expenditure	2001 SAT verbal/math
Maine	7,783	506/500
North Dakota	6,321	592/599
Iowa	7,015	593/603
New Hampshire	7,048	520/516
Montana	6,525	539/539
Wisconsin	8,385	584/596
Minnesota	7,860	580/589
Nebraska	7,423	562/568

The evidence seems to point to this conclusion: Learning is complex. It cannot be linked to a single variable. The chart shows the top 10 states ranked according to per-pupil expenditures in 1998-99. The "rank" figures come from a RAND[11] study that ranked 44 states according to improvement on NAEP tests between 1990 and 1996. RAND found that NAEP scores are "higher in states with higher per-pupil expenditures, lower pupil-teacher ratio in lower grades, [and] higher percentages of teachers reporting adequate resources for teaching."

The table shows RAND's top eight states and their per-pupil expenditures in 1998-99. Both the chart and the table show 2001 SAT scores.

Gerald Bracey contends that disparities in SAT scores cannot be used to deny a relationship between money spent on education and higher scores. He says: "the principal source of differences among states is the proportion of seniors taking the SAT. In Utah and Mississippi, only 4% of the seniors take the test and this tiny elite does well [2001 SAT results: 575/570 and 566/561, respectively]. In Connecticut, 82% of the senior class huddles in angst on Saturday mornings to bubble in answer sheets. With 4/5 of its senior class taking the test, Connecticut is digging much deeper into its talent pool and that excavation shows up in lower scores," (509/510, as shown on the chart).

A study of Texas schools found only "weak" increases in student achievement on standardized tests — despite a steady increase in federal, state, and local dollars for education. The researchers stated: "It is difficult to attribute an increase in student learning to any one factor because so many forces influence student learning, including factors outside the school environment."

Standard & Poor's weighs in from a business perspective. Their Performance Cost Indicator (PCI) "quantifies the return on a school district's resources by directly linking district spending with student results, including standardized test scores and nontest data such as graduation and dropout rates… PCIs can be used to identify districts that yield a particularly strong return on resources." At least two states have signed on for the multimillion-dollar S&P program. Early results for one Michigan district: "Relative to other K-12 school districts in Michigan, Bloomfield Hills School District achieves ex-

---

[11] A California-based think tank.

ceptionally above-average student results with spending that is among the highest in the state." Coincidence? — Or is it related to a combination of factors in addition to money?

When Californians passed Proposition 13, all schools received less money. People saved billions on property taxes. School performance declined. Coincidence? — Or as Pacific Research Institute claims, "a failure in the way education services are delivered?"

Critics of the "more money for schools" movement complain that schools mismanage their funds. A *USA Today* analysis contends that big cities "are increasingly inefficient in providing basic services. It costs New York, Chicago, Los Angeles, Philadelphia, and other big cities twice as much to educate a child."

Whether or not more money brings better results, for now at least, states that do not perform will be penalized by the federal government. President George W. Bush promises: "Taxpayer dollars will only go to states that have standards and expectations for improving schools or teaching a solid academic curriculum."

Sources: Chart: U.S. Bureau of the Census. Annual Survey of Government Finances, Table 11. Online. Available: http://www.census.gov/govs/www/school99.html. May 3, 2002. David W. Grissmer, Ann Flanagan, et al., "Improving Student Achievement: What State NAEP Test Scores Tell Us." RAND. Online. Available: http://www.rand.org/. May 3, 2002. SAT scores, Online. Available: http://www.collegeboard.com. May 8, 2002. Vinovskis, Maris A. "Do Federal Compensatory Education Programs Really Work? A Brief Historical Analysis of Title I and Head Start." *American Journal of Education.* (May 1999). v107. i3. p.187. Moore, Stephen and Dean Stansel. "Can We Stop the Decline of Our Cities?" *USA Today* (Magazine) March 1994, p.1. Standard & Poor's. Online. Available: http://www.ses.standardandpoors.com/. May 3, 2002. "California Schools Fail While Spending Increases." Online. Available: http://www.heartland.org/education/apr97/californ.htm. May 3, 2002. Alexander, Ph.D., Celeste D. "Resource Allocation Practices and Student Achievement: An Examination of District Expenditures by Performance Level with Interviews from Twenty-One Districts." Southwest Educational Development Laboratory (SEDL) and Charles A. Dana Center. The University of Texas at Austin. Online. Available: http://www.sedl.org/pubs/policy24/allocation-practices.pdf. May 7, 2002. Gluckman, Amy. "Tests and Money: Where Does U.S. Public Education Stand?" *Dollars and Sense* (March-April 1998) p.1. Gerald W. Bracey, "Public Education and Its Discontents." Online. Available: http://www.america-tomorrow.com/ati/gb71221.htm. May 8, 2002.

Litigating School Funding Equity

Per-pupil Expenditures in 10 Michigan School Districts in 1994 and 2001

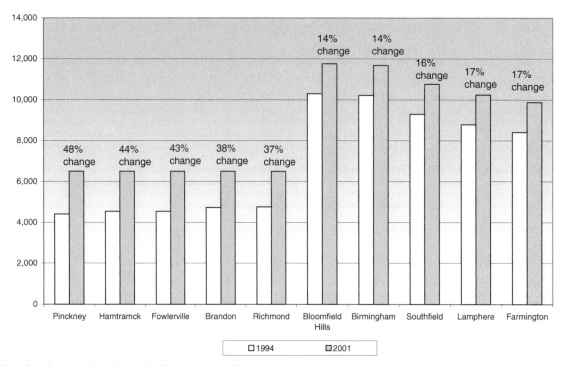

1994   2001

Beginning in the late 1960s, school-funding gaps between wealthy and poor districts — arising from reliance on property taxes — led to litigation. Lawsuits challenged the constitutionality of state school finance systems. One by one, state judges are telling state legislatures to find more equitable ways to fund education, and/or to ensure that every child receives an "adequate," "efficient," or "effective" education.

The states usually respond by shifting the burden from local property taxes to state sales taxes. Other levies are used too. Strictly local control of schools, the American way since the 19th century, is giving way to more state control. This trend is likely to continue as state equalization efforts increase.

On the plus side, when the states assume responsibility for funding schools, property taxes go down. Voters stop seeing local millage increases. On the minus side, wealthier school districts, whose voters are more than willing to raise their own taxes — for better schools, *in their own district* — are unable to do so. They say the quality of their schools is declining.

In 1994, Michigan became the first state to voluntarily move away from property taxes as the root source of education funding. The issue was not equity so much as very-high property taxes. The graphic shows what happened to per-pupil expenditures in Michigan between 1994, when Proposal A was adopted, and 2001. Proposal A boosted revenues for Michigan's poorest school districts. It limited annual increases for the wealthiest districts.

The chart shows the top five winners and losers in terms of the difference between dollars received per student in 1994 and 2001. Bloomfield Hills, an affluent district, had its budget cut by the state every year. The city sends more than $111 million a year in school taxes to the state — only to see two-thirds of it go to other districts. Bloomfield Hills and numerous other cities complain that rising costs force program cutbacks and threaten the quality of their educational offerings. Meanwhile, poorer school districts saw their allocation per pupil rise by up to 48%.

Governor John Engler, a prime mover behind Proposal A, has no sympathy for complaints from wealthy districts. "We need better managers in many districts," he told *The Detroit News*. "The education problems in Michigan are not due to lack of resources."

In his book *Savage Inequalities: Children in America's Schools*, Jonathan Kozol wrote: "One searches for some way to understand why a society as rich and, frequently, as generous as ours would leave [the children of East Saint Louis] in their penury and squalor for so long — and with so little public indignation. Is this just a strange mistake of history? Is it unusual? Is it an American anomaly?" As a practical matter, Kozol asks us to consider this: 90% of male jail prisoners in New York City are public school dropouts. Incarceration costs the city nearly $60,000 a year per person, far more than it would cost to provide a decent education.

There are well-meaning people on both sides of the "equitable funding" issue. Critics call laws like Michigan's "Robin Hood" laws, taking money from wealthy districts to give to poorer ones. Defenders say a child's education should not depend on geography. On a loftier level, the issue is discussed as a clash between local freedom and mass democracy.

Meanwhile, in the words of Stephen Smith, manager of the National Center for Education Finance at the National Conference of State Legislatures: "Adequacy has trumped equity as the biggest issue in education finance." The latest theory is that states must define what an adequate education means — then figure out how much money is needed to achieve the standard.

Sources: Jodi Upton et al. "Wealthy districts hit hardest." *Detroit News*. Online. Available: http://detnews.com. April 30, 2002. Charles V. Tines, "Bloomfield Hills: Standard-setting programs wither away." *Detroit News*. Online. Available: http://detnews.com. April 30, 2002. Michele Moser and Ross Rubenstein. "The Equality of Public School District Funding: A National Status Report." *Public Administration Review*. January-February 2002. *Savage Inequalities*. Online. Available: http://www-unix.oit.umass.edu/~kastor/walking-steel-95/ws-savage.html. May 8, 2002. Phil Magers. "Cost of high standards studied." *Washington Times*. 6 April 2002. Online. Available: http://www.washtimes.com. May 8, 2002.

Trends in Early Childhood Education

Number of 3-5-Year Olds, Number Enrolled in Preprimary School, and Number Enrolled in Head Start: 1965-1999

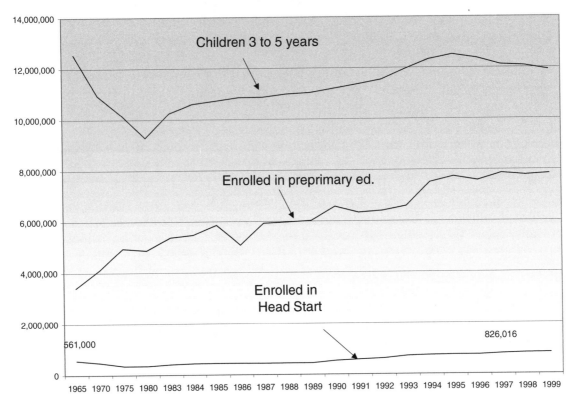

In 1965, there were 12.5 million children between the ages of 3 and 5. Only 27% of them (3.4 million) were enrolled in preprimary education.[12] By 1999, the number of children in the age group had declined to 11.9 million, but 66% (7.8 million) were enrolled in preprimary education. In 1970, 17% of children in the age group attended preprimary programs for a full day; by 1999 the figure was 53%. In 34 years, we moved from a society where very young children stayed at home with Mom to a society in which a majority of very young children head off every weekday morning for a full day at school.

During this period, the federal government got involved in education in a very big and radical way. The Head Start program, a component of President Lyndon Johnson's War on Poverty, assumed parental obligations by delivering educational, health, nutritional, and social services to poor children and their families. The idea dates back to the "infant schools" movement of the early 19th century. Infant schools were designed for the moral training of poor children while their mothers worked. It was believed that infant schools would reduce poverty and welfare costs. The infant school movement died out for various

---

[12]Preprimary means elementary education programs for children who are too young for first grade. Includes center-based programs and kindergarten.

reasons. One was lack of funding, another teacher complaints about the disruptive nature of the young "students."

Widespread interest in preschool education revived in the 1960s, just when poverty became a focus of attention and legislation. Head Start was formed based on the theory that an early investment in nurturing at-risk children will pay off later in fewer strains on social services and the justice system. The assumption is that the federal government can be an appropriate and effective provider of this nurturing.

Head Start began as a summer-only program. It was soon converted to a year-round program. Similar programs for advantaged children sprang up (the little ones got a leg up in the college admissions race and Moms went off to work). In 1995 Head Start began offering services to pregnant women and low-income families with infants and toddlers.

While the federal government took on the job of helping the youngest of the poor, state and local governments got more involved in preprimary education at the kindergarten level. Kindergartens were established in Germany in 1837; the idea soon caught on in the United States. But at the time Head Start began, 32 states didn't have kindergartens. Today 39 states are required to offer kindergarten, but attendance is mandatory in only 15 states.[13] The National Education Association (NEA) was an early supporter of kindergartens and currently endorses mandatory kindergarten in every state. By no means does this issue enjoy universal support. Conservative columnist Phyllis Schlafly, for one, is firmly opposed, as is the National Center for Home Education. Commenting on an NEA proposal for public school education of children from birth through age 8, Schlafly called it "babysitting"; she is equally scornful of an NEA call for mandatory kindergarten.

Still, early childhood education and Head Start enjoy wide support. How far behind have we left the days when most little children stayed home with Mom? One of the National Education Goals for the year 2000, adopted by Congress, is that "all children will have access to high-quality and developmentally appropriate preschool programs that help prepare children for school."

In the next panel we will look at the specifics of Head Start's bipartisan financial support. Most studies have found that the initial positive effects of the Head Start program are short-lived. One proposed solution? Make Head Start programs longer than one year, and make them better — a very expensive proposition indeed, as we shall see.

Sources: Charts: U.S. Bureau of the Census. *Statistical Abstract of the United States 2001*. Table 225. Current Population Reports, P20-533. Current Population Survey Poverty and Health Statistics Branch/HHES Division. Nancy Stevenson. "A modest proposal: Raising children by barnyard standards." Online. Available: http://www.lib.niu.edu/ipo/ii940721.html. May 15, 2002. "The NEA Proves Itself Extremist Again." *The Phyllis Schlafly Report*. Vol. 29. No. 1. August 1995. Online. Available: http://www.eagleforum.org/. May 15, 2002. "Mandatory Kindergarten Is Unnecessary." National Center for Home Education. Online. Available: http://www.hslda.org. May 14, 2002. Bowen, Ezra. "Trying to jump-start toddlers; experts blast the parental push for preschool 'hothouses.' *Time* 7 April 1986, p.66.

---

[13] Source: Indiana Department of Education survey: October, 1999; retrieved May 15, 2002, from http://ideanet.doe.state.in.us/legwatch/2000/a_kinder_issues.html

Funding Early Childhood Education

Funding for Head Start (in millions of dollars): 1965-2000

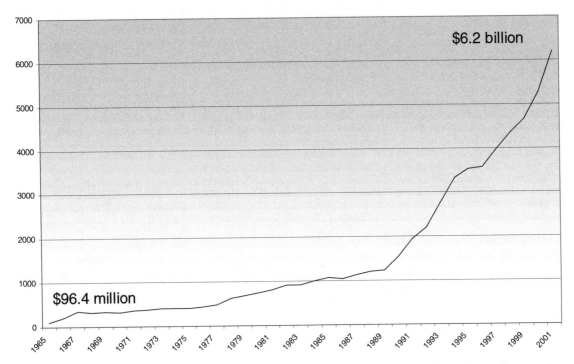

Head Start is supported by both Democrats and Republicans. The chart shows that monetary support for the program has increased steadily. Since the program began in 1965, more than $35 billion has been invested. Funding nearly tripled in the 1990s under the Bush and Clinton administrations. George W. Bush proposed only a 2% increase for Head Start in 2003, with a portion of the funds earmarked for literacy training of all Head Start teachers in "scientifically-based" methods (how to teach a child to hold a book, for example).

Funding covers 50 states, the District of Columbia, territories, American Indians, and migrant programs. The 1994 reauthorization of the Head Start Act established the Early Head Start program for low-income families with infants and toddlers. In fiscal year 2001, $558 million of the $6.2 billion appropriated for Head Start went to Early Head Start programs.

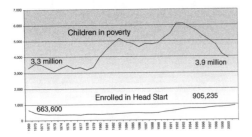

Children Under 6 in Poverty and Children Enrolled in Head Start (thousands): 1969-2000

The average expenditure per Head Start child was $6,633 in 2000-01. The money covers a paid staff of 195,000 (often parents of enrolled children) and support activities such as training. In 2000-01 there were 18,735 centers and 48,512 classrooms.

Some 18 million children have enjoyed Head Start since its inception. Despite the billions of dollars appropriated, Head Start has always been underfunded. It serves only about one-third of eligible children. The small chart shows the number of children under 6 in poverty; Head Start serves children 3-5 years old. The Children's Defense Fund estimates that for $3.3 billion more a year, Head Start could be fully funded.

Head Start opponents like John Hood, an adjunct scholar with the conservative Mackinac Center for Public Policy, contend the money would be better spent on child care in the private or nonprofit sector and later for vouchers for private or parochial schools. Hood asks: "Why not fix the school system itself, rather than devise new and expensive Federal supplements to it? ... Early intervention never could make as much of a difference to a child as 13 years of quality education could." He questions the assumption that it is possible to overcome the influence of heredity and environment through a brief early intervention. So far, though, Head Start remains the most politically palatable way to help poor children so they can start public school on a more level footing.

Head Start departed from the usual way of delivering federal dollars by bypassing public bureaucracies and sending the money to community social service groups deemed best able to identify children in need. Parents are expected to contribute to the program in some way, usually by volunteering.

Some Head Start programs have been hugely successful (particularly those with high parental involvement), some have underperformed, some have become entrenched bureaucracies. Some have been downright crooked: a Cleveland group allegedly invented dozens of children and gave them fake names to bring in extra funds. In the mid-1990s Congress demanded accountability from Head Start grantees in exchange for more funding.

One frequent criticism of Head Start grantees: they rely too heavily on undertrained teachers. Little wonder: the average pay for teachers in early education programs is $16,000 a year, about the median annual earnings of manicurists and pedicurists (Head Start teachers average $21,000). The trend is toward universal, mandatory kindergarten and expansion of all early childhood education. Any hope of such expansion will depend on overcoming opposition to spending money to raise teacher salaries. The National Center for Education Statistics predicts a shortage of more than 2 million teachers between 1998-2008, with 700,000 of them needed in rural and high-poverty areas.

President Bush's No Child Left Behind Act of 2001 authorized $2.85 billion for Improving Teacher Quality State Grants. Will this contribute to teacher satisfaction and retention? There is some evidence that raising standards can help to alleviate teacher shortages, provided there is an accompanying rise in pay.

The next panel looks at how the federal government is looking out for the big kids.

Sources: Charts: Head Start data. Online. Available: http://www2.acf.dhhs.gov/programs/hsb/research/. May 15, 2002. Poverty data. Online. Available: http://wwwcensusgov/hhes/poverty/histpov/hstpov20html. May 15, 2002. Hood, John. "Caveat emptor: the Head Start scam." *USA Today* (Magazine). May 1993. p. 75. "Children Deserve A Fair Share of the Federal Budget Surplus." Children's Defense Fund. Online. Available: http://www.cdfactioncouncil.org. May 15, 2002. Debra Viadero. "Education Researchers Unsure of Federal Attention to Field." Education Week. 12 April 2002 Online. Available: http://www.edweek.org. May 17, 2002.

Federal Government in the Child Care Business

Funding for 21st Century Community Learning Centers (in thousands): 1994-2002

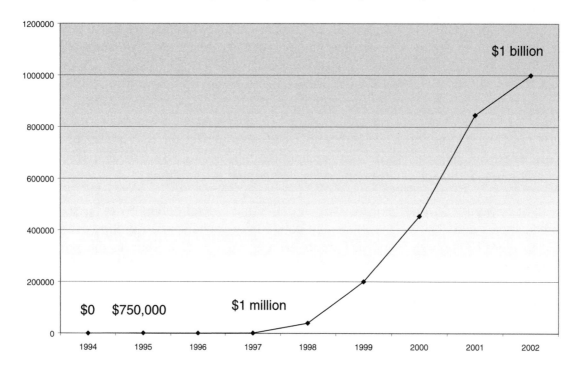

The chart shows how annual appropriations for 21st Century Community Learning Centers have risen. The assumption behind this initiative is that idle minds are the devil's workshop and the federal government can do something about it. Brought to life under the Clinton administration, CLCs were embraced by George W. Bush. He appropriated a record $1 billion for them in his 2002 budget.

CLCs provide before- and after-school academic enrichment opportunities to the latchkey generation. The U.S. Departments of Education and Justice report *Working for Children and Families*[14] points out these statistics to explain the need for afterschool programs: in 69% of married-couple families with children ages 6-17, both parents work outside the home. In 71% of single-mother families and 85% of single-father families, the parent with custody works. There can be a gap of 20 to 25 hours a week between the parental work schedule and the child's school schedule. Studies estimate that between 8 and 15 million latchkey children go home after school to an empty house. The FBI tells us that the time between 2 p.m. and 8 p.m. is prime time for juvenile crime and victimization.

Mott Foundation/JC Penney afterschool surveys show overwhelming support on the part of voters for afterschool programs; the federal government has obliged with funding.

---

[14] Cited in *21st Century Community Learning Centers*; see Source notes.

Not everyone agrees that government-funded after-school initiatives are a good idea. Opponent Darcy Olsen, writing for *USA Today*, cites Department of Education and Census data as sources for her objections: "No more than 12% of children aged five through 12 ever care for themselves, and those who do are alone for about one hour per day on average. Data show that a child's age, not the family's income, is the primary determinant of whether a youngster spends time alone... the assertion that there is an urgent need for taxpayer-subsidized afterschool programs is not convincing."

The federal government is also involved in child care and has its own Child Care Bureau. It was created in 1995 to provide a central focus for federal child care programs. Welfare reform legislation of the 1990s required most low-income single mothers to work. According to former Health and Human Services Secretary Donna Shalala: "Affordable, accessible and quality child care is critical to help move families from welfare to work." To assist in the cause of welfare reform, the Child Care Bureau distributes block grants to the states: $1.2 billion in 1999 for child care for low-income families. According to www. whitehouse.gov, federal and state governments provide more than $18 billion annually in child care money in one form or another to low-income families. Darcy Olsen weighs in on this issue too: "Child care should remain safe from government intrusion." Her contention: If government really wanted to help families, it would lower their taxes.

Sources: Chart: U.S. Department of Education. Education Budget History Table. Online. Available: from http://www. ed.gov/offices/OUS/budnews.html#statetables. May 15, 2002. Information on child care funds obtained from various press releases. Online. Available: http://www.hhs.gov/news/press/. May 17, 2002. Olsen, Darcy. "Government Should Stay Out of Afterschool Care." *USA Today* (Magazine) Sept. 2000. Olsen, Darcy. "Government and child care." *World and I* (March 1998) Vol. 13. No. 3. p. 72. "Almanac of Policy Issues: Child Care." Online. Available: http://www.policyalmanac.org/social_welfare/childcare.shtml. May 17, 2002. U.S. Department of Education. 21st Century Community Learning Centers: Providing Quality Afterschool Learning Opportunities for America's Families. September 2000. Online. Available: http://www.ed.gov/21stcclc/. May 17, 2002.

Chapter 10

School Performance

In this great country, children of every race, class, ethnic background, or handicap can get a primary and secondary education free of charge. It used to be that the overwhelming majority of parents considered our public schools quite good enough. This is not the case anymore. America's schools, especially those in our largest cities, are branded failures, and the public education system is undergoing revolutionary changes.

The perceived failure of America's schools used to be blamed on lack of funding. To this old theory has lately been added the belief that schools are organized according to a stifling bureaucratic model that does not allow for innovations. What can be done? The current buzzwords are schools of choice: charter schools and voucher schools.

Noam Chomsky says that charter schools and voucher schools undermine "the conception that I should care if the kid down the street has an education." George W. Bush says: "We must not trap students in low-performing schools. It is time to see if it works: Let's try a pilot voucher program." Jersey City Mayor Bret Schundler calls school choice "the civil rights struggle of this generation."

Today, more parents are opting for chosen public and private schools over neighborhood schools. Vouchers for low-income children in failing public schools have been adopted in a handful of cities. These initiatives generate tremendous controversy and have created some unlikely bedfellows. Supporters include conservatives, who agree with economist Milton Friedman that a voucher system would improve the efficiency of schools and would increase parental liberty; the political left, who would like to see poor children get a fair shake; and the people who have the most at stake: inner-city parents whose children attend the poorest schools.

Supporters of charter schools see them as a breath of fresh air — innovative and full of opportunity. On the other hand are those who see the choice movement as an untried and unproven threat to longstanding, monopolistic ways of educating children. Some oppose the drain of public funds from already struggling public schools, and some object to teachers who work in alternative schools for less than union wage. Some call vouchers a thinly disguised form of "parochiad" and a gross violation of the principle of separation of church and state. Some wonder if vouchers are fair.

In the first panel that follows, we look at the rapid rise of alternative forms of education: charter schools, for-profit schools, and homeschooling. We also explore the question of which type of school educates our children better. Our second panel examines the question whether there really can be school choice. Finally, we will look at safety in our schools. Are they safe enough? We will look at the perennial problem of bullying and see how technology is putting new weapons into the hands of children.

Tracking the Charter School Movement

Estimated Number of Charter Schools Opening in September: 1992-1999

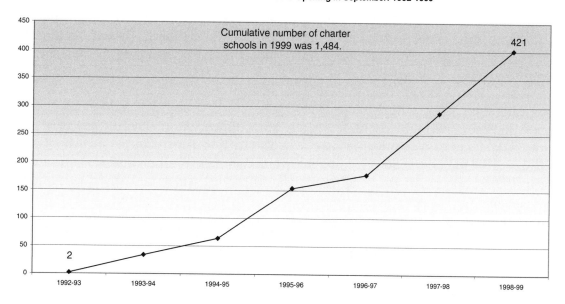

The chart shows U.S. Department of Education (DOE) data. Between 1992, when Minnesota opened the nation's first two schools, and 1999, the number of operating charters rose to 1,484, with 252,009 students enrolled. Charter School Resource Center reports 467 new schools for the 2001-02 school year, for a total of 2,370 charters, with 67 more already authorized to start in the fall of 2002. Obviously, charter schools are catching on.

Charter School Resource Center defines charter schools as "independent public schools of choice, free from rules but accountable for results and customer satisfaction." DOE says they are formed "to realize an alternative vision for schooling." Just about anyone can apply for a charter. Funding depends on how many students a charter school can attract and retain. Success depends on how satisfied parents are with results.

2001-02 Estimated Enrollment

School Type	Enrollment
Public & Private	53,000,000

About 2% of schools are charter schools. They serve about 1% of public school students. Parents and teachers devise curricula. In a survey of 305 charter schools operating in 1999, the Center for Education Reform found that the top five programs were science/ math/tech, core knowledge, thematic instruction, back-to-basics, and college prep. The table shows an estimated enrollment of 576,000 in 2001, a 129% increase over 1999.

In 1988 American Federation of Teachers' (AFT) President Albert Shanker called charter schools "the best answer so far" to the lack of autonomy and flexibility that teachers faced. By 2000, 36 states and the District of Columbia had adopted charter school laws.

Such a challenge to the educational establishment must have its opponents. Ironically, it is the 1-million-member AFT/AFL-CIO that is one of the most outspoken foes of charter schools. The AFT Web site declares: "If the goal is improved student achievement, students in some charter schools are not faring very well. Studies of charter schools in Texas and Arizona show that there has been no evidence of improved student performance..."

The 2.6-million-member National Education Association favors charter schools but cautions that many schools have a racial/ethnic composition similar to the surrounding district. Racial balance is not improved. Thus schools may be "creaming the students that are the least costly to educate."

Time calls the charter school movement a "grassroots revolt." The first charter school served 35 inner-city high school "dropouts." Since then, the movement has been most active in large cities where low-income schools (25% of American public schools), are conspicuously failing to educate children. More than half of all charter students are enrolled in three states: Arizona, California, and Michigan, where the largest cities have a high percentage of minority enrollments.

In 1997, under the stewardship of Governor George W. Bush, Texas adopted one of the most progressive charter school laws in the country. As "Education President," Bush can be expected to continue his support for charter schools, which, under the rubric "public school choice," have wide support from both political parties. The dean of the Harvard Graduate School of Education calls this a welcome contrast to longstanding Republican Party opposition to federal aid to education. Still, according to DOE, most charter schools cite lack of resources as their most serious challenge. Federal legislation authorized $60 million for fiscal year 2002 for public charter schools.

Are charter schools the solution to failing public schools? It's too soon to tell. But they certainly generate enthusiasm. Recent research shows problems with accountability. Once that problem is solved, charter schools may end up with the same bureaucracy as the systems they replaced. Back in Minnesota, where it all began, more than 20% of charter schools faced financial problems so serious that state legislators called for an oversight board. Several schools were forced to close under a cloud of financial and academic problems. There are plenty of opportunities for abuse. In California, a surprise inspection of a public charter school found that it was teaching the tenets of Islam and may have been charging $350 to $400 per month in tuition.

Could anyone have foreseen that after charter schools would come the privatization of public schools? The next panel looks at for-profit charter schools.

Source: U.S. Department of Education. Office of Educational Research and Improvement. *The State of Charter Schools 2000*. Online. Available: http://www.ed.gov/ April 17, 2002. Duchesne Paul Drew and Anthony Lonetree. "Charter schools face a tougher test." *Star Tribune* (Minneapolis), 9 January 2001 p.01A. "Islamic charter school may have violated California regulations." *Church & State*. February 2002 vol. 55, i2, p.18. Center for Education Reform. "Charter Schools Today: Changing the Face of American Education." Online. Available: http://www.edreform.com. April 17, 2002. American Federation of Teachers. "Charter Schools." Online. Available: www.aft.org. April 8, 2002. "What the Research Reveals About Charter Schools." The Center for Education Reform. August 2001. Online. Available: www.edreform.com. April 18, 2002. Gary Miron and Christopher Nelson, "Student Academic Achievement in Charter Schools: What We Know and Why We Know So Little," National Center for the Study of Privatization in Education, Occasional Paper No. 41. Online. Available: http://ncspe.org/. April 17, 2002. "Charter Schools Overview." National Education Association. Online. Available: http://www.nea.org. April 18, 2002. "Envisioning the Ideal Education President: An Historical Perspective." Online. Available: http://www.gse.harvard.edu/news/ April 18, 2002.

Schools for Sale

Number of Edison Schools Operating: 1995-2002

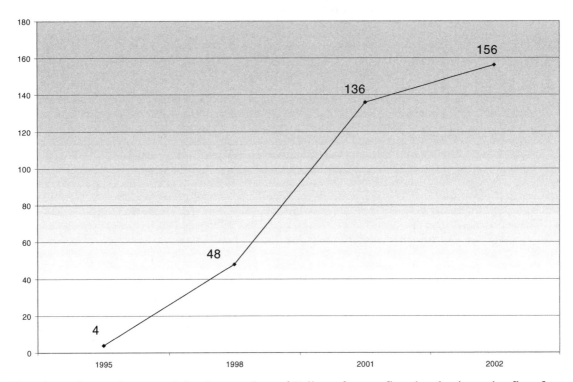

The chart shows the growth in the number of Edison for-profit schools since the first four opened in 1995. The Edison Project is the country's leading for-profit public school management company. When Philadelphia decided in April 2002 to turn over 42 of its lowest performing schools to outside managers, Edison got 20. Management companies like Edison either take over public schools (conversion) or open new charter schools.

Education is big business. Eduventures.com, a Boston market research firm, happily reported industry revenues of $96 billion in 1999, an 11% increase over 1998. The traditional industry sectors—for-profit schools, learning products, and educational services — posted growth rates ranging from 8% to 12.3%.

Education management companies promise to improve student achievement and make money at the same time. Edison's Web site claims: "Student achievement in Edison schools has been heading steadily upward." The American Federation of Teachers is watching Edison closely; they report "mediocre" reading results. Is Edison making money? Not as of February 2002, when the company reported a net loss of 15 cents per share. CEO Chris Whittle, who started the trend, remains optimistic, however.

Source: Chart: The Edison Project. Online. Available: www.edisonproject.com/ April 19, 2002. Susan Snyder and Martha Woodall. "42 schools to be privatized." *Philadelphia Inquirer*, 18 April 2002. Online. Available: http://www.philly.com/. April 19, 2002. "The for-profit education industry is quickly adding clicks to bricks." Online. Available: http://www.edweek.org. April 19, 2002.

Homeschooling

Ten Reasons for Homeschooling and the Percentage of
Homeschooled Students Whose Parents Gave Each Reason: 1999

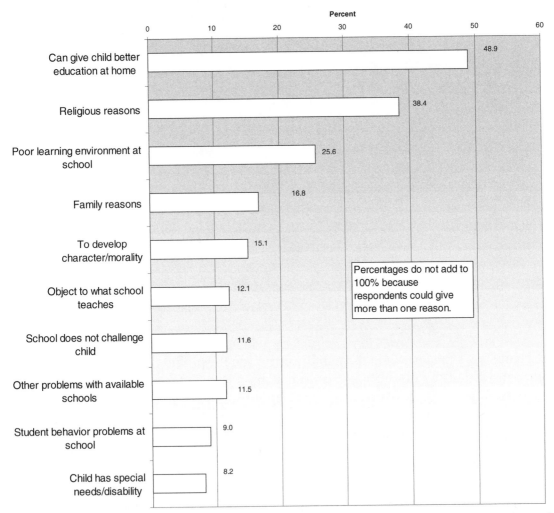

Homeschooling — by necessity the educational method of the pioneers and since the 1980s the choice of more and more concerned parents — is a fine example of what's old being new again. Homeschooling is often dismissed as the province of reactionaries and hippies. It's true that the most vocal and organized homeschoolers have tended to be religiously motivated, usually conservative Christians. But as the graphic above shows, there are other reasons for homeschooling.

In a 1999 National Center for Education Statistics (NCES) survey of homeschool parents, "religious reasons" and "character/morality" are mentioned, but today's homeschoolers also are motivated by concerns about poor academic quality in schools and by issues like violence and peer pressure.

The same survey describes the homeschooled child of the 1990s as most likely to be a white urbanite in grades K-5, from a two-parent household with three or more children, with only one parent in the labor force and a family income of $50,000 or less.

There are no long-term studies of homeschooling, only estimates. NCES estimated that 850,000 students were being homeschooled in the spring of 1999. Other analysts estimated 300,000 in 1990, 700,000 in 1995-96, and at least 1 million in 1999

Homeschooling is legal in all 50 states and the District of Columbia. *Newsweek* informs us that in 1998, 41 states had no minimum academic requirements for parents who wanted to homeschool their children. Nevertheless, says *Newsweek*, homeschooled children managed to average 23 of 36 on the ACT, compared to an average score of 21 for traditionally schooled students. A 23 qualified a student for a "selective" college. In 2000, home-schooled students scored an average of 1,100 on the SAT, 81 points above the national average.

According to Lawrence M. Rudner's 1998 study of 20,760 homeschooled students, half were born to Baptist or Independent Fundamentalist mothers. The table shows two other interesting characteristics of homeschooled children from the survey.

Characteristics of Fourth Graders: 1998

Characteristic	Homeschooled kids	Regular kids
% watching TV 1 hour or less daily	65.3	25.1
% using computer several times per week	21.6	62.5

Another of Rudner's findings: "Home school student achievement test scores are exceptionally high. The median scores … at every grade … are well above those of public and Catholic/Private school students."

Is homeschooling the answer to our educational woes? Consider these demographics. Rudner's study "clearly shows that home school students and their families are a select population. Family income and education levels are well above national averages. The family structure is traditional with married couples as parents, several children, father as breadwinner, and a stay-at-home mother. A large percent of home school students have a parent that has held a state-issued teaching certificate."

Evidence that homeschooling has entered the mainstream: Patrick Henry College of Purceville, Virginia, was established in 2000 as the nation's first devoted to homeschooled students. In 2002, three of its first 14 graduates were accepted into law schools before the college was even accredited. Harvard University, which once only considered applicants with high school diplomas, has assigned an admissions officer to review applications from homeschoolers.

Homeschoolers have their own lobbyist, too. The conservative Home School Legal Defense Association (which funded the Rudner study) is seeking to scale back the National Assessment of Educational Progress (NAEP; see Chapter 7). Rewards are proposed for states that show improvement on NAEP scores ("accountability"), but homeschoolers complain that states are being encouraged to revise their testing programs to match NAEP. They fear this will result in a national curriculum, "a definitive step toward centralized control of education and abrogation of its local governance." Might it also put a damper on educational methods that seem to be working?

Source: Chart: Stacy Bielick et al.. "Homeschooling in the United States: 1999," *Education Statistics Quarterly*. Online. Available: http://nces.ed.gov April 23, 2002; National Center for Education Statistics. Parent Survey of the National Household Education Surveys Program, 1999 (Parent-NHES: 1999). Kantrowitz, Margaret and Pat Wingert, "Learning at Home: Does It Pass the Test?" *Newsweek*, 5 October 1998, p. 64. "Home Schooling." Online. Available: http://www.edweek.org. April 23, 2002. Lawrence M. Rudner. "Scholastic Achievement and Demographic Characteristics of Home School Students in 1998." Online. Available: http://epaa.asu.edu April 23, 2002. Home School Legal Defense Association. "National Testing." Online. Available: http://www.hslda.org/ April 24, 2002.

Which Type of School Does the Best Job?

**Average Mathematics Proficiency of 17-year-olds in
Public and Private Schools: 1978 to 1999**

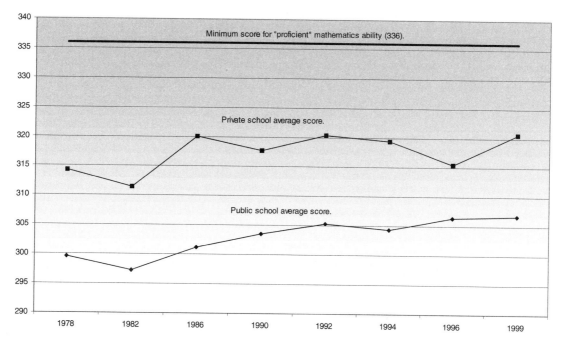

Private schools, unencumbered as they are by bureaucracies, unions, and burdensome state rules and regulations, are widely regarded as doing a better job of educating students. Judging by the mathematics proficiency scores shown on the chart above, this would appear to be so.[1] But it is highly motivated and higher-income families that are more likely to send their children to private schools. Can the better achievement of their children be attributable to parental motivation, education, or income?

Private-school students may score higher in mathematics proficiency, but as the chart shows, neither public-school nor private-school students perform at the "proficient" level in mathematics (see Chapter 7).

We saw in the preceding panel that homeschooled children perform best of all on standardized tests; we also saw that homeschooling is not a practical option for most students.

It is difficult to assess student achievement in charter schools because of their newness and because of variations in assessing schools. Overall, charter schools get mixed reviews. Keep in mind that charter schools tend to serve urban minority students whose test scores tend to be lower. Farrell et al. made the point in 1994, and it is still relevant: "The effective instruction of disadvantaged students is not subject to quick fixes."

---

[1] (See Chapter 7 for a discussion of the meaning of these scores.)

Does the competition afforded by initiatives such as charter schools improve school performance? Proponents claim that wherever there is a cluster of charter schools, traditional schools have been forced to improve. Will charter schools last, or will they fizzle out in favor of the next school reform novelty? Time will tell. Already there is talk of "cyber charter schools" for the twenty-first century.

Sources: Chart: U.S. Department of Education. National Center for Education Statistics. National Assessment of Educational Progress. *NAEP Trends in Academic Progress,* various years, by Educational Testing Service, in *Digest of Education Statistics 2000.* Online. Available: http://nces.ed.gov/April 19, 2002. Walter C. Farrell, Jr. et al. "Will privatizing schools really help inner-city students of color?" *Educational Leadership.* September 1994, p. 72. "Selected Readings on School Reform." Thomas B. Fordham Foundation. Online. Available: http://www.edrs.com/ April 18, 2002.

School Choice: Is It For Real?

Percentage Distribution of Students in Grades 3-12 who Attended an Assigned Public School, a Chosen Public School, or a Private School:
1993, 1996, and 1997

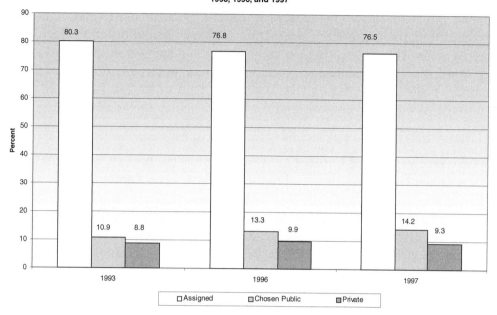

The overwhelming majority of American schoolchildren attend public schools. But, as the chart shows, between 1993 and 1997, the percentage who attended assigned (neighborhood) public schools dropped from 80.3% to 76.8%. The remaining students (19.7% in 1993, 23.2% in 1997) were at schools of choice — public or private. In numerical terms, this means that 10 million children attended schools of choice in 1993; in 1997 it was 12 million. Students at chosen schools were more likely to be at a public school selected by their parents than at a private school.

In 1999, one child in four in elementary and high school was going to school somewhere other than in his or her own neighborhood. More than 13 million children were involved. Parents are more and more inclined to take advantage of school choice.

Education Week defines school choice as: "Any proposal that allows children to attend schools outside their local district boundaries. Such schools may be public institutions other than that school that is assigned in their district or they may be private and/or religious schools. Often these proposals include public funding for all or some of the tuition costs."

The school choice movement gained impetus in the 1980s when test results began to show that private schools were doing a better job. Most people don't have a problem with the concept of school choice — it's a free country. In fact, the middle and upper classes have always had school choice. The objections arise when it comes to funding school choice with public dollars.

Those who advocate extreme forms of school choice want tax dollars in the form of vouchers to be paid to parents. These dollars should come from public schools, they argue. Parents could add their own money and send their kids to schools of their own choosing.

Some cities and states have already created voucher or scholarship programs that allow public school students to attend schools of choice. Most current programs focus on disadvantaged students. Milwaukee, the first city to provide major subsidies to private schools, showed mixed results in student achievement after four years. The Cleveland Scholarship and Tutoring Program provides annual vouchers of up to $2,250 for the city's poorest children, most of whom chose to attend Catholic schools, essentially their only alternative.

State courts have consistently ruled against the use of vouchers for religious schools. At the request of the George W. Bush administration, the U.S. Supreme Court heard arguments on the Cleveland program in 2002. The administration hopes for a ruling that the inclusion of religious schools in educational choice programs doesn't violate the Constitution. A ruling against vouchers could end or limit the programs already in place and possibly close the door on the voucher movement for the foreseeable future.

Time gave its assessment of Cleveland's experiment under the headline: "Cleveland's program gets mixed grades. Parents are happier, but students may not be learning more. And vouchers may be dividing the city."

Vouchers cover only a fraction of the cost of private school tuition. Even with vouchers, those denied educational choices are from the poorest, least motivated, most troubled families. As a practical matter, consider that there are some 50+ million children in public schools — and there are not nearly enough good alternative schools with openings and qualified people to teach in them. If these alternative schools accepted vouchers, would they be trapped in a web of bureaucracy that would destroy their independence and quality? Will competition force public schools to improve?

AFT President Albert Shanker said of vouchers that they "are not an experiment, the conclusion of which is unknown. The result is inevitable — the end of public schools and the establishment of a system of tax-financed private education." Is this what Americans want? The next panel looks at that question.

Source: Chart: National Center for Education Statistics. *The Condition of Education 2001*. Online. Available: http://nces.ed.gov April 22, 2002; National Household Education Surveys Program (NHES), 1993 (School Safety and Discipline survey), 1996 (Parent Interview Survey), and 1999 (Parent Interview Survey); Roberts, Nanette M. and Charles L. Glenn. "School Vouchers: Two Views." *Sojourners*, Jan/Feb 1998 p. 22. Cohen, Adam. "A First Report Card On Vouchers." *Time* (April 1999). "Outcomes Milwaukee Parental Choice Program Study." Online. Available: dpls.dacc.wisc.edu. April 23, 2002. Mark Walsh. "U.S. Asks High Court To Review Voucher Case." Online. Available: http://www.edweek.org/. April 23, 2002.

Public Schools & Vouchers: All in Favor...

The Public's Attitude Toward Public Schools (Answers to Poll Questions): 1999

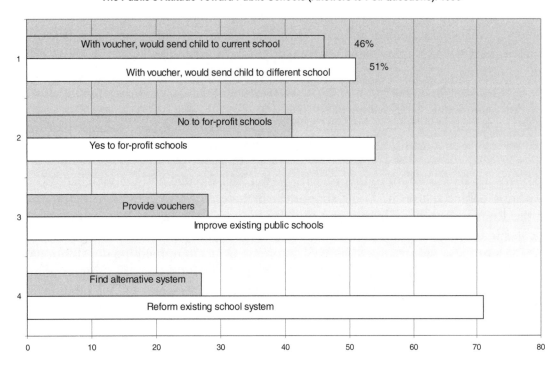

This chart shows the responses to Phi Delta Kappa/Gallup poll questions. (1) "[With tuition paid by the government] would you send your oldest child to the school he or she now attends, or to a different school?" (2) "Do you favor or oppose ... private, profit-making corporations [contracting] to operate schools within certain jurisdictions?" (3) "Which one of these two plans would you prefer — improving and strengthening the existing public schools or providing vouchers for parents to use in selecting and paying for private and/or church-related schools?" (4) "Which approach do you think is preferable [to improve public education] — reforming the existing public school system or finding an alternative to the existing public school system?"[2]

With regard to questions (2), (3), and (4), asked of the general public, respondents showed considerable divergence in their opinions. African-Americans were more likely than whites to favor for-profit schools. The pollsters' conclusion? In general, "The results clearly affirm the public's belief that our national commitment to educating all our children through the public schools should be maintained." But on the question of choice:

As to question (1), which was asked only of public-school parents, respondents were split fairly evenly on the question of whether they would send their oldest child to a different school if tuition were paid by the government, with 46% saying yes and 51% saying they

---

[2]National telephone survey of 1,103 adults (18 years of age and older).

---

would keep their oldest child in his/her current school. In the pollsters' opinion: "Public school advocates can derive satisfaction or feel alarm from the response of public school parents to a question asking where they would send their oldest child if tuition were paid by the government."

Vouchers have been available in Milwaukee and Cleveland since the early 1990s and they have received extensive media coverage and high court challenges in those cities. Yet a 1999 Public Agenda study showed that 60% of parents polled in the two cities knew "very little" or "nothing" about vouchers. Results from an NSBA/Zogby International Poll conducted in 2001 suggested that "the more people know about how voucher programs operate, the less they like them." The pollsters found, for example, that many people withdrew support if it meant that public schools lose tax dollars.

Do poll results like these mean that parents do not fuel the demand for vouchers? If not, then who is behind the push? Some supporters include the George W. Bush administration; the Roman Catholic Church; and big-city mayors, who argue that if middle-class residents are to be lured back from the suburbs, the monopoly over urban schools must be broken. All of these groups urged the U.S. Supreme Court to uphold the constitutionality of Cleveland's voucher program.[3] Voucher opponents include the Bill Clinton administration, the major teachers' unions and groups such as the American Civil Liberties Union, People for the American Way, Americans United for Separation of Church and State, the NAACP, and the Anti-Defamation League.

Judging by test scores (see Chapter 7), it appears our schools *do* need improvement. We have tried charter schools and vouchers, with mixed results. Homeschooling is not a practical option for our 50+ million population of K-12 students. What will we try next?

Next we will look at the issue of safety in our schools. Are our schools failing to keep our children safe?

Source: Chart: Lowell C. Rose and Alec M. Gallup. "The 31st Annual Phi Delta Kappa/Gallup Poll Of the Public's Attitudes Toward the Public Schools." Online. Available: http://www.pdkintl.org/kappan. April 23, 2002. NSBA/Zogby International Poll: "School Vouchers: What the Public Thinks and Why." Online. Available: http://www.nsba.org/novouchers/. April 23, 2002.

---

[3] On June 27, 2002, the U.S. Supreme Court upheld the use of public money for religious school tuition in a 5-4 ruling, calling the Cleveland voucher plan "a program of true private choice."

Death at School

Homicides/Suicides of Students at School: 1992-1999

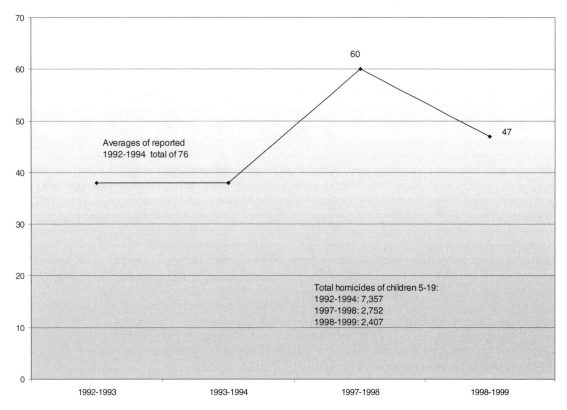

Columbine, Littleton: Who will ever forget the name of this high school in this once obscure Colorado town? It was there, on April 20, 1999, that two heavily armed boys massacred 12 students and a teacher and wounded 23 others before killing themselves. There had been other school shootings, but this one was the bloodiest. The call for gun control legislation became urgent.

There is no national system for reporting on injuries or violence associated with schools. The chart shows data presented in three annual reports on school crime and safety. President Clinton requested the reports in 1998 in response to the extreme school violence of the late 1990s.

The chart shows numbers of homicides and suicides involving students that took place at school. The first report to the president combined numbers for 1992 through 1994, for a total of 76. From July 1, 1997, through June 30, 1998, of 60 school-associated violent deaths, 47 were homicides, 12 were suicides, and 1 involved a student killed by a police officer. In the next July-June period, of 47 school-associated violent deaths, 38 were homicides, 6 suicides, 2 were killed by police officers, and 1 death was unintentional.

After a rash of school shootings in the 1997-98 school year, the school violence rate went down the next year. This good news came during a decade when the male population aged 10-19 increased by 12% and experts predicted a wave of violent crimes committed by a new generation of youthful "super-predators." Youth homicide arrests actually fell to fewer than 1,000 in 1999 from more than 3,000 in 1993. The number of all homicides with child victims also declined between 1992 and 1999. The government data indicate that about 2% of child and adolescent homicides and suicides were school-associated

Characteristics of Student Deaths at School: 1994-1999

Item	Number
Student victims	**172**
Female	52
Male	120
Race/ethnicity	
White, non-Hispanic	66
Black, non-Hispanic	59
Hispanic	37
Asian/Pacific Islander	6
Homicides	**146**
Suicides	**24**

JAMA, The Journal of the American Medical Association, published an independent study of school-related violence that used information collected from newspaper clipping services and police reports. The table shows some of the findings. Of a total of 253 people killed while attending or traveling to and from school between 1994 and 1999, 68% were students.

JAMA found that the average annual rate of school-associated violent deaths was 0.068 per 100,000 students, that multiple-victim events were more common in the late 1990s, and that fewer than 1% of homicides and suicides among school-aged children were school associated. Firearms were the chosen weapons in the majority of incidents. A homicidal event was most likely to involve an African-American male in a senior high school or a combined school in an urban area.

JAMA found a strong link between bullying and violent behavior. Perpetrators were more likely than their victims to have been bullied or to have been suicidal. We will look at bullying later in this discussion.

In the same issue of *JAMA*, Stevens et al. conclude: "Violence among adolescents and children remains an important problem in US schools. Although the rate of single-victim homicides (murders) in schools went down between 1994 and 1999, the number of events in which more than 1 victim was killed increased. Teenagers are 2 1/2 times more likely than adults to be victims of violence." Still, according to the U.S. Department of Education, school is one of the safest places that children can be.

The Secret Service has prepared a report for school officials in an effort to prevent Columbine-style violence at schools. Using the same methods they use to identify potential assassins, they report that the typical school shooter is neither spontaneous nor impulsive but has typically spent at least two days planning the event. Many shooters communicated their plan to others beforehand — as a result, students are being encouraged to report such threats. School violence is not a new phenomenon. The earliest incident examined by the Secret Service took place in 1974. In more than half of the cases studied, the target was someone other than a student.

Sources: Chart: U.S. Departments of Education and Justice. *Indicators of School Crime and Safety, 2000.* Online. Available: http://www.ojp.usdoj.gov/bjs/ April 24, 2002. Anderson, Mark, Joanne Kaufman et al. "School-Associated Violent Deaths in the United States, 1994-1999. *JAMA, The Journal of the American Medical Association.* 5 December 2001, p. 2695. "U.S.S.S. Safe School Initiative: An Interim Report on the Prevention of Targeted Violence in Schools." Online. Available: http://www.ustreas.gov/usss/. April 25, 2002.

How Safe Are Our Schools?

**Non-fatal Crimes Occurring at School or on
the Way to or From School, per 100,000 Students Aged 12-18: 1992-1998**

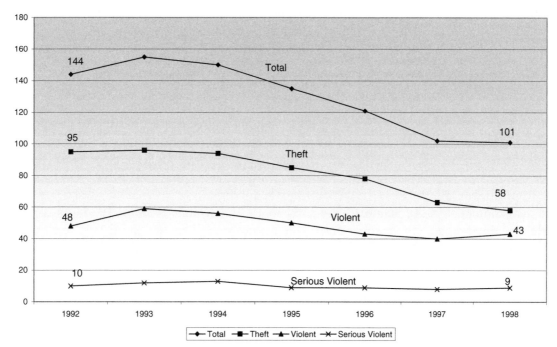

In 1998, students aged 12-18 were victims of more than 2.7 million total crimes at school, including 253,000 serious violent crimes (rape, sexual assault, robbery, and aggravated assault). But schools seem to be getting safer than they were. As we see from the chart, the non-fatal victimization rate declined between 1992 and 1998, from 144 incidents per 100,000 students to 101. Most school crimes involve thefts. Students are about two times as likely to be victims of serious violent crime away from school.

Children get hurt at school. The Centers for Disease Control reports that about 4 million children and adolescents suffer mainly minor injuries each year at school — sports injuries, playground falls and the like. Fatalities are rare: fewer than one in 400 injury-related deaths among children aged five to 19 years occurs in schools.

School safety was on the minds of legislators when Congress passed the Improving America's Schools Act of 1994. That act included the Gun-Free Schools Act (GFSA), which requires that each state receiving federal funds under the Elementary and Secondary Education Act have a state law that requires all local educational agencies in the state to expel from school for at least one year any student found bringing a firearm to school.

The table shows data related to expulsions in 1998-99. There were 3,371 expulsions: 59% (1,991) involved handguns, 12% (418) involved rifles or shotguns, and the remaining 29% (962) involved other types of firearms (bombs, grenades, starter pistols, and rockets). Alabama had the highest number of expulsions per 1,000 students. Most expulsions

States with the Most Students Expelled for Violations of the GFSA: 1998-1999

State	Expulsions
1. Texas	294
2. California	290
3. Georgia	208
4. New York	206
5. Alabama	174
6. Missouri	171
7. Tennessee	152
8. Pennsylvania	145
9. North Carolina	141
10. Virginia/Washington	115

were at the senior high school level (57%), followed by junior high school (33%) and elementary school (10%).

A report released in 2000 by the Hamilton Fish Institute, a federally financed research group affiliated with George Washington University, claimed that school principals are underreporting the problem of guns at schools. The authors claimed that there were "100 times more guns in the hands of children attending American schools than principals have been reporting to Congress." William Modzeleski, the director of the U.S. Department of Education's safe and drug-free schools office, called the report "foolhardy," according to *Education Week on the Web*.

The government says our schools were safer in 1999 than they were in 1995. As we saw in the previous panel, it is a cause for concern that homicides at school now tend to involve multiple victims. Next we will look at perceptions of school safety. Finally, we will look at the problem of bullying.

Sources: Chart: *U.S.* Departments of Education and Justice. *Indicators of School Crime and Safety, 2000*. Online. Available: http://www.ojp.usdoj.gov/bjs/ April 24, 2002. "New CDC Guidelines Help Schools Prevent Injuries In Children." *Medical Letter on the CDC & FDA*. 30 December 2001 p. 3. "Report on State Implementation of the Gun-Free Schools Act — School Year 1998-99." Online. Available: http://www.ed.gov/offices/OESE/SDFS/GFSA/report_2000/part1.html. April 26, 2002. Jessica Portner, "Report Claims Guns More Plentiful at Schools," *Education Week on the Web*, 27 September 2000. Online. Available: http://www.edweek.org/ April 26, 2002.

Perceptions of School Safety

**Percentage of Students who Feared Attack or Harm at School or
who Avoided Places at School in the Last 6 Months: 1989, 1995, and 1999**

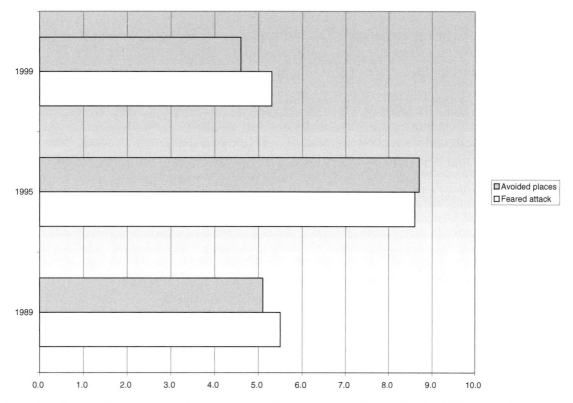

Despite the media attention that accompanied school violence in the 1990s, students felt safer at school in 1999 than they did in 1995. The percentage who reported that they avoided one or more places at school for their own safety fell from 9% to 4.6%. The percentage who reported that they feared being attacked or harmed at school experienced a similar pattern. Students in seventh and eighth grade were more fearful than older or younger students, and students in urban schools were more fearful than students in suburban or rural schools. The source cautions that comparisons between the 1989 data and later data must be made with caution because of changes in the questionnaire. School shooting incidents took place in 1992 and 1993.

While students feel more secure, their parents grow more anxious. A *Wall Street Journal/CNN* poll one year after the Columbine incident showed that 71% of Americans thought shootings were likely in their schools. The government tells us that the odds of a school-aged child being killed in school are one in 2 million.

School-related violence may be down, but bomb threats are up (often called in on cell phones). The National School Safety Center reported at least 5,000 bomb threats in the six months after the Columbine incident, costing schools thousands of lost classroom hours. That trend shows little sign of abating.

Adults' fears of school-related violence have resulted in the stationing of more police officers in schools. Locker searches, surveillance cameras and metal detectors are now commonplace. Zero Tolerance Policies bring suspensions from school for infractions both major and trivial.

Are our schools becoming more like prisons? Kids seem to think so. In the report *School House Hype*, students complained: "Too much security makes you wonder whether it is safe." "When I get up to go to school in the morning, I don't want to feel like I'm going to a correctional facility."

In 1996-97, the most recent year for which data are available, more than half of American K-12 public schools reported a criminal incident to the police. The chance of bad things happening in your child's school is greater if you live in a bad neighborhood. *Preventing Crime* tells us that "Schools in urban, poor, disorganized communities experience more disorder than other schools." Nevertheless, polls show that rural parents (54%) are more fearful of their children's safety than are urban parents (46%) or suburban parents (44%).

Students who fear for their safety at school are not in a mood conducive to learning. They are more prone to absences. We turn now to a widespread and insidious form of frightening behavior — bullying.

Sources: Chart: U.S. Departments of Education and Justice. *Indicators of School Crime and Safety, 2000.* Online. Available: http://www.ojp.usdoj.gov/bjs/April 24, 2002. "Are U.S. Schools Safe?" Online. Available: http://www.cnn. com/SPECIALS/1998/schools/. Lawrence W. Sherman, Denise Gottfredson, et al., *Preventing Crime: What Works, What Doesn't, What's Promising, A Report to the United States Congress.* Prepared for the National Institute of Justice. Online. Available: http:// www.ncjrs.org/works/. April 24, 2002. "NCES: More Than Half the Nation's Schools Report Criminal Incidents." *Curriculum Administrator* (April 2001) p. 16. Brooks, Kim, Vincent Schiraldi, et al., *School House Hype: Two Years Later, A Policy Report.* Justice Policy Center and Children's Law Center.

Will Children Ever Be Safe From Bullies?

**Responses of Readers of TIME FOR KIDS Magazine to the Question
Asked in an Online Poll: Has A Bully Ever Picked on You in School?**

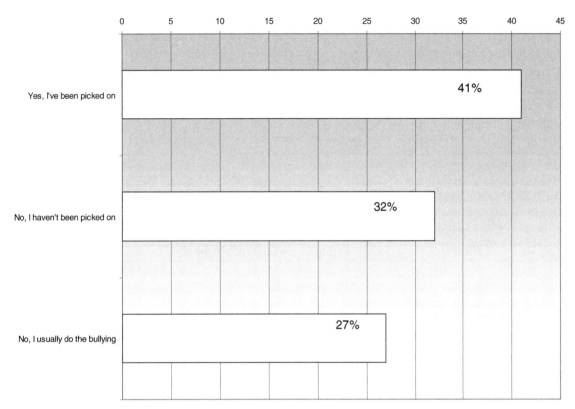

The school crime rate seems to be down, believe it or not. But what about bullying? It has always been with us. Until the 1990s, little attention was paid to bullying; it was considered an inevitable part of childhood. The school shootings focused attention on bullying. According to the U.S. Secret Service, in more than two-thirds of the shooting incidents they studied, the attackers felt persecuted or bullied prior to the attack, suggesting a link between bullying and violence.

The chart shows responses to an online poll. *Time for Kids* asked kids whether a bully had ever picked on them in school (4,109 respondents). 41% said yes, they had been bullied, and more than a quarter responded frankly that they usually did the bullying.

The Nickelodeon/Talking with Kids National Survey of Parents and Kids[4] found that 55% of 8-11-year-olds said that teasing and bullying is a "big problem" for people their age; 68% of 12-15-year-olds said the same thing.

---

[4] Telephone survey of 1,249 parents of children age 8-15 and 823 children age 8-15, "including oversamples of African Americans and Latinos."

The results of the first nationally representative survey on the frequency of bullying in America were reported in *JAMA* in 2001. Of 15,686 children in grades 6 through 10, 30% reported they were involved in bullying, either as perpetrator or victim. Boys were more likely to be involved than girls, and bullying was more common in grades 6-8 than in grades 9-10.

ERIC Digest reported on a study of younger children (fourth- through eighth-graders). "About 15 percent reported being severely distressed by bullying and 22% reported academic difficulties stemming from mistreatment by peers." Students who are bullied may become homicidal or suicidal. Bullies are liable to turn into troubled or criminal adults.

The American Medical Association (AMA) recently recognized bullying as a public health problem. Researchers estimate that 7% of eighth graders and a total of 160,000 children stay home from school each day because they fear being bullied.

Bullies are not loners. A 1999 study by Dorothy Espelage at the University of Illinois found that four out of five students at a Midwestern middle school said, "they act like bullies at least once a month." Why? Because, said one, "it's fun. These kids, they're like helpless — I mean they've got the big glasses and fat stomachs."

UNESCO says that bullying is a worldwide problem and exists in countries both rich and poor. "It's chiefly a male phenomenon, hitting a peak when boys turn 16 years old in some countries and 13 in others." CNN.com reports on an emerging trend in London. Called high-tech bullying, it involves tormenting by Internet text messages, e-mail, and chat rooms. Some vulnerable children have been driven to suicide by these online attacks. Can we look forward to this type of activity making its way to America?

How can bullying be stopped? Studies suggest that incidents can be cut in half through school awareness programs, increased supervision, rules, and support for victims and perpetrators. Teachers must intervene: to ignore is to condone. When teachers intervene, they foster trust (more than one planned act of violence has been stopped because a student reported it to a teacher). Research shows that where bullying is considered "cool," it is hard to stop it. Somehow, a way must be found to make it not "cool."

More and more schools are adopting antibullying policies. In a suggestion apparently aimed at the Boy Scouts of America, the AMA suggests that it would be helpful if youth organizations adopted nondiscrimination policies that include sexual orientation. The AMA recognizes that gay and lesbian young people are frequent targets for bullying.

Sources: Chart: "Let Bullies Beware: Politicians are going after them. But what works best? Banishing them — or changing the culture?" *Time*, 2 April 2001, p. 46. "Study: Bullying rampant in U.S. middle schools." 20 August 1999 and "High-tech school bullies work round the clock." 16 April 2002. Online. Available: CNN.com. April 19, 2002. Stagg Elliott, Victoria. "AMA recognizes bullying as a public health problem." *American Medical News* 9 July 2001, p. 32. Debarbieux, Eric. "Violence in schools a world wide affair." *UNESCO Courier* (April 2001) p 10. Nansel, Tonja R., Mary Overpeck, et al. "Bullying Behaviors Among US Youth: Prevalence and Association With Psychosocial Adjustment." *JAMA: The Journal of the American Medical Association*. 25 April 2001, p2094. Linda Lumsden. "Preventing Bullying." *ERIC Digest* 155 (March 2002) Online. Available: http://ericcass.uncg.edu. April 26, 2002. "Talking with kids about tough issues: A National Survey of Parents and Kids." Online. Available: http://www.nick.com/. April 26, 2002.

Chapter 11

Trends in Elementary and Secondary Education

For decades parents and educators have sought ways to reverse a perceived decline in the quality of America's public schools and to boost the academic achievement of American schoolchildren. The education reform movement gained momentum with the 1983 publication of *A Nation at Risk*, a book that called American schools so mediocre that the economic future of the country was in danger. A more recent wake-up call was the 1996 release of the Third International Mathematics and Science Study (TIMSS), which showed American schoolchildren lagging behind most of the world in math and science achievement.

Numerous remedies have been prescribed to fix our schools. Among the most popular current remedies are the assignment of more homework and the lengthening of the school year. The first two panels present an overview of the amount of time spent by American schoolchildren on homework and attending school. The homework data show that popular perceptions are sometimes at odds with what's actually happening. We'll see that the heaviest burden of homework seems to fall on the youngest shoulders. We'll also see how American students compare to students around the world in terms of time spent on homework and in school.

Thomas Jefferson saw public education as a way "to enable every man to judge for himself what will secure or endanger his freedom." There was a time when Americans believed that the job of schools was to teach students how to think. Today it is generally accepted that the primary purpose of public schools is to prepare students academically for the workplace so that the economy is productive and competitive throughout the world.

Increasingly, the opinions of business leaders are being considered when school reform is discussed. Businesses complain that public-school graduates enter the work world with little understanding of business skills. Colleges say that many entering students have insufficient reading, writing, and math skills to do college-level work.

In the panels that follow, we will see what programs are in place for college- and non-college-bound high school students to prepare them for the world beyond high school. We'll also take a look at wired schools and see how government and business are behind the rush to connect America's classrooms to the Internet.

Why So Much Homework?

Homework Assigned and Done: 1984 and 1999

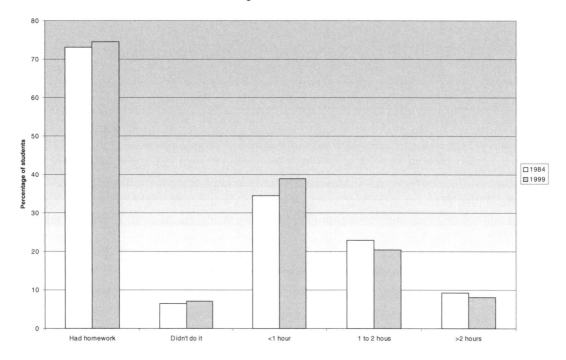

Too much homework? Most kids would say yes. The media report that in the race to keep up with the world's highest academic achievers, kids are overloaded with homework and are in danger of burning out. But the numbers don't show a remarkable increase in the amount of homework assigned or done over a 20-year period. In 1984, an average of 73% of 9-, 13-, and 17-year-olds reported being assigned homework; by 1999, the figure had risen by only 1.5%.

The chart also shows that teachers are assigning a little more homework, but students aren't spending any more time doing it. There was little change in the amount of time students reported spending on homework. How much time should they be spending? The National PTA recommends 10-20 minutes per day for grades K-2, 30-60 minutes for grades 3-6, and an amount that will vary by subject for junior and senior high school students.

The following table shows the breakdown of homework data by age. Among 13-year-olds, there was little change in the percentage who were assigned homework, and there was a decrease in the percentage of 17-year-olds assigned any homework. Only 9-year-olds got more homework. Other studies also have shown that the heaviest burden of homework seems to fall on the youngest students. A study by the University of Michigan, discussed in *NEA Today*, found that of 3,600 young children surveyed, 9-year-olds spent 217 minutes studying each week in 1997, compared to 169 minutes in 1981. Homework-time by 6- to 8-year-olds nearly tripled during that period, from 44 to 123 minutes.

Percentage of 17-, 13- , and 9-year olds, by amount of time spent each day on homework, 1984 and 1999

Year	Age	Any homework assigned	Didn't do homework	Less than 1 hour	1 to 2 hours	More than 2 hours
1984	17	77.5	11.4	26.2	26.8	13.2
1999	17	73.6	13.1	26.4	22.6	11.5
1984	13	77.4	3.7	35.9	29.2	8.6
1999	13	75.9	4.5	37.2	26.3	7.9
1984	9	64.4	4.2	41.5	12.7	6.1
1999	9	74.2	3.8	53.1	12.4	4.9

In 1999, more 13- and 17-year-olds were skipping homework. Fewer spent time on it when they did do it. NCES reports that in 1999 more than half of all students spent less than five hours a week to homework. What were they doing instead? Watching TV, playing electronic games, working on computers, or working.

Does it make any difference how much time children spend on homework? NCES says: "Homework may have a positive effect on older students' achievement, but no discernible effect on the achievement of younger students." Professor Harris Cooper of the University of Missouri, Columbia, who has researched the homework question, claims there is a 15-year cycle to the homework issue. Every 15 years there is a call to abolish it, followed 15 years later by a call for more of it.

How do American kids stack up against kids in other countries? The table below comes from the Third International Mathematics and Science Study (TIMSS), considered one of the most comprehensive and rigorous such tests ever conducted. 4th-, 8th-, and 12th-graders took the exam and completed a survey about their homework and other habits. The table shows average time spent on homework by 12th-grade test-takers in 19 countries compared to the United States. We've included 12th-graders' average test scores in mathematics general knowledge.

Average hours spent by 12th-grade test-takers on homework each day and average scores in mathematics general knowledge and achievement

Country	Average hours of homework	Average test score
United States	1.7	461
International	2.6	500

American 4th-graders scored above average in math and near the top in science. American 8th-graders were about average in both. By 12th grade, American students scored below the international average and ranked nearly at the bottom. Newspaper headlines called the American scores "dismal" and American performance "mediocre." Next we look at another trend in educational reform: a long school year.

Sources: Chart and Table 1. National Center for Education Statistics. NCES, National Assessment of Educational Progress (NAEP), 1984 and 1999 Long-Term Trend Assessment, in *The Condition of Education 2001*, Indicator 22. Online. Available: http://nces.ed.gov/. March 18, 2002. Table 2: "Responses to Selected Student Questionnaire Items: Responses of Students Participating in Mathematics and Science General Knowledge Assessments," *Pursuing Excellence: A Study of U.S. Twelfth Grade Mathematics and Science Achievement in International Context*, NCES 98-049. Online. Available: http://nces.ed.gov March 18, 2002 and *Mathematics & Science Achievement in the Final Year of Secondary School.* Mullis, Ina V. et al., cited in *Congressional Digest*, August-September 1999, p. 205. "Homework: Time To Turn It In? *NEA Today*, April 1999, p. 21. National PTA. Online. Available: http://www.pta.org. February 20, 2002. Hellmich, Nancy. "Author argues amount of homework adds pressure on kids." *Detroit News*, 12 October 2000. Online. Available: http://detnews.com. February 20, 2002.

Should We Lengthen the School Year?

Average Number of School Days per Year and Hours per Day for 13-year-olds: 1991

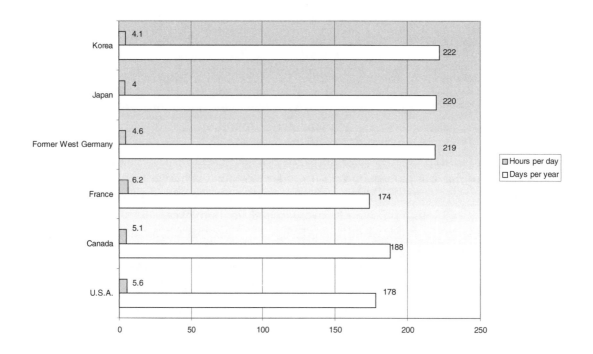

The chart shows the average number of days per year that 13-year-olds in industrialized nations spent in school in 1991. In every country except France, children spent more days in school than did their American counterparts. But there's more to this issue than at first meets the eye. A closer look reveals that American students have a relatively high number of hours of instruction in a day compared to their international counterparts. Only France had more hours in a day.

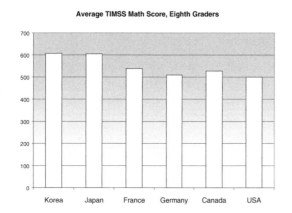

Average TIMSS Math Score, Eighth Graders

Still, U.S. mathematics test scores were the lowest in the six countries shown, as seen on this chart. TIMSS[1] gave momentum to the movement for an extended school year. Proponents point out that the current school calendar is based on the outdated notion that children are needed on the family farm to till the fields during the summer. They point, too, to encouraging research showing that students who attend summer school, after-school programs, or year-round school outscore their peers

---

[1] Third International Mathematics and Science Study.

when tested. Opponents counter that children learn important nonacademic lessons through summer camping and travel (if they can afford it).

The table below demonstrates the growth of year-round education over a nine-year period. The number of states offering year-round education nearly tripled between 1988 and 2001, and the number of students attending year-round school grew by 409%. Today, more than 2 million children attend more than 3,000 public schools operating year-round in 44 states. None of this comes cheaply. When California Governor Gray Davis proposed adding 30 extra days to the middle school calendar, the estimated cost was $1.45 billion.

Growth of Public Year-Round Education in the United States

School Year	States	Schools	Students	Enrollment[2]
1988-89	16	494	428,961	58,254,000
1992-93	23	1,646	1,345,921	62,686,000
1996-97	38	2,400	1,766,642	65,762,000
2001-2002	44	3,011	2,184,596	68,516,000

One final note about whether more homework or lengthening the school year would improve math and science test scores. Educators and parents will continue to debate that issue. TIMSS researchers concluded that the major reason for the disparity in test scores was the nature of the instruction that American students receive in classrooms. They concluded that American teachers stress breadth of learning rather than depth. Richard Riley, U.S. Secretary of Education, opined: "Our problem is not merely the amount of time U.S. students or teachers spend on mathematics and science but what they do with the time they have."

The next four panels look at how high schools are preparing students for life after graduation.

Source: Chart 1: National Center for Education Statistics. *Education in States and Nations*. 2nd ed. NCES 96-160, Phelps, Richard P., Thomas M. Smith and Nabeel Alealam. Washington, DC.: 1996, pp. 144-45. Online. Available:http://nces.ed.gov/. February 15, 2002. Chart 2: IEA Third International Mathematics and Science Study (TIMSS), 1994-95,. Online. Available: http://timss.bc.edu/ timss1995i/Highlights.html. February 21, 2002. Table: Excerpted from "Growth of Public Year-Round Education in the United States Over a 15-Year Period." Statistics compiled by the National Association for Year-Round Education (NAYRE). Online. Available: http:// www.NAYRE.org/about.html February 15, 2002. Total enrollment figures: *Statistical Abstract of the United States 2001*. "Summertime and School Isn't Easy: As the School Calendar Continues to Grow, Will the Lazy, Hazy Days of Summer Be No More?" *Time*, 31 July 2000, p. 18. National Center for Education Statistics. *Pursuing Excellence: A Study of U.S. Fourth-Grade Mathematics and Science Achievement in International Context*, 1997 and *Pursuing Excellence: A Study of U.S. Twelfth-Grade Mathematics and Science Achievement in International Context*, 1998. "A Matter of Time: Politicians Discuss Lengthening the School Year." *Current Events* 16 March 2001, p. 3. Fiske, Edward B. "Insights Into Why U.S. Students Lag Behind in Global Academic 'Horse Race.'" *International Herald Tribune* 11 February 1997 p 17.

---

[2] Public and private school total.

Paths to Work: Vocational Education

**Percentage of Public High School Graduates Concentrating (Accumulating 3 or More Credits) in
Vocational Education, by Program: 1982, 1990, 1994, and 1998**

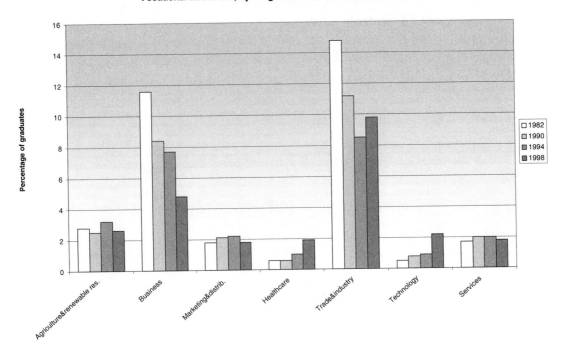

Recent educational reform efforts have emphasized preparing students for college. This has had some implications for vocational education.[3]

Federal support of vocational education in public schools began in 1917. Programs were intended to train students for entry-level jobs. But good Vo-Tech curricula cost money. Students and parent's perceptions today are that traditional vocational education doesn't prepare students for good jobs, although that's where the demand really is (see *Work & Leisure* in this series). Students expect to go to college. Their course selections show this. Enrollment in Vo-Tech courses has declined. In 1982, 34% of high school graduates were following a vocational curriculum; by 1998, the number had fallen to 25%.

As the graphic shows, "trade and industry" and "business" have long been the most popular areas of Vo-Tech concentration. The percentage of graduates choosing those areas declined between 1982 and 1998; "trade and industry" took an upswing thereafter. The decline in this category accounts for the overall decline in Vo-Tech participation.

---

[3] Vocational education at the high school level includes courses in agriculture and natural resources, business services, business management, marketing and distribution, health care, public and protective services, trade and industry, technology and communications, food services and hospitality; child care and education, and personal and other services.

Most other vocational areas did not experience a significant decline. "Health care" and "technology and communications" have seen increases in recent years.[4]

Labor market trends might influence students' choice — the general talk on the media. The service-providing sectors have grown; manufacturing jobs are eroding away. Possibly reflecting this shift, students have been concentrating in the areas of health care, technology/communications, and food service/hospitality. Participation in "marketing and distribution" has not risen although the specialty is also growing, perhaps because students see that area as needing college preparation.

Students have chosen academic curricula since 1982, as shown in the table below. The shift is at least in part due to a 1983 proposal by the National Commission on Excellence in Education urging students to complete a New Basics curriculum. This curriculum includes more coursework in academic subjects — mathematics, science, English, and social studies. Students today are earning more credits across the board than did their peers in 1982.

Average Number of Credits Accumulated by Public High School Graduates, By Type of Coursework, 1982 and 1998

	1982	1998
Total	21.6	25.1
Academic	14.3	18.3
Vocational	4.7	4.0
Enrichment/other	2.6	2.9

Students graduated from high school in 1982 with an average of 21.6 total credits, 14.3 in academic subjects, 4.7 in vocational education. By 1998 students were earning an average of 25.1 total credits — 18.3 in academic and 4.0 in vocational subjects. Overall credits rose about 20%. The number of academic credits rose 28%; Vo-Tec credits declined 15%. The share of vocational education credits was 22% in 1982, 16% by 1998.

In the next panel we look at the students who elect a concentration in vocational education.

Source: Chart: National Center for Education Statistics. High School and Beyond Sophomore Cohort 1982 High School Transcript Study and 1990 and 1994 National Assessment of Educational Progress High School Transcript Studies, and Lisa Hudson et al., "Changes in High School Vocational Coursetaking in a Larger Perspective." *Education Statistics Quarterly*. Online. Available: http://nces.ed.gov/pubs. February 21, 2002. Table: National Center for Education Statistics. High School and Beyond Longitudinal Study of 1980 Sophomores (HS&B-So:1980/1982), "High School Transcript Study" and 1998 High School Transcript Study (HSTS).

---

[4] The "Services" category falls under the formal heading of "Occupational Home Economics" and is comprised of personal and other services, food service and hospitality, and childcare and education.

Who Elects Vocational Education Courses?

Average Number of Vocational Education Credits Accumulated by Public High School Graduates: 1982, 1990, and 1994

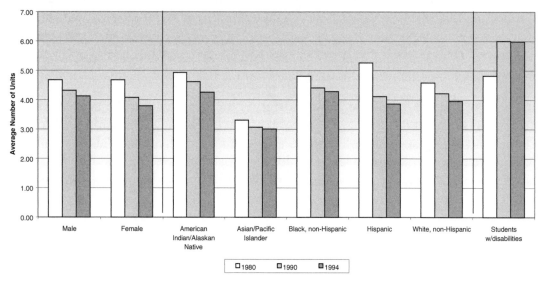

The chart shows the average number of vocational education credits earned by students who chose the vocational track in 1980, 1990, and 1994. Numbers are down for nearly every group shown, with one exception.

Males earned about the same number of vocational education credits as females in 1982. By 1990 a decline was evident for both males and females, but the number for females declined at a faster rate. Hispanic students completed more vocational credits than any other group in 1982; by 1994 their numbers showed the most dramatic decline, from an average of more than 5 credits to fewer than 4. Asians/Pacific Islanders consistently earned fewer vocational credits than any other group, going from a little more than 3 to fewer than 3. The dramatic increase in vocational coursetaking by students with disabilities — from fewer than 5 credits to 6, by far the highest number for any group throughout the survey period — is attributed to the passage of the 1990 Perkins Act, which emphasized serving students with special needs.

Today, vocational education is at a crossroads. There is a small but growing movement, encouraged by federal legislation like the 1998 Perkins Act, to get schools to focus on providing students with a strong foundation in marketable work skills and at the same time maintain college entry as an option. Until that happens on a much wider scale, people are looking at postsecondary education as the desirable path to better jobs.

In the next panel we look at progress along this trajectory.

Source: Chart: U.S. Department of Education, NCES, High School and Beyond Sophomore Cohort 1982 High School Transcript Study and 1990 and 1994 National Assessment of Educational Progress High School Transcript Studies, in *Vocational Education in the United States: Toward the Year 2000*, NCES 2000–029, by Karen Levesque et al., Project Officer: Dawn Nelson. Washington, D.C.: 2000, Tables 17, 18, 19; A. J. Vogl, "Schools: Should Business Set Their Agenda?" *Across the Board*, June 1995, p16-23.

Who's Taking Advanced Classes?

Percentage of High School Graduates Who Took Advanced Classes, By Race-Ethnicity and Gender: 1998

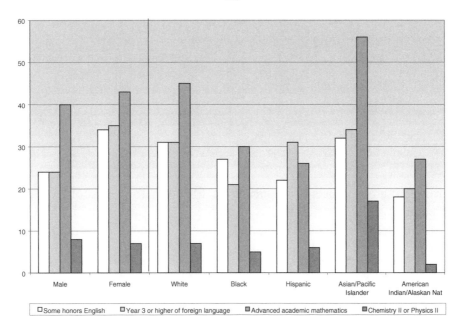

Students expect to go to college. In line with this expectation, they are taking more advanced courses. They are concentrating on mathematics, science, English, and foreign languages. They are going beyond what New Basics curriculum requires. In 1998, young women were generally more likely to take advanced courses than young men — except in the areas of chemistry or physics. White and Asian/Pacific Islander high school graduates were more likely to complete advanced mathematics and science classes than were graduates from other racial/ethnic groups. The racial/ethnic pattern in English and foreign languages is not as marked as the mathematics and science pattern.

The table on the next page shows how the course-taking pattern in mathematics and science has changed since 1982.

The most rigorous advanced placement mathematics curriculum includes such courses as trigonometry, calculus, and calculus/analytic geometry (Advanced Levels II and III). The percentage of high school graduates who achieved these levels went up between 1982 and 1998 from 4.8% and 5.9% to 14.4% and 11.8%. The percentage of students taking any advanced mathematics increased from 26.2% to 41.4%. Students who elect the rigorous curricula are those who are most likely to go to college, and to succeed. These students expect their hard work to pay off with the best jobs and higher income. (Some say that these students may be overeducated. See: "Are We Too Educated for the Future Job Market?" in *Work & Leisure*, Chapter 3.)

**Percentage Distribution of High School Graduates According to the Highest Level
of Advanced Mathematics and Science Courses Taken: Selected Years 1982-1998**

	Mathematics					Science		
	Middle academic		Advanced academic			Chemistry I or Physics I	Chemistry I and Physics I	Chemistry II or Physics II
Year	Level I	Level II	Level I	Level II	Level III			
1982	30.6	18.2	15.5	4.8	5.9	18.4	7.4	4.8
1987	26.8	23.1	12.9	9.0	7.6	23.3	11.8	5.1
1990	25.4	26.2	12.9	10.4	7.2	28.2	13.7	5.6
1992	22.7	26.4	16.4	10.9	10.7	29.9	14.3	6.9
1994	22.4	26.9	16.3	11.6	10.2	32.1	15.0	6.4
1998	20.8	27.7	14.4	15.2	11.8	33.8	18.5	7.3

What about hedging one's bets – preparing for life after high school by electing both a vocational education concentration and a college preparatory curriculum? There is a small but growing trend in that direction. We explore the topic in the next panel.

Source: Graphic: U.S. Department of Education, NCES, The Condition of Education 2001, Indicators 34 and 39, retrieved May 28, 2002, from http://nces.ed.gov/programs/coe/2000/. Table: U.S. Department of Education, NCES, 1998 National Assessment of Educational Progress (NAEP) High School Transcript Study.

Who's Preparing for Both College and a Vocation?

Percentage Distribution of Public High School Graduates According to Curriculum Specialization in High School: 1982, 1990, and 1994

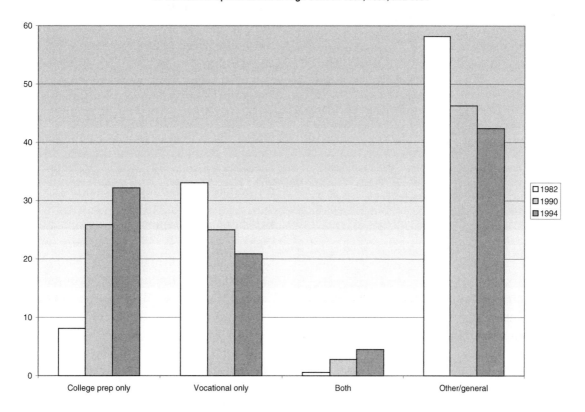

Traditionally, secondary schools prepared students either for entry-level jobs or for college. A new trend is to prepare for either or both. An increasing number of students are completing both a college preparatory curriculum and a vocational concentration. College preparatory graduates complete a course of study consistent with the entrance requirements of public four-year colleges. Vocational program graduates are prepared for manufacturing jobs, for jobs in the services and information industries, or for jobs in business.

The chart shows that more and more students are preparing only for college. In a mirroring fashion, the number of those preparing for future jobs immediately out of high school is dwindling. But there is a new trend. Out of about 2.6 million students who graduated in 1982 and in 1994, less than a percent (0.6%) went for a "mixed" preparation in 1982 — and 4.5% in 1994. The trend is so new, the tabulators haven't had a chance yet to collect much data about this phenomenon.

This group can be viewed through two lenses. Of those who concentrated on the college preparatory curriculum, *7% also* took a Vo-Tech concentration in 1982. In 1994, this number had risen to 12%. Of those who concentrated on vocational education, *2% also* took the college preparatory curriculum. In 1994, this number had risen to 18%.

Which vocational education students were most likely *also* to elect a college preparatory curriculum? As the chart below demonstrates, technology and business specialists were most likely to complete a college preparatory curriculum (43% and 27% respectively), while a food service and hospitality specialist was least likely to do so (only 3% completed a college preparatory curriculum).

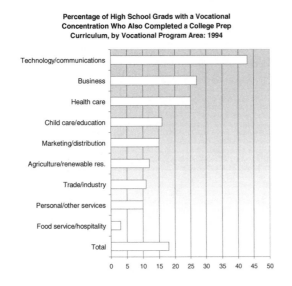

Percentage of High School Grads with a Vocational Concentration Who Also Completed a College Prep Curriculum, by Vocational Program Area: 1994

Why do vocational education students interested in the business and technology programs take college preparatory classes? Perhaps because they think there are better job opportunities in these fields for people with college credentials.

Business and technology programs are the areas most likely to use modern equipment such as computers. In general, the media describe traditional vocational education programs as archaic, underfunded, and neglected, especially those operating in large urban areas. This is beginning to change as businesses and government get more involved in school business.

Employers are vocal about what they expect from schools — and willing to act. For example, the California Business Roundtable, an organization composed of chief executive officers of leading California businesses, is working to require exit exams, finance new facilities, and integrate technology into the state's classrooms as a way of ensuring qualified future employees.

The 1994 passage of the School-to-Work Opportunities Act encouraged employer involvement in schools and led to job shadowing, mentoring, internships, and apprenticeships. More signs of the new order? It is largely thanks to donations from businesses and their pressure for more federal and state funding that nearly every school in the country now has an Internet connection (see the last panel in this chapter, "Tracking the Digital Divide"). As schools incorporate modern technology, vocational education programs are benefiting. This may make them more appealing to more students.

Sources: Chart: Lisa Hudson and David Hurst. "Students Who Prepare for College and a Vocation." *Education Statistics Quarterly*. Winter 2000; *Vocational Education in the United States: Toward the Year 2000* (NCES 2000-029). Online. Available: http://nces.ed.gov. February 25, 2002. California Business Roundtable. "Education." Online. Available: http://www.cbrt.org/education.html. February 27, 2002. "Hire Education." *City Limits*, May 1999, p17-21. Goldman, Abigail. "Schools Tackling Job Training Needs." *Los Angeles Times*. 6 September 1994, pB1.

Tracking the Digital Divide

Percentage of Students in Grades 7-12 Who Used a Computer
at School or Home, by Race-ethnicity: 1984, 1989, 1993, and 1997

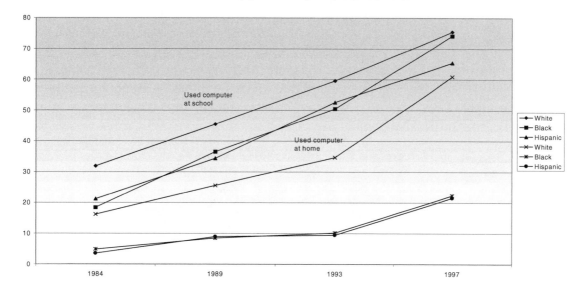

In June 1996, U.S. Education Secretary Richard Riley released *Getting America's Students Ready for the 21st Century: Meeting the Technology Literacy Challenge.* In it he stated: "Computers are the 'new basic' of American education, and the Internet is the blackboard of the future." He expressed a national goal of connecting every classroom in America to the "information superhighway with computers and good software and well-trained teachers." At the time, the wiring of America's classrooms was well underway.

The chart above illustrates that computer learning opportunities in schools have not been equal. There is a digital divide in computer usage by race-ethnicity. According to www.whatis.com, "the digital divide describes the fact that the world can be divided into people who do and people who don't have access to — and the capability to use — modern information technology, such as the telephone, television, or the Internet."

White students are more likely than African-American or Hispanic students to use the Internet at school and at home, although the school-use gap between black and white is narrowing at a faster rate than is the gap between those two groups and Hispanics. Home use of the Internet allows some students to be more prepared than others to understand and make use of technology-based education.

The digital divide is also evident when income is taken into account, as the following table illustrates. Low income in 1997 was below $13,000; high income was $60,801 and over.

**Percentage of Students in Grades 7-12 Who Used a Computer
at School and/or Home, by Family Income: 1984, 1989, 1993, and 1997**

	1984		1989		1993		1997	
	Used a computer at		Used a computer at		Used a computer at		Used a computer at	
Family income	School	Home	School	Home	School	Home	School	Home
Low income	20.0	3.3	36.7	5.7	49.0	5.6	67.6	14.9
Middle income	28.4	10.1	42.6	17.0	57.3	22.2	74.1	44.2
High income	34.1	24.8	47.2	38.3	60.7	51.2	75.4	78.6

Students from high-income families were more likely to use a computer at home and school than were students from low- and middle-income families. Computers and Internet access cost money. But why do fewer low-income students use the Internet at school? The table below clarifies that point.

**Percentage of Public Schools and Instructional Rooms
with Internet Access, by School Characteristics: Fall 1998**

School characteristic	Schools with access	Classrooms with access
Total	89	51
71%+ of students eligible for reduced-price lunch	80	39
50% or more minority enrollment	82	37

In 1998, 89% of public schools had Internet access in 51% of their classrooms. The poorest schools had Internet access in 39% of classrooms. The schools with the highest minority enrollment had access in only 37% of classrooms. While a high percentage of schools may have Internet access, poor and minority schools have fewer Internet access points. Poor schools are also more likely to have outdated equipment and provide slow, frustrating experiences. An article in *Popular Science* states that about 40,000 of the 70,000 computers in New York City public schools are obsolete. The cost to modernize the system: $2.1 billion.

The Bureau of Labor Statistics predicted that by 2000, 60% of all jobs would require high-tech computer skills. In response to labor-market predictions like this, the federal government has sought ways to speed the rate at which computers are delivered to the classroom. Laws enacted in the 1990s and in 2001 guarantee a continued emphasis on technology in schools and funding for it.

Corporate America is deeply involved in the effort to wire every classroom. This has set off a national debate about the role of business in education. Critics complain that donated computers and software usually come with strings attached. For example, they often feature advertising. Such advertising suggests a school's endorsement of products and raises serious ethical questions among child advocates.

In discussing the pros and cons of businesses donating computers to schools, the media repeatedly cited the example of an Internet company called ZapMe! Corp. In the late 1990s, ZapMe! began loaning to schools a package of 15 computers, along with a satellite dish and an Internet server, in exchange for a promise to use the machines at least four hours a day. Each donated monitor featured an on-screen box that continuously alternated public service materials with advertising. In what critics called an invasion of privacy, ZapMe! required students to receive an electronic ID in order to use the computers (a way of conducting market research).

By mid-1999, ZapMe! was operating in 200 schools in about a dozen states (some of them poor and minority schools) and hoped to be in 2,000 schools by year-end. In the face of criticism by consumer groups like Commercial Alert, who called the company a "corporate predator," in late 2000 ZapMe! told 2,300 schools that they had to either give back the equipment or start paying for it.

In the 2000 report "Fools Gold: A Critical Look at Computers in Childhood, " a national group of educators, doctors, and children's advocates claimed that the billions spent on wiring classrooms is fueled more by parental fears of their children being left behind and corporate sales pitches than any real evidence of computers helping children learn. The report stated: "Wiring and computerizing America's schools is an urgent priority — not for children, but for high-tech companies that need to constantly expand their markets." The report recommended that older students be taught the ethical and social implications of technology.

Speaking for business, in 2000 Sun Microsystems Vice President Kim Jones told a San Jose reporter that industry needs to make classroom computers simpler to use. She opined: "I agree 100 percent that technology has not been very effective in the classroom." Jones denied that profit is the only reason for corporate involvement in schools.

Despite the criticism and thanks to businesses and government, the wiring of America's classrooms is proceeding pell-mell. Whereas in 1984, 29.7% of K-12 children used a computer at school, by 1997, 76.4% of them did. The wiring won't stop anytime soon.

Does the use of technology equal better academic performance and does it promise better qualified future employees? Opinions are divided, but the billions of dollars being infused into the schools for technology and teacher training indicate that a lot of people think so. Perhaps those dollars will eventually eliminate the digital divide.

Source: Chart and Table: U.S. Department of Education. The Condition of Education 2001. Indicator 45. Online. Available: http://nces.ed.gov/programs/coe/. May 27, 2002: U.S. Bureau of the Census. October *Current Population Surveys*; Fisher, Arthur. "High Tech, High Grades?" *Popular Science*. (January 1999), p. 64. Trotter, Andrew. "Cyber Learning at Online High." *Education Week*. 24 January 2001, p.28. Corcoran., Katherine. "Report: Computers in Schools Harmful." *San Jose Mercury News*. 13 September 2000. Hardy, Lawrence. "The Lure of School Marketing." *American School Board Journal* (October 1999), p. 22. Commercial Alert. Online. Available: http://www.commercialalert.org/zapme/. March 4, 2002. "ZapMe zaps its school PC program. *The Houston Chronicle*, 6 December 2000 p2.

Chapter 12

Trends in Postsecondary Education

The second half of the twentieth century saw explosive growth in the number of people attending college, the number of educational institutions built to accommodate them, and the cost of a college education. The media continually remind us that the price of a college education is going up and up. At the same time, the college degree becomes ever more desirable. Parents and young people see the degree as a milestone on the path to economic success.

In the 1960s President Lyndon Johnson's Great Society initiatives led to unprecedented numbers of students from low-income families acquiring a college education. But federal dollars haven't kept up with rising costs, and new government initiatives seem to favor students who are better able to pay. At the same time, it is predicted that the pool of college applicants will include more poor students. This leads to the question: Is college now out of the reach of all but the most well-off among us?

The first panels in this chapter offer an overview of the costs of a college education — how people finance their education and how financial options have changed. We'll see that perceptions of the cost of college do not always match the reality. We'll explore the question whether financial aid packages favor those who need them most.

The second set of panels looks at funding and endowments at the college level. Where does the money come from? Where does it go? Next, we look at recipients of college degrees to learn who our new professionals are and who is being left behind in the baccalaureate scramble. We will see how grade inflation is casting doubt on the quality of college diplomas and will also try to determine the value of a college degree.

Finally, we will examine the rapidly growing phenomenon of technology-based distance learning. The cost of higher education is soaring as fast as the cost of health care. Is it possible that distance education will actually replace the university?

Just How Much Has Tuition Gone Up?

**Tuition/fees at Public and Private Institutions of Higher Education,
Consumer Price Index All Items and College Tuition/Fees: 1990-2000**

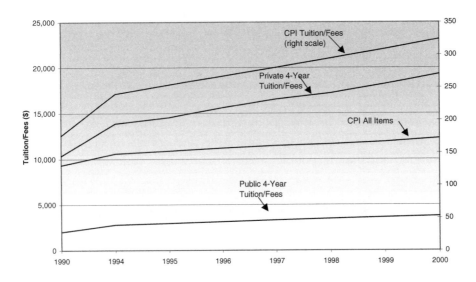

Tuition and fees rose during the 1990 to 2000 decade. They rose both at private and at public institutions of higher learning. Obviously, costs went up. The average price tag for a year at a private college rose from $10,348 to $19,312, an increase of 86%. Costs for a year at a public college rose 85%, from $2,035 to $3,774.

Keep in mind that these tuition figures are averages. A year at the "best" colleges is going to cost much more. Tuition at Stanford University (undergraduate alma mater of four of the nine justices on the U.S. Supreme Court) would have set you back $26,192 for the 2001-2002 school year. That year at MIT would have cost $26,960.

The figures on the right scale of the chart are from the Consumer Price Index (CPI). They represent annual averages of monthly out-of-pocket payments for college tuition/fees. These figures reinforce what we already see on the left scale — that tuition just keeps going up. Between 1990 and 2000, the Consumer Price Index for tuition plus fees rose 355%, compared to a 109% rise in the cost of all other goods and services.

American Express Financial Advisors reports that annual tuition increases of 5% will probably continue into the foreseeable future. By 2020, they say, tuition, fees, room and board at a four-year *public* school could approach $100,000.

Is it worth it? Considering the value of an education in monetary terms, the College Board reports that a person with a Bachelor of Arts degree can expect to earn more than $1 million more over a lifetime than a person with a high school diploma.

Is it worth it to pay more than $100,000 for four years at a selective college? Maybe so. In a widely quoted 1999 working paper for the National Bureau of Economic Research, the authors concluded: "Students who attend colleges with higher average tuition costs or spending per student tend to earn higher incomes later on." On the other hand, *Atlantic Monthly* notes: "The four richest people in America, all of whom made rather than inherited their wealth, are a dropout from Harvard, a dropout from the University of Illinois, a dropout from Washington State University, and a graduate of the University of Nebraska."

What's behind the tuition increases? Is it incompetence on the part of college administrators, as some critics charge? Colleges counter that their buildings are crumbling, faculty clamor for raises, technology needs updating.

A 2002 report released by the National Center for Education Statistics found that tuition increases at public four-year institutions were largely due to decreases in state appropriations. Tuition increases at private institutions were due to increases in faculty salaries and the provision of more financial aid to students and to decreases in endowment revenue and private gifts.

Tuition and the state of the economy are inextricably intertwined. In good times, state legislatures appropriate more money. Some of the money goes to students in the form of grants and aid. Tuition stays flat. When the economy sours, state support for higher education drops. Students must bear a higher share of the college costs. In the late 1980s and early 1990s, a period of recession, states reduced their budget allotments to higher education. Funding fell from an average of 13% in 1988 to less than 9% in 1996. The graphic above shows what happened to tuition in that period — it went up.

Tuition at a private school is affected by the size of the school's endowment. Booming markets make endowments bloom. When the market goes bust, endowment returns are sickly — tuition goes up.

At the time of writing, preliminary reports were that tuition would go up significantly in the 2002-2003 school year at both public and private institutions.

Tuition goes up, but maybe not as much as people think it does. The next panel looks at peoples' perceptions of college costs.

Sources: Chart: *Statistical Abstract of the United States: 2001*, Table 278, "Institutions of Higher Education — Charges: 1985 to 2000," and Table 694, "Consumer Price Indexes for All Urban Consumers (CPI-U) for Selected Items and Groups: 1980 to 2000"; National Center for Education Statistics, *Digest of Education Statistics*, annual, and Bureau of Labor Statistics, *Monthly Labor Review* and *CPI Detailed Report*, January issues. American Express Financial Advisors. Online. Available: http://finance.americanexpress.com/finance/fshub.asp. March 10, 2002. Zhao, Yilu. "As Endowments Slip at Colleges, Big Tuition Increases Fill the Void." *New York Times*. 22 February 2002, p.1A. "Estimating the Payoff to Attending a More Selective College: An Application of Selection on Observables and Unobservables." Stacy Berg Dale, Alan B. Krueger. NBER Working Paper No. 7322. August 1999. Online. Available: http://papers.nber.org/papers/. March 7, 2002. Fallows, James. "The Early-Decision Racket." *Atlantic Monthly*. (September 2001), p. 37. "New ED Report Shows College Tuition Increases Related to Many Factors." U.S. Department of Education Press Release, February 15, 2002. Online. Available: http://www.ed.gov/PressReleases. April 9, 2002.

Perceptions of the Price of College

Percentage Distribution of Tuition and Fees Charged at Public 4-year Institutions and Estimates Reported
by 6th- to 12th Graders and Their Parents: 1999

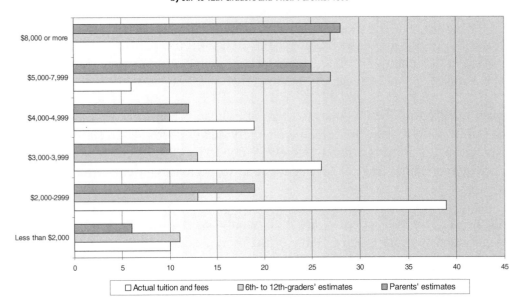

The graphic presents students' and parents' perceptions of the price of a public college — and the actual price of attendance in 1999. Here is the way to read the chart. At 39% of 4-year colleges, tuition and fees totaled less than $3,000 a year. At 84% of colleges, tuition and fees were less than $5,000 a year. A majority of students and parents overestimated the price of college. The average cost of attending any public 4-year college was $3,243. Students' average estimate was $5,664; their parents' average estimate was $5,970.

Why are the perceptions and reality so far apart? Blame the media. The headlines might read like this: "College tuition continues to outpace inflation," unless they are more sensational, like this: "The Scary Cost of College."

It's true that the price of going to college keeps getting higher. What's worse, the steepest tuition increases come during times of economic hardship. Under the circumstances, it's not surprising that many students and their parents think that college is unaffordable. In the next panel we look at other costs of college "beyond tuition."

Source: Chart: National Center for Education Statistics. "The Condition of Education 2001 in Brief." Wirt, John and Andrea Livingston; NCES National Household Education Surveys Program (NHES). 1999 (Parent and Youth Interview Surveys): The College Board: Trends in College Pricing, 1998 (for actual tuition and fees). Online. Available: http://www.nces.gov. March 7, 2002.

Tuition Isn't Even the Half of It

College/University Costs Borne by Students/Families at a High-Priced Public Institution: 1998-1999

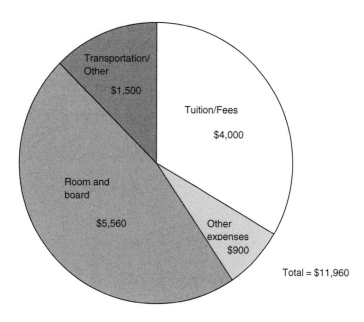

Transportation/ Other $1,500

Tuition/Fees $4,000

Room and board $5,560

Other expenses $900

Total = $11,960

The pie chart shows estimated costs that would have been borne by students and their families if the student attended a relatively high-priced public college in 1998-99. "Other expenses" includes the cost of books and computers. "Transportation/other" includes entertainment. The total cost for a year at this hypothetical college: nearly $12,000. This is the equivalent of the mean annual earnings of a waiter or waitress working full-time that year.

These total costs are probably what parents have in mind when they lament the high cost of college today. However, it could be argued that about half of this $12,000 annual cost is not college costs but simply ordinary living costs, such as room and board.

Estimated Average Cost For a Year at a Public 4-Year College: 1985 to 2000

Year	Tuition/fees	Board	Dorm charges	Total
1985	971	1,241	1,196	3,408
1990	1,356	1,635	1,513	4,504
1994	1,942	1,880	1,873	5,677
1996	2,179	2,020	2,057	6,256
1998	2,360	2,228	2,225	6,813
2000	2,507	2,361	2,434	7,302

The table tracks changes in the average cost of a year at a public institution (which most students attend) over a 15-year period. Transportation and entertainment are excluded. The average total charges for a year at college in 1985 were $3,408. In 2000 the year cost $7,302, a 114% increase.

The median household income in 1985 was $23,618. A year at college for a member of the household would have consumed 14% of the family's income. The median household income in 2000 was $42,100. College costs would have consumed 17%. Of course, for the half of all households whose income is below the median, the share for college would be higher.

The New York Times reported the results of a study of college costs for the year 2000. The study, called "Losing Ground," found that on average, poor families spent 25% of their annual income for their children to attend a public four-year college, compared to 13% in 1980. For middle-class families, the figures went from 4% to 7%. There was no increase for wealthy families from the 2% they spent in 1980 — wealthy families enjoyed a healthy increase in overall income (see *Work & Leisure,* Chapter 4, "Income").

The next two panels look at trends in the financing of a college education in an attempt to answer the question: Is college affordable?

Sources: Chart: U.S. Department of Education, *Study of College Costs and Prices, 1988–89 to 1997–98*, Volume 2: Commissioned Papers, NCES 2002–158; estimates by D. Bruce Johnstone. Online. Available: http://www.nces.gov. March 1, 2002; *Statistical Abstract of the United States: 2001*, Table 278: "Institutions of Higher Education — Charges: 1985 to 2000; NCES. *Digest of Education Statistics*. Steinberg, Jacques. "More Family Income Committed to College." *New York Times,* 2 May 2002. Online. Available: http://www.nytimes.com. May 2, 2002.

Students Like Grants

Average Federal Grant Amount (dollars): 1995-2001

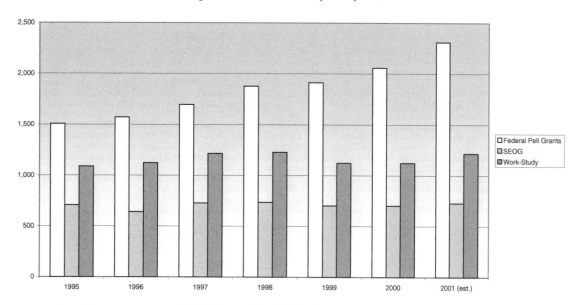

As much as three-quarters of all financial aid for higher education comes from the federal government. The largest federal aid program is the Pell Grant. It is sometimes supplemented by a Federal Supplemental Educational Opportunity Grant (SEOG). The graph shows that the dollar amount of the average Pell Grant rose steadily throughout the 1990s, from $1,507 in 1995 to an estimated $2,310 in 2001, a 53% increase. Most Pell Grants go to low-income students with annual family incomes below $20,000 (see table, below).

Between 1985 and 2000, college costs rose more than 150%. Considering average annual total college costs (tuition, room and board, fees, etc.) of upwards of $7,000, we see from this chart that grants are a drop in the big tuition/fees bucket. They have to be supplemented by some other kind of aid. These days, that means loans (see next panel).

Government assistance for college is a fairly recent phenomenon. It started with the 1944 Serviceman's Readjustment Act, better known as the GI Bill. At the time of its passage, more than half of Americans had no more than an eighth-grade education. Remembering how millions of veterans had returned from World War I to face unemployment, Congress provided funds to help the economy by educating and training veterans. The GI Bill, regarded by historians as one of the most enlightened pieces of legislation ever enacted by Congress, offered veterans up to $500 a year for college tuition and fees ($5,051 in 2002 dollars).

College enrollments soared. By 1950, 1.7% of the population was enrolled in college (it's 5.6% today). After the Russians launched *Sputnik* in 1957, a need to extend higher education to more Americans was seen. Great Society initiatives of the 1960s made it possible for low-income students to earn a college degree. These programs were never intended to pay the entire cost of college, but for a while, a federal grant took a lot of the pain out of financing an education.

From the recipient's point of view, aid in the form of a grant is always preferable to a loan. Grants don't need to be repaid. Pell Grants reached their peak value in the 1970s. According to *Business Week*, in 1975 the maximum Pell Grant covered 85% of the cost of four years at a public college.

Despite a continued federal commitment to assisting every qualified person willing to make the effort, federal grants haven't kept up with tuition costs. By 2000, the maximum Pell Grant of $3,300 covered an average of 39% of the cost of a year at college.

Percentage of Undergraduates Receiving Any Federal Aid and Receiving Federal Grants: 1999-2000

	Any aid	Grants
Total	39.1	23.1
Dependency and 1998 income level		
Dependent	43.7	20.1
Less than $20,000	70.0	65.9
$20,000-39,999	56.3	43.6
$40,000-59,999	40.8	8.9
$60,000-79,999	36.9	1.4
$80,000-99,999	32.5	0.5
$100,000 or more	24.5	0.4
Independent	34.6	26.0
Less than $10,000	67.4	63.1
$10,000-19,999	50.4	37.9
$20,000-29,999	35.1	24.9
$30,000-49,999	20.4	11.6
$50,000 or more	7.8	0.2

The table shows the income status of 1999-2000 undergraduates who received federal grants. "Dependent" means dependent on the family. Nearly 40% of all students received some type of federal aid. Federal grants averaging $2,281 went to 23% of those students. Fifty-five percent of undergraduates received aid (loans, grants, scholarships) averaging $6,265. As tuition goes up, the purchasing power of grants dips. Loans must supplement grants to a greater degree than ever before.

Analysts predict that the college applicant pool in the first decade of the 21st century will include a larger proportion of students from low-income families than ever before. At the same time, college will become increasingly less affordable for the lower and middle classes. How will they finance the part of their education not covered by grants?

The next panel looks at student loan activity. It's way up.

Source: Chart: *Statistical Abstract of the United States: 2001.* Table 276. Table: NCES. *National Postsecondary Student Aid Study: Student Financial Aid Estimates for 1999– 2000.* NCES 2001-209. Malizio, Andrew G., Project Officer; Table 3. "College Crunch." *Business Week.* 27 August 2001, p. 126. Sanchez, Yojairy. "The Top 4 Sources of Aid." *Careers & Colleges.* (November 2000), p. 20. Brownstein, Andrew. "Tuitions Rise Sharply, and This Time Public Colleges Lead the Way." *Chronicle of Higher Education.* 2 November 2001. Online. Available: http://chronicle.com. March 12, 2002. Ikenberry, Stanley O. "Higher Education and Market Forces." *USA Today* (Magazine) March 2001, p. 34. Snyder, Tom. *120 Years of American Education: A Statistical Portrait.* NCES. (1993).

... But Students Get Loans

Percentage of 1992-93 Bachelor's Degree Recipients
Who Borrowed for Higher Education, by Borrowing Status

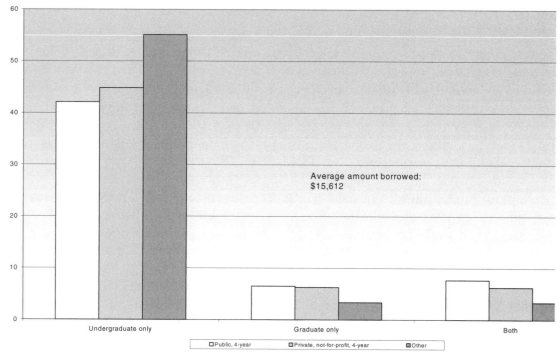

A majority of 1992-93 bachelor's degree recipients (56.3%) resorted to borrowing at some point in their undergraduate or graduate years to finance their education. The graphic shows their borrowing status: 42% borrowed as undergraduates only, 6.5% borrowed only as graduate students, and 7.7% borrowed at both points in their careers.

In 1980, grants accounted for about 55% of federal aid to students and loans for about 42%. By 2000, the figures were reversed, with loans accounting for 58% and grants for 40%. According to The College Board, the amount of federal student loans more than doubled between 1989-90 and 1995-96, from $13 billion to $28 billion. This represents a huge increase in student indebtedness.

Money Borrowed for Undergraduate Education by 1992-1993 Bachelor's Degree Recipients

Item	Average amount
Total	15,612
Bachelor's degree-granting institution	
Public, 4-year	13,623
Private, not-for-profit, 4-year	19,528
Other	13,266

The table shows the average dollar amount owed by 1992-93 bachelor's degree recipients by type of institution. The amount borrowed keeps going up. Today, students who borrow to finance their education can expect to leave a 4-year institution with an average debt of $15,000 to $20,000. A student who pursues an advanced degree can expect to be paying on that loan for up to 20 years. A new doctor or psychiatrist will begin practicing with an average debt of $90,745. Defaulting on student loans became a major scandal when the default rate peaked at 22.4% in 1990.

Federal loans are no longer going to those who need the money most. Legislation enacted in 1992 made it easier for middle-class families to qualify for federal loans by eliminating the consideration of family assets such as home equity. More federal loan money flowed to middle-income students. And *Newsweek* reports that lately, schools have been directing more aid to smart kids, "whether they need it or not," to make their rankings look better.

There is plenty of money out there for the borrowing. Octameron Associates, college financial aid advisors, reports: "Billions in low-interest, subsidized federal student loan money goes unused each year simply because students think they are ineligible, don't bother to go through the paper work hassle, or just don't know about the program." But a Congressional advisory committee warned in 2001 that if loan money continues to go to middle-income students, the financial needs of many among the increasing college-going population will have to go unmet.

Is college affordable today? One answer: People continue to enroll in college. Apparently they think the product is worth the price. It may take longer to finish a degree because students have to work their way through, but Americans are graduating in record numbers.

D. Bruce Johnstone, Professor of Higher and Comparative Education, University at Buffalo, has this to say about affordability: "In spite of tuition increases, it can still be said that any student who is of traditional college-age, who is at all academically able, and who is willing to borrow and/or work part time can probably get into several colleges or universities regardless of the financial status of his or her family." Whether that student can stay the course and bear the burden of debt is up to the student to decide. In the next panel, we look at a special case: Medical School.

There are barriers other than money to attaining a college degree. They include lack of academic preparation, race, and personal barriers, such as the fears that go along with being the first in one's family to attend college. These are issues that educators are well aware of and are seeking ways to address.

Source: Chart and table: *Statistical Abstract of the United States: 2001.* Table 277. U.S. Center for Education Statistics. *Debt Burden Four Years After College.* NCES 200-188 (August 2000). "Trends in Undergraduate Borrowing: Federal Student Loans in 1989-90, 1992-93, and 1995-96." *Education Statistics Quarterly.* (Summer 2000). Online. Available: http://nces.ed.gov. March 12, 2002. Bell, Julie Davis, and Demaree K. Michelau. "Making College Affordable." *State Legislatures.* (October/November 2001), p. 19. Hartigan, Rachel, and Ben Wildavsky. "A School's Free-Lunch Program." *U.S. News & World Report.* 12 February 2001, p. 50. "Octameron Associates. www.octameron.com. Johnstone, D. Bruce. "Higher Education and Those 'Out of Control' Costs." NCES 2002-158. *Study of College Costs and Prices, 1988-89 to 1997-98, Volume 2*: *Commissioned Papers.* Online. Available:http://nces.ed.gov/. March 13, 2002. "Degree Attainment Rates at Colleges and Universities." Online. Available: http://www.gseis.ucla.edu/heri/press_darcu.htm. March 20, 2002. "Colleges Strive to Bring Aid to Poorer Families." *USA Today*, 20 March 2002, p.6D. Kantrowitz, Barbara, "How to Win the College Game." *Newsweek,* 8 April 2002, p. 46.

Medical School Debt: A Special Case

Tuition Costs in Constant 2000 Dollars, 1987-2000

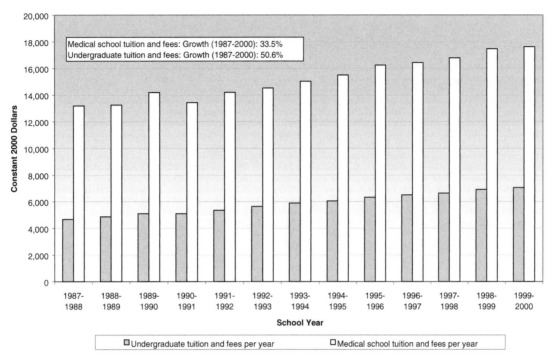

In the context of high tuition costs — the need for loans — and the long haul to repay them, a look at medical education is tempting.

In order to become a doctor, a student must complete 4 years of college and 4 years of medical school. The graphic charts the rise of undergraduate and medical school tuition rates. This trend, of course, has led students to seek educational loans in this specialty, too. According to the Association of American Medical Colleges, about 81% of medical students incur some educational debt. The average debt in 2000 was $95,000 — a 58% increase from 1993 when the average medical school student owed $60,000.[1]

Of course, tuition isn't the only expense for future doctors. The cost of room and board also has gone up (32.5%[2] from 1992-1993 to 1999-2000). In the 1992-1993 school year, the average cost for undergraduate room and board at a 4-year college or university was $4,006 a year. By the 1999-2000 school year, the cost rose to $5,308. This expense can be alleviated if students have the luxury of living with their parents. But, if living with mom and dad is not an option, and living in a dorm is unappealing, living in an apartment (even with a roommate sharing the expenses) may cost even more.

---

[1] In 2000 constant dollars, the increase was 34% (from $71,036 in 1993 to $95,000 in 2000).

[2] In 2000 constant dollars, the increase was 12% (from $4,743 in 1992-1993 to $5,308 in 1999-2000).

After graduation, doctors must complete a 3-5 year residency, and, depending on the specialty, another 1-5 years of a fellowship. The good news: working on a residency pays a salary (about $35,000 a year in 1999). The bad news: medical school debt rose an average of 6% from 1993-1999. Residents' salaries rose only 2%.[3] Many graduates deferred repaying their loans (if they could) until after finishing their residency. Interest accumulated, the debt grew, and deductions for interest paid could not be taken. Since 1986, there has been a 5-year limit on this deduction. Even if graduates went into private practice before the 5-year limit was over, there was a good chance that they would be earning too much to be eligible for the deduction. As part of the Economic Growth and Tax Relief Reconciliation Act of 2001 the 5-year limit on tax deductions for education loans was eliminated and the income limitations were also modified. This law took effect with the 2002 tax year. Thus it remains to be seen if this will truly help graduates pay off their loans.

In the meantime, there are other ways medical school graduates can eliminate their debt. They can commit to serve for two-years in medically under-served areas as a part of the National Health Service Corps. In exchange, primary care physicians can eliminate $50,000 in loan debt. The longer the time commitment, the greater the debt that is erased. Established physicians can join the U.S. Navy or Army Reserves. They offer loan repayment of up to $20,000. If neither public service nor the military is appealing, there is always debt consolidation. Educational consolidation loans, offered through the federal government, banks, and other lenders, lower monthly payments by combining the amount owed on all loans into a single loan and charging a lower rate of interest.[4]

Sources: National Center for Education Statistics. *Digest of Education Statistics, 2001*. Association of American Medical Colleges. "Total Enrollment by Gender and Race/Ethnicity, 1992-2001." and "How much does medical school cost and can I afford it?" Online. Available: http://www.aamc.org/data/facts/famg82001.htm. August 12, 2002. "The Inflation Calculator." Online. Available: http://www.westegg.com/inflation. August 13, 2002. Albert, Tanya. "Bills Offer Relief from Medical School Debt." *Education Update Online* (April 2001). Online. Available: http://www.educationupdate.com/april01/medbills.html. August 20, 2002. Mangan, Doreen. "Say goodbye to your med school debt." *Medical Economics*, 6 December 1999. Online. Available: http://www.findarticles.com. August 12, 2002. Bianco, M.D., Carl. "How Becoming a Doctor Works." Online. Available: http://www.howstuffworks.com/becoming-a-doctor.htm. August 20, 2002. "Bill Summary & Status for the 107th Congress." Online. Available: http://thomas.loc.gov. August 20, 2002. "How Medicare Calculates GME Payments, Part I." *JAMA*. 26 May 1999. Online. Available: http://jama.ama-assn.org/issues/v281n20/fpdf/jrf90014.pdf. August 18, 2002.

---

[3] Since 1965, Medicare paid part of this salary. Direct graduate medical education payments are inflation adjusted based on the average per-resident amount in 1984 and upon the number of residents and the proportion of inpatient days used by Medicare patients. Congress has since modified the formula to reduce Medicare reimbursement payments.

[4] The interest rate is based on a weighted average of the loans being consolidated, and rounded up to the next highest one-eighth of 1%. This is a federally mandated interest rate for educational consolidation loans, and will be the same whether the consolidation loan is financed through the federal government, banks, or other lenders.

Higher Education: Where Does the Money Come From?

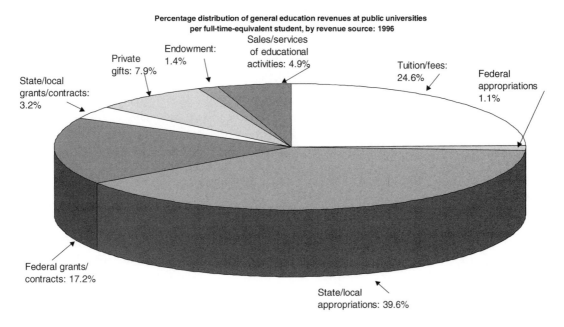

Percentage distribution of general education revenues at public universities per full-time-equivalent student, by revenue source: 1996

Endowment: 1.4%

Private gifts: 7.9%

State/local grants/contracts: 3.2%

Sales/services of educational activities: 4.9%

Tuition/fees: 24.6%

Federal appropriations 1.1%

Federal grants/ contracts: 17.2%

State/local appropriations: 39.6%

Federal, state, and local government appropriations (taxes) pay the bulk of public higher education. Despite increasing enrollment, government appropriations for public universities have been steadily declining for decades, falling from 63% of revenue in 1980-81 to 40.7% in 1996 (state/local and federal appropriations). During that same period, tuition and fees increased as a share of all revenue from 13% to nearly 25%.

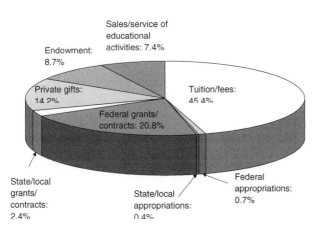

Sales/service of educational activities: 7.4%

Endowment: 8.7%

Private gifts: 14.2%

Federal grants/ contracts: 20.8%

Tuition/fees: 45.4%

State/local grants/ contracts: 2.4%

State/local appropriations: 0.4%

Federal appropriations: 0.7%

Private institutions (pie on the left) derive a bigger share of their revenue from tuition and fees (45.4% compared to 24.6%), and a much smaller share from government appropriations (1.1% compared to 41.6%). Only about 5% of students attend the most select private colleges, but their high sticker prices command a lot of media attention. One explanation for why private schools can charge such high prices was offered by the *Philadelphia Inquirer*: "An attitude, prevalent among the wealthy — which holds that a school charging less than its competitors must not be as good."

When a school's financial circumstances change — as when revenue from grants, contracts, and gifts goes down or the costs go up — tuition increases are the result. Schools are trying to limit tuition increases by broadening their range of revenue sources. Acquiring research dollars from businesses is one way to do this. For example, Carnegie Mellon University and Stanford University get about 40% of their revenue from sponsored research. This path has led to accusations that research institutions are captives of the businesses whose research helps to support them.

In this same vein, concerns have been voiced about the increasing number of institutions that have turned to commercial ventures to help pay off their debts. For example, some colleges now allow corporate sponsors to support their athletic departments in return for displaying company names, logos, and signs. This trend "creates an additional income gap between large and small colleges, reinforces the entertainment culture that now pervades college sports, and leaves schools dependent on a highly volatile source of income," complains the *Philadelphia Inquirer*.

10 Largest Private Gifts to Higher Education Institutions Since 1967

Recipient Institution	Gift
California Institute of Technology	$600 million
Stanford University	$400 million
Rensselaer Polytechnic Institute	$360 million
Massachusetts Institute of Technology	$350 million
Vanderbilt University	$300 million
Emory University	$295 million
New York University	$250-$500 million (art, real estate)
University of Colorado System	$250 million
Franklin W. Olin College of Engineering	$200 million+

As shown on the charts and in the table, private institutions are much more dependent than public institutions on gifts and donations. All but one of the institutions listed (University of Colorado) are private. Private gifts and endowments accounted for 23% of 1996 revenue for the private sector, compared to only 9% for public universities. *The Chronicle of Higher Education* recently reported that philanthropic organizations are shifting their focus away from higher education because of a perception that colleges aren't "needy." This doesn't bode well for keeping tuition costs down.

In the 1990s, with the stock market at record highs, a growing number of colleges began investing their endowments, hoping that the higher yields would hold down soaring tuition costs. Then came the downturn. By January 2002 the average rate of return on college endowment investments dropped to minus 3% in the first year of declines since 1984. The bigger the endowment, the harder the fall. Then, of course, came the talk of big tuition hikes.

Source: Chart: National Center for Education Statistics. *The Condition of Education 1999*, Table 39-1. Table: "Largest Private Gifts to Higher Education Since 1967." *Chronicle of Higher Education Almanac*. Online. Available: http://chronicle.com/stats/big_gifts.htm. March 13, 2002. Gaul, Gilbert M., and Frank Fitzpatrick. "The Price of Winning: The Business of College Sports — What Was...." *Philadelphia Inquirer*. 14 September 2001, p. A1. Hartigan, Rachel, and Ben Wildavsky. "A School's Free-Lunch Program." *U.S. News & World Report*, 12 February 2001, p. 50. Zhao, Zilu. "As Endowments Slip at Colleges, Big Tuition Increases Fill the Void." *New York Times*. 22 February 2002, p1A. Pulley, John L. "For Investment Managers, Boom Years Are Over." *Chronicle of Higher Education*. 25 January 2002. Online. Available: http://chronicle.com. March 13, 2002. Marklein, Mary Beth. "College Endowments Follow Steep Downward Curve." *USA Today*, 14 January 2002, p. 5D. "Crumbling Support." *Chronicle of Higher Education*. Online. Available: http://chronicle.com. March 25, 2002.

Higher Education: Where Does the Money Go?

**Per-Student Educational and General Expenditures (Constant 1995-96 Dollars)
by Type of Higher Education Institution: 1980-1995**

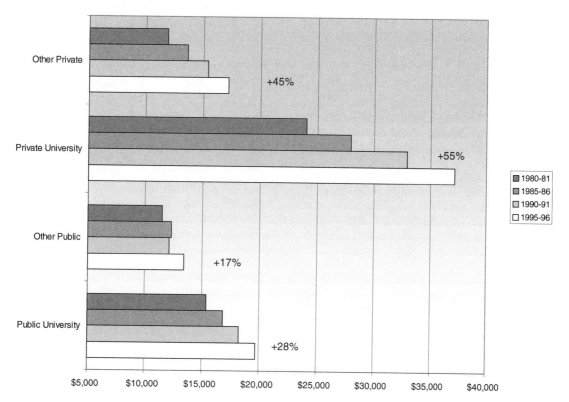

We have seen that higher education is costly for students. Providing that education is costly for colleges. Educators are quick to point out that tuition does not cover anywhere near the actual cost of educating a student.

The chart above bears out that contention. We saw in the first panel of this chapter that average tuition at a public institution in 1995-96 was about $2,000, yet we see from the chart that it cost the public university nearly $20,000 to educate a student that year. Tuition at a private university in 1995-96 was about $12,000, yet it cost the university $37,200 to educate the student.

Between 1980 and 1995, college expenditures per student rose at all types of institutions at rates ranging from 17% to 55%, while state appropriations declined. These increases are related to increases in instructional, administrative, and research costs; scholarships and fellowships; student services; and plant operations and maintenance. At hearings before the Senate Governmental Affairs Committee in February 2000, educators cited the cost of complying with government regulations, recruiting faculty, and building facilities as other factors in driving up college expenditures.

Education is labor-intensive. The "better" the college, i.e., the more its faculty is paid, the more prestigious its research facilities, the more generous the financial aid it offers to at-

Average Annual Percent Increase Previous 5 Years in Per Student Educational and General Expenditures: 1980-1995

Year	Public Sector		Private Sector	
	University	Other 4-Year	University	Other 4-Year
1995-96	1.6	2.2	2.6	2.3
1990-91	1.6	0.3	3.5	2.7
1985-86	1.9	1.4	3.3	2.9
1980-81	0.4	1.0	1.1	0.7

tract the "best" students, the finer its library and computing capabilities, and so on, the more the college spends. Yet, as the table shows, average annual increases in spending by colleges[5] have been relatively modest.

D. Bruce Johnstone wrote about these data: "Although the data are limited, [they do] not seem to support the notion of 'out of control' instructional costs," as critics of the spending policies of higher education institutions often claim. Johnstone opined: "Faculty and administrators of many colleges and universities feel as though they have been living amid almost perpetual financial challenges, constantly cutting, reallocating, downsizing, outsourcing, and chasing new revenues."

In 1997 the public outcry over the rising cost of college led Congress to appoint a National Commission on the cost of Higher Education to find out what could be done to rein in tuition costs. The Commission was unable to explain why the cost of college has risen so fast. The Commission's extensive report complained of the "veil of obscurity" that many institutions have allowed to settle over their financial operations and warned: "If colleges and universities do not take steps to reduce their costs, policymakers at the Federal and state levels will intervene and take up the task for them."

Some states have frozen tuitions. Others are contemplating tuition caps. But analysts say that these are temporary solutions and that higher education financing must be restructured so that it does not rely so heavily on tuition.

In the next panel we look at enrollment trends to find out who our new professionals are.

Source: Chart and Table: U.S. Department of Education. National Center for Education Statistics. *Study of College Costs and Prices, 1988–89 to 1997–98, Volume 2: Commissioned Papers,* NCES 2002–158, by Alisa F. Cunningham, Jane V. Wellman, Melissa E. Clinedinst, and Jamie P. Merisotis. Project Officer: C. Dennis Carroll. Washington, DC: 2001; primary source: NCES, 1999, *Condition of Education 1999,* Washington, DC: U.S. Government Printing Office, Supplemental Table 40-2; retrieved 3/12/02 from http://nces.ed.gov. "Straight Talk About College Costs and Prices: Report of the National Commission on the Cost of Higher Education," January 21, 1998; retrieved 3/21/02 from http://www.acenet.edu/. Tony Pugh, "No Answers on Why College Costs Are Increasing So Fast..." *Philadelphia Inquirer,* Feb. 11, 2000.

---

[5] Instructional, administrative, and research costs; scholarships and fellowships; student services; and plant operations and maintenance.

Trends in Conferred Degrees: Gender

Degrees Conferred by Sex of Student: 1970-1997 and Projections 1998-2011

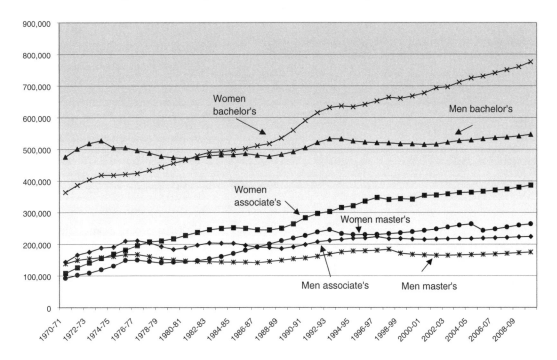

Two remarkable trends evolved during the 20th century. More and more Americans completed college, and starting in the last third of the century, a larger percentage of completers was female. A record 29% of all Americans aged 25 and older held at least a bachelor's degree in 2000 (28% of males, 24% of females), compared to just 5% in 1940 and 21% in 1990. Among people aged 25 to 29, more women (30%) than men (28%) had completed a bachelor's degree or higher.

The graphic shows trends and projections in degree awards. The number of degrees granted at all levels rose steadily in spite of a decline in the traditional college-age population of 18- to 24-year-olds in the 1980s and 1990s. The increase in degree earners was largely due to growing enrollments of women and older people. However, it is projected that from 1999 to 2010, enrollment of people under 25 will rise 24% while it will increase only 9% for older people. The number of students earning degrees is expected to rise between 2001-02 and 2010-11. The number of bachelor's degrees should reach a peak of 1.3 million in 2010-11, reflecting an increase of 13% compared to 2001-02.

In 1970, women earned 25% to 30% fewer degrees than men. By the 1980s women had reached parity with men at all three degree levels. Women's share kept rising. It is projected that women will continue to outperform men. Gains will be especially pronounced among older women. Women are now such a presence on campuses that colleges must compete for the best-qualified men. The drop in the number of men applying to college is attributed to boys doing less well academically in high school and to their higher high school dropout rates.

It now takes an average of five years to get a college degree, and it takes men longer than women to complete. A 1996 UCLA study showed that only 36.8% of men earned their degree in four years, compared to 43.2% of women. After nine years, the numbers increased to 43% of men and 48.6% of women.

Top 10 Fields of Study for 1996-1997 Bachelor's Degree Recipients and Percentage of Male/Female Recipients

Field of study	Total	Men	Women
Business management/Admin. Services	221,875	51.6	48.4
Social sciences/History	124,891	51.3	48.7
Education	105,233	25.0	75.0
Health professions/Related sciences	85,631	18.5	81.5
Psychology	74,191	26.1	73.9
Biological sciences/Life sciences	63,975	46.1	53.9
Engineering	61,185	81.8	18.2
Visual & performing arts	50,083	41.4	58.6
English language & literature/letters	49,345	33.5	66.5
Communications	47,230	41.1	58.9

This table shows the top ten fields of study in 1996-97 at the bachelor's level and the percentages of men and women graduates. Business tops the list. Notice that women dominate in less lucrative fields where they have always been overrepresented notably the education and health professions. In the year 2000, women earned less than men at every degree level.

Enrollment in computer science and engineering declined in the late 1980s to mid-1990s (master's enrollment was up). Women have shown little interest in engineering and IT — due, perhaps, to societal bias: there are many female engineers in Russia and Europe. Women earned 21% of engineering bachelor's degrees awarded in 1995, up from practically zero in 1971. Women's share of bachelor's degrees in computer/information sciences grew from 14% in 1971 to 27% in 1997.

The number of bachelor's degrees awarded grew 31% from 1972 to 1997. The most remarkable upward trend has been in technical fields other than computer science and engineering. Why? Increasing numbers of women concentrated in those other technical areas. Biological and physical science degrees rose about 40% between 1992 and 1998.

The most popular fields at the master's level are education and business. The fields showing the greatest gain between 1983 and 1995 were park, recreation, leisure, and fitness studies (up 189%); engineering (117%); and engineering technologies (108%).

Many future jobs will not require a college degree. *Futurist*, the magazine of the World Future Society, complains: "We are educating people for the wrong futures." (See *Work & Leisure*, Chapter 3, for more on this counter-intuitive finding.)

Source: Chart: National Center for Education Statistics. Earned Degrees Conferred; Projections of Education Statistics to 2010; Higher Education General Information Survey (HEGIS), "Degrees and Other Formal Awards Conferred" surveys; and Integrated Postsecondary Education Data System (IPEDS), "Completions" survey. Table: Morgan, Frank B. "Degrees and Other Awards Conferred by Title IV Eligible, Degree-Granting Institutions: 1996-97." *Education Statistics Quarterly* (Spring 2000). Online. Available: http://nces.ed.gov. March 15, 2002. Clayton, Mark. "Engineering 100: No Men Allowed." *Christian Science Monitor*. 4 January 2000, p.14. "Degree Attainment Rates at Colleges and Universities." Online. Available: http://www.gseis.ucla.edu/heri/press_darcu.htm. March 20, 2002. Clayton, Mark. "The Gender Equation — Part 2." *Christian Science Monitor*, 29 May 2001, p. 17. Gordon, Edward E. "Help Wanted: Creating Tomorrow's Work Force." *Futurist* (July/August 2000), p. 48.

Trends in Conferred First-Professional/ Doctoral Degrees: Gender

First-Professional and Doctor's Degrees Conferred by Sex of Student: 1977-97 and Projections to 2010

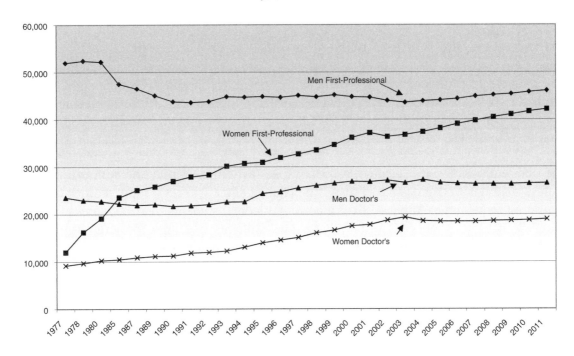

In 1999, slightly more than 1% of Americans held a professional degree and 1% held a doctor's degree. Between 1977 and 1998, the number of first-professional degrees and doctor's degrees awarded grew 22% and 29% respectively. Women's share went from 23% and 28% to 44% and 38%. The number of first-professional degrees awarded to men fell 13.9%; the number of doctor's degrees rose 11%.

Unlike the pattern we saw with the lower degrees, women have not reached parity with men in the higher degrees. This may be due to their facing choices about marriage and children or to the fact that women have only recently increased their high school study of math and science, which will allow them to enter professions previously closed to them. Women's share of higher degrees is projected to increase; they will receive 48% of first-professional degrees and 44% of doctor's degrees by 2010.

Doctor's Degrees Awarded, Percentages, by Sex: 1996-97

Field	Men	Women
Education	36.7	63.3
Engineering	87.6	12.4
Humanities	51.9	48.1
Life sciences	55.0	45.0
Physical sciences	77.9	22.1
Mathematics	76.5	23.5
Business & management.	69.4	30.6
Social sciences & psychology	47.3	52.7

The most popular fields at the doctor's degree level are education, engineering, biological and life sciences, and physical sciences. In this table, we see that, as with bachelor's degree recipients, women dominate in education but lag behind in lucrative fields like engineering, mathematics, and business and management.

Between 1983 and 1995, the doctor's degree fields showing the most growth were business (up 80%), engineering, (117%), health professions (79%), and mathematics (68%). There was a decline (1%) in education degrees. The first-professional fields showing the greatest gains were pharmacy (up 221%), and osteopathic medicine (41%). Dentistry and theology declined.

The table below shows that more first-professional degrees are awarded in law than any other field. Law has always been a high-status job, lawyer jokes notwithstanding. Each year over the last four decades, the percentage of women entering America's law schools climbed by a point or two, from only 4.2% in 1963 to 48.7% in 1999. The profession is lucrative. The median starting salary for full-time attorney jobs rose from $45,000 for the class of 1998 to $50,000 for the class of 1999.

The job outlook for the health professions is favorable. While the number of first-professional health degrees has shown little change since 1982-83, more women are concentrating in this area. About 43% of incoming medical students in 2000 were female, up from 9% in 1970. About 60% of female medical students specialize in more nurturing but less lucrative fields like family practice, psychiatry, and pediatrics.

With regard to other health professions, pharmacy experienced the largest increase in degrees awarded, and women receive more than twice as many pharmacy degrees as men. The Bureau of Labor Statistics reports that half of all pharmacists made between $52,310 and $80,250 a year in 1998. Similarly, more than twice as many women as men choose veterinary medicine. Women were 43% percent of practicing veterinarians in 1999, up from just 2% in 1989. Median annual earnings of veterinarians were $60,910 in 2000.

Number of First-Professional Degrees: 1995-96

Field	Men	Women
Dentistry	1,701	1,397
Medicine	6,741	6,450
Optometry	482	673
Osteopathic medicine	1,091	714
Pharmacy	709	1,747
Podiatry	339	191
Veterinary medicine	657	1,457
Chiropractic medicine	2,165	996
Law	18,445	17,531
Theology	3,394	1,536
Other	25	56

Increasing numbers of women in theology is a phenomenon that began with the call for the ordination of women in the 1970's. The Web site www.religioustolerance.org tells us that the percentage of female graduate students at 229 North American Christian schools of theology rose from 10% in 1972 to 30% in 1997. In some schools of theology, more than 50% of the students are women. Pay is probably not a motivator for people who choose to study theology.

Source: Chart: U.S. Department of Education, NCES, Higher Education General Information Survey (HEGIS), "Degrees and Other Formal Awards Conferred" surveys, and Integrated Postsecondary Education Data System (IPEDS), "Completions" surveys. Table 2: Digest of Education Statistics 2000; primary source: National Academy of Sciences, National Research Council, Office of Scientific and Engineering Personnel, Summary Report 1997: Doctorate Recipients from United States Universities. Salary figures for attorneys retrieved 3/26/02 from http://www.nalp.org/press/jjd99.htm. Jane Easter Bahls, "The New Majority," *Student Lawyer*, Sept. 2000, p. 20-24. Julie Marquis, "A Huge Dose of Change," *Los Angeles Times*, March 10, 2000, p. A1+. Jonathan W. Kelinson, "Trends in College Degrees," U.S. Department of Labor, Bureau of Labor Statistics, Fall 1998, retrieved 3/26/02 from http://www.pueblo.gsa. gov.

College Trends:
Race/Ethnicity and Residency

Bachelor's Degrees Conferred by Race/Ethnicity and Residency: 1977-1996

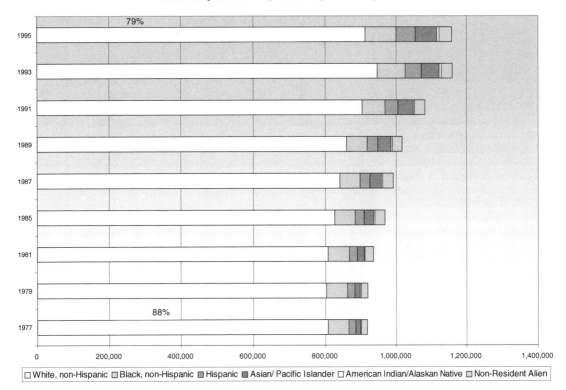

American campuses are becoming more diverse. In 1976, 16% of college students were members of a minority group; by 1996 the figure was 27%. The increase is due to increasing enrollments of Hispanic and Asian/Pacific Islander students. Minorities (including non-resident aliens) made up 12% of bachelor's degree recipients in 1977; they earned 21% of bachelor's degrees awarded in 1995.

In 1999, 17.5% of the African-American population aged 25 to 29 held a bachelor's degree or higher. The figure for Asians/Pacific Islanders was 54%. The figure for American Indians was 9.4%.[6] The figure for Hispanics was 10%. Even though it is projected that the percentage of Hispanics aged 25 to 29 with a bachelor's degree will increase to 12% by 2010, the educational gap between Hispanics and other groups is a cause for concern because they are the fastest growing minority group. Studies show that in the late 1990's, half of Hispanics living in the United States were born and educated in their native countries, had low levels of education there, and never enrolled in American schools. American-born children of Hispanic immigrants tend to drop out of high school at very high rates (29% compared to 7% for non-Hispanic whites in 1996).

---

[6] Based on the 1990 census, the most recent data available. Educational attainment data for Alaska Natives are not available.

The table below provides 1997-98 degree data by racial ethnic group. Minorities received their highest proportion of degrees at the associate's level (22.4%), and their individual shares dropped at each successive level, except for Asians/Pacific Islanders. The preferred field of study at the associate's level was the same for every group: liberal arts and sciences, a field that usually permits a transfer to a four-year institution.

**Percentage Distribution of Degrees Conferred
by Racial Ethnic Group: 1997-98**

Degree Level	White, non-Hispanic	Black, non-Hispanic	Hispanic	Asian or Pacific Islander	American Indian/ Alaskan Native
Associate	76.7	10.0	7.7	4.5	1.1
Bachelor's	79.5	8.3	5.5	6.0	0.7
Master's	82.6	7.7	4.1	8.0	0.5

In the 1990s, the most striking dissimilarities between whites and minority groups at both the bachelor's and master's degree levels were (1) black students were more likely to earn degrees in business management; (2) Hispanic students were more likely to earn bachelor's degrees in humanities and master's degrees in social and behavioral sciences; (3) Asians/Pacific Islanders were more likely to earn degrees in life sciences, computer and information sciences, and engineering; (4) American Indians/Alaskan Natives were more likely to earn bachelor's degrees in education and engineering technologies and master's degrees in social and behavioral sciences; and (5) non-resident aliens were far more likely to earn bachelor's degrees in computer sciences and engineering.

On the topic of non-resident aliens, the Institute of International Education reported a record 547,867 foreign students enrolled at American colleges and universities in 2001, a 6.4% increase over the previous year and the biggest increase since 1980. Where do they come from? In the 1960s Canada was the leader, sending nearly 20% of all international students to the United States. In the late 1970s Iran and Nigeria were the leading countries. In the mid-1980s Taiwan, Malaysia, and Korea were the leading places of origin. In the 1990s the majority of students came from China and India. Coming up next? Most likely, Latin America. Once here, many immigrants decide to stay, offering America "access to the world's best and brightest talent," according to the INS.

Source: Chart: U.S. Department of Education, NCES, Higher Education General Information Survey (HEGIS), "Degrees and Other Formal Awards Conferred" surveys, and Integrated Postsecondary Education Data System (IPEDS), "Completions" surveys. Table: "Percentage Distribution of Degrees Conferred, by Racial Ethnic Group: 1997-98," NCES Fast Facts, retrieved 3/27/02 from http:// nces.ed.gov; primary source, *Digest of Education Statistics*, 2000, Tables 263, 265, 268, 271, and 274. U.S. Census Bureau, "Percent of High School and College Graduates of the Population 15 Years and Over, by Age, Sex, Race, and Hispanic Origin: March 2000," and "Selected Social and Economic Characteristics for the 25 Largest American Indian Tribes: 1990, retrieved 3/27/02 from http:// www.census.gov/population. Table: "Georges Vernez and Lee Mizell, "Goal: To Double the Rate of Hispanics Earning a Bachelor's Degree," retrieved 3/27/02 from http://www.rand.org/publications. Institute of International Education data retrieved 3/27/02 from http://www.opendoorsweb.org/.

Trends in Conferred Doctor's/First-Professional Degrees: Race/Ethnicity and Residency

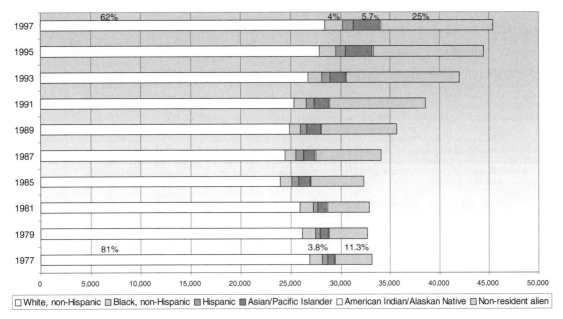

Doctor's Degrees by Race/Ethnicity and Residency: 1977-1998

☐ White, non-Hispanic ☐ Black, non-Hispanic ☐ Hispanic ■ Asian/Pacific Islander ☐ American Indian/Alaskan Native ☐ Non-resident alien

The chart shows the numbers of doctor's degrees earned from 1977 to 1997. The most striking trends are the decline in the percentage share for non-Hispanic whites and the dramatic increase (202%) in the share earned by non-resident aliens. Little progress has been made in narrowing the educational gap at the highest degree levels between whites and minorities other than Asians/Pacific Islanders.

Foreign students comprise fewer than 4% of all students in American higher education but are 33% of doctoral students. They earned 25% of doctor's degrees awarded in 1997. Their specialties were biological sciences/life sciences (28% of degrees awarded), engineering (48%), and physical sciences/science technologies (35%). Fewer American students are concentrating in these areas, and the American scientific community is increasingly dominated by foreign-born scientists who are either educated here and stay or who immigrate.

Another notable trend in the awarding of doctor's degrees is the fact that African-Americans continue to lag behind whites and other minority groups in mathematics. The American Mathematical Society reports that the number of mathematics doctoral degrees that have gone to blacks since 1980 has rarely exceeded 10 each year, and only 15 (1.3%) of 1,119 awarded in 2000 went to blacks (who are 12.9% of the population).[7] In contrast, Asians/Pacific Islanders, who make up 3.8% of the population, received 16.7% of mathematics doctorates.

---

[7] Reported in the *Christian Science Monitor;* see source notes.

The table below shows the number of first-professional degrees conferred by racial/ethnic group, and field of study, in the 1996-97 year. One-fifth of the degrees went to minorities. Notice that Asians/Pacific Islanders earned 15% of medical degrees while blacks earned 7%. Fifty-eight percent of American Indians/Alaskan Native degrees were in law, compared to 51% for the general population.

Perhaps you've noticed that you are being seen by more foreign-born doctors lately. More than half of non-resident aliens in the class of 1997 chose a medical specialty, and many decided to remain in the United States. Nineteen percent of foreign students devoted themselves to the study of theology.

First-Professional Degrees Conferred by
Racial/ethnic Group and Major Field of Study: 1996-97

Field	Total	White, non-Hispanic	Black, non-Hispanic	Hispanic	Asian/ Pacific Islander	American Indian/ Alaskan Native	Non-resident alien
All fields	77,815	59,852	5,251	3,553	7,037	511	1,611
Dentistry	3,784	2,498	190	185	659	19	233
Medicine	15,571	11,095	1,123	703	2,377	111	162
Optometry	1,264	929	31	41	198	5	60
Osteopathic	2,011	1,676	72	50	181	17	15
Pharmacy	2,708	1,829	265	58	466	12	78
Podiatry	614	473	27	24	65	3	22
Veterinary	2,188	1,988	54	71	45	14	16
Chiropractic	3,654	2,986	62	90	196	18	302
Law	40,079	31,672	2,951	2,211	2,534	298	413
Theology	5,859	4,632	472	120	311	14	310

America's most educated individuals are a more diverse lot than they were in 1977. The first-professional class of 1997 was 77% white, 42% female, 6.7% black, 4.6% Hispanic, 9% Asian/Pacific Islander, 0.6% American Indian/Alaskan Native, and 2% foreign-born. They preferred by far the lucrative specialties of medicine and law, with theology a distant runner-up.

Source: Chart: "Doctor's degrees conferred by institutions of higher education, by racial/ethnic group and sex of student: 1976-77 to 1996-97," primary source, U.S. Department of Education, NCES, Higher Education General Information Survey (HEGIS), "Degrees and Other Formal Awards Conferred" surveys, and Integrated Postsecondary Education Data System (IPEDS), "Completions" surveys; retrieved 3/27/02 from http://nces.ed.gov/pubs2000. Table: U.S. Department of Education, National Center for Education Statistics, Integrated Postsecondary Education Data. "Racial disparities especially acute in math PhD programs," *The Christian Science Monitor,* April 2, 2001, p. 20.

Distance Education: Get a Degree From the Comfort of Home

Enrollment in College-Level Distance Education Courses by Type of Institution and Number of Students Enrolled in Institution: 1995 and 1997

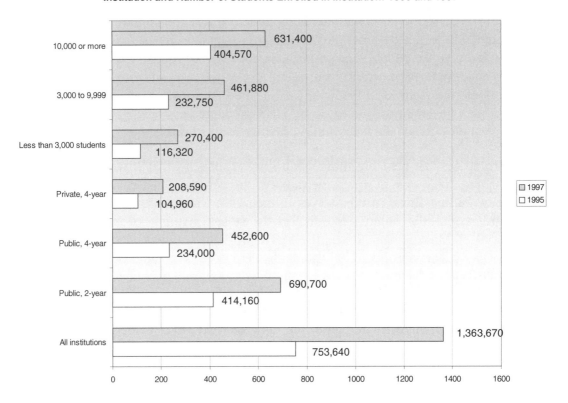

One-third of higher education institutions offered distance education courses in 1994; in 1997 it was 44%. As shown on the graphic, there were an estimated 753,640 students enrolled in distance education in 1995; by 1997, the number had grown to 1.3 million, an increase in just two years of 81%. According to Market Data Retrieval (MDR), in 2002, 84% of colleges surveyed offered distance learning programs, up from 70% a year earlier. Public institutions are more likely to offer these courses, and public four-year institutions are the most likely to offer degrees that can be earned entirely from a distance.

Distance education is nothing new — St. Paul gave lessons by way of epistles (letters). Distance learning took off in the 19th century with the development of the postal service. The 1914 Cooperative Agricultural Extension Act gave a boost to college education by correspondence. The intent was to diffuse "useful and practical information on subjects relating to agriculture, home economics, and rural energy." Correspondence courses opened college doors for many who would not otherwise have been able to attend, especially country dwellers. In modern times, Ben and Jerry learned how to make ice cream through a Penn State correspondence course.

California defines modern distance education as "the non-traditional form of education in which the teacher and student are not located in the same physical space and each is expected to interact through the assistance of technology." The student might be in a dorm room or studio on campus or somewhere on the other side of the world. The technology has evolved from print to include television (telecourses), interactive video and prerecorded video, computers ("e-learning") and beyond (digital services from cable, satellite and wireless companies, interactive TV services, HDTV).

Recent widespread access to modern technology led to an explosion of interest in online college courses followed by an explosion of online diploma mills and other scams.[8] In 1999 the *Chronicle of Higher Education* declared: "For an industry that barely existed three years ago, the level of activity is dizzying."[9] Online, you can learn how to become a psychic, a doctor of vibrational medicine, or a United Nations peacekeeper. Even as you read this, it may become possible to earn a Harvard degree entirely from a distance. But preliminary studies do not show any tuition savings for distance learners. Darn.

Will e-learning be "the next big thing," fulfilling prophecies that it will grow 80% between 2002 and 2007, or will it join the ranks of the dot.coms? There are signs that colleges may be getting ahead of themselves in their rush to offer distance learning. MDR reports some spectacular failures, like that of the State University of New York at Buffalo's School of Management. Its online MBA program was forced to close its doors when only 35 students enrolled; 1,000 students were expected. Little is known about the quality of the online education experience, but the dropout rate may be as high as 50%.

The U.S. Army is so confident that online learning programs will help them recruit and retain soldiers, it has invested $550 million over six years to develop Army University Access On-Line. Distance education also shows promise in helping professionals keep up-to-date on developments in their fields. But the most promising application of this on-demand education may be the same as it ever was: Making it easy for more students to take courses, including those who live far from campuses, the physically handicapped, the homebound, and working students.

Critics of distance education argue that online learning could lead to a system in which rich students earn prestigious degrees on campus while the less fortunate get online degrees — a twist on the digital divide we encountered in an earlier panel. Even as they're pressured to modernize, teachers (and students too) express nostalgia for the old-fashioned and arguably more educational give and take of the traditional classroom.

Source: Chart: NCES, *Distance Education at Postsecondary Education Institutions*, December 1999, NCES 2000-013; NCES, Postsecondary Education Quick Information System, *Distance Education in Higher Education Institutions*, 1997. "MDR: Brick and Mortar Campuses Embracing Distance Learning," *Educational Marketer*, March 18, 2002, v33 i9. California State-Sacramento Distance and Distributed Education FAQ Web Site, http://www.csus.edu/distance/faq.htm, retrieved April 9, 2002. Richard T. Cooper, "Soldier by Day, Online Student by Night," *Los Angeles Times*, July 10, 2000, p. A1+. Eyal Press and Jennifer Washburn, "Digital Diplomas," Mother Jones, January/February 2001, retrieved April 9, 2002, http://www.motherjones.com.

---

[8] The government is looking at ways to extend federal aid to students for distance education. Restrictions on aid were put in place in response to abuses relating to program quality. See http://www.ed.gov/offices/OPE/PPI/DistEd/ (April 9, 2002).

[9] Quoted in NCES, *Distance Education*... See source notes.

There Are No Average Students Here: The Quality of a Higher Education Degree

Percentage of Harvard Students Graduating with Honors: 1946-2001

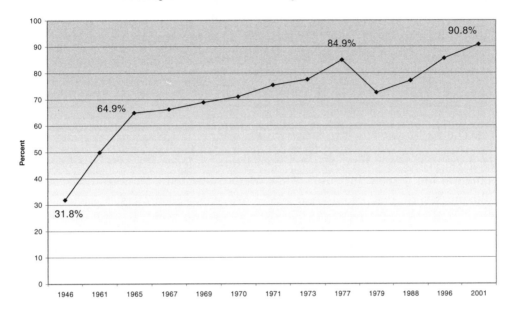

"To be an honors student is to create your own intellectual work in a thesis or a science lab — to have had a transformative experience." — Jamshed Bharucha, dean of the faculty at Dartmouth, where 40% of students graduated with honors in the spring of 2001. Bharucha was speaking to a reporter for *The Boston Globe* for a two-part story on decades of grade inflation at Harvard. The graph shows data compiled by the *Globe* staff for the story. If Bharucha's definition is correct, the percentage of Harvard graduates who had a "transformative experience" rose from 31.8% in 1946 to 90.8% in 2001.

In a follow-up story, the *Globe* reported that 48.5% of Harvard grades in 2000 were A's and A-minuses, compared to 33.2% in 1985. C grades fell from 10% in 1985 to 4.9%. This remarkable academic achievement happened the same year the College Board announced that between 1991 and 2000, the percentage of SAT test takers with high school grade averages in the A range soared from 28% to 41%. Are we getting smarter? Not according to standardized test scores. The College Board reports that SAT scores have declined since the 1960s. ACT scores were flat through the 1990s (see Chapter 7), and Koretz et al. reported no increase in achievement on the Graduate Record Exam.

By way of contrast, the table on the next page shows percentages of seniors graduating with honors from selected schools (data compiled by *The Boston Globe*). MIT does not award graduating honors on the theory that a diploma is distinction enough.

It seems that grade inflation is rampant. Grade inflation is defined by the American Academy of Arts and Sciences as "an upward shift in the grade point average (GPA) of students over an extended period of time without a corresponding increase in student achievement." The Academy's report on colleges, *Evaluation and the Academy: Are We*

Doing the Right Thing?, released in 2002, stated: "Most investigators agree that grade inflation began in the 1960s and continued through, at least, the mid-1990s." The report added that grade inflation is especially noticeable in Ivy League Schools.

Institution	Honors grads
Yale	51
Princeton	44
Brown	42
Columbia[1]	25
Cornell	8
Tufts	52
Boston U	39
Johns Hopkins	35
Boston College	29
Duke	28
MIT	0
Stanford	20

The most frequently advanced explanation for grade inflation is that sympathetic faculty inflated grades to keep failing students from being drafted for service in the Vietnam War. A more controversial explanation links grade inflation to the introduction of affirmative action. Also offered as explanations are the self-esteem movement and academics' preference for concentrating on research over teaching and their willingness to trade good grades for favorable reviews from students. Another, perhaps more cynical explanation links grade inflation to the view of students as consumers and colleges as big businesses. Students with good grades are happy customers.

Once the practice began, there seemed to be no stopping it. In 1977 Harvard toughened its rules for honors awards and, as the chart shows, the numbers declined for a while.

Reports about widespread grade inflation came as no surprise to educators, but the news about Harvard was greeted with derision in the halls of academe. Harvard accepts only the cream of the crop from the world's high schools. Should we assume that all but 9% of Harvard's students do equally superior work?

What are the ramifications of grade inflation in the outside world? There is one less way to distinguish between competence and incompetence. Employers have already turned to personal references as a better judge of ability, leading some to fear a return to the "old-boy old-girl" network (assuming we ever left it behind). The *Dallas Morning News* said bluntly: "The parents of graduating high school seniors … who are preparing to pay the freight on a $30,000-a-year Harvard education have a right to know whether the commodity is worth the asking price." As to Harvard, for the first time, it recently asked its professors to justify the grades they award students.

Sources: Chart: Patrick Healy, "Matters of Honor: Harvard's quiet secret: rampant grade inflation," *The Boston Globe*, October 7, 2001, Patrick Healy, "Harvard figures show most of its grades are A's or B's," The Boston Globe, November 21, 2001. Both stories retrieved May 9, 2002, from http://www.boston.com/globe/metro/packages/harvard_honors/. Henry Rosovsky and Matthew Hartley, *Evaluation and the Academy: Are We Doing the Right Thing? Grade Inflation and Letters of Recommendation,* Academy of Arts & Sciences, 2002, retrieved May 8, 2002, www.amacad.org/publications/occasional.htm. Daniel M. Koretz and Mark Berends, "Changes in High School Grading Standards in Mathematics, 1982-1992," RAND Education, retrieved May 13, 2002, from http://www. rand.org/publications/. "Academic politics: Harvard shouldn't duck grade inflation," *Dallas Morning News*, January 10, 2002.

Was It Worth It? The Value of a College Degree

Mean Earnings of Workers 18 Years Old and Over, by Educational Attainment: 1975 to 1999

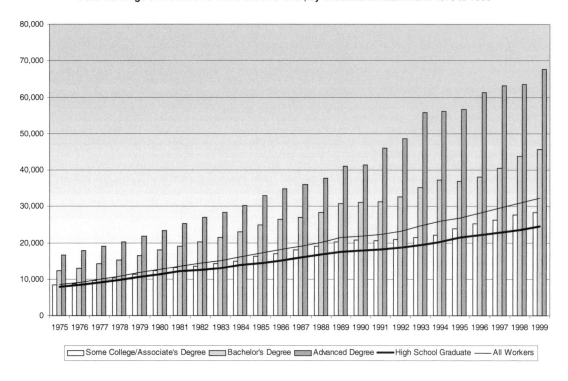

It's plain to see that earnings are higher at higher education levels. According to The College Board, the lifetime premium of a bachelor's degree over a high school diploma is $1 million. The steepest rise in earnings between 1975 and 1999 was for holders of advanced degrees. The General Social Survey, a measure of overall job satisfaction, finds that higher income workers (over $40K) are happier in their work than lower income workers (under $40K).

The table below shows dollar figures and percent change at the beginning and the end of the charted period and presents data by sex. *Inflation rose 204% during this period.* The more educated a person was, the better able he or she was to keep up with inflation.

Mean Annual Earnings by Educational Attainment and Sex: 1975 and 1999

Year/% change	Total	Non-h.s. grad	H.s. grad	Some college/ Assoc. deg	Bachelor degree	Advanced degree
Total Both Sexes						
1975	8,552	6,198	7,843	8,388	12,332	16,725
1999	32,536	16,121	24,572	28,403	45,678	67,697
% change	280%	160%	213%	237%	270%	305%
Male						
1975	11,091	7,843	10,475	10,805	15,758	19,672
1999	40,257	18,855	30,414	35,326	57,706	84,051
% change	263%	140%	181%	226%	266%	327%
Female						
1975	4,968	3,438	4,802	5,019	6,963	9,818
1999	23,551	12,145	18,092	21,644	32,546	46,307
% change	374%	253%	277%	331%	367%	372%

While the contrast in earnings between college graduates and those at other education levels is dramatic for both sexes, the biggest gain in earnings was for women. Since college-educated women were making less than 50% of what college-educated men were making in 1975, they had nowhere to go but up. They are not equal yet. The average annual 1998 income for a man with a bachelor's degree was $51,405; for a woman it was $36,559.

Occupational Groups with Highest Mean Hourly Wages, 2000

Field	Wage
Legal	33.14
Management	32.78
Computer/mathematical	27.91
Architecture/engineering	25.99
Business/finance	23.30

Who earns the top dollars? People in the legal professions earned about four times more than the lowest-paid service workers in 2000. According to the BLS, all but two of the 50 highest paying occupations require a college degree. (The exceptions are air traffic controllers and nuclear power reactor operators. Their median salary in 2000: $82,520 and $57,220 respectively.) The table shows mean hourly wages in 2000 for some of the highest-paid professionals. It seems we will need more teachers to accommodate the students entering college. According to the American Federation of Teachers, the average teacher salary in 1999-2000 was $41,820 (about $29 an hour for a nine-month, 40-hour-week schedule).

The gap between the earnings of higher and lower paid workers has been rising for decades, although the good economic times of the 1990s did see a sharp rise in income for those in the bottom 20% of the earnings scale. Earnings inequality receives a lot of media attention — we've seen the headlines trumpeting the news that CEOs make 500 times more in salary than average workers.

Numerous theories have been advanced to try to explain the gap — education and urbanization mean higher pay, the quality of jobs is changing as we move away from a goods-producing economy, it has something to do with women entering the labor force, it has everything to do with the computer age and the digital divide. George Bernard Shaw said: "If all economists were laid end to end, they would not reach a conclusion" — and they haven't. Meanwhile, the media warn that class warfare is inevitable if the trend continues.

Can the trend of high earnings for high skills continue? Economists do not agree on whether the demand for educated workers will rise faster than the supply. Robert Reich says yes. Dan Luria warns that "most of the new jobs being created are relatively low wage jobs in companies that are not investing in their workers, or in their plants" and that these "low-wage, low-investment firms are winning in the marketplace." (See the *Work & Leisure*, Chapters 2 and 3 for a discussion of labor market predictions.)

Sources: U.S. Bureau of the Census. Online. Available: http://www.census.gov. April 12, 2002. Bureau of Labor Statistics. Online. Available. http://www.bls.gov. April 12, 2002. American Federation of Teachers. Online. Available: http:// www.aft.org. April 12, 2002. Ryscavage, Paul. "A surge in growing income inequality?" *Monthly Labor Review*. August 1995. Online. Available: http://www.bls.gov. April 12, 2002. Reich, Robert B. "How Selective Colleges Heighten Inequality." Luria, Dan. "But Where Are the Jobs?" American Prospect. Online. Available: http://www.prospect.org. April 12, 2002. "Frontline: Does America Still Work?" Online. Available: http://www.pbs.org/wgbh/pages/frontline/america/americandream.html. April 12, 2002.

Chapter 13

Special Needs, Gifts, and Issues

In this final chapter, we take a look at students with special needs and gifts and some issues in education — single-sex education, parental involvement, and the commercialization of the classroom.

The first two panels deal with special education. There are some 6 million children in our schools who require special attention. A portion of these children are retarded, have hearing or other impairments, speech defects, or developmental disorders. Such children have always been with us. But a growing number are simply "learning disabled" or suffer from "emotional disturbances." Over the last quarter century, special education has become both "federalized" and "medicalized." The subject is vast and complicated and we do not do it justice. But we attempt to show some highlights in two panels — and then deal with the popular pharmaceutical solution to hyperactive children, Ritalin. One stands in awe at yet another instance of the pervasive tendency of out times: when a social trauma is encountered, we first nationalize it. Then we turn it into a medical conditions. Finally we prescribe the pill.

While some children suffer from disabilities, others display superior gifts and talents — another kind of challenge. We discuss the current trends in helping (or ignoring) the gifted. A portion of the population sees special education for the talented as "elitist."

In the next panel we present a recent innovation — arising from a popular upswell in California — that may become a national trend: to teach students who speak a foreign language at home English in immersion programs. This phenomenon is part of the reaction to large increases in Spanish-speaking students due to changes in immigration policy. This trend is a counter-current to the pervasive "multicultural" tendency in the society. Next we look at another attempt to improve education: grouping children in same-sex schools and classrooms — where they can concentrate on learning better.

In the last two panels we look at parental involvement in schools — and attempts by corporations to "reach the consumer early" — commercialization of the classroom. Some school systems cooperate with such programs for budgetary gain. But reactions against advertising and products in the school are now emerging.

Special Ed: What's Going On?

Children (0 to 21) in Federally Funded Programs for the Disabled

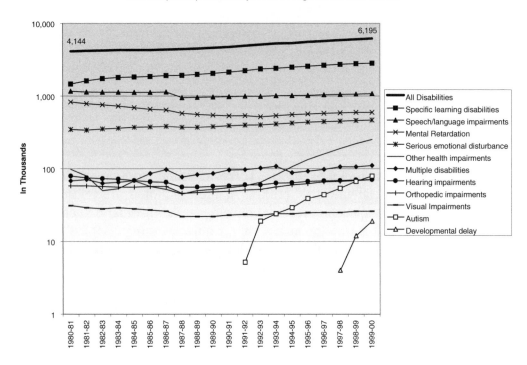

In the 20-year period between 1980 and 2000, children with disabilities increased at a rate more than five times faster than the population of children aged 0 to 19. The graphic shows major types of disabilities (in thousands) while the table shows the growth rates. In gross numbers, 4.1 million children were enrolled in federally-supported special education programs in the 1980-81 school year, 6.2 million in the 1999-00 school year, an increase of nearly 50%, growing at a rate of 2.1% a year. The leading category is "Specific learning disabilities," which grew at a rate 10 times as fast as school age children. We shall devote a special panel to that subject. Here the aim will be to start sorting out this phenomenon and see what's going on. Is something wrong with our children? With our educa-

	Overall Growth Rate - %	Annual Growth Rate - %	Number of Years Measured
Total population of children 0 to 19	9.1	0.4	20
All disabilities of children 0 to 21	49.5	2.1	20
Specific learning disabilities	93.8	3.5	20
Speech or language impairments	-7.5	-0.4	20
Mental retardation	-27.7	-1.7	20
Serious emotional disturbance	35.2	1.6	20
Hearing impairments	-10.1	-0.6	20
Orthopedic impairments	22.4	1.1	20
Other health impairments	158.2	5.1	20
Visual impairments	-16.1	-0.9	20
Multiple disabilities	63.2	2.6	20
Deaf-blindness	-33.3	-2.1	20
Autism and traumatic brain injury	1416.3	40.5	9
Developmental delay	375.0	117.9	3

tional system? Are we better at diagnosing? Or are these results some combination of multiple factors? That's the usual explanation.

Focus on this issue at the national level began with the passage of the All Handicapped Children Act of 1975, since 1990 called the Individuals with Disabilities Education Act (IDEA). The act itself appears to have been a response to satisfy, on the one hand, civil rights advocates fighting to end the segregation and exclusion of children with disabilities and, on the other, parents who argued that children's problems in achieving academic standards were caused by "learning disabilities"; these came to be defined in medical terms requiring special interventions. The federal role was justified using both civil rights and education goals. Since 1975, special education has thus become federalized, with partial federal funding.

	Number of students (000)			Percent of students		
	76-77	80-81	99-00	76-77	80-81	99-00
Specific learning disabilities	796	1,462	2,834	21.6	35.3	45.7
Speech/language impairment	1,302	1,168	1,080	35.3	28.2	17.4
Mental retardation	959	830	600	26.0	20.0	9.7
Serious emotional disturbance	283	347	469	7.7	8.4	7.6

Specific learning disabilities initially ranked third among the top five categories. They reached top rank five years into the act, and commanded nearly 46% of the cases by the 1999-2000 school year, as shown in the table above. This one cluster of disabilities largely accounts for the significant growth in cases in the history of this phenomenon.

What are these specific learning disabilities? There are seven. A child is judged to have normal intelligence but fails to achieve at the expected level in speaking, listening, writing, reading, reading comprehension, mathematical calculation, and mathematical reasoning. The definition thus is very broad. Classifying children as "learning disabled" is therefore relatively subjective. We shall discuss LD in more detail in the next panel.

Notice on the first table, one page back, that growth rates in disabilities that are most subject to direct measurement have had negative or low growth rates — speech impairment, mental retardation, hearing impairments, orthopedic impairments, visual impairments, and deafness/blindness. These seemingly reflect the efficacy of interventions. Disabilities more difficult to measure have grown: specific learning disabilities, emotional disturbance, other health impairments, multiple disabilities, and, in recent years, rather astronomical increases in autism and "developmental delay."

We continue this discussion, under the specific rubric of learning disabilities on the next panel.

Sources: National Center for Education Statistics. U.S. Department of Education. *Digest of Education Statistics,* 1992 and U.S. Department of Education, Office of Special Education and Rehabilitative Services, *Annual Report to Congress on the Implementation of The Individuals with Disabilities Education Act,* various years, and unpublished tabulations; and National Center for Education Statistics, Common Core of Data survey. April 2001. *Rethinking Special Education for a New Century,* Chester E. Finn, Andrew J. Rotterham, and Charles R. Hokanson, editors, Thomas B. Fordham Foundation, May 2001.

Learning Disabilities

LD and Other Selected Disabilities

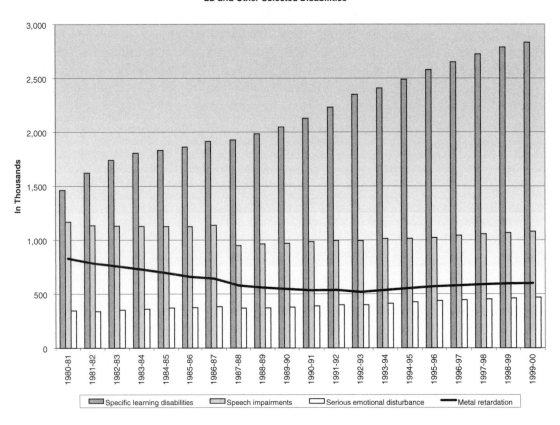

Specific learning disabilities □ Speech impairments □ Serious emotional disturbance ▬ Metal retardation

In the last panel we looked at disabilities funded by the federal government under the Individuals with Disabilities Education Act (IDEA). Here we look at specific learning disabilities (LDs). The graph shows total students enrolled from 1980-2000. Note first of all that students with speech and language impairments are down; as are the mentally retarded. Those with serious emotional disturbance are up — those with specific learning disabilities are *way* up.

In the last panel we learned that students with LD appear intelligent yet cannot communicate orally or in written form in line with their evident intelligence, cannot read well or comprehend what they are reading, and cannot do math or reason abstractly.

The causes of LD are unknown. The condition was once thought to be caused by one or more neurological problems, but these explanations have given way to vague speculations suggesting flaws in fetal brain development. These are thought to be caused by toxins in the environment; tobacco, alcohol, and drug abuse; genetic problems; and so on.[1] But it's clear that *no* conclusive answers are offered by science — which is *not* to say that these speculations are wrong. But ignorance prevails.

At the same time, it has been observed that 80% of children with learning disabilities have problems with reading, that this problem appears early — and if not corrected early, is difficult to reverse. As one of the more insightful papers on this subject states: "The poor first-grade reader almost invariably becomes a poor middle school reader, high school reader, and adult reader. In short, children who get off to a poor start in reading rarely catch up. We wait — they fail."[2] Yet most diagnoses of LD take place at a time when it is already too late to help the students.

To oversimplify somewhat, it might be said that much of the dramatic increase in students with disabilities is due largely to a failure to detect reading problems early and to teach children with reading problems using intensive methods.

Another contributing cause to the rise in disabilities is the growing number of children with serious emotional disturbances. This may be due to medical conditions or possibly, to the "medicalization" of behavioral problems by government agencies and the educational establishment. The problems equally may stem from failures in child raising, inappropriate nutrition, pollution, and societal causes which we're *not* facing squarely but hiding behind medical jargon. In the case of emotional disturbances, as in the case of special LDs, the causes remain vague although the symptoms are quite evident to frustrated teachers.

The rise in the special ed population is not, as some might believe, due to the availability of federal funding. IDEA was to provide up to 40% of funding for special education. During its history, the legislation has provided only 12% of the cost. School systems *lose money* on each child put into special ed. The pressure to put children into special ed classes arises not from the schools but from teachers who wish to find places for unresponsive, frustrated, or disruptive children.

All this has led calls for reform. A summary of reforms is listed in the source. "Medication" is another solution. We deal with that next panel. It is clear, however, that special education needs a new approach. One hopes that the right way will eventually emerge.

Sources: National Center for Education Statistics. *Digest of Education Statistics,* 1992. Department of Education, Office of Special Education and Rehabilitative Services. *Annual Report to Congress on the Implementation of The Individuals with Disabilities Education Act,* various years. National Center for Education Statistics, Common Core of Data survey. April 2001. *Rethinking Special Education for a New Century,* Chester E. Finn, Andrew J. Rotterham, and Charles R. Hokanson, editors, Thomas B. Fordham Foundation, May 2001.

---

[1] For more, see National Institute of Mental Health's web site at http://www.nimh.nih.gov/publicat/learndis.htm#learn5

[2] G. Reid Lyon, Jack M. Fletcher, Salle E. Shaywitz, Bennett A Shaywitz, Joseph K. Torgesen, Frank B. Wood, Anne Schulte, and Richard Olson, "Rethinking Learning Disabilities," Chapter 12 of *Rethinking Special Education for a New Century,* see source note.

Ritalin: Keeping Kids Cool and in School

Estimated Number of Children on Ritalin

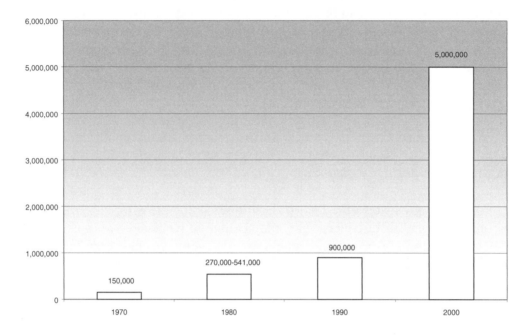

Ritalin — also known as methylphenidate — is the most popular drug prescribed to treat children with behavior disorders. The drug is a stimulant, in the same class as amphetamines and cocaine. It works by stimulating the neurotransmitters in the brain and helps the child with attention deficit/hyperactivity disorder (ADHD) focus and become less fidgety. Ninety percent of all Ritalin is produced and used in the United States.

Labels for hyperactive children change. In the 1940s, children who were hyperactive, inattentive or too impulsive were said to have Hyperkinetic Disorder of Childhood. In 1968, the American Psychiatric Association published a section on children in its handbook of mental disorders for the first time; they used the term hyperkinetic to describe rambunctious children. The term Attention Deficit Disorder (ADD) began to be used in 1980. This label put a finer point on the problem: a child who could not focus or pay attention. In 1987, the term Attention Deficit/Hyperactivity Disorder began to be used, a term that casts a bigger net (and label) over problem children in the classroom. An ADHD child can show a variety of symptoms: can't sit still, can't concentrate, performs poorly academically, is hyperactive, is difficult to control.

The disorder was not discovered the way illnesses are. It was voted into existence by the American Psychiatric Association for its official book of mental disorders. What causes ADHD? No one is certain. In 1998, the National Institute of Mental Health attempted to quell debate about the disorder by finding a biological reason but was unable to do so. Experts have pointed their fingers at nearly everything: stress at home, hearing/vision problems, and lead poisoning have all been thought to play a role (including being gifted and becoming bored with material the child already knows). There is no test for ADHD; a child is diagnosed by being observed. If a child exhibits a collection of symptoms — can't sit still, can't listen, can't follow directions — he may be diagnosed with ADHD.

According to the Drug Enforcement Administration, about 80% of the 11 million prescriptions written for Ritalin each year are for childhood ADHD. Roughly 3-5% of school-age children are thought to be affected by this disorder. Disturbingly, no one is certain how many children are actually on Ritalin. The panel shows what are considered good guesses: an estimated 150,000 children were on the drug in 1970, with figures roughly doubling each decade (according to some estimates). There are currently an estimated 5 million school-age children on the drug. Another 2 million children are thought to be on other psychiatric drugs, such as Adderall and Dexedrine. Production of these drugs has grown 2000%, according to the Drug Enforcement Agency.

Some sources cite such contradictory numbers that the issue of the drug being overprescribed becomes difficult to address. In 1996, the National Association of School Nurses claimed 3 million school children took Ritalin, while a study in *Pediatrics* that same year put the figure closer to 1.5 million.

Another point needs to be made: Ritalin is a useful tool for some troubled students. Children on Ritalin have shown improved levels of concentration. A study in the journal *Experimental and Clinical Psychopharmacology* found the drug improved the social skills of ADHD teenagers and improved their test scores an average of 17%.

What's going on here? An increasing number of parents and physicians are calling the treatment of (and, indeed, the ADHD disorder itself) into question. We seem to expect a classroom of 30 children to behave in the same way and learn at the same rate. Of course, some children have real problems that need to be addressed biochemically. But one can't help but wonder if we're more interested in changing the behavior than the reason for it. Dr. Lawrence Diller, author of *Running on Ritalin*, claims that Ritalin can help "round-and octagonal-peg kids fit into rather rigid square educational holes." Are these children with "special needs" that we aren't addressing? Is hyperactivity and inability to concentrate the problem, or are they the symptom of one?

The next panel will look at a different segment of special education — gifted students.

Sources: Chart data comes from "Children and Psychiatric Drugs: Colorado's Concern Should Be Ours As Well." Retrieved from http://www.wildestcolts.com; Sax, Leonard. "Ritalin – Better Living Through Chemistry." World and I, November 2000, p. 286; "Alternative Treatments for Children Who Have Been Prescribed Psychiatric Medication." Retrieved May 3, 2002 from http://www.alternativementalhealth.com; "Statistics Confirm Rise in Childhood ADHD and Medication Use." Retrieved from http://www.education-world.com; "What is behind the Alarming Increase in Ritalin Use Among US Children?" Retrieved from http://www.wsws.org. "Better Children Through Chemistry." Retrieved from http://www.columbia.edu; "Does ADHD Even Exist?" Retrieved from http://www.naturalchild.com; "ADHD Statistics." Retrieved from http://www1.adhdguide.net.

The Status of Our Gifted Students

"Special" Indeed: The Gifted in Our Schools, 2000

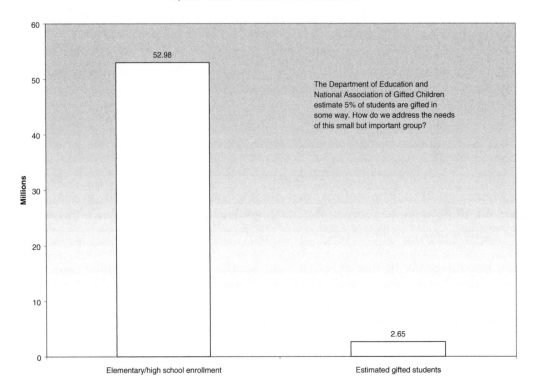

The Department of Education and National Association of Gifted Children estimate 5% of students are gifted in some way. How do we address the needs of this small but important group?

In 1972, U.S. Commissioner of Education, Sidney P. Marland Jr., made this statement in a report to Congress on the state of education for the gifted and talented: "Gifted and talented children are those identified by professionally qualified persons who by virtue of outstanding abilities are capable of high performance. These are children who require differentiated educational programs and/or services beyond those normally provided by the regular school program in order to realize their contribution to self and society."

Just how many students *are* gifted? The Marland Report went on to estimate that gifted students make up 3 to 5% of the student population, and these gifts and talents could appear in many forms: general intellectual ability (high IQ scores), skills in a particular academic field, leadership ability, excellence in the arts, and creative thought (putting ideas together in innovative ways to develop meanings with social merit). The U.S. Department of Education and the National Association of Gifted Children estimate that 5% of the general population are gifted. An additional 3% are academically talented.

We seem to recognize exceptional children when we seem them: the child who reads at an early age, can solve math problems or exhibits artistic talents above the level of his or her age group. Giftedness cannot be taught. Nor is intellect its only marker. In the early 1900s, Lewis Terman began a longitudinal study of 1,500 children with IQs above 140. He noted that giftedness was a complex combination of intellect, emotions, and perception. He wrote in 1905: "Heroic effort is made to boost every child just as near to the top of the intellectual ladder as possible. ... Meanwhile the child's own instincts and emotions ... are allowed to wither away." A century later, we're still arguing about improving education and holding children to high standards.

But what kind of education are gifted students getting? Often they get what all others do too. Topics aren't covered in sufficient depth. The material isn't challenging enough. In one study, nearly half of elementary schools had to eliminate their curriculum when it was discovered that most students already knew the material. Specialized programs are only available a few hours a week. More troubling is the fact that our brightest may lack support. Some people see programs for the gifted as elitist. In a recent Gallup Poll, 61% said schools should do more to provide educational opportunities for gifted youngsters. 35% said nothing should change. And 2% said schools should do *less* to support the gifted. 84% of respondents said they support special funding for gifted students. 16% frowned on such a plan.

What kind of funding do gifted programs get? The Bush administration is planning to repeal funding for the only program specifically aimed at educating the gifted. The Jacob J. Javits Gifted and Talented Education Program received only $11.2 million in grants for fiscal year 2002, a drop in the bucket in a $46.7 billion education budget. The funds would be rolled into block grants for states which may actually mean increased dollars for gifted students. But advocates for the gifted aren't so sure. They point out that a program aimed at the gifted has tremendous symbolic value.

Educating the gifted has always been left up to the states. But standards are inconsistent. Not every state collects data on its gifted students. According to the National Association for Gifted Students, only 32 states have mandates to identify gifted students and 29 provide gifted education programs. Funding varies as well. Texas spent $56 million on gifted education. Massachusetts spent $437,970. That works out to $179 per student in Texas, $6 in Massachusetts. Other than a trip to a museum, what kind of education will $6 bring the young people of Massachusetts?

What should be our answer to the gifted? Should we challenge them or let them rise by their own merits?

Source: *Chart*: figures come from National Center for Education Statistics and each state's Department of Education. Current data is for 2000, except for Texas (1998) and Illinois (1999); Goldberg Goff, Karen. "More Choices For Gifted." *The Washington Times*, October 14, 2001, p. 1. Lewis Terman quote from Delisle, James R. "Neither Freak Nor Geek: The Gifted Among Us." *Education Week*, October 27, 1999, p. 1. Lisa Fine. "Advocates Say Bill Leaves Gifted Students Behind." *Education Week*, June 13, 2001, p. 1. *National Excellence: A Case for Developing America's Talent*, retrieved http://www.ed.gov; "Giftedness and the Gifted: What's It All About?" retrieved from http://www.kidsource.com.

The Growing Numbers of LEP Students

Students With Limited English Skills

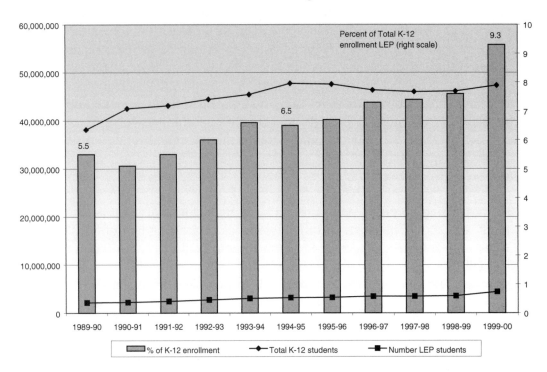

Percent of Total K-12 enrollment LEP (right scale)

Legend: % of K-12 enrollment — Total K-12 students — Number LEP students

The formal definition of Limited English Proficient (LEP): "Students who were not born in the United States or whose native language is not English and cannot participate effectively in the regular curriculum because they have difficulty speaking, understanding, reading and writing in English."

There were more than 4.4 million LEP students in 2000, double the 2.1 million in 1990. LEP students are concentrated at the K-3 grade level. They are a growing share of the total elementary and secondary school enrollment, increasing from 5.5 to 9.3% in the last decade. Why the increase? Immigration. The number of immigrants in recent years has fallen but was on the increase in 1980s, climbing from 530,639 in 1980 to 1.82 million in 1991. Children of these immigrants are now attending school. The efforts to educate them is complicated by the fact many still speak their native language at home. Census data show that the number of children who speak a second language at home has been on the increase, from 6.4 million in 1992 to 6.7 million in 1995 to 8.8 million in 1999.

In traditional bilingual education classes, students with limited command of English are assigned to speak, read, and write in their home language first. Once they have proficiency in Spanish, say, they are taught in English. But some students were spending too long in their native language classes and reported feeling they had lost ground in gaining English language skills. Some educators feel that the gap never gets closed.

It isn't as simple as teaching children in Spanish either. Spanish is the native language for LEP students. But over 400 languages are spoken by LEP students nationwide. Spanish is the native language of 75% of the students. In most states the second language varies wildly. States cite such tongues as Navajo, Vietnamese, Arabic, Russian, Serbo-Croatian. In some states, such as Alaska, Montana, Maine, Vermont and Minnesota, Spanish is not even the top language spoken by LEP students.

We are beginning to rethink how we educate our immigrant students. In 1998, California voters passed Proposition 227. It mandated that all English learners be educated "over-whelmingly" in English immersion programs. Supporters of bilingual education argued that this would harm students. The president of the National Association of Bilingual Education claimed it would be an "evil day" if the initiative passed.

The predicted disaster never came. The opposite happened — test scores went up. The *New York Times* reported in 2000 that for second graders the average score in reading for an LEP student increased 9% over the previous two years. Math scores increased 14 points during the same period. One school, Oceanside Unified School District, saw such a dramatic improvement in reading scores (from the 32nd to the 12th percentile) that its superintendent — the founding president of the California Association for Bilingual Edu-cation — became a convert to English immersion programs. Oceanside's improvement was particularly striking compared to the nearby Vista school. Half of Vista's students were granted waivers to remain in bilingual education. Vista, similar to Oceanside in size and economic background, saw much smaller improvement.

Is English immersion an unqualified success in California? Well, to be fair, other factors were at work at work as well. Class sizes had shrunk in many elementary grades. New teaching styles had been implemented in schools, such as a return to basic sound-it-out phonics programs. Also, not all schools saw impressive gains in test scores.

The developments in California — a state that has always been a trend setter — are being felt elsewhere. Voters in Arizona recently gave overwhelming support to Proposition 203, a proposal similar to 227. Legislation to dismantle bilingual education has surfaced in Colorado.

Is bilingual education doomed? Some of the anecdotal evidence coming out of schools suggests that English immersion — a "sink or swim" policy — may be the way to go. It seems ironic. This is happening just as some schools are seeing their foreign language programs disappear and are striving to be "multicultural" in their curriculum.

Sources: Chart comes from Kindler, Anneka. National Clearinghouse for English Language Acquisition, *Survey of the States' Limited English Proficient Students & Available Educational Programs and Services 1999-2000 Summary Report*, May 2002, prepared for the U.S. Department of Education. "Facts About Limited English Proficient Students." Retrieved May 29, 2002 from http://www.ed.gov; Jacques Steinberg. "Test Scores Rise, Surprising Critics of Bilingual Ban." *New York Times*, August 20, 2000, p. A1; Ken Noonan. "I Believed That Bilingual Education Was Best…Until the Kids Proved Me Wrong." *Washington Post*, September 3, 2000.

The Merits of Single-Sex Education

Should Single-Sex Education be an Option?

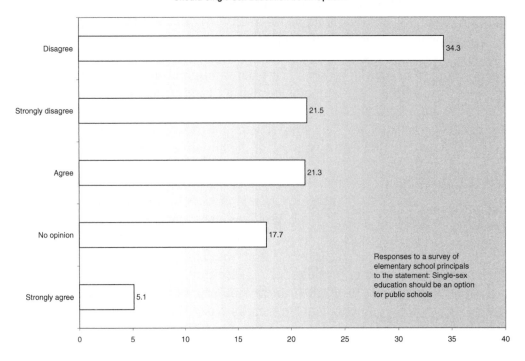

Responses to a survey of elementary school principals to the statement: Single-sex education should be an option for public schools

Much of the debate about single-sex education gets tripped up on its legality under Title IX, the federal law requiring gender equity in public education. But things are changing. In May 2000, as a result of a bipartisan amendment to President Bush's No Child Left Behind Act, the Bush Administration has taken to steps to change the way it enforces this law. Single-sex public schools would be eligible for up to $450 million per year in specially targeted funds. The ACLU and women's advocacy groups have already made noise about this development, just as they have ended up protesting earlier efforts for all boy and girl schools. Separate, they argue, can never be equal.

The graphic illustrates the split on the issue. In this 1997 survey, 1,350 elementary school principals were asked about their feelings on single-sex education. More than half regard the policy as undesirable, while more than a quarter think the policy has a merit. 20% could offer no opinion on the matter. One can't help but wonder if the survey's numbers offer a reasonably accurate picture of society's attitude to this idea.

Perhaps the debate exists because educators, critics and parents have so little evidence to draw on. There are currently 11 public or charter schools that are exclusively single-sex or offer same-sex classes. What are their merits? They often feature smaller class size. Girls often report feeling less intimidated without boys around, and more willing to ask questions. Boys have access to good role models and, more importantly, age-appropriate material. (For all the talk of girls' science and math scores being lower than boys' scores, girls tend to outperform boys in reading and writing performance tests.) Single-sex education also cuts down on typical boy-girl distractions. One potential drawback? Mixing with the opposite sex is a crucial part of a young person's social development.

One of the most ambitious experiments in single-sex education took place in California in 1997. Governor Pete Wilson initiated a program with three sets of schools for both boys and girls. Its intent was to provide school choice, replicate the success of some private girls' schools, and to offer urban boys positive role models. Students were drawn from the ranks of young people who needed the most help: those who had fallen behind in school, were experiencing trouble at home, or had already entered the correctional system. All but one closed within two years (a school in East Palo Alto remains). Only one study was done of the experiment: *Is Single Gender Schooling Viable in the Public Sector? Lessons from California's Pilot Program.* Its authors concluded that it was not the single-sex system that doomed the schools. They failed because the program was implemented poorly, had poorly trained teachers, inadequate funds.

Do these schools work? Most of the studies come from other countries where single-sex education is often freely available. In a study published by the Australian Council for Education Research, a study of 270,000 students over six years found boys and girls in single-sex classrooms scored an average of 15 to 22 percentile ranks higher than did boys and girls in co-educational settings. Graham Able of Dulwich College in London, England found children in single-sex education outperformed those in co-educational settings. In his research, widely published in British newspapers, boys seemed to benefit more than girls, challenging the traditional notions that it is the girls who get short-changed in public school settings.

Other reports suggest that the programs don't really have any effect on student performance. Some argue that if these schools do show academic improvement, it's become single-sex programs tend to attract young people who are driven and want to learn; scores therefore are bound to go up.

Perhaps the issue is best summarized by a quote from someone who has actually been there. A math teacher at the Arthur Ashe Academy for Boys and the Sally Ride Academy for Girls offered up this assessment in the *San Francisco Chronicle*: "In the boy's classes, if they were having trouble with something, they were much less embarrassed to say so. And the girls did much better in math." This is really the point of education, one could argue. It isn't about test scores; it's about stimulating the intellect and providing an atmosphere where a child is free to ask questions. Single-sex education isn't for everyone, of course — but it could very well benefit some.

Sources: Chart comes from the National Association of Elementary School Principals Retrieved May 31, 2002 from http://www.naesp.org; Asimov, Nanette. "Same Sex Schools a Failure, Study Says." *San Francisco Chronicle*, May 23, 2001, p. A3. Karen Stabiner. "Boys Here, Girls There: Sure, If Equality 's The Goal." May 12, 2002, p. B1. "Get the Facts on Single-Sex Schools." Retrieved from http://www.suntimes.com; "National Association for the Advancement of Single Sex Public Education." Retrieved from http://www.singlesexschools.org.

Corporate America Goes Back to School

The Three Rs in Schools: Reading, Writing, and Revenues?

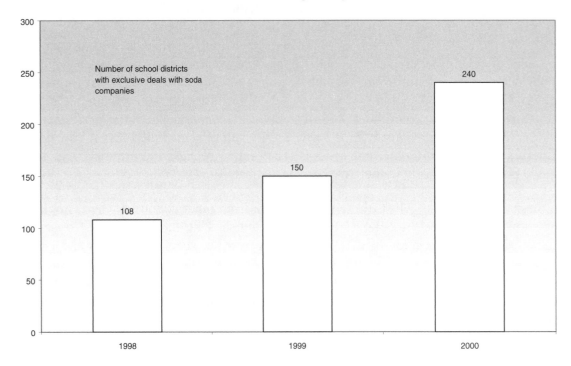

Number of school districts with exclusive deals with soda companies

Schools have entered into deals with soda bottlers to sell their product exclusively at school vending machines, cafeterias, and extracurricular functions. Each district earns a "sponsorship" fee for signing the contact. The figure varies — three South Bay, California districts recently earned between $200,000 to $275,000 for recently signing with Pepsi. They also earn annual fees, and a share of vending sales — loosely translated, the more soda sold, the more money for schools. Some contracts give districts some control about what gets sold in vending machines — water and juice is sold along with soft drinks, for example. But some contracts can be highly specific. The Public Health Institute reports that one soft drink firm stipulated that a district must have a vending machine for every 150 students, can't limit the hours of operation and that 85% of the items sold must be large, 20 ounces bottles of the firm's product.

Fast-food advertising in schools seems to have begun in 1993, according to Eric Schlosser in *Fast Food Nation*. District 11 in Colorado Springs became the first public school district to place ads for Burger King in its hallways and on the sides of its buses. The district had sold the advertisements in the face of a revenue crunch. Initially, their efforts were a disappointment. However, in 1996, the district turned to DD Marketing Inc. to help them renegotiate this deal. By putting together special advertising packages, the firm's president Dan DeRose was able to triple the district's ad revenues. In 1997, he went on to broker a 10 year deal with Coca-Cola to bring the district's revenues up to $11 million over the life of the contract.

Schools get $750 million a year from companies that sell snack or processed food in schools. What do kids usually purchase from vending machines? According to a vending survey done by *Automatic Merchandiser*, soda was the most purchased item, followed by chips and candy. Junk food has become a staple of young people's diets — it's fast, easy and tastes good. A California high schooler described her typical lunch — and perhaps the lunch of more than a few classmates — in a *New York Times* article: "Lunch for me is chips, soda, maybe a chocolate ice cream taco." Diabetes and heart disease? Showing up in alarming rates in teenagers? She shrugs. "That's all I like to eat — the bad stuff."

Bad stuff indeed. Young people now drink twice as much soda as milk. Children are consuming more of these beverages, and have begun to do so at a younger age. Almost half of the children between 6 and 11 drank pop in 1996-97, with the average drinker consuming 15 ounces a day. Teenage boys are the top drinkers. In 1977-78 they consumed roughly 16 ounces daily; by 1994-96, that figure jumped to 28 ounces, according to the Department of Agriculture. Girls have increased consumption as well, from 15 to 21 ounces in the same period. Consumption has gone up in part because serving size has increased, notes the report *Liquid Candy*. A standard serving was 6.5 ounces in the 1950s. We are now looking at 20 ounces bottles — three times the sugar and calories.

Big business isn't just in the halls and cafeteria, either. It's shaping the curriculum as well. The rising cost of textbooks has forced some districts into using corporate-sponsored teaching materials. *Fast Food Nation* cites a few examples: Procter & Gamble's Decision Earth program taught that clear-cut logging was good for the environment. A study guide from the American Coal Foundation dismissed the greenhouse effect claiming that "the earth could benefit rather than be harmed from increased carbon dioxide." Not all the materials had such one-sided viewpoints, of course. Even in states-sponsored material, commercialism shows up. A math textbook published by McGraw Hill, *Mathematics: Applications and Connections* asked students how much money they needed to save to buy Nike sneakers. The book also taught fractions by using M&M candies. Media and brands mushroom all around these kids. Channel One beams 12 minutes of news and advertising into 12,000 middle school and high schools daily. But many companies also sponsor contests that pay for badly needed equipment and computers.

Things are changing in some districts. More districts are refusing solicited soda deals. 10 districts refused in October 1998, 21 in July 1999, and 43 in July 2000. The Oakland school district banned all snack food sales in February 2002 and is looking at losing $650,000 in the process. Senator Charles Schumer has called for the U.S. Department of Agriculture to promote milk vending machines in schools as a way of boosting the nutrition in students' diets.

Sources: Chart data comes from the Center for Commercial-free Public Education and is quoted in Henry, Tamara. "Coca-Cola Rethinks School Contracts." *USA Today*, March 14, 2001, p. 1. Timothy Egan. "In Bid to Improve Nutrition, Schools Expel Soda and Chips." *New York Times*, May 20, 2002, P. A1. Stacey Meacham. "K-12 School Market." *Automatic Merchandiser*, April 2002, p. 12; Eric Schlosser, *Fast Food Nation: The Dark Side of the All-American Meal*, 2002.

Part II

Data Presentation

Data used to create graphics in the first part of this book are present in Part II in tabular format. The tables are arranged by chapter and follow the same sequence as the panels in the chapters. Locating the appropriate table should, therefore, be easy.

In most instances, the data shown are the same as those used to generate the graphics. From time to time, however, additional time series are presented or data are presented for more years. For an explanation of the data, please consult the panel in which they are used. The tables carry some explanatory notes, but the relevance of the data — and the reasons they were selected — are not spelled out.

Tables carry source notes. However, for more information on the subject, including other sources of information, please consult the source notes and (if present), the footnotes shown in the relevant panel in Part I of this volume.

Chapter 1
WHO ARE WE?

Births of a Nation

Live births are in actual counts. Birth rate is births per 1,000 population. Fertility rate is births per 1,000 women aged 15 to 44.

Year	Live Births Actual Total Count	Birth Rate Births per 1,000 Population	Fertility Rate Birth per 1,000 Women aged 15-44
1909	2,718,000	30.0	126.8
1910	2,777,000	30.1	126.8
1911	2,809,000	29.9	126.3
1912	2,840,000	29.8	125.8
1913	2,869,000	29.5	124.7
1914	2,966,000	29.9	126.6
1915	2,965,000	29.5	125.0
1916	2,964,000	29.1	123.4
1917	2,944,000	28.5	121.0
1918	2,948,000	28.2	119.8
1919	2,740,000	26.1	111.2
1920	2,950,000	27.7	117.9
1921	3,055,000	28.1	119.8
1922	2,882,000	26.2	111.2
1923	2,910,000	26.0	110.5
1924	2,979,000	26.1	110.9
1925	2,909,000	25.1	106.6
1926	2,839,000	24.2	102.6
1927	2,802,000	23.5	99.8
1928	2,674,000	22.2	93.8
1929	2,582,000	21.2	89.3
1930	2,618,000	21.3	89.2
1931	2,506,000	20.2	84.6
1932	2,440,000	19.5	81.7
1933	2,307,000	18.4	76.3
1934	2,396,000	19.0	78.5
1935	2,377,000	18.7	77.2
1936	2,355,000	18.4	75.8
1937	2,413,000	18.7	77.1
1938	2,496,000	19.2	79.1
1939	2,466,000	18.8	77.6

[Continued]

Births of a Nation
[Continued]

Year	Live Births Actual Total Count	Birth Rate Births per 1,000 Population	Fertility Rate Birth per 1,000 Women aged 15-44
1940	2,559,000	19.4	79.9
1941	2,703,000	20.3	83.4
1942	2,989,000	22.2	91.5
1943	3,104,000	22.7	94.3
1944	2,939,000	21.2	88.8
1945	2,858,000	20.4	85.9
1946	3,411,000	24.1	101.9
1947	3,817,000	26.6	113.3
1948	3,637,000	24.9	107.3
1949	3,649,000	24.5	107.1
1950	3,632,000	24.1	106.2
1951	3,820,000	24.9	111.4
1952	3,909,000	25.1	113.8
1953	3,959,000	25.1	115.0
1954	4,071,000	25.3	117.9
1955	4,097,000	25.0	118.3
1956	4,210,000	25.2	121.0
1957	4,300,000	25.3	122.7
1958	4,246,000	24.5	120.0
1959	4,286,000	24.2	119.9
1960	4,257,850	23.7	118.0
1961	4,268,326	23.3	117.1
1962	4,167,362	22.4	112.0
1963	4,098,020	21.7	108.3
1964	4,027,490	21.1	104.7
1965	3,760,358	19.4	96.3
1966	3,606,274	18.4	90.8
1967	3,520,959	17.8	87.2
1968	3,501,564	17.6	85.2
1969	3,600,206	17.9	86.1
1970	3,731,386	18.4	87.9
1971	3,555,970	17.2	81.6
1972	3,258,411	15.6	73.1
1973	3,136,965	14.8	68.8
1974	3,159,958	14.8	67.8
1975	3,144,198	14.6	66.0
1976	3,167,788	14.6	65.0
1977	3,326,632	15.1	66.8
1978	3,333,279	15.0	65.5
1979	3,494,398	15.6	67.2
1980	3,612,258	15.9	68.4
1981	3,629,238	15.8	67.3
1982	3,680,537	15.9	67.3

[Continued]

Births of a Nation

[Continued]

Year	Live Births Actual Total Count	Birth Rate Births per 1,000 Population	Fertility Rate Birth per 1,000 Women aged 15-44
1983	3,638,933	15.6	65.7
1984	3,669,141	15.6	65.5
1985	3,760,561	15.8	66.3
1986	3,756,547	15.6	65.4
1987	3,809,394	15.7	65.8
1988	3,909,510	16.0	67.3
1989	4,040,958	16.4	69.2
1990	4,158,212	16.7	70.9
1991	4,110,907	16.3	69.6
1992	4,065,014	15.9	68.9
1993	4,000,240	15.5	67.6
1994	3,952,767	15.2	66.7
1995	3,899,589	14.8	65.6
1996	3,891,494	14.7	65.3
1997	3,880,894	14.5	65.0
1998	3,941,553	14.6	65.6
1999	3,959,417	14.5	65.9
2000	4,064,948	14.8	67.6

Source: Vital Statistics of the United States, 1998, Volume I, Natality, National Center for Health Statistics (NCHS), U.S. Department of Health and Human Services, updated from later issues of National Vital Statistics Reports and Monthly Vital Statistics Report also published by NCHS.

Total Fertility Rate - 1940 to 2000

Total Fertility Rate is defined as the all children likely to be born to 1,000 women (or 1 woman) in the 15-44 age period if "current" fertility rates continue. A rate of 2,100 per 1,000 women or 2.1 per woman is considered to be the "replacement rate," meaning that at such a rate, the population will be completely replaced. The 0.1 fraction is necessary to account for infertile parents and infant deaths.

Year	Rate per 1,000 Women	Rate per Woman
1940	2,301.3	2.30
1941	2,399.1	2.40
1942	2,628.2	2.63
1943	2,718.3	2.72
1944	2,567.6	2.57
1945	2,491.2	2.49
1946	2,942.7	2.94
1947	3,273.5	3.27
1948	3,108.6	3.11
1949	3,110.1	3.11
1950	3,090.5	3.09

[Continued]

Total Fertility Rate - 1940 to 2000

[Continued]

Year	Rate per 1,000 Women	Rate per Woman
1951	3,269.3	3.27
1952	3,358.4	3.36
1953	3,424.1	3.42
1954	3,542.6	3.54
1955	3,578.5	3.58
1956	3,689.0	3.69
1957	3,767.0	3.77
1958	3,700.5	3.70
1959	3,712.4	3.71
1960	3,653.6	3.65
1961	3,620.3	3.62
1962	3,461.3	3.46
1963	3,318.8	3.32
1964	3,190.5	3.19
1965	2,912.6	2.91
1966	2,721.4	2.72
1967	2,557.7	2.56
1968	2,464.2	2.46
1969	2,455.5	2.46
1970	2,480.0	2.48
1970	2,480.0	2.48
1971	2,266.5	2.27
1971	2,266.5	2.27
1972	2,010.0	2.01
1972	2,010.0	2.01
1973	1,879.0	1.88
1973	1,879.0	1.88
1974	1,835.0	1.84
1974	1,835.0	1.84
1975	1,774.0	1.77
1975	1,774.0	1.77
1976	1,738.0	1.74
1976	1,738.0	1.74
1977	1,789.5	1.79
1977	1,789.5	1.79
1978	1,760.0	1.76
1978	1,760.0	1.76
1979	1,808.0	1.81
1979	1,808.0	1.81
1980	1,839.5	1.84
1980	1,839.5	1.84
1981	1,812.0	1.81
1982	1,827.5	1.83
1983	1,799.0	1.80
1984	1,806.5	1.81
1985	1,844.0	1.84

[Continued]

Total Fertility Rate - 1940 to 2000

[Continued]

Year	Rate per 1,000 Women	Rate per Woman
1986	1,837.5	1.84
1987	1,872.0	1.87
1988	1,934.0	1.93
1989	2,014.0	2.01
1990	2,081.0	2.08
1991	2,073.0	2.07
1992	2,065.0	2.07
1993	2,046.0	2.05
1994	2,036.0	2.04
1995	2,019.0	2.02
1996	2,027.0	2.03
1997	2,032.5	2.03
1998	2,058.5	2.06
1999	2,075.0	2.08
2000	2,133.5	2.13

Source: Vital Statistics of the United States, 1998, Volume I, Natality, National Center for Health Statistics (NCHS), U.S. Department of Health and Human Services, updated from later issues of National Vital Statistics Reports and Monthly Vital Statistics Report also published by NCHS.

Total Fertility Rate, Whites and Blacks, 1940 to 1997

Total Fertility Rate is defined as the all children likely to be born to 1,000 women (or 1 woman) in the 15-44 age period if "current" fertility rates continue. A rate of 2,100 per 1,000 women or 2.1 per woman is considered to be the "replacement rate," meaning that at such a rate, the population will be completely replaced. The 0.1 fraction is necessary to account for infertile parents and infant deaths.

Year	Lifetime Births per 1,000 Women 15-44			
	All Races	White	Black	White-Black Difference
1940	2,301.3	2,229.1	2,870.2	641.1
1941	2,399.1	2,328.0	2,956.3	628.3
1942	2,628.2	2,577.3	3,022.1	444.8
1943	2,718.3	2,664.3	3,128.2	463.9
1944	2,567.6	2,500.5	3,075.0	574.5
1945	2,491.2	2,421.2	3,016.7	595.5
1946	2,942.7	2,900.9	3,238.3	337.4
1947	3,273.5	3,229.5	3,575.3	345.8
1948	3,108.6	3,021.7	3,742.1	720.4
1949	3,110.1	3,008.7	3,854.8	846.1
1950	3,090.5	2,976.8	3,928.3	951.5
1951	3,269.3	3,156.9	4,091.2	934.3
1952	3,358.4	3,249.9	4,146.9	897.0
1953	3,424.1	3,306.4	4,283.4	977.0
1954	3,542.6	3,415.1	4,473.9	1,058.8

[Continued]

Total Fertility Rate, Whites and Blacks, 1940 to 1997

[Continued]

Year	Lifetime Births per 1,000 Women 15-44			
	All Races	White	Black	White-Black Difference
1955	3,578.5	3,466.5	4,546.0	1,079.5
1956	3,689.0	3,545.5	4,729.9	1,184.4
1957	3,767.0	3,625.2	4,797.8	1,172.6
1958	3,700.5	3,559.9	4,726.9	1,167.0
1959	3,712.4	3,567.4	4,774.3	1,206.9
1960	3,653.6	3,532.9	4,541.8	1,008.9
1961	3,620.3	3,496.9	4,496.8	999.9
1962	3,461.3	3,341.3	4,340.1	998.8
1963	3,318.8	3,193.5	4,203.0	1,009.5
1964	3,190.5	3,065.0	4,138.6	1,073.6
1965	2,912.6	2,783.4	3,828.5	1,045.1
1966	2,721.4	2,602.9	3,545.3	942.4
1967	2,557.7	2,446.9	3,311.8	864.9
1968	2,464.2	2,365.6	3,099.8	734.2
1969	2,455.5	2,360.3	3,042.8	682.5
1970	2,480.0	2,385.0	3,099.5	714.5
1971	2,266.5	2,160.5	2,902.0	741.5
1972	2,010.0	1,906.5	2,601.0	694.5
1973	1,879.0	1,783.0	2,411.0	628.0
1974	1,835.0	1,748.5	2,298.5	550.0
1975	1,774.0	1,686.0	2,243.0	557.0
1976	1,738.0	1,652.0	2,187.0	535.0
1977	1,789.5	1,703.0	2,251.0	548.0
1978	1,760.0	1,667.5	2,218.0	550.5
1979	1,808.0	1,715.5	2,263.2	547.7
1980	1,839.5	1,748.5	2,176.5	428.0
1981	1,812.0	1,748.0	2,266.0	518.0
1982	1,827.5	1,767.0	2,106.5	339.5
1983	1,799.0	1,740.5	2,066.0	325.5
1984	1,806.5	1,748.5	2,070.5	322.0
1985	1,844.0	1,787.0	2,109.0	322.0
1986	1,837.5	1,776.0	2,135.5	359.5
1987	1,872.0	1,804.5	2,198.0	393.5
1988	1,934.0	1,856.5	2,298.0	441.5
1989	2,014.0	1,931.0	2,432.5	501.5
1990	2,081.0	2,003.0	2,480.0	477.0
1991	2,073.0	1,995.5	2,480.0	484.5
1992	2,065.0	1,993.5	2,442.0	448.5
1993	2,046.0	1,982.0	2,384.5	402.5
1994	2,036.0	1,985.0	2,300.0	315.0
1995	2,019.0	1,989.0	2,175.0	186.0
1996	2,027.0	2,005.5	2,144.0	138.5
1997	2,032.5	2,009.0	2,154.0	145.0

Source: Total Fertility Rates and Birth Rates by Race, 1940-1980 and 1981- 1997, National Center for Heath Statistics, U.S. Department of Health and Human Services, obtained from http:// www.cdc.gov/nchs/default.htm.

Total Fertility Rate by Ethnicity and Race, 1989 to 1997

Total Fertility Rate is defined as the all children likely to be born to 1,000 wo-men (or 1 woman) in the 15-44 age period if "current" fertility rates continue. A rate of 2,100 per 1,000 women or 2.1 per woman is considered to be the "re-placement rate," meaning that at such a rate, the population will be completely replaced. The 0.1 fraction is necessary to account for infertile parents and in-fant deaths.

| Year | Lifetime Births to Women Aged 15 to 44 | | | | | |
	All Origins	Hispanics	African Americans	Asians/ Pacific Islanders	American Indians	Whites
1989	2,014.0	2,903.5	2,424.0	1,947.5	2,247.0	1,770.0
1990	2,081.0	2,959.5	2,547.5	2,002.5	2,183.0	1,850.5
1991	2,073.0	3,002.5	2,551.0	1,956.0	2,169.0	1,826.5
1992	2,065.0	3,043.0	2,514.0	1,942.0	2,190.0	1,810.5
1993	2,046.0	3,020.5	2,454.5	1,935.5	2,141.0	1,792.5
1994	2,036.0	3,014.0	2,365.0	1,943.0	2,080.0	1,792.0
1995	2,019.0	3,019.5	2,245.0	1,924.0	2,033.5	1,786.5
1996	2,027.0	3,047.5	2,204.0	1,907.5	2,030.0	1,795.5
1997	2,032.5	2,999.5	2,210.5	1,925.5	2,047.5	1,801.0

Source: National Vital Statistics Report, Vol. 47, No. 18, April 29, 1999, National Center for Health Statistics, U.S. Department of Health and Human Services.

Live Birth and Abortions by Races, 1975 to 1997

The ratio per 1,000 birth is to be understood as follows: in 1975, for all races, for every 1,000 live births, there were 329 abortions.

| Year | All Races | | | Whites | | | Blacks and Other Races | | |
	Live Births (000)	Abor-tions (000)	Ratio per 1,000 Births	Live Births (000)	Abor-tions (000)	Ratio per 1,000 Births	Live Births (000)	Abor-tions (000)	Ratio per 1,000 Births
1975	3,144.2	1,034	329	2,552.0	701	275	539.1	333	618
1976	3,167.8	1,150	363	2,567.6	791	308	543.5	359	660
1977	3,326.6	1,266	381	2,691.1	882	328	574.7	384	668
1978	3,333.3	1,382	415	2,681.1	972	362	584.7	410	700
1979	3,494.4	1,498	429	2,808.4	1,062	378	612.1	435	711
1980	3,612.3	1,554	430	2,936.4	1,094	373	671.8	460	685
1981	3,629.2	1,577	435	2,947.7	1,108	376	679.2	470	692
1982	3,680.5	1,574	428	2,984.8	1,095	367	694.1	479	690
1983	3,638.9	1,575	433	2,946.5	1,084	368	691.2	491	710
1984	3,669.1	1,577	430	2,967.1	1,087	366	700.3	491	701
1985	3,760.6	1,589	423	3,037.9	1,076	354	720.5	513	712
1986	3,756.5	1,574	419	3,019.2	1,045	346	734.9	529	720
1987	3,809.4	1,559	409	3,043.8	1,017	334	763.1	542	710
1988	3,909.5	1,591	407	3,102.1	1,026	331	804.7	565	702
1989	4,041.0	1,567	388	3,192.4	1,006	315	845.7	561	663
1990	4,158.2	1,609	387	3,290.3	1,039	316	865.0	570	659
1991	4,110.9	1,557	379	3,241.3	982	303	866.8	574	662
1992	4,065.0	1,529	376	3,201.7	943	295	863.3	585	678

[Continued]

Live Birth and Abortions by Races, 1975 to 1997
[Continued]

Year	All Races			Whites			Blacks and Other Races		
	Live Births (000)	Abortions (000)	Ratio per 1,000 Births	Live Births (000)	Abortions (000)	Ratio per 1,000 Births	Live Births (000)	Abortions (000)	Ratio per 1,000 Births
1993	4,000.2	1,500	375	3,149.8	911	289	850.4	589	693
1994	3,952.8	1,431	362	3,121.0	861	276	831.8	570	685
1995	3,899.6	1,364	350	3,098.9	820	265	800.7	544	679
1996	3,891.5	1,366	351	3,093.1	800	259	798.4	566	709
1997	3,880.9	1,328	342	3,072.6	773	252	808.3	555	687

Source: Statistical Abstract of the United States, 2001, U.S. Bureau of the Census, Table 92, p. 71. Data are originally from the Centers of Disease Control. Abortions in 1983 and 1986 are extrapolations. Data for 1976-1978 are not available. The trend between 1975 and 1979, however, is estimated. All birth data, from National Center for Health Statistics, show actual counts.

All Births and Abortion Rates by Two Groups:
Women Aged 15 to 44

Year	Rate per 1,000 Women 15 to 44			
	Births All Races	Abortions		
		All Races	Whites	Black & Other
1975	66.0	21.7	17.2	49.3
1976	65.0	23.5	18.9	51.0
1977	66.8	25.3	20.6	52.8
1978	65.5	27.0	22.3	54.5
1979	63.4	28.8	24.0	56.2
1980	65.6	29.3	24.3	56.5
1981	64.8	29.3	24.3	55.9
1982	64.8	28.8	23.8	55.5
1983	63.4	28.5	23.3	55.5
1984	63.2	28.1	23.1	54.3
1985	64.1	28.0	22.6	55.5
1986	63.1	27.4	21.8	55.9
1987	63.3	27.1	21.1	56.0
1988	64.5	27.3	21.2	57.3
1989	66.4	26.8	20.9	54.7
1990	68.3	27.4	21.5	54.4
1991	67.0	26.3	20.3	53.8
1992	66.5	25.9	19.6	53.9
1993	65.4	25.4	18.9	53.5
1994	64.9	24.1	17.9	51.1
1995	64.4	22.9	17.0	48.1
1996	64.3	22.9	16.6	49.2
1997	63.9	22.2	16.1	47.8

Source: Statistical Abstract of the United States, 2001, U.S. Bureau of the Census, Table 92, p. 71. Date are originally from the Centers of Disease Control. Abortions in 1983 and 1986 are extrapolations. Data for 1976-1978 are not available. Trend data between 1975 and 1979 have been extrapolated. Underlying population data are from the U.S. Bureau of the Census.

Changing Components of the Female Population Aged 15 to 44

Between 1980 and 1997, the two younger age groups have lost population share to the oldest age group in this population.

Year	Population of Age Groups				Percent of 15-44 Age Group		
	15-24	25-34	35-44	Total	15-24	25-34	35-44
1980	20,953	19,864	13,223	54,040	38.8	36.8	24.5
1981	20,738	20,324	13,619	54,681	37.9	37.6	25.2
1982	20,430	20,778	14,436	55,644	36.7	38.4	26.7
1983	20,112	21,128	15,042	56,282	35.7	39.1	27.8
1984	19,815	21,408	15,673	56,896	34.8	39.6	29.0
1985	19,566	21,618	16,251	57,435	34.1	40.0	30.1
1986	19,288	21,742	16,906	57,936	33.3	40.2	31.3
1987	18,919	21,658	17,488	58,065	32.6	40.1	32.4
1988	18,530	21,546	17,954	58,030	31.9	39.9	33.2
1989	18,149	21,308	18,579	58,036	31.3	39.4	34.4
1990	18,041	21,156	19,092	58,289	31.0	39.1	35.3
1991	17,804	20,652	19,845	58,301	30.5	38.2	36.7
1992	17,708	20,088	20,144	57,940	30.6	37.2	37.3
1993	17,682	19,544	20,593	57,819	30.6	36.2	38.1
1994	17,670	19,104	21,030	57,804	30.6	35.4	38.9
1995	17,687	18,922	21,455	58,064	30.5	35.0	39.7
1996	17,693	18,980	21,855	58,528	30.2	35.1	40.4
1997	17,893	18,892	22,173	58,958	30.3	35.0	41.0

Source: U.S. Bureau of the Census, *Quarterly Population Estimates.* See http://www.census.gov.

Contraceptive Use by Women, 15 to 44 Years of Age: 1995

	All Women[1]	Age			Race			Marital Status		
		15-24 Years	25-34 Years	35-44 Years	White	Black	Hispanic	Never Married	Married	Formerly Married
Contraceptive status and method										
All women (1,000)	60,201	18,002	20,758	21,440	42,522	8,210	6,702	22,679	29,673	7,849
PERCENT DISTRIBUTION										
Sterile[2]	29.7	2.6	25.0	57.0	30.2	31.5	28.4	6.9	43.2	45.1
Surgically sterile	27.9	1.8	23.6	54.0	28.5	29.7	26.3	5.7	41.1	42.5
Nonsurgically sterile[3]	1.7	0.7	1.3	2.8	1.6	1.8	2.0	1.1	2.0	2.2
Pregnant, postpartum	4.6	5.9	6.9	1.3	4.3	4.5	6.3	3.1	6.4	1.9
Seeking pregnancy	4.0	2.1	6.2	3.5	3.7	4.6	4.0	1.5	6.4	2.1
Not using contraceptives	22.3	44.4	13.3	12.6	21.1	23.1	26.3	46.8	4.7	18.4
Never had intercourse	10.9	30.8	3.4	1.4	10.4	8.9	12.1	28.9	-	-
No intercourse in last month[4]	6.2	7.0	5.3	6.5	5.7	7.2	8.6	11.5	0.5	12.7
Had intercourse in last month[4]	5.2	6.6	4.6	4.7	5.0	7.0	5.6	6.4	4.2	5.7
Using nonsurgical contraceptives	39.7	45.0	49.1	26.1	41.2	36.1	35.1	41.8	39.7	32.4
Pill	17.3	23.1	23.7	6.3	18.8	14.8	13.6	20.4	15.6	14.6
IUD	0.5	0.1	0.6	0.8	0.5	0.5	0.9	0.3	0.7	0.4
Diaphragm	1.2	0.2	1.2	2.0	1.5	0.5	0.4	0.5	1.8	0.9
Condom	13.1	13.9	15.0	10.7	13.0	12.5	12.1	13.9	13.3	10.1
Periodic abstinence	1.5	0.5	1.8	2.0	1.6	0.7	1.3	0.6	2.3	0.7
Natural family planning	0.2	-	0.3	0.3	0.3	-	0.1	-	0.4	-

[Continued]

Contraceptive Use by Women, 15 to 44 Years of Age: 1995

[Continued]

	All Women[1]	Age			Race			Marital Status		
		15-24 Years	25-34 Years	35-44 Years	White	Black	Hispanic	Never Married	Married	Formerly Married
Withdrawal	2.0	1.6	2.3	1.9	2.1	0.9	2.0	1.5	2.3	1.8
Other methods[5]	3.9	5.6	4.2	2.1	3.4	6.2	4.7	4.6	3.3	3.9

Source: U.S. National Center for Health Statistics, special tabulations from the 1995 National Survey of Family Growth, appearing in *Statistical Abstract of the United States, 2001*, Table 87, p. 69. *Notes:* 1. Includes other races, not shown separately. 2. Total sterile includes male sterile for unknown reasons. 3. Persons sterile from illness, accident, or congenital conditions. 4. Data refer to no intercourse in the 3 months prior to interview. 5. Includes implants, injectables, morning-after-pill, suppository, Today TM sponge, and less frequently used methods.

Life-Expectancy and Birth and Deaths (in Thousands) - 1900 to 1998

Year	Life-expectancy at Birth Years	By Sex		By Races		Differences Between		All Deaths (000)
		Females Years	Males Years	Whites Years	Blacks Years	Women/Men Years	Whites/Blacks Years	
1900	47.3	48.3	46.3	47.6	33.0	2.0	14.6	343.2
1901	49.1	50.6	47.6	49.4	33.7	3.0	15.7	332.2
1902	51.5	53.4	49.8	51.9	34.6	3.6	17.3	318.6
1903	50.5	52.0	49.1	50.9	33.1	2.9	17.8	327.3
1904	47.6	49.1	46.2	48.0	30.8	2.9	17.2	349.9
1905	48.7	50.2	47.3	49.1	31.3	2.9	17.8	345.9
1906	48.7	50.8	46.9	49.3	32.9	3.9	16.4	531.0
1907	47.6	49.9	45.6	48.1	32.5	4.3	15.6	550.2
1908	51.1	52.8	49.5	51.5	34.9	3.3	16.6	567.2
1909	52.1	53.8	50.5	52.5	35.7	3.3	16.8	630.1
1910	50.0	51.8	48.4	50.3	35.6	3.4	14.7	696.9
1911	52.6	54.4	50.9	53.0	36.4	3.5	16.6	749.9
1912	53.5	55.9	51.5	53.9	37.9	4.4	16.0	745.8
1913	52.5	55.0	50.3	53.0	38.4	4.7	14.6	802.9
1914	54.2	56.8	52.0	54.9	38.9	4.8	16.0	810.9
1915	54.5	56.8	52.5	55.1	38.9	4.3	16.2	815.5
1916	51.7	54.3	49.6	52.5	41.3	4.7	11.2	925.0
1917	50.9	54.0	48.4	52.0	38.8	5.6	13.2	981.2
1918	39.1	42.2	36.6	39.8	31.1	5.6	8.7	1,430.1
1919	54.7	56.0	53.5	55.8	44.5	2.5	11.3	1,072.3
1920	54.1	54.6	53.6	54.9	45.3	1.0	9.6	1,118.1
1921	60.8	61.8	60.0	61.8	51.5	1.8	10.3	1,009.7
1922	59.6	61.0	58.4	60.4	52.4	2.6	8.0	1,084.0
1923	57.2	58.5	56.1	58.3	48.3	2.4	10.0	1,174.1
1924	59.7	61.5	58.1	61.4	46.6	3.4	14.8	1,151.1
1925	59.0	60.6	57.6	60.7	45.7	3.0	15.0	1,191.8
1926	56.7	58.0	55.5	58.2	44.6	2.5	13.6	1,257.3
1927	60.4	62.1	59.0	62.0	48.2	3.1	13.8	1,211.6
1928	56.8	58.3	55.6	58.4	46.3	2.7	12.1	1,362.0
1929	57.1	58.7	55.8	58.6	46.7	2.9	11.9	1,369.8
1930	59.7	61.6	58.1	61.4	48.1	3.5	13.3	1,327.2
1931	61.1	63.1	59.4	62.6	50.4	3.7	12.2	1,307.3
1932	62.1	63.5	61.0	63.2	53.7	2.5	9.5	1,293.3

[Continued]

Life-Expectancy and Birth and Deaths (in Thousands) - 1900 to 1998

[Continued]

Year	Life-expectancy at Birth Years	By Sex		By Races		Differences Between		All Deaths (000)
		Females Years	Males Years	Whites Years	Blacks Years	Women/Men Years	Whites/Blacks Years	
1933	63.3	65.1	61.7	64.3	54.7	3.4	9.6	1,342.1
1934	61.1	63.3	59.3	62.4	51.8	4.0	10.6	1,396.9
1935	61.7	63.9	59.9	62.9	53.1	4.0	9.8	1,392.8
1936	58.5	60.6	56.6	59.8	49.0	4.0	10.8	1,479.2
1937	60.0	62.4	58.0	61.4	50.3	4.4	11.1	1,450.4
1938	63.5	65.3	61.9	65.0	52.9	3.4	12.1	1,381.4
1939	63.7	65.4	62.1	64.9	54.5	3.3	10.4	1,387.9
1940	62.9	65.2	60.8	64.2	53.1	4.4	11.1	1,417.3
1941	64.8	66.8	63.1	66.2	53.8	3.7	12.4	1,397.6
1942	66.2	67.9	64.7	67.3	56.6	3.2	10.7	1,385.2
1943	63.3	64.4	62.4	64.2	55.6	2.0	8.6	1,459.5
1944	65.2	66.8	63.6	66.2	56.6	3.2	9.6	1,411.3
1945	65.9	67.9	63.6	66.8	57.7	4.3	9.1	1,401.7
1946	66.7	69.4	64.4	67.5	59.1	5.0	8.4	1,395.6
1947	66.8	69.7	64.4	67.6	59.7	5.3	7.9	1,445.4
1948	67.2	69.9	64.6	68.0	60.0	5.3	8.0	1,444.3
1949	68.0	70.7	65.2	68.8	60.6	5.5	8.2	1,443.6
1950	68.2	71.1	65.6	69.1	60.8	5.5	8.3	1,452.5
1951	68.4	71.4	65.6	69.3	61.2	5.8	8.1	1,482.1
1952	68.6	71.6	65.8	69.5	61.4	5.8	8.1	1,496.8
1953	68.8	72.0	66.0	69.7	62.0	6.0	7.7	1,517.5
1954	69.6	72.8	66.7	70.5	63.4	6.1	7.1	1,481.1
1955	69.6	72.8	66.7	70.5	63.7	6.1	6.8	1,528.7
1956	69.7	72.9	66.7	70.5	63.6	6.2	6.9	1,564.5
1957	69.5	72.7	66.4	70.3	63.0	6.3	7.3	1,633.1
1958	69.6	72.9	66.6	70.5	63.4	6.3	7.1	1,647.9
1959	69.9	73.2	66.8	70.7	63.9	6.4	6.8	1,656.8
1960	69.7	73.1	66.6	70.6	63.6	6.5	7.0	1,712.0
1961	70.2	73.6	67.1	71.0	64.5	6.5	6.5	1,701.5
1962	70.1	73.5	66.9	70.9	64.2	6.6	6.7	1,756.7
1963	69.9	73.4	66.6	70.8	63.7	6.8	7.1	1,813.5
1964	70.2	73.7	66.8	71.0	64.2	6.9	6.8	1,798.1
1965	70.2	73.8	66.8	71.1	64.3	7.0	6.8	1,828.1
1966	70.2	73.9	66.7	71.1	64.2	7.2	6.9	1,863.1
1967	70.5	74.3	67.0	71.4	64.9	7.3	6.5	1,851.3
1968	70.2	74.1	66.6	71.1	64.1	7.5	7.0	1,930.1
1969	70.5	74.4	66.8	71.4	64.5	7.6	6.9	1,922.0
1970	70.8	74.7	67.1	71.7	64.1	7.6	7.6	1,921.0
1971	71.1	75.0	67.4	72.0	64.6	7.6	7.4	1,927.5
1972	71.2	75.1	67.4	72.0	64.7	7.7	7.3	1,963.9
1973	71.4	75.3	67.6	72.2	65.0	7.7	7.2	1,973.0
1974	72.0	75.9	68.2	72.8	66.0	7.7	6.8	1,934.4
1975	72.6	76.6	68.8	73.4	66.8	7.8	6.6	1,892.9
1976	72.9	76.8	69.1	73.6	67.2	7.7	6.4	1,909.4

[Continued]

Life-Expectancy and Birth and Deaths (in Thousands) - 1900 to 1998
[Continued]

Year	Life-expectancy at Birth Years	By Sex		By Races		Differences Between		All Deaths (000)
		Females Years	Males Years	Whites Years	Blacks Years	Women/Men Years	Whites/Blacks Years	
1977	73.3	77.2	69.5	74.0	67.7	7.7	6.3	1,899.6
1978	73.5	77.3	69.6	74.1	68.1	7.7	6.0	1,927.8
1979	73.9	77.8	70.0	74.6	68.5	7.8	6.1	1,913.8
1980	73.7	77.4	70.0	74.4	68.1	7.4	6.3	1,989.8
1981	74.1	77.8	70.4	74.8	68.9	7.4	5.9	1,978.0
1982	74.5	78.1	70.8	75.1	69.4	7.3	5.7	1,974.8
1983	74.6	78.1	71.0	75.2	69.4	7.1	5.8	2,019.2
1984	74.7	78.2	71.1	75.3	69.5	7.1	5.8	2,039.4
1985	74.7	78.2	71.1	75.3	69.3	7.1	6.0	2,086.4
1986	74.7	78.2	71.2	75.4	69.1	7.0	6.3	2,105.4
1987	74.9	78.3	71.4	75.6	69.1	6.9	6.5	2,123.3
1988	74.9	78.3	71.4	75.6	68.9	6.9	6.7	2,168.0
1989	75.1	78.5	71.7	75.9	68.8	6.8	7.1	2,150.5
1990	75.4	78.8	71.8	76.1	69.1	7.0	7.0	2,148.5
1991	75.5	78.9	72.0	76.3	69.3	6.9	7.0	2,169.5
1992	75.8	79.1	72.3	76.5	69.6	6.8	6.9	2,175.6
1993	75.5	78.8	72.2	76.3	69.2	6.6	7.1	2,268.6
1994	75.7	79.0	72.4	76.5	69.5	6.6	7.0	2,279.0
1995	75.8	78.9	72.5	76.5	69.6	6.4	6.9	2,312.1
1996	76.1	79.1	73.1	76.8	70.2	6.0	6.6	2,314.7
1997	76.5	79.4	73.6	77.2	71.1	5.8	6.1	2,314.2
1998	76.7	79.5	73.8	-	-	5.7	-	2,337.3

Source: U.S. Department of Health and Human Services, *National Vital Statistics Report*, Vol. 47, No. 28, December 13, 1999.

Women as a Percent of Total Population by Age Group - 1990

Age	Women as % of Population
0-19	48.8
20-39	49.9
40-59	51.2
60-79	56.1
80-84	65.3
85-89	70.2
90-94	75.4
95+	78.6

Source: U.S. Bureau of the Census, 1990 Census of the U.S. Population.

Old and Young as Percent of Total Population - 1850 to 2000, Selected Years, and Dependency Ratio

The Dependencey Ratio is the number of people that must be supported by 100 people in their productive years.

Year	65 and Older as % of Population	0-19 as % of Population	Both Groups as % of Population
1850	2.5	52.4	54.9
1900	4.1	44.3	48.4
1950	8.1	33.9	42.1
2000	12.7	28.4	41.1

Source: Population Estimates, U.S. Bureau of the Census, U.S. Department of Commerce. *Historical Statistics of the United States*, by the same agency.

Ratio: Black Death Rate to White Death Rate by Age Group

White death rate is taken as 1. Values higher than 1 mean a higher death rate than whites, values below 1 a lower death rate. Blacks only have a lower death rate than whites in the 85 and older age group.

Age Group	Males	Females
<1	2.5	2.4
1-4	2.2	2.0
5-14	1.7	1.5
15-24	1.8	1.4
25-34	2.1	2.2
35-44	2.1	2.3
45-54	2.2	2.1
55-64	1.8	1.7
65-74	1.3	1.4
75-84	1.2	1.2
85+	0.9	0.9

Source: National Center for Health Statistics, Vital Statistics of the United States, as shown in *Statistical Abstract of the United States, 2001*, Table 104, p. 78.

Population Composition of the United States, 1900 to 2000 by Decades

Hispanics may be of any race. They are also included in the other three groups.

Year	Percent of Total Population		
	Whites	Blacks	Other
1900	87.9	11.6	0.5
1910	88.9	10.7	0.4
1920	89.7	9.9	0.4
1930	89.8	9.7	0.5
1940	89.8	9.8	0.4
1950	89.5	10.0	0.5
1960	88.6	10.5	0.9
1960	88.8	10.6	0.6
1970	87.5	11.1	1.4
1980	85.9	11.8	2.2
1990	83.9	12.3	3.8
2000	82.2	12.8	5.0

Source: U.S. Bureau of the Census, U.S. Department of Commerce. Historical data from *Historical Statistics of the United States*, published by the same agency.

Actual and Projected Composition of the Population, Selected Years, as Percent of Total Population

Hispanics may be of any race. They are also included in the other three groups.

Year	Percent of Total Population			
	Whites	Blacks	Other	Hispanics
1980	85.9	11.8	2.2	6.4
2000	82.2	12.8	5.0	11.5
2025	78.5	13.9	7.5	18.2
2050	74.9	14.7	10.4	24.3

Source: U.S. Bureau of the Census, U.S. Department of Commerce.

Chapter 2
WHERE DO WE LIVE?

Urban, Rural, and Suburban Population - 1790 to 2000, by Decade

Year	Urban Population	Rural Population	Urban as % of Total	Suburban Population	Suburban as % of Urban
1790	201,655	3,727,559	5.1	-	-
1800	322,371	4,986,112	6.1	-	-
1810	525,459	6,714,422	7.3	-	-
1820	693,255	8,945,198	7.2	-	-
1830	1,127,247	11,733,455	8.8	-	-
1840	1,845,055	15,218,298	10.8	-	-
1850	3,574,496	19,617,380	15.4	-	-
1860	6,216,518	25,226,803	19.8	-	-
1870	9,902,361	28,656,010	25.7	-	-
1880	14,129,735	36,059,474	28.2	-	-
1890	22,106,265	40,873,501	35.1	-	-
1900	30,214,832	45,997,336	39.6	-	-
1910	42,064,001	50,164,495	45.6	-	-
1920	54,253,282	51,768,255	51.2	-	-
1930	69,160,599	54,042,025	56.1	-	-
1940	74,705,338	57,459,231	56.5	-	-
1950	96,846,817	54,478,981	64.0	-	-
1960	125,268,750	54,045,425	69.9	-	-
1970	149,646,617	53,565,309	73.6	88,173,947	55.09
1980	167,050,992	59,494,813	73.7	104,888,482	59.09
1990	187,053,487	61,656,386	75.2	120,651,559	60.81
2000	225,981,679	55,440,227	80.3	140,637,509	62.24

Source: Historical and 2000 population data from U.S. Bureau of the Census, *1990 Census Tabulations, Population and Housing Unit Counts, August 23, 1993 and* Population Change and Distribution, Census 2000 Brief, April 2001. Data on suburbs from the SOCDS database, distributed by U.S. Department of Housing and Urban Development, accessible at socds.huduser.org/index.html and from Statistical Abstract of the United States, 2001, Census Bureau, Appendix II, p. 892.

Metro and Nonmetro Population and Population Density

Year	Population (000)			People per Square Mile		
	Metro Areas	Suburbs	Nonmetro Areas	Metro Areas	Nonmetro Areas	United States
1960	136,737	-	42,586	193.8	15.0	50.6
1970	160,045	88,174	43,257	226.8	15.3	57.4
1980	177,505	104,888	49,037	251.5	17.3	64.0
1990	198,407	120,652	50,311	281.2	17.8	70.3
2000	225,968	140,638	55,453	320.2	19.6	79.6

Source: *Statistical Abstract of the United States, 2001*, U.S. Bureau of the Census, Appendix II, p. 892. Data on suburbs from the SOCDS database, distributed by U.S. Department of Housing and Urban Development, accessible at socds.huduser.org/index.html.

The 1997 Housing Stock - Smallest and Largest

Period	% of Housing Built in Period	
	Less Than 1,000 sq. ft.	3,000 sq. ft. or More
1949 or before	32.9	2.9
1950-1959	27.2	1.6
1960-1969	31.0	2.1
1970-1979	34.4	3.6
1980-1989	23.0	4.6
1990-1997	16.5	13.4

Source: U.S. Department of Energy, Energy Information Administration, Office of Energy Markets and End Use, *A Look at Residential Energy Consumption in 1997*, November 1999, Washington, DC 20585. New construction data from *Statistical Abstracts of the United States, 2001*, U.S. Bureau of the Census, Table 938, p. 597.

Square Foot Distribution of 1997 Housing Stock

Square Feet	% of Total Units
Fewer than 600	7.8
600 to 999	21.2
1,000 to 1,599	30.0
1,600 to 1,999	15.1
2,000 to 2,399	7.8
2,400 to 2,999	5.2
3,000 or More	4.0
No Estimate Provided	9.0

Source: U.S. Department of Energy, Energy Information Administration, Office of Energy Markets and End Use, *A Look at Resi-dential Energy Consumption in 1997*, November 1999, Washington, DC 20585.

Owners and Renters of Housing in 1999

Group	Owners %	Renters %	Total Units (000)
All	66.9	33.1	102,803
Black	46.5	53.5	12,936
Hispanic	45.2	54.8	9,042
Elderly	80.3	19.7	21,423
Below Poverty	44.0	56.0	14,264

Source: Statistical Abstract of the United States, 2001, Table 961, p. 609. Data drawn from U.S. Census Bureau, Current Housing Reports.

Regional Shares of the Population - 1900 to 2000, by Decades

Year	Percent of Population			
	Northeast	Midwest	South	West
1900	27.6	34.6	32.2	5.7
1910	28.0	32.4	31.9	7.7
1920	28.0	32.1	31.2	8.7
1930	27.9	31.3	30.7	10.0
1940	27.2	30.4	31.5	10.9
1950	26.1	29.4	31.2	13.3
1960	24.9	28.8	30.7	15.6
1970	24.1	27.8	30.9	17.1
1980	21.7	26.0	33.3	19.1
1990	20.4	24.0	34.4	21.2
2000	19.0	22.9	35.6	22.5

Source: U.S. Bureau of the Census, *Population and Housing Unit Counts*, August 27, 1993, and *Census 2000*.

People Moving as a Percent of Total Population

	Percent of Total Population Moving				
	Total	Within County	County to County	State to State	From Abroad
1947-48	20.2	13.6	6.4	3.1	0.3
1948-49	19.2	13.0	5.8	3.0	0.3
1949-50	19.1	13.1	5.6	2.6	0.3
1950-51	21.2	13.9	7.1	3.5	0.2
1951-52	20.3	13.2	6.6	3.4	0.4
1952-53	20.6	13.5	6.6	3.6	0.5
1953-54	19.3	12.2	6.4	3.2	0.6
1954-55	20.4	13.3	6.6	3.1	0.6
1955-56	21.1	13.7	6.8	3.1	0.6

[Continued]

People Moving as a Percent of Total Population

[Continued]

	Percent of Total Population Moving				
	Total	Within County	County to County	State to State	From Abroad
1956-57	19.9	13.1	6.2	3.1	0.5
1957-58	20.3	13.1	6.7	3.3	0.5
1958-59	19.7	13.1	6.1	3.0	0.5
1959-60	19.9	12.9	6.4	3.2	0.5
1960-61	20.6	13.7	6.3	3.2	0.6
1961-62	19.6	13.0	6.1	3.1	0.5
1962-63	20.0	12.6	6.8	3.6	0.6
1963-64	20.1	13.0	6.6	3.3	0.5
1964-65	20.7	13.4	6.8	3.3	0.5
1965-66	19.8	12.7	6.6	3.3	0.5
1966-67	19.0	11.6	6.7	3.4	0.7
1967-68	19.5	11.8	7.0	3.6	0.7
1968-69	19.0	11.7	6.6	3.4	0.7
1969-70	19.1	11.7	6.7	3.6	0.8
1970-71	18.7	11.4	6.5	3.4	0.8
1975-76	17.7	10.8	6.4	3.0	0.6
1980-81	17.2	10.4	6.2	2.8	0.6
1981-82	17.0	10.3	6.2	3.0	0.5
1982-83	16.6	10.1	6.0	2.7	0.4
1983-84	17.3	10.4	6.4	2.8	0.5
1984-85	20.2	13.1	6.5	3.0	0.6
1985-86	18.6	11.3	6.7	3.0	0.5
1986-87	18.6	11.6	6.5	2.8	0.5
1987-88	17.8	11.0	6.2	3.0	0.5
1988-89	17.8	10.9	6.3	3.0	0.6
1989-90	17.9	10.6	6.6	3.3	0.6
1990-91	17.0	10.3	6.1	2.9	0.6
1991-92	17.3	10.7	6.0	2.9	0.5
1992-93	17.0	10.7	5.8	2.7	0.6
1993-94	16.7	10.4	5.8	2.6	0.5
1994-95	16.4	10.8	5.3	2.2	0.3
1995-96	16.3	10.3	5.6	2.5	0.5
1996-97	16.5	10.5	5.5	2.4	0.5
1997-98	16.0	10.2	5.4	2.4	0.5
1998-99	15.9	9.4	5.9	2.8	0.5
1999-00	16.1	9.0	6.4	3.1	0.6

Source: U.S. Bureau of the Census, *Annual Geographical Mibility Rates, By Type of Movment: 1947-2000,* July 12, 2000 (Internet release), see http://www.census.gov/population/www/socdemo/migrate.html.

Chapter 3
THE FAMILY

Average Number of People per U. S. Household in the 20th Century

Year	Ave. Size of Household	Households (000)	Family Households (000)	Total Population (000)
1900	4.76	15,964	-	75,989
1910	4.54	20,256	-	91,962
1920	4.34	24,352	-	105,688
1930	4.11	29,905	-	122,910
1940	3.67	34,949	31,491	128,263
1950	3.37	43,554	38,838	146,777
1960	3.33	52,799	44,905	175,821
1970	3.14	63,401	51,456	199,079
1980	2.76	80,776	59,550	222,942
1990	2.63	93,347	66,090	245,503
2000	2.62	104,705	72,025	274,327

Source: Data for the chart are from four reports all published by the U.S. Bureau of the Census. Current Population Reports, Series P20-537, *America s Families and Living Arrangement: March 2000*. An historical compilation table entitled *Households by Type: 1940 to Present*, Internet release date June 29, 2001, available at http://www.census.gov/population/socdemo/hh-fam/tabHH- 1.txt. *Historical Statistics of the United States - Colonial Times to 1970*, p. 15. *Statistical Abstract of the United States: 2001*, pp. 14 and 15.

Family Households with Their Own Children Under 18, 1970 to 2000 by Decade

Year	Percent of Households			% of Population 19 or Younger
	With Own Children	With Two Parents	With Single Parent	
1970	47	41	6	37.9
1980	40	31	9	31.8
1990	37	27	10	28.8
2000	36	25	11	28.4

Source: U.S. Bureau of the Census, *All Parent Child Situations by Type, Race, and Hispanic Origin of Householder or Reference Person, 1970 to Present*, Internet release date June 29, 2001, data based on the Current Population Survey. U.S. Census Bureau, *America's Families and Living Arrangements 2000*, a Current Population Report issued in June 2001.

Family Households with Children, 1970 to 2000, by Decade

| Year | % of Families w/Children | |
	Married Couples	Single Parent Households
1970	87.2	12.8
1980	78.5	21.5
1990	71.9	28.1
2000	68.7	31.3

Source: U.S. Bureau of the Census, *All Parent Child Situations by Type, Race, and Hispanic Origin of Householder or Reference Person, 1970 to Present*, Internet release date June 29, 2001, data based on the Current Population Survey. U.S. Census Bureau, *America's Families and Living Arrangements 2000*, a Current Population Report issued in June 2001.

Number of Children, Under the Age of 18, by Living Arrangement in 2000

	Married Couples Households (000)	Single-Parent Households (000)	Single-Parent Households as % of Total
1 child family	9,682	6,539	40.3
2 child family	20,904	6,994	25.1
3 child family	12,228	3,477	22.1
4 or more children	6,868	2,332	25.3
Total Children (000)	49,682	19,342	-
Percent of Children	72.0	28.0	-

Source: U. S. Census Bureau, *America s Families and Living Arrangements 2000*, Current Population Report issued June 2001.

Poverty Rates - Children and Families with Children

Year	Percent Below Poverty Line		
	All Children Under 18	Married Couple Families	Female-Headed Single-Parent Families
1980	18.3	7.7	42.9
1985	20.7	8.9	45.4
1990	20.6	7.8	44.5
1995	20.8	7.5	41.5
2000	16.1	6.0	32.5

Source: U.S. Bureau of the Census, *Poverty in the U.S. 2000*, Current Population Reports, September 2001, accessible at http://www.census.gov/hhes/poverty/histpov/hstpov3.html.

Marriages, Divorces, and Marriage and Divorce Rates, 1900 to 2000

Year	Number of Marriages	Number of Divorces	Marriage Rate Per 1,000 Population	Divorce Rate Per 1,000 Population	Prime Marriage Age Popul. As % of Total
1900	709,000	56,000	9.3	0.7	25.6
1901	742,000	61,000	9.6	0.8	-
1902	776,000	61,000	9.8	0.8	-
1903	818,000	65,000	10.1	0.8	-
1904	815,000	66,000	9.9	0.8	-
1905	842,000	68,000	10.0	0.8	-
1906	895,000	72,000	10.5	0.8	-
1907	937,000	77,000	10.8	0.9	-
1908	857,000	77,000	9.7	0.9	-
1909	897,000	80,000	9.9	0.9	-
1910	948,000	83,000	10.3	0.9	26.3
1911	955,000	89,000	10.2	1.0	-
1912	1,005,000	94,000	10.5	1.0	-
1913	1,021,000	91,000	10.5	0.9	-
1914	1,025,000	101,000	10.3	1.0	-
1915	1,008,000	104,000	10.0	1.0	-
1916	1,076,000	114,000	10.6	1.1	-
1917	1,144,000	122,000	11.1	1.2	-
1918	1,000,000	116,000	9.7	1.1	-
1919	1,150,000	142,000	11.0	1.3	-
1920	1,274,000	171,000	12.0	1.6	25.0
1921	1,164,000	160,000	10.7	1.5	-
1922	1,134,000	149,000	10.3	1.4	-

[Continued]

Marriages, Divorces, and Marriage and Divorce Rates, 1900 to 2000

[Continued]

Year	Number of Marriages	Number of Divorces	Marriage Rate Per 1,000 Population	Divorce Rate Per 1,000 Population	Prime Marriage Age Popul. As % of Total
1923	1,230,000	165,000	11.0	1.5	-
1924	1,185,000	171,000	10.4	1.5	-
1925	1,188,000	175,000	10.3	1.5	-
1926	1,203,000	185,000	10.2	1.6	-
1927	1,201,000	196,000	10.1	1.6	-
1928	1,182,000	200,000	9.8	1.7	-
1929	1,233,000	206,000	10.1	1.7	-
1930	1,127,000	196,000	9.2	1.6	24.3
1931	1,061,000	188,000	8.6	1.5	-
1932	982,000	164,000	7.9	1.3	-
1933	1,098,000	165,000	8.7	1.3	-
1934	1,302,000	204,000	10.3	1.6	-
1935	1,327,000	218,000	10.4	1.7	-
1936	1,369,000	236,000	10.7	1.8	-
1937	1,451,000	249,000	11.3	1.9	-
1938	1,331,000	244,000	10.3	1.9	-
1939	1,404,000	251,000	10.7	1.9	-
1940	1,596,000	264,000	12.1	2.0	25.0
1941	1,696,000	293,000	12.7	2.2	-
1942	1,772,000	321,000	13.2	2.4	-
1943	1,577,000	359,000	11.7	2.6	-
1944	1,452,000	400,000	10.9	2.9	-
1945	1,613,000	485,000	12.2	3.5	-
1946	2,291,000	610,000	16.4	4.3	-
1947	1,992,000	483,000	13.9	3.4	-
1948	1,811,000	408,000	12.4	2.8	-
1949	1,580,000	397,000	10.6	2.7	-
1950	1,667,000	385,000	11.1	2.6	23.4
1951	1,595,000	381,000	10.4	2.5	-
1952	1,539,000	392,000	9.9	2.5	-
1953	1,546,000	390,000	9.8	2.5	-
1954	1,490,000	379,000	9.2	2.4	-
1955	1,531,000	377,000	9.3	2.3	-
1956	1,585,000	382,000	9.5	2.3	-
1957	1,518,000	381,000	8.9	2.2	-
1958	1,451,000	368,000	8.4	2.1	-
1959	1,494,000	395,000	8.5	2.2	-
1960	1,523,000	393,000	8.5	2.2	18.7
1961	1,548,000	414,000	8.5	2.3	-
1962	1,577,000	413,000	8.5	2.2	-
1963	1,654,000	428,000	8.8	2.3	-
1964	1,725,000	450,000	9.0	2.4	-

[Continued]

Marriages, Divorces, and Marriage and Divorce Rates, 1900 to 2000

[Continued]

Year	Number of Marriages	Number of Divorces	Marriage Rate Per 1,000 Population	Divorce Rate Per 1,000 Population	Prime Marriage Age Popul. As % of Total
1965	1,800,000	479,000	9.3	2.5	-
1966	1,857,000	499,000	9.5	2.5	-
1967	1,927,000	523,000	9.7	2.6	-
1968	2,069,000	584,000	10.3	2.9	-
1969	2,145,000	639,000	10.6	3.2	-
1970	2,159,000	708,000	10.6	3.5	20.3
1971	2,190,000	773,000	10.6	3.7	-
1972	2,282,000	845,000	10.9	4.0	-
1973	2,284,000	915,000	10.8	4.3	-
1974	2,230,000	977,000	10.5	4.6	-
1975	2,153,000	1,036,000	10.0	4.8	-
1976	2,155,000	1,083,000	9.9	5.0	-
1977	2,178,000	1,091,000	9.9	5.0	-
1978	2,282,000	1,130,000	10.3	5.1	-
1979	2,331,000	1,181,000	10.4	5.3	-
1980	2,390,000	1,189,000	10.6	5.2	25.7
1981	2,422,000	1,213,000	10.6	5.3	-
1982	2,456,000	1,171,000	10.6	5.1	-
1983	2,446,000	1,158,000	10.5	5.0	-
1984	2,477,000	1,169,000	10.5	5.0	-
1985	2,413,000	1,190,000	10.1	5.0	-
1986	2,407,000	1,178,000	10.0	4.9	-
1987	2,403,000	1,166,000	9.9	4.8	-
1988	2,396,000	1,167,000	9.8	4.8	-
1989	2,403,000	1,157,000	9.7	4.7	-
1990	2,443,000	1,182,000	9.8	4.7	25.0
1991	2,371,000	1,187,000	9.4	4.7	-
1992	2,362,000	1,215,000	9.3	4.8	-
1993	2,334,000	1,187,000	9.0	4.6	-
1994	2,362,000	1,191,000	9.1	4.6	-
1995	2,336,000	973,000	7.6	4.1	-
1996	2,344,000	1,150,000	8.8	4.3	-
1997	2,384,000	1,163,000	8.9	4.3	-
1998	2,244,000	1,135,000	8.3	4.2	-
1999	2,251,000	1,146,369	8.3	4.2	-
2000	2,376,000	1,129,025	8.7	4.1	20.2

Source: U.S. Center for Disease Control, National Center for Health Statistics, Fast Stats A to Z Marriage, available online at http://www.cdc.gov/nchs/fastats/marriage.htm. U.S. Center for Disease Control, National Vital Statistics Report from August 22, 2001, *Births, Marriages, Divorces, and Deaths: Provisional Data for January-December 2000.* U.S. Center for Disease Control, National Vital Statistics Report from July 6, 1999, *Births, Marriages, Divorces, and Deaths: Provisional Data for 1998.* U.S. Bureau of the Census, *Statistical Abstract of the United States: 2001,* p. 59, Table 68. U.S. Department of Health, Education and Welfare, Public Health Service, Vital and Health Statistics Series 21, number 24 from December 1973, *Marriages, divorces, and rates: United States, 1867- 1967.*

Median Age of First Marriage, 1890 to 2000 by Decades

Year	Median Year of Marriage		% of Women in Labor Force	
	Men	Women	20 & Older	Married
1890	26.1	22.0	NA	NA
1900	25.9	21.9	NA	6.0
1910	25.1	21.6	NA	NA
1920	24.6	21.2	NA	NA
1930	24.3	21.3	NA	12.0
1940	24.3	21.5	27.0	17.0
1950	22.8	20.3	33.3	25.0
1960	22.8	20.3	37.6	32.0
1970	23.2	20.8	43.3	NA
1980	24.7	22.0	51.3	NA
1990	26.1	23.9	58.0	NA
2000	26.8	25.1	60.9	NA

Source: U.S. Bureau of the Census, *Estimated Age at First Marriage: by Sex, 1890 to Present*, released online in January 1999, available at http://www.census.gov/population/socdemo/ms-la/tabms-2.txt.

Cohabiting Couples, 1960 to 2000, by Decades

Year	Cohabiting Couples (Number)	Cohabiting Couples as % of all Married Coupes	Cohabiting Couples as % of all House-holds
1960	439,000	1.0	0.8
1970	523,000	1.1	0.8
1980	1,589,000	3.0	2.0
1990	2,856,000	5.0	3.1
2000	5,283,000	8.7	5.0

Source: U.S. Census Bureau, *America's Families and Living Arrangements 2000*, Current Population Report, issued June 2001. U.S. Census Bureau. *Estimated Age at First Marriage: by Sex, 1890 to Present*, released online in January 1999, available online at http://www.census.gov/population/socdemo/ms- la/tabms-2.txt. Kenney, Catherine T., "Marriage Delayed or Marriage Forgone? New Cohort Forecasts of First Marriage for U.S. Women," *American Sociological Review*, 2001, vol.66, August, pp 506-519.

Adult Population Never Married, 1950 to 2000 by Decade

Year	Percent Never Married			
	Black Men	White Men	Black Women	White Women
1950	28.5	26.1	20.7	19.9
1960	32.4	24.5	21.6	18.7
1970	35.6	27.2	27.7	21.3
1980	41.1	28.1	33.6	21.0
1990	43.4	28.0	36.9	20.6
2000	44.9	29.1	42.4	22.1

Source: U.S. Census Bureau, *Marital Status of the Population 15 Years Old and Over by Sex and Race: 1950 to Present,* Internet release date, June 29, 2001. U.S. Census Bureau, United States Census 2000, *Race and Hispanic or Latino Origin by Age and Sex for the United States: 2000,* available online at http://www.census.gov/population/www/cen2000/briefs.html.

Gender Distribution of Whites and Blacks Aged 20 to 54, 1950 and 2000

	White Males	White Females	Black Males	Black Females
1950	49.4	50.6	47.1	52.9
2000	50.3	49.7	47.3	52.7

Source: U.S. Census Bureau, United States Census 2000, *Race and Hispanic or Latino Origin by Age and Sex for the United States: 2000,* available online at http://www.census.gov/population/www/cen2000/briefs.html. 1950 data from *Historical Statistics of the United States*, U.S. Census Bureau.

Interracial Married Couples, 1960 to 2000 by Decades

Year	Interracial as % of All Married Couples	Black and White Couples (Number)	White and Non-black Couples (Number)	Black and Non-white Couples (Number)
1960	0.4	51,000	NA	NA
1970	0.6	65,000	233,000	12,000
1980	1.3	167,000	450,000	34,000
1990	1.8	211,000	720,000	33,000
2000	2.6	363,000	1,051,000	50,000

Source: Data are from the U.S. Census Bureau, *Race of Wife by Race of Husband: 1960, 1970, 1980, 1991 and 1992*, detail table available online at http://www.census.gov/population/socdemo/race/interracttab1.txt. For figures on the year 2000, U.S. Census Bureau, *America s Families and Living Arrangements 2000*, Current Population Report, issued June 2001.

Children in Single Parent Households and Marital Status of Parent, 1960, 1968 to 2000

Year	Children Living with One Parent (Thousands)					% of Children in Single-Parent Household
	Total	Parent Never Married	Parent Divorced	Married, Spouse Absent	Widowed	
1960	5,829	243	1,339	2,711	1,540	9.1
1968	8,332	504	2,231	3,732	1,865	-
1969	8,509	469	2,274	3,977	1,784	-
1970	8,438	597	2,506	3,652	1,683	11.9
1971	9,478	810	2,780	4,176	1,706	-
1972	9,634	644	3,017	4,205	1,769	-
1973	10,093	916	3,376	4,007	1,785	-
1974	10,489	986	3,591	4,033	1,873	-
1975	11,243	1,198	4,032	4,238	1,777	-
1976	11,121	1,157	4,407	4,026	1,531	-
1977	11,311	1,368	4,583	3,832	1,527	-
1978	11,711	1,705	4,752	3,794	1,461	-
1979	11,529	1,607	4,752	3,792	1,377	-
1980	12,466	1,820	5,281	3,898	1,469	19.7
1981	12,619	1,919	5,526	3,836	1,339	-
1982	13,702	2,882	5,761	3,791	1,267	-
1983	14,006	3,366	5,881	3,640	1,120	-
1984	14,025	3,360	5,883	3,712	1,069	-
1985	14,635	3,756	6,030	3,750	1,101	-
1986	14,759	3,924	6,146	3,643	1,047	-
1987	15,071	4,295	6,139	3,720	916	-
1988	15,329	4,673	5,871	3,814	970	-
1989	15,493	4,791	6,030	3,687	985	-
1990	15,867	4,853	6,122	3,767	1,125	24.7
1991	16,624	5,568	6,122	4,045	890	-
1992	17,578	6,004	6,439	4,281	853	-
1993	17,872	6,258	6,637	4,214	763	-
1994	18,590	6,655	6,876	4,249	809	-
1995	18,938	6,558	7,201	4,348	830	-
1996	19,752	7,202	7,315	4,453	782	-
1997	19,799	7,553	7,204	4,347	693	-
1998	19,777	7,746	7,101	4,136	794	-
1999	19,899	7,701	7,228	4,144	826	27.8
2000	19,220	7,597	6,985	3,794	845	26.7

Source: U.S. Census Bureau, *Unmarried-Couple Households, by Presence of Children, 1960 to Present*, Internet release date: January 7, 1999, available online at http://www.census.gov/population/socdemo/ms-la/tabad- 2.txt. For figures on the year 2000, U.S. Census Bureau, *Census 2000 Supplementary Survey Profile*, Table 1, available on-line at http://www.cen sus.gov/c2ss/www/Profiles/2000/Tabular/010/01000US1.htm.

Children's Living Arrangements by Race, March 2000

Hispanics may be of any race. They are included in the other three groups as well.

Living Arrangement	Percent of Children			
	Whites	African Americans	Asian/Pacific Islanders	Hispanic Origin
Living with both parents	75.3	37.6	80.5	65.1
Living with mother only	17.3	49.0	14.0	25.1
Living with father only	4.3	4.2	2.5	4.4
Living with neither parent	3.1	9.2	2.9	5.4
% of children in this group	78.4	15.8	4.2	16.1
Number of children (000)	56,455.0	11,412.0	3,047.0	11,613.0

Source: U.S. Census Bureau, *Household Relationship and Living Arrangements of Children under 18,* March 2000, available online at http://www.census.gov/population/socdemo/hh-fam/p20- 537/2000/tabC2.txt.

Black Children's Living Arrangements, 1996 and 2000

Living Arrangement	% of Children		
	1996	2000	Change
Living with both parents	33.6	37.6	4.0
Living with Mother only	53.3	49.0	-4.2
Living with Father only	4.4	4.2	-0.2
Living with neither parent	9.3	9.2	-0.1

Source: U.S. Census Bureau, *Household Relationship and Living Arrangements of Children under 18,* March 2000, available online at http://www.census.gov/population/socdemo/hh-fam/p20-537/2000/tabC2.txt. U.S. Census Bureau, *Household Relationship and Presence of Parents for Persons Under 18 Years,* March 1996.

Expenditures on a Child to Age 18 by Middle-Income, Husband-Wife Families

Costs are in constant 2000 dollars.

Category	Percent of Cost		% Change	Actual Cost		$ Change
	1960	2000		1960	2000	
Housing	32	33	1	46,970	54,658	7,688
Food	24	18	-6	35,227	29,813	-5,414
Transportation	16	15	-1	23,485	24,845	1,360
Health Care	4	7	3	5,871	11,594	5,723
Clothes	11	6	-5	16,146	9,938	-6,208

[Continued]

Expenditures on a Child to Age 18 by Middle-Income, Husband-Wife Families

[Continued]

Category	Percent of Cost		% Change	Actual Cost		$ Change
	1960	2000		1960	2000	
Child Care & Education	1	10	9	1,468	16,563	15,095
Miscellaneous	12	11	-1	17,614	18,219	606

Source: U.S. Department of Agriculture, Center for Nutrition Policy and Promotion, *Expenditures on Children by Families*, 2000 Annual Report, accessible at http://www.cnpp.usda.gov/cnpp/Crc/Crc2000.pdf.

Gay-Couple Households by Selected States

The table shows the 20 states with the highest number of gay-couple households. States are shown in rank order.

State	Number of Gay Couple Households	Gay Couple Households as % of all Households
California	92,138	0.80
New York	46,490	0.66
Texas	42,912	0.58
Florida	41,048	0.65
Illinois	22,887	0.50
Pennsylvania	21,166	0.44
Georgia	19,288	0.64
Ohio	18,937	0.43
Massachusetts	17,099	0.70
New Jersey	16,604	0.54
North Carolina	16,198	0.52
Washington	15,900	0.70
Michigan	15,368	0.41
Virginia	13,802	0.51
Arizona	12,332	0.65
Maryland	11,243	0.57
Indiana	10,219	0.44
Tennessee	10,189	0.46
Colorado	10,045	0.61
Missouri	9,428	0.43

Source: U.S. Department of Commerce, Bureau of the Census, *Census 2000*, Summary File 1 (SF 1) 100-Percent Data.

Chapter 4
ETHNICITY & IMMIGRATION

Population by Race/Ethnicity in 2000

People of Hispanic/Latino origin are included in the top portion of the table. Terms like "some other race" and "two or more races" were provided by the Bureau of the Census on the Census forms. People who used these categories in self-reporting are shown in this table.

	Number	Percent
Total	281,421,906	100.0
White	211,460,626	75.1
Black or African American	34,658,190	12.3
American Indian and Alaska Native	2,475,956	0.9
Asian	10,242,998	3.6
Native Hawaiian and Other Pacific Islander	398,835	0.1
Some other race	15,359,073	5.5
Two or more races	6,826,228	2.4
Hispanic or Latino (of any race)	35,305,818	12.5

Source: U.S. Census Bureau, Census 2000 Redistricting Data (P.L. 94-171) Summary File for states, Tables PL1, PL2, PL3, and PL4.

Top 10 American Indian Tribes, 1980 and 1990

Total tribal population was 1,478,523 in 1980, 1,937,391 in 1990, and 2,475,956 in the 2000 Census.

	Population		% of All Indians		Population Share Change
	1980	1990	1980	1990	1980 to 1990
Cherokee	232,080	369,035	15.7	19.0	3.3
Navajo	158,633	225,298	10.7	11.6	0.9
Sioux	78,608	107,321	5.3	5.5	0.2
Chippewa	73,602	105,988	5.0	5.5	0.5
Choctaw	50,220	86,231	3.4	4.5	1.1
Pueblo	42,552	55,330	2.9	2.9	0.0
Apache	35,861	53,330	2.4	2.8	0.4
Iroquois	38,218	52,557	2.6	2.7	0.1
Lumbee	28,631	50,888	1.9	2.6	0.7
Creek	28,278	45,872	1.9	2.4	0.5

Source: Racial Statistics Branch, Population Division, Bureau of the Census, based on 1980 and 1990 Census data.

Top Eleven Asian Groups in the U.S.

Total Asian population in 2000 was 10,242,998 or 3.6% of the total United States population in 2000 of 281,421,906. Of the 10.2 million members of the Asian population, 7.2 million were foreign born.

	2000 Population	% of Asian Population
Chinese/Taiwanese	2,432,585	23.7
Filipino	1,850,314	18.1
Asian Indian	1,678,765	16.4
Vietnamese	1,122,528	11.0
Korean	1,076,872	10.5
Japanese	796,700	7.8
Cambodian	171,937	1.7
Hmong	169,428	1.7
Laotian	168,707	1.6
Pakistani	153,533	1.5
Thai	112,989	1.1

Source: The Asian Population: 2000, Census 2000 Brief, United States Census 2000, U.S. Census Bureau, U.S. Department of Commerce. Note: The source separately lists populations of those originating in Mainland China and on Taiwan.

Selected Foreign Languages Spoken in the U.S. - 1990

Table shows number of speakers of the language.

	Number of Speakers	% of Non-English Speakers
Total nonenglish	31,844,979	100.0
Spanish	17,339,172	54.4
French	1,702,176	5.3
German	1,547,099	4.9
Italian	1,308,648	4.1
Chinese	1,249,213	3.9
Tagalog	843,251	2.6
Polish	723,483	2.3
Korean	626,478	2.0
Vietnamese	507,069	1.6
Portuguese	429,860	1.3
Japanese	427,657	1.3
Greek	388,260	1.2
Arabic	355,150	1.1
Hindi (Urdu)	331,484	1.0
Russian	241,798	0.8
Yiddish	213,064	0.7

Source: U.S. Bureau of the Census, 1990 Census of Population, CPHL-133.

Measures of Segregation, African Americans, 1990

For an explanation of the categories, please see Chapter 4, Measuring Segregation.

| Metropolitan Areas | Total Population | African Americans | | | | | |
		Population	Dissimi-larity	Isolation	Centrali-zation	Cluster-ing	Concentrat-tion
Los Angeles-Long Beach, CA	8,856,074	991,581	0.730	0.696	0.494	2.9	0.722
New York, NY	8,546,583	2,249,997	0.815	0.820	0.220	1.3	0.865
Chicago, IL	7,410,858	1,427,357	0.842	0.814	0.067	4.5	0.797
Philadelphia, PA-NJ	4,919,786	939,124	0.769	0.720	0.566	5.0	0.712
Detroit, MI	4,266,490	942,794	0.874	0.823	0.623	4.0	0.918
Atlanta, GA	2,959,950	747,219	0.685	0.667	0.432	0.8	0.678
Washington, DC-MD-VA-WV	4,223,484	1,072,422	0.655	0.657	0.135	2.3	0.632
Houston, TX	3,321,973	613,786	0.671	0.644	0.380	0.7	0.629
Boston, MA-NH	3,227,097	213,607	0.695	0.546	0.622	8.5	0.778
Atlanta, GA	2,959,950	747,219	0.685	0.667	0.432	0.8	0.678
Dallas, TX	2,676,248	422,323	0.633	0.575	0.181	1.2	0.723

Source: U.S. Census Bureau, Housing and Household and Economic Statistics Division, accessible at census.gov/hhes.www.housing/resseg/def.htm. Presentation is from the work of Roderick J. Harrison and Daniel H. Weinberg, *Racial and Ethnic Residential Segregation: 1990.*

Cities with the Lowest and Highest African American Population: Measures of Concentration and Isolation

Concentration values nearest to zero mean that minotiries occupy as much space as the same number of whites. Negative values mean that minotrities occupy more space than whites. An isolation figure of 0.7 for a minority means that 7 minorities live with 3 whites. API stands for Asian or Pacific Islander. Hispanics may be of any race.

| Metropolitan Areas | Black Concentration | Isolation Measures | | |
		Black	Hispanic	API
Cities with the Lowest Black Population				
Bismarck, ND	0.908	0.002	0.007	0.006
Wausau, WI	0.448	0.002	0.009	0.115
Laredo, TX	-0.333	0.044	0.946	0.082
Missoula, MT	0.854	0.005	0.014	0.019
Eau Claire, WI	0.603	0.007	0.007	0.075
Medford-Ashland, OR	0.536	0.005	0.057	0.016
Dubuque, IA	0.750	0.010	0.009	0.014
Provo-Orem, UT	0.411	0.003	0.045	0.026
Grand Junction, CO	0.232	0.010	0.129	0.012
Cities with the Highest Black Population				
Houston, TX	0.629	0.644	0.496	0.160
Baltimore, MD	0.792	0.709	0.046	0.054
Atlanta, GA	0.678	0.667	0.093	0.074
Philadelphia, PA-NJ	0.712	0.720	0.427	0.110
Detroit, MI	0.918	0.823	0.128	0.056
Los Angeles-Long Beach, CA	0.722	0.696	0.716	0.406
Washington, DC-MD-VA-WV	0.632	0.657	0.227	0.128

[Continued]

Cities with the Lowest and Highest African American Population: Measures of Concentration and Isolation

[Continued]

Metropolitan Areas	Black Concentration	Isolation Measures		
		Black	Hispanic	API
Chicago, IL	0.797	0.814	0.492	0.152
New York, NY	0.865	0.820	0.666	0.328

Source: U.S. Census Bureau, Housing and Household and Economic Statistics Division, accessible at census.gov/ hhes.www.housing/resseg/def.htm. Presentation is from the work of Roderick J. Harrison and Daniel H. Weinberg, *Racial and Ethnic Residential Segregation: 1990.*

Cities with the Lowest and Highest Hispanic Population: Measures of Concentration and Isolation

Concentration values nearest to zero mean that minotiries occupy as much space as the same number of whites. Negative values mean that minotrities occupy more space than whites. An isolation figure of 0.7 for a minority means that 7 minorities live with 3 whites. API stands for Asian or Pacific Islander. Hispanics may be of any race.

Metropolitan Areas	Hispanic Concentration	Isolation Measures		
		Hispanic	Black	API
Cities with the Lowest Hispanic Population				
Owensboro, KY	0.203	0.006	0.146	0.015
Gadsden, AL	0.217	0.009	0.526	0.036
Jonesboro, AR	-0.288	0.017	0.147	0.017
Cumberland, MD-WV	0.302	0.014	0.075	0.012
Pine Bluff, AR	-0.124	0.023	0.697	0.015
Jackson, TN	0.443	0.019	0.580	0.009
Altoona, PA	0.030	0.005	0.039	0.007
Bismarck, ND	0.829	0.007	0.002	0.006
Dubuque, IA	0.374	0.009	0.010	0.014
Cities with the Highest Hispanic Population				
San Diego, CA	0.320	0.438	0.359	0.292
Orange County, CA	0.493	0.506	0.087	0.228
San Antonio, TX	0.662	0.690	0.417	0.044
Riverside-San Bernardino, CA	0.436	0.433	0.244	0.108
Houston, TX	0.662	0.496	0.644	0.160
Chicago, IL	0.718	0.492	0.814	0.152
Miami, FL	0.417	0.737	0.754	0.063
New York, NY	0.857	0.666	0.820	0.328
Los Angeles-Long Beach, CA	0.710	0.716	0.696	0.406

Source: U.S. Census Bureau, Housing and Household and Economic Statistics Division, accessible at census.gov/ hhes.www.housing/resseg/def.htm. Presentation is from the work of Roderick J. Harrison and Daniel H. Weinberg, *Racial and Ethnic Residential Segregation: 1990.*

Cities with the Lowest and Highest Asian/Pacific Islander Population: Measures of Concentration and Isolation

Concentration values nearest to zero mean that minotiries occupy as much space as the same number of whites. Negative values mean that minotrities occupy more space than whites. An isolation figure of 0.7 for a minority means that 7 minorities live with 3 whites. API stands for Asian or Pacific Islander. Hispanics may be of any race.

Metropolitan Areas	API Concentration	Isolation Measures		
		API	Black	Hispanic
Cities with the Lowest API Population				
Owensboro, KY	0.476	0.015	0.146	0.006
Victoria, TX	0.528	0.009	0.286	0.513
Jackson, TN	0.750	0.009	0.580	0.019
Casper, WY	0.562	0.006	0.025	0.054
Bismarck, ND	0.282	0.006	0.002	0.007
St. Joseph, MO	0.387	0.009	0.091	0.025
Florence, AL	0.621	0.005	0.338	0.006
Rocky Mount, NC	0.614	0.010	0.598	0.024
Florence, SC	0.571	0.010	0.604	0.060
Cities with the Highest API Population				
Washington, DC-MD-VA-WV	0.718	0.128	0.657	0.227
Orange County, CA	0.231	0.228	0.087	0.506
Chicago, IL	0.542	0.152	0.814	0.492
San Jose, CA	0.571	0.369	0.146	0.473
Oakland, CA	0.217	0.322	0.608	0.335
San Francisco, CA	0.794	0.460	0.479	0.413
Honolulu, HI	0.168	0.754	0.182	0.284
New York, NY	0.715	0.328	0.820	0.666
Los Angeles-Long Beach, CA	0.649	0.406	0.696	0.716

Source: U.S. Census Bureau, Housing and Household and Economic Statistics Division, accessible at census.gov/ hhes.www.housing/resseg/def.htm. Presentation is from the work of Roderick J. Harrison and Daniel H. Weinberg, *Racial and Ethnic Residential Segregation: 1990.*

Cities with the Lowest and Highest American Indian Population: Measures of Concentration and Isolation

Concentration values nearest to zero mean that minotiries occupy as much space as the same number of whites. Negative values mean that minotrities occupy more space than whites. An isolation figure of 0.7 for a minority means that 7 minorities live with 3 whites. API stands for Asian or Pacific Islander. Hispanics may be of any race.

Metropolitan Areas	Indian Concentration	Isolation measures		
		Indian	Black	Hispanic
Cities with the Lowest American Indian Population				
Cumberland, MD-WV	-0.123	0.002	0.075	0.014
Dubuque, IA	0.466	0.003	0.010	0.009
Jackson, TN	0.045	0.004	0.580	0.019
Owensboro, KY	0.358	0.002	0.146	0.006
Sharon, PA	0.121	0.003	0.337	0.009
Danville, VA	0.291	0.003	0.453	0.016
Altoona, PA	0.014	0.002	0.039	0.005

[Continued]

Cities with the Lowest and Highest American Indian Population:
Measures of Concentration and Isolation
[Continued]

Metropolitan Areas	Indian Concentration	Isolation measures		
		Indian	Black	Hispanic
Hattiesburg, MS	0.066	0.005	0.586	0.019
Auburn-Opelika, AL	-0.189	0.003	0.425	0.011
Cities with the Highest American Indian Population				
Minneapolis-St. Paul, MN-WI	0.615	0.099	0.296	0.057
Riverside-San Bernardino, CA	-0.462	0.041	0.244	0.433
Flagstaff, AZ-UT	-2.422	0.750	0.093	0.218
New York, NY	0.691	0.135	0.820	0.666
Albuquerque, NM	-17.356	0.504	0.117	0.533
Los Angeles-Long Beach, CA	0.109	0.050	0.696	0.716
Oklahoma City, OK	-0.224	0.082	0.468	0.102
Tulsa, OK	-0.750	0.110	0.514	0.038
Phoenix-Mesa, AZ	-3.971	0.355	0.242	0.407

Source: U.S. Census Bureau, Housing and Household and Economic Statistics Division, accessible at census.gov/hhes.www.housing/resseg/def.htm. Presentation is from the work of Roderick J. Harrison and Daniel H. Weinberg, *Racial and Ethnic Residential Segregation: 1990.*

U.S. Foreign-born Population, 1850 to 2000

Year	Population	
	Millions	%
1850	2.2	9.7
1860	4.1	13.2
1870	5.6	14.4
1880	6.7	13.3
1890	9.2	14.8
1900	10.3	13.6
1910	13.5	17.7
1920	13.9	13.2
1930	14.2	11.6
1940	11.6	8.8
1950	10.3	6.9
1960	9.7	5.4
1970	9.6	4.7
1980	14.1	6.2
1990	19.8	7.9
2000	28.4	10.4

Source: Schmidley, A. Dianne, U.S. Census Bureau, Current Population Reports, Series P23-206, "Profile of the Foreign-Born Population in the United States: 2000," U.S. Government Printing Office, Washington, DC, 2001.

Foreign-Born Population by Citizenship Status

Year	Foreign-born Population (millions)	Noncitizen (millions)	Naturalized Citizen (millions)	Noncitizen as % of Foreign-born
1970	9.7	3.5	6.2	36.1
1980	14.1	7.0	7.1	49.6
1990	19.8	11.8	11.8	59.6
2000	28.4	17.8	17.8	62.7

Source: Schmidley, A. Dianne, U.S. Census Bureau, Current Population Reports, Series P23-206, "Profile of the Foreign-Born Population in the United States: 2000," U.S. Government Printing Office, Washington, DC, 2001.

Citizenship of Foreign-Born by Region in 2000

Region of Origin	% Naturalized Citizens	% of Foreign-born
Europe	52.0	15.5
Asia	47.1	25.4
Northern America	43.1	2.5
Africa	37.0	2.5
Latin America	28.3	51.1

Source: Schmidley, A. Dianne, U.S. Census Bureau, Current Population Reports, Series P23-206, "Profile of the Foreign-Born Population in the United States: 2000," U.S. Government Printing Office, Washington, DC, 2001.

Foreign-Born Population and Illegal Immigrants - 2000

The 33.1 million figure for the foreign-born population is some 4.7 million higher than shown in the last three tables which were based on the March 2000 Current Population Survey data, not 2000 Census results.

Category	Foreign-born Population
Legal immigrants	21,612,023
Temporary migrants	1,200,000
Others of known status	1,789,474
Illegal immigrants	8,490,491
Total	33,091,988

Source: Robinson, J. Gregory, *ESCAP II - Demographic Analysis Results,* Executive Steering Committee for A.C.E. Policy II, Report No. 1, October 13, 2001, U.S. Bureau of the Census and 1999 Statistical Yearbook of the Immigration and Naturalization Service, obtainable at http://www.ins.usdoj.gov/graphics/aboutins/statistics/Illegals.htm.

Chapter 5
THE POLITICAL WORLD: VOTING, TOLERANCE, AND CIVILITY

Voting in Presidential Elections, 1932-2000

Year	Voting Age Population	Turnout	% Turnout
1932	75,768,000	39,816,522	52.6
1936	80,354,000	45,646,817	56.8
1940	84,728,000	49,646,817	56.8
1944	85,654,000	48,025,684	56.1
1948	95,575,000	48,833,680	51.1
1952	99,929,000	61,551,919	61.6
1956	104,515,000	62,033,908	59.4
1960	109,159,000	68,838,204	63.1
1964	114,090,000	70,644,592	69.3
1968	120,328,186	73,211,875	67.8
1972	140,336,000	77,718,554	63.0
1976	158,373,000	81,555,789	59.2
1980	169,597,000	86,515,221	59.2
1984	174,466,000	92,652,680	59.9
1988	182,778,000	91,594,693	57.4
1992	189,529,000	104,405,155	61.3
1996	196,511,000	96,456,345	54.2
2000	205,815,000	105,586,274	54.7

Source: Census data cited in *Committee for the Study of the American Electorate.* Retrieved April 2, 2002 from http://wwww.gspm.org/csae/cgans12.html; U.S. Census Bureau. *Current Population Reports. Voting and Registration in the Election of November 2000,* February 2002, p. 12.

Party Identification of Voters, 1952 to 2000

Year	% of Voters Identifying as			
	Democrats	Republicans	Independents	Apolitical
1952	57	34	6	3
1954	56	33	7	4
1956	50	37	9	4
1958	56	33	7	4
1960	52	36	10	2
1962	54	35	8	4
1964	61	30	8	1

[Continued]

Party Identification of Voters, 1952 to 2000

[Continued]

Year	% of Voters Identifying as			
	Democrats	Republicans	Independents	Apolitical
1966	55	32	12	1
1968	55	33	11	1
1970	54	32	13	1
1972	52	34	13	1
1974	52	31	15	3
1976	52	33	15	1
1978	54	30	14	3
1980	52	33	13	2
1982	55	32	11	2
1984	48	39	11	2
1986	51	36	12	2
1988	47	41	11	2
1990	52	36	10	2
1992	50	38	12	1
1994	47	41	11	1
1996	52	38	9	1
1998	51	37	11	2
2000	50	37	12	1

Source: The NES Guide to Public Opinion and Electoral Behavior. Retrieved April 4, 2002 online from http://www.umich.edu.

Voters' Party Affiliation by Sex

Data include those who "lean" toward one of the parties shown.

Year	Percent of Females and Males Identifying As					
	Democrats		Republicans		Independents	
	Female	Male	Female	Male	Female	Male
1952	56	58	35	33	5	7
1954	53	60	35	31	7	8
1956	47	54	40	35	8	10
1958	55	57	33	33	7	7
1960	50	53	36	36	9	10
1962	51	57	37	32	7	9
1964	61	61	30	30	7	8
1966	55	54	31	33	12	12
1968	57	53	31	35	11	10
1970	54	54	32	32	13	13
1972	54	49	33	35	12	15
1974	53	50	29	33	14	16
1976	52	50	33	33	13	17
1978	55	53	30	30	12	16
1980	55	49	32	34	11	15

[Continued]

Voters' Party Affiliation by Sex
[Continued]

Year	Percent of Females and Males Identifying As					
	Democrats		Republicans		Independents	
	Female	Male	Female	Male	Female	Male
1982	59	51	29	35	10	13
1984	50	46	38	42	11	12
1986	53	48	34	39	11	12
1988	50	43	38	45	10	11
1990	53	50	33	40	11	9
1992	54	45	34	42	11	12
1994	53	41	36	48	10	11
1996	58	45	32	45	9	9
1998	53	49	34	40	11	10
2000	53	46	34	41	12	12

Source: The NES Guide to Public Opinion and Electoral Behavior. Retrieved online April, 4, 2002 from http://www.www.umich.edu.

Registration and Voting in Presidential Elections by Women and Men, 1968 to 2000

Year	% Registered		% Voting	
	Women	Men	Women	Men
1968	72.8	76.0	66.0	69.8
1972	71.6	73.1	62.0	64.1
1976	66.4	67.1	58.8	59.6
1980	67.1	66.6	59.4	59.1
1984	69.3	67.3	60.8	59.0
1988	67.8	65.2	58.3	56.4
1992	69.3	66.9	62.3	60.2
1996	67.3	64.4	55.5	52.8
2000	65.6	62.2	56.2	53.1

Source: U.S. Bureau of the Census, *Reported Voting and Registration by Race, Hispanic Origin, Sex and Age Groups.* Retrieved online from http://www.census.gov.

Eligible Population Voting - By Age Group - 1964 to 2000

Year	Percent of Those Eligible Voting				Total Voting
	Those Aged:				
	18 to 24	25 to 44	45 to 64	65 and Older	
1964	50.9	69.0	75.9	66.3	69.3
1968	50.4	66.6	74.9	65.8	67.8
1972	49.6	62.7	70.8	63.5	63.0
1976	42.2	58.7	68.7	62.2	59.2

[Continued]

Eligible Population Voting - By Age Group - 1964 to 2000

[Continued]

| Year | Percent of Those Eligible Voting | | | | Total Voting |
| | Those Aged: | | | | |
	18 to 24	25 to 44	45 to 64	65 and Older	
1980	39.9	58.7	69.3	65.1	59.2
1984	40.8	58.4	69.8	67.7	59.9
1988	36.2	54.0	67.9	68.8	57.4
1992	42.8	58.3	70.0	70.1	61.3
1996	32.4	49.2	64.4	67.0	54.2
2000	32.3	49.8	64.1	67.6	54.7

Source: U.S. Census Bureau, Current Population Reports, *Voting and Registration in the Election of November 2000*, February 2002, p.12.

Percent of Those Eligible Voting - By Race/ Ethnicity - 1964 to 2000

Hispanics may be of any race and are included under whites and blacks as well.

Year	Whites	Blacks	Hispanics
1964	70.7	58.5	-
1968	69.1	57.6	-
1972	64.5	52.1	37.5
1976	60.9	48.7	31.8
1980	60.9	50.5	29.9
1984	61.4	55.8	32.6
1988	59.1	51.5	28.8
1992	63.6	54.0	28.9
1996	56.0	50.6	26.7
2000	56.4	53.5	27.5

Source: U.S. Bureau of the Census. Current Population Reports. *Voting and Registration in the Election of November 2000,* February 2002, p. 12.

How the Races Voted - 1980 to 2000

Data for Asians not available for 1980, 1984, and 1988.

| | Percent Voting for Parties: | | | |
	Whites	Blacks	Hispanics	Asians
1980				
Republican	56	11	33	-
Democrat	36	85	59	-
Independent	7	3	6	-

[Continued]

How the Races Voted - 1980 to 2000
[Continued]

	Percent Voting for Parties:			
	Whites	Blacks	Hispanics	Asians
1984				
Republican	64	9	37	-
Democrat	38	90	62	-
1988				
Republican	59	12	30	-
Democrat	40	86	69	-
1992				
Republican	39	83	61	31
Democrat	40	10	25	55
Independent	20	7	14	15
1996				
Republican	46	12	21	48
Democrat	43	84	72	43
Independent	9	4	6	8
2000				
Republican	54	8	31	41
Democrat	42	90	67	54
Independent	3	1	2	4

Source: Connelley, Marjorie. *Who Voted: A Portrait of American Politics, 1976-2000. New York Times,* November 12, 2000, p. 4. Data for 2000 were collected by Voter News Service based on questionnaires completed by 13,279 voters leaving 300 polling places on Election Day. 1996 data came from a survey of 16,627 voters. 1992 came from a survey of 15,490 voters. Data from 1980 - 1988 came from the *New York Times* and CBS News: 11,645 in 1998, 9,174 in 1984, 15,201 in 1980.

Presidential Election Voting by Religious Affiliation

	Percent Voting for Party:		
	White Protestant	Catholic	Jewish
1976			
Republican	58	44	34
Democrat	41	54	64
1980			
Republican	63	50	39
Democrat	31	42	45
Independent	6	7	15
1984			
Republican	72	54	31
Democrat	27	45	67
1988			
Republican	66	52	35
Democrat	33	47	64
1992			
Republican	47	35	11

[Continued]

Presidential Election Voting by Religious Affiliation

[Continued]

	Percent Voting for Party:		
	White Protestant	Catholic	Jewish
Democrat	33	44	80
Independent	21	20	9
1996			
Republican	53	37	16
Democrat	36	53	78
Independent	10	9	3
2000			
Republican	63	47	19
Democrat	34	49	79
Independent	2	2	1

Source: Connelley, Marjorie. *Who Voted: A Portrait of American Politics, 1976-2000. New York Times*, November 12, 2000, p. 4. Data for 2000 were collected by Voter News Service based on questionnaires completed by 13,279 voters leaving 300 polling places on Election Day. 1996 data came from a survey of 16,627 voters. 1992 came from a survey of 15,490 voters. Data from 1980 - 1988 came from the *New York Times* and CBS News: 11,645 in 1998, 9,174 in 1984, 15,201 in 1980.

Top Reasons for Not Voting in 2000

Reason Given	Percent
Bad weather	0.6
Transportation problems	2.4
Inconvenient	2.4
Forgot	4.0
Registration problems	6.9
Refused, don't know	7.5
Didn't like candidates	7.7
Out of town	10.2
Not interested	12.2
Illness or emergency	14.8
Too busy	20.9

Source: U.S. Census Bureau, "Voting and Registration in the Election of November 2000," February 2002, p. 10.

How People Classify Themselves on the Political Spectrum

| Year | Percent of Those Who Describe Themselves as: | | | | | | | Summary | | | |
	Moderate, Middle of the Road	Conser-vative	Slightly Conser-vative	Slightly Liberal	Liberal	Extremely Conser-vative	Extremely Liberal	All Conser-vatives	All Liberals	Moderates	No Opinion
1972	27	10	15	10	7	1	1	26	18	27	29
1974	26	12	12	8	11	2	2	26	21	26	27
1976	25	11	12	8	7	2	1	25	16	25	34
1978	27	11	14	10	8	2	2	27	20	27	26
1980	20	13	13	9	6	2	2	28	17	20	35
1982	22	12	13	8	6	2	1	27	15	22	36
1984	23	13	14	9	7	2	2	29	18	23	30
1986	28	13	15	11	9	2	1	30	21	28	21
1988	22	14	15	9	6	3	2	32	17	22	29
1990	24	10	14	8	7	2	1	26	16	24	34
1992	23	13	15	10	8	3	2	31	20	23	26
1994	26	19	14	7	6	3	1	36	14	26	24
1996	24	15	15	10	7	3	1	30	18	28	25
1998	28	13	15	9	7	2	2	30	18	28	24
2000	23	15	12	9	9	3	2	30	20	23	27

Source: The NES Guide to Public Opinion and Electoral Behavior. Retrieved April 4, 2002 online from http://www.umich.edu.

How We See Men and Women - Opinion Poll

	% Describing Trait as:	
	More True of Women	More True of Men
Emotional	90	3
Affectionate	86	5
Talkative	78	10
Creative	65	15
Patient	72	19
Intelligent	36	21
Ambitious	33	44
Easygoing	38	45
Courageous	27	50
Aggressive	20	68

Source: Americans See Women as Emotional and Affectionate, Men as More Aggressive. Retrieved online April 17, 2002 from: http://www.gallup.com.

Fortune 500 Firms Offering Domestic Partner Benefits to Employees

Year	Number Offering Benefits
1993	7
1994	13
1995	15
1996	19
1997	34
1998	60
1999	77
2000	99
2001	116

Source: Unmarried, with Benefits. U.S. News & World Report, February 26, 2001, p. 10; *Domestic Partner Benefits Doubled From 1997. Research Alert*, February 26, 2001, p. 8.

Gays in the Military: Discharges and Harrassment Complaints

Year	Dis- charges	Harrassment Complaints
1994	617	62
1995	772	127
1996	870	132
1997	1,007	182
1998	1,163	400
1999	1,046	968
2000	1,231	871
2001	1,250	1,075

Source: Stone, Andrea. "Military Discharges of Gays, Rising, Report Says." *USA Today*, March 14, 2002, p. 10A. *Gays and the Military Timeline.* Retrieved online April 24, 2002 from http://www.glimm.com; *Army Base Acknowledges Under-Reporting Gay Discharges.* Retrieved online from http://www.sldn.org.

Chapter 6
RELIGION IN AMERICA

Religious Affiliation in the United States, 1990 and 2001

Percent of adult population.

	1990	2001
Christianity	81.7	76.0
Nonreligious/Secular	7.1	13.2
Other	11.2	10.8

Source: "Top 20 Religions in the United States." Retrieved February 28, 2002 from http://www.adherents.com/rel_USA.html. 1990 and 2000 Population data: U.S. Census Bureau.

10 Largest Denominational Families, 1990 and 2001

Percent of U.S. population.

	1990	2001
Catholic	26.2	24.5
Baptist	19.4	16.3
Methodist/Wesleyan	8.0	6.8
Lutheran	5.2	4.6
Presbyterian	2.8	2.7
Pentecostal/Charismatic	1.8	2.1
Episcopalian/Anglican	1.7	1.7
Judaism	1.8	1.3
Mormon/Latter-Day Saints	1.4	1.3
Churches of Christ	1.0	1.2

Source: "Largest Religious Groups in the United States of America." Retrieved February 28, 2002 from http://www.adherents.com/rel_USA.html.

Net % Gain or Loss of Members Due to Switching Religions, 2001

	% Net Gain/Loss
Non-denominational	27
Evangelical/Born Again	26
No religion	18
Pentecostal	11
Buddhist	10
Christian, no denomination specified	8
Jehovah's Witnesses	7
Muslim/Islamic	7
Seventh Day Adventist	7
Assemblies of God	6
Church of God	4
Episcopalian/Anglican	3
Mormon	0
Baptist	-1
Lutheran	-1
Presbyterian	-1
Churches of Christ	-2
Judaism	-4
Congregational/UCC	-5
Methodist	-6
Catholic	-9
Protestant	-13

Source: "Exhibit 7: Number of Adults by Current and Prior Religious Identification, 2001." *American Religious Identification Survey.* Retrieved March 5, 2002 from http://www.gc.cuny.edu/studies/images/image019.gif.

Top 20 Religions in the United States Based on Growth Rate, 1990-2001

	% Change 1990-2001
Wiccan	1,575.0
Deity (Deist)	717.0
Sikhism	338.0
New Age	240.0
Hindu	237.4
Baha'i	200.0
Buddhism	170.0
Congregational/UCC	130.1
Native American Religion	119.0
Nonreligious/secular	110.0
Muslim/Islamic	109.5
Christian, no denomination specified	75.8

[Continued]

Top 20 Religions in the United States Based on Growth Rate, 1990-2001

[Continued]

	% Change 1990-2001
Taoist	74.0
Humanist	69.0
Assemblies of God	67.6
Churches of Christ	46.6
Eckankar	44.0
Pentecostal/Charismatic	38.1
Unitarian Universalist	25.3
Scientology	22.0

Source: Mayor, Egon and Barry Kosmin. "A Measure of Faith." *USA Today*, December 24, 2001. "Top 20 Religions in the United States, 2001." Retrieved February 28, 2002 from http://www.adherents.com/rel_USA.html.

Denominations With the Most Churches in 1999

	1980	1990	1999	% Growth or Decline 1980-1999
Southern Baptist Convention	35,552	37,992	40,870	14.9
United Methodist Church	38,465	37,238	35,609	-7.4
Roman Catholic Church	22,348	22,441	19,627	-12.2
Churches of Christ	12,719	13,097	15,000	17.9
Assemblies of God	9,447	11,149	12,055	27.6
Church of Jesus Christ of Latter-Day Saints	6,771	9,208	11,315	67.1
Jehovah's Witnesses	NA	8,547	11,257	31.7
Presbyterian Church (U.S.A.)	12,701	11,433	11,216	-11.6
Evangelical Lutheran Church in America	10,842	10,912	10,851	0.1
Episcopal Church	7,291	7,333	7,390	1.4

Source: U.S. Census Bureau. *Statistical Abstract of the United States: 2001.* American Religion Data Archive. "Denominational Groupings: Full U.S. Report." Retrieved March 6, 2002 from http://www.thearda.com. "Top 10 Religious Bodies with Most Churches in the U.S., 1990." Retrieved February 28, 2002 from http://www.adherents.com/rel_USA.html. *Note:* NA stands for data not available.

Denominations With the Most Churches in 1999: Average Adherents per Church

	1980	1990	1999
Southern Baptist Convention	458	499	385
United Methodist Church	300	298	235
Roman Catholic Church	2,126	2,379	3,179
Churches of Christ	126	128	100
Assemblies of God	171	194	214
Church of Jesus Christ of Latter-Day Saints	397	385	452

[Continued]

Denominations With the Most Churches in 1999: Average Adherents per Church

[Continued]

	1980	1990	1999
Jehovah's Witnesses	NA	161	88
Presbyterian Church (U.S.A.)	316	311	317
Evangelical Lutheran Church in America	496	479	475
Episcopal Church	387	333	314

Source: U.S. Census Bureau. *Statistical Abstract of the United States: 2001.* American Religion Data Archive. "Denominational Groupings: Full U.S. Report." Retrieved March 6, 2002 from http://www.thearda.com. "Top 10 Religious Bodies with Most Churches in the U.S., 1990." Retrieved February 28, 2002 from http://www.adherents.com/rel_USA.html. *Note:* NA stands for data not available.

Non-Christian Houses of Worship in the United States, 2002

Jewish data are for 1990. Baha'i data are for 2001.

	2002
Jewish	3,419
Islamic	1,835
Buddhist	1,654
Baha'i	1,200
Hindu	647
Sikh	213
Taoist	9

Source: U.S. Census Bureau. *Statistical Abstract of the United States: 1994.* The Pluralism Project. "Geographic Distribution of Religious Centers in the U.S." Retrieved March 6, 2002 from http://www.pluralism.org/resources/statistics/distribution.php. "Welcome to The Baha'i Faith—Community." Retrieved March 6, 2002 from http://www.us.bahai.org/community/index.html. "Taoist Temples and Centers in the West." Retrieved March 7, 2002 from http://www.ReligionQuest.com.

Top 10 Online Activities of "Religion Surfers", 2001

	% of "Religion Surfers"
Looked for info about own faith	67
Looked for info about another faith	50
Downloaded religious music	38
Emailed a prayer request	38
Given spiritual guidance via email	37
Bought religious items online	34
Planned religious activities via email	29
Gotten idea for religious ceremonies	28

[Continued]

Top 10 Online Activities of "Religion Surfers", 2001

[Continued]

	% of "Religion Surfers"
Subscribed to a religious listserv	27
Downloaded sermons	25

Source: Larsen, Elena. *CyberFaith: How Americans Pursue Religion Online.* Pew Internet & American Life Project: Washington D.C., December 23, 2001. Retrieved online at http://www.pewinternet.org/.

Top 10 Things Congregations Do With Their Web Sites, 2000

	% That Currently Offer This Feature
Encourage visitors to attend their church	83
Post mission statements, sermons, or other text	77
Link to denomination and faith-related sites	76
Link to scripture studies or devotional material	60
Post schedules, meeting minutes, internal communications	56
Post photos of congregational events	50
Post youth group material	44
Link to sites to help with congregational administration	40
Link to community sites	33
Have material promoting missionary/evangelical work	31

Source: Larsen, Elena, et. al. *Wired churches, wired temples: Taking congregations and missions into cyberspace.* Pew Internet & American Life Project: Washington D.C., December 20, 2000.

Chapter 7
HOW EDUCATED ARE WE?

Percentage of High School Graduates, 1870-2000

	Public High School	Private High School	Graduates as % of 17-year Olds
1870	NA	NA	2.0
1880	NA	NA	2.5
1890	50.0	50.0	3.5
1900	65.3	34.7	6.4
1910	71.2	28.8	8.8
1920	74.3	25.7	16.8
1930	88.8	11.2	29.0
1940	93.6	6.4	50.8
1950	88.6	11.4	59.0
1960	87.6	12.4	69.5
1970	89.6	10.4	76.9
1980	90.3	9.7	71.4
1990	89.7	10.3	73.8
2000	89.6	10.4	70.6

Source: National Center for Education Statistics. U.S. Department of Education. *Digest of Education Statistics: 2000.* Retrieved March 19, 2002 from http://nces.ed.gov. *Note:* NA stands for data not available.

Higher Education: Enrollment and Degrees Conferred, 1870-1998

	Total Enrollment	Public Enrollment	Private Enrollment	Degrees Conferred
1870	52.0	NA	NA	9.4
1880	116.0	NA	NA	13.8
1890	157.0	NA	NA	16.7
1900	238.0	NA	NA	29.4
1910	355.0	NA	NA	39.8
1920	598.0	NA	NA	53.5
1930	1,101.0	NA	NA	139.8
1940	1,494.0	NA	NA	216.5
1950	2,281.3	1,139.7	1,141.6	496.9
1960	4,145.1	2,561.4	1,583.6	476.7

[Continued]

Higher Education: Enrollment and Degrees Conferred, 1870-1998

[Continued]

	Total Enrollment	Public Enrollment	Private Enrollment	Degrees Conferred
1970	8,580.9	6,428.1	2,152.7	1,271.0
1980	12,096.9	9,457.3	2,639.5	1,731.0
1990	13,818.6	10,844.7	2,973.9	1,940.0
1998	14,549.2	11,176.2	3,373.0	2,298.0

Source: U.S. Census Bureau. *Historical Statistics of the United States: Colonial Years to 1970.* National Center for Education Statistics. U.S. Department of Education. *Digest of Education Statistics: 1999.* U.S. Census Bureau. *Statistical Abstract of the United States: 2001.* Enrollment data for 1960 is actually enrollment data for 1961. Source did not provide data for 1960. Enrollment data for 1950-1998 are from the *Digest of Education Statistics.* Degree-conferred data for 1870-1960 are from *Historical Statistics.* Data from 1970-1998 are from *Statistical Abstract.* *Notes:* NA stands for data not available.

Percentage of 25+ Year Olds Who Have Completed At Least 4 Years of High School, 1960-2000

	1960	1965	1970	1975	1980	1985	1990	1995	2000
Total	41.1	49.0	52.3	62.5	66.5	73.9	77.6	81.7	84.1
White	43.2	51.3	54.5	64.5	68.8	75.5	79.1	83.0	84.9
Black	20.1	27.2	31.4	42.5	51.2	59.8	66.2	73.8	78.5
Hispanic	NA	NA	32.1	37.9	44.0	47.9	50.8	53.4	57.0
Asian/Pacific Islander	NA	NA	NA	NA	NA	NA	80.4	NA	85.7

Source: U.S. Census Bureau. *Statistical Abstract of the United States: 1994* and *2001. Notes:* NA stands for data not available.

Percentage of 25+ Year Olds Who Have Completed At Least 4 Years of College, 1960-2000

	1960	1965	1970	1975	1980	1985	1990	1995	2000
Total	7.7	9.4	10.7	13.9	16.2	19.4	21.3	23.0	25.6
White	8.1	9.9	11.3	14.5	17.1	20.0	22.0	24.0	26.1
Black	3.1	4.7	4.4	6.4	8.4	11.1	11.3	13.2	16.5
Hispanic	NA	NA	4.5	NA	7.6	8.5	9.2	9.3	10.6
Asian/Pacific Islander	NA	NA	NA	NA	NA	NA	39.9	NA	43.9

Source: U.S. Census Bureau. *Statistical Abstract of the United States: 1994* and *2001. Notes:* NA stands for data not available.

Literacy Rates in the United States, by Race, 1870-1979

	Total	White	Black & Other
1870	80.0	88.5	20.1
1880	83.0	90.6	30.0
1890	86.7	92.3	43.2
1900	89.3	93.8	55.5
1910	92.3	95.0	69.5
1920	94.0	96.0	77.0
1930	95.7	97.0	83.6
1940	97.1	98.0	88.5
1952	97.5	98.2	89.8
1959	97.8	98.4	92.5
1969	99.0	99.3	96.4
1979	99.3	99.6	98.4

Source: U.S. Census Bureau. *Historical Statistics of the United States: Colonial Times to 1970.* National Center for Education Statistics. U.S. Department of Education. "Literacy from 1870 to 1979: Illiteracy." *National Assessment of Adult Literacy.* Retrieved March 21, 2002 from http://nces.ed.gov/naal/historicaldata/illiteracy.asp. Notes: Data for 1969 and 1979 "Black & Other" include only the rate for Blacks.

Adult Functional Literacy in the United States, by Educational Attainment, 1992

Data are in percentages.

	Total	Still in School	Less Than High School	Some High School	GED or High School Diploma	Some College (no Degree)	College Degree
Level 1	21.0	16.0	75.0	42.0	16.0	8.0	3.0
Level 2	27.0	36.0	20.0	38.0	36.0	23.0	11.0
Level 3	32.0	37.0	4.0	17.0	37.0	45.0	33.0
Level 4	17.0	11.0	0.0	2.0	10.0	22.0	41.0
Level 5	3.0	0.0	0.0	0.0	1.0	3.0	12.0
% of literacy tasks performed correctly	54.4	54.2	35.4	46.2	54.0	58.8	65.0

Source: Kaestle, Carl F., et. al. "Adult Literacy and Education in America." *Education Statistics Quarterly*, Winter 2001. Retrieved March 21, 2002 from http://nces.ed.gov.

Adult Functional Literacy in the United States, by Employment Status, 1992

Data are in percentages.

	Total	Full-Time	Part-Time	Unemployed	Out of Workforce	Retired
Level 1	21.0	13.0	14.0	24.0	29.0	41.0
Level 2	27.0	24.0	26.0	36.0	20.0	32.0
Level 3	32.0	36.0	36.0	29.0	29.0	21.0
Level 4	17.0	23.0	20.0	11.0	13.0	5.0

[Continued]

Adult Functional Literacy in the United States, by Employment Status, 1992

[Continued]

	Total	Full-Time	Part-Time	Unemployed	Out of Workforce	Retired
Level 5	3.0	5.0	4.0	1.0	2.0	1.0
% of literacy tasks performed correctly	54.4	57.6	56.8	52.0	51.2	47.0

Source: Kaestle, Carl F., et. al. "Adult Literacy and Education in America." *Education Statistics Quarterly*, Winter 2001. Retrieved March 21, 2002 from http://nces.ed.gov.

Average 17-Year Old Reading Proficiency Scores, by Race, 1971-1999

	1971	1975	1980	1984	1988	1992	1996	1999
Average score, overall	285.2	285.6	285.5	288.8	290.1	290.2	289.7	288.1
White, non-Hispanic	291.4	293.0	292.8	295.2	294.7	297.4	295.1	294.6
Black, non-Hispanic	238.7	240.6	243.1	264.3	274.4	260.6	266.1	263.9
Hispanic	NA	252.4	261.4	268.1	270.8	271.2	265.4	270.7
Minimum score for "proficient" reading ability	302.0	302.0	302.0	302.0	302.0	302.0	302.0	302.0
Minimum score for "basic" reading ability	265.0	265.0	265.0	265.0	265.0	265.0	265.0	265.0

Source: National Center for Education Statistics. U.S. Department of Education. *Digest of Education Statistics, 2001. Notes:* NA stands for data not available.

Average Student Reading Proficiency Scores for 13 Year Olds, 1971-1999

	1971	1975	1980	1984	1988	1992	1996	1999
Average score, overall	255.2	255.9	258.5	257.1	257.5	259.8	257.9	259.4
White, non-Hispanic	260.9	262.1	264.4	262.6	261.3	266.4	265.9	266.7
Black, non-Hispanic	222.4	225.7	232.8	236.3	242.9	237.6	234.0	238.2
Hispanic	NA	232.5	237.2	239.6	240.1	239.2	238.3	243.8
Minimum score for "proficient" reading ability	281.0	281.0	281.0	281.0	281.0	281.0	281.0	281.0
Minimum score for "basic" reading ability	243.0	243.0	243.0	243.0	243.0	243.0	243.0	243.0

Source: National Center for Education Statistics. U.S. Department of Education. *Digest of Education Statistics, 2001. Notes:* NA stands for data not available.

Average Student Mathematics Proficiency Scores for 17 Year Olds, 1973-2000

	1973	1978	1982	1986	1990	1992	1994	1996	1999	2000
Average score, overall	304.0	300.4	298.5	302.0	304.6	306.7	306.2	307.2	308.2	301.0
White, non-Hispanic	310.0	305.9	303.7	307.5	309.5	311.9	312.3	313.4	314.8	308.0
Black, non-Hispanic	270.0	268.4	271.8	278.6	288.5	285.8	285.5	286.4	283.3	274.0
Hispanic	277.0	276.3	276.7	283.1	283.5	292.2	290.8	292.0	292.7	283.0
Minimum score for "proficient" reading ability	336.0	336.0	336.0	336.0	336.0	336.0	336.0	336.0	336.0	336.0
Minimum score for "basic" reading ability	288.0	288.0	288.0	288.0	288.0	288.0	288.0	288.0	288.0	288.0

Source: National Center for Education Statistics. U.S. Department of Education. *Digest of Education Statistics, 2001.* National Center for Education Statistics. U.S. Department of Education. *The Nation's Report Card: Mathematics 2000.*

Average Student Mathematics Proficiency Scores for 13 Year Olds, 1973-2000

	1973	1978	1982	1986	1990	1992	1994	1996	1999	2000
Average score, overall	266.0	264.1	268.6	269.0	270.4	273.1	274.3	274.3	275.8	275.0
White, non-Hispanic	274.0	271.6	274.4	273.6	276.3	278.9	280.8	281.2	283.1	286.0
Black, non-Hispanic	228.0	229.6	240.4	249.2	249.1	250.2	251.5	252.1	251.0	247.0
Hispanic	239.0	238.0	252.4	254.3	254.6	259.3	256.0	255.7	259.2	253.0
Minimum score for "proficient" reading ability	299.0	299.0	299.0	299.0	299.0	299.0	299.0	299.0	299.0	299.0
Minimum score for "basic" reading ability	262.0	262.0	262.0	262.0	262.0	262.0	262.0	262.0	262.0	262.0

Source: National Center for Education Statistics. U.S. Department of Education. *Digest of Education Statistics, 2001.* National Center for Education Statistics. U.S. Department of Education. *The Nation's Report Card: Mathematics 2000.*

Expenditures per Pupil at the Elementary and Secondary Levels and Student Test Scores, 1970-2000

Expenditures in constant 2000-01 dollars. Expenditures per pupil based on average daily attendance. Expenditures per pupil, 2000 data are estimated.

	1970	1975	1980	1985	1990	1995	2000
Expenditure per pupil	4,427	5,222	5,617	6,161	7,653	7,829	8,787
Federal on-budget support (mil.)	25,106	32,133	32,778	25,773	28,790	38,070	44,959
Average composite SAT scores	1,049	1,010	994	1,009	1,001	1,010	1,019

Source: National Center for Education Statistics. U.S. Department of Education. *Digest of Education Statistics, 2001.*

Parents' Opinions on Higher Academic Standards and Standardized Tests, 2000

	% Agreeing With State- ment
Support higher academic standards with consequences for students and teachers	81
Their school district is careful and reasonable in implementing higher standards	82
Standardized tests are a good way to spot struggling students	76
Students pay more attention and study harder if they must pass a test to graduate	75
It's OK for teachers to spend a significant amount of time to prepare students for standardized tests	55
Schools place too much emphasis on standardized test scores	59

Source: "Survey Finds Little Sign of Backlash against Academic Standards or Standardized Tests." Retrieved April 24, 2002 from http://www.publicagenda.org.

Average Scholastic Assessment Test (SAT) Scores For College-Bound High School Seniors, 1967-2001

All scores are recentered.

	Total		Male		Female	
	Verbal	Math	Verbal	Math	Verbal	Math
1967	543	516	540	535	545	495
1968	543	516	541	533	543	497
1969	540	517	536	534	543	498
1970	537	512	536	531	538	493
1971	532	513	531	529	534	494
1972	530	509	531	527	529	489
1973	523	506	523	525	521	489
1974	521	505	524	524	520	488
1975	512	498	515	518	509	479
1976	509	497	511	520	508	475
1977	507	496	509	520	505	474
1978	507	494	511	517	503	474
1979	505	493	509	516	501	473
1980	502	492	506	515	498	473
1981	502	492	508	516	496	473
1982	504	493	509	516	499	473
1983	503	494	508	516	498	474
1984	504	497	511	518	498	478
1985	509	500	514	522	503	480
1986	509	500	515	523	504	479
1987	507	501	512	523	502	481
1988	505	501	512	521	499	483
1989	504	502	510	523	498	482
1990	500	501	505	521	496	483
1991	499	500	503	520	495	482
1992	500	501	504	521	496	484
1993	500	501	504	524	497	484
1994	499	504	501	523	497	487
1995	504	506	505	525	502	490
1996	505	508	507	527	503	492
1997	505	511	507	530	503	494
1998	505	512	509	531	502	496
1999	505	512	509	531	502	495
2000	505	514	507	533	504	498
2001	506	514	509	533	502	498

Source: Gams, Janice, et. al. The College Board. "2001 College Bound Seniors Are The Largest, Most Diverse Group in History." Retrieved April 11, 2002 from http://www.collegeboard.com/sat/cbsenior/yr2001/pdf/CompleteCBSReport.pdf.

American College Testing (ACT) Average Scores, 1967-2001

	English	Math
1967	18.5	20.0
1970	17.7	17.6
1975	17.9	17.4
1980	17.8	17.3
1982	17.9	17.2
1983	17.8	16.9
1984	18.1	17.3
1985	18.1	17.2
1986	18.5	17.3
1987	18.4	17.2
1988	18.5	17.2
1989	18.4	17.1
1990	20.5	19.9
1991	20.3	20.0
1992	20.2	20.0
1993	20.3	20.1
1994	20.3	20.2
1995	20.2	20.2
1996	20.3	20.2
1997	20.3	20.6
1998	20.4	20.8
1999	20.5	20.7
2000	20.5	20.7
2001	20.5	20.7

Source: National Center for Education Statistics. U.S. Department of Education. *Digest of Education Statistics, 1992* and *2001* editions.

Scholastic Achievement vs. College Performance

	%
Student test results:	
% of ACT test takers ready for college level courses, 2001	82.0
% of 17 year olds proficient in reading, 1999	40.0
% of 17 year olds proficient in math, 1999	60.7
Professors' opinions in 2000:	
% of high school graduates who write clearly	18.0
% of high school graduates who use proper grammar and spelling	21.0
% of high school graduates who have basic math skills	39.0

Source: "Reality Check 2000." *Education Week*, February 16, 2000. National Center for Education Statistics. U.S. Department of Education. *Digest of Education Statistics, 2001.*

Median Income and Poverty Level in 2000 Constant Dollars, 1965 to 2000

	1965	1970	1975	1980	1985	1990	1995	2000
No high school diploma	17,160	18,782	17,217	15,707	14,241	14,235	13,389	14,474
High school diploma	20,991	23,515	23,248	22,001	20,821	20,779	19,880	21,395
Bachelor's degree	30,409	33,842	32,805	31,284	34,495	35,658	35,428	39,835
Poverty threshold, four person family with two children	17,619	17,611	17,604	17,452	17,449	17,462	17,463	17,463

Source: U.S. Census Bureau. "Table P-16. Educational Attainment—People 25 Years Old and Over by Median Income and Sex: 1991 to 2000", "Table P- 17. Years of School Completed—People 25 Years Old and Over by Median Income and Sex: 1958 to 1990.", and "Table 1. Weighted Average Poverty Thresholds for Families of Specified Size 1959 to 2000." Retrieved April 8, 2002 from http://www.census.gov.

Chapter 8
TEACHERS AND TEACHING

Number of Teachers, Number of Students, and Pupil-Teacher Ratio, 1870-2010

Data for public elementary and secondary schools. Data for 1955 and later are from *Digest of Education Statistics, 2001*. Teacher data from 1870-1950 includes nonsupervisory staff, such as librarians and guidance staff.

	Number of Teachers (000)	Number of Students Enrolled (000)	Pupil-Teacher Ratio
1870	201	6,872	34.2
1875	258	8,786	34.1
1880	287	9,868	34.4
1885	326	11,398	34.9
1890	364	12,723	35.0
1895	398	14,244	35.8
1900	423	15,503	36.7
1905	460	16,468	35.8
1910	523	17,814	34.1
1915	604	19,705	32.6
1920	680	21,578	31.7
1926	814	24,741	30.4
1930	854	25,678	30.1
1936	871	26,367	30.3
1940	875	25,434	29.1
1946	831	23,300	28.0
1950	914	25,111	27.5
1955	1,141	30,680	26.9
1960	1,408	36,281	25.8
1965	1,710	42,173	24.7
1970	2,059	45,894	22.3
1975	2,198	44,819	20.4
1980	2,184	40,877	18.7
1985	2,206	39,422	17.9
1990	2,398	41,217	17.2
1995	2,598	44,840	17.3
2000 est.	2,953	47,160	16.0

[Continued]

Number of Teachers, Number of Students, and Pupil-Teacher Ratio, 1870-2010

[Continued]

	Number of Teachers (000)	Number of Students Enrolled (000)	Pupil-Teacher Ratio
2005 proj.	3,142	47,536	15.1
2010 proj.	3,192	47,131	14.8

Source: U.S. Census Bureau. *Historical Statistics of the United States: Colonial Times to 1970.* National Center for Education Statistics. U.S. Department of Education. *Digest of Education Statistics, 2001.* National Center for Education Statistics. U.S. Department of Education. *Projections of Education Statistics to 2011. Notes:* est. stands for estimated. proj. stands for projected.

Number of Teachers by Gender

Data prior to 1961 include all nonsupervisory instructional staff and librarians.

	Number		Percentage	
	Female	Male	Female	Male
1870	123	78	61.3	38.7
1880	164	123	57.2	42.8
1890	238	126	65.5	34.5
1900	296	127	70.1	29.9
1910	413	110	78.9	21.1
1920	585	93	85.9	14.1
1930	703	140	83.4	16.6
1940	681	195	77.8	22.2
1950	724	196	78.7	21.3
1961	967	441	68.7	31.3
1966	1,178	532	68.9	31.1
1971	1,350	705	65.7	34.3
1976	1,474	722	67.1	32.9
1981	1,462	723	66.9	33.1
1986	1,518	688	68.8	31.2
1991	1,729	669	72.1	27.9
1996	1,610	554	74.4	25.6

Source: National Center for Education Statistics. U.S. Department of Education. *Digest of Education Statistics, 1996* and *2001.*

Highest Degree Held by Public School Teachers, 1961-1996

Numbers in thousands. Figures based on number of public school teachers surveyed.

	1961	1966	1971	1976	1981	1986	1991	1996
Less than bachelor's degree	205.6	119.7	59.6	19.8	8.7	6.6	14.4	6.5
Bachelor's degree	871.6	1,190.1	1,430.3	1,352.7	1,094.7	1,065.5	1,110.3	943.5
Master's or specialist degree	325.2	396.7	556.9	814.7	1,077.2	1,118.4	1,261.3	1,179.4
Doctor's degree	5.6	1.7	8.2	8.8	6.6	15.4	12.0	36.8
Total no. of teachers surveyed	1,408.0	1,710.0	2,055.0	2,196.0	2,185.0	2,206.0	2,398.0	2,164.0

Source: National Center for Education Statistics. U.S. Department of Education. *Digest of Education Statistics, 2001.*

Teacher Certification, School Year 2000

	Teachers Who are Not Certified (%)	Average Number of Students Being Taught by Non-Certified Teachers (000)	Total Number of Teachers	Number of Teachers Not Certified
Total	6.2	2,921	2,948,444	182,566
High-poverty districts	8.8	997	709,366	62,308
Elementary ed.	4.7	833	1,101,739	52,047
Bilingual ed./ESL — all levels	5.2	179	217,302	11,204
Special ed. — all levels	9.1	560	384,899	35,013
English/lang. arts — secondary	4.8	211	273,381	13,217
Mathematics — secondary	5.7	182	198,421	11,387
Science — secondary	7.3	198	170,011	12,350
Social studies — secondary	4.8	144	188,960	9,031

Source: "Title II State Report 2001—Waivers," all states and Washington D.C.. Retrieved May 9, 2002 from http://www.title2.org.

Projected Number of Job Openings and Projected Number of Graduates to Fill Them, 2000-2010

	Job Openings, 2000-2010	Number of Degrees Conferred, 2000-2010	Number of Graduates Still in the Teaching Profession After 1 Year
Elementary education	551,000	601,022	516,578
Secondary education (including middle school)	676,000	616,590	529,959
Special education	197,000	213,422	183,436

Source: National Center for Education Statistics. U.S. Department of Education. *Digest of Education Statistics*, 1996-2001 editions. Daniel E. Hecker. "Occupational employment projections to 2010." *Monthly Labor Review*, November 2001.

Top Reasons for Teacher Dissatisfaction, 1993-1994

Data are in percent.

	All Schools	Urban, High-Poverty Public Schools	Small, Private Schools
Poor salary	45	46	73
Lack of student motivation	38	50	14
Student discipline problems	30	27	12
Inadequate administrative support	30	18	34
Inadequate time to prepare	23	8	18
Unsafe environment	2	26	0
Poor opportunity for advancement	10	24	9
Class size too large	13	7	13

Source: Ingersoll, Richard M. Center for the Study of Teaching and Policy. University of Washington. *Teacher Turnover, Teacher Shortages, and the Organization of Schools,* January 2001.

Average Teacher Salaries Compared to All Workers and All Government Workers, 1956-2000

	Teachers	All Workers	All Government Workers
1956	25,564	25,535	24,112
1958	27,521	26,311	26,028
1960	29,165	27,663	27,272
1962	31,566	28,958	28,546
1964	33,434	30,655	30,572
1966	34,298	31,522	31,369
1968	36,383	32,592	32,886
1970	37,751	33,031	34,983
1972	39,733	35,210	38,556
1974	36,134	33,451	35,625
1976	37,643	34,701	36,337
1978	36,514	34,073	35,320
1980	32,461	31,790	32,100
1982	33,775	32,923	33,671
1984	36,310	33,249	34,630
1986	39,776	34,542	36,587
1988	40,534	34,725	36,315
1990	40,765	34,015	36,038
1992	41,602	35,176	37,586
1994	41,569	34,893	38,265
1996	41,211	35,067	38,370

[Continued]

Average Teacher Salaries Compared to All Workers and All Government Workers, 1956-2000

[Continued]

	Teachers	All Workers	All Govern- ment Workers
1998	41,760	37,170	39,497
2000	41,820	38,074	39,772

Source: Nelson, F. Howard. The Research & Information Services Department. American Federation of Teachers, AFL-CIO. *Survey & Analysis of Teacher Salary Trends 2000.*

Average Class Size and Pupil-Teacher Ratio, 1987-2000

Ideal class size is 17.

	1987-1988	1990-1991	1993-1994	1999-2000
Class size, public	24.2	23.4	23.9	22.3
Class size, private	20.9	19.8	20.4	18.9
Pupil-teacher ratio, public	17.3	17.3	17.3	16.0
Pupil-teacher ratio, private	15.2	14.9	14.7	13.9

Source: National Center for Education Statistics. U.S. Department of Education. *The Condition of Education, 1997* and *2002* editions. National Center for Education Statistics. U.S. Department of Education. *Digest of Education Statistics, 2001.*

Top Serious Problems in Schools According to Teachers, 1993-1994

Data in percentage.

	Public	Private
Students come unprepared to learn	28.8	4.1
Lack of parental involvement	27.6	4.0
Student apathy	23.6	4.5
Poverty	19.5	2.7
Student disrespect for teachers	18.5	3.4
Student use of alcohol	9.3	3.1

Source: National Center for Education Statistics. U.S. Department of Education. *Digest of Educational Statistics, 2001.*

National Assessment of Educational Progress (NAEP) Reading Achievement for 4th Graders, 1992-2000

Percentage of students at reading level.

	Below Basic	Basic	Proficient	Advanced
1992	38	34	22	6
1994	40	31	22	7
1998	38	32	24	7
2000	37	31	24	8

Source: National Center for Education Statistics. U. S. Department of Education. *The Nation's Report Card: Fourth Grade Reading Highlights 2000, 2001.*

National Assessment of Educational Progress (NAEP) Mathematics Achievement for 12th Graders, 1990-2000

Percentage of students at reading level.

	Below Basic	Basic	Proficient	Advanced
1990	42	46	10	1
1992	36	49	13	2
1996	31	53	14	2
2000	35	48	14	2

Source: National Center for Education Statistics. U.S. Department of Education. "The Nation's Report Card: National Mathematics Achievement- Level Results, Grade 12: 1990-2000." Retrieved June 11, 2002 from http://nces.ed.gov/nationsreportcard/mathematics/results/natachieve-g12- pf.asp.

Percentage of High School Students Who Agree With the Following Statements, 1998

	1998
It's important for me to be a person with good character	97.1
I am satisfied with my own ethics and character	90.8
Within the last year, I lied to a parent	92.1
Within the last year, I lied to a teacher	81.8
Within the last year, I cheated on a test in school	70.2
Stolen something from parents and relatives	31.1
Stolen something from a store	47.1
Within the last year, I hit a person because I was angry	69.7

Source: Josephson Institute of Ethics. *1998 Report Card on the Ethics of American Youth, October 1998.*

Chapter 9
TRENDS IN EDUCATIONAL FUNDING

Revenues for Public Elementary and Secondary Schools, by Source of Funds (Thousands of Dollars): 1919-20 to 1998-99

Beginning in 1980-81, revenues for state education agencies are excluded. Beginning in 1988-89 data reflect new survey collection procedures and may not be entirely comparable with figures for earlier years. Detail may not sum to totals due to rounding.

School year	Total	Federal	State	Local (including intermed.)[1]
1919-20	970,121	2,475	160,085	807,561
1929-30	2,088,557	7,334	353,670	1,727,553
1939-40	2,260,527	39,810	684,354	1,536,363
1941-42	2,416,580	34,305	759,993	1,622,281
1943-44	2,604,322	35,886	859,183	1,709,253
1945-46	3,059,845	41,378	1,062,057	1,956,409
1947-48	4,311,534	120,270	1,676,362	2,514,902
1949-50	5,437,044	155,848	2,165,689	3,115,507
1951-52	6,423,816	227,711	2,478,596	3,717,507
1953-54	7,866,852	355,237	2,944,103	4,567,512
1955-56	9,686,677	441,442	3,828,886	5,416,350
1957-58	12,181,513	486,484	4,800,368	6,894,661
1959-60	14,746,618	651,639	5,768,047	8,326,932
1961-62	17,527,707	760,975	6,789,190	9,977,542
1963-64	20,544,182	896,956	8,078,014	11,569,213
1965-66	25,356,858	1,996,954	9,920,219	13,439,686
1967-68	31,903,064	2,806,469	12,275,536	16,821,063
1969-70	40,266,923	3,219,557	16,062,776	20,984,589
1970-71	44,511,292	3,753,461	17,409,086	23,348,745
1971-72	50,003,645	4,467,969	19,133,256	26,402,420
1972-73	52,117,930	4,525,000	20,699,752	26,893,180
1973-74	58,230,892	4,930,351	24,113,409	29,187,132
1974-75	64,445,239	5,811,595	27,060,563	31,573,079
1975-76	71,206,073	6,318,345	31,602,885	33,284,840
1976-77	75,322,532	6,629,498	32,526,018	36,137,018
1977-78	81,443,160	7,694,194	35,013,266	38,735,700
1978-79	87,994,143	8,600,116	40,132,136	39,261,891
1979-80	96,881,165	9,503,537	45,348,814	42,028,813

[Continued]

Revenues for Public Elementary and Secondary Schools, by Source of Funds (Thousands of Dollars): 1919-20 to 1998-99

[Continued]

	Total	Federal	State	Local (including intermed.)[1]
1980-81	105,949,087	9,768,262	50,182,659	45,998,166
1981-82	110,191,257	8,186,466	52,436,435	49,568,356
1982-83	117,497,502	8,339,990	56,282,157	52,875,354
1983-84	126,055,419	8,576,547	60,232,981	57,245,892
1984-85	137,294,678	9,105,569	67,168,684	61,020,425
1985-86	149,127,779	9,975,622	73,619,575	65,532,582
1986-87	158,523,693	10,146,013	78,830,437	69,547,243
1987-88	169,561,974	10,716,687	84,004,415	74,840,873
1988-89	192,016,374	11,902,001	91,768,911	88,345,462
1989-90	208,547,573	12,700,784	98,238,633	97,608,157
1990-91	223,340,537	13,776,066	105,324,533	104,239,939
1991-92	234,581,384	15,493,330	108,783,449	110,304,605
1992-93	247,626,168	17,261,252	113,403,436	116,961,481
1993-94	260,159,468	18,341,483	117,474,209	124,343,776
1994-95	273,149,449	18,582,157	127,729,576	126,837,717
1995-96	287,702,844	19,104,019	136,670,754	131,928,071
1996-97	305,065,192	20,081,287	146,435,584	138,548,321
1997-98[2]	325,925,708	22,201,965	157,645,372	146,078,370
1998-99	347,329,664	24,521,817	169,298,232	153,509,615

Source: U.S. Department of Education, National Center for Education Statistics, *Statistics of State School Systems; Revenues and Expenditures for Public Elementary and Secondary Education;* and Common Core of Data surveys. Retrieved May 24, 2002, from http://nces.ed.gov/pubs2002/digest2001/tables/dt157.asp *Notes:* 1. Includes a relatively small amount from nongovernmental private sources (gifts and tuition and transportation fees from patrons). These sources accounted for 2.5% of total revenues in 1998-99.

Public Financial Support: Indicators of Public Effort to Fund Education, by Level: Selected School Years Ending 1930-97

In constant 1998 dollars. NA Not available.

	Per Capita Personal Income	Public Education — Revenue per Student		Per Student Revenue as a Percentage of Per Capita Personal Income	
		Elementary/ Secondary	Postsecondary Education	Elementary/ Secondary	Postsecondary Education
School Year Ending					
1930	6,609	709	1,490	10.7	22.5
1940	6,958	949	1,671	13.6	24.0
1950	9,536	1,325	2,745	13.9	28.8
1960	12,784	2,021	3,881	15.8	30.4

[Continued]

Public Financial Support: Indicators of Public Effort to Fund Education, by Level: Selected School Years Ending 1930-97

[Continued]

	Per Capita Personal Income	Public Education		Per Student Revenue as a Percentage of Per Capita Personal Income	
		Revenue per Student			
		Elementary/ Secondary	Postsecondary Education	Elementary/ Secondary	Postsecondary Education
1966	15,703	2,697	4,923	17.2	31.3
1970	17,340	3,435	5,390	19.8	31.1
1980	20,153	4,400	4,742	21.8	23.5
1984	21,506	4,531	4,492	21.1	20.9
1988	23,723	5,293	5,225	22.3	22.0
1992	24,169	5,910	4,929	24.5	20.4
1994	24,538	5,982	5,043	24.4	20.6
1996	25,376	6,066	5,223	23.9	20.6
1997	25,954	6,145	NA	23.7	NA

Source: NCES, *The Condition of Education 2000*, Table 62-1; primary source: *Digest of Education Statistics 1999* and *120 Years of American Education: A Statistical Portrait*, retrieved May 2, 2002, from http://nces.ed.gov

Finances of Public Elementary and Secondary School Systems by Enrollment-Size Group: 1997-98

Data are in millions of dollars (327,202 represents $327,202,000,000), except as indicated. Data are estimates, subject to sampling variability.

	All school systems	School Systems With Enrollment of						
		50,000 or more	25,000 to 49,999	15,000 to 24,999	7,500 to 14,999	5,000 to 7,499	3000 to 4,999	Under 3,000
Fall enrollment (1,000)	46,127	9,113	5,302	4,431	6,896	4,219	5,427	10,738
General revenue	327,202	64,456	35,698	28,854	48,238	30,513	39,100	80,343
From federal sources	21,790	5,338	2,474	1,782	2,946	1,634	2,108	5,508
Through state	19,753	4,972	2,277	1,653	2,612	1,513	1,889	4,838
Compensatory programs	6,995	2,036	811	592	915	519	653	1,469
Handicapped programs	2,790	476	292	238	400	235	273	875
Child nutrition programs	5,961	1,623	761	556	809	475	585	1,154
Direct	2,037	366	197	130	334	121	219	670
From state sources[1]	160,178	30,978	18,535	15,940	24,184	14,063	17,586	38,893
General formula assistance	112,205	19,549	12,550	11,556	17,246	10,091	12,942	28,271
Handicapped programs	9,426	2,056	1,185	861	1,380	760	909	2,274
From local sources	145,234	28,140	14,689	11,132	21,108	14,816	19,406	35,942
Taxes	97,932	14,754	10,051	7,291	14,780	10,856	14,004	26,196
Contributions from parent government	24,369	9,839	2,114	1,862	3,012	1,866	2,570	3,107
From other local governments	3,047	382	285	196	285	233	441	1,225
Current charges	8,653	1,336	905	770	1,313	824	1,088	2,416
School lunch	4,770	671	508	456	770	492	652	1,220
Other	11,233	1,828	1,335	1,014	1,718	1,037	1,303	2,998
General expenditure	331,445	65,157	35,965	29,110	48,607	30,997	39,777	81,833
Current spending	287,075	56,989	30,774	25,000	42,101	26,801	34,171	71,239

[Continued]

Finances of Public Elementary and Secondary School Systems by Enrollment-Size Group: 1997-98

[Continued]

	All school systems	School Systems With Enrollment of						
		50,000 or more	25,000 to 49,999	15,000 to 24,999	7,500 to 14,999	5,000 to 7,499	3000 to 4,999	Under 3,000
By function:								
Instruction	174,709	34,955	18,494	15,306	25,871	16,567	21,117	42,398
Support services	96,100	18,390	10,405	8,199	13,859	8,848	11,283	25,115
Other current spending	16,267	3,643	1,875	1,495	2,372	1,385	1,771	3,726
By object:								
Total salaries and wages	186,092	36,769	20,416	16,609	27,644	17,662	22,354	44,638
Total employee benefits	48,626	10,284	5,146	4,218	7,373	4,544	5,712	11,348
Other	52,357	9,936	5,213	4,172	7,085	4,594	6,104	15,253
Capital outlay	35,874	6,659	4,322	3,403	5,248	3,333	4,453	8,456
Interest on debt	7,402	1,480	821	664	1,079	695	1,016	1,648
Payments to other governments	1,094	28	48	43	178	168	137	491
Debt outstanding	144,057	28,024	15,279	12,964	21,378	13,974	20,258	32,180
Long-term.	141,591	27,944	15,131	12,815	21,045	13,744	19,823	31,088
Short-term	2,466	80	147	149	333	230	435	1,092
Long-term debt issued	32,648	5,502	3,027	2,747	5,307	3,748	5,317	7,000
Long-term debt retired	15,573	3,192	1,402	1,064	2,515	1,663	2,354	3,383

Source: Statistical Abstract of the United States: 2001, Table 241; primary source: U.S. Census Bureau, Internet site http://www.census.gov/govs/www/school.html. *Note:* 1. Includes other sources, not shown separately.

States Ranked According to Per Pupil Elementary-Secondary Public School System Finance Amounts: 1998-99

(Dollars. Detail may not add to total because of rounding.)

	Elementary-Secondary Revenue				Current Spending for Selected Categories					
						Instruction			General Administration	School Administration
	Total	From Federal Sources	From State Sources	From Local Sources	Total[1]	Total[1]	Salaries Only	Benefits Only		
	US 7,504	US 520	US 3,715	US 3,269	US 6,458	US 3,979	US 2,897	US 729	US 130	US 370
1	NJ 11,430	DC 1,711	VT 6,442	DC 8,834	NJ 10,230	NY 6,369	NY 4,757	NY 1,244	AK 439	DC 651
2	DC 10,545	AK 1,382	HI 6,205	NJ 6,383	DC 9,645	NJ 6,225	NJ 4,353	NJ 1,137	NJ 287	NJ 549
3	NY 10,448	NM 844	DE 5,709	NH 6,140	NY 9,373	CT 5,537	CT 4,050	IN 1,115	ND 263	MD 520
4	CT 9,864	ND 801	MI 5,534	CT 5,673	CT 8,632	MA 5,424	RI 3,746	WI 1,113	NH 243	VT 508
5	AK 9,182	MT 720	AK 5,468	NY 5,443	AK 8,472	AK 5,208	MA 3,692	RI 1,104	IL 221	AK 499
6	RI 8,733	HI 694	WA 4,706	PA 4,787	MA 8,106	RI 5,120	AK 3,471	WV 1,092	PA 221	CT 488
7	DE 8,659	LA 693	NJ 4,626	RI 4,555	RI 7,878	VT 4,837	VT 3,412	ME 1,073	NE 215	MI 442
8	MA 8,647	MS 676	WI 4,606	MA 4,505	VT 7,541	ME 4,738	PA 3,410	MD 1,043	KS 212	OR 431
9	PA 8,576	SD 640	NM 4,593	MD 4,499	DE 7,536	PA 4,714	DC 3,345	DE 993	VT 208	CA 424
10	MI 8,535	WV 635	WV 4,557	IL 4,480	PA 7,502	DE 4,678	DE 3,225	CT 990	OK 200	ME 416
11	VT 8,471	NY 624	MN 4,523	NE 4,136	WI 7,413	WI 4,642	WI 3,188	MA 973	NY 195	NV 405
12	WI 8,385	WY 609	KS 4,431	OH 4,140	MI 7,234	DC 4,370	ME 3,154	MI 952	WI 194	WY 403
13	WY 8,181	CA 607	NC 4,430	ME 3,856	MD 7,176	MD 4,349	MN 3,145	AK 948	MN 183	DE 402
14	MD 8,133	MI 592	AR 4,427	VA 3,827	ME 7,119	MN 4,230	MD 3,035	OR 905	AR 181	HI 399
15	IN 8,046	AZ 584	NY 4,381	IN 3,525	WY 6,836	MI 4,198	IL 3,016	PA 894	IA 179	OH 392
16	MN 7,860	KY 579	WY 4,287	CO 3,520	OR 6,809	NH 4,197	NH 2,993	WY 843	SD 177	KS 392
17	IL 7,838	TX 548	NV 4,258	WI 3,410	IL 6,760	WY 4,101	MI 2,958	VT 819	MT 174	RI 392
18	OH 7,812	DE 543	OR 4,237	SD 3,335	MN 6,674	WV 4,090	WY 2,891	VA 781	CT 173	NY 386
19	ME 7,783	FL 542	IN 4,140	TX 3,309	WV 6,626	IL 4,079	VA 2,852	GA 765	DC 171	WI 385
20	OR 7,452	IL 542	CA 3,998	WY 3,285	IN 6,625	IN 4,072	HI 2,825	WA 747	MO 171	CO 385
21	NE 7,423	OK 530	KY 3,942	GA 3,251	OH 6,572	OR 4,024	IN 2,825	MN 736	WV 170	IN 379
22	GA 7,405	AL 526	CT 3,808	MO 3,092	NH 6,373	VA 3,879	GA 2,818	OH 732	MI 168	VA 379
23	WV 7,360	OR 524	FL 3,730	IA 3,077	VA 6,285	NE 3,874	OH 2,791	FL 715	RI 167	NC 376

[Continued]

States Ranked According to Per Pupil Elementary-Secondary Public School System Finance Amounts: 1998-99

[Continued]

| | Elementary-Secondary Revenue | | | | Current Spending for Selected Categories | | | | | |
| | | | | | | Instruction | | | | |
	Total	From Federal Sources	From State Sources	From Local Sources	Total[1]	Total[1]	Salaries Only	Benefits Only	General Administration	School Administration
24	VA 7,325	NE 519	MA 3,712	FL 3,040	IA 6,229	OH 3,862	WV 2,779	HI 713	OH 164	WA 371
25	FL 7,312	SC 515	AL 3,680	ND 3,022	WA 6,116	HI 3,818	IA 2,745	NE 703	KY 162	WV 370
26	WA 7,254	AR 514	RI 3,674	MN 2,961	HI 6,082	GA 3,803	TX 2,704	MT 696	OR 157	MA 368
27	KS 7,133	PA 506	GA 3,674	MT 2,891	GA 6,074	MT 3,691	NC 2,683	NV 693	WY 145	GA 364
28	HI 7,062	RI 503	IA 3,565	AZ 2,704	NE 6,016	WA 3,651	NE 2,655	IL 687	ME 145	NH 358
29	NH 7,048	VT 502	ID 3,546	OR 2,691	KS 5,919	IA 3,645	NE 2,655	IA 665	MA 145	FL 356
30	IA 7,015	WA 487	ME 3,506	SC 2,611	MT 5,880	MO 3,577	MT 2,653	UT 664	NM 143	IL 354
31	CA 6,811	GA 480	OK 3,434	TN 2,487	CO 5,876	CA 3,539	KS 2,641	LA 658	MS 141	MO 349
32	MO 6,779	TN 462	SC 3,429	MI 2,409	CA 5,797	NC 3,534	OR 2,636	NH 650	AL 139	SC 346
33	NC 6,754	NC 444	PA 3,283	DE 2,407	MO 5,787	CO 3,436	CA 2,587	ND 630	ID 121	IA 326
34	CO 6,722	MD 442	OH 3,280	AK 2,332	FL 5,651	TX 3,418	KY 2,582	ID 619	IN 119	PA 325
35	NV 6,703	MO 441	MO 3,245	KS 2,274	SC 5,647	KY 3,411	CO 2,556	SC 604	LA 117	AL 317
36	TX 6,595	MA 430	MD 3,192	LA 2,266	TX 5,632	KS 3,368	WA 2,533	NC 600	NC 110	KY 317
37	SC 6,555	OH 428	VA 3,125	CA 2,205	KY 5,628	SC 3,345	SC 2,472	CA 590	TN 98	NE 314
38	MT 6,525	KS 427	UT 3,079	WV 2,168	NC 5,623	NV 3,339	NV 2,449	KY 590	TX 98	MT 314
39	KY 6,384	NJ 421	LA 3,076	NV 2,149	NV 5,576	TN 3,323	AL 2,442	NM 554	CO 93	TX 313
40	ND 6,321	ME 421	MT 2,915	WA 2,061	LA 5,420	ND 3,314	LA 2,410	TN 517	WA 89	NM 303
41	NM 6,290	ID 395	CO 2,866	OK 2,054	NM 5,417	LA 3,313	ND 2,399	AR 516	NV 83	LA 301
42	SD 6,206	CT 383	IL 2,816	NC 1,881	ND 5,411	FL 3,256	TN 2,390	OK 516	AZ 82	ID 297
43	LA 6,036	IN 382	NE 2,768	KY 1,863	OK 5,255	SD 3,208	SD 2,336	DC 507	DE 81	AR 295
44	OK 6,019	MN 376	TX 2,738	ID 1,797	AR 5,205	AL 3,208	NM 2,268	MO 503	GA 80	OK 282
45	AL 5,972	IA 373	MS 2,737	AL 1,767	AL 5,184	AR 3,150	AR 2,248	SD 496	SC 73	MN 276
46	AZ 5,952	VA 372	AZ 2,664	MS 1,622	SD 5,175	ID 3,119	FL 2,230	KS 487	FL 65	AZ 270
47	AR 5,867	WI 368	TN 2,617	UT 1,597	TN 5,109	OK 3,078	ID 2,213	AL 485	VA 63	SD 267
48	ID 5,739	UT 362	ND 2,498	VT 1,527	ID 5,009	NM 3,037	OK 2,155	MS 480	MD 60	TN 263
49	TN 5,566	CO 336	SD 2,232	AR 927	AZ 4,629	MS 2,742	AZ 2,059	CO 462	UT 43	ND 260
50	UT 5,038	NV 296	NH 624	NM 854	MS 4,544	UT 2,732	MS 2,021	AZ 378	HI 39	MS 255
51	MS 5,034	NH 284	DC -	HI 163	UT 4,169	AZ 2,679	UT 1,871	TX 358	CA 35	UT 247

Source: U.S. Census Bureau, Annual Survey of Government Finances, Table 11, retrieved May 3, 2002, from http://www.census.gov/govs/www/school99.html *Notes:* 1. Includes amounts not shown separately. Revenue from and expenditure to other school systems are excluded to avoid double counting. Expenditure for adult education, community services, and other nonelementary-secondary programs are also excluded. Some data appear under local sources for Hawaii's state-operated school system for consistency with data presented for all other school systems.

Per Pupil Expenditures in 10 Michigan School Districts: 1994 and 2001

District	1994 Dollars Per Student	2001 Dollars Per Student	1994-2001 Percent Change
Pinckney	4,403	6,500	48
Hamtramck	4,536	6,500	44
Fowlerville	4,534	6,500	43
Brandon	4,719	6,500	38
Richmond	4,758	6,500	37
Bloomfield Hills	10,294	11,755	14
Birmingham	10,217	11,678	14
Southfield	9,298	10,759	16

[Continued]

Per Pupil Expenditures in 10 Michigan School Districts: 1994 and 2001

[Continued]

District	1994 Dollars Per Student	2001 Dollars Per Student	1994-2001 Percent Change
Lamphere	8,777	10,237	17
Farmington	8,407	9,868	17

Source: Jodi Upton et al., "Wealthy districts hit hardest," *The Detroit News*, retrieved April 30, 2002, from http://detnews.com.

Number of Children 3 to 5 Years Old, Number Enrolled in Preprimary Education, Number Enrolled in Head Start, and Number of Children Under 6 in Poverty: 1965-2001

NA Not Available.

	Total Children Age 3-5	Enrolled in Preprimary Education	Enrolled in Head Start	Under 6 in Poverty
1965	12,549,000	3,407,000	561,000	NA
1970	10,949,000	4,104,000	477,400	3,561,000
1975	10,185,000	4,955,000	349,000	3,460,000
1980	9,284,000	4,878,000	349,000	3,986,000
1983	10,254,000	5,384,000	414,950	5,164,000
1984	10,612,000	5,480,000	442,140	4,938,000
1985	10,733,000	5,865,000	452,080	4,832,000
1986	10,866,000	5,081,000	451,732	4,619,000
1987	10,872,000	5,931,000	446,523	4,818,000
1988	10,993,000	5,978,000	448,464	4,800,000
1989	11,039,000	6,026,000	450,970	4,868,000
1990	11,207,000	6,569,000	540,930	5,198,000
1991	11,370,000	6,334,000	583,471	5,483,000
1992	11,545,000	6,402,000	621,078	6,082,000
1993	11,954,000	6,581,000	713,903	6,097,000
1994	12,328,000	7,514,000	740,493	5,878,000
1995	12,518,000	7,739,000	750,696	5,670,000
1996	12,378,000	7,580,000	752,077	5,333,000
1997	12,121,000	7,861,000	793,809	5,049,000
1998	12,078,000	7,788,000	822,316	4,775,000
1999	11,920,000	7,844,000	826,016	4,170,000

[Continued]

Number of Children 3 to 5 Years Old, Number Enrolled in Preprimary Education, Number Enrolled in Head Start, and Number of Children Under 6 in Poverty: 1965-2001

[Continued]

	Total Children Age 3-5	Enrolled in Preprimary Education	Enrolled in Head Start	Under 6 in Poverty
2000	NA	11,419,000	857,664	3,917,000
2001	NA	11,392,000	905,235	NA

Source: Statistical Abstract of the United States, 2001, Table 225. Primary Source: U.S Census Bureau, Current Population Reports, P20-533; Current Population Survey Poverty and Health Statistics Branch/HHES Division. Head Start data retrieved May 21, 2002, from http://www2. acf.dhhs.gov/programs/hsb/research. Poverty data retrieved May 15, 2002, from http://wwwcensusgov/hhes/poverty/histpov/hstpov20html.

Head Start Enrollment History

Fiscal Year	Enrollment	Appropriation ($)
1965	561,000	96,400,000
1966	733,000	198,900,000
1967	681,400	349,200,000
1968	693,900	316,200,000
1969	663,600	333,900,000
1970	477,400	325,700,000
1971	397,500	360,000,000
1972	379,000	376,300,000
1973	379,000	400,700,000
1974	352,800	403,900,000
1975	349,000	403,900,000
1976	349,000	441,000,000
1977	333,000	475,000,000
1978	391,400	625,000,000
1979	387,500	680,000,000
1980	376,300	735,000,000
1981	387,300	818,700,000
1982	395,800	911,700,000
1983	414,950	912,000,000
1984	442,140	995,750,000
1985	452,080	1,075,059,000
1986	451,732	1,040,315,000
1987	446,523	1,130,542,000
1988	448,464	1,206,324,000
1989	450,970	1,235,000,000
1990	540,930	1,552,000,000
1991	583,471	1,951,800,000
1992	621,078	2,201,800,000

[Continued]

Head Start Enrollment History

[Continued]

Fiscal Year	Enrollment	Appropriation ($)
1993	713,903	2,776,286,000
1994	740,493	3,325,728,000
1995	750,696	3,534,128,000
1996	752,077	3,569,329,000
1997	793,809	3,980,546,000
1998	822,316	4,347,433,000
1999	826,016	4,658,151,448
2000	857,664	5,267,000,000
2001	905,235	6,200,000,000

Source: Head Start data, retrieved May 15, 2002, from http://www2.acf.dhhs.gov/programs/hsb/research

President's Education Budget: Budget for 21st Century Learning Centers: 1994-2002

	1994	1995	1996	1997	1998	1999	2000	2001	2002
Budget ($000)	825	130	190	350	370	370	480	845,614	1,000,000

Source: U.S. Department of Education, Education Budget History Table, retrieved May 15, 2002, from http://www.ed.gov/offices/OUS/budnews.html#statetables.

Chapter 10
SCHOOL PERFORMANCE

Estimated Number of Charter Schools in Operation as of September 1999, by State

- indicates zero. The study reports the number of charters given to individual entities, though some charters may use space within another school or be connected to another school by another arrangement. The number of charters shown does not include the total number of school sites operating under a charter. Some charters, particularly in Arizona, run similar programs in several sites. In those cases, the study only counts the charter once. Several charters in California were awarded to districts or complexes of schools. Since previously each school within the group was a separate school, the study counts each school as a separate charter school. Taking into account multiple school sites operating under a single charter (121), the study estimates that the total number of school sites operating under charters was 1,605 (1,484 + 121) as of September 1999. The column "Total schools closed as of Sept. 1999" reflects the cumulative number of charter schools closed since 1992. The number of schools that opened in the 1998-99 school year is slightly different for some states from the number of schools reported as of September 1998. The 1998-99 column includes several schools that opened later in the 1998-99 school year.

	Number of Charter Schools Starting in the Year							Total Schools Closed as of Sept. 1999	New Schools as of Sept. 1999	Total Schools Operating Sept. 1999
	1992-93	1993-94	1994-95	1995-96	1996-97	1997-98	1998-99			
Total	2	34	64	154	178	289	401	59	421	1,484
Minnesota	2	5	7	3	3	8	12	3	17	54
California	-	28	36	30	21	19	29	9	56	210
Colorado	-	1	13	10	8	19	10	1	8	68
Michigan	-	-	2	41	33	36	24	5	15	146
New Mexico	-	-	4	0	1	0	0	3	1	3
Wisconsin	-	-	2	3	6	7	12	1	11	40
Arizona	-	-	-	47	58	45	44	16	44	222
Georgia	-	-	-	3	9	9	7	1	4	31
Hawaii	-	-	-	2	0	0	0	0	0	2
Massachusetts	-	-	-	15	7	3	10	1	5	39
Alaska	-	-	-	-	2	13	2	1	2	18
Delaware	-	-	-	-	2	1	1	0	1	5
District of Col.	-	-	-	-	2	1	17	2	10	28
Florida	-	-	-	-	5	28	42	4	38	109
Illinois	-	-	-	-	1	7	6	1	7	20
Louisiana	-	-	-	-	3	3	5	0	7	18
Texas	-	-	-	-	17	21	71	5	64	168
Connecticut	-	-	-	-	-	12	4	1	2	17
Kansas	-	-	-	-	-	1	14	0	0	15
New Jersey	-	-	-	-	-	13	17	0	19	49
North Carolina	-	-	-	-	-	34	26	5	23	78
Pennsylvania	-	-	-	-	-	6	25	0	17	48
Rhode Island	-	-	-	-	-	1	1	0	0	2
South Carolina	-	-	-	-	-	2	3	0	5	10
Idaho	-	-	-	-	-	-	2	0	6	8
Mississippi	-	-	-	-	-	-	1	0	0	1
Nevada	-	-	-	-	-	-	1	0	0	1
Ohio	-	-	-	-	-	-	15	0	31	46
New York	-	-	-	-	-	-	-	-	5	5
Missouri	-	-	-	-	-	-	-	-	15	15
Utah	-	-	-	-	-	-	-	-	6	6
Oklahoma	-	-	-	-	-	-	-	-	2	2

Source: The State of Charter Schools 2000, Fourth-Year Report, January 2000, retrieved April 18, 2002, http://www.ed.gov/. Primary source: The study contacted officials at each state department of education and supplemented their information from a variety of sources, including the Common Core of Data Survey (1997-98), charter school directories, and state charter school resource centers.

Average Mathematics Proficiency, by Age and Selected Characteristics of Students and by Control of School: 1978 to 1999

All age groups exclude persons not enrolled in school. These test scores are from the National Assessment of Educational Progress (NAEP). Performers at the 150 level know some basic addition and subtraction facts, and most can add two-digit numbers without regrouping. They recognize simple situations in which addition and subtraction apply. Performers at the 200 level have considerable understanding of two-digit numbers and know some basic multiplication and division facts. Performers at the 250 level have an initial understanding of the four basic operations. They can also compare information from graphs and charts and are developing an ability to analyze simple logical relations. Performers at the 300 level can compute decimals, simple fractions and percents. They can identify geometric figures, measure lengths and angles and calculate areas of rectangles. They are developing the skills to operate with signed numbers, exponents and square roots. Performers at the 350 level can apply a range of reasoning skills to solve multi-step problems. They can solve routine problems involving fractions and percents, recognize properties of basic geometric figures, and work with exponents and square roots. Scale ranges from 0 to 500.

Selected Characteristics of Students	1978	1982	1986	1990	1992	1994	1996	1999
9-year-olds								
Total								
Male	217.4	217.1	221.7	229.1	230.8	232.2	232.9	232.9
Female	219.9	220.8	221.7	230.2	228.4	230.0	229.0	231.2
Race/ethnicity								
White	224.1	224.0	226.9	235.2	235.1	236.8	236.9	238.8
Black	192.4	194.9	201.6	208.4	208.0	212.1	211.6	210.9
Hispanic	202.9	204.0	205.4	213.8	211.9	209.9	214.7	212.9
Control of school								
Public	217.2	217.0	220.1	228.6	227.7	229.3	229.7	230.6
Private	230.5	231.8	230.0	238.1	241.5	244.5	239.1	242.0
13-year-olds								
Total	264.1	268.6	269.0	270.4	273.1	274.3	274.3	275.8
Male	263.6	269.2	270.0	271.2	274.1	276.0	276.3	277.2
Female	264.7	268.0	267.9	269.6	272.0	272.7	272.4	274.5
Race/ethnicity								
White	271.6	274.4	273.6	276.3	278.9	280.8	281.2	283.1
Black	229.6	240.4	249.2	249.1	250.2	251.5	252.1	251.0
Hispanic	238.0	252.4	254.3	254.6	259.3	256.0	255.7	259.2
Control of school								
Public	262.6	267.1	268.7	269.3	271.7	273.0	272.9	274.2
Private	279.2	281.1	275.7	279.9	283.3	284.6	285.5	288.5
17-year-olds								
Total	300.4	298.5	302.0	304.6	306.7	306.2	307.2	308.2
Male	303.8	301.5	304.7	306.3	308.9	308.5	309.5	309.8
Female	297.1	295.6	299.4	302.9	304.5	304.1	304.9	306.8
Race/ethnicity								
White	305.9	303.7	307.5	309.5	311.9	312.3	313.4	314.8
Black	268.4	271.8	278.6	288.5	285.8	285.5	286.4	283.3
Hispanic	276.3	276.7	283.1	283.5	292.2	290.8	292.0	292.7
Control of school								
Public	299.6	297.3	301.2	303.5	305.3	304.4	306.4	306.7
Private	314.3	311.4	320.1	317.7	320.4	319.4	315.5	320.6

Source: U.S. Department of Education, National Center for Education Statistics, National Assessment of Educational Progress, NAEP Trends in Academic Progress, various years, by Educational Testing Service, in *Digest of Education Statistics 2000*, retrieved April 19, 2002, from http://nces.ed.gov/.

Percentage Distribution of Students in Grades 3-12 Who Attended a Chosen or Assigned School, by Child's Race/Ethnicity, Parents' Highest Education Level, and Household Income: 1993, 1996, and 1999

Upgraded students and homeschoolers were excluded from the estimate. Percentages may not add to 100.0 due to rounding.

Child Race/Ethnicity, Parent Highest Education, Household Income	1993			1996			1999		
	Public		Private	Public		Private	Public		Private
	Assigned	Chosen		Assigned	Chosen		Assigned	Chosen	
Total	80.3	10.9	8.8	76.9	13.3	9.9	76.5	14.2	9.3
Race/ethnicity									
White	81.4	8.5	10.2	78.0	10.7	11.3	77.7	11.1	11.2
Black	77.4	18.9	3.7	74.2	20.8	5.1	72.0	22.5	5.6
Hispanic	79.7	13.6	6.7	76.4	16.1	7.5	77.3	18.2	4.5
Other	73.4	14.5	12.1	70.4	18.6	11.1	74.1	16.3	9.6
Parents' highest education level									
Less than high school	84.4	13.3	2.3	79.1	17.4	3.5	79.3	18.1	2.6
High school diploma or equivalent	83.6	11.2	5.2	83.0	11.6	5.4	81.0	13.8	5.2
Some college including technical/vocational	80.1	11.1	8.8	77.0	14.6	8.4	77.9	15.1	7.0
Bachelor's degree	76.9	8.7	14.3	71.4	13.4	15.3	72.4	12.8	14.9
Graduate/advanced degree	73.1	9.9	16.9	68.3	11.3	20.4	69.2	12.5	18.3
Household income									
$10,000 or less	82.9	14.0	3.0	76.6	19.5	3.9	73.7	22.2	4.1
$10,001-20,000	82.3	13.9	3.8	80.0	15.3	4.7	77.4	17.9	4.8
$20,001-35,000	81.8	10.6	7.7	78.7	14.0	7.4	79.4	15.1	5.4
$35,000-50,000	80.4	9.7	9.9	78.0	11.9	10.1	77.4	13.2	9.4
More than $50,000	75.9	8.5	15.6	73.6	10.2	16.3	75.0	10.3	14.6

Source: The Condition of Education 2001, retrieved April 22, 2002, from http://nces.ed.gov; primary source: NCES, National Household Education Surveys Program (NHES), 1993 (School Safety and Discipline Survey), 1996 (Parent Interview Survey), and 1999 (Parent Interview Survey).

Number of Nonfatal Crimes Against Students Ages 12 Through 18 Occurring at School or on the Way to or From School Per 1,000 Students, by Type of Crime and Selected Student Characteristics: 1992 to 1998

NA Not reported. Serious violent crimes include rape, sexual assault, robbery, and aggravated assault. Violent crimes include serious violent crimes and simple assault. Total crimes include violent crimes and theft. "At school" includes inside the school building, on school property, or on the way to or from school. Population sizes are 23,740,295 students ages 12 through 18 in 1992; 26,151,364 in 1996; and 26,806,268 in 1998. Because of rounding or missing data, detail may not add to totals.

	1992				1996				1998			
	Total	Theft	Violent	Serious Violent[1]	Total	Theft	Violent	Serious Violent[1]	Total	Theft	Violent	Serious Violent[1]
Student characteristics												
Total	144	95	48	10	121	78	43	9	101	58	43	9
Gender												
Male	168	105	64	15	134	78	56	11	111	59	52	10
Female	117	85	32	5	107	77	30	6	91	58	33	8
Age												
12-14	172	105	67	16	151	91	60	9	125	65	60	14
15-18	120	87	33	6	119	81	38	9	97	67	30	8
Race/ethnicity												
White, non-Hispanic	156	105	52	9	129	83	45	7	105	60	45	9
Black, non-Hispanic	114	67	46	18	105	73	32	12	111	64	48	12
Hispanic	113	72	41	10	137	74	63	22	109	58	51	15
Other, non-Hispanic	129	110	19	NA	108	72	36	11	89	57	32	4
Urbanicity												
Urban	141	92	50	15	126	76	50	14	117	68	49	13
Suburban	155	105	50	10	130	82	48	8	97	56	40	7

[Continued]

Number of Nonfatal Crimes Against Students Ages 12 Through 18 Occurring at School or on the Way to or From School Per 1,000 Students, by Type of Crime and Selected Student Characteristics: 1992 to 1998

[Continued]

	1992				1996				1998			
	Total	Theft	Violent	Serious Violent[1]	Total	Theft	Violent	Serious Violent[1]	Total	Theft	Violent	Serious Violent[1]
Rural	124	80	44	6	95	71	24	4	93	50	43	11
Household income												
Less than $7,500	123	65	57	14	86	55	31	8	110	56	53	17
$7,500-14,999	111	65	46	13	92	54	38	9	97	38	59	12
$15,000-24,999	125	60	65	16	120	68	52	15	126	64	62	10
$25,000-34,999	137	94	43	5	130	78	52	10	102	50	52	15
$35,000-49,999	180	133	47	9	131	84	48	9	86	57	29	6
$50,000-74,999	150	119	31	4	138	95	43	7	110	68	42	10
$75,000 or more	206	136	70	17	139	104	35	5	112	75	37	6

Source: U.S. Departments of Education and Justice, *Indicators of School Crime and Safety, 2000*, retrieved April 24, 2002, from http://www.ojp.usdoj.gov/bjs/.
Note: 1. Serious violent crimes are also included in violent crimes.

Percentage of Students Ages 12 Through 18 Who Reported Fearing Being Attacked or Harmed at School or on the Way to and From School During the Previous 6 Months, by Selected Student Characteristics: 1989, 1995, and 1999

Comparisons between the 1989 data and the 1995 and 1999 data should be made with caution due to changes in the questionnaire. "At school" means in the school building, on the school grounds, or on a school bus. Population sizes are 21,554,000 students ages 12 through 19 in 1989, 23,601,000 students ages 12 through 18 in 1995, and 24,614,000 students ages 12 through 18 in 1999.

	Feared Attack/Harm at School[1]			Feared Attack/Harm Going to School[1]		
	1989[2]	1995	1999	1989[2]	1995	1999
Student Characteristics						
Total	5.5	8.6	5.3	4.4	6.5	3.9
Gender						
Male	5.7	8.3	4.9	3.8	5.3	3.4
Female	5.4	8.9	5.7	5.1	7.9	4.5
Race/ethnicity						
White, non-Hispanic	4.4	6.3	3.9	2.8	3.8	2.1
Black, non-Hispanic	6.8	13.4	9.0	7.9	13.1	8.2
Hispanic	11.4	15.5	8.1	10.1	13.4	7.6
Other, non-Hispanic	8.0	9.4	4.2	6.0	8.2	3.8
Grade						
6th	8.8	11.8	9.3	7.3	7.2	4.7
7th	9.4	11	7.5	6.4	8.9	4.7
8th	5.4	9.2	6	3.9	6.9	3.8
9th	5.0	9.1	5.2	4.5	6.2	3.6
10th	5.0	7.5	4.5	3.6	6.3	4.4
11th	3.4	5.8	3.3	3.8	5.5	3.0
12th	2.5	5.9	2.5	2.7	4.2	3.2
Urbanicity						
Urban	7.5	12.3	7.3	8.2	11.7.0	7.5
Suburban	4.8	7.4.0	4.9	3.5	5.1	2.9

[Continued]

Percentage of Students Ages 12 Through 18 Who Reported Fearing Being Attacked or Harmed at School or on the Way to and From School During the Previous 6 Months, by Selected Student Characteristics: 1989, 1995, and 1999

[Continued]

	Feared Attack/Harm at School[1]			Feared Attack/Harm Going to School[1]		
	1989[2]	1995	1999	1989[2]	1995	1999
Rural	4.8	7.0	3.8	2.2	4.0	1.8
Control						
Public	5.9	9.1	5.7	4.5	6.7	4.0
Private	1.7	3.3	1.7	4.3	5.0	2.8

Source: U.S. Departments of Education and Justice, *Indicators of School Crime and Safety, 2000*, retrieved April 24, 2002, from http://www.ojp.usdoj.gov/bjs/. *Notes:* 1. Includes students who reported that they sometimes or most of the time feared being victimized in this way. 2. Students ages 12 through 19.

Students' Use of Time: Percentage of 9-, 13-, and 17-Year-Olds Who Were Watching 3 or More Hours of Television, Assigned Homework, and Reading for Fun Daily: 1984 and 1999

Age and Year	Watched TV 3 or More Hours	Homework Assigned/Done		Time on Homework			Read Daily for Fun
		Had Homework Assigned	Didn't Do Homework	Less Than 1 Hour	1 to 2 Hours	More Than 2 Hours	
Age 9							
1984	66.7	64.4	4.1	41.5	12.7	6.1	53.3
1999	51.1	74.2	3.8	53.1	12.4	4.9	54.1
Age 13							
1984	63.4	77.4	3.7	35.9	29.2	8.6	35.1
1999	45.9	75.9	4.5	37.2	26.3	7.9	28.2
Age 17							
1984	43.7	77.5	11.4	26.2	26.8	13.2	30.8
1999	34.3	73.6	13.1	26.4	22.6	11.5	24.8

Source: U.S. Department of Education, NCES, National Assessment of Educational Progress (NAEP), 1984 and 1999 Long-Term Trend Assessment, in *The Condition of Education 2001*, Indicator 22, retrieved 3/18/02 from http://nces.ed.gov/.

Achievement in Mathematics

Eighth and seventh grades in most countries. Latvia is annotated LSS for Latvian Speaking Schools

Country	Eighth Grade Average Achievement	Country	Seventh Grade Average Achievement
Singapore	643	Singapore	601
Korea	607	Korea	577
Japan	605	Japan	571
Hong Kong	588	Hong Kong	564
Belgium	565	Belgium	558
Czech Republic	564	Czech Republic	523
Slovak Republic	547	Netherlands	516
Switzerland	545	Bulgaria	514
Netherlands	541	Austria	509
Slovenia	541	Slovak Republic	508

[Continued]

Achievement in Mathematics

[Continued]

Country	Eighth Grade Average Achievement	Country	Seventh Grade Average Achievement
Bulgaria	540	Belgium	507
Austria	539	Switzerland	506
France	538	Hungary	502
Hungary	537	Russian Federation	501
Russian Federation	535	Ireland	500
Australia	530	Slovenia	498
Ireland	527	Australia	498
Canada	527	Thailand	495
Belgium	526	Canada	494
Thailand	522	France	492
Israel	522	Germany	484
Sweden	519	Sweden	477
Germany	509	England	476
New Zealand	508	United States	476
England	506	New Zealand	472
Norway	503	Denmark	465
Denmark	502	Scotland	463
United States	500	Latvia	462
Scotland	498	Norway	461
Latvia (LSS)	493	Iceland	459
Spain	487	Romania	454
Iceland	487	Spain	448
Greece	484	Cyprus	446
Romania	482	Greece	440
Lithuania	477	Lithuania	428
Cyprus	474	Portugal	423
Portugal	454	Iran, Islamic Rep.	401
Iran, Islamic Rep.	428	Columbia	369
Kuwait	392	South Africa	348
Colombia	385		
South Africa	354		

Source: IEA Third International Mathematics and Science Study (TIMSS), 1994-95.

Percentage of Public High School Graduates Concentrating in Vocational Programs

Concentrating means to accumulate 3 or more credits in a specialty.

Year	Agriculture and Renewable Resources	Business	Marketing and Distribution	Health Care	Trade and Industry	Technology and Communications	Occupational Home Economics			
							Total	Personal and Other Services	Food Service and Hospitality	Child Care and Education
1982	2.8	11.6	1.8	0.6	14.8	0.5	1.7	1.3	0.2	0.2
1990	2.5	8.4	2.1	0.6	11.2	0.8	2.0	1.3	0.5	0.3
1994	3.2	7.7	2.2	1.0	8.5	0.9	2.0	1.1	0.4	0.6
1998	2.6	4.8	1.8	1.9	9.8	2.2	1.8	0.8	0.5	0.6

Source: U.S. Department of Education, National Center for Education Statistics, High School and Beyond Sophomore Cohort 1982 High School Transcript Study and 1990 and 1994 National Assessment of Educational Progress High School Transcript Studies.

Average Number of Vocational Education Credits Accumulated by Public High School Graduates: 1982, 1990, and 1994

	1980	1990	1994
Male	4.68	4.32	4.13
Female	4.68	4.08	3.80
American Indian/Alaskan Native	4.93	4.62	4.26
Asian/Pacific Islander	3.31	3.07	3.01
Black, non-Hispanic	4.81	4.41	4.29
Hispanic	5.26	4.12	3.87
White, non-Hispanic	4.59	4.22	3.96
Students with Disabilities	4.82	6.01	5.99

Source: U.S. Department of Education, NCES, High School and Beyond Sophomore Cohort 1982 High School Transcript Study and 1990 and 1994 National Assessment of Educational Progress High School Transcript Studies, in Vocational Education in the United States: Toward the Year 2000, NCES 2000 029, by Karen Levesque et al., Project Officer: Dawn Nelson. Washington, D.C.: 2000, Tables 17, 18, 19.

Percentage Distribution of High School Students Who Took Advanced Mathematics or Science Classes or Advanced English Classes and a Foreign Language, by Race-Ethnicity and Sex: 1998

	Advanced Academic Mathematics	Chemistry II or Physics	Some Honors English	3+ Years Foreign Language
Male	40	8	24	24
Female	43	7	34	35
White	45	7	31	31
Black	30	5	27	21
Hispanic	26	6	22	31

[Continued]

Percentage Distribution of High School Students Who Took Advanced Mathematics or Science Classes or Advanced English Classes and a Foreign Language, by Race-Ethnicity and Sex: 1998

[Continued]

	Advanced Academic Mathematics	Chemistry II or Physics	Some Honors English	3+ Years Foreign Language
Asian/Pacific Islander	56	17	32	34
American Indian/Alaskan Native	27	2	18	20

Source: U.S. Department of Education, NCES, *The Condition of Education 2001*, Indicators 34 and 39, retrieved May 28, 2002, from http://nces.ed.gov/programs/coe/2000/.

Percentage of Students in Grades 1-12 Who Had Potential Access to a Computer and Used the Internet for Various Purposes at Various Locations, by Race-Ethnicity and Family Income: 1998

Included in the total but not shown separately are students from other racial-ethnic groups. Low income is the bottom 20 percent of all family incomes, high income is the top 20 percent of all family incomes, and middle income is the 60 percent in between. Analysis includes only those students in grades 1-12 who were ages 5-18.

Accessibility, Location	Total	Race-Ethnicity			Family Income		
		White	Black	Hispanic	Low	Middle	High
Students who had potential access to:							
Computer in household	57.6	70.1	27.7	28.4	21.2	53.7	87.7
WEBTV in household	1.3	1.5	0.8	0.3	0.3	1.2	2.1
Anyone from household use Internet from home	34.3	43.7	10.8	13.2	7.7	28.5	63.2
Students who used the Internet:							
At school	78.4	82.7	70.1	70.5	68.4	77.9	85.5
At home	25.0	32.2	8.4	8.0	4.9	20.4	47.6
Outside the home	19.8	22.4	13.0	15.5	15.0	20.4	21.1
At public library	2.4	2.5	2.0	2.3	1.8	2.6	2.1
At community center	0.1	0.1	0.0	0.2	0.4	0.1	0.0
At someone else's computer	3.0	3.7	0.9	2.6	2.9	3.4	2.1
Purpose of Internet use at home is:							
E-mail	14.9	19.6	3.5	4.4	2.8	11.7	29.3
Contacting friends/family	13.9	18.4	2.8	4.2	2.6	10.8	27.6
Educational purposes	5.8	7.5	1.0	2.0	1.1	4.4	12.1
Hobbies	3.8	5.0	1.1	0.8	0.6	2.9	8.0
Educational courses/research for school	19.3	25.1	6.4	6.1	4.0	15.2	37.5
News, weather, sports	5.3	6.9	1.8	1.8	0.8	4.2	10.3
Search for information	9.2	11.8	2.9	3.3	1.8	7.3	18.1
Games, entertainment, fun	1.9	2.6	0.2	0.5	0.4	1.7	3.4

Source: U.S. Department of Commerce, Bureau of the Census, October Current Population Surveys.

Chapter 12
TRENDS IN POSTSECONDARY EDUCATION

Institutions of Higher Education-Charges: 1985 to 2000

In dollars. Estimated. For the entire academic year ending in year shown. Figures are average charges per full-time equivalent student. Room and board are based on full-time students.

Institutions	Tuition and Required Fees[1]				Board Rates[2]				Dormitory Charges			
	All Colleges	2-Year Colleges	4-Year Schools	Other 4-Year Institutions	All Colleges	2-Year Colleges	4-Year Schools	Other 4-Year Institutions	All Colleges	2-Year Colleges	4-Year Schools	Other 4-Year Academic Control and Year
Public:												
1985	971	584	1,386	1,117	1,241	1,302	1,276	1,201	1,196	921	1,237	1,200
1990	1,356	756	2,035	1,608	1,635	1,581	1,728	1,561	1,513	962	1,561	1,554
1994	1,942	1,125	2,820	2,360	1,880	1,681	1,993	1,828	1,873	1,190	1,897	1,958
1995	2,057	1,192	2,977	2,499	1,949	1,712	2,108	1,866	1,959	1,232	1,992	2,044
1996	2,179	1,239	3,151	2,660	2,020	1,681	2,192	1,937	2,057	1,297	2,104	2,133
1997	2,271	1,276	3,323	2,778	2,111	1,789	2,282	2,025	2,148	1,339	2,187	2,232
1998	2,360	1,314	3,486	2,877	2,228	1,795	2,438	2,130	2,225	1,401	2,285	2,312
1999	2,427	1,323	3,645	2,974	2,346	1,828	2,576	2,245	2,328	1,450	2,408	2,407
2000	2,507	1,336	3,774	3,090	2,361	1,844	2,624	2,234	2,434	1,542	2,514	2,512
Private:												
1985	5,315	3,485	6,843	5,135	1,462	1,294	1,647	1,405	1,426	1,424	1,753	1,309
1990	8,174	5,196	10,348	7,778	1,948	1,811	2,339	1,823	1,923	1,663	2,411	1,774
1994	10,572	6,370	13,874	10,100	2,434	1,970	2,946	2,278	2,490	2,067	3,277	2,261
1995	11,111	6,914	14,537	10,653	2,509	2,023	3,035	2,362	2,587	2,233	3,469	2,347
1996	11,864	7,094	15,605	11,297	2,606	2,098	3,218	2,429	2,738	2,371	3,680	2,473
1997	12,498	7,236	16,552	11,871	2,663	2,181	3,142	2,520	2,878	2,537	3,826	2,602
1998	12,801	7,464	17,229	12,338	2,762	2,785	3,132	2,648	2,954	2,672	3,756	2,731
1999	13,368	7,852	18,226	12,809	2,865	2,884	3,188	2,765	3,074	2,581	3,914	2,849
2000	14,175	8,107	19,312	13,467	2,882	2,922	3,157	2,791	3,219	2,739	4,063	2,973

Source: Statistical Abstract of the United States: 2001, Table 278, Institutions of Higher Education-Charges: 1985 to 2000. *Notes:* 1. For in-state students. 2. Beginning 1990, rates reflect 20 meals per week, rather than meals served 7 days a week.

Perceptions of College Costs: Percentage Distribution of Tuition and Fees Charged at Public 4-Year Institutions and Estimates Reported by 6th- to 12th-Graders and Their Parents: 1999

	Actual Tuition/Fees 1998-99 ($)	6th- to 12th-Graders' Estimates ($)	6th- to 12th-Graders' Parents' Estimates ($)
Less than $2,000	10	11	6
$2,000-2999	39	13	19
$3,000-3,999	26	13	10
$4,000-4,999	19	10	12
$5,000-7,999	6	27	25
$8,000 or more	0	27	28
Average	3,243	5,664	5,970

Source: U.S. Department of Education, NCES, *The Condition of Education 2001 in Brief*, John Wirt and Andrea Livingston; Primary source: NCES National Household Education Surveys Program (NHES), 1999 (Parent and Youth Interview Surveys).

Total Costs/Expenses Borne by Students and Families, U.S. Colleges and Universities: 1998-99

	Public ($)		Private ($)	
	High Expense	Low Expense	High Expense	Low Expense
Tuition and Required Fees	4,000	1,200	20,000	10,000
Other Educational Expenses	850	700	900	900
Room and Board	5,650	1,800	6,600	5,600
Transportation/Other	1,500	2,000	1,500	1,500
Total	12,000	6,000	29,000	18,000

Source: U.S. Department of Education, *Study of College Costs and Prices, 1988- 89 to 1997- 98*, Volume 2: Commissioned Papers, NCES 2002 158; primary source: estimates by D. Bruce Johnstone (author); retrieved 3/1/02 from http://www.nces.gov.

Federal Student Financial Assistance: 1995 to 2001

35,450 represents $35,450,000,000. For award years July 1 of year shown to the following June 30. Funds utilized exclude operating costs, etc., and represent funds given to students. NA Not available. X Not applicable.

Award Year Impact Data	1995	1996	1997	1998	1999	2000	2001, est.
FUNDS UTILIZED ($ mil.)							
Total	35,450	38,849	40,074	43,072	43,469	46,933	NA
Federal Pell Grants	5,445	5,764	6,331	7,233	7,191	7,883	9,095
Federal Supplemental Educational Opportunity Grant	764	762	811	855	784	799	875
Federal Work-Study	764	776	906	913	1,044	1,123	1,216
Federal Perkins Loan	1,029	1,022	1,062	1,070	1,058	1,058	1,058
Federal Direct Student Loan (FDSL)	8,296	9,796	9,873	10,933	10,972	10,960	NA
Federal Family Education Loans (FFEL)	19,152	20,729	21,091	22,068	22,420	25,110	NA
NUMBER OF AWARDS (000)							
Total	13,667	14,516	14,652	15,187	15,257	15,822	NA

[Continued]

Federal Student Financial Assistance: 1995 to 2001

[Continued]

Award Year Impact Data	1995	1996	1997	1998	1999	2000	2001, est.
Federal Pell Grants	3,612	3,666	3,733	3,855	3,759	3,832	3,937
Federal Supplemental Educational Opportunity Grant	1,083	1,191	1,116	1,163	1,118	1,139	1,203
Federal Work-Study	702	691	746	744	930	1,000	1,000
Federal Perkins Loan	688	674	679	669	698	698	676
Federal Direct Student Loan (FDSL)	2,339	2,762	2,775	3,017	3,026	2,915	NA
Federal Family Education Loans (FFEL)	5,243	5,531	5,603	5,739	5,726	6,238	NA
AVERAGE AWARD ($)							
Total	2,594	2,676	2,735	2,836	2,849	2,966	NA
Federal Pell Grants	1,507	1,572	1,696	1,876	1,913	2,057	2,310
Federal Supplemental Educational Opportunity Grant	706	640	727	735	701	701	727
Federal Work-Study	1,087	1,123	1,215	1,228	1,123	1,123	1,215
Federal Perkins Loan	1,497	1,516	1,564	1,600	1,516	1,516	1,565
Federal Direct Student Loan (FDSL)	3,548	3,547	3,558	3,624	3,626	3,760	NA
Federal Family Education Loans (FFEL)	3,653	3,748	3,764	3,845	3,916	4,025	NA
COHORT DEFAULT RATE[1]							
Federal Perkins Loan	12.6	13	12.5	11.5	11.5	X	X
FFEL/FDSL Combined Rates	10.4	9.6	8.8	6.9	X	X	X

Source: Statistical Abstract of the United States: 2001, Table 276. Primary source: U.S. Department of Education, Office of Postsecondary Education, unpublished data. *Notes:* 1. As of June 30. Represents the percent of borrowers entering repayment status in year shown who defaulted in the following year.

Enrollment and Tuition Costs in Medical School, 1987-2000

School Year	Degrees Conferred	Enrollment	Actual Dollars		Constant 2000 Dollars	
			Undergraduate Tuition & Fees Per Year	Medical School Tuition & Fees Per Year	Undergraduate Tuition & Fees Per Year	Medical School Tuition & Fees Per Year
1987-1988	15,358	-	3,201	9,034	4,677	13,200
1988-1989	15,460	-	3,472	9,439	4,873	13,248
1989-1990	15,075	-	3,800	10,597	5,089	14,193
1990-1991	15,043	-	4,009	10,571	5,094	13,432
1991-1992	15,243	-	4,385	11,646	5,347	14,202
1992-1993	15,531	65,575	4,752	12,265	5,626	14,521
1993-1994	15,368	66,175	5,119	13,074	5,884	15,028
1994-1995	15,537	66,788	5,391	13,834	6,040	15,499
1995-1996	15,341	66,942	5,786	14,860	6,324	16,242
1996-1997	15,571	66,926	6,118	15,481	6,492	16,428
1997-1998	15,424	66,896	6,351	16,075	6,627	16,773
1998-1999	15,562	66,539	6,723	17,011	6,905	17,470
1999-2000	15,286	66,377	7,044	17,627	7,044	17,627

Source: National Center for Education Statistics. U.S. Department of Education. *Digest of Education Statistics, 2001.* Association of American Medical Colleges. "Total Enrollment by Gender and Race/Ethnicity, 1992- 2001." Retrieved August 12, 2002 from http://www.aamc.org/data/facts/famg82001.htm. "The Inflation Calculator." Retrieved August 13, 2002 from http://www.westegg.com/inflation.

Percentage Distribution of General Education Revenues of Higher Education Institutions Per Full-Time-Equivalent (FTE) Student, by Revenue Source and Control and Type of Institution: Academic Years Ending 1977-96

Federally supported student aid received through students (e.g., Federal Student Loan Programs) is included under tuition and fees. Data for academic years 1976-77 through 1985-86 include only institutions that provided both enrollment and finance data. FTE students include both undergraduate and graduate students. Details may not add to 100 due to rounding.

Academic Year Ending	Total	Tuition and Fees	Federal Appropriation	State/Local Appropriation	Federal Grant/ Contract	State/Local Grant/ Contract	Private Gifts	Endowment	Sales/Service of Educational Activities
Private, Not-for-Profit Universities									
1977	100	40.3	2.2	1.8	27.7	2.5	12.9	8.0	4.6
1978	100	40.6	2.0	1.6	27.4	2.2	13.4	7.7	5.1
1979	100	40.8	2.0	1.5	27.4	2.2	12.9	8.2	4.9
1980	100	40.1	1.9	1.4	27.8	2.6	12.4	8.3	5.4
1981	100	40.8	1.8	1.5	27.4	2.1	12.8	8.4	5.2
1982	100	42.5	1.7	1.4	25.6	1.9	12.7	8.7	5.3
1983	100	45.0	1.8	1.4	23.2	2.2	12.9	7.7	5.7
1984	100	44.2	1.6	1.3	22.8	2.2	13.4	8.4	6.1
1985	100	44.4	1.5	1.2	22.8	2.1	13.5	8.7	5.7
1986	100	44.2	1.4	1.2	23.2	2.2	13.6	8.6	5.7
1987	100	43.8	1.1	1.1	23.9	2.8	13.3	8.2	5.7
1988	100	44.0	1.1	1.0	22.3	3.6	13.5	8.5	6.0
1989	100	44.0	1.1	0.9	21.9	3.7	13.2	8.6	6.5
1990	100	43.9	1.1	0.9	21.9	3.7	13.4	8.6	6.4
1991	100	45.1	0.9	0.8	21.1	3.2	13.6	8.5	6.8
1992	100	45.2	0.9	0.5	21.0	3.4	13.5	8.1	7.4
1993	100	44.9	0.8	0.4	21.0	3.4	14.0	8.1	7.4
1994	100	45.1	0.8	0.4	21.5	2.6	14.1	7.9	7.6
1995	100	45.2	0.7	0.4	21.1	2.7	14.0	8.1	7.8
1996	100	45.4	0.7	0.4	20.8	2.4	14.2	8.7	7.4
Public Universities									
1977	100	16.4	2.9	52.4	17.0	2.1	4.7	0.7	3.7
1978	100	16.3	3.0	52.5	16.7	2.1	4.8	1.0	3.5
1979	100	15.9	3.0	52.1	16.9	2.3	4.7	1.0	4.0
1980	100	15.9	2.6	51.8	17.4	2.1	5.0	1.1	4.1
1981	100	16.4	2.3	51.3	17.3	2.3	5.0	1.1	4.3
1982	100	17.6	2.1	51.4	15.8	2.2	5.3	1.1	4.4
1983	100	19.0	2.0	50.3	15.0	2.1	5.9	1.2	4.5
1984	100	19.1	2.0	50.6	14.9	1.9	5.8	1.3	4.4
1985	100	18.3	2.1	51.2	14.8	2.0	5.9	1.3	4.4
1986	100	18.6	2.1	50.5	14.8	2.0	6.2	1.4	4.4
1987	100	19.5	1.9	49.3	15.0	2.4	6.4	1.0	4.5
1988	100	19.8	1.5	48.7	15.4	2.4	6.6	1.0	4.5
1989	100	20.0	1.5	47.7	15.6	2.6	7.0	1.0	4.6
1990	100	20.4	1.4	46.8	15.6	2.9	7.4	1.0	4.6
1991	100	21.1	1.4	45.6	16.0	3.0	7.2	1.1	4.8
1992	100	22.3	1.3	43.0	16.7	2.8	7.5	1.2	5.0
1993	100	23.3	1.3	41.3	17.2	2.7	7.7	1.3	5.1
1994	100	23.8	1.3	40.4	17.7	3.0	7.7	1.2	4.8
1995	100	24.0	1.2	40.3	17.7	3.1	7.6	1.3	4.9
1996	100	24.6	1.1	39.6	17.2	3.2	7.9	1.4	4.9
Private, Not-for-Profit 4-Year Colleges									
1977	100	61.7	0.9	2.1	10.8	2.0	15.6	5.8	1.0
1978	100	62.5	1.0	2.0	10.5	2.0	15.2	5.8	1.0
1979	100	62.2	1.0	1.9	11.0	2.0	14.7	6.2	1.0
1980	100	61.0	1.0	1.9	11.5	2.3	14.5	6.6	1.1
1981	100	61.6	1.1	1.9	10.7	2.3	14.3	6.9	1.2
1982	100	63.0	0.8	1.7	9.2	2.3	14.2	7.6	1.0
1983	100	64.6	0.6	1.7	7.7	2.4	14.4	7.5	1.0
1984	100	65.0	0.5	1.7	7.7	2.4	14.2	7.4	1.1
1985	100	64.8	0.5	1.6	7.7	2.5	14.3	7.5	1.1
1986	100	64.9	0.5	1.6	7.8	2.6	14.1	7.4	1.1
1987	100	65.2	0.6	1.6	7.4	2.9	14.1	7.2	1.1
1988	100	65.5	0.5	1.6	7.4	3.1	13.4	7.3	1.1
1989	100	66.0	0.4	1.4	7.1	3.6	13.0	7.5	1.1
1990	100	66.9	0.4	1.2	7.1	3.8	12.4	7.3	1.0
1991	100	68.1	0.4	1.1	6.8	3.5	12.1	7.1	0.9

[Continued]

Percentage Distribution of General Education Revenues of Higher Education Institutions Per Full-Time-Equivalent (FTE) Student, by Revenue Source and Control and Type of Institution: Academic Years Ending 1977-96

[Continued]

Academic Year Ending	Total	Tuition and Fees	Federal Appropriation	State/Local Appropriation	Federal Grant/ Contract	State/Local Grant/ Contract	Private Gifts	Endowment	Sales/Service of Educational Activities
1992	100	68.9	0.4	0.8	7.0	4.1	11.5	6.5	0.9
1993	100	69.2	0.3	0.7	7.1	3.8	11.3	6.1	1.5
1994	100	69.6	0.2	0.7	7.0	4.0	11.2	5.8	1.5
1995	100	69.9	0.2	0.5	7.2	3.7	11.6	5.9	1.0
1996	100	68.9	0.2	0.5	6.6	3.7	12.5	6.5	1.0
Public 4-Year Colleges									
1977	100	16.4	4.9	60.7	11.6	2.1	2.4	0.3	1.7
1978	100	16.0	4.9	61.4	10.9	2.2	2.5	0.2	1.8
1979	100	15.2	4.9	61.6	11.2	2.3	2.5	0.3	1.9
1980	100	14.9	5.0	61.5	11.3	2.2	2.6	0.3	2.1
1981	100	15.4	5.3	60.8	10.9	2.2	2.7	0.4	2.3
1982	100	16.1	4.7	61.5	9.7	2.1	2.9	0.4	2.5
1983	100	17.0	4.8	61.2	8.7	2.1	3.2	0.4	2.5
1984	100	18.2	4.7	59.8	8.5	2.3	3.3	0.4	2.7
1985	100	17.6	4.6	60.7	8.3	2.1	3.4	0.4	2.8
1986	100	17.7	4.3	60.0	8.4	2.6	3.6	0.4	3.0
1987	100	18.0	4.3	58.8	8.4	3.0	3.8	0.5	3.3
1988	100	18.4	4.3	58.4	8.3	2.9	3.7	0.5	3.5
1989	100	19.2	2.8	58.1	8.6	3.0	4.1	0.6	3.7
1990	100	19.7	4.2	55.6	8.6	3.2	4.3	0.6	3.8
1991	100	20.7	3.8	53.8	8.9	3.4	4.8	0.3	4.2
1992	100	22.3	3.6	51.3	9.4	3.7	4.9	0.6	4.2
1993	100	23.8	3.4	48.9	9.8	4.0	4.9	0.7	4.4
1994	100	24.4	3.6	47.6	10.1	4.2	5.0	0.6	4.6
1995	100	24.1	3.4	46.9	10.4	4.9	5.0	0.6	4.7
1996	100	24.8	3.5	45.9	10.7	5.5	5.1	0.4	4.1
Public 2-Year Colleges									
1977	100	16.8	2.0	72.5	5.8	2.0	0.5	0.1	0.4
1978	100	16.1	1.8	73.3	5.5	2.3	0.5	0.1	0.4
1979	100	15.8	1.9	72.7	6.0	2.5	0.5	0.1	0.5
1980	100	16.1	1.3	72.6	6.3	2.6	0.5	0.1	0.5
1981	100	16.8	1.2	71.7	6.3	2.8	0.5	0.1	0.6
1982	100	18.0	1.1	71.7	5.2	2.9	0.5	0.1	0.5
1983	100	19.3	0.8	71.4	4.3	2.9	0.6	0.1	0.5
1984	100	19.5	0.9	71.0	4.4	2.9	0.6	0.1	0.5
1985	100	19.1	0.7	70.9	4.6	3.4	0.6	0.1	0.5
1986	100	18.6	0.6	71.4	4.5	3.7	0.6	0.1	0.6
1987	100	18.5	0.7	70.4	4.1	4.8	0.6	0.1	0.6
1988	100	18.7	0.7	70.5	4.1	4.7	0.7	0.1	0.5
1989	100	19.1	0.7	68.7	4.2	6.0	0.8	0.1	0.5
1990	100	19.6	0.7	67.7	4.2	6.3	0.9	0.1	0.5
1991	100	20.4	0.7	67.4	4.2	5.7	0.9	0.1	0.5
1992	100	22.1	0.8	65.2	4.5	5.8	1.0	0.1	0.5
1993	100	23.4	0.6	63.7	5.0	5.4	1.0	0.1	0.7
1994	100	23.8	0.6	63.0	5.3	5.4	1.0	0.1	0.8
1995	100	23.4	0.5	63.0	5.5	5.7	1.1	0.1	0.7
1996	100	23.2	0.4	61.5	5.6	7.4	1.1	0.1	0.7

Source: U.S. Department of Education, NCES, *The Condition of Education 1999*, Table 39-1; Primary source: NCES Higher Education General Information Survey (HEGIS) Financial Statistics of Institutions of Higher Education survey and Integrated Postsecondary Education Data System (IPEDS) Institutional Characteristics, Financial Statistics, and Fall Enrollment surveys.

Educational and General Expenditures of Institutions of Higher Education Per Full-Time-Equivalent (FTE) Student (in Constant 1995-96 Dollars), by Expenditure Categories and Control and Type of Institution: Academic Years Ending 1981-96

	Public Sector				Private Sector			
	University		Other 4-Year Colleges		University		Other 4-Year Colleges	
	E&G Spending per Student	Avg. Annual % Increase Previous 5 Years	E&G Spending per Student	Avg. Annual % Increase Previous 5 Years	E&G Spending per Student	Avg. Annual % Increase Previous 5 Years	E&G Spending per Student	Avg. Annual % Increase Previous 5 Years
1995-96	$19,700	1.6	$13,403	2.2	$37,200	2.6	$17,177	2.3
1990-91	18,237	1.6	12,102	0.3	32,945	3.5	15,417	2.7
1985-86	16,868	1.9	12,283	1.4	27,983	3.3	13,605	2.9
1980-81	15,391	0.4	11,482	1.0	24,040	1.1	11,876	0.7

Source: U.S. Department of Education. National Center for Education Statistics. *Study of College Costs and Prices, 1988-89 to 1997-98*, Volume 2: Commissioned Papers, NCES 2002-158, by Alisa F. Cunningham, Jane V. Wellman, Melissa E. Clinedinst, and Jamie P. Merisotis. Project Officer: C. Dennis Carroll. Washington, DC: 2001, p23; primary source: NCES, 1999, *Condition of Education 1999*, Washington, DC: U.S. Government Printing Office, Supplemental Table 40-2; retrieved 3/12/02 from http://nces.ed.gov.

Earned Degrees Conferred by Degree-Granting Institutions, by Level of Degree and Sex of Student: 1970-71 to 2009-10

	Associate's Degrees			Bachelor's Degrees			Master's Degrees		
	Total	Men	Women	Total	Men	Women	Total	Men	Women
1970-71	292,014	166,227	125,787	839,730	475,594	364,136	251,633	149,550	102,083
1971-72	316,174	175,413	140,761	887,273	500,590	386,683	263,371	154,468	108,903
1972-73	343,924	188,591	155,333	922,362	518,191	404,171	277,033	157,842	119,191
1973-74	360,171	191,017	169,154	945,776	527,313	418,463	292,450	161,570	130,880
1974-75	391,454	209,996	181,458	922,933	504,841	418,092	311,771	167,248	144,523
1975-76	406,377	210,842	195,535	925,746	504,925	420,821	317,164	167,783	149,381
1976-77	412,246	204,718	207,528	919,549	495,545	424,004	311,620	161,212	150,408
1977-78	402,702	192,091	210,611	921,204	487,347	433,857	301,079	153,370	147,709
1978-79	400,910	183,737	217,173	921,390	477,344	444,046	298,081	150,749	147,332
1979-80	416,377	188,638	227,739	929,417	473,611	455,806	295,739	147,043	148,696
1980-81	434,526	196,944	237,582	935,140	469,883	465,257	295,546	145,532	150,014
1981-82	449,620	203,991	245,629	952,998	473,364	479,634	289,921	144,697	145,224
1982-83	452,240	202,704	249,536	969,510	479,140	490,370	284,263	143,595	140,668
1983-84	454,712	202,932	251,780	974,309	482,319	491,990	286,251	143,390	142,861
1984-85	446,047	196,166	249,881	979,477	482,528	496,949	288,567	143,508	145,059
1985-86	436,304	190,839	245,465	987,823	485,923	501,900	289,349	141,269	148,080
1986-87	435,085	190,047	245,038	991,264	480,782	510,482	299,317	145,163	154,154
1987-88	436,764	186,316	250,448	994,829	477,203	517,626	310,621	149,354	161,267
1988-89	455,102	191,195	263,907	1,018,755	483,346	535,409	324,301	153,653	170,648
1989-90	481,720	198,634	283,086	1,051,344	491,696	559,648	337,168	156,482	180,686
1990-91	504,231	207,481	296,750	1,094,538	504,045	590,493	352,838	161,842	190,996
1991-92	514,756	211,964	302,792	1,136,553	520,811	615,742	369,585	169,258	200,327
1992-93	530,632	215,261	315,371	1,165,178	532,811	632,297	387,070	176,085	210,985
1993-94	539,691	218,352	321,339	1,169,275	532,422	636,853	397,629	178,598	219,031
1994-95	555,216	219,514	335,702	1,160,134	526,131	634,003	406,301	179,081	227,220
1995-96	571,226	223,948	347,278	1,164,792	522,454	642,338	419,401	180,947	238,454
1996-97	558,555	217,613	340,942	1,172,879	520,515	652,364	430,164	184,375	245,789
1997-98	561,000	218,000	343,000	1,184,406	519,956	664,450	405,000	172,000	233,000
1998-99	559,000	216,000	342,000	1,200,303	518,746	681,557	398,000	168,000	230,000
1999-00	569,000	215,000	354,000	1,237,875	530,367	707,508	396,000	166,000	230,000

[Continued]

Earned Degrees Conferred by Degree-Granting Institutions, by Level of Degree and Sex of Student: 1970-71 to 2009-10

[Continued]

	Associate's Degrees			Bachelor's Degrees			Master's Degrees		
	Total	Men	Women	Total	Men	Women	Total	Men	Women
2000-01	571,000	216,000	355,000	1,209,000	524,000	685,000	396,000	165,000	231,000
2001-02	577,000	217,000	359,000	1,227,000	529,000	698,000	399,000	165,000	233,000
2002-03	581,000	218,000	363,000	1,241,000	527,000	714,000	402,000	166,000	236,000
2003-04	583,000	218,000	364,000	1,251,000	535,000	716,000	406,000	167,000	239,000
2004-05	587,000	219,000	367,000	1,275,000	538,000	737,000	411,000	168,000	243,000
2005-06	591,000	220,000	371,000	1,294,000	544,000	750,000	417,000	169,000	248,000
2006-07	596,000	221,000	374,000	1,318,000	549,000	769,000	425,000	171,000	254,000
2007-08	603,000	223,000	380,000	1,337,000	553,000	784,000	432,000	173,000	260,000
2008-09	611,000	224,000	387,000	1,355,000	558,000	797,000	439,000	175,000	264,000

Source: U.S. Department of Education, NCES, Earned Degrees Conferred; *Projections of Education Statistics to 2010*; Higher Education General Information Survey (HEGIS), Degrees and Other Formal Awards Conferred surveys; and Integrated Postsecondary Education Data System (IPEDS), Completions survey.

Earned Degrees Conferred by Degree-Granting Institutions, by Level of Degree and Sex of Student: 1970-71 to 2009-10

	First-Professional Degrees			Doctor's Degrees		
	Total	Men	Women	Total	Men	Women
1970-71	43,411	40,723	2,688	33,363	28,090	5,273
1971-72	50,018	46,489	3,529	34,777	28,571	6,206
1972-73	53,816	48,530	5,286	33,816	27,365	6,451
1973-74	55,916	48,956	6,960	34,083	26,817	7,266
1974-75	62,649	52,892	9,757	34,064	26,267	7,797
1975-76	64,359	52,374	11,985	33,232	25,142	8,090
1976-77	66,581	52,270	14,311	32,131	23,658	8,473
1977-78	68,848	52,652	16,196	32,730	23,541	9,189
1978-79	70,131	52,716	17,415	32,615	22,943	9,672
1979-80	71,956	52,792	19,164	32,958	22,711	10,247
1980-81	72,032	52,223	19,809	32,707	22,224	10,483
1981-82	73,054	51,250	21,804	32,775	21,902	10,873
1982-83	74,468	51,378	23,090	33,209	22,064	11,145
1983-84	75,063	50,455	24,608	32,943	21,700	11,243
1984-85	73,910	49,261	24,649	33,653	21,819	11,834
1985-86	71,617	46,523	25,094	34,041	22,061	11,980
1986-87	70,735	45,484	25,251	34,870	22,615	12,255
1987-88	70,856	45,046	25,810	35,720	22,648	13,072
1988-89	70,988	43,961	27,027	38,371	24,401	13,970
1989-90	71,948	43,846	28,102	39,294	24,756	14,538
1990-91	74,146	45,071	29,075	40,659	25,557	15,102
1991-92	75,387	45,153	30,234	42,132	26,073	16,059
1992-93	75,418	44,707	30,711	43,185	26,552	16,633
1993-94	75,800	44,853	30,947	44,446	26,916	17,530
1994-95	76,734	44,748	31,986	44,652	26,841	17,811
1995-96	78,730	45,564	33,166	45,876	27,146	18,730

[Continued]

Earned Degrees Conferred by Degree-Granting Institutions, by Level of Degree and Sex of Student: 1970-71 to 2009-10

[Continued]

	First-Professional Degrees			Doctor's Degrees		
	Total	Men	Women	Total	Men	Women
1996-97	78,598	44,911	33,687	46,010	26,664	19,346
1997-98	80,300	45,600	34,700	45,900	27,300	18,600
1998-99	78,400	44,700	33,600	45,200	26,700	18,500
1999-2000	76,500	43,200	33,300	45,000	26,500	18,500
2000-01	75,400	42,100	33,300	44,900	26,400	18,500
2001-02	75,200	41,600	33,600	45,000	26,400	18,600
2002-03	75,400	41,500	33,900	45,100	26,400	18,700
2003-04	75,900	41,500	34,400	45,300	26,500	18,800
2004-05	76,700	41,800	35,000	45,600	26,600	19,000
2005-06	77,700	42,100	35,600	46,000	26,700	19,300
2006-07	78,700	42,300	36,400	46,400	26,800	19,600
2007-08	80,100	42,700	37,400	46,800	27,000	19,800
2008-09	81,600	43,200	38,400	47,100	27,100	20,000

Source: U.S. Department of Education, NCES, Earned Degrees Conferred; *Projections of Education Statistics to 2010*; Higher Education General Information Survey (HEGIS), Degrees and Other Formal Awards Conferred surveys; and Integrated Postsecondary Education Data System (IPEDS), Completions survey.

Bachelor's Degrees Conferred by Institutions of Higher Education, by Racial/ Ethnic Group and Sex of Student: 1976-77 to 1995-96

For years 1984-85 to 1995-96, reported racial/ethnic distributions of students by level of degree, field of degree, and sex were used to estimate race/ethnicity for students whose race/ethnicity was not reported. Because of rounding, percents may not add to 100.0. Data exclude men and women whose racial/ethnic characteristics were not ascertainable.

	Number of Degrees Conferred						
	Total	White, non-Hispanic	Black, non-Hispanic	Hispanic	Asian/Pacific Islander	American Indian/Alask. Native	Non-Resident Alien
1976-77	917,900	807,688	58,636	18,743	13,793	3,326	15,714
1978-79	919,540	802,542	60,246	20,096	15,407	3,410	17,839
1980-81	934,800	807,319	60,673	21,832	18,794	3,593	22,589
1984-85	968,311	826,106	57,473	25,874	25,395	4,246	29,217
1986-87	991,264	841,818	56,560	26,988	32,624	3,968	29,306
1988-89	1,016,350	859,703	58,078	29,918	37,674	3,951	27,026
1989-90	1,048,631	884,376	61,063	32,844	39,248	4,392	26,708
1990-91	1,081,280	904,062	65,341	36,612	41,618	4,513	29,134
1991-92	1,129,833	936,771	72,326	40,761	46,720	5,176	28,079
1992-93	1,159,931	947,309	77,872	45,376	51,463	5,671	32,240
1993-94	1,165,973	936,227	83,576	50,241	55,660	6,189	34,080
1994-95	1,158,788	913,377	87,203	54,201	60,478	6,606	36,923
1995-96	1,163,036	904,709	91,166	58,288	64,359	6,970	37,544

[Continued]

Bachelor's Degrees Conferred by Institutions of Higher Education, by Racial/Ethnic Group and Sex of Student: 1976-77 to 1995-96

[Continued]

	Number of Degrees Conferred						
	Total	White, non-Hispanic	Black, non-Hispanic	Hispanic	Asian/Pacific Islander	American Indian/Alask. Native	Non-Resident Alien
Men							
1976-77	494,424	438,161	25,147	10,318	7,638	1,804	11,356
1978-79	476,065	418,215	24,659	10,418	8,261	1,736	12,776
1980-81	469,625	406,173	24,511	10,810	10,107	1,700	16,324
1984-85	476,148	405,085	23,018	12,402	13,554	1,998	20,091
1986-87	480,782	406,749	22,501	12,865	17,253	1,817	19,597
1988-89	481,946	407,154	22,370	13,950	19,260	1,730	17,482
1989-90	490,317	413,573	23,262	14,941	19,721	1,859	16,961
1990-91	496,424	415,505	24,328	16,158	20,678	1,901	17,854
1991-92	516,976	429,842	26,956	17,976	23,248	2,182	16,772
1992-93	530,541	435,084	28,883	19,865	25,293	2,449	18,967
1993-94	530,804	429,121	30,648	21,807	26,938	2,616	19,674
1994-95	525,174	417,006	31,775	23,600	28,973	2,736	21,084
1995-96	521,439	408,829	32,852	24,994	30,630	2,885	21,249
Women							
1976-77	423,476	369,527	33,489	8,425	6,155	1,522	4,358
1978-79	443,475	384,327	35,587	9,678	7,146	1,674	5,063
1980-81	465,175	401,146	36,162	11,022	8,687	1,893	6,265
1984-85	492,163	421,021	34,455	13,472	11,841	2,248	9,126
1986-87	510,482	435,069	34,059	14,123	15,371	2,151	9,709
1988-8	534,404	452,549	35,708	15,968	18,414	2,221	9,544
1989-90	558,314	470,803	37,801	17,903	19,527	2,533	9,747
1990-91	584,856	488,557	41,013	20,454	20,940	2,612	11,280
1991-92	612,857	506,929	45,370	22,785	23,472	2,994	11,307
1992-93	629,390	512,225	48,989	25,511	26,170	3,222	13,273
1993-94	635,169	507,106	52,928	28,434	28,722	3,573	14,406
1994-95	633,614	496,371	55,428	30,601	31,505	3,870	15,839
1995-96	641,597	495,880	58,314	33,294	33,729	4,085	16,295

Source: U.S. Department of Education, NCES, Higher Education General Information Survey (HEGIS), Degrees and Other Formal Awards Conferred surveys, and Integrated Postsecondary Education Data System (IPEDS), Completions surveys.

Doctor's Degrees Conferred by Institutions of Higher Education, by Racial/ Ethnic Group and Sex of Student: 1976-77 to 1996-97

For years 1984-85 to 1996-97, reported racial/ethnic distributions of students by level of degree, field of degree, and sex were used to estimate race/ethnicity for students whose race/ethnicity was not reported. Because of rounding, percents may not add to 100.0. Data exclude men and women whose racial/ethnic characteristics were not ascertainable.

| | Number of Degrees Conferred | | | | | | |
	Total	White, non-Hispanic	Black, non-Hispanic	Hispanic	Asian/Pacific Islander	American Indian/Alask. Native	Non-Resident Alien
1976-77	33,126	26,851	1,253	522	658	95	3,747
1978-79	32,675	26,138	1,268	439	811	104	3,915
1980-81	32,839	25,908	1,265	456	877	130	4,203
1984-85	32,307	23,934	1,154	677	1,106	119	5,317
1986-87	34,041	24,434	1,057	751	1,098	105	6,596
1988-89	35,659	24,884	1,066	629	1,323	85	7,672
1989-90	38,113	25,880	1,153	788	1,235	99	8,958
1990-91	38,547	25,328	1,211	732	1,459	102	9,715
1991-92	40,090	25,813	1,223	811	1,559	118	10,566
1992-93	42,021	26,700	1,352	827	1,582	106	11,454
1993-94	43,149	27,156	1,393	903	2,025	134	11,538
1994-95	44,427	27,826	1,667	984	2,690	130	11,130
1995-96	44,645	27,756	1,636	999	2,646	158	11,450
1996-97	45,394	28,344	1,847	1,098	2,607	173	11,325
Men							
1976-77	25,036	20,032	766	383	540	67	3,248
1978-79	23,488	18,433	734	294	646	69	3,312
1980-81	22,595	17,310	694	277	655	95	3,564
1984-85	21,296	15,017	561	431	802	64	4,421
1986-87	22,061	14,812	485	441	794	57	5,472
1988-89	22,597	14,541	491	350	945	50	6,220
1989-90	24,248	15,105	533	423	871	49	7,267
1990-91	24,333	14,565	581	387	987	58	7,755
1991-92	25,168	14,674	576	458	1,062	65	8,333
1992-93	25,980	14,902	615	439	1,041	51	8,932
1993-94	26,531	15,126	631	465	1,373	66	8,870
1994-95	26,898	15,354	731	488	1,758	58	8,509
1995-96	26,836	15,101	730	516	1,693	80	8,716
1996-97	26,826	15,339	786	572	1,606	86	8,437
Women							
1976-77	8,090	6,819	487	139	118	28	499
1978-79	9,187	7,705	534	145	165	35	603
1980-81	10,244	8,598	571	179	222	35	639
1984-85	11,011	8,917	593	246	304	55	896
1986-87	11,980	9,622	572	310	304	48	1,124
1988-89	13,062	10,343	575	279	378	35	1,452
1989-90	13,865	10,775	620	365	364	50	1,691
1990-91	14,214	10,763	630	345	472	44	1,960
1991-92	14,922	11,139	647	353	497	53	2,233
1992-93	16,041	11,798	737	388	541	55	2,522

[Continued]

Doctor's Degrees Conferred by Institutions of Higher Education, by Racial/Ethnic Group and Sex of Student: 1976-77 to 1996-97

[Continued]

	Number of Degrees Conferred						
	Total	White, non-Hispanic	Black, non-Hispanic	Hispanic	Asian/Pacific Islander	American Indian/Alask. Native	Non-Resident Alien
1993-94	16,618	12,030	762	438	652	68	2,668
1994-95	17,529	12,472	936	496	932	72	2,621
1995-96	17,809	12,655	906	483	953	78	2,734
1996-97	18,568	13,005	1,061	526	1,001	87	2,888

Source: U.S. Department of Education, NCES, "Doctor's degrees conferred by institutions of higher education, by racial/ethnic group and sex of student: 1976-77 to 1996-97"; primary source, U.S. Department of Education, NCES, Higher Education General Information Survey (HEGIS), Degrees and Other Formal Awards Conferred surveys, and Integrated Postsecondary Education Data System (IPEDS), Completions surveys; retrieved 3/27/02 from http:// nces.ed.gov/pubs2000.

Total Number of Students Formally Enrolled in Distance Education Courses, by Selected Institutional Characteristics: 1995 and 1997

Type of institution	1995	1997
Total[1]	753,640	1,661,100
Public, 2-year	414,160	714,160
Public, 4-year	234,020	711,350
Private, 4-year	104,960	222,350
Less than 3,000 students	116,320	382,060
3,000 to 9,999	232,750	477,470
10,000 or more	404,570	801,570

Source: NCES, Distance Education at Postsecondary Education Institutions, December 1999, NCES 2000-013; NCES, Post-secondary Education Quick Information System, Distance Education in Higher Education Institutions, 1997. *Notes:* 1. Includes private 2-year institutions, not reported separately. Too few offered distance education to make a reliable estimate.

Mean Earnings of Workers 18 Years Old and Over, by Educational Attainment and Sex: 1975 to 1999

Mean annual earnings [dollars]. Total number with earnings in thousands.

	Total		Not a High School Graduate		High School Graduate		Some College/Associate Degree		Bachelor's Degree		Advanced Degree	
	Mean	Number with Earnings	Mean	Number with Earnings	Mean	Number with Earnings	Mean	Number with Earnings	Mean	Number with Earnings	Mean	Number with Earnings
Total Both Sexes												
1975	8,552	97,881	6,198	24,916	7,843	39,827	8,388	16,917	12,332	9,764	16,725	6,457
1976	9,180	100,510	6,720	25,035	8,393	40,570	8,813	17,786	13,033	10,132	17,911	6,985
1977	9,887	103,119	7,066	24,854	9,013	41,696	9,607	18,905	14,207	10,357	19,077	7,309
1978	10,812	106,436	7,759	23,787	9,834	43,510	10,357	20,121	15,291	11,001	20,173	8,017
1979	11,795	110,826	8,420	23,783	10,624	45,497	11,377	21,174	16,514	11,751	21,874	8,621
1980	12,665	111,919	8,845	23,028	11,314	46,795	12,409	21,384	18,075	12,175	23,308	8,535
1981	13,624	113,301	9,357	22,296	12,109	47,332	13,176	21,759	19,006	12,579	25,281	9,336
1982	14,351	113,451	9,387	20,789	12,560	46,584	13,503	22,602	20,272	13,425	26,915	10,051
1983	15,137	115,095	9,853	20,020	13,044	47,560	14,245	23,208	21,532	13,929	28,333	10,377

[Continued]

Mean Earnings of Workers 18 Years Old and Over, by Educational Attainment and Sex: 1975 to 1999

[Continued]

	Total		Not a High School Graduate		High School Graduate		Some College/ Associate Degree		Bachelor's Degree		Advanced Degree	
	Mean	Number with Earnings	Mean	Number with Earnings	Mean	Number with Earnings	Mean	Number with Earnings	Mean	Number with Earnings	Mean	Number with Earnings
1984	16,083	118,183	10,384	20,206	13,893	48,452	14,936	24,463	23,072	14,653	30,192	10,410
1985	17,181	120,651	10,726	19,692	14,457	49,674	16,349	25,402	24,877	15,373	32,909	10,510
1986	18,149	122,757	11,203	19,665	15,120	50,104	17,073	26,113	26,511	15,788	34,787	11,087
1987	19,016	124,874	11,824	19,748	15,939	50,815	18,054	26,404	26,919	16,497	35,968	11,411
1988	20,060	127,564	11,889	19,635	16,750	51,297	19,066	27,217	28,344	17,308	37,724	12,109
1989	21,414	129,094	12,242	19,137	17,594	51,846	20,255	28,078	30,736	17,767	41,019	12,265
1990	21,793	130,080	12,582	18,698	17,820	51,977	20,694	28,993	31,112	18,128	41,458	12,285
1991	22,332	130,371	12,613	17,553	18,261	46,508	20,551	35,732	31,323	20,475	46,039	10,103
1992	23,227	130,860	12,809	16,612	18,737	45,340	20,867	37,339	32,629	21,091	48,652	10,479
1993	24,674	133,119	12,820	16,575	19,422	44,779	21,539	39,429	35,121	21,815	55,789	10,521
1994	25,852	135,096	13,697	16,479	20,248	44,614	22,226	40,135	37,224	22,712	56,105	11,155
1995	26,792	136,221	14,013	16,990	21,431	44,546	23,862	40,142	36,980	23,285	56,667	11,258
1996	28,106	138,703	15,011	17,075	22,154	45,908	25,181	40,410	38,112	24,028	61,317	11,281
1997	29,514	140,367	16,124	16,962	22,895	45,976	26,235	40,802	40,478	25,035	63,229	11,591
1998	30,928	142,053	16,053	16,742	23,594	45,987	27,566	41,412	43,782	25,818	63,473	12,095
1999	32,356	144,640	16,121	16,737	24,572	46,082	28,403	42,860	45,678	26,215	67,697	12,749
Male												
1975	11,091	57,297	7,843	15,613	10,475	21,347	10,805	9,851	15,758	5,960	19,672	4,526
1976	11,923	58,419	8,522	15,634	11,189	21,499	11,376	10,282	16,714	6,135	21,202	4,868
1977	12,888	59,441	8,939	15,369	12,092	21,846	12,393	10,848	18,187	6,341	22,786	5,038
1978	14,154	60,586	9,894	14,550	13,188	22,650	13,382	11,352	19,861	6,611	24,274	5,422
1979	15,430	62,464	10,628	14,711	14,317	23,318	14,716	11,781	21,482	6,889	26,411	5,765
1980	16,382	62,825	11,042	14,273	15,002	24,023	15,871	11,663	23,340	7,132	27,846	5,733
1981	17,542	63,547	11,668	13,701	15,900	24,435	16,870	11,784	24,353	7,393	30,072	6,235
1982	18,244	63,489	11,513	12,868	16,160	24,059	17,108	12,103	25,758	7,865	32,109	6,594
1983	19,175	63,816	12,052	12,376	16,728	24,449	18,052	12,261	27,239	8,010	33,635	6,719
1984	20,452	65,005	12,775	12,325	18,016	24,827	18,863	12,818	29,203	8,387	35,804	6,648
1985	21,823	66,439	13,124	12,137	18,575	25,496	20,698	13,385	31,433	8,794	39,768	6,627
1986	23,057	67,189	13,703	12,208	19,453	25,562	21,784	13,502	33,376	8,908	41,836	7,009
1987	24,015	67,951	14,544	12,117	20,364	25,981	22,781	13,433	33,677	9,286	43,140	7,134
1988	25,344	69,006	14,551	11,993	21,481	26,080	23,827	14,019	35,906	9,466	45,677	7,449
1989	27,025	69,798	14,727	11,774	22,508	26,649	25,555	14,384	38,692	9,737	50,144	7,434
1990	27,164	70,218	14,991	11,412	22,378	26,753	26,120	14,844	38,901	9,807	49,768	7,402
1991	27,494	70,145	15,056	10,679	22,663	24,110	25,345	18,076	38,484	11,126	54,449	6,154
1992	28,448	70,409	14,934	10,335	22,978	23,610	25,660	18,768	40,039	11,353	58,324	6,344
1993	30,568	71,183	14,946	10,151	23,973	23,388	26,614	19,532	43,499	11,810	68,221	6,302
1994	32,087	72,246	16,633	9,981	25,038	23,418	27,636	19,859	46,278	12,324	67,032	6,663
1995	33,251	72,634	16,748	10,312	26,333	23,473	29,851	19,918	46,111	12,251	69,588	6,679
1996	34,705	73,955	17,826	10,583	27,642	23,966	31,426	20,208	46,702	12,562	74,406	6,636
1997	36,556	74,596	19,575	10,348	28,307	24,152	32,641	20,359	50,056	13,008	78,032	6,728
1998	38,134	75,213	19,155	10,085	28,742	24,155	34,179	20,545	55,057	13,486	77,217	6,942
1999	40,257	76,233	18,855	9,917	30,414	24,235	35,326	21,173	57,706	13,683	84,051	7,225
Female												
1975	4,968	40,584	3,438	9,303	4,802	18,480	5,019	7,066	6,963	3,804	9,818	1,931
1976	5,373	42,091	3,723	9,401	5,240	19,071	5,301	7,504	7,383	3,997	10,345	2,117
1977	5,804	43,678	4,032	9,485	5,624	19,850	5,856	8,057	7,923	4,016	10,848	2,271
1978	6,396	45,850	4,397	9,237	6,192	20,860	6,441	8,769	8,408	4,390	11,603	2,595
1979	7,099	48,362	4,840	9,072	6,741	22,179	7,190	9,393	9,474	4,862	12,717	2,856
1980	7,909	49,094	5,263	8,755	7,423	22,772	8,256	9,721	10,628	5,043	14,022	2,802
1981	8,619	49,754	5,673	8,595	8,063	22,897	8,811	9,975	11,384	5,186	15,647	3,101
1982	9,403	49,962	5,932	7,921	8,715	22,525	9,348	10,499	12,511	5,560	17,009	3,457
1983	10,111	51,279	6,292	7,644	9,147	23,111	9,981	10,947	13,808	5,919	18,593	3,658
1984	10,742	53,178	6,644	7,881	9,561	23,625	10,614	11,645	14,865	6,266	20,275	3,762
1985	11,493	54,212	6,874	7,555	10,115	24,178	11,504	12,017	16,114	6,579	21,202	3,883
1986	12,214	55,568	7,109	7,457	10,606	24,542	12,029	12,611	17,623	6,880	22,672	4,078
1987	13,049	56,923	7,504	7,631	11,309	24,834	13,158	12,971	18,217	7,211	24,004	4,277
1988	13,833	58,558	7,711	7,642	11,857	25,217	14,009	13,198	19,216	7,842	25,010	4,660
1989	14,809	59,296	8,268	7,363	12,468	25,377	14,688	13,694	21,089	8,030	26,977	4,831
1990	15,493	59,862	8,808	7,286	12,986	25,224	15,002	14,149	21,933	8,321	28,862	4,883
1991	16,320	60,226	8,818	6,875	13,523	22,398	15,643	17,657	22,802	9,348	32,929	3,948
1992	17,145	60,451	9,311	6,277	14,128	21,730	16,023	18,571	23,991	9,738	33,814	4,135
1993	17,900	61,937	9,462	6,425	14,446	21,391	16,555	19,897	25,232	10,005	37,212	4,218
1994	18,684	62,850	9,189	6,498	14,955	21,195	16,928	20,276	26,483	10,388	39,905	4,493
1995	19,414	63,587	9,790	6,678	15,970	21,073	17,962	20,224	26,841	11,034	37,813	4,578
1996	20,570	64,748	10,421	6,492	16,161	21,942	18,933	20,202	28,701	11,466	42,625	4,646
1997	21,528	65,771	10,725	6,614	16,906	21,824	19,856	20,442	30,119	12,027	42,744	4,863
1998	22,818	66,840	11,353	6,657	17,898	21,832	21,056	20,867	31,452	12,332	44,954	5,153
1999	23,551	68,409	12,145	6,819	18,092	21,847	21,644	22,687	32,546	12,533	46,307	5,523

Source: U.S. Census Bureau Internet Release date: December 19, 2000; retrieved April 11, 2002, from http://www.census.gov/population/socdemo/education/tableA- 3.txt.

Chapter 13
SPECIAL NEEDS, GIFTS, AND ISSUES

Students Supported by Special Education Programs of the Federal Government

Values are in thousands. 4,144 is 4,144,000.

	All Disabili- ties	Specific Learning Disabili- ties	Speech or Language Impair- ments	Mental Retarda- tion	Serious Emotional Distur- bance	Hearing Impair- ments	Ortho- pedic Impair- ments	Other Hearing Impair- ments	Visual Impair- ments	Multiple Disabi- lities	Deaf- Blind- ness	Autism and Traumatic Brain Injury
1980-81	4,144	1,462	1,168	830	347	79	58	98	31	68	3	-
1981-82	4,198	1,622	1,135	786	339	75	58	79	29	71	2	-
1982-83	4,255	1,741	1,131	757	352	73	57	50	28	63	2	-
1983-84	4,298	1,806	1,128	727	361	72	56	53	29	65	2	-
1984-85	4,315	1,832	1,126	694	372	69	56	68	28	69	2	-
1985-86	4,317	1,862	1,125	660	375	66	57	57	27	86	2	-
1986-87	4,374	1,914	1,136	643	383	65	57	52	26	97	2	-
1987-88	4,439	1,928	950	580	371	56	46	45	22	77	1	-
1988-89	4,529	1,984	964	560	372	56	47	50	22	83	1	-
1989-90	4,631	2,047	971	547	380	57	48	52	22	86	2	-
1990-91	4,761	2,129	985	535	390	58	49	55	23	96	1	-
1991-92	4,941	2,232	996	537	399	60	51	58	24	97	1	5
1992-93	5,111	2,351	994	518	400	60	52	65	23	102	1	19
1993-94	5,309	2,408	1,014	536	414	64	56	82	24	108	1	24
1994-95	5,378	2,489	1,015	555	427	64	60	106	24	88	1	29
1995-96	5,573	2,579	1,022	570	438	67	63	133	25	93	1	39
1996-97	5,729	2,649	1,043	579	445	68	66	160	25	98	1	44
1997-98	5,903	2,725	1,056	589	453	69	67	190	25	106	1	54
1998-99	6,054	2,789	1,068	597	462	70	69	221	26	106	2	67
1999-00	6,195	2,834	1,080	600	469	71	71	253	26	111	2	79

Source: National Center for Education Statistics. U.S. Department of Education. *Digest of Education Statistics, 1992* and U.S. Department of Education, Office of Special Education and Rehabilitative Services, Annual Report to Congress on the Implementation of The Individuals with Disabilities Education Act, various years, and unpublished tabulations; and National Center for Education Statistics, Common Core of Data survey. April 2001.

Growth Rates of Students Supported by Federal Special Education Programs

	Overall Growth Rate - %	Annual Growth Rate - %	Number of School Years Measured
Total population of children 0 to 21	9.1	0.4	20
All disabilities	49.5	2.1	20
Specific learning disabilities	93.8	3.5	20
Speech or language impairments	-7.5	-0.4	20

[Continued]

Growth Rates of Students Supported by Federal Special Education Programs

[Continued]

	Overall Growth Rate - %	Annual Growth Rate - %	Number of School Years Measured
Mental retardation	-27.7	-1.7	20
Serious emotional disturbance	35.2	1.6	20
Hearing impairments	-10.1	-0.6	20
Orthopedic impairments	22.4	1.1	20
Other health impairments	158.2	5.1	20
Visual impairments	-16.1	-0.9	20
Multiple disabilities	63.2	2.6	20
Deaf-blindness	-33.3	-2.1	20
Autism and traumatic brain injury	1,416.3	40.5	9
Developmental delay	375.0	117.9	3

Source: National Center for Education Statistics. U.S. Department of Education. *Digest of Education Statistics, 1992* and U.S. Department of Education, Office of Special Education and Rehabilitative Services, Annual Report to Congress on the Implementation of The Individuals with Disabilities Education Act, various years, and unpublished tabulations; and National Center for Education Statistics, Common Core of Data survey. April 2001.

Number of Children on Ritalin

	Number of Cases
1970	150,000
1980	541,000
1990	900,000
2000	5,000,000

Source: "Does Ritalin Even Exist? The Ritalin Sham." Retrieved from http://www.naturalchild.com.

Limited English Proficiency Students in the Kindergarden Through 12th Grade Age Group

	Total K-12 Students	Number of LEP Students	% of K-12 Enrollment
1989-90	38,125,896	2,154,781	5.5
1990-91	42,533,764	2,232,500	5.1
1991-92	43,134,517	2,430,712	5.5
1992-93	44,444,939	2,735,952	6.0
1993-94	45,443,389	3,037,922	6.6
1994-95	47,745,835	3,184,696	6.5
1995-96	47,582,665	3,228,790	6.7
1996-97	46,375,422	3,452,073	7.3

[Continued]

Limited English Proficiency Students in the Kindergarden Through 12th Grade Age Group

[Continued]

	Total K-12 Students	Number of LEP Students	% of K-12 Enrollment
1997-98	46,023,969	3,470,268	7.4
1998-99	46,153,266	3,540,673	7.6
1999-00	47,356,089	4,416,580	9.3

Source: Kindler, Anneka. *National Clearinghouse for English Language Acquisition, Survey of the States* Limited English Proficient Students & Available Educational Programs and Services 1999-2000 Summary Report, May 2002, prepared for the U.S. Department of Education. *Facts About Limited English Proficient Students.* Retrieved May 29, 2002 from http://www.ed.gov;

KEYWORD INDEX

This index allows users to locate all subjects, issues, government agencies, companies, programs, associations, schools, educational institutions, books, reports, personal names, and locations cited in *Social Trends & Indicators USA: Community & Education*. Page references do not necessarily identify the page on which a topic begins. In the cases where the topic spans two or more pages, page numbers point to where the index term appears-which may be the second or subsequent page on the topic. Cross-references have been added to index citations for ease in locating related topics.

Medicine, veterinary
— *See:* Veterinary medicine
Men
— advanced classes, p. 259
— age at first marriage, p. 50
— cancer, p. 18
— causes of death, p. 21
— cholesterol levels, p. 18
— degree recipients, pp. 283, 285
— drownings, p. 18
— heart disease, p. 18
— homicides, p. 18
— life expectancy, pp. 18-19
— political-party affiliation, pp. 100-101
— strokes, p. 18
— suicides, p. 18
— teachers, p. 182
— traffic deaths, p. 18
— vocational education credits accumulated, p. 258
Mentally retarded children, pp. 298-299
Methodists, pp. 130-133, 135
Methylphenidate, p. 302
Metropolitan areas, pp. 27-28, 30, 330*t*
Metropolitan Statistical Areas, p. 29
— *See also:* MSA
Miao, p. 77
Michigan
— gay-couple households, p. 63
— litigation for school funding, pp. 220-221
— NAEP rankings, p. 217
— per-pupil expenditures, p. 217
— uncertified teachers, p. 187
Michigan Educational Assessment Program test, p. 169
Military, pp. 122, 357*t*
Million Man March, p. 61
Minnesota, pp. 187, 218
Missouri, pp. 63, 246
MIT
— grade inflation, p. 293
— honor graduates, p. 294
— private gifts, p. 280
— tuition costs, p. 268
Moderates, p. 114
Moldova, p. 163
Mon-Khmer (language), p. 77
Monaco, p. 30
Mongolia, p. 30
Montana, pp. 75, 218
Morehouse College, pp. 53, 61
Mormons, pp. 130-133
Morning-after pill, p. 15
Motor vehicle accidents, p. 21
MSAs, p. 29
Murphy Brown, p. 62
Muslims, pp. 132-135, 145
NAEP rankings, pp. 217-218, 376*t*
A Nation At Risk, pp. 162, 167, 176, 199, 204
National Adult Literacy Survey, pp. 156-157
National Assessment of Educational Progress survey, pp. 159,

National Assessment of Educational Progress survey continued: 162, 203, 235-236
— *See also:* NAEP
National Association of Bilingual Education, p. 307
National Association of Gifted Children, p. 304
National Association of School Nurses, p. 303
National Center for Education Statistics, pp. 234-235, 269
National Coalition for Parent Involvement in Education, p. 198
National Commission on Excellence in Education, p. 257
National Council of Teachers of Mathematics, p. 205
National Defense Act, p. 204
National Health Service Corps, p. 278
National Institute of Child Health and Human Development, p. 201
National Institute of Mental Health, p. 302
National Literacy Act, p. 191
National Reading Panel, pp. 201-202
National School Safety Center, pp. 247-248
Native American religion, pp. 134-135
Native Americans, p. 55
Native Hawaiians, pp. 70-71
Native North Americans, pp. 6-7, 24
Navajo Indian tribe, pp. 72-73
Nebraska, p. 218
Netherlands, pp. 163-165
Nevada, p. 64
Never-married parents, pp. 59-60
Never-married population, p. 339*t*
New Age religions, pp. 134-135
New Basics curriculum, pp. 257, 259
New Hampshire
— gay-couple households, p. 64
— NAEP rankings, p. 218
— uncertified teachers, p. 187
New Jersey, p. 217
— gay-couple households, p. 63
— NAEP rankings, p. 217
— uncertified teachers, p. 187
New Math movement, p. 204
New Mexico, p. 64
New York (City)
— Asian population, p. 75
— population density, p. 30
New York (State), pp. 36, 217
— Asian population, p. 75
— expulsions from school, Gun-Free Schools Act, p. 246
— gay-couple households, pp. 63-64
— NAEP rankings, p. 217
New York University, p. 280
New Zealand, pp. 163-164
Nickelodeon/Talking with Kids National Survey of Parents *and Kids*, p. 249
Niger, p. 5
No Child Left Behind Act, pp. 169, 195, 199, 202, 225, 308
Non-Christian houses of worship, pp. 140-141
Nonfamily households, p. 42
Nonfatal crimes in schools, p. 245
Nonmetropolitan areas, pp. 27-28, 30, 330*t*

This index allows users to locate all subjects, issues, government agencies, companies, programs, associations, schools, educational institutions, books, reports, personal names, and locations cited in *Social Trends & Indicators USA: Work & Leisure*; *Social Trends & Indicators USA: Community & Education*; *Social Trends & Indicators USA: Health & Sickness*; and *Social Trends & Indicators USA: Crime & Justice*. Page references do not necessarily identify the page on which a topic begins. In cases where the topic spans two or more pages, page numbers point to where the index term appears-which may be the second or subsequent page on the topic. Cross-references have been added to index citations for ease in locating related topics.

African-Americans continued:
— *See also:* Blacks
— arrests, p. IV:53
— births, pp. II:6, II:321*t*
— causes of death, pp. III:8, III:31, III:33, III:35-36, III:43
— diseases, pp. III:14, III:97
— employment, p. I:16
— families, pp. II:53, II:62
— homicides, pp. IV:217-218
— hospital closings, p. III:370
— income, p. II:21
— infant mortality, pp. II:21, III:313
— law enforcement personnel, p. IV:204
— life expectancy, p. II:20
— population, pp. II:24, II:70-71, II:345*t*
— population mobility, p. II:39
— risk behaviors, p. III:17
— single-parent households, p. II:61
— specialized museums, p. I:229
— Total Fertility Rates, p. II:8
African wastewater treatment, p. III:326
Age-based discrimination, pp. I:161, I:163, I:167
Age groups
— abortion rates, p. III:307
— book purchases, p. I:220
— death rates, 1917-1918, p. II:17
— depression, p. III:64
— disabled population, p. III:226
— employment, pp. I:20, III:296
— first marriages, p. II:338*t*
— high-school completion rates, p. I:39
— illegal labor, pp. I:43, I:301*t*
— Internet use, pp. I:272-273, I:378*t*
— mathematics proficiency, p. II:161
— population, p. I:345*t*
— psychiatric treatment, p. III:262
— reading proficiency, p. II:159
— retirement, pp. I:139, I:344*t*
— sexual activity, p. III:270
— suicides, p. III:261
— volunteering, pp. I:239-240, I:370*t*
— voter turnout, p. II:104
— work hours, p. I:44
Agency for Healthcare Research and Quality, p. III:361
Aggravated assaults, p. IV:135
— by sex, pp. IV:36, IV:38
— juveniles arrested, pp. IV:133, IV:137-138
— recidivism, p. IV:260
— reported, p. IV:5
— victimization, p. IV:31
Aging population, p. III:485*t*
— *See also:* Elderly population
— *See also:* Senior citizens
— causes of disability, p. III:228
— health problems, pp. III:203-204
— living arrangements, pp. III:191-192
— Medicaid, p. III:386
— perceptions of quality of life, pp. III:205-206
Agoraphobia, pp. III:252-253

Agriculture, pp. II:256-257, II:262
— child labor, p. I:46
— employment, pp. I:3-4, I:291*t*
— workplace injuries, p. I:156
The AGS Foundation for Health in Aging, p. III:344
Aides
— *See:* personal home care aides
AIDS
— attendant diseases, pp. III:3, III:61, III:333
— by race/ethnicity, pp. III:52, III:54
— causes of death, pp. III:53, III:131, III:440*t*
— Centers for Disease Control and Prevention (CDC), p. III:287
— cyclical patterns, p. III:51
— disability benefits, p. III:243
— funding, pp. III:400-402
— new cases, p. III:506*t*
— origins, pp. III:62, III:95
— total occurrences reported, pp. III:444*t*
— treatment, p. III:286
AIDS Coalition to Unleash Power
— *See:* ACT UP
Air pollution, pp. III:316-320, III:518*t*
Air Rage: Crisis in the Skies, p. III:140
Aircraft hijacking, p. IV:245
Aircraft pilots and flight engineers, pp. I:27-28
— *See also:* airline pilots
Airline passenger screening, pp. IV:232-234, IV:367*t*
Airline pilots, pp. I:22, I:296*t*
— *See also:* aircraft pilots and flight engineers
Airplane crashes, p. III:4
al-Rahman, Abd, p. IV:184
Alabama, pp. II:246, IV:284, III:370
Alaska, pp. IV:121, II:217, III:409
Alaska Natives, pp. IV:159-160
— diseases, pp. III:288-289
— educational attainment, pp. II:258-259, II:287-290
— low birth weight, p. III:40
— physicians, p. III:337
— population, pp. II:70-72
— risk behaviors, p. III:136
Albuterol, p. III:167
Alcohol
— adults, p. III:121
— cirrhosis, pp. III:6, III:108
— mouth cancer, p. III:161
— North America, p. III:64
— teenagers, pp. III:117-118
Alcohol consumption, pp. III:108, IV:173, IV:352*t*
Alcohol-related arrests, pp. IV:112, IV:334*t*
Alcohol-related crimes, p. IV:334*t*
— crime rate, p. IV:10
— Prohibition era, p. IV:29
— public-order crimes, pp. IV:101, IV:104, IV:111-112
— rate fluctuation, p. IV:174
Alcohol-related deaths, pp. IV:115-116, III:125, III:131, IV:174, IV:335*t*
Aleuts, p. II:24
All Handicapped Children Act, p. II:299
Allegra, p. III:178

Allergies, p. III:229
Alliance for Aging Research, p. III:341
Allopaths, p. III:336
Alternative medicine practitioners
— by specialization, pp. III:78-82, III:450*t*
— clinical trials, pp. III:162-163
— herbal medicines, p. III:75
Altruistic suicides, p. III:35
Alzheimer's Disease (AD), p. III:5
— aging population, p. III:204
— causes of death, pp. III:4, III:7-8, III:71-72, III:449*t*
— disabled population, pp. III:225, III:243
— fluoride, p. III:328
— hormone replacement therapy, p. III:168
— hospice care, p. III:376
— mental illnesses, pp. III:248-249
Amber, pp. IV:142-143
American Academy of Arts and Sciences, p. II:293
American Academy of Dermatology, p. III:147
American Academy of Family Physicians, p. III:339
American Academy of Pediatrics, pp. III:46, III:96
American Association of Colleges of Nursing, p. III:347
American Association of Law Libraries, p. IV:96
American Attitudes Toward Physical Activity & Fitness, p. III:93
American Bar Association, p. IV:284
American Booksellers Association, p. I:220
American Civil Liberties Union (ACLU)
— hate crimes, p. IV:287
— hospital closings, p. III:363
— prison population, p. IV:247
— single-sex education, p. II:308
— use of force by police, p. IV:214
— women's reproductive health care, p. III:366
American College Testing program
— *See:* ACT
American Dietetic Association, p. III:84
American Federation of Teachers, pp. II:231-232, II:240
American Front Skinheads, p. IV:181
American Hospital Association, p. III:82
American Housing Survey, p. III:191
American Indians, p. II:343*t*
— abortions, pp. II:12-13
— births, pp. II:10, II:321*t*
— causes of death, pp. III:8, III:27
— drug arrests, p. IV:161
— drug use, pp. IV:159-160
— educational attainment, pp. II:151, II:258-259, II:287-290
— health problems, pp. III:40, III:288-289
— juveniles arrested, p. IV:137
— law enforcement personnel, p. IV:203
— population, pp. II:24, II:70-72, II:347*t*
— risk behaviors, p. III:136
— Total Fertility Rates, p. II:8
American Medical Association, pp. III:75, III:79, III:82, II:250, IV:276
— community health centers, p. III:101
— elder abuse, p. III:197
— emergency medical technicians, p. III:357

American Medical Association continued:
— medical malpractice jury awards, p. III:416
— physician-assisted suicide, p. III:216
American Medical Student Association, p. III:395
American Nurses Association, p. III:350
American Psychiatric Association, pp. III:170, III:251, II:302
American Psychological Association, p. IV:290
American Society of Criminology, p. IV:243
American Society of Health-System Pharmacists, p. III:390
American Society of Plastic Surgeons, p. III:277
Americans with Disabilities Act, pp. III:223, III:245
America's Missing: Broadcast Emergency Response, p. IV:141
America's Most Wanted, p. IV:142
Amharic, p. II:76
Amino acid dietary supplements, p. III:75
Amnesty International, p. IV:248
Amoxil, pp. III:166-167
Amphetamines, p. III:125
Amputations, p. I:155
Amusement industries, p. I:7
Amyl nitrite, p. III:120
Anabolic steroids, p. IV:153
Analgesics, p. III:128
Analytic geometry, p. II:259
Androstenedione, p. III:130
Anemia, pp. III:39-40
Anesthesiology, p. III:341
Angiocardiography, p. III:152
Angioplasty, balloon, pp. III:25, III:151
Anglicans, pp. II:130-133, II:135
Animal Liberation Front, p. IV:181
Annual Report on Eating Patterns in America, p. I:180
Anomic suicides, p. III:35
Anorexia nervosa, pp. III:115, III:248-249, III:256-257
Anthrax, p. III:392
Anti-Defamation League, p. IV:287
Anti-inflammatory steroid injections, p. III:390
Antibiotics, pp. III:166, III:329-331, III:390-392
Antidepressants, pp. III:63-64, III:165, III:169-170, III:445*t*
Antiques, p. I:286
Antitrust violations sentencing, p. IV:108
Anxiety disorders, pp. III:247-248, III:250, III:252, III:262
AOL, p. I:282
Apache Indian tribe, pp. II:72-73
Apples, p. III:87
Aquariums, p. I:229
Arabic, p. II:76
Arabs, p. IV:184
Archer, Dennis, p. IV:288
Architecture-related occupations, p. II:296
Arizona, pp. II:63-64, IV:121, IV:277
Arizona State University, p. IV:118
Armed Forces of Puerto Rican Liberation, p. IV:181
Armed robbery, pp. IV:36, IV:38
Armenia, p. II:163
Arrests, pp. IV:294*t*
— alcohol-related crimes, pp. IV:112-113
— Border Patrol, pp. I:49, I:302*t*
— by race/ethnicity, p. IV:53

Blacks continued:
   III:32, III:34, IV:53
— mathematics proficiency, pp. II:161-162
— Medicare, p. III:380
— murders, pp. III:37-38
— physicians, p. III:337
— political-party affiliation, p. II:108
— Population Replacement Rate, p. II:6
— poverty, p. IV:53
— racial profiling, p. IV:222
— risk behaviors, pp. III:16, III:135-137
— risk factors, p. III:20
— single-parent households, p. II:61
— suicides, pp. III:260, III:434*t*
— Total Fertility Rates, pp. II:6-7
— unemployment, p. IV:53
— volunteering, p. I:241
— voter turnout, p. II:106
Bladder cancer, p. III:156
Blindness, pp. III:227, III:229, III:231, III:386
Blood-alcohol concentration (BAC), p. IV:115
Blood clots, p. III:168
Body Mass Index (BMI), p. III:16
Bok, Sissela, p. IV:145
Bombs, p. II:245
Bones, broken, p. III:227
Bookkeeping, accounting, and auditing clerks, pp. I:61-62
Bookmobiles, pp. I:254, I:374*t*
Books, pp. I:185, I:220-221, I:268, I:286, I:366*t*
Border Patrol, pp. IV:24, I:49
Born Again Christians, pp. II:132-133
Boston College, p. II:294
The Boston Globe, p. II:293
Boston Public Schools, p. IV:131
Boston University, p. II:294
Botanicals, p. III:75
Botox, p. III:279
Botulinum toxoids, p. III:392
Bowling, p. I:200
Bowling Alone, p. III:93
Box-office revenues, pp. I:222, I:366*t*
Boy Scouts, p. I:205
Brady Handgun Violence Prevention Act, pp. IV:46-47
Brady, James, p. IV:46
Branch libraries, p. I:254
Brand-name prescription drugs, pp. III:175-176, III:179
Breakfast, pp. III:139-140
Breast cancer
— causes of death, pp. III:3, III:12-13, III:18, III:67-68
— Fred Hutchinson Cancer Research Center, p. III:144
— hormone replacement therapy, p. III:168
— survival rates, pp. III:19, III:158, III:426*t*
— work-related stress, p. III:144
Breastfeeding, pp. III:41-42, III:435*t*
Bribery sentencing, p. IV:108
Britney Spears, p. I:283
Broadway shows, pp. I:224-225
Broken bones, p. III:227
Bronchial cancer, pp. III:67, III:156, III:158

Bronchitis, p. III:3
Broward County (FL), p. IV:267
Brown University, p. II:294
Bruises, p. I:155
BuddhaNet, p. II:145
Buddhism, pp. II:132-135, I:252-253
— Internet, p. II:145
— non-Christian houses of worship, pp. II:140-141
Bulgaria, pp. II:5, II:163-164
Bulimia nervosa, pp. III:115, III:248-249, III:256-257
Bullying, pp. II:249-250
Bureau of Alcohol, Tobacco, and Firearms, pp. IV:24, IV:227
Bureau of Diplomatic Security, p. IV:227
Bureau of Education of the Handicapped, p. III:232
Bureau of Health Professions, pp. III:338, III:349, III:355
Bureau of Justice Assistance, p. IV:266
Bureau of Justice Statistics, pp. IV:243, IV:272, IV:283
Bureau of Labor Statistics, pp. I:54, III:141, III:146, III:351
Bureau of Prisons, p. IV:227
Bureau of the Census, p. IV:159
Burglaries
— arrests, p. IV:67
— by location, pp. IV:73-74
— by time of day, p. IV:325*t*
— corrections expenditures, p. IV:249
— decrease in rates, p. IV:65
— reported to police, pp. IV:4, IV:7-8, IV:77, IV:373*t*
Burns, p. I:155
Bush administration (President George W.), pp. III:106, II:242, III:416
Business
— education, pp. II:256-257, II:262
— productivity, pp. I:122, I:326*t*
— profits, p. I:122
— salaries and wages, pp. I:122, II:296
Business management and administrative services, p. II:284-285
Business services, p. I:7
Business trips, pp. I:190-191, I:359*t*
Businesses
— *See:* Home-based businesses
— home-based,
Butchers and meat cutters, p. I:54
Bypass, coronary
— *See:* Coronary bypass
Cable television, p. I:226
Cadmium, p. III:324
Cafeteria plans, p. I:135
Calculus, p. II:259
California
— Asian population, p. II:75
— cigarette smoking, p. III:409
— class size reduction programs, p. II:196
— community hospital beds, p. III:369
— distribution of elderly population, p. III:190
— expulsions from school, p. II:246
— gay-couple households, pp. II:63-64
— hate crimes, p. IV:290
— law enforcement deaths, p. IV:211

California continued:
— nursing legislation, p. III:349
— prison population, p. IV:248
— racial profiling, p. IV:223
— sex offender registry, p. IV:122
— vacation time, p. I:190
— youth gangs, p. IV:138
California Business Roundtable, p. II:262
California Department of Developmental Services, p. III:258
California Highway Patrol, pp. IV:200, IV:202, IV:223
California Institute of Technology, p. II:280
California Obesity Prevention Initiative, p. III:407
Calorie Control Council, p. III:115
Calories, pp. III:89-90
CAM
— *See:* Complementary and alternative medicine
Cambodia, p. III:332
Cambodian population, p. II:74
Camel cigarettes, p. III:138
Campylobacter infections, p. III:111
Canada, pp. I:47, IV:125, II:254, III:334
— literacy, p. II:163
— mathematics class characteristics, p. II:165
— mathematics proficiency, p. II:164
— mathematics scores, TIMSS, p. II:254
Cancer, pp. III:3, III:5, II:18
— *See also:* Malignancies
— *See also:* Melanomas
— *See also:* Neoplasms
— *See also:* Specific cancers
— by race/ethnicity, p. III:18
— causes of death, pp. III:2-4, III:8-9, III:67, III:69-70, III:401
— causes of disability, p. III:227
— contributing factors, pp. III:68, III:160-161, III:328
— deaths, pp. III:446*t*
— detection, p. III:156
— digestive organs, p. III:3
— elderly population, p. III:210
— funding, pp. III:400-401
— hospice care, p. III:376
— survival rates, pp. III:19, III:156-158, III:478*t*
— treatment, p. III:159
Cannabis sativa, p. IV:153
— *See:* Marijuana
Capital punishment
— *See:* Death penalty
Capitol Police, pp. IV:226-227
Car-rental firms, p. I:196
Carbon monoxide (CO), pp. III:316, III:318
Cardiac catheterization, p. III:151
Cardiovascular disease, pp. III:2, III:150, III:168, III:210, III:310, III:341, III:405
— *See also:* heart disease
Caribbean wastewater treatment, p. III:326
Carpal Tunnel Syndrome, pp. I:155, III:236
Carrots, p. III:87
Cars, p. I:190
Case resolutions, pp. I:163, I:167-168, I:353*t*
Cashiers, pp. I:61-62

CAT
— *See:* Computerized axial tomography
Catheterization, cardiac
— *See:* Cardiac catheterization
Catholic Church, p. IV:56
Catholic Family and Human Rights Institute, p. IV:125
Catholic hospitals, pp. III:366-367
Catholics, pp. II:110, II:130-133, II:135
Catholics for a Free Choice, pp. III:366-367
Cats, p. I:191
Caucasians, pp. II:24-25
Causes of death
— accidents, pp. III:1-2, III:4, III:32
— alcohol, pp. III:125, III:131
— Baby Boom generation, pp. III:69-70
— black-white death ratio, p. II:21
— by race/ethnicity, pp. III:8-9, III:31
— by sex, pp. III:6-7, III:12, III:32-34, III:43
— diseases, pp. III:3, III:53, III:67-72, III:475*t*
— elderly population, p. III:448*t*
— government health funding, p. III:401
— heart failure, pp. III:3, III:12
— homicides, pp. III:4, III:8-9, III:36-38, III:131
— immunizations, p. III:99
— leading causes by year, pp. III:421*t*
— leading causes, by sex, pp. III:6-7, III:13, III:24-30
— perinatal conditions, p. III:9
— research funding, p. III:401
— risk behaviors, pp. III:4, III:125, III:131
— shootings, p. III:4
— suicides, pp. III:4, III:6, III:8, III:34-36, III:131
Causes of disability, pp. III:227-228
CD4 lymphocyte, p. III:53
CDC
— *See:* Centers for Disease Control
Celebrex, pp. III:178, III:275
Celera Genomics, p. III:105
Cendant Corp., p. IV:84
Center for Budget and Policy Priorities, p. III:387
Center for Nutrition Policy and Promotion, pp. II:66-67
Centers for Disease Control, pp. III:16, III:36, III:43, III:49, III:66, III:95, III:97-99, IV:190
— abortions, p. III:306
— active community environments, pp. III:405-406
— antibiotics, pp. III:329, III:331
— *Best Practices for Comprehensive Tobacco Control, Programs*, p. III:408
— bioterrorism, pp. III:392-393
— birth defects, p. III:310
— diseases, pp. III:109, III:161, III:287-288
— food poisoning, pp. III:111-112
— infant mortality, p. III:310
— maternal mortality, p. III:23
— risk behaviors, pp. III:135, III:147
— sexual activity of teenagers, p. III:284
Centers for Medicare and Medicaid Services, p. III:382
Central America, p. I:47
Central cities, pp. II:27-28
Central Intelligence Agency (CIA), pp. IV:186, IV:188-189,

Cisco Systems Inc., p. I:59
Cities, central, p. II:27
Citizens for Safe Drinking Water, p. III:328
Citizenship, p. II:349t
Civil liberties, p. IV:185
Civil Rights Act, p. IV:284
Civil Rights movement, p. IV:286
Civil rights violations, pp. IV:108-110
Civil Unions Law, p. II:65
Civilian employment, p. I:13
Claritin, pp. III:167, III:178, III:276
Class Size Reduction Program, pp. II:195-197
Classical music, p. I:218
Clean Air Act, p. III:316
Clean Water Act, pp. III:315, III:321
Clergy, p. II:143
Cleveland Scholarship and Tutoring Program, p. II:240
Clinical laboratory technologists, pp. III:359-360
Clinical nurse specialists, p. III:351
Clinton administration, pp. IV:95, III:106, IV:128, I:166
A Clockwork Orange, p. I:231
Clothing, pp. II:66-67
Club drugs, pp. III:120, IV:154
Clubs, p. I:185
CO
— *See:* Carbon Monoxide
— *See:* Carbon monoxide (CO)
Coaches' salaries, pp. I:206-207
Coalition Against Insurance Fraud, p. IV:94
Coalition for the Prevention of Economic Crime, p. IV:91
Coast Guard Law Enforcement Detachments, p. IV:24
Coca-Cola, p. II:310
Cocaine, p. IV:147
— arrests, p. IV:11
— emergency room visits, p. III:124
— illicit substance use, adults, p. III:121
— lifetime use reported, pp. IV:151-152
— school-based health centers, p. III:104
— trafficking, pp. IV:167-168
— use by race/ethnicity, pp. III:126-127
— use by teenagers, pp. III:117-119
— youth gangs, p. IV:34
Code Red, p. I:280
Coffee consumption, p. III:139
Cohabitation, pp. II:51, II:57-58, II:338t
Collagen injections, pp. III:277-279
Collectibles, p. I:286
College, p. II:151
College affordability, pp. II:275-276
College athletics, p. I:363t
College Board, pp. II:172, II:293, II:295
College completion rates, p. I:300t
College costs, pp. II:271-273, II:275, II:395t
College degrees, pp. I:24, I:57, I:61, I:114-116
College education, pp. I:51, I:67, I:94, I:264-265
College enrollment, pp. II:150-151
College preparatory curricula, pp. II:261-262
College sports, pp. I:199, I:206, I:208
Colonoscopy, p. III:31

Colorado, pp. II:63-64
Colorectal cancer, pp. III:67-68, III:430t
— causes of death, p. III:30
— obesity, p. III:405
— screening, pp. III:31, III:211
— survival rates, pp. III:156, III:158
Columbia University, p. II:294
Columbine High School, p. II:243
Commerce, p. I:280
Commercial Alert, p. II:265
Commercial participant amusements, p. I:185
Commercialized vice, p. IV:136
Commission on Pornography, p. III:280
Common Good Fear of Litigation Study, p. III:417
Communications, p. II:284
Communications Industry Forecast, p. I:268
Community foundations, pp. I:242, I:245-246
Community health centers, pp. III:100-101, III:436t
Community Learning Centers, pp. II:226-227
Community Protection Act (Washington state), p. IV:121
Community water systems, pp. III:326-327, III:519t
Commuting, pp. I:135, III:140
Complementary and alternative medicine (CAM), pp. III:74, III:82
Compliance officers, p. I:45
Comprehensive Drug Abuse and Control Act, pp. IV:12, IV:149
Computed tomography, p. III:355
Computer cracker, p. I:281
Computer hacking, pp. IV:92, I:280-281, I:379t
Computer learning opportunities, pp. II:263, II:393t
Computer products, p. I:185
Computer-related occupations, pp. I:32, I:52, I:54-55, I:58-59, I:61-62, II:296
Computer systems administrators
— *See:* Network and computer systems administrators
Computer use, p. II:264
Computer viruses, p. I:280
Computer worms, p. I:280
Computerized axial tomography, p. III:152
— *See also:* CAT scans
Computerized axial tomography (CAT) scans, p. III:152
Computerized Axial Tomography (CAT) scans, p. III:155
Computers, p. I:286
Concerts, p. I:216
The Condition of America's Schools: 1999, p. II:199
Condoms, pp. II:15, III:104, III:304-305
Congenital malformations, pp. III:10, III:236, III:312
Congregationals, pp. II:132-135, II:144
Congressional Budget Office, p. III:387
Connecticut, pp. II:217, III:338, III:373-374
Conservatives, p. II:114
Construction, p. II:32
— employment, p. I:34
— injuries in the workplace, p. I:156
— occupational fatalities, p. I:151
— productivity, pp. I:104-107, I:329t
Consumer Research Study on Book Purchasing, p. I:220
ConsumerSentinel, p. IV:82
Continuing care retirement communities, p. III:194

Contraceptive practices, pp. II:14-15, III:161, III:304-305, II:323t

Contracts, p. I:14

Contusions, p. I:155

Convict labor, pp. IV:254-255

Conyers, Jr., John, p. IV:287

Cook County (IL), pp. IV:266-267

Copyright infringement, pp. IV:95-97, IV:328t

Cornell University, pp. III:195, II:294

Coronary bypass, p. III:25

Corporate profits, pp. I:122, I:124, I:339t

Correctional population, pp. IV:19-20, IV:299t

Corrections Corporation of America (CCA), pp. IV:251-252

Corrections system employment, pp. IV:21-22

Corrections system expenditures, pp. IV:249-250, IV:373t

Cosmetic surgery, pp. III:179, III:277-279, III:504t

Cough syrup, p. III:130

Coughlin, Lt. Paula, p. I:166

Council on Graduate Medical Education, p. III:344

Counterfeiting, pp. IV:88-89, IV:99-100, IV:105, IV:108, IV:327t

County mental hospitals, p. III:264

Court trials, pp. IV:273-274

Crack cocaine, pp. IV:151, IV:162

Cream products, p. III:83

Creatine, p. III:130

Creative writing, pp. I:218-219

Creditcards.com, p. IV:91

Creek Indian tribe, pp. II:72-73

Creole, French
— See: French Creole

Crib death, pp. III:45-46
— See also: Sudden Infant Death Syndrome (SIDS)

Crime Act, p. IV:206

Crime and Punishment: Women in Prison, p. IV:243

Crime control costs, pp. IV:23-24

Crime Index, pp. IV:3, IV:6, IV:14

Crime prevention, p. IV:206

Crime rate
— arrests, pp. IV:102, IV:149, IV:175-176, IV:354t
— history, p. IV:15
— justice system employment, p. IV:21

Crimes Against Children, p. IV:139

Crimes against the family, p. IV:136

Crimes cleared by arrest, p. IV:379t

Crimes in schools, pp. II:245, II:387t

Croatia, p. II:163

Crocheting, p. I:218

Cross-country sports, pp. I:208-209

Cruises, p. I:196

Crystal Cathedral, p. II:145

Cuba, p. II:163

Culture and humanities
— See also: arts, culture, and humanities p. I:242

Curfew violations, pp. IV:106-107, IV:136

Curriculum specialization, p. II:261

Cuts, p. I:155

Cyberchurches, p. II:145

Cyberstalking, p. IV:120

Czech Republic, pp. II:163-165, I:187

Dance, pp. I:218-219

Danish, pp. II:76-77

D.A.R.E.
— See: Drug Abuse Resistance Education

Database administrators, p. I:52

Date-rape drugs, pp. IV:56, IV:154
— See also: Rohypnol

Dating online, pp. I:284-285

DAWN
— See: Drug Abuse Warning Network

DCBE
— See: Double-Contrast Barium Enema
— See: Double-contrast barium enema (DCBE)

DDT, p. III:323

Deaconess-Waltham Hospital (MA), p. III:370

Dead Rabbits, p. IV:43

Deafness, pp. III:227, III:229, II:298

Death penalty, pp. IV:245-246

Death row inmates, pp. IV:244, IV:246, IV:371t

Death With Dignity Law, p. III:216

Deaths
— by cause, pp. III:1-2
— by race/ethnicity, p. II:21
— diseases, pp. III:15, III:18, III:423t
— influenza epidemic, p. II:17
— life expectancy, pp. II:324t
— police officers, pp. IV:210-212, IV:217-218, IV:361t
— schools, p. II:243
— terrorism, pp. IV:190-191, IV:358t

Defense Department, pp. I:13, I:293t

Defense research and development, p. III:398

Degree completion, pp. I:260-262, I:265

Degrees conferred, pp. I:58, II:283, I:296t II:399t

Degrees conferred, professional
— See: professional degrees conferred

Deism, pp. II:134-135, I:252-253

Delaware, pp. II:64, II:187, II:217

Dementia, pp. III:71, III:198, III:204, III:243

Democratic Republic of the Congo, pp. III:332, III:334

Democrats, p. II:98

Denmark, p. IV:125

Dental care benefits, pp. III:103, I:131, I:133, III:210

Dentists, pp. III:79, IV:93, II:286, II:290

Department of Education, pp. IV:290, II:304

Department of Health and Human Services, p. III:63

Department of Justice, pp. IV:203, IV:207, IV:270, IV:290

Department of Labor, p. I:45

Dependency ratio, pp. II:22, I:141

Depressants, p. IV:153

Depression, pp. III:445t
— age groups, p. III:262
— cases, pp. III:247-248
— senior citizens, p. III:204
— treatment, pp. III:63-64, III:169
— treatments, pp. III:75-76

Dermabrasion, pp. III:277-278

Desktop publishers, p. I:52

Drug-related arrests continued:
— trafficking, p. IV:245
Drug-related crimes, pp. IV:101-104
— Baby Boom generation, p. IV:29
— firearms-related crimes, p. IV:40
— not included in crime rate, p. IV:10
— possession and trafficking, p. IV:109
— recidivism, p. IV:260
— state prisons population, pp. IV:236-237
Drug-resistant bacteria, p. III:329
Drug shortages, pp. III:389-391, III:530*t*
Drug treatment programs, p. IV:263
Drug use, pp. IV:157-158, IV:345*t*
— by race/ethnicity, pp. IV:159, IV:162
— by type of drug, pp. IV:169-170
DrugFreeTeenagers.com, p. III:133
Drugs distributed, pp. IV:349*t*
Drunk driving, pp. IV:101, IV:104, IV:206
— *See also:* Driving under the influence
DTP, p. III:96
— *See:* Diphtheria, Tetanus, and Pertussis (DTP)
DUI
— *See:* Driving under the influence
— *See:* Driving under the influence (DUI)
DUKE NUKEM, p. IV:145
Duke University, pp. III:81, I:171, III:237, II:294, III:345
Durable goods, p. I:102
Durex [company], pp. III:271, III:273
Durham versus United States, p. IV:276
Durkheim, Emile, p. III:35
Dutch, p. II:77
DVD players, p. I:227
Dyslexia, p. III:243
E-learning, p. II:292
E-mail, pp. I:273, I:278
E-tailers, p. I:284
Ear infections, p. III:229
Ear surgery, pp. III:150, III:277-279
Earnhardt, Dale, p. I:211
Earnings, p. III:498*t*
— by educational attainment and sex, p. II:295
— by race/ethnicity and sex, p. I:71
— by sex, p. I:318*t*
— college degrees, pp. I:114-116
— disabilities, pp. III:244-245
— doctoral degrees, p. II:404*t*
— householders, pp. I:322*t*
— independent contractors, pp. I:71, I:307*t*
— workforce, p. I:342*t*
Earth First!, pp. IV:177, IV:181
Earth Liberation Front, p. IV:181
Eastern equine encephalitis, p. III:392
Eating habits, pp. II:211, III:466*t*
— disease prevention, p. III:90
— eating disorders, pp. III:256-257
— mental health, p. III:247
— stress, pp. III:139-140
— U.S. Surgeon General's recommendations, p. III:83
— weight, pp. III:89, III:115-116

eBay, pp. IV:100, I:282, I:380*t*
Ebola virus, pp. III:62, III:95
Echinacea, p. III:75
Eckankar, pp. II:134-135, I:252-253
Economic Growth and Tax Relief Reconciliation Act of 2001, p. II:278
Economic sectors, pp. I:3, I:104, I:291*t*
Ecstasy, pp. III:119-120, III:124, IV:147, IV:153
Ectopic pregnancy, p. III:23
Edison project, p. II:233
Education
— accountability, p. II:166
— adults, p. I:233
— attainment, pp. II:284-285
— charitable giving, pp. I:242-244
— college preparatory, p. II:262
— costs of universities, p. II:281
— elementary and secondary, pp. II:189-190
— employment, pp. I:1, I:10-12
— enrollment, p. I:292*t*
— expenditures, p. II:399*t*
— funding, pp. II:377*t*
— grants, p. II:273
— job advancement, pp. I:260-262
— volunteering, pp. I:245-246
Education administrators, pp. I:22, I:24-25, I:58-59
Education assistance, p. I:135
Education budget, p. II:384*t*
Education for All Handicapped Children Act, p. III:232
Education of the Handicapped Act, p. III:232
Education revenues, pp. II:212, II:279, II:397*t*
Educational achievements, pp. II:293, II:369*t*
Educational attainment, pp. IV:53, I:56, IV:264, I:335*t*
— adults, pp. I:264-265, I:332*t*
— Asians, pp. I:118-119
— blacks, pp. I:112, I:118-119
— breastfeeding mothers, p. III:42
— disabled population, p. III:497*t*
— earnings, pp. I:114-116, II:295, I:318*t* 405*t*
— exercise habits, p. III:92
— Hispanics, pp. I:112, I:118-119
— householders, pp. I:322*t*
— income, pp. I:94-95, II:177
— labor force, p. I:304*t*
— literacy, p. II:155
— men, p. I:94
— productivity, pp. I:110-111
— race/ethnicity, pp. II:152-153
— smoking, p. III:136
— teachers, pp. II:184-185
— volunteering, pp. I:238, I:370*t*
— whites, pp. I:112, I:118-119
— women, p. I:94
— workforce, p. I:56
Educational services, pp. I:104-105
EEOC
— *See:* Equal Employment Opportunity Commission (EEOC)
Eggs, p. III:83

Egoistic suicides, p. III:35
Eight-ball chicks, p. IV:134
El Salvador, p. I:47
E.L.A., p. II:169
Elder abuse, pp. IV:10, III:198, III:486t
— Adult Protective Services, p. III:199
— American Medical Association, p. III:197
— nursing homes, pp. III:201-202
— perpetrators, p. III:200
Elderly population, pp. II:22, II:35, IV:83, III:189, III:196, IV:241
— causes of death, p. III:448t
— diseases, p. III:210
— geographic distribution, pp. III:189-190
— health care, p. III:379
— health problems, pp. III:210-211
— immunizations, p. III:463t
— living arrangements, p. III:195
— living wills, p. III:211
— Medicare benefits, p. III:207
— prisoners, pp. I:141, IV:240
Elders, Jocelyn, p. III:107
Electrical and electronics engineers, p. I:58
Electronic commerce, pp. I:196, I:280
Electronic Communications Privacy Act, p. IV:229
Electronic fetal monitoring, p. III:302
Electronic surveillance
— See: wiretapping
Electronics, pp. I:286, I:367t
Electronics engineers
— See: electrical and electronics engineers
Electronics purchases, p. I:227
Elementary and Secondary Education Act, p. II:199
Elementary education, pp. I:11, II:189-190, I:292t
Elementary school principals, p. II:308
Elementary school teachers
— job openings, pp. I:24-25, I:58, I:61-62
— retirement, pp. I:22-23
— worker shortages, p. I:59
Eli Lilly & Co., p. III:170
Eligibility clerks, p. I:27
Elliptical motion trainers, p. I:200
Embezzlement, pp. IV:105, IV:108, IV:136
Eme Edict, p. IV:40
Emergency medical technicians (EMTs), pp. III:357-358
Emergency medicine physicians, p. III:341
Emergency room visits, pp. III:124-125, III:130, III:471t
Emory University, p. II:280
Emotional abuse of elderly, p. III:199
Emotional problems, pp. III:227, III:229-231, III:264
Emotionally disturbed children, pp. II:298-299
Emphysema, pp. III:3, III:5-6
Employee benefits, pp. I:127-130, I:133, I:135-138
Employee contributions, p. I:132
Employees, pp. I:127, I:296t
Employer costs, pp. I:127-128, I:131
Employment, pp. I:1, I:16, IV:22
— administrative support occupations (including clerical), pp. I:20, I:296t
— by industry, pp. I:1, I:3-7, I:9-14, I:20, I:34, III:141-143, III:234,

Employment continued:
III:244-245, I:291t
— by race/ethnicity and sex, p. I:16
— disabled workers, p. III:233
— Fair Labor Standards Act, p. II:146
— high school diplomas, p. II:177
— high school education, pp. I:11-12
— justice system, p. IV:21
— literacy, pp. II:157-158
Employment-practice liability cases, p. I:170
EMTs
— See: Emergency medical technicians
— See: Emergency medical technicians (EMTs)
End-stage renal disease, p. III:380
Endocrine system, pp. III:150-151, III:236
Endometrial cancer
— See: Uterine cancer
Endoscopy, p. III:151
Endotracheal tube insertion, p. III:152
Endowments, p. II:279
Engineering occupations, pp. II:284-285, II:296
Engineering services, p. I:7
Engineers, p. I:32
— See also: computer engineers
Engineers (industrial), pp. I:22-25, I:296t
England, pp. IV:125, II:165
English language, p. II:284
English Language Arts test
— See: E.L.A.
English literature, p. II:284
English, honors
— See: Honors English
Enrollment, pp. II:222-223, II:231
— elementary education, p. I:292t
— high school sports, pp. I:204-205
— Medicaid, p. III:386
— Medicare, pp. III:490t
Enron Corp., pp. IV:85, IV:109
Entertainment, p. I:268
— See also: arts and entertainment
Environment, pp. I:242-246, III:315
Environmental crimes and sentencing, p. IV:108
Environmental interest organizations, p. IV:181
Environmental Protection Agency, pp. III:322, III:327
Epidemic-related deaths, p. III:463t
Epilepsy, pp. III:229, III:231
Episcopalians, pp. II:130-133, II:135-138
Episiotomy, p. III:151
Equal Employment Opportunity Commission (EEOC), p. I:159, I:163, I:165, I:167, I:169, I:353t
Equipment and software, p. I:102
Equipment cleaners and laborers
— See: handlers, equipment cleaners, and laborers
Erectile dysfunction treatments, pp. III:275-276
Escherichia coli infections, p. III:111
Eskimos, p. II:24
Esophageal cancer, pp. III:156, III:161
Estonia, p. II:163
Estrogen, p. II:18

Estuaries, pp. III:323, III:325

Ether, p. III:120

Ethical and Religious Directives for Catholic Health Education, p. III:367

Ethiopia, p. III:332

Ethnicity, pp. II:10, II:12-13
— *See also:* Race/ethnicity
— abortions, pp. II:10, II:12-13, II:321*t*
— advanced classes, p. II:259
— Bachelor's Degree recipients, pp. II:287-288
— births, pp. II:10, II:321*t*
— college enrollment, p. II:151
— computer learning opportunities, p. II:263
— doctoral degrees conferred, pp. II:289-290
— educational attainment, pp. II:152-153
— fertility rates, p. II:321*t*
— home ownership, p. II:35
— honors English classes, p. II:259
— population, pp. II:24, II:70, II:343*t*
— Population Replacement Rate, p. II:8
— reading proficiency, p. II:159
— single-parent households, p. II:61
— Total Fertility Rates, pp. II:6-8
— vocational education credits accumulated, p. II:258

Euro RSCG [company], pp. III:271, III:273

Europe, pp. II:5, II:24, I:41, III:326

Euthanasia, pp. III:214-215, III:218
— *See also:* Physician-assisted suicide

Evaluation and the Academy: Are We Doing the Right Thing?, pp. II:293-294

Evangelicals, pp. II:132-133, II:136-138

Excessive force, pp. IV:213-214, IV:363*t*

Executive, administrative, managerial occupations, pp. I:20, I:69-70, I:296*t*

Exercise habits, pp. III:20-21, III:92, III:161, I:203

Expenditures, pp. II:215-217
— defense of the indigent, pp. IV:283-284
— drug control, pp. IV:171-172
— fast food, p. III:109
— health care, pp. I:130, III:484*t*
— Medicare, pp. III:490*t*
— prescription drugs, p. III:484*t*
— psychotherapy, p. III:263
— restaurant, p. III:109
— worker's compensation claims, p. I:153

Expulsions from school, pp. II:245-246

Extortion and sentencing, p. IV:108

Eye treatments, pp. III:150, III:277-279

Fabricators and laborers
— *See:* Operators, fabricators, and laborers

Fair Labor Standards Act (FLSA), pp. I:43, II:146

Families
— income, pp. I:92, II:264
— leisure time, p. I:173
— mealtimes, p. I:180
— poverty rates, pp. I:92-93, I:315*t*

Family and Medical Leave Act (FMLA), pp. I:137-138, I:344*t*

Family entertainment concerns, p. I:231

Family households, pp. II:42, II:44, II:53, II:333*t*

Family leave, pp. I:135, I:137

Family Violence Prevention and Services Act of 1992, p. III:199

Fanning, Shawn, p. IV:95

Farmers and ranchers, p. I:54

Farmers' markets, p. III:87

Farming, forestry, and fishing occupations, pp. I:20, I:31, I:69-70, I:200, I:296*t*

Farmlands, p. III:458*t*

Fast-food expenditures, pp. III:109-110

Fast Food Nation, pp. III:110, III:112, II:310-311

Fast-pitch softball, p. I:200

Fat injections, p. III:279

Fatalistic suicides, p. III:35

Fatalities, pp. I:149, I:151, I:156

Fathers, pp. II:53, II:62, I:183

Fats, pp. III:20-21, III:83

Fecal occult blood test (FOBT), p. III:31

Federal appropriations, p. II:279

Federal Aviation Administration, p. IV:232

Federal Bureau of Investigation (FBI)
— arrests, p. IV:272
— arson, p. IV:81
— burglaries, pp. IV:73-74
— crime index, pp. IV:9-10, IV:14, IV:293*t*
— curfew violations, p. IV:107
— federal law enforcement, pp. IV:226-227
— hate crimes, pp. IV:289-290
— property crime index, p. IV:8
— terrorism, pp. IV:180-181, IV:186, IV:188-189
— *Uniform Crime Report*, pp. IV:3, IV:5

Federal Bureau of Prisons, p. IV:226

Federal Correctional Institute Morgantown, p. IV:248

Federal financial aid, pp. II:211, II:226-227, II:273-274

Federal Firearms Act, p. IV:46

Federal government employment, pp. I:1, I:9-10, I:13, I:292*t* 293*t*

Federal government funding, p. I:256

Federal government grants and contracts, pp. III:100, II:279

Federal Interstate Anti-Stalking Law, p. IV:120

Federal law enforcement personnel, pp. IV:226-227, IV:365*t*

Federal Prison Industries, p. IV:255

Federal prisons, pp. IV:237, IV:245, IV:248, IV:370*t*

Federal Protective Service, p. IV:227

Federal Trade Commission, pp. IV:82, IV:90-91

Federal Wire Act, p. IV:118

Felony defendants
— released or detained until case disposition, pp. IV:379*t*
— trial dates, pp. IV:270-274

Female-male teacher ratio, pp. II:182-183

Females, pp. III:137, III:150, III:154, III:304, II:322*t*
— *See also:* Women
— athletes, p. I:204
— childbearing years, p. II:21
— gangsters, p. IV:135
— larcenies, p. IV:136
— law enforcement personnel, p. IV:203
— murdered, pp. IV:314*t*
— prisoners, p. IV:17

Females continued:
— violent crimes, pp. IV:135-136
— vocational education, pp. II:258-259
Fertility rates
— birth rate, pp. III:507t
— by decade, pp. II:2, II:4
— by race/ethnicity, p. I:40
— European community, p. II:5
— live births, pp. II:315t
— population replacement rates, p. II:4
— reproductive patterns, pp. III:292-295
Fibril injections, pp. III:277-278
Fiction, p. I:220
Filipinos, pp. III:40, II:74
Finance, insurance, and real estate, pp. I:6, I:104-105, I:292t
Financial aid, p. II:273
Financial Executives International, pp. IV:84, I:171
Financial exploitation of elderly, p. III:199
Financial managers, pp. I:22, I:24-25, I:58
Financial restatements, p. IV:84
Finland, p. II:163
Finnish, p. II:76
Firearms, p. II:245
Firearms-related crimes, pp. IV:45, IV:47-48, IV:314t
Fires, p. III:4
First Church of Cyberspace, p. II:145
First-line supervisors and managers, pp. I:61-62
First marriages, p. II:338t
Fishing occupations
— *See:* farming, forestry, and fishing occupations
Fitness centers, p. I:135
Fitness trainers and aerobics instructors, p. I:52
Five Point Gang, p. IV:43
The Fix, p. IV:30
Flexible spending accounts, p. I:136
Flexible workplace, p. I:135
Flight engineers
— *See:* aircraft pilots and flight engineers
Florida
— gay-couple households, pp. II:63-64
— geographic distribution of elderly population, p. III:190
— hate crimes, p. IV:289
— hospital beds, p. III:369
— malpractice litigation, pp. III:415, III:417
— sex offender registries, pp. IV:121-122
— smoking prevalence, p. III:409
— vacation travel, p. I:190
— youth gangs, p. IV:138
Florida State Department of Health, p. III:392
Flour, p. III:83
Flowers, pp. I:185, I:284
FLSA
— *See:* Fair Labor Standards Act
— *See:* Fair Labor Standards Act (FLSA)
Flu epidemic
— *See:* influenza epidemic
Fluid cream products, p. III:83
Fluoride, pp. III:315, III:327-328

FOBT
— *See:* Fecal occult blood test
— *See:* Fecal occult blood test (FOBT)
Food and Drug Administration, pp. III:176, III:330, III:389-391
Food Guide Pyramid, p. III:83
Food poisoning, pp. III:111-112
Food preparation workers, pp. I:61-62
Food services, p. II:262
— *See:* accommodations and food services
FoodNet, p. III:111
Foods, pp. II:66-67
— bioterrorism, p. III:88
— consumption of major commodities, pp. III:451t
— nutrient levels, pp. III:459t
— pesticide use, pp. III:87-88
— phytochemicals, p. III:90
Foods, organic
— *See:* organic foods
Fools Gold: A Critical Look at Computers in Childhood, p. II:265
Football, p. I:209
Foreign-born physicians, p. III:337
Foreign-born population, pp. I:301t
Foreign-educated physicians
— *See:* IMGs
Foreign Intelligence Surveillance Act (FISA), p. IV:230
Foreign languages used in the United States, pp. II:76-77, II:344t
Forensic pathology physicians, p. III:341
Forestry and fishing occupation
— *See:* farming, forestry, and fishing occupations
Forestry and fishing occupations
— *See:* farming, forestry, and fishing occupations
Forgery, pp. IV:105, IV:108
Fortune 500 firms, p. II:120
Foundations, pp. I:242, I:245-246
Fourth graders, p. II:200
Fractures, p. I:155
France
— breastfeeding, p. III:42
— duration of school year, p. II:254
— entertainment, p. I:187
— literacy, pp. II:163-165
— prostitution, p. IV:125
— terrorism, p. IV:184
— tuberculosis, p. III:334
— vacation time, p. I:192
Franklin W. Olin College of Engineering, p. II:280
Fraternal organizations, p. I:185
Fraud, pp. IV:64, IV:82, IV:85, IV:101, IV:104-105, III:376
Fred Hutchinson Cancer Research Center, p. III:144
Free weights, p. I:202
French, p. II:76
French (language), p. II:77
French Creole, p. II:77
Fresno (CA), p. IV:72
Friends Don't Let Friends Drive Drunk, p. IV:113
Frost & Sullivan, p. IV:117
Fruits, p. III:83
Funding, pp. II:211, II:224-225, I:256, II:377t

Fuqua School of Business, p. I:171
G-ratings, p. I:230
GAAP
— *See:* Generally Accepted Accounting Principles (GAAP)
GAD
— *See:* Generalized Anxiety Disorder
Gallbladder cancer, p. III:161
Gambling, pp. IV:10, IV:101, IV:105, IV:108
Games, p. I:282
Gangs, pp. IV:39, IV:43, IV:206, IV:313*t*
— *See also:* Street gangs
— *See also:* Youth gangs
Garlic, p. III:75
Gasoline, p. III:120
Gastroesophageal Reflux Disease (GERD), p. III:167
Gays, pp. III:54, II:63-64, II:122, I:191, II:342*t*
— *See also:* Homosexuals
— *See also:* Lesbians
GDP
— *See:* Gross Domestic Product
GEDs
— *See:* General equivalency diplomas (GEDs)
General equivalency diploma
— *See:* GED
General Equivalency Diplomas (GEDs), p. I:264
General managers and top executives, pp. I:58, I:61-62
General office clerks, pp. I:61-62
The General Social Survey, p. II:295
General surgeons' medical malpractice premiums, p. III:415
Generalized Anxiety Disorder (GAD), p. III:252
Generally Accepted Accounting Principles (GAAP), p. IV:85
Generic prescription drug prices, p. III:175
Genetic engineering, pp. III:105-106
Genital cancer, p. III:3
Genital herpes, p. III:95
Genital surgery, pp. III:150-151
Genitourinary system diseases, pp. III:236, III:310
Genome research centers, p. III:105
Geographic distribution of population, pp. III:189-190
Geographic maldistribution of physicians, p. III:344
Geometry, analytic
— *See:* Analytic geometry
Georgia, pp. I:50, II:63-64, II:163, II:246, IV:248, IV:284
German (language), p. II:76
German measles, p. III:57
— *See also:* Rubella
Germany, pp. II:163, I:187, II:254, III:334
Getting America's Students Ready for the 21st Century, p. II:263
Ghettos, p. IV:162
GI Bill, pp. II:273-274
— *See also:* Serviceman's Readjustment Act
Gideon v Wainwright, p. IV:281
Gift shopping, p. I:284
Gifted children, pp. II:304-305, II:406*t*
Ginkgo Biloba, p. III:75
Ginseng, p. III:75
Girl Scouts, p. I:205
Giuliani, Mayor Rudy, p. IV:216

Glandular surgery, p. III:151
Global Tuberculosis Control: WHO Report 2002, p. III:332
Glucophage, p. III:167
Golf, pp. I:200, I:211
Gonorrhea, pp. III:51-52
Goods-producing industries, p. I:291*t*
Government, p. II:193
Government drug-control budget, pp. IV:350*t*
Government expenditures on crime control, p. IV:24
Government funding, p. I:256
— Human Genome Project, pp. III:464*t*
— National Institutes of Health, pp. III:400-401, III:535*t*
— research and development, pp. III:397-399, III:532*t*
Grade inflation, p. II:293
Grandtravel, p. I:191
Grants, pp. III:100, II:273
Grapes, p. III:87
Great Britain, pp. III:42, I:187, I:192
Great Lakes water pollution, p. III:321
Greek (language), p. II:76
Greeting cards, p. I:284
Grenades, p. II:245
Griffin v Illinois, p. IV:282
Grocery expenditures, pp. III:85-86, III:457*t*
Gross Domestic Product (GDP), pp. I:102, I:143, I:328*t*
Grossman, Lt. Colonel David, p. IV:145
Groundskeeping laborers
— *See also:* landscaping and groundskeeping laborers p. I:61
Guards and watch guards, pp. I:61-62
Guatemala, p. I:47
Gun Control Act, p. IV:46
Gun-Free Schools Act, pp. IV:129-132, II:245-246
Gun-related homicide arrests, pp. IV:311*t*
Gun-related violent crime, pp. IV:39, IV:45, IV:47
Guyana, p. II:163
Gym classes
— *See:* physical education classes
Gynecologists, pp. III:341, III:415
H-1B visas, p. I:59
Hacking, p. I:208
Hair salons, p. I:54
Hair transplantation for men, pp. III:277-278
Haiti, p. I:47
Hallucinogens, pp. IV:151-153
Hamm, Mia, p. I:209
Hand packers and packagers, pp. I:61-62
Handguns, pp. IV:40, II:245
Handlers, equipment cleaners, and laborers, pp. I:20, I:296*t*
Hanta virus, pp. III:62, III:95
Happy Meals, p. III:110
Harassment, pp. I:19, I:149, I:159, I:161, I:163, I:169, I:353*t*
Hard Pack, p. III:138
Harrison Act, p. IV:12
Harry Potter and the Sorcerer's Stone, pp. I:221, I:283
Harvard Mental Health Letter, p. III:135
Harvard School of Public Health Department of Nutrition, p. III:109
Harvard University, pp. III:75, II:293
Harvest Christian Fellowship, p. II:144

Hashish, pp. III:118, III:121, III:124, IV:152
— illicit substance use, teenagers, p. III:117
Hate crimes, pp. IV:286-290, IV:382t
— *See also:* Bias-related crimes
Hawaii, p. II:64
Hawaiian Natives, p. II:72
Hay fever, p. III:229
Hayflick Limit, p. III:48
Hazelden Foundation, p. III:123
HBV immunizations, p. III:97
HDL
— *See:* High-Denisty Lipoprotein (HDL)
Head injuries, pp. III:227, III:243
Head Start, pp. II:222-225, II:383t
Heaemophilus influenzae type b
— *See:* Hib
Health assessments, pp. III:488t
Health care, pp. I:242-244, III:484t
— costs for children, pp. II:66-67
— employment, pp. I:7, I:34
— expenditures, p. I:342t
— fraud, pp. IV:93-94, IV:328t
— Medicare enrollment, p. III:379
— productivity, pp. I:104-105
— vocational education, pp. II:256-257, II:262
— volunteering, pp. I:245-246
Health Care Financing Administration, p. III:374
Health clubs, pp. I:200-201
Health information technicians
— *See:* medical records and health information technicians
Health insurance, p. I:131
— employee benefits, pp. I:128-130, I:132
— independent contractors, p. I:72
— same-sex partners, p. I:136
Health Maintenance Organizations (HMOs), pp. III:345, III:382-383
Health Professional Shortage Areas, p. III:338
Health professions, p. II:284
Health sciences, p. II:284
Health services, pp. III:394-395, III:531t
Health violations in community water systems, p. III:326
Healthy Eating Index, p. III:84
Healthy People, pp. III:73, III:303, III:403-404, III:408
Hearing impairments, pp. III:203, III:227, III:229, II:298, III:487t
Hearing screenings, p. III:103
Heart attacks, pp. III:3, III:275-276
Heart disease, pp. III:5, III:14, II:18
— *See also:* Cardiovascular disease
— aging population, p. III:203
— Baby Boom generation, p. III:69
— causes of death, pp. III:4, III:6, III:8-9, III:12, III:24-25, III:69, III:401
— causes of disability, p. III:227
— funding, pp. III:400-401
— risk behaviors, p. III:136
— risk factors, pp. III:12, III:328
— treatments, pp. III:25, III:155
Heat burns, p. I:155

Hebrew, p. II:77
Helpers and laborers, p. I:43
Hemic system surgical procedures, pp. III:150-151
Hemorrhages in maternal mortality, p. III:23
Henderson, Charles, p. II:145
Hepatitis, pp. III:6, III:61, III:96, III:148, III:444t
Herbal therapies, pp. III:75, III:77, III:82, III:450t
Herbs, medicinal
— *See:* medicinal herbs
Hero Syndrome, p. IV:81
Heroin, p. IV:147
— control legislation, p. IV:11
— description, pp. IV:151-152
— emergency room visits, pp. III:124-125
— trafficking, pp. IV:12, IV:167-168
Herpes, genital
— *See:* Genital herpes
Heterosexuals, pp. III:53, III:289
Hib vaccinations for children, pp. III:96-97
High blood pressure
— *See also:* Hypertension
— causes of disability, pp. III:227-228
— obesity, p. III:405
High-Density Lipoprotein (HDL), pp. III:20-21
High school
— diplomas, pp. I:39, II:148, II:177, I:300t
— dropouts, pp. II:148-149
— sports, pp. I:199, I:204-205, I:362
— students, pp. I:250-251
— vocational education, pp. II:256-257, II:260-262, II:363t
High school education
— adults, p. I:264
— earnings, pp. I:114-116
— employment, pp. I:11-12
— enrollment, pp. I:292t
— income, p. I:94
— staff, p. I:292t
— workforce, p. I:57
High-speed pursuits, pp. IV:219, IV:364t
Highly Active Anti-Retroviral Therapy, p. III:54
Hill, Anita, pp. I:162, I:165
Hinckley, John, pp. IV:277, IV:280
Hindi (language), p. II:76
Hinduism, pp. II:134-135, II:140-141, I:252-253
Hispanics, p. I:47
— abortions, pp. II:12-13
— births, pp. II:10, I:40, II:321t
— breastfeeding, p. III:41
— causes of infant mortality, pp. III:44, III:313
— computer learning opportunities, p. II:263
— deaths, pp. III:8-9, III:15
— diseases, pp. III:97, III:289
— drug use, pp. IV:159-160
— earnings, p. I:71
— education, pp. II:161-162, II:259
— educational attainment, pp. I:39, I:112, I:118-119, II:151-153, II:258, II:287-290
— employment, pp. I:16, I:30, I:37, I:67-68
— families, p. I:38

Hispanics continued:
— federal law enforcement officers, p. IV:227
— housing, p. II:35
— immunizations, p. III:99
— income, pp. I:82-83
— Internet use, pp. I:270-271
— law enforcement personnel, pp. IV:203-204
— learning disabilities, p. III:66
— literacy, p. II:159
— low birth weight, p. III:309
— Medicare, p. III:380
— physicians, p. III:337
— population, pp. II:24-25, II:39, II:70-71, II:346t
— risk behaviors, p. III:137
— single-parent households, p. II:61
— Total Fertility Rates, pp. II:6-8
— volunteering, p. I:241
— voter turnout, p. II:106
— youth gangs, p. IV:43
Historical diseases, pp. III:442t
History museums, p. I:229
HIV, pp. III:51, III:286, III:288-290
— attendant diseases, pp. III:3, III:333
— by race/ethnicity and sex, p. III:54
— Centers for Disease Control, p. III:288
— deaths, pp. III:8, III:53, III:289
— number of cases, p. III:506t
Hmong population, p. II:74
Hobson, Senator Cal, p. IV:253
Holidays, p. I:133
Holland, p. III:215
Holy Anorexia, p. III:115
Home-based businesses, pp. I:51, I:73-74, I:308t
Home care aides, p. I:53
— *See also:* personal home care aides
Home-cooked meals, p. I:357t
Home-entertainment products, p. I:226
Home health agencies, pp. III:207-209, III:393
Home health aides, p. I:52
Home health care, p. I:131
Home ownership, pp. II:35, III:191-192, I:194-195, II:331t
Home School Legal Defense Association, p. II:235
Home security, p. I:171
Home theatre in a box, p. I:227
Homeland Defense, p. IV:357t
Homeland Security Council, p. IV:187
Homelessness, p. IV:7
Homeopathy, pp. III:78, III:80, III:82
Homes, p. I:194
Homeschooling, p. II:234
Homework, pp. II:252-253, I:278, II:390t
Homicides, p. IV:41
— *See also:* Murders
— by age, pp. IV:308t
— by location, p. IV:319t
— by race/ethnicity, pp. IV:52-53, IV:217-218
— by sex, pp. II:18, IV:35, IV:310t
— children, p. II:243
— Columbine High School, p. II:24

Homicides continued:
— deaths, pp. III:4, III:8-9, II:21, III:131, III:432t
— domestic, pp. IV:48-49
— firearms-related, pp. IV:45, IV:311t
— incarcerations, pp. IV:306t
— population density, pp. IV:57-58
— rate fluctuation, pp. IV:28-30
— recidivism, p. IV:260
— reported to the police, pp. IV:4, IV:6
— students at school, p. II:243
— terrorism, pp. IV:190-191
— victims, pp. IV:34, IV:315t
Homosexuals, pp. III:53, III:287
— *See also:* Gays
— *See also:* Lesbians
— *See also:* Same-sex partners
Honda Accord, p. IV:71
Honduras, p. I:47
Honest Cannabis Information Foundation, p. III:134
Hong Kong, pp. II:5, II:31, II:163-165, I:187
Honolulu, p. II:75
Honor graduates, pp. II:293-294
Honors English, p. II:259
Hormone replacement therapy (HRT), pp. III:161, III:168
Horoscopes, p. I:282
Hospice care, pp. III:213, III:363, III:373, III:375
— diseases, p. III:376
— Hospice Home Care movement, p. III:373
— Kubler-Ross, Elisabeth, pp. III:212, III:374
— Medicare, pp. III:214, III:374, III:377-378
— pain control, pp. III:213-214
— patients, pp. III:525t
— Saunders, Dr. Cicely, pp. III:376, III:378
— United Government Services, pp. III:377-378
Hospitality, p. II:262
Hospitals, pp. I:131, III:212, III:264, III:364-365, III:525t
— *See also:* Catholic hospitals
— admissions, pp. III:369-370
— closings, pp. III:363, III:367, III:369-372
— expenditures, p. III:395
— medical procedures, pp. III:477t
— mergers, pp. III:366, III:525t
Hosting meals, pp. I:187, I:358t
Hot Network, p. III:280
Hotels and lodging, pp. I:7, I:196
Hotmail, p. I:282
House Select Committee on Aging, p. III:198
Household activities, pp. I:181-182, I:357
Household expenditures, pp. I:145, I:347t
Household income, pp. I:309t
— benefits, p. I:145
— college tuition, pp. II:271-272
— infant mortality, p. III:313
— Internet use, pp. I:270, I:378t
— life expectancy, p. II:21
— victimization rates, pp. IV:31-32
— weekend travel, p. I:192
Household service occupations, pp. I:20, I:32, I:296t
Households, pp. II:42-43, II:45, II:333t

Infant mortality continued:
517*t*
— rates, pp. III:43, III:312-313
— selected years, pp. III:44-45
Infants, pp. III:10-11, III:41
— *See also:* Children
— *See also:* Juveniles
— *See also:* Teenagers
— *See also:* Youth
Infectious diseases, pp. III:94, III:236, III:462*t*
— *See also:* Diseases
Infertility, p. III:299
Influenza, p. III:5
— causes of death, pp. III:2, III:4, III:8-9, III:69-70, III:99, III:401
— epidemic of 1918, pp. III:2, II:17, II:20, III:94
— immunizations, pp. III:96, III:98-99
Information clerks
— *See:* receptionists and information clerks
Information scientists (research)
— *See also:* computer and information scientists p. I:52
Information services, pp. I:104-105
Information systems managers
— *See:* computer and information systems managers
Information technology, p. IV:188
Inglewood Unified School District (CA), p. IV:131
Inhalants, pp. III:119-120, IV:151
Injectables, p. II:15
Injuries, pp. I:153, III:228, III:235, III:238
Ink jet printers and counterfeiting, p. IV:88
Inpatient hospitals, pp. III:207-209
INS
— *See:* Immigration and Naturalization Service
Insanity defense, pp. IV:275, IV:277-280, IV:381*t*
Insanity Defense Reform Act, p. IV:277
Inspectors
— *See:* machine operators, assemblers, and inspectors
Instant messaging, p. I:278
Institute on Race and Poverty, p. IV:222
Instrumental activities of daily living, pp. III:203-204
Insurance
— *See:* finance and insurance
Insurance claims and policy processing clerks, p. I:54
Insurance companies, p. III:416
Insurance fraud, p. IV:80
Insurance Information Institute, p. IV:79
Integrative medicine, p. III:82
Integumentary system, pp. III:150-151
Intellectual property, p. IV:97
Interest and dividend income, pp. I:145-146
Internal Revenue Service (IRS), pp. IV:91, IV:226, I:283
International Anti-Counterfeiting Coalition, p. IV:100
International Chamber of Commerce, p. IV:100
International Classification of Diseases, p. III:22
International Intellectual Property Association, p. IV:97
International Parental Kidnapping Crime Act, p. IV:141
International Task Force on Euthanasia and Assisted Suicide, p. III:217
Internet
— *See also:* Worldwide Web

Internet continued:
— charitable giving, p. I:235
— computer hacking, p. I:280
— counterfeiting, p. IV:100
— dating, pp. I:284-285
— entertainment, pp. I:226, I:233, I:268
— missing children, p. IV:143
— online travel spending, p. I:196
— productivity, p. I:97
— religion, pp. II:142-143, II:145
— schools, p. II:264
— search terms, pp. I:282-283, I:379*t*
— volunteering, p. I:246
Internet copyright piracy, pp. IV:95, IV:98
Internet fraud, pp. IV:82, IV:91
Internet gambling, pp. IV:101, IV:117-118
Internet Public Library, pp. I:257-258
Internet use, pp. I:276, I:377*t*
— age groups, p. I:378*t*
— by race/ethnicity and sex, pp. I:270-276, I:377*t*
— children, pp. I:278, I:379*t*
— household income, p. I:378*t*
Internists' medical malpractice premiums, p. III:415
Interracial marriages, pp. II:54-55, II:339*t*
Interuterine devices (IUDs), pp. II:15, III:304-305
Interviewers and clerks
— *See:* loan interviewers and clerks
Intrauterine Devices
— *See:* IUDs
Iowa, p. II:218
Ireland, pp. III:42, II:163-165
Irish gangs, p. IV:43
Iron lung, p. III:95
Iroquois, pp. II:72-73
Irradiation, p. III:112
IRS, p. I:283
Is Love Colorblind?, p. II:55
Is Single Gender Schooling Viable in the Public Sector?, p. II:309
Ischemic heart disease (IHD), pp. III:4, III:8, III:424*t*
Islam, pp. II:140-141
— fastest-growing religions, pp. I:252-253
— increase/decrease in membership, pp. II:132-135
— terrorism, p. IV:184
Israel, pp. II:164, IV:184
Italian (language), p. II:76
Italian gangs, p. IV:43
Italy, pp. II:163, I:187, I:192, III:334
Items stolen, p. IV:326*t*
Jackson-Lee, Sheila, p. IV:287
Jacob Wetterling Act, p. IV:121
Jails, pp. III:265-266
Japan, pp. II:5, II:163-165, I:187, II:254
Japanese, pp. III:43, II:74, II:76-77
Jazz concerts, p. I:216
Jehovah's Witnesses, pp. II:132-133, II:136-138
Jenkins, Henry, p. IV:145
Jewelry making, p. I:218
Jewish Defense League, p. IV:181

Jewish gangs, p. IV:43
Jews, pp. II:110, II:145
Jobs, pp. I:52-53
— advancement, pp. I:260-262, I:265
— college education, pp. I:51, I:58, I:61-62
— entrants, p. I:37
— gains, pp. I:32-33, I:299*t*
— leavers, p. I:37
— losses, pp. I:33, I:299*t*
— openings, pp. II:189-190, I:296*t*
— satisfaction, p. II:295
— training, pp. I:260-262
— worker supply, pp. I:24-25, I:27-28
Joe Camel, p. III:138
Jogging, p. I:202
Johns Hopkins University, p. II:294
Joint Legislative Task Force on Government Oversight, p. IV:223
Jones, Paula, p. I:166
Jonesboro (AR), p. IV:129
Jordan, Michael, p. I:211
Journal of the American Medical Association, pp. III:81, III:168, III:273-274, III:405
Judaism, pp. II:130-133, II:135, II:140-141
Judges, p. I:32
Jupiter Communications, p. I:196
Jury awards, p. I:170
Justice Policy Institute, pp. IV:129, IV:134, IV:237
Justice system employment
— arrests, pp. IV:266, IV:378*t*
— by government level, p. IV:302*t*
— crime rate, pp. IV:21-23
Justice system expenditures, pp. IV:303*t*
Justifiable homicides, pp. IV:217, IV:363*t*
Juveniles, pp. IV:39-40, IV:70, IV:101, I:221
— *See also:* Children
— *See also:* Infants
— *See also:* Teenagers
— *See also:* Youth
— arrests by race/ethnicity, pp. IV:133-137
— by sex, pp. IV:340*t*
— drugs, p. IV:149
— poverty, p. IV:134
— special units of police departments, p. IV:206
— violent crimes, pp. IV:340*t*
Kaczynski, Theodore, p. IV:181
Kaiser Family Foundation, p. I:231
Kanner, Leo, p. III:259
Kansas, p. IV:276
Kanzai, Amil, p. IV:182
Kazakhstan, p. II:163
Kennedy School of Government, p. III:75
Kennedy, President John F., p. IV:46
Kennedy, Robert F., p. IV:46
Kentucky, pp. II:187, III:409
Kenya, p. III:332
Kerr-Mills Act, p. III:384
Ketamine, p. IV:154
Kevorkian, Dr. Jack, p. III:216

Kidnapping, pp. IV:142, IV:245, IV:260
Kidney diseases, pp. III:8, III:40, III:161
— *See also:* Nephritis, nephrosis, and nephrotic syndrome
Kids Walk-to-School Program, p. III:406
Kilpatrick, William Heard, p. II:204
King, Jr., Dr. Martin Luther, p. IV:46
King, Rodney, pp. IV:204, IV:288
KKK
— *See:* Ku Klux Klan
Klaas, Polly, p. IV:142
Koppel, Ted, p. IV:243
Korea, pp. II:164-165, II:195, II:254
Korean population, pp. II:74, II:76-77
Kozol, Jonathan, p. II:221
Kru, p. II:77
Ku Klux Klan (KKK), pp. IV:181, IV:286
Kubler-Ross, Elisabeth, pp. III:212, III:374
Kurdistan Workers Party, p. IV:183
Kyrgyzstan, p. II:163
Labor force distribution, pp. I:299*t*
Labor law violations, p. I:45
Labor relations managers
— *See:* personnel and labor relations managers
Laboratory animal caretakers
— *See:* veterinary assistants and laboratory animal caretakers
Laboratory technologists
— *See:* Clinical laboratory technologists
Lacerations, p. I:155
Lakes and water pollution, pp. III:323, III:325
Landscaping and groundskeeping laborers, pp. I:61-62
Language-impaired children, pp. II:298-299
Lanoxin, p. III:167
Laotian population, p. II:74
Larcenies
— arrests, pp. IV:68-69
— by type, pp. IV:322*t*
— corrections system expenditures, p. IV:249
— females, p. IV:136
— property crime, pp. IV:7-8
— reported to police, p. IV:373*t*
Larsen, Elena, p. II:142
Las Vegas (NV), p. IV:124
Laser skin resurfacing, pp. III:277-279
Last Tango in Paris, p. I:231
Latin America, pp. II:25, I:47, III:326
Latinos, pp. I:41, II:70-71
Latter-Day Saints, pp. II:130-131
Latvia, pp. II:5, II:163-164
Law, pp. II:286, II:290
Law enforcement, pp. IV:30, I:157-158, IV:201-202, IV:205
— by race/ethnicity and sex, pp. IV:203-204, IV:360*t*
— deaths, pp. IV:361*t*
— departments, p. IV:199
— employment, p. IV:359*t*
— salaries, p. IV:209
— timeline, pp. IV:197-198
Lawyers, pp. I:22-25, I:32, I:58
LDP
— *See:* Low-Density Lipoprotein

Machine operators, assemblers, and inspectors continued:
  I:296*t*

MADD
— *See:* Mothers Against Drunk Driving (MADD)

Mail and message distributing occupations, p. I:32

Maine, pp. II:64, II:218

Major League Baseball (MLB), pp. I:210-211

Making Weight, p. III:116

Malaria, pp. III:58-59, III:442*t*

Malaysia, pp. II:5, I:187

Malcolm X, p. IV:46

Male-female teacher ratio, pp. II:182-183

Males, pp. IV:17, IV:136, III:137, III:150-151, I:204
— *See also:* Men

Malignancies, pp. III:2-4
— *See also:* Cancer
— *See also:* Neoplasms

Mammograms, pp. III:18, III:156, III:210, III:425*t*

Managed care, pp. III:207-209, III:344

Management analysts, pp. I:22-25, I:296*t*

Managerial and professional specialty occupations, pp. I:31-32

Managerial occupations
— *See:* executive, administrative, managerial occupations

Manhattan Project, p. III:105

Manic depression
— *See:* Bipolar disorder

Manslaughter, p. IV:135

Manufacturing
— compensation, p. I:326*t*
— employees, pp. I:329*t*
— employment, p. I:34
— income, p. I:120
— injuries in the workplace, p. I:156
— productivity output, pp. I:98-99, I:104-105

Maps, p. I:185

Marihuana Tax Act, p. IV:12

Marijuana, pp. III:126, III:133, IV:173
— adults, p. III:121
— consumption, p. III:104
— drug-related arrests, pp. IV:11, IV:147, IV:175
— emergency room visits, p. III:124
— lifetime drug use reported, pp. IV:151-153
— teenagers, pp. III:117-118, III:132
— trafficking, pp. IV:167-168

Marital status, pp. I:65-68

Marketing, pp. II:256-257, II:262

Marketing, advertising, public relations managers, p. I:58

Marriage, pp. II:48-49, II:335*t*
— age at first marriage, p. II:50
— Baby Boom generation, p. II:51
— by race/ethnicity, pp. II:52-54

Married-couple households, pp. II:45-47, I:92, III:269-270, I:315*t*

Maryland, pp. II:63-64, IV:223, III:338

The Maryland Report, p. II:304

Massachusetts, pp. II:63-64, IV:121, II:217, IV:287, II:305, III:338, III:370, III:409

Massachusetts Institute of Technology, p. IV:145
— *See:* MIT

Massachusetts Institute of Technology (MIT)
— grade inflation, p. II:293
— honor graduates, p. II:294
— private gifts, p. II:280
— tuition costs, p. II:268

Massage therapy, pp. III:78-79, III:162

Master's degrees, pp. I:94, II:283

Match.com, p. I:284

Matchmaker.com, p. I:284

Material exploitation of elderly population, p. III:199

Material moving occupations
— *See also:* transportation and material moving occupations

Maternal age at conception, p. III:40

Maternal complications of pregnancy, p. III:10

Maternal mortality, pp. II:21, III:22-23, IV:53, III:427*t*

Maternity leave, p. I:137

Mathematics, p. II:392*t*
— achievement, pp. II:390*t*
— class characteristics, pp. II:165, II:195
— doctoral degrees conferred, p. II:285
— proficiency, pp. II:161-162, II:164, II:203, II:237, II:366*t* II:386*t*
— salaries, p. II:194
— scores, p. II:254

Mathematics-related occupations, p. II:296

Mayhem: Violence as Public Entertainment, p. IV:145

MBA, p. I:212

McDonald's restaurants, pp. III:110, IV:184

McNaughtan, Daniel
— *See:* M'Naghten, Daniel

McVeigh, Timothy, pp. IV:179-181

Mealtimes, p. I:180

Measles, pp. III:55, III:94-95, III:97

Measles, German
— *See:* German measles

Meat cutters
— *See:* butchers and meat cutters

Meats, p. III:83

Media images, p. III:221

Medicaid
— elderly population, pp. III:220, III:363
— enrollment, pp. III:529*t*
— fraud, p. IV:94
— health care expenditures, p. I:131
— nonelderly population, pp. III:384-388

Medical assistants, pp. I:52-53

Medical care, p. I:133

Medical ethics, p. III:188

Medical hospitals, pp. III:364-365

Medical Injury Compensation Reform Act (CA), p. III:418

Medical liability reform legislation, p. III:418

Medical malpractice, pp. III:303, III:415-417, III:540*t*

Medical procedures, pp. III:477*t*

Medical professionals, pp. IV:93, I:157-158, III:520*t*

Medical records and health information technicians, pp. I:52-53

Medical review boards, p. III:418

Medical schools, pp. III:82, II:277, II:396*t*

Medical technologists
— *See:* Clinical laboratory technologists

Medicare
— Baby Boom generation, pp. III:380, III:382
— benefits, pp. III:207-209, III:214, III:489*t*
— elderly population, p. III:219
— enrollment, pp. III:380, III:527*t*
— expenditures, p. III:528*t*
— fraud, pp. IV:93-94
— hospice care, pp. III:374, III:376-379, III:526*t*
— income, p. III:381
— legislation, p. III:341
— medical infrastructure, p. III:363
— per-capita expenditures, p. I:131
— risk behaviors, pp. III:490*t*
— solvency, pp. III:381-382
Medicare+Choice program, pp. III:382-383
Medications, pp. III:102, II:301-302
Medicine, pp. III:75, II:286, II:290
Medicine, alternative
— *See:* Alternative medicine
Medicine, chiropractic
— *See:* Chiropractic medicine
Medicine, veterinary
— *See:* Veterinary medicine
Meditation, pp. III:162-163
Megan's Law, p. IV:121
Melanomas, pp. III:147-148, III:476*t*
— *See also:* Cancer
— *See also:* Skin cancer
Melissa, p. I:280
Membership organizations, pp. I:7, I:205, I:247-249, I:371*t*
Men
— *See also:* Males
— accidents, p. II:18
— activities of daily living, p. III:204
— age at first marriage, p. II:50
— art purchases, p. I:219
— athletic programs, p. I:206
— cancer survival rates, p. III:158
— causes of death, pp. III:6-7, III:12, II:18, II:21, III:24-26, III:30, III:32, III:34, III:37-38, III:53, III:422*t*
— coaches' salaries, pp. I:206-207
— cosmetic surgery, pp. III:277-278, III:504*t*
— creative writing, p. I:219
— disabled, pp. III:225, III:236
— diseases, pp. III:13, II:18, III:28, III:54, III:116, III:147, I:155, III:160, III:247, III:249, III:262, III:288
— domestic homicides, pp. IV:48-49
— earnings, p. I:71
— education, pp. II:259, I:262
— educational attainment, pp. I:94, II:258, II:283, II:285
— employment, pp. I:16, I:29-30, I:33, I:65-67, I:69, I:174-175
— homicides, p. II:18
— household activities, pp. I:181-182
— income, pp. I:84, I:94
— injuries at work, pp. I:155-156
— Internet use, p. I:276
— job training, p. I:262
— life expectancy, pp. II:18-19, III:47
— living arrangements, p. III:192

Men continued:
— Medicare, p. III:380
— modern dance, p. I:219
— occupational fatalities, p. I:156
— occupations, pp. I:31-32, I:156
— online shopping, p. I:277
— police officers, p. IV:200
— political-party affiliation, pp. II:100-101
— pottery, p. I:219
— prisoners, pp. IV:18, IV:238-239
— risk behaviors, pp. III:16-17, III:135-136
— risk factors, pp. II:18, III:20
— sexual activity, pp. III:269-270
— Social Security benefits, p. I:29
— sports scholarships, p. I:206
— suicides, pp. II:18, III:260, III:432*t*
— teachers, p. II:182
— violent crime, pp. IV:35-38
— volunteering, pp. I:236-237
— writing, p. I:219
Mental health, pp. III:103, III:107, III:247
— facilities, pp. III:264-265, III:501*t*
— professionals, pp. I:157-158
— services, p. I:131
Mental Health Systems Act, p. III:251
Mental illness, p. III:499*t*
— disabilities, pp. III:227, III:235, III:248-251, III:265-266
— educational attainment, p. III:241
— workforce disabilities, pp. III:238-239
Mental retardation, pp. III:229-231, III:243
Mental Retardation Facilities and Community Mental Health Centers Construction Act, p. III:265
Mercury, p. III:324
MergerWatch, p. III:366
Merit resolutions, pp. I:167-168
Message distributing occupations
— *See:* Mail and message distributing occupations
Metals, pp. III:323-325
Metalworking, p. I:218
Meter readers, pp. I:54-55
Meth Tour, p. IV:156
Methadone Control Act, p. IV:12
Methamphetamines, pp. III:124-125, III:129
— drug-related arrests, pp. IV:11, IV:147
— drug trafficking, pp. IV:167-168
— laboratories, pp. IV:155-156
— lifetime use reported, pp. IV:151-153
Methodists, pp. II:130-133, II:135
Methylphenidate, p. II:302
Metropolitan areas, pp. II:27-28, II:30, II:330*t*
Metropolitan Statistical Areas (MSAs), p. II:29
Mexican Mafia, p. IV:40
Mexico, pp. I:47, III:334
Miami (FL), p. IV:72
Miao, p. II:77
Michigan
— gay-couple households, p. II:63
— geographic distribution of elderly population, p. III:190
— insanity defense, p. IV:277

Phytochemicals, p. III:90

Piaget, Jean, p. II:203

The Pill, pp. II:15, III:304-305

Pineal gland surgeries, p. III:151

Pipefitters and steamfitters
— *See:* plumbers, pipefitters, and steamfitters

Pistols, p. II:245

Pituitary gland surgeries, p. III:151

Placebos, p. III:76

Plague, pp. III:58, III:60, III:392, III:442*t*

Planes, p. I:190

Plants, p. I:185

Plastic surgery
— *See:* Cosmetic surgery

The Playboy Channel, p. III:280

Plays (nonmusical), p. I:216

Playstation 2, p. I:283

Plug Uglies, p. IV:43

Plumbers, pipefitters, and steamfitters, pp. I:22, I:27-28

PM-10
— *See:* Particulate matter
— *See:* Particulate matter (PM-10)

PMDD
— *See:* Premenstrual dysphoric disorder

Pneumonia, pp. III:5, II:22
— Baby Boom generation, pp. III:69-70
— by century, p. III:2
— by race/ethnicity, pp. III:8-9
— childhood immunizations, pp. III:96, III:98
— funding, p. III:401
— immunizations, p. III:99
— leading diseases, p. III:4

Pocket-picking, p. IV:69

Podiatry degrees conferred, pp. II:286, II:290

Pokemon, p. I:283

Poland, pp. I:47, II:163, I:187

Police and detective supervisors, pp. I:22-23, I:27

Police department technology, pp. IV:208-209

Police forces, pp. IV:23, IV:43-44
— by sex, p. IV:200
— deaths, pp. IV:210-212, IV:217-218
— employment, pp. IV:21-22
— excessive force, pp. IV:213-214

Police pursuits, pp. IV:220-221

Police shootings, pp. IV:363*t*

Policy processing clerks
— *See:* insurance claims and policy processing clerks

Polio, pp. III:55-56, III:94-96

Polish, p. II:76

Political organizations, pp. I:245-246

Political-party affiliation, pp. II:99, II:350*t*
— by party, pp. II:98, II:114
— by race/ethnicity, p. II:108
— by sex, pp. II:100-101

Pollution, pp. III:315-316, III:326-328

Ponds, pp. III:323, III:325

Population, pp. II:70-72, II:343*t*
— births, p. II:4
— by sex, p. II:323*t*

Population continued:
— central cities, pp. II:27-28
— dependency ratio, p. II:22
— foreign-born, pp. II:348*t*
— geographic distribution, pp. II:24-25, II:30, II:36, II:331*t*
— growth rates, pp. II:37, I:302*t*
— households, pp. II:333*t*
— metropolitan areas, pp. II:27-28, II:330*t*
— Metropolitan Statistical Areas (MSAs), p. II:29
— MSAs, p. II:29
— never-married adults, p. II:339*t*
— nonmetropolitan areas, pp. II:27, II:330*t*
— over age 65, p. I:347*t*
— rural areas, p. II:329*t*
— suburban areas, pp. II:27-28, II:329*t*
— Total Fertility Rates, p. II:4
— urban areas, p. II:329*t*
— youth, pp. II:327*t*

Population changes in geographic areas, p. II:39

Population density, pp. II:30-31, IV:57-58, II:330*t*

Population mobility, pp. II:38-39, II:331*t*

Population Replacement Rate, pp. II:4, II:6, II:8

Pornography, pp. IV:108, III:280-281, I:282

Portland (OR), p. IV:124

Portuguese (language), p. II:76

Posse Comitatus Act of 1878, p. IV:24

Post-traumatic stress disorder, pp. III:247, III:252-253

Postal Inspection Service, p. IV:227

Postal Service clerks, pp. I:1, I:13, I:22-23, I:27-28, I:293*t*

Postneonatal deaths, p. III:312

Pottery, p. I:218

Poultry, p. III:83

Poverty rate
— by race/ethnicity, p. IV:53
— children, p. II:335*t*
— family demographics, pp. I:315*t*
— juveniles arrested, p. IV:134
— living arrangements, p. II:47
— minimum wage, p. I:91
— single-parent households, p. II:60
— U.S. Government definition, pp. I:88-89
— working families, pp. I:92-93

Powdered cocaine, p. IV:162

Powell v Alabama, p. IV:281

Precision, production, craft, repair occupations, pp. I:20, I:31, I:43, I:69-70, I:296*t*

Pregnancy-based discrimination, pp. I:161, I:164, I:167

Pregnancy, ectopic
— *See:* Ectopic pregnancy

Premarin, p. III:167

Premarital sex, pp. III:267-268, III:502*t*

Premenstrual dysphoric disorder (PMDD), p. III:170

Prepress technicians and workers, p. I:54

Preprimary schools, pp. II:222-223, II:382*t*

Presbyterian Church (U.S.A.), pp. II:136-138

Presbyterians, pp. II:130-133, II:135

Preschool teachers, pp. I:58-59

Prescription drug plans, p. I:133

Prescription drugs, p. III:75

Religions, pp. II:358*t*
— attendance at services, pp. I:233, I:249-250, I:343*t*
— Christian churches, p. II:134
— gains/losses in membership, pp. II:359*t*
— membership, pp. I:252-253, II:358*t*
— traditional denominations, pp. II:130-133
— volunteering, pp. I:242, I:244-246
— voting preferences, p. II:110
Religious activities, p. II:142
Religious diversity, p. I:164
Religious organizations, pp. I:247-249, I:371*t*
Renal disease, pp. III:2, III:380
Reno, Janet, p. I:50
Rensselaer Polytechnic Institute, p. II:280
Rental households, pp. II:35, III:195, II:331*t*
Repair occupations
— *See:* precision, production, craft, repair occupations
Repeat offenders, p. IV:206
Repetitive-strain injuries, p. III:236
Report on Smoking and Health, pp. III:107, III:136
Reproduction, p. III:291
Republicans, p. II:98
Research grants, p. III:81
Reservoirs, pp. III:323, III:325
Residency, pp. II:287-290
Residential treatment centers, p. III:264
Resistance machines, pp. I:200, I:202
Respiratory diseases, p. III:5
— birth defects, p. III:310
— causes of death, pp. III:3-4, III:8-10
— causes of disability, pp. III:227-228, III:235-236, III:238
— children, p. III:229
— surgical procedures, p. III:150
— therapeutic procedures, p. III:152
Restaurant dining, pp. I:180, I:357*t*
Restaurant expenditures, pp. III:109-110
Retail buyers
— *See:* wholesale and retail buyers
Retail trade, pp. I:6, I:61, I:104-105, I:157-158, I:292*t*
Retirement, pp. I:23, I:344*t*
— age group, pp. I:22, I:24, I:27, I:127, I:139, I:344*t*
— dependency ratio, p. I:142
— employee benefits, p. I:136
— household expenses, p. I:145
— income, pp. I:128-129, I:133
— occupations, pp. I:22-23, I:296*t*
Rett's Syndrome, p. III:258
Rheumatism, pp. III:227-228
Rhode Island, pp. II:64, II:217, IV:224, III:338
Ridge, Tom, p. IV:188
Rifles, p. II:245
Riley, Richard, p. II:263
Risk behaviors, pp. III:489*t*
Ritalin, pp. III:129, III:165, III:171-174, II:302-303, II:407*t*
III:483*t*
River water pollution, pp. III:323, III:325
R.J. Reynolds, p. III:138
Road rage, p. III:140
Robbery, p. IV:373*t*

Robbery continued:
— corrections expenditures, p. IV:249
— household income, pp. IV:31, IV:38
— juveniles arrested, pp. IV:133, IV:135, IV:137-138
— murders, p. IV:58
— rate fluctuation, pp. IV:25-26
— recidivism, p. IV:260
Robert Wood Johnson Medical School, p. III:167
Rockets, p. II:245
Rocky Mountain Spotted Fever, p. III:95
Roe v. Wade, p. III:306
Rohypnol, pp. III:120, IV:154
Roman Catholic Church, pp. II:136-138, II:242
Romania, p. II:163
Room and board, pp. II:271, II:277
Roosevelt, President Franklin D., p. IV:230
Roper Starch Worldwide, p. I:187
Rose, Mike, p. II:155
Rowing, p. I:208
Rubella, pp. III:55-56, III:94-95
— *See also:* German measles
Rubeola, p. III:56
Rudolph, Eric Robert, p. IV:181
Runaways, pp. IV:101, IV:136
Running, p. I:202
Running on Ritalin, p. II:303
Rural population, pp. II:27, II:329*t*
Russia, pp. II:5, I:187
Russian (language), pp. II:76-77
Russian Federation, pp. II:163-165, III:334
RVs, p. I:190
— *See:* Recreational vehicles (RVs)
Sacramento (CA), p. IV:72
SAD
— *See:* Social anxiety disorders
Safety in schools, pp. II:247-248
Safety issues, pp. I:171-172
Sailer, Steven, p. II:55
St. John's Wort, pp. III:75-76, III:81, III:87, III:162-163
Salaries
— athletes, pp. I:212, I:364*t*
— baggage screeners, p. IV:233
— law enforcement personnel, p. IV:209
— medical school graduates, p. III:414
— net worth, p. I:38
— productivity, p. I:120
— teachers, pp. II:182, II:193-194
— weekly, p. I:128
Sales occupations, pp. I:20, I:32, I:61-62, I:69-70, I:296*t*
Sales of educational services, p. II:279
Salk, Dr. Jonas, p. III:95
Sally Ride Academy for Girls, p. II:309
Salmonella infections, p. III:111
Salts, pp. III:20-21
Same-sex partners, pp. II:64, I:136
— *See also:* Gays
— *See also:* Homosexuals
— *See also:* Lesbians
Sarafem, p. III:170

Satellite television receivers, p. I:227
SATs, pp. II:166, II:171, II:217, II:293, II:368*t*
Saudi Arabia, p. IV:184
Saum, William, p. IV:118
Saunders, Dr. Cicely, pp. III:376, III:378
Savage Inequalities: Children in America's Schools, p. II:221
Savings, pp. I:347*t*
Savings & loans fraud, p. IV:109
Saw palmetto, p. III:75
Schistosomiasis, p. III:326
Schizophrenia, pp. III:247-249
Schlafly, Phyllis, p. II:223
Schlosser, Eric, p. III:110
Scholastic Aptitude Test
— *See:* SATs
Scholastic Assessment Test
— *See:* SATs
School-based health centers, pp. III:102-104, III:464*t*
School choice, pp. II:239-240
School finances, pp. II:220-221, II:379*t*
School performance, p. II:385*t*
School-to-Work Opportunities Act, p. II:262
School vending machines, p. II:310
School vouchers, pp. II:241-242
School-year duration, p. II:254
Schools, p. I:34
— bullying, pp. II:249-250
— by type, pp. II:211, II:222-223, II:231, II:233, II:237
— crime, pp. IV:128, IV:130, II:245
— expulsions, pp. IV:131-132
— problems perceived by teachers, p. II:198
— problems perceived by the general public, p. II:199
— youth gangs, pp. IV:42-43
Schools and Staffing Survey, pp. II:191, II:198
Science museums, p. I:229
Sciences, advanced
— *See:* Advanced sciences
Scientific and technical services
— *See:* professional, scientific, and technical services
Scientology, pp. II:134-135, I:252-253
Scofflaws, p. IV:266
Search engines, p. I:278
Seasonal workers, p. I:46
Seconal, p. III:129
Second homes, p. I:194
Secondary education, pp. I:11, II:189-190
Secondary school teachers, pp. I:58-59, I:61-62
Secret Service, p. IV:228
Secretaries, stenographers, and typists, pp. I:32, I:61-62
Secularism, pp. I:252-253
Securities and Exchange Commission, pp. IV:84-85, IV:109
Security measures, p. I:281
Sedatives, pp. III:119, III:128
Seeds, p. I:185
Segregation, p. II:345*t*
Seizure disorders, pp. III:229, III:231
Self-employment income, p. I:145
Senior citizens, pp. III:187-188

Senior citizens continued:
— *See also:* Aging population
— *See also:* Elderly population
— living arrangements, pp. III:193-194
— media images, pp. III:221-222
— Medicaid expenditures, p. III:220
— Medicare expenditures, p. III:219
— quality of life, p. III:210
— risk behaviors, pp. III:489*t*
— suicides, p. III:260
Sentencing, pp. IV:108-110, IV:333*t*
SEOG, p. II:273
Sepsis, bacterial
— *See:* Bacterial sepsis
September 11, 2001
— airline passenger screening, p. IV:232
— corporate responses, p. I:171
— deaths, p. IV:190
— food-borne terrorism, p. III:112
— genetic engineering, p. III:106
— Immigration and Naturalization Service, p. IV:227
— racial profiling, p. IV:224
— terrorism, pp. IV:177, IV:182
— timeline, pp. IV:192-194
— workplace safety, p. I:150
Septicemia, pp. III:4-5, III:7-8
Service occupations
— employment, pp. I:31-32, I:291*t*
— independent contractors, pp. I:69-70
— injuries in the workplace, p. I:156
Serviceman's Readjustment Act, pp. II:150, II:273
— *See also:* GI Bill
Services industry, pp. II:256-257, II:262
— employment, pp. I:1, I:3-4, I:6
— productivity, p. I:102
Seventh Day Adventists, p. II:132
Severance pay, p. I:134
Sewing, p. I:218
Sewing machine operators, p. I:54
Sex-based crimes, pp. IV:10, IV:101
Sex-based discrimination
— case resolutions, pp. I:163, I:167
— charges filed with the EEOC, p. I:161
Sex education, p. III:103
Sex information, pp. III:282-283, III:505*t*
Sex offenders, pp. IV:121, IV:336*t*
Sex on TV, p. I:231
Sexes
— *See also:* Females
— *See also:* Males
— *See also:* Men
— *See also:* Women
— deaths, pp. II:17, II:21
— earnings, pp. I:71, II:295
— educational attainment, pp. II:258-259, I:262, II:283, II:285, I:318*t*
— employment, pp. I:65-67, I:69, I:174, I:298*t* I:355*t*
— high school athletes, p. I:362*t*

Special education programs continued:
   407*t*

Special education teachers, pp. I:22, I:24-25, I:58

Special units of police departments, pp. IV:206-207

Special weapons and tactics (SWAT), p. IV:211

Specialized museums, p. I:229

Specialty hospitals, p. III:365

Speech impairments, pp. III:229-231, II:298-299

Speed, p. III:124

Spending on sports, p. I:206

The Spice Channel, p. III:280

Spinal problems, pp. III:227-228

Sponges, p. II:15

Sports, pp. I:199-200
— high school athletes, p. I:204
— injuries, p. I:205
— marketing, p. I:213
— online auctions, p. I:286
— professional, p. I:210
— scholarships, p. I:206
— supplies, p. I:185
— teenagers, pp. I:201-202, I:361*t*
— television, p. I:211

Sports Illustrated, p. I:213

Spouse abuse, p. IV:10

Sprains, p. I:155

Springfield (OR), p. IV:129

Stalking, pp. IV:119-120, IV:336*t*

Standardized tests, pp. II:168, II:170, II:218, II:367*t*

Stanford Sleep Disorders Clinic, p. III:144

Stanford University, pp. II:268, II:280, II:294

Starter pistols, p. II:245

State and local grants, p. II:279

State Department, p. IV:183

State government, pp. I:1, I:9-10, II:211, I:256, I:292*t*

State mental hospitals, p. III:264

State prisoners, pp. IV:236, IV:369*t*

State University of New York at Buffalo, p. II:292

STDs
— *See:* Sexually transmitted diseases

Steamfitters
— *See:* plumbers, pipefitters, and steamfitters

Stenographers and typists
— *See:* Secretaries, stenographers, and typists

Stents, pp. III:25, III:151

Sterility, p. II:14

Sterilization, pp. III:304-305

Steroid use, p. III:104

Stimulants, pp. IV:11, III:119, III:128, IV:151-152, III:173

Stock performance, p. I:103

Stomach cancer, pp. III:67-68, III:156

Streams, pp. III:323, III:325

Street gangs, p. IV:44

Street, Picabo, p. I:209

Stress
— cancer, p. III:161
— morning habits, pp. III:139-140
— nighttime habits, pp. III:143-144
— noonday habits, pp. III:141-142

Stress continued:
— risk behaviors, p. III:108
— vacations, p. III:145

Strikes, p. I:210

Strokes, p. II:18
— *See also:* Cerebrovascular disease
— Baby Boom generation, p. III:69
— causes of death, pp. III:2-5, III:8-9
— disabilities, pp. III:227, III:243, III:401
— women, pp. III:12-13

Students
— *See also:* Children
— *See also:* Juveniles
— *See also:* Teenagers
— *See also:* Youth
— deaths in school, pp. II:243-244
— disabilities, p. II:258
— financial assistance, pp. II:395*t*
— indebtedness, pp. II:275, II:277-278, III:414
— LEP, pp. II:306-307
— limited English proficiency, p. II:306

Students Against Drunk Driving, p. IV:113

Subsidized commuting, p. I:135

Substance abuse, pp. IV:53, III:102, III:411, III:471*t*

Substance Abuse and Mental Health Services Administration
  (SAMHSA), pp. IV:157, IV:159, III:412

Substance use, pp. III:121-123

Suburbs, pp. II:27-28, II:30, II:329*t*

Sudden Infant Death Syndrome, pp. III:10, III:437*t*
— *See also:* Crib death
— *See also:* SIDS

Sudden Sniffing Death Syndrome, p. III:120

Sugars, pp. III:20-21

Suicide, p. III:35

Suicides, pp. III:431*t*
— aging population, pp. III:204, III:261
— causes of death, pp. III:4, III:8, II:21, III:131
— Columbine High School, p. II:243
— firearms-related, p. IV:39
— men, pp. II:18, III:34-36, III:260
— mental health, pp. III:248-249
— school-based health centers, p. III:103
— terrorists, p. IV:190

Suicides, altruistic
— *See:* Altruistic suicides

Suicides, anomic
— *See:* Anomic suicides

Suicides, egoistic
— *See:* Egoistic suicides

Suicides, fatalistic
— *See:* Fatalistic suicides

Sulfa drugs, pp. III:2, II:22

Sulfur dioxide, pp. III:316-317

Sunbeam Corp., p. IV:84

Super Nintendo, p. IV:145

Supplemental Educational Opportunity Grants
— *See:* SEOG

Supplemental income, p. II:183

Supplemental pay, p. I:129

Support staff
— *See:* teachers and support staff
Suppositories, p. II:15
Supreme Court, pp. IV:24, IV:277, IV:281-282
Surfing, p. I:200
Surgeon General of the United States, pp. III:83, III:403
Surgeons
— *See:* Physicians and Surgeons
— *See:* physicians and surgeons
Surgical hospitals, pp. III:364-365
Surgical procedures, pp. III:150-151, III:154-155
Survival rates for cancers, pp. III:13, III:19, III:447*t*
   III:478*t*
Sweden, pp. III:42, II:163-164, III:334
Swedish (language), p. II:77
Swimming, pp. I:200, I:208-209
Switch operators
— *See:* railroad brake, signal, and switch operators
Switchboard operators (including answering service)
— occupations in decline, p. I:54
Switzerland, pp. II:163-165
Symbionese Liberation Army, p. IV:181
Symphonies, pp. I:224-225
Synthroid, pp. III:167-168
Syphilis, pp. III:51-52, III:58, III:442*t*
Systematic phonics, pp. II:200-202
Systems analysts, pp. I:58-59, I:61-62
— *See also:* computer systems analysts
Tagalog, pp. II:76-77
T'ai chi, pp. I:200-201
Tailhook, pp. I:162, I:166
Taiwanese population, p. II:74
Tajikistan, p. II:163
Talking Back to Prozac, p. III:64
Tanning, p. III:147
Taoism, pp. II:134-135, II:140-141, I:252-253
Task Force on Antimicrobial Resistance, p. III:330
Tattoos, pp. III:148, I:283
Tax evasion and sentencing, p. IV:108
Taxes, pp. II:211, II:213
TB
— *See:* Tuberculosis
Teacher Followup Survey, p. II:191
Teacher-pupil ratio, pp. II:180, II:371*t*
Teachers, p. II:371*t*
— by sex, pp. II:182, II:372*t*
— certification, pp. II:186, II:373*t*
— dissatisfaction, p. II:374*t*
— educational attainment, pp. II:184-185, II:373*t*
— elementary schools, pp. I:24-25, I:58, I:61-62
— preschool, pp. I:58-59
— problems perceived in schools, p. II:198
— retirement, pp. I:22-23
— salaries, pp. II:182, II:193-194, II:374*t*
— secondary schools, pp. I:58-59, I:61-62
— shortages, p. II:189
— Singapore, p. II:188
— special education, pp. I:22, I:24-25, I:58, I:296*t*
— supplemental income, p. II:183

Teachers continued:
— turnover, pp. II:191-192
— uncertified, p. II:187
— worker shortages, p. I:59
— workplace assaults, pp. I:157-158
Teachers' aides, pp. I:22-23, I:296*t*
Teachers and support staff, p. I:11
Team Marketing Report, p. I:212
Technical and related support occupations, pp. I:20, I:296*t*
Technical services
— *See:* professional, scientific, and technical services
Technical, sales, and administrative support occupations, p.
   I:31-32
Technicians and related support occupations, pp. I:32, I:69
Technology and communications, pp. II:256-257, II:262
Teenagers, pp. IV:33, IV:75, IV:106, IV:325*t*
— *See also:* Children
— *See also:* Juveniles
— *See also:* Students
— *See also:* Youth
— illegal labor, p. I:43
— illicit substance use, pp. III:117-120, III:132, III:134
— Internet use, pp. I:278-279, I:379
— physical education classes, p. I:203
— reading habits, p. I:221
— religious services attendance, p. I:373*t*
— sedatives, p. III:119
— sexual activity, pp. III:282-285, III:505*t*
— smoking, pp. III:137-138
— sports, pp. I:199, I:201-202, I:204
Telemarketing, p. IV:82
Telemedicine, pp. III:361-362, III:524*t*
Telephone operators, p. I:54
Television, pp. III:221-222, I:226-227, I:231, I:268, III:280,
   III:491*t*
Tellers, p. I:54
Tendinitis, p. I:155
Tennessee, pp. II:63, II:196, II:246
Tennis, pp. I:202, I:208-209
Terrorism
— civil liberty, p. IV:185
— deaths, pp. IV:183, IV:190-191, IV:356*t*
— domestic, pp. IV:180, IV:182
— global, p. IV:177
— timeline, pp. IV:178-179
Terrorism Information and Prevention System (TIPS), p.
   IV:186
Test scores, pp. II:171-175
Testosterone levels, pp. III:6, III:29, III:151, IV:153
Tests, standardized
— *See:* standardized tests
Tetanus, pp. III:94-95
Texas, pp. IV:122, IV:284, III:415, III:417
— Asian population, p. II:75
— education for gifted children, p. II:305
— expulsions from school, p. II:246
— gay-couple households, pp. II:63-64
— geographic distribution of elderly population, p. III:190
— hospital beds, p. III:369

Texas continued:
— standardized tests, p. II:218
— vacation spending, p. I:190
— youth gangs, p. IV:138
Thai population, p. II:74
Thailand, p. III:42
Theatres, pp. I:185, I:217, I:224-225
Theft, p. II:245
— arrests, pp. IV:68-70
— by property stolen, p. IV:76
— correction expenditures, p. IV:249
— crimes reported to the police, p. IV:373*t*
— juveniles, p. IV:136
— property crime, pp. IV:4, IV:7-8
Theology degrees conferred, pp. II:286, II:290
Therapeutic procedures, pp. III:152-154
They Say You're Crazy, p. III:170
Third International Mathematics and Science Study
— *See:* TIMSS
Third National Incidence Study of Child Abuse and Neglect, p. IV:107
Thomas, Clarence, pp. I:162, I:165
Thomas, Timothy, p. IV:204
Thompson, Tommy, pp. III:73, III:112
Thyroid gland surgeries, p. III:151
Ticket prices, pp. I:212-213, I:222, I:364*t*
Time for Kids, p. II:249
Time for Life: Surprising Ways Americans Use Their Time, p. I:181
Timelines
— drug-control legislation, p. IV:12
— hate crimes, p. IV:286
— law enforcement, pp. IV:197-198
— September 11, 2001, pp. IV:192-194
— terrorism, pp. IV:178-179
TIMSS, pp. II:188, II:195, II:253-254
Title IX, pp. I:204, II:308
Tobacco advertising, p. III:138
Tobacco consumption, pp. IV:12, IV:148, IV:352*t*
Tobacco control programs, pp. III:102, III:408-409
Tomatoes, p. III:87
Tonsillitis, p. III:229
Tort reform, p. III:417
Total Fertility Rate, p. III:295
Total Fertility Rates, pp. II:5-8
Touch football, p. I:202
Toxemia, p. III:23
Toxic Shock Syndrome, pp. III:61-62, III:444*t*
Toyota Camry, p. IV:71
Toys, pp. II:66, I:286
Toys and sports supplies, p. I:185
Tracheal cancer, p. III:67
Track and field, p. I:209
Trade, pp. I:6, II:256-257, II:262
Traditional workers, pp. I:71-72
Traffic deaths, pp. II:18, IV:115-116
Train robbery, p. IV:245
Tranquilizers, pp. III:119, III:128, IV:151
Trans fat, p. III:109

Transportation
— assaults in the workplace, pp. I:157-158
— child rearing costs, pp. II:66-67
— college costs, p. II:271
— injuries in the workplace, p. I:156
— occupational fatalities, p. I:151
Transportation and material moving occupations, pp. I:20, I:43, I:296*t*
— *See also:* material moving occupations
Transportation and public utilities, pp. I:6, I:292*t*
Transportation and warehousing, pp. I:104-105
Transportation Security Administration, p. IV:233
Traumatic brain injury, p. II:298
Travel, pp. I:190-192
Travel agencies, pp. I:194, I:196-197, I:360*t*
Treadmill exercise, p. I:200
Treason, p. IV:245
Tricyclic antidepressants, p. III:64
Trigonometry, p. II:259
Trimox, pp. III:166-167
Trinidad and Tobago, p. II:163
Triplets, pp. III:39, III:299-300
Truancy, p. IV:101
The Truly Disadvantaged, p. II:53
Trust fund assets of Medicare, p. III:528*t*
Tuberculosis, pp. III:2-3, III:58-59
— cases and rates, pp. III:442*t*
— foreign countries, pp. III:332-334
Tufts University, pp. III:175, II:294
Tuition and fees, pp. II:151, II:269-270, II:272, II:394*t* III:539*t*
— Consumer Price Index, p. II:268
— medical school, p. II:277
— public universities, p. II:279
Tularemia, p. III:392
Turkey, p. I:187
Turkmenistan, p. II:163
Turning the Corner on Father Absence in Black America, p. II:53
Twinkie Defense, p. IV:276
Twins, pp. III:39, III:299-300
Two-parent households, pp. II:46, II:67
Typhoid fever, pp. III:58-59, III:442*t*
Typists
— *See also:* word processors and typists p. I:54
U. S. Customs Service, p. IV:329*t*
Uganda, p. III:332
Ukraine, p. II:163
Ultrasound, p. III:152
Umbilical cord complications, p. III:10
Uncertified teachers, p. II:187
Underemployment, p. I:57
Unemployment, pp. IV:53, I:145
UNESCO, p. II:250
UNICOR, p. IV:255
Uniform Crime Report, pp. IV:3-5, IV:7, IV:9, IV:14, IV:139
Uninsured population, pp. III:384-385
Unions, pp. I:1, I:14, I:16, I:294*t*
Unitarian Universalism, pp. II:134-135, I:252-253

United Church of Christ, pp. II:132-135
United Government Services, pp. III:377-378
United Kingdom, pp. II:163, III:334
United Methodist Church, pp. II:136-138
United Nations building, p. IV:184
United Nations Human Rights Committee, p. III:218
United Republic of Tanzania, p. III:332
U.S. Administration on Aging, p. III:199
U.S. Army, p. II:292
U.S. Army Reserves, p. II:278
U.S. Customs Service, pp. IV:99, IV:226-227
U.S. Department of Education, p. I:61
U.S. Department of Energy, p. III:105
U.S. Department of Justice, p. IV:3
U.S. Navy, p. II:278
U.S. Office of Dietary Supplements, p. III:75
U.S. Surgeon General, p. III:107
University of Colorado system, p. II:280
University of Michigan, pp. II:57, I:183, III:257
University of Utah Drug Information Service, p. III:389
Unsafe School Choice Option, p. IV:129
Up the IRS, Inc., p. IV:181
Urban Policy Institute, p. IV:134
Urban population, pp. II:27, II:329*t*
Urdu, p. II:76
Urinary tract cancer, pp. III:3, III:156
Urinary tract surgeries, p. III:150
Urologists, p. III:275
Uruguay, p. II:163
USDA, pp. III:84, III:87-90, III:109, III:113
Usef, Ramzi, p. IV:183
Utah, p. IV:276
Uterine cancer, pp. III:19, III:68, III:158, III:161, III:168
Utilities, pp. I:104-105
Uzbekistan, p. II:163
Vacation homes, pp. I:194, I:359*t*
Vacation spending, p. I:190
Vacation time, pp. I:128, I:133, I:187, I:189, I:191-192, I:359*t*
Vacations, pp. III:145-146
Vaccinations, pp. III:94-95
Vaccines, pp. III:389-392, III:463*t*
Vaccinia (cell culture), p. III:392
Vagrancy, pp. IV:101, IV:106-107, IV:112
Valium, p. III:129
Valley State Prison, p. IV:243
Vancomycin-Resistant Enterococci
— *See:* VRE
Vandalism, pp. IV:80, IV:105
Vanderbilt University, p. II:280
Varicella, p. III:96
Vasotec, p. III:167
VCRs, p. I:226
Vegetables, p. III:83
Venezuelan encephalitis, p. III:392
Vermont, pp. II:64-65, III:338
Very-low birth weight, p. III:310
Veterans, p. II:150
Veterans Administration, pp. I:131, III:264
Veterinary assistants and laboratory animal caretakers, p. I:52

Veterinary medicine degrees conferred, pp. II:286, II:290
Viagra, pp. III:267, III:275-276, III:504*t*
Victim assistance, p. IV:206
Victimization
— by race/ethnicity, pp. IV:316*t*
— by sex, race/ethnicity, and income, pp. IV:309*t*
— children, pp. IV:136, IV:139-140, IV:337*t*
— homicides, p. IV:35
— household income, pp. IV:31-32
— workplace, p. IV:320*t*
Video games, pp. IV:144-145, I:227, I:231, I:268, IV:342*t*
Video products, p. I:185
Video rentals, pp. I:222, I:366*t*
Video Vigilante, p. IV:125
Videocassette recorders
— *See:* VCRs
Vietnam, p. III:332
Vietnamese (language), pp. II:76-77
Vietnamese population, p. II:74
Violence in schools, pp. IV:128, II:245
Violent crime, pp. I:151-152, I:351*t*
— actual crimes reported, pp. IV:4-6
— arrests, pp. IV:16, IV:266, IV:273
— by race/ethnicity, p. IV:52
— by sex, pp. IV:35, IV:135
— crimes reported to the police, p. IV:77
— drug-related, p. IV:13
— firearms-related, p. IV:39
— household income, p. IV:31
— juveniles, p. IV:133
— not included in crime index, pp. IV:9-10
— prisoners, pp. IV:236-237
— rate fluctuation, pp. IV:26-27
— recidivism, p. IV:260
— victimization rates, p. IV:305*t*
Violent Crime Control and Law Enforcement Act, p. IV:47
Violent Offender Incarceration and Truth-in-Sentencing Incentive Grant (VOITIS) program, pp. IV:250, IV:252
Vioxx, p. III:178
Viral hepatitis, p. III:61
Virginia, pp. II:63, II:187, II:246
Virginia Slims cigarettes, p. III:136
Virtual doctors
— *See:* Telemedicine
Virtual libraries, p. I:257
Virtual volunteering, p. I:246
Viruses, pp. I:280, III:323
Vision care, p. I:133
Vision impairments, pp. III:203, III:227, III:229, III:231, II:298, III:487*t*
Vision screenings, p. III:103
Visual arts, p. II:284
Vitamins, p. III:75
VOC
— *See:* Volatile Organic Chemicals
Vocational education, pp. IV:264, II:392*t*
— adult education, pp. II:256-257, I:264-265
— by specialization, pp. II:261-262
— credits accumulated, p. II:258

Volatile organic chemicals, pp. III:316, III:318
Volleyball, pp. I:202, I:208-209
Volpe, Justin, p. IV:204
Volunteering, pp. I:233-234, I:369*t*
— age group, pp. I:239-240, I:370*t*
— by organization type, pp. I:245-246, I:370*t*
— by sex, pp. I:236-237
— educational attainment, p. I:238
— race/ethnicity, pp. I:241, I:370*t*
— work-related organizations, pp. I:245-246
Voter registration, p. II:352*t*
Voter turnout, pp. II:112, II:355*t*
— age, pp. II:104, II:353*t*
— presidential elections, pp. II:96, II:350*t*
— race/ethnicity, pp. II:106, II:353*t*
— religion, pp. II:110, II:354*t*
— women, p. II:102
Vouchers, school, pp. II:241-242
VRE, p. III:330
Wackenhut Corrections, pp. IV:251-253
Wages, pp. I:16, I:120, I:122, I:128, I:295*t*
— by occupational group, p. II:296
— manufacturing, pp. I:336*t*
Waiters and waitresses, pp. I:61-62
Wakeboarding, pp. I:200-201
Walking
— 200,
The Wall.org, p. II:145
Walsh, Adam, p. IV:142
War on Drugs
— arrests by race/ethnicity, p. IV:163
— murders, pp. IV:28, IV:30
— Nixon, President Richard, p. IV:147
— timeline, p. IV:12
— wiretapping, p. IV:230
— youth, p. III:118
Washington (DC), pp. II:64, IV:124, IV:132, IV:215
Washington (State), pp. II:63-64, II:246
Waste Management Inc., pp. IV:84, IV:109
Wastewater treatment in selected countries, p. III:326
Watch guards
— *See also:* guards and watch guards p. I:61
Water pollution, pp. III:315, III:321-325, III:518*t*
Waterways, pp. III:321-322
Weapons crimes, pp. IV:10, IV:101, IV:104
Weather Underground, p. IV:181
Weaving, pp. I:218-219
Weekend travel, p. I:192
Weight-control habits, p. III:115
Weight machines, pp. I:200, I:202
Welfare clerks, p. I:296*t*
Welfare Reform Act, p. II:47
Wellness programs, p. I:135
Wesleyans, pp. II:130-131, II:135
West Germany (former), p. II:254
West Paducah (KY), p. IV:129
West Virginia, pp. II:75, II:187, III:369-370, III:409, III:417
Western equine encephalitis, p. III:392
Western Sahara, p. II:30

Western United States, p. III:189
*What Works? Questions and Answers About Prison
   Reform*, p. IV:262
White-black death rate ratio, p. II:327*t*
White collar crime, pp. IV:108-109
White families, p. I:38
White House budget, p. IV:188
White, Dan, p. IV:276
Whites, p. III:28
— abortions, pp. II:12-13, II:321*t*
— activities of daily living, p. III:204
— arrests, p. IV:53
— births, pp. II:10, III:23, I:40, II:319*t*
— breastfeeding, p. III:41
— cancer survival rates, pp. III:156-158
— causes of death, pp. III:8-9, II:21, III:24-27, III:32, III:34, III:36, III:43-44
— computer learning opportunities, p. II:263
— correctional population, p. IV:19
— crib death, pp. III:45-46
— deaths, pp. III:15, III:18, II:21
— diseases, pp. III:14, III:18, III:28, III:52, III:54, III:64, III:288-290
— drug arrests, pp. IV:161, IV:163-164
— drug convictions, pp. IV:164-166
— drug use, pp. III:126-127, IV:159-160
— earnings, p. I:71
— educational attainment, pp. I:39, I:112, I:118-119, II:151-153, II:258-259, II:287-290
— employment, pp. I:16, I:30, I:37, I:67-68
— family net worth, p. I:38
— gender distribution, p. II:339*t*
— homicides, pp. IV:52, IV:217-218
— housing, p. II:35
— income, pp. II:21, I:82-83
— infant mortality, pp. II:21, III:313
— Internet use, pp. I:270-271
— interracial marriages, pp. II:54-55
— juveniles arrested, p. IV:137
— learning disabilities, p. III:66
— life expectancy, pp. II:20, III:47-48, III:403-404
— literacy, pp. II:154, II:159
— low birth weight, pp. III:40, III:308-309
— mammograms, p. III:18
— marriage, pp. II:52-53
— maternal mortality, pp. II:21, III:22
— mathematics proficiency, pp. II:161-162
— Medicare, p. III:380
— physicians, p. III:337
— political-party affiliation, p. II:108
— population, pp. II:24-25
— population mobility, p. II:39
— Population Replacement Rate, p. II:6
— risk behaviors, pp. III:16-17, III:135-136
— risk factors, p. III:20
— single-parent households, p. II:61
— suicides, pp. III:260, III:434*t*
— Total Fertility Rates, pp. II:6-8
— volunteering, p. I:241

Writing, pp. I:218-219

Wrongful termination, p. I:162

WWF, p. I:283

www.buddhanet.org, p. II:145

www.godweb.org, p. II:145

Wyoming, pp. II:75, IV:278

X-rated movies, p. I:231

Yahoo!, p. I:282

Yale University, p. II:294

Yates, Andrea, p. IV:279

Yiddish, pp. II:76-77

Yoga, pp. III:163, I:200-201

Young Adult Literacy Survey, p. II:154

Youth, pp. II:22, I:141, I:242, I:244-246

— *See also:* Children

— *See also:* Infants

— *See also:* Juveniles

— *See also:* Teenagers

Youth gangs, pp. IV:137, IV:206, IV:313*t*

— *See also:* Gangs

— *See also:* Street gangs

— by race/ethnicity, pp. IV:40-43

— cocaine, p. IV:34

— selected states, p. IV:138

Zantac, p. III:167

ZapMe! Corp., pp. II:264-265

Zero tolerance, p. IV:195

Zimbabwe, p. III:332

Zoloft, pp. III:63-64, III:167, III:170, III:276, III:445*t*

Zoological gardens, p. I:7